A. J. Anthony Morris

War, 1906–1914

The Advocacy
of Peace
and Retrenchment

Chapters 2 and 6, and parts of other chapters, are based largely on the unpublished Oxford thesis: RADICAL LIBERAL CRITICISM OF BRITISH FOREIGN POLICY 1906–1914 (1964) by A. J. Dorey.

Rowman and Littlefield
Totowa, New Jersey 07512

First published in the United States 1972
by Rowman and Littlefield, Totowa, New Jersey

ISBN 0 – 87471 – 108 – 8

Printed in Great Britain by
Butler and Tanner Limited
Frome and London

Contents

PREFACE   ix

PROLOGUE   1
Themes   1
Beginnings   13

Chapter 1.   FORGING THE ENTENTES, 1905–07   29
Sir Edward Grey   29
France and Germany   34
The Anglo-Russian Convention   52

Chapter 2.   THE MINISTER FOR WAR DECEIVES HIS CRITICS   71
A change in military strategy   71
Haldane and the Cabinet   78
Haldane and the Commons   84

Chapter 3.   THE SECOND HAGUE CONFERENCE   97

Chapter 4.   THE NAVAL CRISIS, 1908–10   122
Prelude, 1908   122
Panic and collapse, 1909–10   140

Chapter 5.   THE RISE AND FALL OF THE TRIPLE ENTENTE,
1908–11   169
Dubious partners   169
Friendship with Germany   198
A false dawn   223

Chapter 6.   THE FOREIGN SECRETARY IS CENSURED FOR HIS
PAINS   235

The *Panther's* leap   235
Persia and Tripoli   251
The gathering of Grey's critics   259
Grey disarms some of his critics   272

Chapter 7.   A CABINET INTERLUDE—THE DIE IS CAST   282
A packed Defence Committee   282
Confrontation   295

Chapter 8.   HOPES OF PEACE: DESIGNS FOR WAR   303
Pourparlers   303
Keeping faith—friendship with Germany and another
    disarmament campaign   323
The Suicide Club   333

Chapter 9.   A LAST EXERCISE IN DELUSION   348
Two Balkan wars   348
Balance or concert?   361

Chapter 10.   WAR: A QUESTION OF INTEREST OR MORAL
    OBLIGATION?   376
A minor irritation   376
A decent reticence   386
'Fight . . . against this incipient madness'   403
'Let every man look into his own heart . . .'   415

SELECT BIBLIOGRAPHY OF PRINTED SOURCES   421

INDEX   435

O passi graviora dabit deus his quoque finem

for Cis, Anthony and Fiona

Preface

Usually more concerned about domestic problems than the conduct of foreign affairs, Radicals and their allies, even those for whom questions of war and peace were their primary concern, rarely offered coherent and never constant criticism of the Liberal Government's foreign policy and the related problems of military and naval disarmament. If 'Peace, Retrenchment and Reform' was a common cry, when Radicals pursued their particular 'crusade' of the moment they paid little attention to the equally earnest efforts of their neighbours. Thus, small groups of Radical politicians—'The Trouble Makers', as A. J. P. Taylor has felicitously described them—were as often in opposition to one another as to the Government they 'supported'. Undoubtedly this added much to 'the rich pattern of dissent', but it immeasurably increased my difficulties in attempting to write the story of their campaigns before the 1914 war.

Dissent does not make for a comfortable life in politics. The dissenter knows instinctively what is right and what is wrong. He assumes that what is morally wrong can never be politically right. His moral indignation is readily summoned, and though this may illuminate some evils with startling clarity, it can thrust others deep into the shadows. The conscience of dissent has always been the product of paradox and tension, of the uneasy coupling of emotion and rationality that has often manifested itself in the belief that pious exhortations or earnest avowals of faith are the necessary and sufficient answer to complex political problems. The dissenting conscience in politics has never readily accepted that moral frontiers seldom match the boundaries of party political programmes. It is as well to remember that when Radicals addressed themselves to the faithful they garbed all with the dignity of conscience and eschewed vulgar notions of conjecture or prejudice. Theirs was not a point of view but an apocalyptic celebration, a triumphant affirmation of revealed truth.

As a beginner in this craft I have tried to follow Bacon's maxim that it is better to excite the judgment briefly rather than inform tediously. This has meant, on occasion, dismissing in perfunctory manner a number of important and attractive themes that if pursued would have blurred the outlines of my story. I hope that at some later date I may return to treat them with the detail they deserve. Wherever possible, I have allowed the Radicals and their friends to speak for themselves. I hope that what is thus lost in clarity—for they often contradicted one another—is more than compensated by the gain in veracity. One of the disappointments in writing this book has been the comparatively few references to foreign policy in the private papers of Radical politicians. Therefore I have been obliged to rely, more than I would have wished, on their public rather than their private confidences. The speeches they made, the questions they asked in Parliament; the articles and books they wrote; the reports of their activities in the Radical press, these have been the major sources of this book.

I could not have completed this work without the generous aid and comfort of many people. I am pleased to have the opportunity to acknowledge the particular debt of gratitude I owe Dr A. J. Dorey whose own researches were both an aid and inspiration in the writing of this book. My friends, David Evans, John Griffith and Cameron Hazlehurst, bore without complaint the burden of reading most of the chapters in their earliest form. Their kindly criticisms and suggestions have, I am sure, added much that is of value to this book while saving me from many errors I otherwise would have made. Likewise, Stephen Koss and Howard Weinroth, afforded me much valued and valuable advice and help with sections of the book. My colleagues of the Government Department of the London School of Economics generously encouraged me in this project, and I am particularly indebted to Richard Greaves and Maurice Cranston.

For their patience, courtesy and help in answering my frequent requests for information on source materials, I wish to thank the staff of the British Library of Political and Economic Science, particularly Mr C. G. Allen and Miss Deirdre McKellar; the staff of the University Library, Warwick, particularly Mr John Pemberton; the staff of the British Museum Library, the National Newspaper Library and the Public Record Office; Mr D. G. Vaisey of the Bodleian Library; Dr William Mitchell of the University Library, Newcastle-upon-Tyne; Dr G. Chandler of the Liverpool City

Libraries; Mr Edward Milligan of the Library of the Religious Society of Friends; and Mr Donald Groome of the National Peace Council. Also, Mrs Helen Bowen Pease, Miss G. M. Cross, Mrs Pauline Dower, Miss Ann Holt, Mrs Penelope Massingham, Sir Felix Brunner, Viscount Harcourt and Mr S. S. Wilson.

I am obliged to the editors of *History* and the *Journal of Modern History* for allowing me to use material previously published in their journals.

Mrs Linda Snowden, with patience and good humour, 'translated' my drafts into the final typescript—a feat of imagination as well as of endurance, for which I am most grateful.

The greatest debt of gratitude I owe to my wife and children. For three years they have suffered, without undue complaint, the threat of our house being submerged under a mountain of old newspapers and books. For their patience and fortitude, their understanding, help and constant encouragement, I dedicate this book to them with my love.

A.J.A.M.

Leamington Spa
August 1971

Prologue

Themes

The Boer War was a catalyst of policy and power, of principle and personality within Liberal ranks. Its outbreak laid bare divisions that had long tormented the party. Its course, aided by Chamberlain's logical extension of his imperialistic principles to attack the ancient shibboleth of Liberalism, free trade, eventually bound the disparate elements in a loose and mutually suspicious yet electorally successful coalition that brought triumph and a decade of power. The Boer War reforged the bonds between Radicals and Labour when it seemed they were about to part and 'turned the tables of morality' upon the imperialists who until then had enjoyed the best of the moral argument with their opponents. Now they found 'the mine-owners of the Rand tied securely to their coat-tails'.[1]

Liberalism owned its critics of imperialism before the war began, but they were a small and curiously hesitant coterie compared with those who unquestioningly supported an idea long purged of its former derogatory interpretation with its connotations of despotism and the unbridled spirit of military adventure. The example of Louis Napoleon's Empire, which the Liberals had held up to the public as an awful warning twenty years before, had long been forgotten. For a few a term of partisan abuse, for most men imperialism was a gospel that had captured their sentiment and allegiance.

The most influential of the early critics of imperialism, John Atkinson Hobson, in two articles in the *Contemporary Review* for 1898, had attacked the notion that British trade profited from an extension of British control.[2] Trade, despite the avowals of the expansionists, did not follow the flag but the price list. Hobson

[1] A. J. P. Taylor, *The Trouble Makers* (1957), 98.
[2] *Contemporary Review*, lxxiv, July and Dec. 1898, 176ff, and 833ff.

rejuvenated the old Cobdenite tradition by showing that the biggest increase in exchange of goods was not, as had been widely supposed, between Britain and her colonies, but between Britain and her European industrial competitors. If this was so, then why insist on colonies at all? Nine years earlier Hobson had formulated his theory of underconsumption. Though a product of Marxist thought, Hobson's remedy was different in degree and method if not in principle from that of Marx. The capitalist, said Hobson, in seeking to invest his profits abroad became an imperialist, as it were, despite himself! Militancy and expansion were the direct result of the existence of social evils at home. Therefore, reform and social progress was incompatible with imperialism.

The theorist having spoken it was the turn of the politician. In January 1899 John Morley, addressing his constituents at Brechin, informed them that he could 'not any longer take an active and responsible part in the formal counsels of the heads of the Liberal party'. Liberalism had reached the dividing line. 'You may call it Jingoism, you may call it Imperialism.' He was willing to recognise that there was a favourable way of interpreting imperialism as 'national duty, not national vain glory . . . the guardianship and guidance of a great State'. But that was not what 'Imperialism is in the sense in which it is now used'. Imperialists acquiesced in the prospect of militarism and gigantic expenditure on armaments that must inevitably lead to war. *The Times* stigmatised Morley for clinging to outdated ideals: 'while the world has not stood still . . . Nations . . . have learned that wealth and progress, like all other good things, have to be guarded by strong hands and stout hearts.'[1]

There followed a protracted discussion, pursued in articles, pamphlets and speeches, as to what exactly imperialism was that did not abate until submerged in the sharper polemical altercation aroused by the outbreak of the Boer War. The arguments canvassed by the enemies of imperialism followed divergent lines. There were those, like Morley and Leonard Courtney, who upbraided the reckless desire for expansion and were disgusted by the braggadocio and bombast of much imperialist sentiment. Others, like Hobson and Greenwood, warned against the creatures of capitalism. For all his noble talk, it was greed that motivated the imperialist.[2] These critics added to the 'commercial interest' the 'service interest'. Thus, they identified the enemy as 'the commercial aristocracy and rich middle class' who now stood to take that place once occupied by

[1] *The Times*, 18 Jan. 1899.
[2] See F. Greenwood, *Nineteenth Century*, lxv, April 1899, 538ff.

feudalism and the landlord system.[1] This indictment was most fully
developed by the Radical, Robert Wallace. He claimed that the
Liberal party had become dependent on 'a thousand firms, financiers,
adventurers and company promoters who seized on every new
market'.[2] Unlike Campbell-Bannerman, Wallace did not wish to
distinguish between so-called *bastard* and *legitimate* imperialism.
The Liberal leader had seized upon this dichotomy as the best available means of countenancing what Morley had said, while avoiding
an overt rift in the Liberal ranks. Wallace was not to be denied.
Imperialism of whatever genre meant 'despotism abroad and more
aristocratic recrudescence at home'.

The debate was no less heated within the parliamentary Liberal
party than outside. As war with South Africa drew nearer, divisions
of opinion widened and animosities were exacerbated. But the
manner in which war was finally declared, initially frustrated a
large section of the party's anti-imperialist lobby. The ultimatum
issued by President Kruger on 9 October followed two days later by
attack, made the Boers appear to be the aggressors. In the circumstances, to suggest that the war was the responsibility of the British
Government, or worse of pecuniary interests countenanced by them,
looked like being unpatriotic and striking an unfair blow at national
morale. And the maintenance of morale was soon put at a high
premium. Any initial optimism about the success of British arms
was dampened by a series of stinging reversals culminating in
December with Black Week.

The divisions and hesitations within the Liberal ranks reflected a
problem of national conscience. To add to the confusion, the language
of debate was muddled and imprecise, if only because the concept of
imperialism now bore a variety of interpretations and evaluations
that had accrued to it. In the Commons, the loudest protests against
the war came from the Welsh and Irish members. Their arguments
were untrammelled by subtleties or niceties in distinguishing between
a false, arrogant, materialistic imperialism, and a true imperialism
allied to common sense, good government and peace.[3] Their arguments were brutal, straightforward, anti-Jewish, anti-capitalist and
often xenophobic.

The agonies of the Liberal conscience played out on a public stage
were not suffered to anything like the same degree within Socialist
ranks. At the turn of the century the causal connection that Hobson

[1] See *Contemporary Review*, lxxvi, Aug. 1899, 172ff.
[2] See *ibid.*, lxxv June, 1899, 782ff.
[3] See, for example, W. T. Stead in his *Review of Reviews*, xx, 329 and 554;
and xxi, 441–9.

had established between capitalism and militant expansion did not attract a significant following among Britain's Socialists.[1] There was a certain unconscious ambivalence in their words on this as on many another issue. But to the end of the first decade of the new century, imperialism did not enjoy an important place in their political vocabulary.[2] The Fabians for their part were more reserved and perplexed than the more Radical sections of British labour.[3] Shaw was convinced that to serve the interests of the workers Britain ought to embrace imperialism.[4] Fred Madison and Burns blamed everything on a handful of German Jews.[5] The Independent Labour party published a pamphlet entitled *Imperialism* which with typical insularity contradicted Marx. The truth was it had been written with an eye more to the approaching elections than as a guide for a moral or economic crusade by the party.[6] Britain's Socialists, as ever, were acting in character.

The simple accident of time released the nascent Labour party from the trammels of tradition that underlay the divisions within Liberalism's ranks. The younger, more pragmatic element in the Liberal leadership—Rosebery, Haldane, Grey and Asquith—in varying degrees favoured imperialism because their eyes were turned not to the past but the future. Why, they asked themselves, should they be impeded by memories of Gladstone's doubts, or the Quaker intransigence of Bright, or the uncompromising isolationism of Cobden? Often enough in the past Rosebery had pronounced their diagnosis of what ailed Liberalism. The party

> 'had become all legs and wings, a daddy long-legs fluttering among a thousand flames: it had to be consumed in order that

[1] The term *Socialist* must be employed with reservation, and particularly in the case of the parliamentary Labour party: see J. Ramsay MacDonald, *The Socialist Movement* (1911), 235. 'The Labour party is not Socialist. It is a union of socialist and trade-union bodies for immediate political work. . . . But it is the only political form which evolutionary socialism can take in a country with the political traditions and methods of Great Britain. Under British conditions, a socialist party is the last not the first form, of the socialist movement in politics.' Compare his comments in *Socialism: Critical and Constructive* (1921), 61–2 and particularly on the Fabians.
[2] See, for example, the review of Hobson's *Imperialism: a study*, in *The Labour Record*, i, no. 11, p. 327; cf. 'Socialist Imperialism' in *New Age*, 27 June 1907, p. 137. The confusion of attitude among Socialists towards imperialism was not helped by a predominantly Tory press as confused as those they sought to criticise. See, for example, *The Standard*, 15 Oct. 1907: 'Mr Bernard Shaw has a better conception of Imperialism . . . but the Fabian view on Empire is that of Karl Marx re-expressed, with the approval of all the Socialist leaders, by Mr Quelch.'
[3] See Beatrice Webb, *Our Partnership* (1948), 190–4.
[4] G. B. Shaw, *Fabianism and the Empire* (1900).
[5] See Madison in *North American Review*, clxx, 523; Burns, *Hansard*, IV: 80:783.
[6] *Imperialism* (1900), I.L.P. pamphlet, no 3.

something more sane, more consistent, and more coherent could take its place . . . it cannot gain victories as a mad mob of dervishes each waving his own flag and howling curses on everyone else's . . . Poor Liberal Party, what a plight it is in . . . for the last thirty years it has leaned absolutely on Mr G. It has been like a man who has been accustomed to get about with a crutch only, and when that crutch is withdrawn, helplessness and hopelessness ensued.[1]

'Away with the old party gods', was the cry of the pretenders to the Liberal leadership. The future seemed to beckon towards a more balanced, independent and constructive view of the role of Empire. Theirs was the rational attitude, and as such implied a critical approach that could reject the chronic, continuous and authoritative nature of an unfortunate tradition. Not only this; their arguments seemed countenanced by the prevailing mood of society. It was in harmony with the nation's beliefs, assumptions and enthusiasm.

Opposed to this thinking stood the older leadership of the party—Harcourt, Morley and Bryce—their philosophy impregnated with and coruscated by atavism. Their ethical judgments of men and issues were made with an air of conscious superiority. They more naturally divined their future course by turning their eyes to the past exemplars of the Liberal faith. They were older men with older ways who viewed themselves as the undoubted heirs of Liberalism and as the trustees of its tried and sacred traditions. Where traditions are trammelled, passions are aroused that drive out reason, and selfishness promotes misrepresentation and the caricaturing of ideas, thus emphasising differences. Imperialism became 'a war cry better calculated to rally one half of the Liberal party against the other than to carry dismay amongst the followers of Lord Salisbury and Mr Chamberlain'.[2]

Nor were the Radicals[3] immune to this split that sundered the Liberal body to which they were so loosely attached. The constant

---

[1] Quoted Robert Rhodes James, *Rosebery* (1964), 386 and 405.
[2] *Edinburgh Review*, cxcv, Jan. 1902, 256.
[3] There is an inescapable ambivalence in the use of the term Radical in that it is a negative description suggesting an attitude of mind rather than indicating attachment to particular limited policies. I have employed the term *Radical* throughout in a generic sense that is not intended to imply any constancy or homogeneity of aims in either domestic or foreign policy by a fixed group of parliamentarians. Individuals described themselves as Radicals, and groupings of such men were constantly forming and reforming in the pursuit of different aims. For the purposes of this book, and for simplification, the term Radical may be taken as implying an anti-imperialist, subscribing to the ideals of universal disarmament, friendly relations with all countries, open diplomacy and the settlement of international disputes by arbitration. A number of Radicals were pacifists, though the majority more by sentiment than conviction.

pressures of seeking an identity of purpose amid such wild and eclectic disparity, exaggerated the dichotomy in their thinking more than in any other group. They were torn between the competing claims of an optimism rooted in their trust in the infinite capacity of human nature to improve, their belief in the ever-imminent Radical millennium, and the counter-attractions of a political tradition that a selective memory invested with virtues and wisdom it had never actually possessed. As Bright had looked back to Fox, the Radicals now wistfully recalled Gladstone's governments, conveniently forgetting the occupation of Egypt and the annexation of Uganda, the threats of war with Russia and the launching of the Spencer naval programme. They honoured the whole host of Liberalism's traditional tribal gods from Fox to Gladstone. Each they summoned in turn to play both prophet for future actions enjoined and justification for attitudes presently indulged in.

As to the Boer War, Radicals were agreed it was wrong. Morley had stated their case in imperishable words. 'Such a war will bring you no glory. It will bring you no profit but mischief, and it will be wrong. . . . You may send the price of Mr Rhodes' Chartereds up to a point beyond the dreams of avarice. Yet even then it will be wrong.' If the war was wrong, then surely it was logical for them to desire a Boer victory? The Irish members had no doubts on this matter. For them Black Week was a triumph to be applauded. But they found no support for this among the Radicals. Imputations of any deficiency of patriotism always touched a sore point in the Radical make-up. It was not Boer victories in the field at the expense of British arms that they sought. Even Lloyd George and his little band of associates who valiantly braved the hysterical excesses of a nation—the greater part of which confused patriotism with imperialism—and who for their pains were dubbed 'pro-Boers', neither deserved this title, nor ever wished for England's military humiliation. They avoided the decisive issue of conscience by claiming the war was unnecessary. There had been no need to go to war at all; the essential points at issue could better have been achieved by negotiation. Thus they resolved all in one stroke. Their patriotism remained untarnished, and the solution they offered enjoyed the imprimatur of prescriptive respectability. This after all, was the course Fox had chosen in the wars with revolutionary France.

So the Liberals publicly wrestled with their consciences. Painful and ponderous attempts to bridge the gulf between the rival factions, such as the Reform Club Concordat of July 1901, were swiftly and lightly broken. In 1898 the nominal leadership of the Liberals in the

Commons was taken from a disillusioned Harcourt by Campbell-Bannerman. It was the new leader who somewhat surprisingly provided, if not the formula for permanent reunification, at least time to allow self-inflicted wounds to heal. Campbell-Bannerman until that moment could never have been accused of displaying undue political acumen. In a major speech he accused the Government of employing 'methods of barbarism' in South Africa. The importance of this speech was that it changed the whole direction of argument away from what had caused the war to the manner in which it was being fought. At one stroke he allowed the kindling of moral fervour within the divided ranks of his party, while avoiding the awkward political problem that had been tearing them apart. What is more, he made sure that Liberalism would be the residuary legatee at a future election, when the populace grew disenchanted with the muddled and prolonged ending of a war which discredited both the principles and adherents of imperialism. With the Peace of Vereeniging the Liberals were some way towards reunification. But the balm that best soothed their wounds was that peace brought politics back to the old well-tried domestic issues where the Unionists could be guaranteed to save the Liberals from themselves.

Though the Radicals could find some measure of comfort in the final outcome of the Boer War, with at least its partial vindication of the censures they had raised against the militant spirit of imperialism, the massive increases in armament expenditure occasioned by that struggle gave a fresh and anxious impetus to their campaign for disarmament. Radical attitudes towards the problems of disarmament should not be viewed in isolation from the other cardinal tenets of their faith. They certainly never saw it as an isolated issue themselves, though there was a considerable degree of difference attached by different groups to the common cry that 'policy and armaments are interdependent'. For the more moderate element it meant no more than that any assessment of Britain's military and naval requirements should always be calculated against the existing relations of Britain with other Powers.[1] But the majority of Radicals believed that it was Britain's aggressive policies that in the first place had promoted the need for large armaments. Hence any government claiming to advocate the pursuit of peace should automatically reduce its armaments.

[1] See, *inter alia*, speech of Campbell-Bannerman, *Hansard*, iv:129:494–5; J. F. Green, 'Peace and foreign policy', *Concord*, xxiv, no. 12, Dec. 1908, 140–2; paper read by Francis Hirst to the Manchester Statistical Society in December 1911, 'The policy and finance of modern armaments: with special reference to Anglo-German rivalry' (1912).

Radical views on disarmament were widely disseminated and are well illustrated by the Cobden Club's publication, *The Burden of Armaments: a plea for retrenchment*.[1] This book was prepared by a committee, among whose members were Shaw-Lefevre as chairman, Algernon West, Francis Hirst, G. H. Perris and Murray Macdonald. Rather less than half the book was given to a review of the period covered by Cobden's pamphlet *The Three Panics*, and the period of economy and remissions of taxation which lasted from 1863 until 1884. There followed a more detailed examination of the period ending 1904–05. From 1884, it was claimed, a change of policy for the worse had begun. The public mind, inflamed by pictures of national danger and the 'always latent fear and suspicion of the foreigner', was played upon with fatal success. Copious tables of statistics in the appendices underlined 'the increasingly rapid plunge into wild extravagance despite the protests of the wider and more far-sighted', among whom Randolph Churchill was particularly favoured. His retirement had 'permanently weakened the cause of economy and strengthened the hands of the professionals in the great spending departments'. The 'increased expenditure in 1885 had the result predicted by those who advised moderation, of inducing a large increase in the naval expenditure of France'. So the vicious circle was completed and the game of beggar-my-neighbour given fresh impetus. In twenty years naval expenditure had quadrupled, 'from $10\frac{1}{2}$ millions to 42 millions, an increase of 25 millions in the last ten years, and by nearly 15 millions in the last five years'. Of such was made the kingdom of the imperialist scaremonger and the naval 'expert'. The Army vote revealed an equally prodigal expenditure, and to what end? 'This enormous increase in our aggregate armaments burden, from nearly £28,000,000 in 1884 to ver £76,000,000 in 1904, has not added substantially to the weight and authority of England in the councils of the nations.'

As might be expected, the book, after bewailing its long catalogue of woe, ends on a note of optimism.

> Events of the greatest importance have occurred in the past five years which in our view, make it far less necessary for this country to maintain its armed forces at a point ready for instant war, and absolutely safe to return to the peace establishment at which they stood immediately before the late war. The first of these is the agreement which has been so happily arrived at with France. . . . The second is the war between Russia and Japan . . . which must, by its exhausting effects, make it difficult, if not impossible, for Russia to embark on another great war for some

[1] Published 1905; quotations are taken from pp. 126, 209–12 and Appendix VII.

time to come. The third is the establishment of the Permanent International Tribunal at the Hague, and the conclusion of arbitration treaties between this country and nearly all the other Great Powers of the world.

Given these changed conditions, it was surely not too audacious to call for 'a return to the standard of strength and numbers, and consequently of expenditure, which was thought amply sufficient six years ago, immediately before the war in South Africa'. Summarising their arguments, the authors then made a confession of faith.

> It has been well said that the military and naval expenditure of a country must be determined mainly by its foreign policy. If that policy is ambitious and Imperialist . . . it is very necessary to back it up with an adequate armed force . . . [but] if a policy of peace is pursued, if there is no craving for expansion, if there is consideration and respect for the rights of other nationalities, if there is a willingness to refer matters in dispute with other Powers to arbitration, there can be no reason for maintaining gigantic armaments on a war footing.

This classical statement of the Radical attitude to disarmament was to be constantly repeated, without modification, in the Commons and the Radical Press up to the outbreak of war in 1914.

The intricacies of the day-to-day conduct of foreign affairs had little attraction for the majority of Liberal and Radical members of the Commons. Their constant preoccupation was with domestic questions. Despite the sinister growth in armaments, there had been unbroken peace for more than thirty years between the Great Powers of Western Europe. There was a widespread, cheerful if illusory, hope that the world would very soon abandon war for arbitration as the means of adjudicating and settling international disputes.[1]

Radical criticism of the manner in which foreign affairs was conducted had been crystallised in a Commons debate initiated by Henry Richard as long ago as March 1886.[2] Richard's motion was an expression of the dissatisfaction felt by backbenchers at their inability to reverse or even affect Government policy because party organisation and the claims of party loyalty had so strengthened the Cabinet's hand. Richard's motion was lost by a mere six votes. Gladstone castigated his unruly backbenchers for their unwonted interference in matters which were not their concern. The motion was impracticable because it sought to bestow what was an executive function upon the legislature. The question of legislative control of

[1] See David Lloyd George, *War Memoirs* (1934), i, 1–2.
[2] For debate, see *Hansard*, iii:33:1386ff.

foreign policy was soon to be submerged in the violent battle between Home-Rulers and Anti-Home-Rulers. For the next twenty years the Unionist party dominated Parliament so that a change of tactics was called for by the Radicals: 'a public campaign of criticism which could be advanced by direct challenges within the existing pattern of Parliamentary debates'.[1] In the period before the Liberal electoral triumph of 1906, Radical criticism concentrated on substantive rather than procedural issues. Radical concern to improve backbench effectiveness was always greater when the party, to which they at least owed nominal allegiance, was in power. Only then could they hope directly to influence policy. However, by the working of some strange political alchemy, during the last years of Balfour's Administration it appeared that the Tories were adopting Radical policies in foreign affairs.

The Radicals abhorred all foreign entanglements. Yet, in a less than perfect world they were prepared to admit that they disliked most of all the thought of joining the Triple Alliance of Germany and Austria. Germany conjured up memories of Bismarck, the enemy of European Liberalism. Austria-Hungary was still remembered as the enemy of Italian unification. On sentimental grounds, if Britain had to be involved in an alliance with anyone, then the best choice was France. There was considerable pro-French sympathy among that body of Radicals who had laboured long and hard to discount the idea that France was Britain's natural enemy. This had been no easy task when the bulk of French and English politicians had viewed the international claims of their several countries with overt and mutual hostility. Radicals, like Randal Cremer, had kept communications open between the countries through correspondence and meetings with members of the French Republican party. They were convinced that an open rupture of relations with France was inconceivable. When on 8 April 1904 the Anglo-French agreement was signed, many Radicals were convinced that the formal mending of relations between the two countries was the climax of *their* campaign, for it was 'difficult to credit a Government whose loudest ideals are conquest and retaliation with a conscious effort towards pacific reconstruction on the largest scale'.[2] The agreement was seen as the triumph of the principles of the peace party over the doubters who unfortunately were not confined within the Unionist ranks alone. 'The peace party was right, and certain pseudo-Liberal statesmen whom the programme of peace frightened more than that of war

[1] Peter Richards, *Parliament and Foreign Affairs* (1967), 22.
[2] *Concord*, xx, no. 4, April 1904, p. 51.

were wrong . . . a world settlement with our most important neighbour was perfectly practicable.'[1] If there was cause for regret it was 'that the Treaty was not concluded by a Liberal Government, a regret which will, however, be alleviated by the knowledge that it is after all only the flower of the historic policy of Liberalism'.[2] The *Morning Post* might regret 'this desperate hurry to make friends with someone',[3] and Rosebery might represent it as 'a humiliation inflicted upon Britain by a one-sided agreement'.[4] But, it was *The Speaker* that echoed the greater part of Radical opinion when it stated: 'We entirely demur to the view that we ought to wince and smart over every acquisition of France, even if this acquisition costs us nothing. It is to the good and not the harm of mankind . . . and for that we rejoice.'[5] Above all, the glory of the Anglo-French agreement was that it was

> unlike the treaties by which the great wars of the past have been closed; it is not like the arbitrary arrangements of power and territory that have occasionally been made by councils of autocratic rulers. It is a compact between the representatives of two democratic states made after a prolonged period of peace without any immediate decisive pressure from without.[6]

It is tempting to assume, with the fashionable cynicism of our own disillusioned age, that moral unctuousness was the hallmark of the Radicals in their criticism of the conduct of foreign affairs. But Radicalism at the opening of the twentieth century was still contained within a greater Liberalism that had not yet abandoned its pretensions to being the sole guardian of the eternal and absolute principle of liberty. Dissent was principled, for the Radicals were children of their age, an age that was both idealist and cynical but never disillusioned. They were enthusiastic, gullible, righteously indignant and surprised when the actions of politicians did not correspond with their words. But above all else, they possessed an unshakeable optimism which was rooted in their simple faith in the good sense of the common man. They believed that it was within their power to change the ends of governments and the tempers of men so that a sense of the iniquity of war would be brought home to each individual. They were convinced that they could create a passion for the pacific settlement of disputes so that all men might dwell together in a brotherhood of nations of the world. Their noble

---

[1] *Ibid.*, p. 52.   [2] *Daily News*, 9 April 1904.
[3] *Morning Post*, 15 April 1904.
[4] Speech by Rosebery at Queen's Hall, 10 June 1905.
[5] *The Speaker*, 16 April 1904.   [6] *Concord, supra*, p. 51.

optimism led them to suppose that, with the formation of a Government led by a Radical Prime Minister, peace might at last become a political actuality.

Never had the omens of success seemed better. Radical policies enjoyed publicists and apologists of the finest literary distinction. It was a period unrivalled in the history of Radical journalism, embracing as it did the diverse talents of men like A. G. Gardiner, H. W. Massingham, Hobhouse, Brailsford, Hirst and a galaxy of other lesser literary luminaries. In the columns of great dailies, the *Manchester Guardian* and the *Daily News*; in journals like *The Speaker* soon to become *The Nation, The Economist*, and a plethora of quarterlies and monthlies, a wide platform was afforded dissenting opinion. There their nostrums and solutions to Britain's problems, both at home and abroad, were dealt with persistently and profoundly.

Though the voice of Radicalism was broadcast widely and loudly, it was always the voice of disagreement that echoed what were the unpopular views of a minority. It was a self-conscious voice that often neither appreciated the true significance nor the limitations of its contribution to political debate. It was not that its declaimers were by nature perverse, but they had the unhappy disposition to suppose a mass audience prepared to accept the universalisation of the Radicals' own moral precepts. Always they clung to their principles with an unflinching tenacity and blind conviction. They cared deeply and unselfishly, and from that care sprang the claim, constantly made, that their voice spoke for a larger, more influential body of opinion than in fact it did.

Because in all political solutions they sought demonstrable moral justification on their own terms, they showed a lack of balance in their appreciation of the size and significance of the actions they censured. They were the victims of an overweening conscience. At a time when opinion was already losing its short-won day in the national Press, when its intrinsic value was fast depreciating, they attempted to bring the self-conscious pietism of the Radical confessional to judge in public the verisimilitude and dissimulation of the conduct of the nation's affairs. They spoke to the committed and alienated the uncommitted, whom they never understood or tried to understand.[1] They deprecated the changes in the methods of journalism, yet they did not envy the success of their opponents, they despised it.[2] They were noble but in the end ineffectual critics.

[1] See, G. P. Gooch, *Life of Lord Courtney* (1920) 501, n.l.
[2] See, *inter alia, The Nation*, 20 July 1907, 'The Worst Journalism'; a series

Beginnings

It was apparent to informed spectators that the days of the Unionist Government were numbered from the first announcement by Chamberlain, in May 1903, of his support of Imperial Union and tariff reform. Perhaps not all Liberals were as immediately sanguine in their appreciation of the significance of this sudden new departure in English politics as Asquith who, on first reading the news excitedly informed his wife, 'It is only a question of time when we shall sweep this country.'[1] A new interest in their personal political fortunes now quickened the Liberal ranks. Even Campbell-Bannerman, who at one point in 1903 for health reasons had contemplated, should the Liberals come in, a post of dignity rather than power, found his flagging enthusiasm for supreme office revived when it became apparent from by-election results there was scarce a safe Unionist seat left in the country.[2]

In the earliest days of 1905, Liberal leaders were urgently discussing the possible structure of a Liberal Administration. Deep differences hardened by the Boer War continued to afflict the leadership, and the best that efforts to effect a reconciliation had achieved was merely to thrust the differences below the surface for the moment. The very leadership of a future Liberal Government was problematical. Spencer, Liberal leader in the House of Lords since 1902, felt that he had a claim to be Prime Minister as of right. His candidature was to be resolved by a timely cerebral seizure. Then there was Rosebery, the last Liberal Prime Minister, whose claims were canvassed by some while he disclaimed the position for himself saying that it was his wish that Asquith should be Premier.[3] Campbell-Bannerman's claim to the title might well have been the most obvious, but he was subject to the misgivings and censures of dangerous and powerful critics within the party. Such confusion, as Edmund Gosse confided to his diary, beggared description. 'It is

---

of articles in *The Nation*, beginning 18 July 1908, dealing with the 'Harmsworth Brand'; Hilaire Belloc, *English Review*, Mar. 1909; cf. Caroline Playne, *The Pre-War Mind in Britain* (1928), 116–17.
[1] Margot Asquith, *Autobiography* (1936), ii, 53.
[2] Thirty seats changed hands at by-elections in the period 1900–05. During the same period 17 M.P.s changed their party allegiance; 11 Unionists took the Liberal whip, including W. S. Churchill. The Unionists altogether lost 25 seats, 20 of these to the Liberals. On two occasions in the Commons, Campbell-Bannerman inquired whether a Government should continue in office in the face of such a massive rejection by the electorate. See *Hansard*, iv:141:123ff and iv: 150:70ff. Leaders of both parties discounted the by-election results in calculating a possible general election result.
[3] See Marquess of Crewe, *Lord Rosebery* (1930), ii, 585–7.

the old quarrelsome leaders who constitute the great difficulty.'[1]
Haldane, at the time, proffered an amusing solution to the problem,
yet six months later in concert with Asquith and Grey he conspired
with some purpose to resolve the issue to suit their own ends.

At the beginning of September 1905, meeting at *Relugas*, Grey's
fishing lodge in the Highlands of Scotland, the three conspirators
concluded a pact that if Campbell-Bannerman did not take a peerage
and leave the leadership of the Commons to Asquith, then they in
turn would refuse to serve under him. Spencer did not enter into
their calculations though he had not been disabled then by illness.
There were two reasons for the so-called Relugas Compact. The
first, and of lesser importance, was that Campbell-Bannerman's
leadership of the Opposition had not been such as to suggest that he
would make an effective Prime Minister. In this not unnatural
mistake, the conspirators' expectations were to be proved wrong.[2]
The second, and major reason, emerges clearly from the letter
Haldane was deputed to write to Knollys, King Edward's Private
Secretary, apprising him of their decision.

> During the South African War he [Campbell-Bannerman] took
> the line that the group represented by Rosebery outside the
> House of Commons and by Asquith and Grey inside did not
> represent the mind of his party, and that he must look to his
> majority as thinking differently. Now we have never admitted
> that this was a sound judgment. The majority of his Liberals in
> the House of Commons are sensible enough though they have
> often been weak and acquiescent. And, as far as we can estimate
> the situation, if . . . the Liberal Party has a majority in the next
> election a very large part of that majority will be in heart with
> us, though it may be timid in the presence of the Liberal
> leaders. . . . It is not from any desire for personal success that
> any of us wish to propose to Sir H. C-B the tenure of these
> offices,[3] as a condition of our joining hands with him, but we
> have a strong feeling that without them we should have no
> sufficient basis from which to exercise real influence in the work
> of the reform of the Liberal party.[4]

The Compact was designed to ensure that the voice of any future

[1] Entry for 13 Feb. 1905, quoted in Dudley Sommer, *Haldane of Cloan* (1960), 143.
This was not unlike the remark made by the Liberal candidate, Dr Hutchinson,
at the Rye by-election. When asked, 'Who is your leader?', he replied, 'For
God's sake don't talk about leaders.'
[2] Compare J. A. Spender, *Life of Rt. Hon. Sir Henry Campbell-Bannerman*
(1924), ii, 404–5: 'There never was a more miraculous change in the form of a
public man than from Campbell-Bannerman as leader of the Opposition to
Campbell-Bannerman as Prime Minister.'
[3] The offices suggested were the Woolsack for Haldane, the Exchequer for
Asquith and the Foreign Office for Edward Grey.
[4] Haldane to Knollys, 12 Sept. 1905, quoted Sommer, 145–6.

Liberal Government should be imperialist rather than Radical in tone.

The King was still at Marienbad when Haldane's letter was received, so that Knollys's reply, written on 16 September, was on his own behalf. He was a little critical of the 'all or nothing' nature of the venture.

> A Cabinet of which Sir H. C-B was the head without the moderates, would, it appears to me, be disastrous both for the country and the Party. The Government would be a weak one, which would probably lead it to adopt very radical measures, possibly to interrupt the continuity of the Foreign policy of the present and former Governments. . . . Of course, what the King would desire would be the presence of a restraining influence in the Cabinet . . . and this could only be effected by the presence in it of men like yourself, Asquith and Sir E. Grey.[1]

Haldane was not the kind of man to be deterred by gentle advice. His mind at least was quite made up.[2] He saw no blemish in the pact which might be described, not unfairly, as political blackmail. His advice to Asquith in a letter on 27 September was that he should see Campbell-Bannerman at the earliest opportunity. Meanwhile, a visit to Balmoral to meet the King was arranged for Haldane in early October. There, to the enormous gratification of Haldane, the seal of royal approval was given to the course of action proposed by the conspirators. Later Haldane was to recall leaving 'the Castle with the feeling that there was no more for me to do, and that the next step must be taken by Asquith when he saw C-B'.[3]

Asquith was unable to implement Haldane's advice until 13 November, when he presented himself at 29 Belgrave Square within hours of Campbell-Bannerman returning from his continental cure. There was an exchange of opinions on Russia and Germany. Asquith noted with satisfaction that Campbell-Bannerman's views on Germany were sound. 'He dislikes the Kaiser and thinks him a dangerous, restless, mischief-making man.' Discussion then turned to the composition of a future Liberal Government. Asquith advertised the claim of Haldane for the Woolsack without success, and more favourably, that of Grey for the Foreign Office. Until that moment

---

[1] Knollys to Haldane, 16 Sept. 1905, quoted Sommer, 147.
[2] Certainly he was more sure than Grey, as is apparent from the ill-ordered letter written by the latter to Asquith on 6 October. See Roy Jenkins, *Asquith* (1964), 146.
[3] R. B. Haldane, *An Autobiography* (1929), 161. The King shared the Liberal imperialist view that Radical policies would be weak, internationalist and philanthropic. Therefore, he agreed to take an active part in executing the compact. See George Monger, *The End of Isolation* (1963), 257–8, nn. 1 and 4; cf. Stephen E. Koss, *Lord Haldane, Scapegoat for Liberalism* (1969), 33.

it seemed that Campbell-Bannerman 'had never before realised how urgently Grey was needed at the Foreign Office'. His own candidate had been Elgin.[1] The subject of the Relugas Compact was never directly broached by Asquith, though Campbell-Bannerman revealed not a little knowledge of what had been going on behind his back. He told Asquith, 'I hear that it has been suggested by that ingenious person Richard Burdon Haldane, that I should go to the House of Lords, a place for which I have neither liking, training nor ambition.' This observation afforded little comfort to Asquith. It was obvious that any move by Sir Henry to the Lords would be made reluctantly and with repugnance.[2]

A few days later, Asquith together with Grey met Campbell-Bannerman to discuss not personalities but policy, and in particular the question of Ireland. At this meeting a compromise approach to Home Rule was worked out to which Campbell-Bannerman gave expression in a speech at Stirling on 23 November. He claimed that it was his wish to see 'the effective management of Irish affairs in the hands of a representative Irish authority'.

Rosebery at the time was engaged on a speaking tour of Cornwall for the Liberal League. He mused upon the true significance of C-B's words, and deciding they indicated a step backward to the 1892 position, on 25 November rehearsed to a wildly enthusiastic audience at Bodmin his objections to what he termed 'this hoisting of the flag of Irish Home Rule'.

> I object to it mainly for this reason: that it impairs the unity of the Free Trade Party, and that it indefinitely postpones legislation on social and educational reform on which the country has set its heart. I will, then, add no more on this subject except to say emphatically and explicitly and once and for all that I cannot serve under that banner.[3]

Rosebery's speech caused acute embarrassment to the Liberals. Most men assumed that Rosebery had spoken not for himself alone but for Grey and Asquith, Fowler and Haldane, his Liberal League Vice-Presidents. Rosebery did not know that Campbell-Bannerman's speech was a carefully prepared statement of a compromise policy worked out in consultation not only with the Irish Party but with

[1] When Morley suggested that Elgin might go to the Foreign Office rather than Grey, Spender commented: 'Speaking as a journalist the double task of explaining why Grey was not appointed and of inventing Elgin from the beginning would break my back and I should not attempt it'. See W. Harris, *J. A. Spender* (1946), 74.
[2] A full account of the conversation, from which the quotations are taken, is in Margot Asquith, ii, 55ff.
[3] Quoted, Rhodes James, 454.

Grey and Asquith as well.[1] Rosebery's eagerness to mark his separation from Campbell-Bannerman had but painfully established that the loyalty once owed him by Grey and Asquith was now a thing of the past. It was he that was isolated from his former acolytes.

From young Henry Paulton, Rosebery heard the bad news that far from being enthusiastic about his speech Asquith and Haldane considered it a 'positive disaster'. Yet worse, Grey repudiated Rosebery's interpretation of Campbell-Bannerman's words, in public by a speech at Newcastle and in private by an uncharacteristically acid letter. Reduced for the moment to savage and despairing temper, Rosebery denounced Grey and Asquith in unmeasured terms.[2] Their personal friendships were not permanently sundered, but Rosebery's maladroit and illtimed performance at Bodmin had once and for all broken the overt political effectiveness of the Liberal League. Nor need Campbell-Bannerman have felt displeased by the final outcome of these events. In October he had written to Herbert Gladstone wondering exactly what game Rosebery was playing. 'Is the great man with us or against us?' he had inquired. Now Rosebery had revealed his hand and done for himself.[3]

Liberal leaders were aware that Balfour's brilliant dialectic obsequies could not much longer delay the inevitable demise of his administration. Yet some chose this moment to show hesitation. If Balfour resigned, would it be wise to come in before a dissolution?[4] But Campbell-Bannerman resisted supported by Ripon and Morley, and the others gave way.

Balfour tendered to the King his resignation as Prime Minister and that of his Cabinet colleagues on 4 December 1905. It had been Balfour's decision to resign despite pressures from all sides advising him to seek dissolution. Whatever determined the actual timing of his decision, Balfour was aware both of the loudly advertised rift in the Liberal party caused by Rosebery's monumental indiscretion, and also of the advantage this might afford the waning Unionist cause.[5]

By 1 December the majority of the Liberal leadership were aware that Balfour was determined on resigning after the weekend. Cables were despatched to summon Campbell-Bannerman, and he arrived

[1] See Sir Sydney Lee, *King Edward the Seventh* (1925–27), ii, 441.
[2] See Sir Charles Mallet, *Herbert Gladstone: a memoir* (1932), 200.
[3] See Rhodes James, 453.
[4] See Jenkins, 150.
[5] See *inter alia* K. Young, *Balfour* (1963), 253–4; Peter Fraser, *Joseph Chamberlain* (1966), 271ff.; J. L. Garvin, *Chamberlain* (1932–33), iii, 583; Oliver Esher and M. V. Brett, eds., *Journals and Letters of Reginald Viscount Esher* (1934–1938), hereafter cited as *E.P.*; also, Viscount Chilston, *Chief Whip*, (1961), 331.

in London a matter of hours before Balfour tendered his resignation. Early visitors to Belgrave Square were Asquith and Grey, to discuss policy in general and Ireland in particular. The three men parted amicably. Campbell-Bannerman was in high good humour that afternoon when visited by Spender bearing a missive from Rosebery. Commanded to the Palace on the morning of 5 December, Sir Henry kissed hands as Prime Minister and set to work to form his Administration.

However, his former good spirits by then had been dashed by a visit from Grey, 'all buttoned up and never undoing one button' and bluntly demanding that if he was to serve, then Campbell-Bannerman must go to the Lords. Leadership in the Commons should be given to Asquith. This strange interview surprised and wounded Campbell-Bannerman. It was not so much Grey's obvious intransigence that worried C-B, as the fact that Asquith appeared to be an active party to the ultimatum. For the moment Campbell-Bannerman refused to yield, though he could not but be aware that it would be extremely difficult, if not impossible, to construct an administration without Asquith. Campbell-Bannerman was not aware that Grey knew when he presented the ultimatum that Asquith had detached himself from the Relugas Compact and had determined to serve the Prime Minister whether he went to the Lords or not.[1]

Asquith was still prepared to bring moral pressures on his leader to try to get him to go to the Lords, but more than that he would not do.[2] As Asquith explained to Haldane, his conscience would not justify his holding out against Campbell-Bannerman. It was his duty to accept. There was also a technical loophole that allowed face-saving escape. 'The conditions are in one respect fundamentally different from those which we . . . contemplated when we talked in the Autumn. The election is before us not behind us.'[3]

The whole unedifying business of Campbell-Bannerman's position was finally resolved by his wife who insisted that there should be 'no surrender' on his staying in the Commons. Morley and Tweedmouth were the first to hear of this decision.[4] It was next morning before Asquith was told. Pale and obviously upset, yet speaking in a determined manner, Campbell-Bannerman told Asquith, 'I'm going to stick to the Commons, Asquith, so will you go and tell Grey he may

[1] Earlier that day Grey had written to Asquith: 'If you go in without me eventually I shall be quite happy outside and I shan't think the least wrong of you'. Quoted Jenkins, 153.
[2] See Margot Asquith, ii, 71, 74.
[3] Asquith to Haldane, Dec. 1905, quoted J. A. Spender and C. Asquith, *Life of Lord Oxford and Asquith* (1932), i, 174–5.
[4] See John Morley, *Recollections* (1917), ii, 142–3.

have the Foreign Office and Haldane the War Office.'[1] This information Asquith duly conveyed, by personal interview with Grey who
remained unshaken in his opposition, and by letter to Haldane.

It is interesting that Campbell-Bannerman was at this stage still
prepared to offer key Cabinet positions to Haldane and Grey, and
this despite their avowed imperialistic sympathies, not to mention
the trouble their attitude was causing him.[2] Later, Haldane was to
claim that the decision to keep himself and Grey rested upon
Campbell-Bannerman's desire to cash the imperialist section of the
Cabinet as an asset in the forthcoming elections. Had Sir Henry
been certain of an overwhelming Liberal victory, he would quite
happily have dispensed with their services.[3] Leonard Courtney had
no doubt in his mind why the Prime Minister chose as he did. C-B
was convinced 'that the Grey section was supported in the country by
men enough to cause the loss of a very appreciable number of seats
if they were not in the Government in force. . . . This alliance is
necessary for a big majority though it may weaken its force.'[4]
Others claimed that it was to avoid the damaging effect of an open
avowal of disunity within the party[5] when the main issue before the
electorate would be Free Trade. As Asquith had put it to Haldane:

> It would be said that we were at issue about Home Rule, the
> Colonies, the Empire, etc., etc., and the defection of the whole
> of our group would be regarded as conclusive evidence. The
> *tertius gaudens* at Dalmeny [Rosebery] would look on with
> complacency. I cannot imagine more disastrous conditions on
> which to fight a Free Trade election.[6]

[1] Margot Asquith, ii, 75.
[2] The claims of Grey and Haldane for office were different. C-B privately
disliked Haldane whom he derisively nicknamed Schopenhauer, and from the
first was determined to frustrate Haldane's ambition to get the Woolsack.
Campbell-Bannerman's offer of the War Office might well have been two-
edged in intent. That position had been the grave of more than one parliamentary reputation in recent years. On the other hand, Campbell-Bannerman
liked Grey. What is more, to fill the Foreign Office satisfactorily without Grey
would have been an exceedingly difficult task. If Grey was left out of consideration, C-B's two possible candidates for the post were Elgin and Cromer.
The former Spender considered 'impossible'; the latter had neither active
experience of British politics nor was he even a member of the Liberal Party.
Given the material available, the only practicable alternative to Grey would
seem to have been Crewe, whom Asquith suggested when writing to C-B,
7 Dec. 1905, unaware that by then the difficulties with Grey were resolved.
[3] See Sir Almeric Fitzroy, *Memoirs* (1927), i, 289. Herbert Gladstone was
quite prepared as the price of electoral victory to see C-B banished to the Upper
House so long as Grey, Asquith and Haldane were in the Cabinet. See A. G.
Gardiner in *The Nation*, 4 June 1921.
[4] Gooch, *Courtney*, 505–6; cf. R. C. K. Ensor, *England 1870–1914* (1936), 384;
and S. Maccoby, *English Radicalism 1886–1914* (1953), 394.
[5] Grey to Munro Ferguson, 8 Dec. 1905, quoted, G. M. Trevelyan, *Grey of
Fallodon* (1937), 101.
[6] Asquith and Spender, i, 175.

Any Radical would have considered this argument more than a little disingenuous. They championed Free Trade not on economic grounds alone but because it taught the sovereign truth of the interdependence of nations. Imperialism and Protection, after all, were both plants of a common poisoned stock. Therefore, to them it was no mere coincidence that Chamberlain was both the main architect of the Boer War, and chief protagonist of commercial exclusiveness.[1]

Grey, at first the most moderate in attitude, at the last was the most implacable. Of the original triumvirate he was the least interested in office.[2] There was, too, a certain awkward inflexibility in his character.[3] In some ways Grey was not unlike Rosebery. With Asquith having capitulated unconditionally, Haldane's sense of political survival was sufficient to overcome his former reservations. Haldane, together with Arthur Acland, thoughtfully sent for by Spender to act as intermediary and pacifier general, laid siege to Grey's scruples. By the morning of 8 December Grey finally capitulated. That hurdle successfully surmounted, Campbell-Bannerman smoothly completed his Cabinet and the final list was published on 11 December. The whole farrago had lasted less than four days and had ended with Campbell-Bannerman the winner.[4]

The Government of fifty-six members with a Cabinet of twenty showed a fine balance, representing as it did all interests within the Liberal party. It was true that the Liberal imperialists had done well occupying four senior positions. But there were Crewe, Carrington, Elgin and Tweedmouth to occupy the middle ground. Ripon, Herbert Gladstone, Morley and poor Bryce, whose reward for political loyalty was that crown of thorns the Irish Secretaryship, represented the old strict Gladstonian tradition. The Radicals could claim the Prime Minister, Reid, now Lord Chancellor Loreburn, and Sinclair. There was the old man of the Left, John Burns, and the new man, Lloyd George. Birrell and Buxton made up the party. Nor was this all, for behind this reassuring phalanx of talent stood an unusual number of new men of rare ability occupying junior offices not yet

---

[1] See for example, Gooch, *Courtney*, 496. A typical formulation of this attitude is illustrated by the motion passed at the 1905 Trade Union Congress concerning Free Trade. 'A system of Preference or Retaliation by creating cause for dispute with other countries would be an hindrance to international progress and peace', *Reformers' Year Book* (1906), 104.
[2] Viscount Grey, *Twenty-Five Years: 1892–1916* (1925), i, 63–5.
[3] A fact that was noted by Arthur Acland in a letter he wrote to Asquith in 1900. 'I think that he [Grey] is a man rather to see difficulties than to help people over them.' Quoted Jenkins, 152.
[4] The Radical Quaker M.P., J. E. Ellis, noted in his diary, 11 Nov. 1905: 'List of Cabinet appointments out. A very good list, too, showing that C-B has evidently held his own—the main point' Quoted A. Tilney Bassett, *Life of John Edward Ellis, M.P.* (1914); 220; see also *E.P.*, ii, 126.

within the Cabinet; McKenna at the Treasury, Churchill at the Colonial Office, Runciman at the Local Government Board, and Samuel at the Home Office.

While Leo Maxse, the irascible, often irrational, ultra-Tory editor of the *National Review*, railed at 'the predominance of pro-Boers',[1] the King, who had sought in September 'the presence of a restraining influence in the Cabinet being aware that many members of it would be men holding extreme views', now wrote to the Prince of Wales: 'It is certainly a strong Government with considerable brain power. Let us only hope that they will work for the good of the country, and indeed, the Empire.'[2]

The majority of Liberals would have subscribed to the editorial view of the *Manchester Guardian* that this was 'not the Cabinet of any section . . . [but] the Cabinet of the Party'.[3] The incredible and erratic Radical editor, W. T. Stead, in his *Review of Reviews*, published a detailed analysis of the new Cabinet's membership. He drew attention to one important feature that many others ignored.

> The most conspicuous feature of the Cabinet is—to perpetuate a bull—the absence of Lord Rosebery. . . . Exit Lord Rosebery with the benedictions of all Liberals. He has done more for the unity of this party by deserting it than he ever did when he endeavoured to hold it together. His self-elimination being an accomplished fact, Sir Henry Campbell-Bannerman had no difficulty [*sic*!] in getting together a political team containing every conspicuous personality and representing every section of the party which recognises him as leader. . . . Taken as a whole, the Cabinet is a strong Cabinet and a good Cabinet. It is symmetrical, well balanced and very representative. It has only one centre, and that is Campbell-Bannerman.[4]

Despite Balfour's gloomy predictions, the formation of this strong Liberal Ministry brought no shudders to the chancelleries of Europe. Consols rose, and the commercial community if anything seemed relieved by the exit of the Unionist administration. The Liberals had successfully and expertly solved a thorny constitutional and political problem, avoiding an overt split between the extremes that

---

[1] *National Review*, Jan. 1906, p. 773.
[2] Quoted Philip Magnus, *King Edward the Seventh* (1964), 347.
[3] *Manchester Guardian*, 11 Dec. 1905. The *Daily News* also proclaimed its satisfaction with a strong and united Cabinet representing 'every section'; cf. Blunt's scathing comments: 'People talk of violent democratic changes. I do not believe in them. The new Cabinet is a Whig Cabinet.' W. S. Blunt *My Diaries* (1919–20), ii, 129.
[4] W. T. Stead, *The Liberal Ministry of 1906* (1906), 21 and 69. This pamphlet was a gossipy enlargement of the 'character sketch' of the Liberal administration which had appeared in the January 1906 issue of the *Review of Reviews*.

made up the party. For the Tories, there remained the now forlorn hope that differences within the Liberal ranks would once again become exacerbated during the period of the election, for the second half of the drama had yet to be played.

In politics nothing succeeds like success. Now that his leadership was unassailed, Campbell-Bannerman seemed at once to acquire the capacity to absorb easily all sections of his party, even those who had been most offended and injured by his 'methods of barbarism' speech. They, quite as eagerly as the Radicals, attended a reception given by the Prime Minister at his house in Belgrave Square.[1] 'Sir Henry', said Stead, 'commands the confidence of the Radicals . . . and is regarded with respect and a certain amount of awe by the Liberal Leaguers. . . . An honest man, a sound Liberal . . . and a deadly hater of all the crimes of the Jingo.'[2] The Radicals delightedly acclaimed Campbell-Bannerman as their own. With such a man at the helm confidence and trust could be placed in the administration. However, there was still some hesitancy in trusting the Liberal imperialists who seemed to enjoy a disproportionate share of Cabinet places. Haldane in particular attracted concern, but Radicals were 'not without hope that the force of events . . . [would] soon compel him to abjure his heresies and support the democratic policies of his chief'.[3]

Sir Edward Grey's name did not attract that obloquy that was so often the unfortunate lot of Haldane. There was not for Grey the enthusiasm that greeted the news of Morley's or Loreburn's appointment. Yet few Radicals, even among those who later were to criticise and vilify Grey, would not have agreed with Stead's estimate.

> He is a much better Liberal than might be inferred from the company he has been keeping for the last ten years. . . . He is regarded as a safe man with a 'judgmatical' head on him. . . . There is a Jingo strain in him, but . . . [it] is well tempered by common sense and the Ten Commandments. In foreign politics he will say ditto to Lord Lansdowne. . . . His policy will be as like that of his predecessor as two peas. . . . We may take it for granted that he will do nothing to pander to the German phobes, and we trust that when the Second Hague Conference meets he may be not less zealous than was Lord Salisbury to use that international parliament for the purpose of securing and consolidating international peace.[4]

Though it was generally agreed that Protection would be the major issue at the forthcoming election, many men were interested in the

---

[1] See Francis Hirst, *In the Golden Days* (1947), 256.   [2] Stead, p. 17.
[3] *Concord*, xxii, no. 1, Jan. 1906, p. 4.   [4] Stead, pp. 27–8.

line the Liberals would adopt in their conduct of foreign affairs. Could they be trusted as a 'safe proposition'? Sir Edward Grey's presence afforded assurance that they could be. His very appearance and manner inspired the confidence of his contemporaries.[1] He was 'the strong silent man whom the generation brought up on Carlyle earnestly sought'.[2]

Almost two months before his appointment as Foreign Secretary, Grey had made an important speech in the City which had achieved a twofold effect. First, it checked a movement among a considerable section of the Press who were claiming that a Liberal Government would revert to a policy of splendid isolation. Second, it put to rest any fears that Cambon, the French Ambassador in London, might have had that the Anglo-French understanding would be weakened. He complacently informed Rouvier that the Liberals were adopting a reassuring line. It was assumed that Grey's speech was a statement of official Liberal policy.[3] In the course of a broad survey, Grey had said:

> I observe in some quarters that there is being industriously circulated an idea that a change of Government in this country would bring some new and welcome change in foreign policy . . . In my opinion there is no foundation whatever for such a suspicion. There are three cardinal features at the present moment of British policy, not one of which does the Liberal party wish to see changed. The first is the growing friendship and good feeling between ourselves and the United States. . . .

[1] See, for example, *Annual Register* (1905), 221. There had been some dismay felt at the Foreign Office at the prospect of a Liberal Government. Mallet in particular was apprehensive, and in October 1905 told Bertie, when they were considering a successor for Sanderson, that it was overwhelmingly important they should appoint someone 'who will keep the Liberals straight'. Mallet very much approved of Grey, considering him 'quite sound' and 'the right man' for Foreign Secretary; see Monger, 257, nn. 1–3. According to Margot Asquith's account: 'The Foreign Office adore Edward Grey, and were in a state of trembling anxiety lest he should stand out' (*Autobiography*, ii, 63).

[2] Lloyd George, i, 56. From a reading of his speeches it is very difficult to understand the extent of Grey's appeal. As early as May 1906, after Grey's speech on Vivian's Disarmament motion, Massingham writing in *The Speaker*, 12 May 1906, declared: 'Sir Edward Grey is one of the four or five men who have at once attained a position of great authority in the New House of Commons. I suppose those who read the speech may not quite realise this force of magnetism which is exercised without any effort, with no recourse to familiar arts of speech, but is rather a pure effect of personality.' See also A. G. Gardiner, *Prophets, Priests and Kings* (1913), 72–3: 'Sir Edward Grey is intrinsically the weightiest speaker of his time. When he sits down in the House of Commons it is as though discussion has ceased. . . . He does not argue; he delivers a judgment. There is no appeal, and no one asks for an appeal.'

[3] It was in fact a personal statement by Grey, which is of particular interest as it expresses opinions formulated while still in Opposition and before contact with Foreign Office advisers; see Trevelyan, 89–92.

Another . . . the alliance between Great Britain and Japan. . . .
Another . . . our French Agreement.

On the improvement of Anglo-German relations, he was quite
specific. Any such improvement depended upon 'the relations of
Germany with France on all matters . . . under the French Agreement . . . [being] fair and good also.' He concluded by re-emphasising

> the need for continuity in foreign policy. There is an impression
> in some quarters that free Government owing to the changes of
> party cannot have the same trustworthy and reliable foreign
> policy as autocratic governments. I believe that to be wrong—
> as regards ourselves, certainly wrong.[1]

Spender's *Westminster Gazette,* regarded both at home and abroad as
the most authoritative expression of Liberalism in the British Press,
at Grey's request, forcefully reiterated the points he had made.
There would be 'no more doubts about the continuity of policy
when the Liberals succeeded the Unionist administration, and should
anyone have needed reassuring on that point Sir Edward Grey's
speech should be final'.[2]

On 21 December 1905, his Government now safely formed,
Campbell-Bannerman, in a speech at the Albert Hall, unfolded his
programme as the curtain-raiser to the general election. It was
bolder in spirit and more comprehensive than many critics had
anticipated. Though the greater part of the speech was concerned
with domestic issues, the Radicals, delighted with the declaration
on foreign affairs, dubbed it the 'League of Peace Speech'. It was
considered a happy augury of things to come, the beginning of a new
epoch, with 'the Babylon of Toryism fallen and all the graven
images of her gods broken to the ground'.[3] Radicals had sought a
disclaimer of the assertions, sadly even made by Liberal candidates
at the recent by-elections, that foreign policy was a subject outside
politics. They could not have been more vigorously opposed to this
attitude.[4] In fact, Campbell-Bannerman had emphatically affirmed

[1] Grey was the only Liberal imperialist who took the notion of 'continuity'
of policy really seriously, though Haldane had spoken of it in his letters to
Knollys, 12 and 19 Sept. 1905, cited above. The tradition of 'continuity' in
foreign policy was supposedly to place the interests of country above the
narrow considerations of party advantage. However, this comfortable dogma
rested on the assumption that there was little difference in attitude between
the parties on questions of foreign policy. While this was by and large true of
the Unionists and the Liberal imperialists, a wide ethical gulf divided them
from the Radical and Labour members.
[2] See Grey to Spender, 19 Oct. 1905, cited Zara S. Steiner, *The Foreign Office
and Foreign Policy, 1898–1914* (1969), 94, n. 2, and 190; and *Westminster
Gazette,* 19 Oct. 1905.
[3] *Concord,* xxii, no. 1, Jan. 1906, p. 3.
[4] *Ibid.,* xxiii, no. 11, Nov. 1907, pp. 109–10.

his adhesion to the policy of the *entente cordiale* with France, and added that he 'saw no cause whatever of estrangement in any of the interests of Germany and Britain because of this'. But, it was the high moral tone Campbell-Bannerman adopted in his forecast of Britain's future rôle that particularly appealed.

> As to our general policy towards our neighbours . . . it will remain the same in Government as it was in opposition. It will be opposed to aggression and adventure, it will be animated by a desire to be on the best terms with all nationalities and to cooperate with them in the common work of civilisation. . . . I rejoice that . . . the principle of arbitration has made great strides, and that today it is no longer counted weakness for any of the Great Powers of the world to submit those issues which would once have been referred to the arbitrement of self-assertion and of passion to a higher tribunal. Ah! but ladies and gentlemen . . . it is vain to seek peace if you do not also ensue it. I hold that the growth of armaments is a great danger to the peace of the world. A policy of large armaments keeps alive and stimulates and feeds the belief that force is the best, if not the only policy that tends to inflame old sores and to create new sores. And I submit to you that as the principle of peaceful arbitration gains ground it becomes one of the highest tasks of a statesman to adjust those armaments to the newer and happier condition of things. What nobler rôle could this great country assume than at the fitting moment to place itself at the head of a league of peace, through whose instrumentality this great work could be effected.

No statement could better have been designed to appeal to Radical sentiment. As Radicals saw it, the speech underlined those differences that they had always emphasised between a Liberal and a Tory view of international relations. There would be no more appeals to the material forces of offence and defence, to the Sophist doctrine of the strong man armed. There would be an end to the ruinous competition in armaments as a pledge of Britain's peaceful intent. At last, a Prime Minister was prepared to base his appeal upon conscience and reason.

To the great mass of the electorate, and for most Liberal candidates, foreign affairs was a background issue in the din of electoral battle that ended 1905. In the forefront stood domestic affairs and particularly the question of Free Trade. The Liberal programme was largely a negative rejection of tariff reform. Those few candidates who chose to mention foreign affairs in their election addresses did so in the most general terms. Most eschewed any reference to the entente with France. While Radical candidates gave some prominence to the burden of armament expenditure and expressed the hope that a new era of peace among men of all nations was about to dawn, the general cry was retrenchment and reform. The wounds inflicted by ten years of Jingo imperialism had to be healed. The first task for men of conscience was an attack upon the mountain of neglected domestic issues.

Estimates by Liberal and Unionist pundits of the probable result of the general election proved grossly incorrect.[1] The final unprecedented Liberal majority was ascribed by contemporaries to a variety of reasons—a reaction against the South African War; the campaign against Chinese 'slave' labour in the Transvaal mines; the disunity of the Tories; the 1902 Education Act; Chamberlain's attack on the sacred principles of Free Trade; Balfour's mistakes as the Tory leader; and a host of other like causes and excuses. Many Radicals sought the explanation in Campbell-Bannerman's personality and record. Ponsonby wrote later: 'There is no doubt that C-B —the man who weathered the storm and stood unflinchingly for his principles in times when it was most difficult to proclaim them— was largely responsible for the tremendous turnover of votes.'[2] However, the facts do not allow this romantic interpretation.

The electorate had increased by 7·9 per cent since 1900, yet the Unionist vote *increased* by 36·3 per cent. The combined Liberal and Labour vote increased by 189·2 per cent. The most startling increase was that of the Labour vote, more than 500 per cent. These figures argue for the operation of a more fundamental agency than the appeal of party programmes, Government records or personalities. In fact, the 1906 election saw for the first time the proper organisation of the mass electorate. The election continued for a fortnight. The early massive successes of the Liberals in the boroughs, which to some extent had been anticipated, were repeated to a lesser extent in the county districts which traditionally were Unionist strongholds. The resultant House of Commons saw the Unionists reduced to a not inconsiderable rump of 157 members temporarily bereft of their leader. The Liberals with 401 members had an absolute majority over all the other parties combined.[3]

This was the most democratic, inexperienced, radical, non-conformist Commons that had yet sat at Westminster. The Government's back benches, suffocatingly crowded, bore the electoral flotsam of

---

[1] For a number of differing contemporary estimates see *The Speaker*, 6 Jan. 1906, *The Times*, 13 Jan. 1906, *Daily Mail*, 27 Dec. 1905; cf. W. T. Stead, who in the June issue of his *Review of Reviews*, p. 573, claimed that the Liberals would enjoy their biggest majority since 1832.
[2] Hirst, *In the Golden Days*, 258.
[3] For a contemporary analysis of the membership of the Commons, see *The Times*, 15 Feb. 1906.

the Radical tidal wave that had helped to sweep the Liberals to power. Here were harboured the champions of a multitude of causes ranging from the normal, philanthropic and religious, to the unusual, forlorn and downright eccentric. So much enthusiasm, so much inexperience, could not help but produce and spread an apocalyptic spirit, and an impatient desire to make all things anew.[1]

Among so much that was new and strange, the most singular feature of the 1906 Parliament could well have been claimed for the success of the Labour party. F. W. Pethick Lawrence in the preface to his *Reformers' Year Book, 1907* wrote: 'Labour [in general sense] increased its numbers from 14 to 49 and in the place of but four Independents a solid section of 30 men pledged to support neither of the historic parties obtained places in the new House of Commons.'[2] Even so, Keir Hardie's dream of a combination of Labour and Irish members holding the balance of power and thus dictating, or at the least influencing Government policy, could not be realised in the face of the massive Liberal majority.[3] The most that could be claimed was that now the Government occupied a central position where it would be the target of sniping from both extremes of the political spectrum.

The exaggerated character of much of Labour's 'politicking', with its emphasis on street-corner propaganda and the loud, frequent and unwarranted advertisements of success and influence, was not guaranteed to engender much support and even less to promote credence for their policies among their potential sympathisers and allies on the Government's back benches. Rather, they were often an embarrassment to their Radical allies.[4] In addition, the simmering

[1] This spirit was not much in evidence in the private comments of the Liberal leaders. See, for example, C-B's remark to Esher that, 'Criticism in opposition is one thing; accomplished fact is another', *E.P.* ii, 128; cf. W. E. Foster's comment: 'Before the Queen made me a Cabinet Minister I was much more of a Radical. After that I did what I could and not what I would.'

[2] Balfour, the defeated Tory leader, took a very gloomy view of the significance of Radical and Labour electoral successes. He wrote: 'C-B is a mere cork dancing on a torrent which he cannot control, and what is going on here is a faint echo of the same movement which has produced massacres in St Petersburg, riots in Vienna and Socialist processions in Berlin.' Blanche Dugdale, *Arthur James Balfour* (1936), i, 335.

[3] *The Times*, 9 Jan. 1906, in an article, 'The working classes and the election', had been concerned at the prospect of a sufficient number of Labour members being returned so as to put that group in the same blancing position formerly enjoyed by the Irish. Ramsay MacDonald had taken a different view from that of Keir Hardie. He maintained that the Liberal majority was to Labour's advantage. It freed them from all the demoralising influences of political compromise enabling them to pursue their own line firmly and frankly without being cajoled by moderate reformers into compliance with half-measures for fear of allowing reactionaries into power—an anticipation of the Radical's dilemma. The situation allowed a distinct Labour point of view to be promoted in the House. See *Labour Record*, i, no. 12, Feb. 1906, p. 369.

[4] See H. W. Massingham, *The Speaker*, 10 Mar. 1906.

internecine conflicts between the cabals that nominally owed allegiance to Labour, were publicised in the differences of emphasis and the solutions offered to various problems in the canon of Socialist works. Thus, from the first, the rôle of Labour's new members was reduced to that of political gadfly. Their individual eccentricities of dress, habit and speech, their ability 'to rub shoulders' with the other members of the Commons, drew more attention and concern, all too often resolved in patronising comment, than any passionate avowal of political faith.[1] In any event, the stamina of Labour members was all but absorbed by domestic problems which were always their primary concern. Little energy was left for the consideration of questions of foreign policy save the occasional flourish of outraged conscience by an individual member. Not that it could be said at this time there was any single, cohesive Labour policy on foreign questions. The internationalism of Socialism prompted some to a spirited and belligerent attitude which rejected non-intervention as 'the natural policy of a Cobdenite Radical who believes the only object of diplomacy is the promotion of trade'. The majority of Labour members 'had no real constructive foreign policy but shared the views which were traditional in Radical circles'. The only safe generalisation that can be made is that their thinking was very simple and expressed in undifferentiated terms. They were all temperamentally unsympathetic towards the traditional objects of British foreign policy.[2]

[1] See, for example, C. T. King, *The Asquith Parliament* (1910), 68ff. How soon the Labour parliamentary party's bubble of revolutionary pretension was dissolved, is apparent from C. F. G. Masterman's comment at the end of the second parliamentary session of the new Government. He wrote in *The Nation*, 24 Aug. 1907: 'Here were no wild revolutionists, harbingers of an uprising of the lower orders, determined to break up the recognised courtesies and hypocrisies of England's benevolent plutocracy. Instead there was discovered a mixture of old-fashioned Trades Unionists with a sprinkling of well behaved and pleasant Socialists . . . the occasional violent speeches of their left wing were received with a pleasant toleration, harder to combat than open contempt.' Militant Socialists were soon to regret this lack of fervour by Labour members of Parliament; see *New Age*, 1 Aug. 1907, p. 209; cf. Cunninghame Graham's remarks to W. S. Blunt, 'When Labour members get into Parliament they are at once bitten with the absurd idea that they are no longer working men, but statesmen, and they try to behave as such. I tell them . . . that they would do more good if they came to the House in a body drunk and tumbling about the floor.' Blunt, ii, 205.
[2] See *New Age*, 9 May 1907, p. 17; and C. R. Attlee, *The Labour Party in Perspective* (1937), 200.

Chapter 1   Forging The Ententes: 1905–07

Sir Edward Grey

When Grey was appointed Foreign Secretary his most convinced supporters were aware that he was subject to divided loyalties. Only a strongly developed sense of political responsibility overcame his desire to retreat from politics altogether—a desire that grew rather than diminished in intensity throughout the period he held office. Critics and friends alike agreed on the man's patent honesty and sincerity. He seemed to have 'inherited something of Gladstone's moral earnestness'.[1] Yet this apparent paragon of selfless virtue was not always as open in his communication with his Cabinet colleagues as was at the time supposed.

Grey's appointment had almost coincided with the beginning of a thorough reorganisation of the Foreign Office aimed at developing responsibility and initiative among the staff, and promoting the devolution of tasks. 'During these formative years of transition . . . Sir Edward Grey was supported by a team of lieutenants whose merits were happily combined.'[2] This happy combination of merits was to become one of the chief counts in the indictment made against Grey in later years by his Radical critics. They were to argue that the Foreign Secretary too often deferred to the judgments of his permanent officials.[3] It is true that Grey was tolerant of opposition,[4]

[1] A. J. P. Taylor, *The Struggle for Mastery in Europe* (1954), 436.
[2] Alwyn Parker, quoted G. M. Trevelyan, *Grey of Fallodon* (1937), 168. On the reorganisation of the Foreign Office, see, *inter alia*, D. Collins, *Aspects of British Foreign Policy, 1904–1919* (1965), chap. II; Zara S. Steiner, *The Foreign Office and Foreign Policy, 1898–1914* (1969), chap. II.
[3] See, for example, Conwell-Evans, *Foreign Policy from a Back Bench* (1932), 47. 'Sir Edward Grey's ignorance of Germany and of foreign countries in general caused him to lean heavily on the officials, and to share their defects, notably their disastrous inability to appreciate the constitutional and peace forces in Germany.' See also Arthur Ponsonby's comment cited by Steiner, 84. 'He trusts the opinions of his permanent officials more than his own judgment, and is therefore capable of making rather serious mistakes.'
[4] See, *inter alia*, Algernon Law, cited Trevelyan, 168; also, Lord Hardinge of Penshurst, *Old Diplomacy* (1947), 192.

but he was never a 'cipher minister directed by his officials'.[1] Grey was happy to seek the advice of his professional advisers, but from the beginning decisions were his own. He 'had a high Whig notion of the position he occupied as the political chief, and he laid it down that —"I do not regard anything except my own letters and official papers as deciding policy" '.[2]

Charles Hardinge, the newly appointed Permanent Under Secretary at the Foreign Office, was the key figure among Grey's advisers in the early years. He was older and more experienced than Grey, but the two men worked amicably together. Hardinge was always loyal to his chief. The time Grey spent in the Commons, the ever increasing volume of his work, meant that his officials were forced to take a more important and active rôle than had their predecessors. Under the new reorganised system, Hardinge became the channel through which almost all the business of the Foreign Secretary flowed. Hardinge, like his master,[3] was committed to stand by France and to find means to contain German power. So from the beginning both men acted on the assumption that it was Germany that presented the major threat to European peace. In their minds Germany's rôle on the European scene was inflexibly cast.[4]

Within the Cabinet Grey enjoyed great independence and freedom of decision. This was strengthened rather than weakened by the ill-patched alliance of imperialists and Radicals within the Liberal party. The 'Limps' held three key ministries. Radical opinion was suspicious of the 'composite character of the Cabinet that suggests in the privacy of many minds . . . if the Imperialists will not fall into line with the overwhelming majority, the sooner they are shed the better'.[5] Morley might have proved an embarrassment to Grey, but he was too engrossed in himself and Asiatic affairs to

---

[1] Steiner, 86.

[2] Trevelyan, 169; see also Steiner, 121; and *E.P.*, ii, 346.

[3] Grey recalls in his Memoirs (*Twenty-five Years*, ii, 43–5), that he left the Foreign Office in 1895, 'full of discontent and apprehensions feeling that we were dependent on Germany and yet had not Germany's good will'. He returned in 1905, 'with a fixed resolve not to lose the one friendship we had made'. Grey also admits (i, 35) that when he re-entered office after a break of more than a decade he was 'much too hard pressed by current work to have leisure to look up old papers and read the records in the Foreign Office of what had been done while I was in Opposition'. Therefore his view of Germany and the Triple Alliance remained what it had been in 1895—i.e. that a policy of friendship with the Triple Alliance would be 'not altogether comfortable' for Britain (see i, 9).

[4] See Hardinge to Grey, 20 Feb. 1906, and his Memorandum, 30 Oct. 1906, quoted Steiner, 94: 'It is generally recognised that Germany is the one disturbing factor owing to her ambitious schemes for a *Weltpolitik* and for a naval as well as a military supremacy in Europe.'

[5] *Concord*, xxi, no. 12, Dec. 1905, p. 170.

appreciate the true significance of European diplomatic stratagems.[1] The rest of the Radicals hastened to bury themselves in the urgent domestic demands of their departments. In truth they took little interest in foreign affairs,[2] and were never encouraged to do otherwise. Lloyd George's account of how the Cabinet dealt with foreign policy in these years is somewhat jaundiced but it has an important core of truth.

> There was in the Cabinet the air of 'hush hush' about every allusion to our relations with France, Russia and Germany. Direct questions were always answered with civility, but were not encouraged. We were made to feel that, in these matters, we were too young in the priesthood to presume to enter into the sanctuary reserved for the elect. So we confined our inquisitiveness and our counsel to the more mundane affairs in which we had taken part in Opposition during the whole of our political careers. Discussions, if they could be called discussions, on foreign affairs, were confined to the elder statesmen who had seen service in some previous ministerial existence. . . . We were hardly qualified to express an opinion . . . for we were not privileged to know any more of the essential facts than those which the ordinary newspaper reader could gather from the perusal of his morning journal.[3]

---

[1] See the survey of foreign policy made by Morley in the Commons, 20 July 1906, *Hansard*, iv:161:571. 'We are no longer concerned in dynastic quarrels in Europe, nor even with territorial divisions in Europe. We see the transformation of our policy into an Asiatic policy.'

[2] See, Irene Cooper Willis, *How We Went into War: a study of Liberal idealism* (n.d.), iii–iv. 'The upbringing and tradition of Liberals must be remembered. Coming in the main from non-conformist element of society, they had been brought up upon humanitarian principles and taught to writhe at the mention of cruelty and oppression. Their political attitude, springing as it has sprung, from a religious attitude, has tended to be one in which wishes are mistaken for horses and beliefs take the place of realities. This has been particularly noticeable in the average Liberal's semi-indifference to foreign policy in the pre-war period. That indifference was to a great extent temperamental and not altogether due to the overwhelming needs of social reform in which he was immersed. The conception of conflict between nations, on which foreign policy was based, was distasteful to him; he had no wish to acknowledge it. He was internationally minded; he believed in concord between nations, and so ardently that he did not question overmuch whether concord between nations actually existed. . . . Few Liberals were students of foreign politics. . . . The Conservatives were much better informed, but in such matters they have always been ahead of the Liberals.' See also Gilbert Murray, *The Foreign Policy of Sir Edward Grey, 1906–15* (1915), 41–3.

Indifference to the conduct of foreign affairs was not confined to the rank and file members of the Liberal Party. Some ministers, even when they were sent information, seemed to exhibit an extraordinary lack of interest. See, for example, the strange anecdote retailed by Grey in his Memoirs, ii, 260. Also J. Tilley and S. Gaselee, *The Foreign Office* (1933), 137–8; and W. F. A. Rattigan, *Diversions of a Diplomat* (1924), 30–1.

[3] Lloyd George, *War Memoirs* (1934), i, 28; see also, Augustine Birrell, *Things Past Redress* (1937), 225–6. Such discussion of foreign affairs that there was, usually was hastened over to grapple with domestic problems. For an example

Radicals reassured themselves that all must be well with the conduct of foreign affairs as long as Campbell-Bannerman was Prime
Minister. They expected him to keep a watchful eye on the Foreign
Secretary. However, it was unrealistic to cast the Prime Minister for
this part. He had never been closely connected with questions of
foreign policy. He subscribed to the general assumptions and philosophy of Radicalism; he was concerned with the evil influence of
certain sections of the Press who seemed intent on worsening Britain's
relations with Germany. He suspected that certain elements even
within his own party supported war as an instrument of policy. But,
as he concluded somewhat lamely in a letter addressed to Bryce just
before taking office, 'These sort of people do not reckon with the
financial state of our country and the unpopularity of war. . . . The
thing in fact is madness, but it exists.'[1]

Grey was convinced that his was the most important rôle in
determining the direction Britain's foreign policy should take. He
believed that the Prime Minister was in this no more than an equal.[2]
Grey's view of his primacy in these matters, explains in part his
reluctance to outline his opinions to his Cabinet colleagues. Add to
this his knowledge that many ministers did not share his views, and
we may more readily understand why he did not seek to spell out
his policy in the Cabinet. Grey knew that even his close friend and
ally, Haldane, did not share all his assumptions, and in particular
those on the nature, real or imagined, of the German threat and the
best manner to combat it.

Two other factors enhanced Grey's independence: the first not his
doing; the second, the direct result of his own actions. The Cabinet
in 1906 was, according to Haldane, 'like a meeting of delegates. It
consisted of a too large body of members, of whom two or three had
the gift of engrossing its attention for their own business. The result
of this and the want of system which it produced was that business
was not always properly discussed, and the general point of view that
vitally required clear definition almost never.' Campbell-Bannerman
did not have the capacity to control discussion. The Government
lived, 'too much from hand to mouth, dependent for . . . [its]
achievements on the initiative, not of the body as a whole, but of
individual members. There ought to have been much more systematic

---

of this, see, Lucien Wolf, *Life of the First Marquess of Ripon* (1921), ii, 294.
Compare this with Grey's assertions, ii, 259–60; and also Asquith's in his
The Genesis of the War (1923), 2–4.
[1] Campbell-Bannerman to Bryce, 31 Oct. 1905, quoted Monger, 261.
[2] See Grey, *Twenty Five Years*, i, 119. Also his article in the *Journal of the Royal
Institute of International Affairs*, 16 July 1930.

consultation among members. . . . Because of imperfect procedures there was insufficient team work.'[1] Grey writing to Ripon in July 1906, observed that 'Foreign policy has been little discussed in the Cabinet'.[2] He might have added that this was in no small part due to himself. The very day he wrote to Ripon, a Foreign Office memorandum provided that the confidential print be rearranged into two classes of special and general interest. The former was to go only to the departments immediately concerned. On Grey's instructions, important despatches were sent usually to Campbell-Bannerman and Ripon, but rarely to anyone else.[3] It is clear that Grey repeatedly sought to exclude information from the Radical members of the Cabinet who otherwise might well have questioned the line he was adopting.[4]

Because of the need for swift decisions, negotiations and compromise with other sovereign states, it was generally accepted that the Cabinet ought to enjoy considerable freedom and discretion. Control to a large extent depended on the determination of broad issues of principle beforehand on which it was expected the Foreign Secretary would act. But in Grey's case, when he took office his interpretation of the European situation and of the direction and temper that British policy should follow, was opposed to that of a significant section both of the Cabinet and the parliamentary Liberal party. There were two quite distinct schools of thought as to how foreign policy ought to be conducted. Grey belonged to that group who had a hardheaded conception of what constituted the national interest. The other group did not approve a forward policy in external relations, and were opposed to the idea of committing Britain to the support of any Power that as a result might involve her in European tensions. There was no secret about this. That is why there was uncertainty in all quarters as to how the Liberal Government would act. The result of the general election ensured that there would

---

[1] R. B. Haldane, *Autobiography* (1929), 217–18.
[2] Grey to Ripon, 27 July 1906, quoted Monger, 307.
[3] For a list of examples, see Monger, 307, n. 2. The Foreign Office adopted their master's strategy. It became almost common practice for them to withhold certain documents from their critics, no matter what their status. Thus, when the Government of India was proving difficult in its opposition to certain features of the proposed Anglo-Russian Agreement, Hardinge informed Nicolson: 'We have left the Government of India entirely out of our account.' When the King became difficult, Hardinge urged Nicolson to observe caution as to what he sent to him. See, on this, Monger, 292. For a general account of the confidential print, see F. Gosses, *The Management of British Foreign Policy before the First World War* (1948), 111–16.
[4] Hardinge admitted to Lascelles that he dreaded the day 'when Grey finds himself face to face with the peace at any price section of the Cabinet headed by the Lord Chancellor', quoted Monger, 297.

be the broadest ever spectrum of interest and opinion on all subjects. In foreign affairs a new element had been introduced with that group of M.P.s who were temperamentally and intellectually unsympathetic towards a conception of national interest resting upon assumptions they rejected, and executed by men who were representatives of a despised class. Their goal was distant, but it was the path of internationalism and not nationalism that they wished to follow. They had 'no selfish mercantile or capitalistic aims to hide under the sounding title of "patriotism" and unspoiled as yet by royal and aristocratic patronage, by "society" intrigue, or by the tyranny of capitalist pressure, they enjoy[ed] . . . an enormous advantage in the way of freshness of mind and detachment of view'.[1] This heady estimate of the rôle of dissenting opinion in foreign affairs unfortunately ignored the fact that before 1914 the dissenters never coordinated their criticisms. The gap between what may be characterised as 'traditionalist' and 'progressive' views on foreign policy was not formalised or comprehensively articulated until the founding of the Union of Democratic Control in September 1914, and thereafter the slow identification in men's minds of the two viewpoints with the Conservative and Labour parties respectively.[2]

France and Germany

On the first day's meeting of the new Parliament in February 1906, Chamberlain noted with pleasure that the statement on foreign affairs in the King's Speech gave the Conservatives 'confirmation of what we have learned from speeches made by Ministers, namely that in our foreign policy there will be continuity. We have nothing to do but to express satisfaction in that matter.'[3] Replying, Campbell-Bannerman said:

> It is right for the people of this country that it should be stated again and again and as emphatically as possible, that the understanding that we have with France remains as strongly entrenched as it was when it was first established, that it has no sinister purpose towards any other nation or Government and that we merely wish to find in it a means of strengthening that good and almost affectionate feeling beween France and Great Britain we are all anxious to encourage. . . . Our relations to the nation and Government of France . . . remain exactly what they were.

The words of this statement had been very carefully chosen, mindful of keeping a balance between friendship with France and good

[1] *Concord*, xxii, no. 2, Feb. 1906, p. 19; see also, January, p. 2.
[2] See, Collins, 100ff; cf. A. J. P. Taylor, *The Trouble Makers*, 96.
[3] *Hansard*, iv:152:153; Campbell-Bannerman's reply, cols. 166:167.

relations with other Powers, particularly Germany.[1] However, in part it was a false statement, and Campbell-Bannerman was one of the few people who knew of the changes that had occurred in Britain's relationship with France in the two months since the Liberal Government had been formed.

The Liberals had taken office at a time of acute international tension. In June 1905 Delcassé, author with Lansdowne of the 1904 Anglo-French Agreement, had accepted the interpretation of Cambon, the French Ambassador in London, that the entente between the two countries was in reality an alliance.[2] Delcassé had attempted to persuade the French Cabinet that England had made overtures with a view to concerted action with France against Germany. Delcassé had enjoyed seven years of virtually unlimited power at the Quai d'Orsay but, surprisingly, his suggestion was rejected by the French Prime Minister, Rouvier, who did not relish the prospect of fighting Germany when he was assured by the War Minister that France was totally unprepared. Delcassé, having vainly warned the Cabinet that their pusillanimity would only encourage German insolence, had been forced to resign.[3] For the moment, the entente seemed to founder, and Delcassé's resignation was seen as nothing less than dismissal at German pressure.[4] France now agreed that an international conference should be convened at Algeciras to handle the Moroccan problem. Undoubtedly Germany had a case for interfering in Morocco, but her bullying of France was out of all proportion to her interests. Germany's actions were specifically designed to effect a breach in the entente. In this she was unsuccessful. By the autumn the French Cabinet seemed to have recovered its nerve and the bond with Britain appeared to be as strong as it had ever been.

The Algeciras Conference was due to begin in January 1906. Meanwhile, Balfour had resigned and the Liberals had taken office.

---

[1] Quoted J. A. Spender, *Life of Sir Henry Campbell-Bannerman* (1924), ii, 258.
[2] See *Documents Diplomatiques Français* (hereafter cited as *D.D.F.*), vi, 465. Here was a classic case of the wish being father to the thought. See Delcassé's conversation with his assistant Paléologue, 1 Feb. 1904, quoted G. P. Gooch, *Studies in Diplomacy and Statecraft* (1942), 68.
[3] For a full account of the Cabinet meeting, see, *D.D.F.* vi; Annexe 1. Rumours were soon circulating in Germany that Britain had offered a defensive and offensive alliance to France and Lansdowne flatly denied this to the German Ambassador. See, *British Documents on the Origins of the War 1898–1914* (hereafter cited as *B.D.*), iii, 98. Again, in October, as the result of a story published in *Le Matin* of Britain offering France armed support, Sanderson repeated Lansdowne's disclaimer to Metternich. See, *Die Grosse Politik der Europäischen Kabinette 1871–1914*, ed. J. Lepsius, A. Mendelssohn-Bartholody, and F. Thimme (Berlin, 1922–27), (hereafter cited as *D.G.P.*), xx.ii, 6873. For Radical comment on these rumours see, *inter alia, Manchester Guardian*, 9, 13 and 14 Oct. 1905; *Daily News*, 10 and 13 Oct. 1905.
[4] See Grey, i, 71; *Manchester Guardian*, 7 June 1905.

Grey considered that the conference would be difficult, probably critical. He required Nicolson, who was to be the British delegate, to give cordial support to France under the terms of the 1904 entente. On 21 December Campbell-Bannerman publicly proclaimed his Government's adhesion to the entente. That same day, Grey told Nicolson that Britain would support France in her efforts to gain a special place in Morocco, because if France should fail, 'the prestige of the entente will suffer and its vitality will be diminished'.[1] Grey attributed the current tension in Anglo-German relations to Germany's dislike of the entente, but, 'even at the risk of sending a little shudder through a German audience' he was determined that the entente should stay.[2] Grey's recollection of the discomfiture and dangers of Britain's isolation before the signing of the entente was, 'vivid and disagreeable . . . I was determined not to slip back into the old quaking bog, but to keep on what seemed then the sounder and more wholesome ground. There was no thought in this of using our better relations with France . . . against Germany; it was hoped that relations with Germany would improve.'[3] As the old year died, to Grey the dangers of war seemed very real. On 3 January, he informed Metternich that if Germany and France went to war over Morocco then public opinion would make it impossible for the British Government to stand aside. Grey wrote to Campbell-Bannerman of this conversation, adding in the margin of his letter, 'Lansdowne I find has also said as much.' Metternich, however, was convinced that Grey had gone much further than his Tory predecessor ever had.[4]

Meanwhile, there was consternation in France that Britain's new Government might once again lapse into a policy of isolation. Cambon, who had been on leave in France, returned to London on 10 January and immediately saw Grey. He told him that 'While it was not necessary nor indeed expedient that there should be any formal alliance . . . it was of great importance that the French Government should know beforehand whether, in the event of aggression against France by Germany, Great Britain would be prepared to render France armed assistance.' Grey refused to give any binding answer, but volunteered as his personal estimate that 'if France were to be attacked by Germany . . . public opinion would be strongly moved in favour of France'.[5] Cambon then asked for

[1] *B.D.* III, 193 and 200.
[2] Grey to Lascelles, 1 Jan. 1906, quoted Monger, 268.
[3] Grey, i, 103.
[4] See *B.D.* III, 296; cf. *D.G.P.* XXI.i, 7018.
[5] Cf. Lord Loreburn, *How the War Came* (1919), 77: 'Those who remember the House of Commons elected in January 1906 . . . will by no means agree that public opinion would in 1906 have rallied to the material support of France.

unofficial communications on naval and military matters 'in case the
two countries find themselves in alliance in such a war', and Grey
agreed to this.[1]

At the time of this conversation, Liberal ministers were scattered
all over the country engaged in electioneering. Grey sent a summary
of his interview with Cambon to Campbell-Bannerman, but omitted
any reference to the military conversations. He concluded his letter:
'I assume that you will have a Cabinet directly the Elections are over
to decide what I am to say.'[2] Ripon also received a copy of this letter.
He wrote to Fitzmaurice who was Under-Secretary for Foreign
Affairs:

> Our engagements with France are, I understand, confined to a
> promise of full diplomatic support, and I have no doubt that
> the French Government understand that we are bound to
> nothing beyond that. But there are indications . . . that the
> French people and many of their public men are expecting
> support of another kind if the Conference breaks down and
> serious trouble with Germany arises. . . . I think we ought to
> decline to go further than diplomacy will reach. . . . The situa-
> tion requires great wariness, but we may trust Grey for that.[3]

Fitzmaurice enclosed Ripon's letter when he wrote to Campbell-
Bannerman on 11 January expressing his own fears that there might
well be a reaction in France when they discovered that, contrary to
their belief, Great Britain was pledged to no more than diplomatic
action. On 14 January Campbell-Bannerman replied to Grey's letter.
'We have happily a little more time for reflection as the French
Ambassador cannot expect an answer during the elections, and
things appear to be looking a little more favourable and therefore
there is less urgency.'[4]

On 11 January Grey had left London for his constituency, meeting
Haldane the next day at Berwick. There, together in a closed carriage, they had discussed the military conversations. Both men had
agreed that the Prime Minister ought to be consulted, and Haldane
undertook that task. But when Campbell-Bannerman was informed,
he proved unhappy about the possible interpretations that might be
placed on the 'communications', as is apparent from the letter he
wrote to Ripon on 2 February. 'I do not like the stress laid upon joint

---

It would have been vehemently opposed to it.' Grey's references to 'public
opinion' are strange in the mouth of a man who was very much the incarnation
of the Great Whig tradition. See Gardiner, 77: 'Sir Edward Grey is . . . the
least democratic, as he is the least demonstrative of men.'
[1] *B.D.* III, 210.   [2] Quoted Monger, 27.
[3] Quoted Wolf, ii, 292–3.   [4] Quoted Spender, ii, 252.

preparations. It comes very close to an honourable undertaking.'[1] However, his reservations were overcome, and he was persuaded 'to give his consent on the understanding that they were provisional and precautionary measures, and that the Government was not bound by their results. Thus limited, he regarded them as raising no new question of policy and therefore within the competence of the War Office.'[2]

When Grey had another interview with Cambon on 31 January, no Cabinet had been held, although Campbell-Bannerman had written ten days earlier asking Grey when he would like a Cabinet to confirm the answer he should give to the French. Cambon again asked whether France could count upon the assistance of England in the event of an attack upon her by Germany. Grey reminded the Ambassador of the military and naval conversations taking place between the two countries that now had been regularised. Since the present arrangements between the two countries were so satisfactory, Grey inquired whether it was really necessary to alter them by a formal declaration. 'To change the entente into a defensive alliance ... was a great and formal change.' The consent of the Cabinet would be required—though Grey hastened to add that he had no doubts concerning their good disposition towards such a change. Parliament would also have to be informed.[3] Grey could not have hinted more clearly to Cambon that in the circumstances France had received as much as could reasonably be expected. To ask for more at the present juncture would involve the Cabinet. That could cause difficulties. Cambon took the hint.

> Certain ministers would be surprised at the opening of official diplomatic conversations between the military services of the two countries and the joint studies which they undertake. We have, therefore, thought it better to keep quiet and to continue discreetly preparations which would place the two Governments in the position of acting quickly in concert when the need arises.[4]

Of the Cabinet's members, only Campbell-Bannerman and Ripon knew what had been said in this conversation between Grey and Cambon. Ripon was decidedly uneasy about possible implications.

---

[1] Quoted, Spender, *Campbell-Bannerman*, ii, 257.
[2] *Ibid.*, ii, 253.
[3] *B.D.* III, 219.
[4] *D.D.F.* XI.i, 106. The French military attaché, Huguet, admitted that he was not a little surprised at the readiness with which authorisation had been given for the military conversations. British ministers must have realised 'that the studies now to be pursued would—whatever the qualifications—constitute a moral engagement', see Gooch, *Studies in Diplomacy and Statecraft*, 70.

He wrote to Sir Henry: 'I am very unhappy about the result of Grey's conversation with C.'[1] He might very well have expressed concern with the manner in which Grey had conducted the affair from the beginning. It is incontestable that the Foreign Secretary had kept his colleagues in the dark because otherwise they certainly would have criticised if not opposed his actions.[2] The military conversations were a political act. They were 'the substitute for an alliance—and in some ways a more decisive one. Once the British envisaged entering a continental war, however remotely, they were bound to treat the independence of France, not the future of Morocco, as the determining factor.'[3] Campbell-Bannerman and Ripon were not blameless for this episode as Grey's biographer is quick to point out.[4] However, the abiding and significant fact was Grey's deviousness with his colleagues in pursuing the policy he desired, and his gross constitutional impropriety in not consulting them.[5]

The conference on Morocco met at Algeciras on 16 January. By February the parties had reached deadlock, primarily over the question of police organisation. At this time Grey was torn between his desire to make some concessions to Germany to avoid war, and his determination to stand by France. It was his opinion that the French should make 'a great effort and if need be some sacrifice' to placate the Germans. But if war should break out, then Britain would support France.[6] 'The entente and still more the constant and

---

[1] Ripon to Campbell-Bannerman, 1 Feb. 1906, quoted Monger, 273.
[2] See the account of Grey's conversation with Gooch, 14 Feb. 1909, in Gooch, *Studies in Diplomacy*, 105.
[3] Taylor, *The Struggle for Mastery in Europe*, 438. The Olympian detachment that Grey affected—'What they settled I never knew'—was supposedly based upon the assumption that the military talks were important at a military level only and did not prejudice Britain's diplomatic freedom. If this was Grey's view, then it reveals an extraordinary naïvety that is not evident in his general diplomatic dealings. Nor does it square with the fact that in July 1907, Grey approved a revised British plan. Compare Grey, i, 94, and J. P. Mackintosh, *The British Cabinet* (2nd edn, 1968), 336. See also, J. E. Tyler, *The British Army and the Continent: 1904–14* (1938), 165. R. C. K. Ensor's suggestion in his *England 1870–1914* (1936), 401, that Grey was motivated by fear of a leakage of information from the Cabinet, is not convincing.
[4] Trevelyan, 139.
[5] Grey's own lame excuses for his conduct (i, 86–7) are effectively dealt with by Loreburn, *How The War Came*, 80–1. Equally, Spender's defence of Campbell-Bannerman (*Campbell-Bannerman*, ii, 258) does not stand up when closely examined.
[6] Grey's constantly repeated concern about a European war breaking out as a result of French intransigence in the face of German demands, is not easy to understand in the light of contemporary evidence of the climate of French opinion. The French Chamber overthrew the Rouvier Cabinet on a question of domestic policy at a critical moment of the Algeciras conference to which they had shown a profound indifference. The General Election that followed resulted in the almost total annihilation of the party which represented bellicose patriotism. Sanderson, who had been present with Grey at the meeting with

emphatic demonstrations of affection . . . have created in France a belief that we should support her in war. . . . If this expectation is disappointed the French will never forgive us.'[1] In March, British support of France's claims hardened,[2] and in the face of such determined opposition, the Germans climbed down. The question of the police was settled in France's favour. Other lesser questions were soon resolved and the conference concluded on 17 April, Germany having suffered a major diplomatic rebuff.

Because at the last the Germans had proved conciliatory over Morocco, conditions now seemed propitious for an improvement in Anglo-German relations. However, almost immediately an incident developed at Akaba on the Turko-Egyptian frontier. This confirmed, in the minds of those who were already suspicious of Germany's true intent, that unease they had felt at the prospect of any *rapprochement* between the two countries. Even observers like Fitzmaurice and Ripon, who were comparatively sympathetic towards Germany, drew the conclusion that the Germans were playing a game that was going to cause trouble all along the line.[3] However, the crisis was swiftly resolved and the movement to improve Anglo-German relations once more gathered impetus. Even King Edward, whose dislike of his nephew was common knowledge, now sought to enjoy better personal relations with the Kaiser.[4]

Haldane was particularly active in his attempts to improve relations between Germany and Britain. He explained in his *Autobiography*:

> As a people we did not like the Germans. We neither knew their history, language or literature well, nor did even our Foreign Office know them. I had made speeches, some of them possibly indiscreet, pointing this out, and those speeches had been

---

Cambon on 10 January, had tried to restrain Grey and regarded the idea of a European war as 'preposterous'. See Elie Halévy, *Imperialism and The Rise of Labour*, 137. *The Speaker*, 17 Jan. 1906, looking at the situation through German eyes, drew the conclusion that 'the question of war may probably be dismissed. The interests of France in Morocco are established, the interests of Germany are not seriously engaged there. The situation does not, therefore, offer the makings of a war.' It is fair to add, that this was reversal of the conclusion *The Speaker* had drawn a fortnight earlier, 13 Jan. 1906.
[1] *B.D.* III, 299.
[2] *Ibid.*, II, 342, 350, 355–7. Grey's support of France at Algeciras was coloured by his determination to effect a *rapprochement* with France. He maintained that Russia would judge Britain's value as a potential partner by the support offered France at a moment of crisis. See, Trevelyan, 143–4 and 181. In fact, in Russian military circles it had the opposite effect. See Halévy, 140.
[3] See, letters of Fitzmaurice, 18 April 1906, and Ripon, 20 April 1906, quoted Monger, 297, n. 2.
[4] See Magnus, *King Edward the Seventh* (1964), 359–60.

appreciated more in Germany than here. Still I thought it my duty to try my best.[1]

In the early summer of 1906, Haldane, in his capacity as War Minister, received an invitation to attend the annual German Army manoeuvres and to inspect the organisation of their War Office. During this period Haldane had friendly conversations with Metternich and von Stumm. In June, Haldane even suggested that Grey might persuade France to show a more friendly attitude towards Germany.[2]

However, in the process of examining the assumptions that underlay his policy, Grey identified Germany as representing the major threat to a European balance of power. In a minute Grey wrote in June he declared, 'The Germans do not realise that England has always drifted or deliberately gone into opposition to any power which establishes a hegemony in Europe.'[3] When, in July, Prince Radolin, the German Ambassador in Paris, approached Bourgeois with the information that a *rapprochement* was proceeding between Germany and Britain, the French asked Grey whether this meant a change in his policy. Grey not only assured the French on this count but added, 'If we were called on to take sides, we must take sides with France as at Algeciras.'[4] This statement reflected a considerable change in the nature of the entente in the eight months since Grey had been Foreign Secretary. Under Lansdowne the purpose of the entente was to protect Britain's interests. Now it had become a means of protecting France against Germany. Independence of diplomatic manoeuvre was no longer possible when Britain's security was considered to rest upon France's strength.

Earlier Grey had doubted the wisdom of sanctioning a meeting between King Edward and the Kaiser, but eventually his doubts were overcome and the subsequent encounter of the two monarchs in August was a success. Hardinge, who had been involved in political discussions with the Germans while the Emperors met, became convinced that the Germans 'now seemed at last to realise that friendly relations with us cannot be at the expense of our entente with France'.[5] Hardinge's views were not shared by the majority of his

---

[1] Haldane, 200–1.   [2] See, Monger, 299.   [3] *B.D.*, III, 419.
[4] *Ibid.* It is interesting to compare the private assurance of Grey with his public comments on the nature of the diplomatic support for France offered by Britain. See, for example, *Hansard*, iv:160:317–318—'I have but two things to say about our relations, our good understanding with France. One is that good understanding is not directed against any other country; and the second is that it must be recognised that the good understanding must not be impaired by any other development of our foreign policy.'
[5] *B.D.* III, 425.

Foreign Office colleagues. Though momentarily checked, the anti-German current there still flowed as strongly as ever.

Haldane was due to arrive in Berlin on 31 August. At the last moment a telegram arrived from the Foreign Office suggesting that, as the French Press was uneasy about the visit, it ought to be cancelled. Supported by the King and Campbell-Bannerman, Haldane determined to carry on. He wrote to Grey to say that he would resign if the consequences of his visit turned out to be evil. Then Grey could claim that 'an erring colleague had expiated his temerity'.[1] Grey's reply to this letter was full of anxious complaints. 'I want to preserve the entente with France, but it isn't easy, and if it is broken up I must go.'[2] Fears, promoted by the querulous observations of some Parisian journalists, were enough for Grey to put his career as a minister at hazard. In the event his concern proved groundless. Haldane's visit was an unqualified success. He had enjoyed particularly cordial relations with the Kaiser. In his conversations with Tschirschky, Haldane had promised that with Grey he would examine possible means by which Britain could exercise her influence in Paris to improve Franco-German relations. Haldane's visit to Berlin was the last in 1906 that caused Grey acute embarrassment. In October, Grey made it clear to Cambon that France might depend upon Britain's support. As at Algeciras 'our support would be just as strong and our attitude as firm'.[3]

During 1907 Britain's relations with Germany followed a similar course to 1906. Grey resisted pressure to show greater friendliness towards Germany because he was constantly concerned with the possibility of an unfavourable French reaction. In April 1907 there was a minor crisis. Campbell-Bannerman, who had been paying a visit to Paris, informed Clemenceau that 'he did not think that English public opinion would allow British troops being employed on the continent of Europe'. Naturally Clemenceau was dismayed by this information and asked Campbell-Bannerman whether he was aware of the military conversations of January 1906. Grey, after consulting with the Prime Minister, did his best to allay Clemenceau's fears by sending the French Premier a reassuring letter. He claimed that while public opinion might be very reluctant to go to war 'it would not place limits upon the use of our forces, if we were engaged in war, and all our forces, naval and military, would then be used in the way in which they would be most effective'.[4] It is obvious, from the different emphasis in what was said to Clemenceau by Grey and

[1] Haldane, 202.
[2] Quoted Monger, 305.
[3] B.D. III, 442.
[4] B.D. III, 9-10.

Campbell-Bannerman, that the British Prime Minister still entertained doubts about Grey's policy.[1] At the same time, Campbell-
Bannerman did not seem to be able to promote those doubts
effectively. The British Foreign Office was apprehensive of the
Prime Minister's views.[2] They also had cause to fear the King's.
Edward was anxious to invite the Kaiser to pay a visit to England.
Grey acceded reluctantly to this request, but in order to minimise its
effect he told the King that the Kaiser must bring no more than one
minister with him and that on no account should Bülow accompany
his master.[3] Grey's niggling attitude can be accounted for only by
his inordinate nervousness at any unfavourable French reaction to
a gesture of Anglo-German friendship. Though Grey had his way
over the exclusion of Bülow, Edward insisted successfully that the
Kaiser should be accompanied by two ministers.[4]

In October 1907 a further trivial incident confirmed the extent of
Grey's unreal anxiety that France should not have any cause for
offence at Anglo-German relations. The Army Council authorised a
visit to Germany by the band of the Coldstream Guards. Earlier,
permission had been refused for a similar visit to France. Grey
angrily protested to Haldane.

> It is really important that the Coldstream Band should not go
> to Germany . . . there has been so much embracing already
> this year and there is so much still to come that our foreign
> policy will not stand any more. . . . I am not at all comfortable
> about the effect of what has been arranged already, and I can't
> be responsible for the consequences if any more Anglo-German
> visits are piled on this year.[5]

Grey wrote to Knollys in similar vein, prompting an angry response
from the King. Edward suggested that if Britain's friendship with

[1] The message of reassurance to Clemenceau, which Campbell-Bannerman saw
and approved, laid emphasis upon the military conversations being sanctioned
'if a crisis arose in connection with the Algeciras Conference'. The conversations, of course, continued after the crisis but it is just possible that Campbell-
Bannerman did not know of this. See Tyler, 76. A sub-committee of the Committee of Imperial Defence, which was to report on the plans evolved from
the military conversations, did not receive those plans until 3 Dec. 1908, and
did not present its findings until 24 July 1909. See Sydenham, 196.
As Chairman of the Committee of Imperial Defence, Campbell-Bannerman
pursued his task with considerably less vigour than either his predecessor or
successor. During his period as Chairman only fifteen sessions were held as
opposed to eighty-two under Balfour. However, more work was undertaken
by sub-committees and as a result Haldane and Sydenham enjoyed a greater
freedom of initiative. See F. A. Johnson, *Defence by Committee* (1960), 82.
[2] Mallet, who was Grey's private secretary, wrote to Bertie, 13 April 1907, 'It
was very stupid of him [Clemenceau] to raise the question . . . with Campbell-
Bannerman of all people', quoted Monger, 325.
[3] *B.D.* vi, 47–8.
[4] *B.D.* vi, 49, 51 and 58. See also Sidney Lee, ii, 553.
[5] Grey to Haldane, 4 Oct. 1907, quoted Monger, 328.

France rested upon 'so trumpery a point', then such slender foundations rendered the entente of 'but little practical value'.[1] The King
was supported by Haldane, but their representations to Grey were
of no avail. The band did not visit Germany. Grey later claimed:
'There was always the risk that these friendly demonstrations,
desirable if made with *arrière pensée* might be resented and used at
Paris to create distrust.'[2] Despite this gloss, Grey's actions remain a
commentary upon his extraordinary concern that France should in
no circumstances be afforded the least cause for worry.

The policy that Grey pursued towards France and Germany during
these years is best represented in Eyre Crowe's memorandum which
was circulated on 1 January 1907.[3] Crowe was the chief authority on
German problems in the Foreign Office. In 1906 he had been made
Senior Clerk and supervising head of the Western Department, an
excellent position from which to exercise influence upon Anglo-
German relations. Crowe's advice—to adopt the doctrine of the
balance of power—was founded upon a suspicious appraisal of
Germany's intentions. He was fearful of the implications of German
expansion. Grey described the memorandum as 'both interesting and
suggestive . . . most helpful as a guide to policy'.[4] Though at the
time the memorandum attracted little attention, it was 'a masterly
statement of the views which Grey and majority opinion in the
Office were coming more and more to adopt, and contributed something to the precision of those ideas, and therefore perhaps to their
hold over the men who subscribed to them'.[5]

In his first two years in office Grey had imparted a new direction
to Britain's relations with France and Germany. This was accepted
in the Cabinet, as even those who had some knowledge of what had
happened, like Campbell-Bannerman and Ripon, seemed incapable
of offering any practicable alternative.[6] For the rest of their Radical
colleagues, they were not aware there had been any changes. In any
event, they were quite content to fall in with a policy which by
eschewing isolation abroad allowed higher social expenditure at
home where their interests were almost exclusively engaged. What
opposition there had been to Grey's policy had come not, as might
have been expected, from the Radical wing of his party, but from his

[1] Sidney Lee, ii, 551–2.   [2] Grey, i, 113
[3] *B.D.* iii: Appendix A.   [4] *B.D.* iii, 428.
[5] Monger, 315. At the time it was not recognised as an epoch-making document.
It was seen by Campbell-Bannerman, Ripon, Asquith, Morley and Haldane.
It appears that neither Morley nor Loreburn paid it much attention at the
time. See Francis Hirst's introduction to Morley's *Memorandum on Resignation*
(1928), xvi. See further, on Memorandum, Steiner, 112, n.1.
[6] See Birrell, 231–2.

friend and imperialist companion, Haldane, and also the King. Neither Edward, because of his constitutional position, nor Haldane, because of friendship, presented a serious obstacle to a determined and independent Foreign Secretary.

More was heard of Russia than of Germany in the opening years of the 1906 Parliament. Radical and Labour members knew as little as the majority of the Cabinet of the manner and direction in which Grey was changing the Anglo-French entente. Their thoughts were absorbed by domestic problems. When they chose to turn their gaze on the international scene they myopically concentrated their attention on the question of armament expenditure.[1] Whenever there was talk of German 'isolation' because of the Anglo-French entente, the leading Radical journals remained complacent. The *Manchester Guardian* had recorded its admiration for Delcassé's 'bold simplicity of diplomatic conception', and viewed him as 'a friend of England and of peace' rudely tumbled from office by unwonted pressure from Germany.[2] The reason for Germany's temporary exclusion from the British sphere of influence was because 'the ideas of Liberalism were once more a great power in the the world'. Unfortunately, the temper of the German Government was still ruled 'by the traditions of Bismarck'. It 'would take time to acclimatise itself to the new pattern of things'.[3] Certainly, nothing could have been more complacent than H. W. Massingham's view that since Germany was now isolated 'no question of her rivalry with the British navy need disturb the present generation of British statesmen'.[4]

However, a small but influential group of Radicals was not happy with the growing evidence of estrangement between Great Britain and Germany. At the Fourteenth Universal Peace Congress held at Lucerne in September 1905 the British delegates, meeting with their

[1] See G. P. Gooch, *Under Six Reigns* (1958), 140. Relations between Germany and Britain were seen by many Radicals as an extension of the greater armaments question. Therefore, as far as they were concerned, their priorities were correct. See, for example, Francis Hirst, *A. G. C. Harvey: A Memoir* (1926), 68.
[2] See *Manchester Guardian*, 7 June 1905. However, there was already in some Radical quarters a view of Delcassé's policy as based upon the demand for *revanche*. See *Concord*, xxi, no. 6, June 1905, 81–2. This view was later to become the classical Radical assessment. See, for example, Bertrand Russell *The Policy of the Entente 1904–1914* (1915), 12ff.
[3] *The Speaker*, 25 Aug. 1906. In June that journal had commented: 'The chief enemy of the reputation of Germany and her friendship with her neighbours is the reactionary tradition of Bismarck. . . . We don't expect to see any intimate alliance of friendship with Germany as long as her present methods of Government exist.' Writing in the same number, 30 June 1906, Massingham categorically stated that 'Tolerably good relations with Germany are all that we can hope for in reason.'
[4] *Contemporary Review*, lxxxix, Feb. 1906, 270.

German counterparts, anxiously considered means for improving relations between their two countries. As a first step towards the organisation of a movement for *rapprochement,* a conciliation committee was formed which issued an address, subsequently published in all the leading British dailies except *The Times* and the *Telegraph.* The address claimed that beneath the apparent antagonism of industrial and commercial competition there was in reality a common interest, each nation providing the other with the good things it could best produce. Similarly, the political interests of the two Empires were not antagonistic provided they were governed by moderation and consideration for popular welfare.

> The efforts of all sensible men in both countries should be directed to the works which both people equally need. . . . Far from believing that the Anglo-French entente is a ground of separation, we believe it gives a new possibility for these three great nations to work together in friendship for their common interest and the peace of the world.

On 1 December 1905, Avebury, as chairman at a meeting at the Caxton Hall, claimed that it was an entire delusion to suppose that the *entente cordiale* with France was a veiled threat to Germany. This claim was greeted with wild applause. 'Our earnest wish is to be friends with both, and not only with them, but with other countries also.' Other speakers, including Leonard Courtney, reiterated this message.[1]

Radical concern with the unfortunate spirit of distrust and even hatred of Germany manifested in some quarters, was well merited. Sections of the popular Press did their best to whip up anti-German feeling. Campbell-Bannerman, together with some of the more Radical of the Liberal leadership, was not tardy in denouncing this Press campaign, and asserted his conviction that the true interests of the German and British peoples were not to be found in conflict. Because the Radicals showed a sensitivity about manifestations of 'Teutophobia' in the 'Randlord' Press, they in their turn were unfairly dubbed 'pro-German'. In fact, in the two-year period between the signing of the entente with France and the conclusion of the

[1] The meeting was fully reported in *The Times,* 2 Dec. 1905, together with a lengthy leader which indulged in some rather cheap sneers at 'the well intentioned people under whose auspices the meeting was held'. At the same time, *The Times* could not resist the opportunity of scolding the German Government. A number of leading members of the Liberal party wrote expressing their sympathy with the objects of the meeting, including Bryce. He condemned 'the noisy provocations of a happily small, though vociferous section of the English Press. There exists no ground for conflict between Germany and Britain.'

Algeciras Conference, Radical opinion, as reflected in its Press, was if anything pro-French and not behindhand in its criticism of the conduct and policies of the German Government.[1] Because they feared the harm that was being done by an irresponsible Press that excused its excesses in the name of patriotism,[2] Radicals actively fostered a host of goodwill resolutions, friendly speeches, visits between German and English editors, working men and priests. Radicals were opposed to any action that might lead to heavy expenditure upon armaments or might increase the likelihood of war.[3] Their motivation compares well with that of someone like Leo Maxse or even Grey who stigmatised their sincere manifestations of friendship towards Germany as 'gush'.[4]

The Radicals were quick to point out that no group in proportion to its strength had done more than they for the Anglo-French entente. No one desired its continuance more than they did. At the same time they could not ignore the inherent dangers of such an agreement. In the wrong hands it might degenerate into mere partisanship. It was possible to consider that Germany had adopted a vexatious attitude at Algeciras. But equally it could be claimed that her demand for an international, as against a one-Power mandate, at least had the form of international law behind it. England's task was to strive to maintain a judicial and unprovocative attitude. The greatest single danger to good international relations was 'the Press polemics on the subject'. These, 'if not a positive danger were certainly an unmitigated nuisance'.[5]

As the Algeciras Conference continued it was noted that the French

---

[1] See, *inter alia, Manchester Guardian*, 7 and 17 June 1905; *The Speaker*, 13 and 27 Jan. 1906; *Daily News*, 6 April 1905.

[2] See Churchill's speech to the Eighty Club, 17 May 1906. 'The Lord deliver a nation from its "patriotic" Press. When the patriotic and fire eating Editors—most of whom are above the military age—are not engaged in showing how patriotic they can be . . . they are engaged in showing how the German people spend their nights and days in looking for some opportunity for burning London to the ground. . . . Against these chimeras, hideous and menacing, we appeal to the good sense of the British and German races.'

[3] Repington, in an article in *The Times*, 27 Dec. 1905, attacked protestations of regard for Germany by Radicals, as undeserved, inopportune and dangerous since they were exploited in Germany to encourage German chauvinism and far from promoting peace were an indirect incentive to war. It is, therefore, no great wonder that the Radicals were contemptuous of *The Times* military correspondent whom they dubbed, 'the gorgeous Wreckington'. See, C. à Court Repington, *Vestigia* (1919), 3. See also the comments made on Repington in *The Nation*, 18 July 1908, p. 558, at the time of the revelation of the Tweed-mouth–Kaiser correspondence.

[4] See and compare, E. B. Baker and P. J. Noel Baker, *J. Allen Baker* (1927), 169ff.; *National Review*, July 1906, p. 707; and Grey, in *B.D.* iii, 419. Grey was not above using these goodwill visits, despite his private views, as evidence of his own Liberal disposition: see *Hansard*, iv:160:318.

[5] *Concord*, xxii, no. 2, Feb. 1906, p. 27.

claims had been maintained steadily throughout a parliamentary crisis and a change of Government, and this at a time when Russia was disabled as a first-class ally. Information from trusted sources suggested that the French were pursuing a bellicose policy in Morocco. The Radicals suspected that this would have been impossible unless Britain had offered her thoroughgoing support. Massingham was expressing a general Radical concern when he said, 'One dislikes the notion that England has been drawn into playing with a situation of great gravity without being able to influence it for good.'[1]

The Conference wound wearily to its conclusion. The Radicals recognised that Germany's diplomacy had been frustrated. *The Speaker* claimed that Germany had obtained 'everything to which she was reasonably entitled, and agreement has only been delayed so long because of her desire to obtain something more'.[2] Generally, the Radicals were pleased with the outcome of the Conference. Though it may have been unduly prolonged and doubtless very boring, they rejoiced 'that the craving for sensation and the passion for mastery were not allowed to spoil the work for humanity which the Conference was summoned to perform. The slow methods of the law are certainly preferable to the scramble of unchecked private interest, ambition or revenge.'[3]

In November 1906 a curious event occurred. At that time rumours were rife in Germany of discussions progressing between the English and French military staffs. When questioned about these rumours in the French Senate, Clemenceau made a statement that could well have been interpreted as an avowal.

> How could I answer yes or no? . . . I have only been President of the Council for three weeks and . . . I have never heard anything of any document of the nature of that Anglo-French military convention you speak of. These are questions so framed that it is the first duty of a government with any sense of responsibility to refuse to answer them.[4]

If this was meant to be a negative reply the *Manchester Guardian* found it 'very unconvincing'. But, what the *Guardian* had sought was a disavowal of 'a guarantee of mutual military assistance in certain eventualities'. This was to look for something more definite than the military conversations.[5] Generally, the Press played the matter

---

[1] *The Speaker*, 10 Mar. 1906.   [2] *Ibid.*, 31 Mar. 1906.
[3] *Concord*, xxii, no. 4, Apr./May, 1906, p. 58.
[4] *Senate*, 20 Nov. 1906, quoted Halévy, *Imperialism and the Rise of Labour*, 191, n. 1.
[5] See *Manchester Guardian*, 23 Nov. 1906. Cf. comments upon the *Matin* revelations in Oct. 1905, that Lansdowne had offered military aid to France· 9, 13 and 14 Oct. 1905. Also *Daily News*, 10 and 13 Oct. 1905.

down.[1] What is more interesting and significant is that no member of Parliament sought to elicit information from the Government.[2]

Radicals sought to disown the need for suspecting Germany's intentions. To counteract the claims of alarmists they were obliged to make an optimistic assessment of Britain's security arrangements. At the same time they found comfort in the hope that Socialist successes eventually would create in Germany a more democratic and Radical Government. Such a Government, they supposed, would naturally be pacific in intent.[3] Therefore, Radical attention was focused with more than usual intensity upon Germany at the beginning of the new year because of the elections for the Reichstag. It was hoped, and confidently asserted in some quarters, that the Socialists would gain a large number of seats and that 'this would limit von Bülow's meddling in foreign affairs'.[4] However, Radical hopes were disappointed, for the election in February led to a marked defeat for the Social Democrats.

> Those who expected a demonstration on the side of the people against the Caesarism of William II and the bureaucratic and military system of government, are fully undeceived by the result of these elections . . . the Germans learn very slowly in the matter of politics . . . No alteration can be expected for some considerable time to come.[5]

Radicals in this difficult period still retained more faith in continental Socialism as a force for peace than in the British Labour Party. They recognised that while Labour talked to the public in terms of internationalism, it spoke with a different temper and attitude in the Commons. As a parliamentary party it hardly seemed to have begun to think about foreign affairs. The German elections were written off as Bülow welding together the middle class parties of Germany into a patriotic coalition against Socialism. Yet, in little more than six

---

[1] See, *inter alia, Morning Post,* 22 Nov. 1906; 'a curiously lame declaration': *Daily News,* 21 Nov. 1906; 'a curious expression'.

[2] Adopting the formula which was to be common when reassuring Radical questioners in Parliament in following years, Haldane and Campbell-Bannerman informed Metternich that there existed no military convention between France and Great Britain, which if true in the letter was not so in spirit. See, *D.G.P.* XIII.i, 125. The Kaiser commented on Haldane's assurance; 'magnificent lies'.

[3] See, *inter alia, Labour Record,* i, July 1905, p. 184: *Concord,* xxii, no. 2, Feb. 1906, p. 26. Radical commentators conveniently ignored the venerable Bebel's words in the Reichstag, that in certain circumstances Social Democrats would fight. Also they ignored the ambiguity of the Social Democrat programme that coupled 'reference of all international disputes to arbitration' with, 'the training for universal capacity to bear arms'.

[4] Report of Berlin correspondent, *Daily Chronicle,* 9 Jan. 1907.

[5] Josef Redlich, *The Speaker,* 9 Feb. 1907; see also H. Beresford Butler in *Contemporary Review,* xci, 399–406.

months it was being confidently stated that Socialism, particularly in Germany, was a growing force. Continental Socialism was seen as beginning to realise with a new seriousness its mission as an international party. Its resolve to combat war by any means available had achieved success in forcing France and Germany, the two Powers most likely to make war, to divert their attention from external problems to combat antimilitarism at home. Perhaps a party that could make victory doubtful would make war impossible? This could well be the best guarantee available in the circumstances for the peace of Europe.[1]

Two months later, Radical hopes that Anglo-German relations might improve, suffered another crippling blow with Bülow's rejection in the Reichstag of Campbell-Bannerman's initiative for the discussion of disarmament at the Hague. A measure of the exceptional depression felt in some Radical circles is revealed by *The Nation's* attack not only upon the German Government, but the German people.

> We cannot console ourselves with the suspicion that the German Government is less enlightened or less friendly than the German nation. . . . There is . . . unfortunately on this question, no division of feeling between the German bureaucracy and the German people, and we have to face the fact that the Radicals . . . are quite as decidedly opposed to the English policy as any of the Conservative groups. . . . It would be folly to minimise the profound differences which separate us. They are neither accidental nor temporary, and for many years to come they are likely to be the decisive factor in European history. . . . Germany believes her isolation to be an artificial creation of an ingenious and hostile diplomacy. . . . What she refuses to recognise is that this isolation is in reality her own work, the consequence . . . of her own reactionary policy.[2]

The *Manchester Guardian* did not show the same pique as *The Nation* at Germany's actions. Bülow's speech had revealed a 'justified and genuine resentment at the representation of Germany as the political pariah of Europe'.[3] This claim was followed four days later by the assertion that it was the Liberal Government's duty to make clear that the Anglo-French entente did not preclude an Anglo-German understanding. There should be 'some concrete manifesta-

---

[1] See, *The Nation*, 12 Oct. 1907. Cf. the earlier statements of *Concord*, xxi, no. 11, Nov. 1905, p. 160. See also, Frédéric Passy 'Victories of Reason' in *Les Documents du Progrès*, Dec. 1908. 'In 1870, two thirds of Germans were unconscious of their rights. Today a general rising of proletarian opinion would render it impossible to begin the butchery.'
[2] *The Nation*, 4 May 1907.
[3] *Manchester Guardian*, 3 May 1907.

tion from Sir Edward Grey that he is conscious of this duty'.[1] The general consensus of Radical opinion was that it was absurd to ignore the changes that had occurred in the international scene in the past few years. There had been an extension of the system of alliances and understandings in which England had played a leading rôle. Two great European Powers now stood outside this network, Germany and Austria. Naturally they were annoyed, felt 'cornered', and 'probably we should have been as much annoyed had we found ourselves in the same position'.[2]

By June, *The Nation* had recovered its composure and turned its attention 'to the painful study' of the relationship of Germany and Britain in an article significantly entitled 'The policy of penning in'. The Anglo-French entente had meant for Germany the collapse of Bismarck's system. The history of the new distribution of forces suggested that behind it was

> Some obscure and general impulse whose scope is larger than any calculation of national interest. . . . M. Delcassé was compelled to resign in 1905 because he had followed too openly and too successfully the policy of isolating Germany. M. Rouvier and M. Pichon have followed him in France; Sir Edward Grey has succeeded Lord Lansdowne, and M. Isvolsky Count Lamsdorff. But still, as if by some inevitable pressure of forces, the process continues. We call it merely a movement of peace, which menaces no one, and seeks only to eliminate, among certain Powers, every possible source of discord. The Germans observing that they alone find no place in the complicated network of *ententes* describe it more bluntly as a system of 'penning-in'.[3]

Radicals still felt some degree of anxiety because of Germany's obvious restlessness. But, as the summer of 1907 progressed, they were prepared to convince themselves that perhaps they had exaggerated the tension between Britain and Germany. In August, when King Edward met the Kaiser at Wilhelmshohe and Francis Joseph at Ischl, *The Nation* concluded that an entente with Germany was not required. Relations had again entered upon a happier, more normal phase.[4]

When the Foreign Office vote was taken on 1 August the great issues involved were debated with a singular listlessness in a thinly

---

[1] *Ibid.*, 7 May 1907. [2] *Concord*, xxiii, no. 5, May 1907, 53–4.
[3] *The Nation*, 1 June 1907.
[4] *Ibid.*, 19 Oct. 1907. At the same time, even the German Socialist Press including the official organ of the party, *Vorwärts*, complained bitterly of Edward's activities as 'not favourable for peace' and begged their 'English comrades to speak up seriously' about this in Parliament. See Montgelas, 26–7.

attended Commons. There was not a word about Anglo-German relations, and Grey in his speech[1] was urbane, cautious and, as always, said as little as was possible. For good measure he threw in a few gratuitous remarks about the difficulties of his office and his determination despite these difficulties 'always to endeavour to give the utmost information in my power' to the House. Presumably, this crumb was a response to the muted chidings of the Radicals. For the moment they were convinced that the problems of Anglo-German relations could be solved if greater publicity were afforded to Britain's 'true policies'. Foreign policy was being conducted with extreme secrecy and Sir Edward was fast developing into the most autocratic and reticent of all Foreign Ministers.[2] Was it any wonder that the Germans had an erroneous view of Britain's intentions when they had to rely for their information upon a jingo Press with editors like Leo Maxse, the 'most egregious *gobemouche* ever'?[3] The Radicals believed that if the lies, innuendoes and insolence of the bellicose Press, of which *The Times* was not the least offender, 'that has been shouting *Delenda est Carthago* ever since the passage of the Navy Act in 1900' could be muted, then this would go a long way towards improving Anglo-German relations which now stood upon such a delicate equipoise. Bülow was showing every sign of reconciliation and acceptance of the solidarity of the entente between France and Britain. It was for Britain to recognise this change of front in Berlin. She should adjust her interests and rivalries and seek to give durable validity to this new policy. If Britain did not respond, the feud would become permanent. This could only result in 'inevitable war' between the two nations. The choice was Britain's. A proper response would effect as its natural consummation a reduction in naval armaments. Reconciliation with Germany could be postponed 'only at the cost of compromising many of the purposes essential to a Liberal policy alike at home and abroad'.[4]

The Anglo-Russian Convention

Grey, even before entering office, had made no secret of the fact that he strongly desired an agreement with Russia. In his 'City Speech' in October 1905, he had claimed that it was

> urgently desirable that Russia's influence should be re-established in the councils of Europe. The estrangement

---

[1] *Hansard*, iv:179:1305ff.
[2] See, *inter alia, Albany Review*, Dec. 1907, 243ff.; *The Nation*, 3 Aug., 19 Oct. and 23 Nov. 1907.
[3] Compare Repington's estimate of Maxse in his *Vestigia*, 262.
[4] *The Nation*, 19 Oct. 1907.

between us and Russia has, in my opinion, its roots not in the present but solely in the past. It may be, perhaps it must be, that confidence between the two countries must be a plant of slow growth; but the conditions should be favourable to its growth and it should be the business of both Governments to foster and encourage those conditions.

In February 1906 Grey wrote to his friend Cecil Spring Rice, then in charge of the Embassy at St Petersburg, 'I am impatient to see Russia re-established as a factor in European politics. Whether we shall get an arrangement with her about Asiatic questions remains to be seen: I will try when she desires it and is ready.'[1]

Among the ruling circle in St Petersburg there was a marked prejudice against Great Britain and suspicion about her intentions. The reactionary pro-German party hoped for the renewal of the historic project of an alliance between the three Emperors, the *Dreikaiserbund*.[2] The British Ambassador in Russia claimed that

> if the Emperor and the Russian Government were free from any other political ties they would gladly form an intimate alliance with Germany. . . . German influence today is predominant both in the Court and in Government circles. . . . The alternate hectoring and cajolery, which are the distinctive features of German diplomacy in other countries, are not employed here. A suave conciliatory attitude and a gentle solicitude are characteristics of German diplomacy in this capital.[3]

When in May Lamsdorff resigned as Russian Foreign Minister and Isvolsky took his place, this was interpreted as a victory for the pro-German party.[4]

In March 1906 Grey had made a tacit agreement with Benckendorff, the Russian Ambassador, to work for a definite understanding between Russia and Britain.[5] That month he wrote to Knollys: 'An entente with Russia is now possible, and it is the thing to be most desired in our foreign policy. It will complete and strengthen the entente with France and add very much to the comfort and strength

[1] Grey to Spring Rice, 19 Feb. 1906, quoted Trevelyan, 143.
[2] Within three weeks of the signing of the Anglo-Russian Convention, certain British diplomats were still concerned about the possibility of the *Dreikaiserbund* becoming a reality, see *B.D.* VI, 41.
[3] *B.D.* IV, 213.
[4] See *B.D.* IV, 219. Also, Morley to Minto, 13 July 1906. 'Lamsdorff, it seems, was driven from office like Delcassé by Germany, exactly because he was for making friends with us', quoted Monger, 282–3. See also E. J. Dillon in *Contemporary Review*, lxxxix, 897. This view was given credence because a tacit word of mouth agreement on accord between the foreign policies of Russia and Britain had been made with Lamsdorff in January. See, *D.D.F.* IV, 223 and 386.
[5] See *B.D.* IV, 212.

of our position.'[1] Meanwhile, Morley in his weekly letter to Minto, the newly appointed Viceroy to India, cautiously urged him to consider the terms that might be exacted from Russia in the event of an understanding between the two countries.[2] In April, Morley, Asquith and Sir Arthur Nicolson, shortly to go to St Petersburg as Ambassador with the express brief to work for an agreement with Russia, met for dinner at Grey's house. For four hours they talked with their host of 'entente, in and out, up and down'.[3] Nicolson for his part was not too optimistic about the outcome of his mission, but promised his fellow diners 'confidence, encouragement and support', he undertook the task 'with great diffidence and considerable misgiving'.[4]

What were Grey's reasons for desiring an Anglo-Russian entente? In his memoirs written nearly twenty years later he claimed:

> If we were to get out of the old bad rut in which we had so often come to the verge of war with Russia, we had to work for a definite agreement. Russia was the ally of France; we could not pursue at one and the same time a policy of agreement with France and a policy of counter alliances against Russia. . . . An agreement with Russia was the natural complement of an agreement with France; it was also the only practical alternative to the old policy of drift, with its continual complaints, bickerings and dangerous friction.[5]

Here Grey is giving his readers but half of the picture, as is revealed by a memorandum that he wrote at the height of the Algeciras crisis. 'An entente between Russia, France and ourselves would be absolutely secure. If it is necessary to check Germany it could then be done.'[6] With the backing of official opinion at the War Office, Grey sought to forge a diplomatic instrument to check Germany. The importance that Grey attached to an agreement between Russia and Britain, and its essential nature as part of his overall diplomatic strategy, is made clear by his record of a conversation with Benckendorff: 'I could not myself pursue any other policy, and if Russia made this policy im-

---

[1] Grey to Knollys, 28 Mar. 1906, quoted Trevelyan, 183.
[2] See Morley to Minto, 23 Mar. 1906, in John Morley, *Recollections* (1917), ii, 167.
[3] *Ibid.*, ii, 169. Haldane probably was also present at the dinner. See, Harold Nicolson, *First Lord Carnock: a study in the old diplomacy* (1930), 206.
[4] Nicolson was a convinced and enthusiastic supporter of an entente between Russia and Britain. Therefore, it is instructive to compare his gloomy summary of English opinion on such an agreement (Nicolson, 206), with Morley's abandoned review of the same subject to Minto. 'H.M.'s Government with almost universal support in public opinion, have decided to attempt . . . to arrange an entente.'
[5] Grey, i, 15?–3.
[6] *B.D.* III, 299.

possible, I should leave it to someone else to adopt and pursue another.'[1]

Russia's weight in the military and diplomatic scales had been dramatically altered with her defeat by Japan. For the better part of a century she had played the rôle of trouble-maker in central Asia and had posed a constant threat to the security of the British in India. Therefore, it was hardly surprising that talk of an Anglo-Russian agreement designed at one stroke to solve the problems of Persia, Tibet and Afghanistan, was met by the Indian Government at Simla with a certain incredulity not to say suspicion and positive dislike. They were opposed to Russia being conceded local relations with the Afghans. They were worried about the military implications of an entente which seemed designed to make permanent a disadvantageous inequality. What possible advantage could there be for Britain in weakening the effectiveness of her ally Japan as the price of friendship with an unreliable Power known for its long history of diplomatic chicanery?

Within the Cabinet, Grey limited the discussion of the negotiations to that small group of ministers—Campbell-Bannerman, Asquith, Ripon and Morley—who were known to be sympathetic. They all accepted the principle of the entente and therefore were not likely to raise any serious objection to Grey's conduct of policy.[2] Unlike the negotiations with France, those with Russia involved Grey in consultation with other Government departments—the Government of India and the India Office. Therefore, of all Grey's Cabinet colleagues, Morley's support for his scheme was a necessary condition of its success. Grey handsomely acknowledged this upon the successful completion of the entente, both in a letter to the Prime Minister,[3] and to Morley himself:

> If you had not taken the strong and clear line which you did, we should have had to go to the Cabinet time after time to get authority to overrule the objections of the Indian government to point after point in the negotiations. The result would have

[1] Grey, i, 169–70.

[2] Morley's statement to his biographer, General Morgan, made in September 1914, that he was 'always opposed to the Russian Agreement' is contrary to his spirited defence of that agreement in the Commons in February 1908, and his contemporary letters both to Minto and Grey, some of which he published in his *Recollections* in 1917. 'Morley may have changed his mind about the Russian Agreement after the outbreak of war in 1914, but there is no shadow of doubt as to what his mind had been at the time when the Agreement was being made', Trevelyan, 185, n. 1.

[3] Grey to Campbell-Bannerman, 31 Aug. 1907. 'Without Morley we should have made no progress at all, for the Government of India would have blocked every point and Morley removed mountains in the path of negotiations.' Quoted Grey, i, 165.

been very slow and difficult and the whole thing might have come to nought.[1]

Morley was not the easiest of colleagues with whom to deal. His personality, like his thinking, had a number of contradictory and divergent strands that are difficult to reconcile. His métier was in literature. Though ill-endowed by nature for the rôle of administrator and man of affairs, it was nevertheless on the political stage that Morley determined to cut a figure of the highest stature. In turn, he considered himself a suitable candidate as Chancellor of the Exchequer and Foreign Secretary, and even seems at one time to have aspired to becoming Prime Minister.[2] Morley was supposedly a Radical. Yet, there was much of the Conservative in his make-up.[3] He was jealous that others should frequently acknowledge his eminence in the Liberal party's hierarchy. Inordinately sensitive, he resented the neglect of his ministerial colleagues whether real or supposed. He was immoderate in his threats of resignation on one pretext or another. Sweet and gentle in private intercourse, in public office he could and often did play the part of autocrat and martinet.[4] Grey therefore had to be cautious and diplomatic in his dealings with Morley. In this he was successful. Morley acknowledged that Grey was invariably considerate and free and constant in consultation.[5]

Morley was no stranger to the workings of the Foreign Office. On occasion, during Grey's brief holidays, he took over as caretaker Foreign Secretary with evident pleasure.[6] But for the greater part of the time he did not receive the despatches on Britain's relations with France and Germany. Thus he lacked the essential key to the understanding of Grey's policy. In his judgment of the general diplomatic scene and in particular the European significance of an agreement with Russia, he had to rely upon what he could glean in conversation with his colleagues, and his critical appreciation might well have been lulled by his own exaggerated estimate of his gifts as a diplomatist.[7]

Morley had earlier assured Minto that he was 'not in the least inclined to let the Foreign Office decide affairs that are specially

---

[1] Grey to Morley, 13 Aug. 1907, quoted Trevelyan, 185.
[2] See *inter alia*, Haldane, *Autobiography*, 96.
[3] Redmond's opinion of Morley was that he was 'a wretched fellow. Morley has no courage, you can't depend upon him', quoted in W. S. Blunt, *My Diaries* (1919–20), ii, 139.
[4] See Haldane, 95ff. W. S. Churchill, *Great Contemporaries* (1941), 84; *E.P.*, ii, 211 and 223.
[5] See Morley to Asquith, 26 Sept. 1906, quoted Monger, 284.
[6] See Grey, I, 14?
[7] See Trevelyan, 144, n. 1.

Indian and on which India will have to smart if they go wrong'. But when Minto raised objections and suggested that the Government of India ought to be fully consulted before any agreement with Russia was completed, Morley quickly and sharply reminded him of his constitutional duties. Whether a policy be 'good or bad, right or wrong . . . H.M.'s Government have determined upon their course and it is for their agents and officers all over the world to accept it'. Some gratuitous advice on the nature of diplomacy was followed by a harsh conclusion. 'The plain truth is . . . this country cannot have two foreign policies. . . . You have set out your views with signal force. They do not convert us—and so, like other Ministers who cannot carry their colleagues, you will make the best of it.'[1]

Minto's arguments about weakening the Anglo-Japanese Treaty were not effective. The Liberal Government to a man were indifferent, even hostile, towards the Treaty.[2] Morley recognised that the proposed local arrangements with Russia, which were causing the Indian Government such concern and offence, would have an instant appeal to the Radicals in Parliament. It might well have been as a sop to his Radical conscience that from the first he went to considerable lengths to stress to Minto the anti-expansionist and anti-Imperialist nature of the Liberal Cabinet and the Radical temper of the Government's back bench supporters.

> The new Parliament and the new Cabinet will be, in the highest degree, jealous both of anything that looks like expansion, extended protectorates, spheres of influence and so forth; and of anything with the savour of militarism about it. I do not dream that the G of I in your hands will follow in the steps of our predecessors as to Tibet, Persia, the Amir . . . of policy of that sort I am incurably suspicious, and the Cabinet will assuredly sympathise with my suspicions, and so, still more loudly will the H. of C. . . . Please to recognise that the centre of gravity is utterly changed for good or evil by this election. Especially will this, as I think, touch frontier matters, wars on tribes, Tibetan wrangles and the like . . . taking new responsibilities will be watched with sharp suspicion for the present at any rate.[3]

Morley's main reason for supporting Grey's policy towards Russia was probably his desire to reduce Army commitments in India. Esher, at Haldane's suggestion, had persuaded Morley to ask

[1] Morley to Minto, 6 July 1906, quoted Morley, ii, 177–8.
[2] No Cabinet Minister despised the Anglo-Japanese Treaty more than did Morley. He wrote to Minto: 'Every day more loudly do I pour out imprecations on the Second Anglo-Japanese Treaty', quoted Monger, 286.
[3] See Morley to Minto 16 and 25 Jan. 1906 in Morley, ii, 157–8 and 162–3.

Campbell-Bannerman to appoint him Chairman of a sub-committee of the Committee of Imperial Defence. The sub-committee's brief was to consider the 'military needs of the Empire'. When in May 1907 it reported, its findings were that any war with Russia for India would involve vast military organisation and expenditure. In the first year of any such engagement one hundred thousand men would have to be sent to India. This, for Morley, was the fundamental argument for a convention with Russia. He informed Minto: 'We have not got the men to spare and that's the plain truth of it.'[1]

But Morley's support for Grey's policy was not limited to considerations that involved India alone. During 1906 his comments to Minto on German diplomacy have 'a rather improbable air, as if he picked them up in the course of gossip'.[2] In August, for instance, he wrote to Minto that for those same reasons that made Germany seek coldness between England and Russia 'we ought to do what we can to baulk her'. Again in September, he wrote of Germany's 'general world policy . . . complicating attempts at an entente between us and Russia'.[3] Morley supported Grey unreservedly because he lacked knowledge of some of the key pieces in the jigsaw of international relations and because of faults in his own character, particularly conceit about his own prescience. In time Morley was to regret his actions, but then it was too late.

Among Grey's permanent advisers at the Foreign Office, none played a more important part in the negotiations with Russia than Hardinge. He had returned from Russia to the Foreign Office in 1906 with the express intent to do all that he could to bring about an Anglo-Russian agreement.[4] He saw that a revived Russia would be a real continental check to German threats.[5] His knowledge of Russia, and the close identification of his views with those of Nicolson, proved invaluable.[6] Grey acknowledged the key part played by his Permanent Under Secretary in the creation of the entente.[7] Hardinge always appreciated the European significance of the proposed agreement.

Grey was to claim that in negotiating with Russia:

> The cardinal British object . . . was to secure ourselves for ever . . . from further Russian advances in the direction of the Indian frontier. Russia was to cease threatening and annoying

[1] Morley to Minto, 31 May 1907, quoted Monger, 285.
[2] Monger, 286.
[3] Morley to Minto, 29 Aug. and 20 Sept. 1906, quoted Monger, 288. Morley in his *Recollections* did not print those letters that revealed a hostile attitude towards Germany.
[4] See *B.D.* IV, 520.   [5] See Steiner, 94.   [6] See Nicolson, 206.
[7] See Grey to Hardinge, 27 Sept. 1907, quoted Steiner, 95.

British interests concerned with India. This had been a formidable diplomatic weapon in her hands. She was now, once and for all to give it up.

Grey makes no mention of Germany in listing the advantages of the Agreement, yet it was fear of Germany and the possibility of a Russo-German *rapprochement* that dominated the negotiations throughout.[1]

Because from the beginning Grey had declared his intention was the improvement of Anglo-Russian relations, the Radicals could not claim that the news of negotiations for a possible agreement between the two countries came as a surprise. However, they assumed that certain necessary conditions would be satisfied before any formal convention was drawn up. The Radicals were assured by Milyoukov, leader of the Constitutional Democratic party in Russia, the Cadets, that 'only after the triumph of the Russian people over their bureaucracy could an agreement be based upon the love of peace of the two peoples'. For the moment 'any alliance between England and the Russian bureaucracy eager for money would be resented by the Russian people'.[2]

There was a large element of the politics of romance in the attitude towards Russia of the more extreme Radicals and their Socialist allies. For them, nothing less than the expulsion of the Russian Government beyond the pale of human society was just reward for its black iniquities. They leaned heavily upon the less than objective accounts of Russian exiles for their knowledge of Russia. Gilbert Murray wrote in 1915: 'All our natural sympathies conspired to make us see with their eyes, their beauty of character often fascinated us and the martyrdoms they endured blotted out from our minds all

---

[1] See *inter alia*, R. P. Churchill, *The Anglo-Russian Convention 1907* (1939), 344; Monger, 288ff.
[2] Quoted *Concord*, xxii, no. 6, June 1906, 77, Russia, desperately requiring a loan to relieve her financial embarrassment, turned to her traditional source, France. Considerable doubts were felt in France about the wisdom of floating yet another loan for Russia. Clemenceau, in particular, warned his countrymen against supplying 'financial resources destined to assure . . . [the Tsar] . . . victory over his own subjects' (*The Times*, 1 Feb. 1906). Liberal opinion in Russia was against the loan. *The Times*, 10 Apr. 1906 reported, 'The Opposition organs continue their campaign against the conclusion of a foreign loan before the Duma meets. . . . They are afraid the Government, having secured a large sum of money will try to terrorise the Duma.' However, a joint Anglo-French loan was floated in April. English Radicals saw this as a subsidy for reaction in Russia and found it difficult to reconcile this with Government talk of non-intervention in Russia's internal affairs. *Concord* claimed that it was, 'an extraordinary transaction . . . a weapon given by foreign countries to the Tsardom for use against an oppressed people striving for liberty'. When less than two months later the Tsar dissolved the Duma, the gloomy forecasts of the Radicals even found support in *The Times*, 23 July 1906. 'The Government's arbitrary step justifies those who besought the friends of constitutional liberty not to lend more money to the autocracy.'

thoughts of their possible errors or crimes.'[1] Sentimentalism invested the Duma with a significance in Russia's affairs that in terms of practical politics it never merited. Sympathy aroused among Radical politicians for the indignities suffered by the members of the Tauride Chamber concealed the reality of illiterate deputies with their conceited, myopic, doctrinaire leaders who preferred propaganda to policy. While Cadets, Octobrists and Social Democrats railed of reform and reformation and squabbled among themselves, the Russian Government ignored them. Nicolson noted that the only views that mattered were those of the Government and the revolutionaries outside the Duma. The latter cared 'nothing for constitutions or Dumas or reforms', and their only wish was 'to make all government impossible'.[2]

Campbell-Bannerman shared his Foreign Secretary's lack of sympathy for the extreme Radical view of Russian affairs. Both men believed that to demonstrate against the Tsar's Government was to injure the cause of Liberalism in Russia by playing straight into the hands of the reactionaries. While Grey was aware that to say as much in public would be fatal, in his private correspondence he referred slightingly to 'Keir Hardie and Co.', as 'people who don't want to know the truth and to do good, but express their own emotions. Dram drinkers I call them . . . for they must be in a state of emotion and when you attempt to dilute their emotions with the truth they are as angry as a drunkard, whose whisky you dilute with water.'[3]

There was no lack of powerful publicists on the Radical side to portray the worse excesses of the Russian Government's treatment of its peoples. In particular, Nevinson and Brailsford formed a close and active alliance determined at any cost to check the movement towards an understanding with Russia. When it was learned it was proposed that a British fleet should visit Kronstadt as part of its Baltic cruise, the tidal gates of Radical criticism burst open.[4] Even the milder sections of the Liberal Press were opposed to such a visit. *The Speaker* claimed that while:

> We are all [sic] in favour of improving Anglo-Russian relations, at a time of crisis in Russia's affairs when liberty is fighting for

[1] Gilbert Murray, *The Foreign Policy of Sir E. Grey* (1915), 82–3.
[2] Nicolson, 223. For a scathing commentary upon the ineffectiveness of the Duma and the inadequacies of its deputies, see E. J. Dillon in *Contemporary Review*, xci, 888ff. Cf. the apologia of Milyoukov, *ibid.*, xcii, 457ff. It has to be remembered that Dillon was a great friend of the Conservative ex-minister, Witte.
[3] Campbell-Bannerman to Grey, 8 Oct. 1906: Grey to Katherine Lyttleton, 28 June and 25 July 1909, quoted Trevelyan, 190–1.
[4] This was an over-hasty initiative by the Foreign Office. Neither the Tsar nor Isvolsky welcomed it. See Lee, ii, 565; and *D.G.P.* xxv. i, 8512–15.

its very life, it would be unfortunate if we should contemplate sending our fleet to Kronstadt to be fêted as the guests of the Tsar. . . . The hand which we proffered to the Russian nation would be seized as a prop by the tottering Russian despotism . . . still red with the fresh blood of Bielostok.[1]

In the Commons at Question Time, Labour members in particular reminded the Foreign Secretary of the atrocities daily perpetrated by the Russian Government. The Government would seem to be countenancing these barbarities if they were determined upon sending the fleet to Kronstadt on a complimentary visit. They criticised both the tardiness and mildness of official representations from the Foreign Office to the Russian Government about the monstrous barbarity of its behaviour. In a debate on 5 July Grey faced his critics and defended his policy. Characteristically, he began and ended his speech with a pious avowal of the virtues of silence. 'The less comment on Russian affairs the better. . . . There is one safe rule to follow, and that is as far as we can to avoid comment and all interference . . . the best help in these matters is the least interference . . . the best sympathy is silence.' To call off the visit of the fleet, he maintained, was to interfere in Russia's internal affairs, a move that certainly would not strengthen the party of reform. 'I ask, would it be possible not to make it seem that there was a taking of sides if the fleet did not visit the Russian ports? I look forward to increasing our good relations with the Russian Government and the Russian people.'[2]

The problem eventually was resolved by the action of the Russian Government. They tactfully requested the abandonment of the visit. On 14 July it was announced publicly that the Baltic cruise was cancelled. The Radicals congratulated themselves on what they considered to be the successful conclusion of their campaign of opposition.[3] Here, happily, was evidence that the British people still believed in liberty and would not 'be compromised by official association with the organisers and apologists of massacre who call themselves the Government of Russia'. The abandonment of the Kronstadt visit was something, but not enough. 'We owe it to our own privileges', claimed *Concord*, 'to show that . . . the Russian people and their embryo parliament have the deep sympathy of all humane men'.[4]

In his speech in the Commons, Grey had spoken of Russia showing 'signs of vitality, energy and ability to work her way through to a great future'. The only possible evidence that offered some validity

---

[1] *The Speaker*, 23 June 1906.   [2] *Hansard*, iv:160:327 and 340.
[3] See H. W. Nevinson, *Fire of Life* (1935), 230–4.
[4] *Concord*, xxii, no. 6, July 1906, 82.

for this singularly optimistic assertion was that the Duma was still in session. To Liberals this afforded the single most important guarantee of an improvement in Russia's polity. Delegates from the nascent Russian Parliament were in London in July to attend for the first time a conference of the Inter-Parliamentary Union. On 23 July, when Campbell-Bannerman was due to address the delegates, the Press announced that the Tsar had suspended the Duma. The British Prime Minister was placed in a difficult situation. The Russian delegates were the object of everyone's attention. He would have to make some comment. Campbell-Bannerman solved the problems by proclaiming: *'La Douma est morte, vive la Douma'*—a trite enough slogan with just sufficient ambiguity to allow Grey to wriggle out of a diplomatic *contretemps* with Benckendorff.[1] However, it caused severe embarrassment to Nicolson in Russia.[2] The Radicals were delighted with Campbell-Bannerman. With pardonable exaggeration, Arthur Ponsonby claimed that out of catastrophe had been made a battle cry of hope.[3] Nevinson was ecstatic. He wrote that Campbell-Bannerman was given

> . . . a new reputation for courage as the champion of freedom. The advocates of reaction were outraged. The supporters of the Russian *Entente* abandoned hope. The 'King's Friends' rebuked . . . [Campbell-Bannerman's words] . . . as disloyal. But the hearts of all who had fought for freedom and peace leapt for joy.[4]

For Grey, the dissolution of the Duma was a severe blow. It increased his difficulties when facing his Radical and Labour critics in the Commons. He knew that some measure of success for the reform movement in Russia was his best argument to obtain support for a policy of *rapprochement*. Hardinge was desolate. It seemed that at one blow the edifice which they had been building up so painfully and with so much care was destroyed.[5] To add to Grey's discomfiture and embarrassment, the Commons had decided to send a congratulatory message to the Duma. Now that the Duma was dissolved the Radicals proposed that a deputation should take the message to the late Duma's President. Grey managed to scotch this idea with the argument that it would constitute an undue interference in the internal affairs of Russia. Grey's words of warning and censure were reinforced by the warnings of a band of reactionary thugs in Moscow

---

[1] See Grey, i, 155.
[2] See Nicolson, 222: 'Two months ago there was every hope [of an agreement] and now very little.'
[3] Quoted, Spender, ii, 264.   [4] Nevinson, 205.
[5] See Hardinge to Nicolson, 21 Aug. 1906, quoted Monger, 287.

called the Black Gang, who threatened to tear limb from limb any members of the deputation who dared to set foot in Russia. This did not deter Brailsford, but he was unable to get a passport and eventually it was left to Nevinson to deliver the message privately.[1] Grey had not been alone in his disapproval of the idea of a deputation. Campbell-Bannerman writing to Grey in October had said: 'I entirely enter into the view expressed by Nicolson and endorsed by H.M. as to the folly of the deputation to Russia.' His disapproval was based upon two grounds. First, that it might, 'set back the tide of reform and liberty'. Second, and more interestingly, it would 'enable the Russian Government to say if this is the sort of friend you are going to be, we prefer the Kaiser. And where should we be then?'[2]

During the spring and summer of 1907, while official negotiations for an agreement between the two Governments were pushed on apace, Radicals and Socialists in their Press and the Commons maintained a shrill barrage of opposition and criticism. Nevinson and Brailsford were particularly active. Convinced that the Russian revolution must eventually succeed, even though the prospects then seemed so poor, Nevinson appealed to his readers' consciences:

> It is at this great crisis in history when the forces of tyranny and freedom in Russia are confronting each other for the last struggle, and a new age is about to open not only for that country but for mankind, that the English people are being trapped by a Liberal Foreign Office into some sort of alliance, agreement or understanding with the forces of Russian tyranny.[3]

For the committed the problem was simple. The *New Age* claimed that if Britain pandered to despotism in Russia how could she hope to preserve that vital allegiance to constitutional principles at home? One could not talk of admiring Pym and Hampden and at the same time be prepared to purchase a diplomatic advantage at the price of the soul of a people.[4] Perhaps most disquieting was the way the general public remained so apathetic, apparently untouched by the internal distress of Russia and unconcerned at the possibility of Britain countenancing despotism by giving support to the Russian Government. 'Not a single mass meeting has been held independent of party: not a single statesman has made a Midlothian campaign: not one great newspaper has taken up the cause of Russian freedom. . . . Where is the quick response which England felt when France

[1] Nevison, 207–9; and in *Albany Review*, Aug. 1907, 516–17. Also Grey, i, 156.
[2] Campbell-Bannerman to Grey, 8 Oct. 1906, quoted Trevelyan, 190.
[3] *Albany Review*, August 1907, 515–16.
[4] *New Age*, 23 May 1907.

was struggling to be free?'[1] But no matter how the Radicals battled to capture the public conscience the people remained unmoved by the trials and tribulations of the Russian Left.[2]

The Nation recognised that the problem of relations with Russia was complicated by a new issue. After the summoning of the Second Duma, progressive opinion in England was as divided and puzzled as it appeared to be in Russia. There, the Cadet party had lost its former buoyancy. Reduced in numbers and bereft of their ablest leaders, the Cadets seemed more intent upon their political survival than anything else. This would explain why many were for an entente with Britain. But they had some strange allies in this policy, like the arch-representative of chauvinism and reaction, *Norve Vremya*. It was certain that any agreement would be prestigious for the Russian Government and would provide it with fresh credit for borrowing. While the agreement remained unsigned there was room for bargaining to improve the temper of the Russian Government and to demand constitutional safeguards. The example of the Russian agreement with France in 1891, which had inaugurated a terrible period of reaction and repression, showed how futile it was to expect to influence Russia's internal affairs after the completion of an agreement. Some critics had claimed that the alternative to an Anglo-Russian agreement was that Russia would throw herself into the arms of Germany, the least liberal of all European Governments. However, *The Nation* dismissed this idea as 'an unreal risk'.[3]

On 11 June a letter signed by a group of intellectuals, Radicals and Socialists including Shaw, Ramsay MacDonald, George Cadbury, John Galsworthy, J. A. Hobson and Cunninghame Graham, was published in *The Times*. It expressed the writers' 'apprehension at a report that an agreement [was] being arranged with . . . the Government of St Petersburg'.

> We cannot but condemn an arrangement which, for a very dubious and temporary advantage, places this country in a false position with regard to the liberation movement which, so far as we can forecast the future, is likely to exert the highest influence on the European history of the present century.

In the Commons, despite the supposed advantage afforded by the new arrangements for the answering of Foreign Office questions, and

[1] *New Age*, 20 June 1907, p. 120.
[2] 'It appears to be impossible to excite even a "sporting" interest in the national tragedy that lies behind the trials of Socialist members of the First Duma and Liberals of the Second. . . . It would seem that politics like charity, is most real round the parish pump.' *Concord*, xxiv, no. 1, Jan. 1908, 3.
[3] *The Nation*, 8 June 1907.

although the Foreign Secretary was a member of the House, Radical members found it all but impossible to extract any information from Grey.[1] The inexperience of new members had operated in Grey's favour, but in October 1906 he had confided to Nicolson that he was not looking forward to meeting the new Parliament because new members had acquired the art of asking questions and raising debates. As far as Grey was concerned, much that attracted back bench attention was far better left alone.[2] However, when he was questioned, Grey's vagueness and circumlocution defeated attempts to expose his thinking and intentions. On 13 June 1907, Grey was asked point blank whether the negotiations with Russia involved 'general political relationships'. He replied:

> The direct object of the negotiations is to prevent conflict and difficulties between the two Powers and in the part of Asia which affects the Indian frontier and the Russian frontiers in that region. If these negotiations result in an agreement, it will deal only with these questions. What the indirect result will be as regard general political relationships must depend on how such an agreement works in practice and what effect it has on public opinion in both countries.[3]

No Radical bothered to pursue in detail the question of possible 'indirect results' despite their experience of the indirect results of the entente with France.

On 16 June, by Imperial decree, the Second Russian Duma was dissolved and a new electoral law was promulgated giving predominance to the landowners and the middle classes. Stolypin, the Russian Prime Minister, was forced to make concessions to autocracy. The revolutionary spirit seemed to have spent its force. Everywhere in Russia there was an atmosphere of suspicion, fear and oppression. It was against this background that the final negotiations for the convention were pursued.

The dissolution of the Second Duma brought another crisis of conscience for the Radicals. The *Spectator* might advise its readers that in the conduct of external affairs the Russian Government ought to be considered as no more than 'a piece of diplomatic machinery', but

---

[1] For procedural arrangements, see *Hansard*, iv:152:340–1 and 802–4. See, also, Spender, *The Public Life*, ii, 40. 'The British House of Commons held Ministers responsible to it, but it seldom or never presumed to press for an answer when the Foreign Secretary put his finger to his lips.' On the limitations of question time in the House as a means of eliciting information on foreign affairs from the Foreign Secretary, see Gosses, 86–9.

[2] See Grey to Nicolson, 3 Oct. 1906, quoted Monger, 287. Grey preferred when possible to make private arrangements with a questioner. See, for example, Austen Chamberlain, 346–7.

[3] *Hansard*, iv:175:1589.

The Nation could not accept this. A modern Government had to be identified with certain principles. 'Democracy may well flatter itself that for all its weaknesses it has no need of such allies.'[1] *New Age* comforted itself with the thought that this would be the end of talk of an entente between Russia and Britain. 'Now one would imagine that even a Liberal Government would stop short of that degree of infamy. . . . Events have made constitutional democracy in Russia a contradiction in terms. . . . We say, "The Duma is dead: long live the Russian Republic!" '[2]

For all the militancy of their journalism, the wiser Radicals soon recognised that they were engaged in fighting a hopeless battle. The Government was determined on concluding a convention with Russia. There was nothing that they could hope to do about it. A correspondent noted bitterly in the columns of the *Manchester Guardian*: 'We shall not hear of this base thing until it is done.'[3] Now it was merely a question of waiting upon the Government. It was not likely that there would be any official information until Parliament had risen for the summer recess.[4]

On Sunday, 14 July, considered by some a singularly appropriate date as it marked the anniversary of the fall of the Bastille, a meeting was organised in Trafalgar Square by the Friends of Russian Freedom.[5] It was to protest against any alliance with the Russian Government. Most of the speakers were Socialists 'determined to make Sir Edward Grey pause before he committed . . . [Britain] to a policy disastrous alike to her interests and honour.'[6] Though the language the speakers employed was for the most part extreme, *The Nation* claimed that the opinions expressed were 'shared by a very large number of Englishmen of all parties'.[7] The meeting itself went off without any incident. Then a group of the more ardent spirits marched down Whitehall to demonstrate in front of the Foreign Office. When Jack Williams attempted to address the crowd from the vantage point of the Foreign Office's railings, he had barely managed to shout, 'Down with the Government', when he was pulled down by the police who then charged the crowd and broke up the meeting.[8]

[1] *The Nation*, 26 June 1907.   [2] *New Age*, 20 June 1907, p. 113.
[3] Letter to *Manchester Guardian*, 27 June 1907.
[4] See *The Nation*, 10 Aug. 1907: 'Treaties are rarely published while Parliament is sitting.'
[5] This long-standing one-time Liberal body was now dominated by Socialists and the more extreme Radicals.
[6] *New Age*, 18 July 1907, p. 177.   [7] *The Nation*, 20 July 1907.
[8] Cf. Reports of meeting in *Manchester Guardian*, 15 July 1907: *Labour Leader*, 19 July 1907, pp. 52 and 60; and *New Age*, 18 July 1907, p. 184. 'The people of England were given another illustration of the devotion of a Liberal Government to the ideal of liberty.'

The Anglo-Russian Convention was signed at the Russian Foreign Office on the afternoon of 31 August. Parliament had risen two days earlier. Among the first to congratulate Grey on the conclusion of the Agreement was Campbell-Bannerman. Apart from its Asian implications, the entente would 'make things easier in Europe'. Ripon also congratulated Grey. There was no reference to the European significance of the entente in his letter.[1]

The French were delighted, the Germans reserved. Von Miquel, the German chargé d'affaires at St Petersburg, claimed: 'These plans need not necessarily be ascribed to any anti-German tendency, yet Germany is the country which is most affected by the Agreement.' The Kaiser minuted this despatch: 'Yes, when taken all round, it is aimed at us.'[2]

When the official terms were published in September, Radical criticism of the Convention was ineffectual. Morley, who among Cabinet members best understood the Radicals' vulnerability, identified the source of their weakness. They were 'of all sorts of political temperament' and agreed on few things in concert. Their energies were 'dissipated upon a number of different projects.' Given the exercise of moderate commonsense they presented no serious difficulty to a determined and single-minded minister.[3]

Those moderates who had disclaimed the relevance of the manner in which Russia conducted her internal affairs to the pursuit of an entente with her by Britain, naturally were not as concerned as the militants. They concentrated their energies upon thwarting any possible Tory criticisms and were satisfied by the evidence of an apparent lack of greed in Britain's international dealings. Above all, they were pleased by the possibility of a reduction of Britain's defence commitments in India.

A Liberal cannot grow lyrical over the Convention, but he can reasonably say that in so far as it promises relief to Indian

---

[1] Campbell-Bannerman to Grey, 3 Sept. 1907; and Ripon to Grey, 6 Sept. 1907, both quoted by Trevelyan, 189.

[2] *D.G.P.* xxv, 8537. What particularly impressed Miquel was 'the meaning of the Anglo-Russian Agreement lies not so much in Asia but much more in Europe where its consequences could be made noticeable for a long time', *ibid.*, xxv, 8536. Public statements by German politicians about the Convention were marked by an insincere optimism, but the nationalist leader, Reventlow, regarded Anglo-Russian reconciliation as more disquieting than the Anglo-French entente. It was the crowning success of *Einkreisungspolitik*, the policy of German encirclement. See Luigi Albertini, *Origins of 1914 War* (1952), i, 189.

[3] See Morley to Minto, 15 June and 11 May 1906 quoted Morley, ii, 172 and 175; Blunt, ii, 191–2. 'The whole thing is abominable, but what fools the Radical members is to have put up with Grey these two years since the General Election.'

finances, secures our honour in relation to Tibet, and checks the pace of actual European attack upon Persia while protecting legitimate British interests there, it serves some substantial ends with the least possible discredit.[1]

Another group of Radicals vigorously denied the assertion that one could accept the Liberal Government's claim, frequently made in the Commons, that Russia's internal affairs were not relevant to the conduct of external questions concerning frontier settlements. Nevinson had angrily dismissed this particular excuse in the *Albany Review*. 'It would be impossible to enter into an arrangement with the Tsar's Government about so much as one yard of mountain territory in Bokhara without taking sides with tyranny against the cause of freedom. . . . We shall have entered into another Holy Alliance for the suppression of Liberty.'[2] Members of the International Arbitration and Peace Association also adopted this view.[3] Socialists had consistently pursued this line of criticism but expressed themselves with such imbalance and violence that they alienated support among the less aggressive Radicals.[4] Criticism of the Convention was cautious among that group of Radicals who were Balkan enthusiasts.[5] They hoped that out of the Anglo-Russian Agreement might be developed the old Liberal policy of bringing pressure upon Turkey, Austria and Germany to remedy affairs in the Balkans.[6] This explains why, after a period of wavering and rather hesitant criticism, C. R. Buxton's *Albany Review* finally subsided into approval of the entente.

There remained two strands of Radical criticism. Both were more consistent and permanent, and were directed towards the general conduct of foreign affairs. The first was a condemnation of secrecy. This was to become a hardy perennial of Radical criticism. Nevinson had initiated the attack by claiming that the secrecy and obscurantism of Britain's foreign policy was endured by the Commons only

---

[1] *Manchester Guardian*, 2 Sept. 1907.
[2] *Albany Review*, Aug. 1907, pp. 516–18.
[3] See *Concord*, xxiii, nos. 9/10, Sept./Oct. 1907. 'The Agreement is bound to give renewed strength to the vile Muscovite despotism and therefore to be a blow to the cause of liberty. . . . This apparently is of no concern to our Whig Foreign Secretary and his colleagues.' See also *The Nation*, 3 Aug. 1907: 'We are adding to the prestige of autocracy, we are condoning political crimes far less pardonable than those which led us to boycott Servia.'
[4] See *New Age*, 3 Oct. 1907: 'Our Honour Cheap Today'; and 'The Anglo-Russian Convention', at pp. 354 and 361. The only attempt to analyse Grey's policy by this Socialist weekly during the period of negotiations presents an extraordinary caricature. See *New Age*, 23 May 1907, p. 52. See also, *ibid.*, comments on Grey, 21 Nov. 1907, p. 65.
[5] See, for example, letter by H. Gregory to *Manchester Guardian*, 25 July 1907.
[6] See *Albany Review*, ii, 7, 243–4, 287 and 716.

because of the personal respect felt for Grey. Foreign Office methods were calculated to conceal commitments until it was too late for anything to be done about them. Most of the Radical journals subscribed to his view, but *Concord* alone reverted to this charge against Grey when the terms of the Anglo-Russian Convention were published. 'It is surely a preposterous thing that in a country supposed to be governed on democratic principles the representatives of the people should be left in the dark until the whole affair has been settled between the Foreign Offices of the two countries.'[1]

The second strand of criticism was pursued by *The Nation*. It noted with concern that Grey seemed to be more interested in the material interests of the British Empire than in keeping faith with the moral ideals of Liberalism. As to the question of more information being made available to members of Parliament, *The Nation* claimed:

> The annual debate in the Commons affords little clue to the larger calculations that in the end dictate Sir Edward Grey's handling of questions of detail. . . . The grouping of States, the making of Ententes, the careful weighing of the balance of power go busily forward . . . a certain mobilisation of Powers is proceeding always with England and France at its centre, always with Germany outside.[2]

The signing of a Convention between Britain and Russia was merely further proof of the anti-German design of Grey's policy. Grey's aim was to 'restore the influence of Russia as a counterpoise to Germany in the Concert of Europe.' Britain had chosen 'in the interests of . . . [its] *Weltpolitik* to cover up weakness and to restore Russia to her old position of influence'.[3]

The Times had welcomed the Anglo-Russian Agreement because it would 'lead to closer and more intimate relations all over the world'.[4] The *Westminister Gazette*, recognised as the official voice of Liberalism, explicitly declared that the agreement had 'no European motive'. But *The Nation* was not to be persuaded by this assurance. A close study of the 'bargain' strengthened their opinion that Grey

[1] *Concord*, xxiii, nos. 9/10, Sept./Oct. 1907, p. 93. See also resolution of International Arbitration Executive Committee on Anglo-Russian Agreement, 8 Oct. 1907: 'Foreign relations of the Empire should be placed under effective Parliamentary supervision and no longer be left to the uncontrolled power of the Executive.' Cf. the Duma's complaint on the same grounds, quoted R. P. Churchill, 333.
[2] *The Nation*, 3 Aug. 1907.
[3] *Ibid.*, 7 Sept. 1907; cf. 'Calchas' (J. L. Garvin) in *Fortnightly Review*, Oct. 1907. There the explanation for Britain's 'movement to settle outstanding differences in the rest of the world' was Germany's 'challenge of our naval supremacy which is the life of our race'.
[4] *The Times*, 2 Sept. 1907.

had interests other than Asiatic upon his mind when it was concluded. 'To win a partner in the game of *Weltpolitik* we have paid a
price which nothing but the expectation of Russian support in other
regions of controversy could have explained.'[1]

When eventually the terms of the Anglo-Russian Convention were
debated in the Commons in February 1908, Grey with Morley's
support successfully routed Tory critics.[2] Radical complaints were
muted. Their attention by then was engaged in other directions and
upon other issues. *The Nation* alone boldly maintained its perceptive
and critical thesis.[3]

[1] *The Nation*, 28 Sept. 1907.
[2] There is an account of the debate in Morley, ii, 244–5.
[3] See, for example, *The Nation*, 22 Feb. 1908: 'The Anglo-Russian Agreement
was for both countries an incident in the development of the ties which our
French entente created. That is its real genesis. . . . We have carried out
M. Delcassé's idea of isolating conservative Germany by embracing reactionary
Russia.'

Chapter 2   The Minister for War
Deceives His Critics

A change in military strategy

Though Haldane was soon to count on Campbell-Bannerman's support as his most influential aid in pushing his proposed reforms of the Army through the Cabinet and Parliament, at the time of his appointment to be Secretary of State for War there was little love lost between the two men. It had been Haldane's wish that Rosebery and not Campbell-Bannerman should have been Prime Minister. The Relugas Plot had failed, but it was still a recent and bitter memory to Campbell-Bannerman who regarded Haldane as having been the prime mover in the intrigue. Therefore, there was a natural vindictive anticipation in the Prime Minister's remark of waiting to see how Schopenhauer got on in the Kailyard. The War Office had been the grave of many reputations. The 'ingenious' Haldane was now Minister for War, a post that C-B had declared no one would touch with a pole.[1]

The Boer War had made it obvious that Britain's military organisation required reforming thoroughly. But what military ardour had not been soured by the war was dampened by peace. The fear of possible enemies, and martial enthusiasm, made way in the public mind for dislike of war and of the military profession. To advocate conscription in whatever guise was to arouse invincible opposition. 'This repugnance to compulsory military service was a sentiment of which the vast majority of English-men had learned to be proud; it came from the heart of their liberalism.'[2]

When Arnold Forster had replaced St John Brodrick at the War Office in September 1903, a war-weary public was already beginning to demand economies rather than reforms. Campbell-Bannerman as leader of the Opposition had clearly enunciated the Radical attitude towards the Army. If a policy of peace towards the rest of the world

[1] Sir Frederick Maurice, *Haldane* (1937), i, 157.
[2] E. Halévy, *The Rule of Democracy*, 155.

was to be pursued then this must mean retrenchment in military spending. The best policy was to leave the Army alone for it was his experience that reform was but a little less expensive than war.[1]

For that small yet determined coterie who were interested in the problems of reforming the British Army, the one bright feature of the new Liberal Government was Haldane's appointment. They approved of the man and trusted him.[2] Esher wrote to Kitchener assuring him: 'The change of Government has produced one great good at least. It has rid us of Arnold Forster. . . . The new Secretary of State cannot fail to do well. Above all he has determined to walk slowly, and has no preconceived ideas. He is adroit, shrewd and exceedingly clever.'[3] Esher's pleasure at the appointment was not surprising. Haldane had professed his willingness to be '"nobbled" by our Committee'.[4]

Grey was acutely conscious of the military implications of the policy that he was pursuing towards France and Germany. His primary concern was that at whatever cost France should not be bullied into Germany's arms. The public saw the problem of Anglo-German relations in terms of the strength of the countries' respective navies. The Army's rôle in Grey's calculations did not attract their attention. But Grey knew that it was imperative that a policy of Army reform should be pursued by Haldane as the necessary complement of the direction which he was imparting to Britain's foreign policy. From the beginning, Grey was 'more aware of the close relationship of foreign policy and military strength than his predecessors of the 1890s'.[5]

Charles Repington, who was military correspondent of *The Times*, recorded: 'The great danger that we ran at this time was that the victorious Radicals should incontinently so cut down the Army, and so reduce the estimates, that reforms would be out of the question.'[6] The problems Haldane faced were enormous.[7] Paul Cambon told

---

[1] See *Hansard*, iv:129:494–5.
[2] See, *inter alia*, Maurice, i, 168; H. Nicolson, *George V* (1952), 93; Fitzroy, i, 288; Repington, 264–5: 'I was pleased because Mr Haldane . . . did not entertain the destructive design which the left wing of his party harboured against the Army.'
[3] *E.P.*, ii, 132.   [4] *Ibid.*, ii, 126.
[5] F. A. Johnson, *Defence by Committee* (1960), 93.   [6] Repington, 266.
[7] The political difficulties of his new post apart, the practical problems that Haldane faced were enormous. Lord Roberts was not exaggerating when, in the summer of 1905, he told the House of Lords that Britain's 'armed forces as a body [were] absolutely unfitted and unprepared for war'. *Hansard*, iv:149:14. Though the War Office had been recently reorganised, no practicable plan of reform had been devised. As had his predecessors at the War Office, Haldane never doubted his ability to achieve successful reform. The major

Repington that there was no hope of Haldane being successful. 'To create an Army, money and men are required. The Liberal Cabinet will not provide the money; the nation will not provide the men.'

Haldane, already distrusted and disliked by the Radicals above all other Cabinet Ministers, by a series of injudicous speeches during the election campaign caused them further offence.[1] The War Minister knew that he could count on very few of his party to support him, and even within the Cabinet most of his ministerial colleagues, while prepared to profit should he succeed, would happily see him dropped if he failed.[2]

However, the prospect that faced Haldane was not one of completely unrelieved gloom. Campbell-Bannerman's public pronouncements in Opposition could not be taken to represent his opinions now that he was Head of Government. Esher foresaw in December 1905 that there would be no difficulty in working with Campbell-Bannerman.[3] In the Cabinet Haldane could count on the support of his fellow Liberal imperialists who occupied key positions of power. There were brilliant talents, both military and civilian, keen to give every encouragement and support to Haldane in his reform measures. Colonel Gerald Ellison, who was Haldane's principal private secretary, and Sir Charles Harris, permanent head of the financial department, were but two who headed a long list of dedicated and loyal administrators. Esher was anxious to give his support. Among Haldane's probable critics in the Cabinet, none could claim more than limited expertise on military matters. Haldane's position as a minister backing a definite scheme which few of his critics understood, made him very strong.[4] Though his party had entered office with a mandate for economy in all fields save the social services, Haldane could expect that the influence exercised by the Treasury inside the Cabinet would tend to be 'somewhat less than in the civil sphere, because of the more technical reasoning and

---

advantage he enjoyed was that his succession to office coincided with the emergence of a new strategic situation and his willingness to operate from first principles in creating his 'Hegelian Army'. See his *Autobiography*, 183–5; and John Ehrman, *Cabinet Government and War 1890–1940* (1958), 34–7.
[1] See Haldane's speeches to City, 4 Jan. 1906, and at East Lothian, 11 Jan. 1906. He 'recognised obligations higher even than that of economy'. The 'business of the Government was to preserve the Army and Navy in as strong a position as possible'. See the motion of censure against Haldane by the Executive Committee of the International Arbitration and Peace Association, 30 Jan. 1906. C-B was very angry with Haldane for his indiscreet speeches. See C-B to Asquith, 5 Jan. 1906, quoted Stephen E. Koss, *Lord Haldane, Scapegoat for Liberalism* (1969), 45.
[2] See Repington, 275.
[3] See *E.P.*, ii, 127–8.
[4] See Lord Sydenham, *My Working Life* (1927), 193.

arguments which the military department could raise against reduction of expenditure'.[1] In the Commons Haldane knew that he could expect determined opposition from Radical members of his party. But again, few of them were experts upon military questions. Haldane knew that if he was prepared to take meticulous concern over the details of his scheme, this would surely defeat arguments that were based on vague assertions of antimilitaristic principles. Haldane could expect the censures of much of the Liberal Press, but he enjoyed the not altogether negligible support of *The Times*, and a special department of the War Office dealt in supplying the Press with propaganda that was favourable to his schemes.[2] Pacifist and antimilitarist opinion was vocal but more superficial than many supposed, and the 'militarisation of the nation, and particulary of the governing classes was more profound'.[3] At all costs, Haldane was determined to make a success of his job and to that end he bent all his formidable physical and intellectual powers.[4]

In a 'rough note' which Haldane had sent on New Year's Day 1906 to the Army Council for their consideration, he had said: 'As regards the purpose of the Army, what is obviously required is a highly organised and well equipped force which can be transported with the least possible delay to any part of the world where it is required.'[5] In less than a month, this general statement of policy had become the precise object.

It has to be remembered that for more than half a century it had been accepted military policy that the primary function of the Army was the garrisoning of the Empire and the protection of its

---

[1] Johnson, 101–2.

[2] War Office public relations activities inspired bitter attacks by Radicals who blustered and stormed at 'The student of Schopenhauer', for becoming 'an indiscriminating coadjutor of the *Daily Mail*'. See particularly the open letter to Haldane by 'Pacificus'(!) in *Concord* xxv, no. 3, Mar. 1909, 27–9. 'Your War Office utters loud raucous cries of "Help!" Help from anywhere, from anybody, from anything. Help from the coercive capitalist; help from the Yellow Press, help from the clap trap doggerel and the faked bioscope pictures of the music-hall stage; help from the inane vapourings of the pantomime "boy". Nothing is too foolish or too degraded to be a friend of your War Office.'

[3] Halévy, *The Rule of Democracy*, 186. See also Fitzroy, i, 395; and Blunt, ii, 299. See also pamphlet by J. A. Farrer, *Moral Cant About Conscription* (1908), for examples of influence in schools, Church, Bar and medical profession. For a Radical pacifist estimate of the balance of forces, see *Concord*, xxiv, no. 1, Jan. 1908, p. 1.

[4] See Haldane to J. A. Spender, quoted Sommer, 169. 'I am enjoying myself hugely. The work of thinking out and executing organisation delights me. My Generals are like angels'. See also Campbell-Bannerman's remark to Esher: 'At the rate of progress made by Haldane . . . [he] would probably resign in about 10 days after having exhausted all possible reforms of the W.O., and of the Army' (ii, 128).

[5] Maurice, i, 169.

land frontiers. Cardwell's system of linked battalions, created in 1871, had been specifically designed to provide sufficient troops for these duties. By far the greatest number of troops, some 76,000, were engaged on garrison duties in India. The protection of that subcontinent, and in particular its North-West frontier, dominated both War Office and Admiralty thinking. Successive War Ministers when presenting their estimates had reiterated constantly that India had been their primary concern when framing their policies. India was 'the only possible place of contact with a great European Army'. The Russian Empire was described as 'our most formidable and also most probable military adversary'.[1] Therefore, in 1906, it was natural that men of all parties should suppose that if a minister talked of despatching troops overseas in a considerable expeditionary force, their destination would be British India to resist possible aggression by Russia.

Grey, anxiously watching developments in Morocco, wrote a discreet note to Haldane on 8 January informing him that there were indications and persistent reports that Germany contemplated attacking France in the spring.

> I don't think these are more than the precautions and flourishes that Germany would naturally make apropos of the Morocco Conference. But they are not altogether to be disregarded. A situation might arise presently in which popular feeling might compel the Government to go to the help of France and you might suddenly be asked what you could do . . . I don't want you to give any definite answer in a hurry but I think you should be preparing one.[2]

When they met at Berwick on 12 January, Haldane and Grey agreed that it might become necessary to implement the entente with France, and that military plans to provide for that eventuality should be prepared. Haldane in his book, *Before the War*, has outlined both the nature of the problem with which he was faced by this information from Grey, and the solution offered.

---

[1] See, *inter alia*, *Hansard*, iv:131:342–3 and 623–4; 136: 1497; 146–78; also L. S. Amery, *The Problem of the Army* (1903), 146. The claim made by Halévy, *Rule of Democracy*, 161, n. 2, that Haldane indicated the change in strategical thinking during a speech to the Commons in March 1906—*Hansard*, iv: 153:675—is not convincing. Haldane was answering an economic argument, and it was to rebutt this point that he directed the rhetorical question cited by Halévy. However, if the most favoured construction is put upon Haldane's words, it still does not amount to a, clear, unequivocal explanation or statement of intent on what was, after all, a fundamental change. A few military 'experts' in 1906 did write articles on the basis that Belgium was a possible area of British military intervention as much as the N.-W. frontier of India. See S. R. Williamson, *The Politics of Grand Strategy* (1969), 92.
[2] Grey to Haldane, 8 Jan. 1906, quoted Maurice, i, 172–3.

Could we . . . reconsider our military organisation so that we might be able rapidly to dispatch . . . say 100,000 men in a well formed army . . . to guard the French frontier of Belgium in case the German Army should seek to enter France in that way . . . I became aware at once[1] that there was a new army problem. It was, how to mobilise and concentrate at a place of assembly to be opposite the Belgian frontier, a force calculated as adequate . . . to make up for the inadequacy of the French armies for their great task of defending the entire French frontier from Dunkirk down to Belfort. . . . An investigation of a searching character presently revealed great deficiencies in the British military organisation. . . . There was, therefore, nothing for it but to attempt a complete revolution in the organisation of the British Army at home. . . . The outcome was a complete recasting, which, after three years work, made it practicable rapidly to mobilise, not only 100,000 but 160,000 men; to transport them, with the aid of the Navy, to a place of concentration which had been settled between the Staffs of France and Britain; and to have them at their appointed place within twelve days, an interval based on what the German Army required on its side for a corresponding concentration.[2]

In this account written after the war, Haldane clearly indicates both the *raison d'être* of the Expeditionary Force that he forged, and its destination. The questions to be asked are: were these Haldane's intentions from the beginning? If they were, did he make his purpose clear either to the Cabinet or to Parliament?

Commentators writing when the 1914–18 war was over, suggest that from the beginning of his tenure at the War Office, Haldane made his intentions clear. For example, J. A. Spender claimed that

The scheme of army reorganisation which Mr Haldane had carried through at the War Office *frankly contemplated* the despatch of an army to the Continent and prepared an Expeditionary Force for that purpose as a means of reinforcing it. As we look back on these times their secrets seem to have been very open ones to those who had eyes to see.[3]

Again, Sir Charles Harris, who was intimately involved in Haldane's reforms, in his account of Haldane's work at the War Office published

---

[1] Ministers when writing their memoirs after the war tended to telescope time to satisfy the small vanity of proving their prescience concerning the 'inevitability' of war with Germany. Therefore, the claim by Haldane that he 'at once' realised the need for a complete change in military thinking, needs treating with a certain amount of caution.

[2] R. B. Haldane, *Before the War* (1920), 29–33.

[3] Spender and Asquith, *Life of Lord Oxford and Asquith*, i, 348 (my italics). Spender wrote this comment in 1931. However, correspondence with Esher, and a leader he wrote in the *Westminster Gazette*, 5 June 1912, strongly suggests that at the time Spender was no more aware of the implications of Haldane's scheme than the next man. The leader concerned the disposition

in 1928 stated that in the autumn of 1906, that is before the 1907–08 Army Estimates were framed, the minister

> had formulated two problems for solution: (a) to produce . . . the strongest possible regular force, not for home defence but capable of taking the field on the Continent, with an adequate second line Army for home defence or expansion in addition; and (b) to make all necessary preparations for putting the Expeditionary Force in the field with a rapidity equal to that of Germany.[1]

However, these statements of the patency of Haldane's intentions compare strangely with Morley's complaint to his biographer made in 1915. 'Haldane *now* says he foresaw the war, . . . Why did he not confide his foresight to his colleagues? He never talked like that in the Cabinet.'[2]

In the period during which Haldane laid the foundations for, and established his Army reforms, he never once said anything to indicate that there had been a revolution in military thinking and that the traditional concept of the strategy of the British Army was no longer relevant. He made no announcement that he perceived the nature of the problems which the Army faced had dramatically changed, from opposing Russia on the North-West frontier of India to supporting France against Germany in Europe. Rather, in the public presentation and explanation of his reforms, Haldane talked as though there had been no change in the strategical problems faced by the War Office, and that the same criteria of judgment were being employed as had served in the immediate past.[3]

---

of the French and British fleets in the Mediterranean and the North Sea, but as Spender's biographer points out, the views Spender held upon this subject were 'a little surprising' if he knew 'this was part of a larger policy arising out of the Anglo-French Entente'. See Wilson Harris, *J. A. Spender* (1946), 119–20.
[1] Sir Charles Harris, 'Lord Haldane at the War Office', in *Viscount Haldane of Cloan: the man and his work* (1928), 11. Cf. Harris to Haldane, 19 Mar. 1916. When Haldane circulated a 'Memorandum of Events between 1906–15' among his friends in *1916*, and asked for their comments, Harris wrote: 'You speak of France as the probable theatre of operations at the very beginning of your term of office. At the time [1906–08] we were deep in the scheme for reinforcing India to meet Russia on the N.W. Frontier; and when in 1908 Churchill attacked your system it was on the hypothesis you defended it. . . . I mention this because your memorandum rather reads as though in 1906 Germany was already the recognised enemy . . .' (The above quotation is taken from Dr Dorey's thesis, p. 80.) Kitchener, who was Commander-in-Chief of the Army in India, throughout this period was convinced that Russia was planning to invade India, and bent all his energies to prepare for this contingency. See Philip Magnus, *Kitchener: portrait of an imperialist* (1958), 238.
[2] J. H. Morgan, *John Viscount Morley: an appreciation and some reminiscences*, (1924), 46–7.
[3] The Committee of Imperial Defence continued to concentrate its attentions upon the Russian 'menace' and did not turn its attention to the problems of British intervention upon the Continent in the event of war against Germany

Haldane and the Cabinet

Because of the size of the task Haldane had undertaken, he was not ready to present his scheme of reforms to the Cabinet until the beginning of 1907. At that time the international situation was not such as would have directed the Cabinet's attention to the possibility of offering military aid to France to repel a possible invasion by the German Army.

The acute international tension of January 1906, which had led to the formalising of secret military conversations between the British and French Staffs to concert plans to resist Germany, was forgotten. In any event, the secret of the military conversations was shared by few ministers—the Prime Minister, Ripon, Grey, Haldane and possibly Asquith.

By November 1906, Haldane had developed on paper the general outlines of his scheme, and Campbell-Bannerman appointed a subcommittee of the Committee of Imperial Defence to report 'whether this scheme thus outlined appears to conform to reasonable national requirements and to be capable of being carried into practical effect'. Haldane defined the main features of his proposals as first, an Expeditionary Force ready for rapid mobilisation at all times. Second, a Territorial Force capable of supporting and if necessary expanding the Expeditionary Force in the event of a great national emergency. The sub-committee was precluded from considering any alternative scheme. When they reported, they did so simply and in guarded terms that the scheme was an improvement on any that had been devised previously.[1]

Esher's aid was invoked to explain the scheme to Campbell-Bannerman, for the Prime Minister had been 'unable to understand Haldane's rhetorical rendering of it'. In the event, Campbell-Bannerman still retained some doubts as to possible weaknesses, but Esher's impression was that the Prime Minister could be expected to back Haldane's scheme. On occasion, Morley was proving himself difficult by raising questions that in Esher's opinion were unnecessary and gave the false impression to the military that the Cabinet was disunited on the merits of the scheme. However, by 21 December Morley's doubts for the moment appeared to have been placated, and

until the reforms instituted by Haldane were well under way. See Hankey's comments on this in *Government Control in War* (1945), 24. It is of interest to note that writers of popular fiction turned earlier and more readily to the consideration of Germany rather than Russia as the most likely threat to Britain's security. For examples, see I. F. Clarke, *Voices Prophesying War* (1966), chap II and IV, *passim.*
[1] See Sydenham, 193–4.

he was giving no more trouble. Haldane received confirmation from Campbell-Bannerman that he could count on his support. The Prime Minister was impressed that Haldane had managed to convert what had appeared to him nebulous ideas into a Bill. 'The fact is,' Esher confided to his son, 'none of the Cabinet understand, or ever will understand, the question.'[1]

Because there were still certain reservations felt, a Cabinet Committee was set up to consider Haldane's scheme. When interviewed, Haldane did not make a good impression on his questioners. Morley again chose to play the part of a prophet of doom. On 1 January 1907 he wrote to Campbell-Bannerman, 'The dangers to the Cabinet and its solidarity seem to be Ireland and Haldane.'[2] Haldane was plunged into deep depression and talked of failure and his return to the Bar. But, a week later he seems to have recovered his nerve and spirits when he wrote to the Prime Minister, 'I am really getting very hopeful. . . . I have confidence enough in myself to be keen to try if you and the Cabinet will let me. You have given me every help.'[3]

Meanwhile, Morley had informed Esher that though the Cabinet Committee was not hostile to Haldane's scheme, they were not enthusiastic about it. They were frightened by 'the length of the Bill and the *bother* which drastic proposals always entail'.[4] So that he might gain Campbell-Bannerman's support, Haldane stressed the thoroughly Cardwellian nature of the reforms he proposed to make. He wrote to the Prime Minister: 'I feel that what we are doing now is so completely the realisation of those intentions of Cardwell with which you were yourself so much associated.'[5] This was much the best ploy to engage the Prime Minister's sympathies. For Campbell-Bannerman, who had been financial secretary at the War Office when Cardwell had been the Minister, the Cardwell System was, 'the ark of the military covenant'.[6]

Though he did not realise it at the time, Haldane's battle for the Cabinet's approval of his scheme was now all but won. His attempts to gather support outside the Cabinet from Milner were unsuccessful,[7]

[1] *E.P.*, ii, 208–9.
[2] Morley to Bannerman, 1 Jan. 1907, quoted, Koss, *Haldane*, 50.
[3] Haldane to Campbell-Bannerman, 8 Jan. 1907, quoted Koss, 51.
[4] *E.P.*, ii, 215.
[5] Haldane to Campbell-Bannerman, 9 Jan. 1907, C.B. Papers, B.M. Add. MSS. 41, 218. See also Koss, 51; and Williamson, 93–4.
[6] Spender, *Campbell-Bannerman*, ii, 325.
[7] See A. M. Gollin, *Proconsul in Politics* (1964), 133. 'I listened to Haldane for nearly 20 minutes the other night. . . . He might have said something if he had a mind to it. It was all *blather*. If that is *the best* we can expect from these fellows, Heaven help us.'

but where previously there had been doubts and uncertainty, even hostility, he now found that his colleagues were prepared to support him. Campbell-Bannerman wrote to Sinclair that Haldane had been to talk with him about the suggested reforms. 'He dwelt on the fact of the Cardwell system being maintained. . . . All is therefore for the best—the soldiers are delighted; the volunteers everywhere enthusiastic; Grey and Asquith very warm for it; Burns and J. M. most appreciative. Every bolthole was thus stopped! I could only congratulate him.' This was a bitter letter for Sinclair to receive. From the beginning he had been hostile to Haldane's scheme and had exerted all his influence on Campbell-Bannerman to warn him of Haldane's 'transparent attempts to conjure with the magic word Cardwell'.[1] Now it was agreed that there would be no useful purpose served by the Cabinet Committee meeting again, and Haldane's scheme was approved by the Cabinet.[2]

As 1907 drew to its close Haldane had every reason to look back with satisfaction at the fortunes which the year had bestowed upon his plans. He had successfully launched his Expeditionary Force and the required legislation for the Territorial Army was safely placed on the statute book. But the ever-present problems of economy still posed a threat, and that despite Spender's all too comfortable assertion in his *Westminster Gazette* that the Liberal Government was 'too much concerned with the success of the scheme to risk it for a few hundred thousand pounds'.[3] A week earlier than Spender's rash prediction, Haldane had been forced to circulate a Memorandum to his fellow ministers assuring them that he had cut everything as close as he dared and that 'unless the Cabinet decides to withdraw troops from overseas I cannot go further without breaking heavily into the efficiency of the Army.' Once again Haldane felt a terrible sense of isolation in the face of his critics. He had lost the support of the King for being too 'progressive', particularly in his attitude towards the Guards. On the other hand, he was deserted by the

---

[1] Sinclair to C-B 27 Jan. 1907; and C-B to Sinclair, 5 Feb. 1907. (C-B Papers, B.M. Add. MSS 42, 130). I am indebted to Dr A. J. Dorey for drawing my attention to these letters.

[2] That Esher's claim, the Cabinet did not understand the import of the proposals in Haldane's scheme, was a correct assessment, is evidenced by Morley's attitude to the sub-committee of the Committee of Imperial Defence of which he was chairman. The Committee's brief was to examine 'the reasonable military requirements of the Empire'. Morley maintained that 'India was the key . . . Indian requirements cover all others.' Morley was under the impression that he was tackling the whole military problem, but a European war and a British commitment upon the Continent were not even considered. So the main point of Haldane's reforms was conceded, or at least ignored. See *E.P.*, ii, 210–13 and 216–18.

[3] *Westminster Gazette*, 21 Nov. 1907.

majority of the Cabinet because they considered that he was too 'moderate' in his pursuit of economy. Esher noted the nature and cause of Haldane's dilemma. 'His weakness is that in wanting to please everybody, he satisfies no one. His strength is that he anxiously desires to create a perfectly equipped military machine, is exceedingly tenacious of main principles, and believes in *force* as the foundation of Empire.'[1]

Campbell-Bannerman's health was failing and by November 1907 it was evident that he was seriously ill. Haldane was not happy with the prospect of a change of Prime Minister. He doubted whether his friend Asquith as Prime Minister would have the capacity to maintain discipline within the Cabinet.[2] Already Lloyd George was showing signs of restlessness about military and naval expenditure. Haldane had managed to repulse Lloyd George's first attack upon the Army Estimates in February with the aid of 'the wonderful old P.M.'. But he feared this was only a temporary victory, and his expectations of survival without Campbell-Bannerman's aid were not sanguine.[3] In April 1908 Haldane wrote a letter of farewell to his dying chief. 'There is no member of your Cabinet who has realised more what he has learned and gained from you than myself.'[4] A relationship that had begun with distrust and hostility ended in confidence, amity and mutual dependence.

When Asquith's new Cabinet was announced, Haldane's worst fears were realised. Lloyd George was given the Exchequer, and Winston Churchill was raised to the Board of Trade. Haldane's potentially most dangerous critics were thus both given more power and independent influence in the Cabinet. As in all Cabinets, alliances were formed between members of kindred spirit. 'Of those the closest and in some ways the most incongruous, was the alliance between Lloyd George and Winston Churchill.'[5] The Tory Press dubbed the pair 'Cleon and Alcibiades'. More unkindly, John Burns referred to them as 'the two Romeos'. Lloyd George was a virtuoso in the art of political manipulation. He dazzled Churchill, but the younger man exercised no influence on Lloyd George. There could not have been a less happy appointment to the Exchequer as far as Haldane was concerned. There was little love lost between the two men. Lloyd George called Haldane 'the Minister for Slaughter'. Haldane considered

---

[1] *E.P.*, ii, 267.
[2] There were some who considered that Haldane would be a better choice as Campbell-Bannerman's successor than Asquith. Perhaps, the strangest of these advocates was *New Age*. See 8 Feb. 1908, p. 281.
[3] See Haldane to his sister, 5 and 7 April 1908, quoted Koss, *Haldane*, 55.
[4] Haldane to Campbell-Bannerman, 6 April 1908, quoted Koss, *ibid.*
[5] Violet Bonham Carter, *Winston Churchill as I knew him* (1967), 166.

Lloyd George to be an 'illiterate with an unbalanced mind'.[1] Haldane, however, did not make the mistake of underestimating his opponent. He sought assurances from Asquith, so he told Esher. They had struck a bargain over the War Office Estimates for the future. When Esher had occasion to meet and talk with Lloyd George, he drew the conclusion that he 'did not contemplate a pointed attack on Haldane'.[2] But then, why should he when he had an able and willing young lieutenant in Winston Churchill to do all his attacking for him?

A sub-committee, hell-bent on armament retrenchment, had been formed with Harcourt, Lloyd George and Churchill. Baulked in their first desire to reduce the Naval Estimates, they now concentrated their energies on the Army. Esher warned Lloyd George that his enquiry would lead him 'to conclude that no large reduction of the cost of the Army is possible'.[3] Haldane, meanwhile, taking a very serious view of this 'economists' ' campaign, offered his resignation to Asquith, but withdrew it when assured by the Prime Minister that the sub-committee would not be allowed to touch upon any question of Army *policy*.[4] When on 14 May Lloyd George requested that Haldane should cut down the Army he had been met by a point-blank refusal. Churchill now submitted a Memorandum for the Cabinet's consideration, but Haldane, maintaining that it would mean 'ruin and confusion to the Expeditionary Force', strongly deprecated any attempt to interfere with his scheme which had been given the Cabinet's approval the previous year.

On 18 June Churchill returned to the attack with a Memorandum that plainly stated the Army was too large. The 'Expeditionary Force was not justified by any legitimate need of British policy'.[5] He ridiculed the manner in which Haldane used the name of Cardwell to buttress his own scheme. 'By a melancholy transition the economic and reforming policy of Mr Cardwell has become the very keystone in the arch of expenditure.' At Windsor on 22 June Esher and Morley studied Churchill's proposals. To Esher it seemed 'as if Lloyd George has managed to get Winston to lead a frontal attack on Haldane, which is bound to be repulsed with heavy losses. This is not a very auspicious move for a young Minister. Haldane will remain in position. But where will Winston be? Not in such force as before.' Esher was convinced that Churchill was motivated by a desire, 'to push to

[1] Maurice, 1, 168.
[2] *E.P.*, ii, 303 and 310.
[3] Esher to Lloyd George, 22 May 1908, *E.P.*, ii, 313.
[4] Esher to Knollys, 26 May 1908, quoted Sommer, 213
[5] Cf. Fisher to Esher, 5 May 1908, *E.P.*, ii, 309

the front of the Cabinet. He thinks himself Napoleon.'[1] But it was the Tory leader Balfour who made the more accurate estimate. 'Winston was just playing his father's part again.' At all events, Churchill was determined to make himself 'damned disagreeable'[2] to Haldane. And Lloyd George continued happily to pull the strings from the wings.

Haldane replied in detail to Churchill's Memorandum on 25 June.

> Some of the problems which Churchill had attacked simply did not exist; the British Army staffs were proportionately lower than those of seven other leading Powers, and the total strength of our Army, compared with the Armies of the Continent of Europe, was smaller than in Wellington's time. . . . He pointed out that Germany possessed expeditionary forces of far greater strength than the infant one with which we were alleged to be 'menacing' our neighbours. After all, we had '*certain Treaty obligations which might compel us to intervene on the Continent.*'[3]

Churchill's original Memorandum makes it clear that the Cabinet had no idea that Haldane's scheme was designed with a possible continental engagement in mind. Haldane knew that he had 'his back to the wall'. He told Esher that 'in the Cabinet he was well supported by Morley, and he relied on Grey', but, 'he did not speak with the confidence of a few weeks before'.[4]

Haldane's hint of continental obligations was ignored as an irrelevant 'puff' by Churchill in a further Memorandum he addressed to the Cabinet on 27 June. Churchill claimed that British forces bore no relation either to 'a struggle with Russia on the Indian frontier or with Germany on the Continent'. The 'formidable and sinister conjunction of dangers' advertised by the War Office to frighten the reductionists into acquiescence could be prevented by 'skilful diplomacy and wise administration'. But, should even these unhappily fail, whether doubled or halved the Army would not be able to cope. Britain's defence was the Navy, and the Army was for 'minor emergencies'. For the control of such emergencies, the Army was 'unnecessarily large'.

Haldane was convinced that Churchill was out to get rid of him.[5] Despite Asquith's attempts to engage Esher's aid in composing the quarrel between the two ministers, if anything the bitterness of the

---

[1] *E.P.*, ii, 323–4 and 327.
[2] Austen Chamberlain, *Politics from Inside* (1936), 50–1.
[3] Frank Owen, *Tempestuous Journey* (1954), 161–2 (my italics).
[4] Esher to Knollys, 26 June 1908, *E.P.*, ii, 324.
[5] Haldane was also worried about rumours that he would be given the Woolsack. He informed Asquith that he wished for nothing more at that juncture than to stay at the War Office.

struggle increased. Haldane knew that he could count on the support of Asquith, Crewe and Grey. His task was how to win over the waverers, and he chose to do this by attacking the strongest part of his opponents' case. Together with Sir Charles Harris, his right hand man in matters of finance, Haldane set out to prove that the forces he required were not unnecessary. However, he chose to base his case upon the requirements for reinforcements in India in the event of an attack by Russia on the North-West frontier. There was no mention of a European theatre of military operations. This ploy was entirely successful. The reductionists were beaten. They could find no flaws in Haldane's logic and even their Treasury official, who checked the War Office costing, could find no loophole. Haldane confided to his mother: 'I am glad to say that I am near the top of the great mountain which has been in my way. I have come to a preliminary agreement with the Chancellor of the Exchequer which frees my hands for the present and relieves me of immediate anxiety. I took the bull by the horns and acted firmly.'[1]

Churchill's final Memorandum of 3 July amounted to capitulation. 'Accepting the rigid data that we have been prescribed', he could make a case for only minor economies. There would be no more talk of drastic savings on the Army Estimates, Cleon and Alcibiades withdrew from the fray to lick their wounds, determined that when next they essayed a sortie for economy upon a service department they would prepare a better brief.

Haldane and the Commons

Haldane knew that he could not expect a sympathetic response in the Commons from the Radical members of his party for any Army reforms he might propose unless he should also provide for massive economies. Haldane's very claim to the title Liberal was questioned by the Radicals. 'His Liberalism is German. It is vague and indeterminate. It breathes expediency rather than the compulsion of principle. It approaches politics purely as a business proposition, and seeks to establish national greatness on scientific and material rather than moral foundations.' It was natural for them to distrust, 'the standard bearer of Lord Rosebery . . . the chief author and inspirer of the Liberal Imperial schism'.[2] Nor were the Radicals and their Labour allies temperamentally disposed to listen to debates about the Army, when to their minds there were far more pressing subjects,

1 Quoted Maurice, i, 230.
2 Gardiner, 285.

more urgent priorities to be dealt with in the social and domestic legislative field.

> Army reorganisation, if safely and fitly pursued, without weak trifling with unsubstantial and reactionary ideas about universal military service, may be well enough in its way; but it is no special problem of Liberalism, whose mastering ideas are intellectual and moral, which has to survey the whole future of democracy.'[1]

When the Liberals had achieved their overwhelming victory in the general election, *The Times*, magnanimously accepting the *fait accompli*, stressed that it would give its support to the new Government if it proposed any measure of military reform.[2] The Radical Press had been quick to reject this 'effrontery' from 'the great organ of Philistinism'. The *Daily News* declared it had suffered 'enough of Government by *The Times* newspaper. We do not want its hypocritical support.'[3] The best security for the integrity of the Liberal majority and for the peaceful era of development and reform was 'not the Punic faith of *The Times* and the patronage of the Whigs, but a fearless handling of the problem of bloated armaments'.[4] *The Speaker* was not alone in its plea for a return to the standards of 1898, so that money might be released for social reform. A watchful eye would have to be kept by the 'progressive element' in the Cabinet upon some of their more reactionary colleagues, for already there were unhappy rumours that a cutting back of the armaments bill might well be a slow process. 'There is a deal of whispering around us to the effect that the new Government cannot reduce expenditure, at all events not at once, not this year. Some colour has been given to this by several recent utterances of the Chancellor of the Exchequer.' However, the comforting words of the Prime Minister about a 'League of Peace' were taken as a pledge of good faith. The Radicals merely wished to point out 'that the right moment to begin was *now*'.[5]

Three months after taking office, on 8 March 1906, Haldane, making his debut as War Minister in the Commons, introduced his Army Estimates. They provided for a negligible saving upon those of the previous year, but he pleaded in justification that he required time to think out the problems of Army reform. To all intents and purposes, Haldane enjoyed a triumph. He received the private congratulations of both front benches and the public acclaim of Leo

---

[1] *The Nation*, 1 June 1907.
[2] *The Times*, 27 Jan. 1906.
[3] *Daily News*, 28 Jan. 1906.
[4] *Concord*, xxii, no. 2, Feb. 1906, p. 18.
[5] *Ibid.*, p. 23.

R A W—D

Maxse in the *National Review*, who declared that Haldane's speech had been a 'conspicuous success'. Haldane had 'disarmed criticism by his candid confession that for the moment his ideas were in a nebulous condition'.[1] The Radical Press adopted a defensive pose. They 'reluctantly acquiesced in thirty millions for the Army—but for this year only'. 'It was clearly not to be expected—at least in these days of the unheroic in politics—that a great scheme of reduction could be brought about by the second week of March . . . this year's estimates must fairly be considered the Estimates of the outgoing Conservative Government.'[2]

H. W. Massingham writing in the *Daily News* wished to make it plain that the Radical desire for economy was something more than a mere passion for thrift. 'It arises first from the moral objection to militarism, and secondly out of the necessities of the programme of social reform to which the Government is committed.'[3] *The Tribune* was convinced that Haldane would not be able to come to the Commons again and request so much.

> The new Parliament has been elected by men whose interest in Estimates is not that of academic debaters or amateur strategists or professional apologists or critics, but of the humble and obscure classes for whom public waste of the resources that might rebuild the strength and vigour of the State means a palpable addition to the burden of their lives.[4]

The *Manchester Guardian*, though it sympathised with the reductionist case, pointed out that they could hardly expect a reduction of £10 million in a single year.[5] But all these statements were merely so many pious avowals of already well advertised attitudes. They were directed to general points of principle, not particular aspects of policy. J. A. Hobson in a letter to the *Westminster Gazette* in April complained that 'it was not a question of meeting obligations incurred by the late Government' that accounted for Haldane's Estimates, but 'a deliberate assuming of new obligations of a similar order'. Such expenditure could only be justified if the Government contended that a grave international emergency had arisen recently. Hobson's judgment was ignored.

On 22 July 1906, in a speech to which *The Times* had 'looked forward . . . with great interest and no small anxiety',[6] Haldane outlined to the Commons his proposals for military organisation. Haldane's style of oratory has been described as 'river of rhetoric

[1] Quoted Koss, *Haldane*, 46.
[2] *Concord*, xxii, no. 3, Mar. 1906, pp. 35–6.
[3] *Daily News*, 9 Mar. 1906.   [4] *Tribune*, 9 Mar. 1906.
[5] *Manchester Guardian*, 7 Mar. 1906.   [6] *The Times*, 23 July 1906.

that flowed on for ever'. Listeners were 'engulfed by wave after wave from the rhetorical ocean, and the waters flowed on in copious unconcern'. No one could invest a subject in 'a more lucid fog'. He spoke invariably at inordinate length and breakneck speed inducing helplessness and confusion in his audience as they lost themselves in the 'amazing labyrinth of his locution'. The only means of attempting to comprehend Haldane was to painfully and painstakingly read him the next day in *Hansard*.[1]

Haldane declared that it was his wish to streamline the Army to provide a force of greater fighting efficiency. There was obviously 'no want of clearness in his conception of the function of the Army',[2] though whether this was immediately apparent to his bemused audience is a matter of conjecture. There was to be maintained in Britain an Expeditionary Force of considerable size, and under a Territorial Army scheme a second-line Army would be provided. The Regular Army was to be reduced by some 20,000 men—a measure that neither placated the Radicals nor pleased Haldane's Tory critics. Leo Maxse's former good opinion of Haldane was abandoned in disgust.

Haldane had claimed in March that it was India which was the direct cause of the necessity to keep up a large establishment of troops.[3] The *Manchester Guardian* had countered this argument by claiming that Russia's collapse in the face of Japanese aggression provided the opportunity for a reduction of the Indian defences.[4] Haldane destroyed this hope in July by pointing out that the Indian Army had two functions. Its first was to resist the aggression of any Great Power. But second, and of equal importance, the Indian Army was the means of preserving internal order in India.[5] No

---

[1] Gardiner, 282–3, and Austen Chamberlain, 54–5; see also C. T. King *The Asquith Parliament* (1910), 32–3; John Buchan, *Memory-Hold-The-Door* (1940), 131–2; and *The Nation*, 2 Mar. 1907. 'The length of Mr Haldane's speech to the House of Commons on Monday lends some colour to the rumour that he means one day to rival Palmerston's achievement and to speak from the dusk of one day to the dawn of the next.' See also *New Age*, 3 April 1913, p. 513: 'Lord Haldane owes a good deal of his reputation as a thinker to the vagueness of his language. He must be profound because he is incomprehensible.'

[2] This, according to the *Manchester Guardian*, 7 Mar. 1906, had been the chief cause of military expenditure, when inviting Haldane to employ 'his natural aptitude for thinking out a problem from first principles'.

[3] *Hansard*, iv:153:663.

[4] *Manchester Guardian*, 22 Mar. 1906 and 17 April 1906.

[5] *Hansard*, iv:160:1082–83. Cf. Kitchener to Lady Salisbury, 30 Dec. 1902, quoted Magnus, *Kitchener*, 240–1: 'The idea that pervades everyone in India is that the army is intended to hold India against the Indians . . . I think this is a wrong policy.' Kitchener was always convinced that the Army's function was not that of supporting the civil power but of guarding India's frontiers against external attack.

argument could have been calculated to be more distasteful to those Radicals who were determined on the rapid progress of India to self-government. They deplored Haldane's argument that the size of the Army in India was to be explained away on the grounds that troops were needed to keep the native population in order. Sir Henry Cotton, the leader of that group of Radicals who were particularly interested in the Indian question, and who was such a thorn in Morley's side, speaking in the debate on the Indian Budget said: 'Now [we are] told that the real reason for a British force in India is to serve the functions of a local militia and to prevent insurrection. I welcome the admission. . . . Our real security in India, the real basis of order in that country, is not the Army we might maintain there, but the contentment of the people in India.'[1] Despite this attack, Haldane maintained his case, but sought to evade responsibility and temper criticism by involving Morley. 'I have all these men . . . to supply drafts for the battalions in India and the Colonies. I have not learned that my Rt. Hon. friend, the Secretary for India, is prepared to ask me to withdraw any of the fifty-two battalions which he has already from me for the purpose of India.'[2]

J. A. Spender, who was known to be close to the secrets of the Cabinet, writing in the *Contemporary Review* of the likely problems a Liberal Government would face, had stated that economy in the Army Estimates was always a matter of 'international weather permitting'. But, if a settlement with Russia was achieved then 'the military situation might be so altered . . . that we should have a fair opportunity of reconsidering some military plans which were laid for a wholly different set of circumstances'.[3] Therefore, when the Anglo-Russian Convention was signed in 1907 it was natural that Radicals should inquire whether it could be cashed in terms of savings upon Indian defence.[4] Had not Morley claimed that the Convention was 'undoubtedly first and foremost an Indian Treaty'?[5] But when Sir John Brunner asked if the Anglo-Russian Agreement had lessened the need for a defensive force against invasion,[6] Haldane had merely reiterated his previous statements. He was entirely in the hands of other ministers. After all, he reminded his critics, Britain was responsible for the protection of 300 million people in India.[7]

---

[1] *Hansard*, iv: 161: 630.   [2] *Ibid.*, iv: 169: 1287–88.
[3] J. A. Spender, 'The new Government and its problems', *Contemporary Review*, lxxxix, 469.
[4] See, for example, *Manchester Guardian*, 30 Nov. 1907.
[5] *Hansard*, iv: 184: 559.   [6] *Ibid.*, iv: 185: 368.   [7] *Ibid.*, iv: 186: 853–4.

In the Commons Haldane had employed a simple argument to justify the organisation of an Expeditionary Force.

> The primary task which rests on the British Army is to maintain the defence of an Empire which extends over 12,000,000 square miles. . . . The first purpose for which we want an Army is for overseas war . . . our Expeditionary Force ought to be moulded for overseas warfare. . . . Our business is to maintain an Expeditionary Force just as large as to form a reserve which may enable us swiftly and resolutely to reinforce the outposts of our forces, which are the outposts of the Empire, and which act as its police . . . the force at which we aim . . . is six big divisions . . . and represents a total of 150,000 men.[1]

What Haldane did not make clear to the House was the *raison d'être* for this organisation. It was not Haldane's Radical critics that seized upon this weakness, but the Tory leader, Balfour.

> What is required, so far as I am able to see, is the power of sending continuous reinforcement to India in a great emergency. That does not mean sending 150,000 men straight off in a few weeks to Bombay. . . . That does not require the sort of expedition the Rt. Hon. Gentleman appeared to contemplate. . . . You will require what is called a striking force to deal with some Continental situation, the defence of Belgium for instance, or some country which our strategy in the world obliges us to defend, and that you require to be ready at a moment's notice.[2]

These must have seemed strange calculations to the ex-Unionist, now Liberal M.P., Guest, who had welcomed Haldane's statement to the House on 8 March precisely because of the minister's abandonment of any idea of taking part in continental warfare.[3] Thoughts of European battles might engage the attentions of so-called military experts and Tory Jingoes, but were no fit concern for a Liberal statesman. The measure of Haldane's scheme was obvious. It was intended 'to provide an efficient and expansible force for frontier wars'. The 'landing of a British Army on the continent of Europe' simply wasn't contemplated.[4]

Balfour's speech was made in July 1906. It was April 1907 before a Radical chose to question the policy behind the Expeditionary Force. Then it was Sir Charles Dilke, thought of by many as something of an expert on military and naval affairs—an opinion not shared by Haldane. 'Everyone agreed', said Dilke, 'that any advance upon India by Russia would be a matter of very slow progress.' If that were so, then it followed that the Expeditionary Force could 'not be

---

[1] *Hansard.*, iv:160:1080ff .   [2] *Ibid*, iv:160:1161–3.
[3] *Ibid*, iv:153:745.   [4] *Yorkshire Observer*, 5 March 1907.

intended for that purpose that Haldane had indicated'. Dilke 'entirely concurred' with Balfour's view, that the force 'could only be intended for European complications'.[1]

Dilke's observations were ignored. If possible, even less attention was paid to the venerable Radical, W. P. Byles, who by the furthest exercise of the imagination could not be supposed by the House to be a perceptive and knowledgeable critic of military affairs. When he rose in his place, the Opposition was reduced to helpless laughter.[2] Nevertheless, he determinedly pressed Haldane for information. Why did Britain need a 'striking force' at all?[3] Haldane sidestepped the issue. What had been called a 'striking force' was 'rather in the nature of a police force of the Empire which we can send on short notice'.[4] He reiterated the point later in the same speech. 'The so-called striking force[5] or as I would call it, the Imperial police force, a force which can be sent on small expeditions on short notice. . . . It cannot be a large force but it ought to be large enough to deal with some sudden emergency.'[6]

In March 1908 the Radicals again returned to the attack when moving an amendment in Committee to the Army Estimates for 1908–09. Haldane had defended his Expeditionary force because, among other grounds, it had not required one extra man. The only cost was the comparatively small one of putting the force into organised form.[7] Luttrell pressed Haldane; whom did they intend to strike with the Expeditionary Force? Byles also rejoined the fray. Admitting that 'the technical details . . . were beyond his ken', nevertheless he claimed, 'the essential question [was], why had they never been told why the country wanted 160,000 men as an Expeditionary Force?' To these inquiries no answer was returned. The Radicals refused to give up and on the Report Stage of the Estimates pressed again for information. This time they concentrated on the value of the Anglo-Russian Convention. Again Luttrell was in the van of the questioners. What had taken place in the last

---

[1] *Hansard*, iv:172:111–12.

[2] See the greeting he received from the House, *Hansard*, iv:176:258. Byles stoutly maintained that while he might be received with derision, he was not in the least ashamed of his opinions on war. See Birrell's comment on the Commons' attitude to 'sincerity' in a speaker in Gardiner, 53.

[3] *Hansard*, iv:170:326.

[4] *Ibid*, iv:170:503.

[5] Repington claimed that it was his suggestion that the title 'Expeditionary Force' was employed rather than 'striking force', as he 'thought this would alarm the Radicals unduly'. See J. Luvaas, *The Education of an Army* (1965), 310.

[6] *Hansard*, iv:170:522.

[7] *Ibid.*, iv:185:1618; 186:829–30, 876, 882–6. See also *The Nation*, 2 Mar. 1907, p. 6.

few years to make it necessary to double the military forces which
Grey, when in Opposition in 1903, had considered quite sufficient?
'Why was it necessary to keep so many troops abroad? . . . Our
policy in India should have the effect of enabling us to reduce rather
than increase the force.' Cotton wanted to know what the supposed
value of the Agreement with Russia was if it did not allow for the
reduction of a single soldier in India. But it was J. M. Robertson
who mounted the strongest attack.

> Why should Hon. Members be asked to spend their time
> considering diplomatic arrangements and to speak of them in
> terms of the highest eulogium when not a farthing of value came
> from them in the long run? . . . No rational arguments had been
> made by the Secretary of State for War to explain the troops in
> India. Were we maintaining the figures in terms of a secret
> agreement with Japan? He wished the Government to give an
> answer on that point. . . . Could it be seriously stated that
> anything had happened to necessitate a striking force of 160,000
> men especially when we were now on good terms with Russia?

Robertson concluded with his own suggestion that the answer
might lie with the 'faceless military experts'. But to all these impassioned requests for information and clarification of intent, the
Government returned no reply. Even when, five days later, F. C.
Mackarness pursuing Robertson's point demanded of Grey whether
an understanding existed between Great Britain and any other
country that required military or naval commitments to be maintained at a determined strength or standard, the Foreign Secretary
replied with a simple negative.[1]

Haldane continued to blunt the ardour of his questioners by a
studied and determined vagueness. He talked of 'Indian garrisons'
and of 'an Imperial police force'. Theatres of possible wars were
always 'distant', and the location of possible operations involving
British troops were invariably 'overseas'. As to what he meant by
'overseas', he made it quite clear that this was not intended as a
euphemism for a short distance. It was India and other like farflung
outposts of the Empire to which he was referring.[2]

Though it might be supposed that the formation and probable
destination of the Expeditionary Force would most have attracted
his critics' attention, it was Haldane's proposed reforms of the
auxiliary forces that caused the greatest furore at the time. While
Haldane on occasion spoke of the possibility of the Territorial Army

[1] *Hansard*, iv:186:1210.
[2] See, for example, *Hansard*, v:11:1037ff.; see also, Williamson, 93, n. 10.

being used to 'expand' the Regular Army,[1] his new scheme was sold to the Commons and the public on the basis of a 'home defence' system. The reason for this was quite simple, as Repington explained.

> We could not at this time so much as hint that we might ever be engaged upon the continent of Europe, because we were immediately treated to every kind of abuse for suggesting such a thing, and no one would look at any argument founded upon it. Our engagements to Belgium were regarded as ancient history, and nobody thought about them, or understood what they meant. So I fell back upon the Hearth-and-Home idea.[2]

Debates on the merits of the new Territorial Army scheme were considered the prerogative of the military 'experts' in the House. The Radicals felt out of their depth. Truth be told, they found such debates boring and considered them a waste of valuable parliamentary time.[3] When they chose to intervene, they concentrated their attacks on points of moral principle, and poured the vials of their wrath on ephemera such as the school cadet corps, rifle clubs, and the rôle afforded the lord-lieutenants of the counties in the new organisation which they considered anti-democratic, reactionary and downright feudal.[4] But, when Dilke attacked Haldane for trying to cover his real activities by 'alleging that home defence was the basis of the new Territorial Army',[5] it was the Labour member John Ward who took the part of Haldane and upbraided Dilke for attempting to gain Radical support against a scheme that obviously had 'nothing to do with the striking force at all'.[6]

Radical criticism was disarmed because the Bill contained features that appealed to many of them. Haldane had been at pains to emphasise this volunteer system.[7] If military responsibility was to be placed on men who could be sent abroad only if they offered to go, then surely this was the best safeguard that the nation could not be led into wars of which it disapproved? For every Radical who feared

---

[1] On what Haldane implied by 'expand', see his speech at Newcastle, reported in the *Manchester Guardian*, 15 Sept. 1906.
[2] Repington, 278.
[3] See, for example, *Concord*, xxiv, no. 1, Jan. 1908, p. 1: 'Mr Haldane managed to waste a large proportion of last year's Parliamentary Session over the details of his revolutionary Army Bill'; also, *The Nation*, 11 Jan. 1908, 521.
[4] See, *inter alia, Hansard*, iv: 160:1136; and iv:172:1592; *Concord*, xxiii, no. 5, May 1907, pp. 55–8. At the Fourth National Peace Congress 27/28 June 1907 a motion protested against, 'the militarisation of educational institutions'. *The Nation*, 13 April, 1907: 'The scheme for county administration rests upon a false foundation. . . . It is conceived in a feudal spirit . . . the encouragement of Cadet Corps and Rifle Clubs shows . . . a childish simplicity in the belief that armies are made by teaching little boys to play at soldiers. . . . The Radical and Labour Party are very rightly hostile to the dangerous spirit lurking in those proposals.'
[5] *Hansard*, iv:176:510–11.   [6] *Ibid.*, iv:172:267.   [7] *Ibid.*, iv:153:679ff.

that the failure of the volunteer scheme would give fresh fuel to the campaign for conscription,[1] there was another who saw in it the best possible guarantee against that awful prospect. It was for this reason that Arnold Lupton, who was an extreme antimilitarist, declared that he would like to see the Territorial Army doubled in size.[2]

The only consistent Radical criticism of Haldane's scheme came from outside the Commons in a series of leading articles from September 1906 to June 1907 in the *Manchester Guardian*.[3] There, the Radicals were soundly rebuked for their disinterest. The *Guardian* attacked Haldane for not admitting the true purpose of his Territorial Army. It was suspected that service overseas was the core of his plan. As one of the chief means by which Parliament controlled foreign policy was the placing of limits upon the size of an Army available for overseas operations, the Commons should refuse to sanction his scheme until Haldane provided an unqualified answer as to what exactly was the intended function of the new forces.

The Radicals were still at odds with themselves when the final division was taken on Haldane's Bill. How had Haldane managed to yet again confuse his potential critics and enemies within his own party? A contemporary article written on Haldane's Army reforms provides part of the solution.

> His sacred principle as Army reformer was to be all things to all men. . . . There was no conceivable point of view to which he did not offer some temptation to agree; and he got his Bill through a House that his long speeches had made too somnolent to disagree and his amazing eclecticism too confused to devise a consistent plan of opposition.[4]

Once the Territorial Army scheme was launched, the Radicals left it strictly alone. The *Daily News* avowed that the Commons had 'no mind to revert to the question in the near future . . . Mr Haldane's efforts to make the scheme a success will command from this point of view, as from others, the general goodwill of the reformers'.[5] Fears of conscription were allayed by the success of the scheme once

---

[1] See, for example, Cremer, *Hansard*, iv:172:1658; and Lea, iv:176:526ff.
[2] *Hansard*, iv:185:1871.
[3] *Manchester Guardian*, 15 Sept., 26 Nov. 1906, 28 Feb., 10 April, 29 May, 6 and 20 June 1907.
[4] H. Sidebottom, 'Mr Haldane's Army Reforms: some general objections', *Albany Review*, Sept. 1907, i, no. 6, p. 619. Dilke and F. E. Smith had made the same point in the Commons, see *Hansard*, iv:172:110ff, and iv:176:254ff. See also Sinclair, 130. 'To differ from him seemed to be denying the existence of God. He could dignify the most prosaic case by giving it a philosophic background. This was no mere forensic trick; it was the consequence of sincere conviction, of a habit of mind which saw everything in organic relations.'
[5] *Daily News*, 19 June 1907.

put into practice. There was no shortage of volunteers for Mr Haldane's new Army.[1] Even the *Manchester Guardian* called off its campaign. Though they had distrusted the Territorial Army at its birth, they were 'now concerned to foster its early growth to enable it to grow to a sound maturity'.[2]

Concern with the possibility of British military intervention upon the Continent increased temporarily after the Bosnian crisis of 1908–09. But by a strange chance this served to protect Haldane from his Labour and Radical critics. It was the militarist section of the Tory party, abandoning Balfour's restrained opposition on military matters, who in attacking Haldane for his economies spoke of war in Europe coupling this with the demand for compulsory military service. Robert Blatchford, jingo and anti-German, joined the Tory assault.[3] In 1909 he went so far as to proclaim that the problem of Britain's defence was the defence of France.[4] But, as Tory criticism of Haldane became shriller in tone and more vindictive in intent, Haldane's stature in the eyes of the Radicals grew. Thus, a strange quirk of fortune converted him to a figure of authority and sanity; an anticonscriptionist who repelled the Tory cries for compulsory service with a cool disdain and unimpeachable logic. Scarce a bleat was heard from the Radical fold. Such occasional grumblings of concern as emerged, were muted and contradictory.[5]

Haldane had achieved his object. He had laid the foundations for the best possible Army that time and circumstance allowed, and this despite the efforts of hostile critics both within and outside his party, in the Cabinet, the Commons and the Press. His success was the result of a singleminded determination coupled with a capacity

[1] See Halévy, *The Rule of Democracy*, 180–1.
[2] *Manchester Guardian*, 13 Aug. 1908; cf. editorial of 19 June 1908.
[3] The Radicals were delighted when Keir Hardie repudiated the arguments of the 'Blatchford–Hyndman axis', in the *Labour Leader*, 14 Aug. 1908, p. 521, 'Socialists and war: in reply to Blatchford, Hyndman, and the Jingo Press'. See also, *The Nation*, 15 Aug. 1908, p. 693. There is a summary of the contents of Blatchford's *Daily Mail* articles in Oron J. Hale, *Publicity and Diplomacy* (1940), 373–7; see also Williamson, 133–4.
[4] See Robert Blatchford, *Germany and England* (1909), *passim*.
[5] See, *inter alia*, *The Nation*, 12 Mar. 1910: 'What is the function of the British Army? Only some obligation to fight upon the Continent could explain Haldane's military planning.' They lamented the fact that the Commons failed to press for clarification, cf. *The Nation*, 31 Dec. 1910. The Army as a 'voluntary long range force' was not suited for continental operations which would require a 'short range' army which could only be raised by conscription, and Haldane was a known opponent of conscription. See Haldane's preface to Sir Ian Hamilton's *Compulsory Service, A Study of the Question in the Light of Experience* (1910), the first edition of which was published a month before the *The Nation* article. See, *inter alia*, Haldane's speech in Commons, *Hansard*, v:22:1971; 2073ff. and reply, 30 Jan. 1908 to Parliamentary Committee of Trade Union Congress.

for prodigious labour. He had provided Grey with the necessary force to implement the entente with France should that eventually arise. He had explained the size of the forces he retained in Great Britain by quoting the Cardwell System at his critics. This system had 'the advantage that it reduced the question of the size of the Army to a single variable . . . the number of troops which it was essential at any given time to keep abroad, in the Colonies and India, and in the Crown possessions'.[1] There was no mention here of Europe, and he always justified the number of troops by talk of India's requirements. In the name of economy his critics could either challenge the 'System' or aim to reduce the overseas forces. Haldane stood by the system, and the *Manchester Guardian* along with most other Radical critics[2] never questioned its retention. The Labour party never developed an effective or cohesive criticism of Haldane's plans.[3]

Haldane's Radical critics always considered that the best and sufficient insurance against jingo intentions the War Minister might harbour was the presence of Campbell-Bannerman at the head of the Administration. Nor would their Radical chief easily succumb to the blandishments of the military 'experts'. 'The Prime Minister', declared *The Nation*, 'is a man of caution and discrimination; he can rise above the mechanical fears of "experts", and survey broadly a political situation that lies open to the gaze of all intelligent men.'[4] Campbell-Bannerman provided the all-important key to Haldane's success both in the Cabinet and the Commons. The Prime Minister's support overcame the disquiet that Radicals felt concerning the soundness of Haldane's Liberal principles. 'The old chief's word was law to the extremists of his party', wrote Churchill. 'They were quite sure he would do nothing more in matters of foreign policy and defence than was absolutely necessary, and that he would do it in the manner least calculated to give satisfaction to jingo sentiments.'[5] Campbell-Bannerman was Haldane's guarantor. The

---

[1] *Hansard*, iv:185:707.

[2] Seely and Dilke were the only two 'experts' who questioned the system, see *Hansard*, iv:185:736ff. But, neither gained support for their military arguments from the Radicals. See, debate, 15 Mar. 1906, *Hansard*, iv:153:1441ff. On arguments for retention of Cardwell System despite its defects, see *Manchester Guardian*, 5 Mar. 1908.

[3] See, for example, *New Age*, 2 May 1907, p. 2: 'We cannot think that Socialists have, in general, adequately thought out the problems involved. Too many of them write and speak as if the questions were not worth considering, or use language implying that the country could be safely left without any means of defence. This is absurd. You don't have to be a Jingo to recognise that sentimental anti-militarism gets you nowhere.'

[4] *The Nation*, 18 Jan. 1908.

[5] W. S. Churchill, *The World Crisis 1911–18* (1923), 34–5.

Prime Minister supported Haldane, as we have seen, on the strength of the Cardwell argument, and his belief that the success of the reform schemes was the only practicable alternative to compulsory military service. 'Beat them we must,' Campbell-Bannerman told Haldane, referring to the activities of the National Service League, 'for an agitation for compulsion is the inevitable result of failure'.[1]

The Radicals never understood the implications of Haldane's scheme. That was some measure of the success of Haldane's deception. But in any event they were ill-equipped to be perceptive critics of the canny War Minister. They were content to indulge in antimilitaristic propaganda, and petulant assertions that both time and money were being wasted on the War Office that could better be spent on social reforms. For his part, Haldane felt, and rightly so, that he had done all he could for the Army.[2]

[1] Quoted, Koss, *Haldane*, 51.   [2] See Fitzroy i, 399.

Chapter 3   The Second Hague Conference

No sooner had their most optimistic hopes been realised by their electoral triumph than the Radicals eagerly turned their attention to the proposed peace conference to be held at the Hague. Their expectations were high. There was a new aggressive confidence in their approach. 'The time has passed for preaching and petitioning on behalf of peace. We are bound to take the aggressive, and we have now, as our French friends have been saying, "To make war on war".' But they were not blind either to the nature or the magnitude of the possible obstacles that lay in their path. 'If the world is not to be again cheated of the boon it so much needs and has so long demanded, the problem of the arrest of armaments will be the chief item upon the programme of the Second Hague Conference. . . . The time for vague promises and pious aspirations is past.'[1]

Radicals believed that the recent results at the polls had considerably and significantly strengthened the hands of those in Britain who sought universal peace. Those who had governed Great Britain's policy in the past, without ever feeling the pinch of social conditions, would do well to study and mark the signs of the times and particularly the growth in Labour's vote. They only deluded themselves if they supposed that the reaction against imperialism had gone as far as it might. Radical peace supporters now sought a substantial as well as a sentimental reward to crown their labours. The Prime Minister had spoken in his great pre-election speech at the Albert Hall of a 'League of Peace'. The time to begin working for such a League had arrived.

February 22 was traditionally the date for demonstrations by peace societies throughout Europe. The recently formed National Council of Peace Societies[2] meeting at Friends' House, passed a

[1] *Concord*, xxii, no. 2, Feb. 1906, p. 17.
[2] A new series of international peace congresses was started in 1889 which met at a different centre each year. The Seventeenth Congress, held in London in 1908, led to the National Peace Council being placed on a permanent

resolution proposed by the Radical M.P., W. P. Byles, that 'a serious effort will be made at the Hague Conference to arrive at an agreement for an arrest, with a view to ultimate reduction, of armaments'. While the party hot for peace in the House of Commons had undoubtedly increased, Hodgson Pratt warned the meeting that it would be foolhardy to underestimate the strength of the opposition.

> We must see clearly that there are two great currents of opinion in direct and intense antagonism—one of which has to secure complete victory over the other. The one has its source in the traditions and ideals of the aristocratic, military and landowning classes, strongly united by ties of tradition and social position. The other current of opinion has its source in the convictions —half democratic and half religious—of the middle and Labour classes, who for nearly four centuries have been taught that righteousness alone exalteth a nation, and alone secures welfare, whether for the individual or for the community.[1]

If the 'immortal achievements of 1899' were to be completed, it was plainly the duty of right thinking men to demand that the limitation of armaments be the primary concern at the Hague meeting.

G. P. Gooch, like other young Radicals recently elected to the Commons, their enthusiasm as yet untempered by bitter experience, might suppose it 'easy to exaggerate the small and unrepresentative part played by the military party' in Britain, and to advise that the best way 'to fight them was to ignore them'. But the first bold yet practicable suggestion for action was made by the veteran Leonard Courtney when in March 1906 he addressed the Russell and Eighty Clubs at Oxford. Perhaps his critical appreciation of the significance of the recent election results had been sharpened by his own rejection at the polls. In the event, he did not allow himself to indulge in the general Radical euphoria. The election in truth had been a conservative reaction, a reversion to the old faith, FreeTrade. Even now there were echoes from the Liberal back benches warning of the necessity for preparation against imminent continental enemies. Now was the time for a bold initiative before it was too late, a time for a little courage in facing the risks of reduced armaments.

> I am sick and tired of the constant presentation of the nations of the world as so many predatory hordes ready at the least

footing. However, four years earlier it had been constituted as a lightly organised body primarily concerned with arranging national annual congresses in Britain. Courtney was the first President, H. S. Perris the first permanent Secretary; see K. Ingram, *Fifty Years of the National Peace Council* (1958), *passim*.
[1] For a report of this meeting, see *Concord*, xxii, no. 3, Mar. 1906, pp. 45–7.

sight of an opportunity to seize upon what belongs to other nations and to snatch, consume and devour what is not their own. I do not believe that is really the temper of the civilised nations of Europe.

Courtney maintained that, as all the countries of Europe appeared to be more or less in genuine alarm of one another, the country that first showed confidence that the best way of preventing attack was not to invite it by distrust, would establish for itself a great reputation and its inhabitants might glory in the formation of a League of Peace of which they would be the real pioneers. He concluded: 'We had better not wait for the cooperation of other nations but must run the glorious risk of leading the way.'[1]

The *Manchester Guardian* approved of Courtney's speech. 'Surely it is a spirit of Pharisaism in politics that holds back the generous impulse to take the lead in the reduction of armaments by the suggestion that it would not be safe?'[2] *Tribune* in a powerful leader supported Courtney's plea. Britain enjoyed

> a peculiarly favourable position to undertake the initiative. . . . It is significant that at the Socialist Congress last week in Brussels, the Socialists of all countries discussed what means were available to make war impossible in practice. The Labour Party in England, widely as it differs in many respects from Labour parties elsewhere, is as wholehearted as the Socialists of France or Germany in its love of peace. Peace is at the bottom the cause of democracy. It is the condition of its growth and power.

However, tucked away in the same edition of *Tribune*, a report telegraphed by the paper's Berlin correspondent sounded an ominous note. 'It would appear that the German Government, at any rate, is seriously disinclined to regard even comparative disarmament as other than a somewhat Utopian proposal of academic interest.'[3]

[1] Report in *Manchester Guardian*, 12 Mar. 1906.
[2] *Ibid.*
[3] *Tribune*, 13 Mar. 1906. The dependence of the extension of democratic government upon disarmament, was a frequently employed theme in Radical writing of the period. See, *inter alia*, *The Speaker*, 12 May 1906. 'The release of Europe from the iron tyranny of its military burdens is more than anything else the condition of the development and success of popular Government. . . . Democracy in Europe has by a sound instinct fastened on a constructive policy of peace as its leading aim.' The emphasis upon the democratic impetus for disarmament was favoured by the Radicals as opposed to the internationalist arguments of the Socialists. In some ways it was an attempt to curb the revolutionary element present among themselves. See, for example, *Concord*, xxi, no. 11, Nov. 1905, p. 159: 'The cry of "Lay down your Arms" . . . is not merely the demand of internationalists . . . it is the demand of Democrats who desire that the popular will should be obeyed.' See also *The Nation*, 'Democracy and the Peace Movement', 1 Aug. 1908.

Campbell-Bannerman had not been slow in giving comfort to Radical hopes. Early in the new parliamentary session, replying to a question from Percy Alden, he had said, 'I have openly expressed my opinion in favour of a general reduction of armaments, and I can assure my honourable friend that no favourable opportunity will be lost for facilitating that result.'[1] Two days earlier he had described to the Commons in simple terms, his policy on the question of armaments limitation.

> It is . . . an inverted Pool of Siloam. Instead of all the people rushing to be the first in the water, they are all to linger on the brink and urge their neighbours to go in. In my judgment we are the country above all others upon whom it is incumbent to show a willingness to check the pace with which these great armaments have been mounting up of late years, with respect to the Navy especially.[2]

Radicals applauded Campbell-Bannerman's unimpeachable sentiments. They had repeatedly argued that international armaments was a vicious, ever-spiralling circle fed by fear. The circle had to be broken. Was it reasonable to expect Powers with comparatively weak navies to make the first move? Because of her overwhelming naval supremacy, it was for Britain to make the first step. Now was not a time for pessimism. In their eyes, conditions had never seemed more favourable for the organisation of peace. Campbell-Bannerman's Radicalism was trusted, his sympathy for the cause of disarmament well known. By his public speeches the Prime Minister had made it plain that he would give a vigorous moral lead to the Ministry on the issue of peace.

On 7 April the Russian Government issued its draft programme for the Hague Conference. Claiming to have 'had in view the necessity of giving a fresh development to the humanitarian principles which served as a basis for the work of the great international meeting of 1899', they did not propose to deal with the question of limitation of armaments. They hoped that 'Governments would see in the points proposed . . . an expression of the desire to approach the lofty ideal of International Justice which is the constant goal of the civilised world'. But, to ignore the armaments question seemed to the Radicals to be playing Hamlet without the Prince.[3] If all that

[1] *Hansard*, iv:162:1064.
[2] *Hansard*, iv: 162: 118.
[3] See, for example, motion of the Executive Committee of the International Arbitration and Peace Association, 10 Apr. 1906. 'This Committee protests against the omission of this great subject as calculated to rob the coming Conference of any substantial interest or importance. It therefore urges the

was proposed was a new code of neutrality and a new set of rules for the Red Cross, it would seem to make a travesty of the Prime Minister's November appeal. Not surprisingly the Radicals were angry with the turn of events. In the Commons they pressed the Government to secure the inclusion of disarmament as a subject upon the Peace Conference agenda. In reply to a supplementary question by Byles, Campbell-Bannerman said that he was not sure whether it would be practicable to make specific proposals with regard to the limitation of armaments, but, he assured his questioner, the matter was one which the Government regarded with sympathetic interest.[1]

In May, the Government accepted for debate a motion on armament limitation proposed by the Lib–Lab member for Birkenhead, the vigorous and breezy Radical, Henry Vivian.[2] The Commons expressed their support for reduction of armaments and directly challenged the Government to make proposals on the subject at the Hague Conference. An attempt to move an amendment by the Liberal navalist, Bellairs, was defeated, though it gained some support even in Liberal quarters.[3] However, the feature that afforded most satisfaction to the Radicals was Grey's reply to the debate. Lightly dismissing Balfour's attack as 'an abstract declaration that ignored . . . the whole point of the Resolution, which is that . . . [decrease in armaments] is a question of degree', he declared that the Government would not be precluded from taking an initiative in the matter.

> Our policy is that national expenditure has grown enormously in the last few years and that now we have reached the turning point and there is a prospect that the expenditure can be

Prime Minister to obtain its insertion upon the programme. . . . Any Power making this proposal will, it believes, win the enthusiastic confidence and support of the labouring masses in all parts of the world.'
[1] *Hansard*, iv:155:984.
[2] *Ibid.*, iv:156:1383–1416. The terms of the final resolution were: 'This House is of the opinion that the growth of expenditure on armaments is excessive and ought to be reduced; such expenditure lessens national and commercial credit, intensifies the unemployed problem, reduces the resources available for social reform, and presses with exceptional severity on the industrial classes, and it therefore calls upon the Government to take drastic steps to reduce the drain on national income, and to this end to press for the inclusion of the question of the reduction of armaments by international agreement in the agenda for the forthcoming Hague Conference.' Many Socialists took a jaundiced view of the Radical penchant for making pious resolutions. They objected to 'theoretic moonshine' as a substitute for direct action. See, for example, letter of James Robson to *New Age*, 23 May 1907, at p. 63. 'Passing resolutions is the paradisaical occupation par excellence for the English Radical.'
[3] See, for example, speech of Charles Wilson, Liberal member for Hull West, *Hansard*, iv:156:1401.

considerably reduced without sacrificing national safety . . .
I hold that a declaration of this kind from a British House of
Commons is something that is worth having if only for the
effect it may have on other Governments. . . . I do not believe
that at any time has the conscious public opinion in the
various countries of Europe set more strongly in the direction
of peace than at the present time, and yet the burden of naval
and military expenditure goes on increasing. . . . There is no
more profitable task to which . . . to aspire than to produce
some practical result of agreement amongst nations as would
lead to reduction of this unproductive expenditure. . . . I trust
this resolution may be taken as an invitation from the British
House of Commons to respond in favour of encouraging a
reduction of armaments.[1]

Bellairs by leave withdrew his amendment and amid cheers
Vivian's resolution was put and agreed to by the House. The Radicals
exulted. Their Press was delighted with Grey's speech. It may not
have been picturesque, epigrammatic or literary, but it 'would stand
out as one of the most important . . . in the history of the present
Parliament'. It meant, 'that the Prime Minister's declaration at the
Albert Hall is not a pious formula but a concrete declaration of
policy'.[2] Altogether it had been, 'a surprisingly good speech, and in
spite of some characteristically diplomatic phrases could be taken as a
definite pledge to action'.[3] Messages of approval and congratulation
flowed in from all over Europe. But in Germany, while the Social
Democrats received the news of the resolution with satisfaction, the
German Government stated that it believed itself justified in keeping
its own counsel until it saw whether the motion of the House of Commons bore any fruit. From Washington it was learned that the
Administration there would gladly support any proposition which
Britain or any other Power might submit to the Hague Conference
on the question of the reduction of armaments. But it was not
prepared to take any initiative in the matter itself and was to stick
to that formula despite appeals made by Grey to Whitelaw Reid, the
American Ambassador in London, in July 1906, and to President
Roosevelt in February 1907.[4]

The Radicals were clear in their own minds as to what would
constitute a practical plan for the Hague Conference. First, that
Britain's own delegates should be convinced of the efficacy of such
conferences and be men both resolute and resourceful in statecraft
and not 'mere service experts'. Second, that irrelevant minor
questions should be postponed for a plan 'simple in operation that

---

[1] *Hansard*, iv. 156: 1412 15.   [2] *The Speaker*, 12 May 1906.
[3] *Concord*, xxii, no. 5, June 1906, p. 65.   [4] See Trevelyan, 206.

will at once appeal to the imagination of the peoples'. The whole appeal should rest on the question of expenditure in the form of a five years' guarantee to limit peace expenditure in armaments. A partial agreement, a naval truce without a military truce, would be better than nothing, and the willing majority had to be prepared for the contingency, unlikely though it might seem to them at the time, of the obstinate opposition of a single great Power. Third, the conference 'should become an annual event', so that 'every year's experience will afford new suggestions for the strengthening of the *entente* and new means of carrying them out'.[1]

Though for the moment the omens seemed excellent, the Radicals did not relax their pressure. Avebury initiated a debate in the House of Lords on 25 May.[2] While Fitzmaurice's reply was exceedingly feeble, the Radicals felt that they had no cause to be unduly concerned.[3] As G. H. Perris claimed: 'I have reason to believe that the thorough peace men in the Cabinet regard the prospect for disarmament with so much confidence that for the time being there seems to be no call for any great supporting agitation.'[4] Nevertheless, the usual memorials on disarmament were got up and signed, and a deputation to Campbell-Bannerman in June headed by the old Radical H. J. Wilson boasted the signatures of some 120 M.P.s.[5] Then with satisfaction it was learned that the Prime Minister had agreed to address the Interparliamentary Union when it met at Westminster Hall in July. This would afford an ideal opportunity for a great statesman to make a strong appeal to the nations of the world on the most pressing of all issues.

Meanwhile, the Third National Peace Congress of Great Britain and Ireland was held on 13 and 14 June at Birmingham—a case of carrying the message into the enemy's camp! Not surprisingly, there were hardly any representatives of local organisations present in the city that was so much under the influence of Chamberlain, but the atmosphere as always was confidently optimistic. There was constant reference to the hope that definite proposals for the limitation of armaments would be placed on the agenda of the forthcoming Hague Conference. Support was reaffirmed for any initiative that

---

[1] See G. H. Perris, *For an Arrest of Armaments* (1906), *passim*.
[2] *Hansard*, iv:157:1517–48.
[3] Fitzmaurice had pointed out the twin difficulties of first, finding a *unit* of disarmament, and second, how that unit should be applied. *The Times*, 25 May 1906, described the debate in the Lords as 'a very practical discussion of what is in the nature of the case a rather academic subject'.
[4] *Concord*, xxii, no 5, June 1906, p. 65.
[5] See *Manchester Guardian*, 9 June 1906 for Cremer's Memorial; and *The Times*, 22 June 1906 for the Wilson deputation to Campbell-Bannerman.

Campbell-Bannerman or Grey might propose in the matter. Nor was it simply a case of waiting on the pleasure of the Government. It was their task 'to fulfil the *mandate* of the general election and the vote of the House of Commons on 9 May by making definite proposals at the Hague for military and naval standstill'.[1] But the general air of comfortable unanimity and accord was rudely shattered in a debate on a motion by W. A. Appleton of the Lace Makers Union calling for 'the working classes in this country to unite with their fellow workmen in other countries in opposing war and militarism as inimical to the vital interests of their class'. H. M. Hyndman for the Social Democratic Federation was not prepared to accept that the horrors of peace were any less than the horrors of war.[2] It was the war between the classes that was the greatest evil, and much worse for the working man than any conflict between the nations of the world. As a supporter of internationalism among working men, he for one would have nothing to do with a bourgeois pacifism that always confined itself to the interests of the moment. In rejecting the comfortable paternalistic assertions of the peace movement towards the

[1] My italics. See in particular the motions of Henry Vivian and Perris. Of course, the Radical plaint that the Government had been given a mandate for retrenchment in military and naval spending, rested upon their particular interpretation of the significance of the 1906 election. In their private reveries many like Morley might have felt that the truth of the matter was that the election had not really settled any great issue. See Morley to Minto, 24 Jan. 1908, quoted Koss, *John Morley at the India Office* (1969), 69.

The Times angrily criticised any claim that the burden of arms was excessive. It did not find it surprising that other nations should feel 'a very natural reluctance to commit themselves to proposals, however admirable, which might jeopardise all the national ideals and interests they hold dear' (22 June 1906). They quoted with approval the views of M. Denis: 'Les pacifistes sont les complices des conquérants parce qu'ils sollicitent leurs cupidités en énervant les résistances' (20 July 1906).

[2] Hyndman was bold enough to suggest to the Congress the formation of a general citizen army. The present Army was 'ineffective and incompetent in war and dangerous in peace', because, 'at present it was in the hands of the capitalist and landlord classes. What we want is a citizen army which will be the army of democracy'. The other delegates were horrified by these martial sentiments. When *The New Age*, 2 May 1907, examining Haldane's Army Bill, mooted the idea that 'the whole population must be provided with arms and trained in their use', there was an outburst from a number of their subcribers. One was moved to observe: 'If this is Socialism, then I say, "Get thee behind me Satan". It is the doctrine of Hell' (16 May, 1907, p. 47); see reply, 23 May 1907, p. 50; and compare with S. Maccoby *English Radicalism: the end?*, p. 29, n. 3. The whole issue of a citizen army was a continuous concern in the pages of *The New Age*; see, for example, Ensor's article, 'Socialism and the Army: another view', 8 Aug. 1907, pp. 233ff. At the Stuttgart International Socialist Congress, August 1907, the resolution on action to be taken against militarism and imperialism stated: 'This Congress sees in the democratic organization of citizen armies in place of the existing standing armies, a real guarantee of peace, making wars of aggression impossible and leading to the disappearance of national antagonisms.' For a contemporary Radical account of the issue, see Ensor, 'The International Socialist Congress', *Albany Review*, Oct. 1907, pp. 18ff.

working classes, Hyndman's Democratic Federation was much closer to continental Socialists than either the parliamentary Labour party or the trade union movement in Britain.[1]

Addressing the Fourteenth Interparliamentary Conference[2] on 23 July, Campbell-Bannerman said: 'Tell your Governments when you return home . . . that example is better than precept, that actions speak louder than words, and urge them in the name of humanity to go into the Hague Congress, as we ourselves hope to go, pledged to

[1] See J. F. Green's report to the Fifteenth Universal Peace Congress at Milan, *Pacifism and the Working Class Movement*, 20 Sept. 1906: 'The Trade Union Congress meeting in September had adopted a resolution proposed by Mr. John Ward, M.P., endorsing the aims of the peace movement.' The Labour Party had affirmed its support and even the Social Democratic Federation while 'adhering to the sacrosanct dogma of Marxism', was prepared to co-operate and had been represented at both National and International Congresses. The Peace Movement found difficulty in adjusting its fundamentally middleclass paternalistic spirit towards the working classes, as is clear from the motion proposed by T. P. Newman and agreed to at the Sixteenth Universal Congress, September 1907 at Munich: 'The Congress, whilst desiring to express its appreciation of the part taken by many labour leaders and trade unions with regard to peace, would confirm its Resolutions of 1905 and 1906, and would still urge upon the various peace organisations in all countries the importance of interesting working men and women . . . in the subject of peace, and of obtaining their cooperation. *Arguments should be based on the grounds not only of material benefit . . . but on the high ideals of brotherhood, law and justice.*' (My italics.) This was the last occasion before the outbreak of war in 1914 that they formally attempted to solve by resolution what proved to be an intractable problem.

For a Socialist view of this problem, see *The New Age*, 30 May 1907, pp. 67–8: 'Universal peace is as remote an event as the absorption of the Solar System in the constellation Hercules . . . nevertheless these excellent idealists would have reformers work for peace and nothing but peace. But . . . the main business of Socialists at this moment . . . is the publication of the horrors of peace. . . . If the mere cessation of war guaranteed any sort of real peace, every Socialist would oppose war with all his might; but since the cessation of devastating industrial war, the choice of the Socialist must plainly be between two evils. . . . How many members of the Peace Society really recognise the industrial war at all? . . . The establishment of industrial peace is a more radical remedy than a thousand Hague Conferences.'

In matters of war and peace, *New Age* constantly urged the Parliamentary Labour party's voice to 'make a more valuable contribution than a feeble echo of Radical negations' (26 July 1907, p. 129). 'Socialism must rid itself of Liberal traditionalism and pseudo-Socialist sentimentalism' (12 Sept. 1907, p. 305); cf. Perris's appeal to the Peace Societies to broaden the basis of their support, in *Concord* xxiv, no. 1, Jan. 1908, p. 2.

[2] The Interparliamentary Union was founded in 1889 after an earlier initiative by Dr Albert Fischoff and the Radical M.P. Henry Richard in 1875 had proved abortive. The aim of the Union was 'to place the dream of the friends of peace within the realms of practical politics'. For many years the Union restricted itself to the problem of arbitration. See *Peace Year Book 1911*, pp. 64–5; also H. Evans, *Sir Randal Cremer: his life and work* (1909), ch. xvi. By 1906 the British group had grown to 350 M.P.s. Weardale was President, Randal Cremer was Secretary, and the Treasurers were Sir John Brunner and Sir Howard Vincent. The Union was not intended to be an exclusively Liberal organisation, but its most active participants were nevertheless drawn from the more Radical section of that Party and, of course, the parliamentary Labour party. See further, Evans, 28off.

diminish the charges in respect of armaments'. All Radicals rejoiced at Campbell-Bannerman's unequivocal statement. The *Manchester Guardian* noted that there was an immense field of enthusiasm waiting for the statesmen and lawyers to reap a harvest. The Prime Minister had been able to assume that the will to serve peace was in the air. All that remained was to devise means.[1] What practical plan, if any, did Campbell-Bannerman have? The Radicals did not have long to wait for their answer.

Balfour, during the election campaign in January, had made great play with the idea that a Liberal Ministry would forfeit Britain's security in the name of economy. Sir Henry had answered these charges with vigour.

> I don't wish Mr Balfour to lie awake o'nights whilst the Liberal Government is in power, listening for the boom of guns in the Thames or the Mersey. They will be able to sleep quite as profoundly under our Administration as they had any reason to do during the last ten years. When we mention that dreadful word economy, we mean economy, not at the cost of security, but such retrenchment as shall make security more secure.[2]

One of the last policy documents issued by the Tories had been a *Statement of Admiralty Policy* forecasting substantial reductions in the Naval Estimates. Balfour had described as 'an heroic stroke of the pen' his Administration's decision in 1905 when reorganising the Fleet, to strike off the active list 'a vast number of vessels many of them comparatively new'. If the Tories could bring themselves to do this much, surely an even bolder initiative might be expected from the Liberals?

On 26 July, the Secretary for the Admiralty, Edmund Robertson, opening for the Government on the 1906–07 Navy Estimates, stated:

> Instead of four 'Dreadnoughts' we propose to lay down only three. Instead of five ocean going destroyers we propose to lay down only two . . . we propose to reduce the number of submarines from twelve to eight. . . . In other words, we reduce the total committal of the new programme from £9,300,000 to £6,800,000. . . . Instead of the four armoured vessels which it was originally intended to lay down in 1907–08, we propose to make provision for two armoured vessels only, but with the proviso to be stated in the estimates that a third armoured vessel is to be laid down if the proposals in regard to the

---

[1] *Manchester Guardian*, 24 July 1906.
[2] Speech to Liverpool Liberals, 9 Jan. 1906.

reduction of armaments laid before the Hague Conference prove abortive.[1]

The Liberal Government had decided to depart from the Cawdor Programme.[2] Was this really as bold a move as at first it appeared to be? Robertson was careful to emphasise in his speech that the Board of Admiralty were unanimous in approving the reductions. In notes that at the time he prepared for the Government, Admiral Fisher defended the reductions primarily on the grounds 'that we are on the threshold of a new era in naval construction. . . . Until the new ships are in commission we have got plenty of the old ones to fight with.' It would be 'not only pernicious but ridiculous in the extreme' if the Board 'was bound to build ships it really does not want'.[3] The abandonment of the Cawdor Plan on this evidence would not seem to have been that 'glorious risk' of which Courtney had spoken at Oxford.[4]

Though Conservatives, such as Arthur Lee, protested violently at the Government's statement because they claimed it must lead inevitably 'to panic in a few years followed by an avalanche of extravagant expenditure', the Radicals and their Labour allies were delighted and scorned Lee's gloomy prognostications. The announcement 'would be welcomed by the friends of peace and arbitration all

[1] *Hansard*, iv:162:69–72.

[2] On 30 Nov. 1905, Cawdor, then First Lord of the Admiralty, had issued a memorandum, *Admiralty Work and Progress*, stating: 'At the present time strategic requirements necessitate an output of four large armoured ships annually.' Pressure for the abandonment of the Cawdor Programme came from two sources within the Cabinet. To retain the Programme was to assume a combination of the French and German navies which Asquith considered 'a myth—not a reliable possibility'. With the new emphasis on closer relations between France and Britain in Grey's policy, there was no longer any need to consider a combination of France and Germany as even a reasonable possibility. In any event the Dreadnought gave Britain for the moment an unassailable advantage even in the face of a Franco-German combination. However, the overwhelming argument was the pressure to effect economies to finance the introduction of Old Age Pensions. This was supported by the majority of the Cabinet. Tweedmouth stubbornly resisted reduction to two Dreadnoughts as Asquith required, until Haldane suggested the compromise, which eventually was accepted, of the building of a third Dreadnought depending on the outcome of the Hague Conference. Therefore within the Cabinet the pace-makers for naval reductions were not the Radicals but the Liberal imperialists. See Monger, 311–12.

[3] Lord Fisher, *Memories and Records* (1920), ii, 110–12.

[4] That there was no element of 'risk' involved in cutting down the programme is emphasised by the fact that while the Foreign Office was preoccupied in this period by the problem of Germany, the Admiralty was still pursuing its isolationist attitude and was concerned for the need for defence against a combination of all Powers.

A few years later, Fisher was to claim that he was satisfied that the best policy to be adopted at the time was to keep the naval building programme back whenever Germany's building permitted so that Britain could then at a later date build better and more powerful modern ships, see R. H. Bacon, *Lord Fisher of Kilverstone*, ii, 104.

over the world', claimed Keir Hardie. Fred Maddison reminded Lee that the time had passed for supposing that 'a proposal to reduce armaments was within the domain of dreams'. Balfour pointed to the inconsistency of a Government that while claiming that the Navy was being kept at the highest pitch of efficiency told its Radical supporters that they were making a significant demonstration of peaceful intent.[1] 'It is sufficient for me to say that the idea that these innocent, naif, unsuspecting statesmen who are going to join in the Hague Conference will be taken in by this noble appeal is really absurd.' Campbell-Bannerman was quick to reject Balfour's charge. 'It may be difficult to realise all the things that are attempted or thought of. But I would rather be one of those who try to realise them than one of those who run them down and point out nothing but difficulties. . . . We desire to stop this rivalry, and to set an example in stopping it.'[2]

This was not an answer to Balfour's criticism, rather a declaration of faith, and the *Manchester Guardian* was nearer the truth when it stated that it was a happy coincidence that the Sea Lords supported the Government's policy because it fitted with their own, while Liberals were satisfied for 'reasons of general policy which are the weightiest of all'.[3] In fact, Campbell-Bannerman was in the vanguard of his party in his attitude towards naval reduction, and only the most eccentric of Radical pacifists would have suggested that Britain should surrender her naval supremacy. The question that the Radicals posed was, 'What constitutes supremacy?' The Tories were after all notoriously 'timid and shrinking persons who naturally went in for panics'. There was 'no more timid and shrinking person than an Imperialist Jingo'.[4]

The Tories in Parliament and their allies in the Press interpreted every reduction in the Navy as a cause for public anxiety and concern. The Radicals in their turn were forced to emphasise the strength of the Navy.[5] The navalists constantly bemoaned supposed defects

[1] Robertson had recognised this difficulty early in his speech, and his arguments were couched to satisfy 'two entirely different schools of critics, each of which may be dissatisfied with our proposals', *Hansard*, iv:162:72.
[2] *Hansard*, iv:162:80 (Lee and Hardie); 105 (Maddison); 110–11. (Balfour); 117–18 (Campbell-Bannerman).
[3] *Manchester Guardian*, 20 Oct. 1906.
[4] *Hansard*, iv:162:100.
[5] As far as the Commons was concerned, most of the argument took place at Question Time. H. W. Massingham noted in *The Speaker*, 17 Mar. 1906, 'A characteristic of the new House of Commons is the complete reversal of the parliamentary habits of its predecessors. Question Time has again become an interesting and dramatic part of the sitting. The House is crowded; the questioning is close; the number of questions is so large that I do not see how it is possible to maintain the present time limit of three quarters of an hour.'

in ship design and in organisation.[1] The Radicals, with their eyes firmly fixed on the Hague Conference and determined that Britain's representatives at all costs should take with them an earnest of peaceful intent, found themselves acting as propagandists for the excellence of Britain's naval preparedness. It was strange inversion of traditional rôles that found them emphasising the incomparable weight and effectiveness of the Navy's fire power.

Meanwhile, at the International Peace Congress held in Milan in September, there was a considerable setback for English Radical opinion in the face of united European opposition. Continental lovers of peace desired the Hague Conference to give priority to the establishment of juridical status between nations. English delegates were convinced that this view was not practical and insisted that the first priority ought to be the arrest of armaments. However, in this wish they were defeated. A French delegate, M. Moch, was convinced that any attempt to discuss armaments at the Hague would lead to certain fiasco. It was not a happy occasion, and G. H. Perris writing of the Congress said that such 'a body of parochial doctrinaires who

---

And the Ministerialists supply the majority of the questions. This practice of a following freely interrogating its chiefs when they form the Executive Government is unprecedented.'

The whole idea of a question was to elicit an answer from a Minister that supported the questioner's own views; see King, 270. The House generally resented questions, and more particularly supplementary questions, for they were considered a waste of time and were often indistinctly heard and badly stated. It took 'considerable courage as well as quick wits to shoot supplementaries and brave the noisily cheered snubs that the Minister can always inflict': J. C. Wedgwood, *Memoirs of a Fighting Life* (1941), 64. The Radicals numbered among their ranks some of the most skilful questioners, but on the issue of the Navy they were generally bested by the Tory, Lee, and the erstwhile Liberal member for King's Lynn, Captain Bellairs. They daily inquired whether 'the naval programme was equal to the Two Powers standard'; or, if the Admiralty considered it was 'equal to the minimum requirements of the country'. A popular object of play was the Dilke Return on the relative size of the fleets of the different Powers.

Outside the House, the Tory Press poured scorn and obloquy both on the Government and on its Admiralty advisers. The Government, according to the *Standard*, 22 Oct. 1906, was 'striking a blow at the vital efficiency of the Navy. . . . The advent of the Liberal Government has in ten months done more damage to the nation than we might anticipate from conflict with a first-class European Power.' As for Fisher, *The Globe*, 21 Sept. 1906, declared: 'We are not speaking at random when we assert that more than any one man the responsibility and the guilt for these reductions lies at his door.' Maxse's *National Review* rebuked Fisher for becoming 'the obedient tool of a cheeseparing Cobdenite Cabinet.'

The Radicals hit back as best they might at this barrage of invective. Shaw Lefevre in particular made a number of contributions, both to *The Speaker*, 15 Sept. 1906, where he roundly criticised 'The Blue Funk School'; and in the *Contemporary Review*, lxxxi, 153ff., and xc, 624ff.

[1] Fisher had nothing but contempt for the 'naval Experts' whom he described as 'false prophets'. Nevertheless, the danger was that 'their arguments appealed to the inherent pessimistic British instinct'; see Fisher, ii, 104.

cannot rise to a great opportunity when it is put before them', were not fit to presume 'to continue the work begun by Cobden and Bright, Victor Hugo and Elihu Burrit. . . . I could not but reflect . . . that if any Labour leader had been present . . . or in fact an accredited statesman of any party . . . he would have gone away laughing at the idea that an alliance with such men as these was worth anything.'[1]

Enter upon the scene W. T. Stead, friend of peace yet a supporter of a strong British Army and Navy, and ever incorrigible optimist. On the first day of the new year a letter of his was published in the world's Press referring to the programme for the forthcoming Hague Conference. In 1899 the one serious failure had been the International Pilgrimage. Not in the least deterred by this experience, he now proposed to revive the project under his own tender care.

> I appeal to the friends of peace everywhere to take steps energetically to support the initiative of the British Government. . . . It is only by pressure from below that those who rule can be stirred to action. In every land the next three months should be utilised for the purpose of evoking an expression of public opinion upon this matter. On the eve of the Conference a Pilgrimage of Peace composed of leading representatives of the advocates of the League of Peace in every nation should proceed from Court to Court, from capital to capital, pleading for this policy.

Some men responded to Stead's incurable romanticism and optimism; the majority of those he approached poured cold water upon his scheme. Stead's personal history and the very times were out of joint with such a grandiose scheme. As Keir Hardie said when declining to join: 'If in the midst of the pilgrimage someone was to quote the *Review of Reviews* as blessing Mr Haldane's scheme for introducing militarism into our schools and Universities and encouraging it in connection with our churches, that would not make for seriousness.'[2]

The Prime Minister had constantly declared his concern with the world problem of escalating competition in armaments and its con-

---

[1] *Concord*, xxii, nos. 8/9, Sept./Oct. 1906, pp. 113–14.
[2] Quoted F. Whyte, *The Life of W. T. Stead* (1925), ii, 289. There are also quoted the replies of *inter alios*, Shaw, Wells and Lord Hugh Cecil. Hardie's objections were not limited to Stead's schemes alone, as a letter to Felix Moschelles, 7 Mar. 1907, makes clear: 'So long as we accept militarism and the system of society of which militarism is an essential and integral part, no great change can ever be accomplished. The Peace movement needs its rebels. . . . Some friends of peace are strangely inconsistent . . . they proclaim the glories of Empire whilst at the same time deploring the natural and inevitable consequences of Empire building. . . . I see no hope of the triumph of peace principles until Society has been reorganised on the communistic, non-competitive basis. It is for this, amongst other reasons, that I am a Socialist' (printed in *Concord*, xxiii, no. 3, March 1907, pp. 37–8).

sequent dangers to European peace. He was determined that his Government should take a bold step for reduction at the Hague. After careful consultation and discussion with Grey,[1] he wrote an article which appeared in the first number of *The Nation*, entitled: 'The Hague Conference and the limitation of armaments.'[2] Campbell-Bannerman's intention was to allay public fears, both at home and abroad, that to raise the question of armaments limitation at the Hague was 'ill-timed, inconvenient or mischievous'.

It was desirable in 1898 to lighten the burden of armaments; but that consummation is no less desirable today when the weight of the burden has been enormously increased. . . . I suggest that only upon one hypothesis can the submission of this grave matter to the Conference be set down as inadmissible: namely that guarantees of peace, be they what they may, are to be treated as having no practical bearing on the scale and intensity of warlike preparation.

That would be a lame and impotent conclusion, calculated to undermine the moral position of the Conference, and to stultify its proceedings in the eyes of the world. It would amount to a declaration that the common interest of peace, proclaimed for the first time by the community of nations assembled at the Hague, and carried forward since then by successive stages, with a rapidity beyond the dreams of the most sanguine, has been confided to the guardianship of the Admiralties and War Offices of the Powers.

. . . We have already given earnest of our sincerity by the considerable reductions that have been effected in our naval and military expenditure, as well as by the undertaking that we are prepared to go further if we find a similar disposition in other quarters. Our delegates, therefore, will not go into the Conference empty handed. It has, however, been suggested that our example will count for nothing, because our preponderant naval position will still remain unimpaired. I do not believe it. The sea power of this country implies no challenge to any single State or group of States. I am persuaded that throughout the world that power is recognised as non-aggressive and innocent of designs against the independence, the commercial freedom, and the legitimate development of other States, and that it is, therefore, a mistake to imagine that the naval Powers will be disposed to regard our position on the sea as a bar to any proposal for the arrest of armaments, or to the calling of a temporary truce. The truth appears to me to lie in the opposite direction.

The *Albany Review* observed: 'The significance of our Prime Minister's article in *The Nation* . . . is that he is the first European statesman

[1] See Spender, *Campbell-Bannerman*, ii, 328.
[2] 2 March 1907. *The Nation* was a remodelled version of *The Speaker*.

to challenge the old fashioned diplomacy, and to voice the great but inarticulate aspiration of the common people.'[1]

Campbell-Bannerman had chosen his words carefully to avoid offence or misunderstanding. But at home from the expected sources,[2] and from Germany, to whom the message had been specially addressed, there came a discouraging response. To the Germans, the Prime Minister's arguments, for all his declarations of good faith, were disingenuous. Here was the world's leading naval power calling for a cessation in naval competition at a time when it enjoyed not only the greatest preponderance of fighting ships but also had invented a battleship infinitely superior in fire power, armour and speed to any other warship afloat. If there was to be a general limitation of armaments upon the basis of the *status quo*, then Britain's naval supremacy would be perpetuated cheaply. Such a scheme was obviously a concerted plan by France and Britain to put pressure on Germany. Instead of opening the door to possible settlement, Campbell-Bannerman found that his initiative had slammed it in his face.[3]

The Prime Minister's article was not the piece of Machiavellian cunning that the Germans supposed.[4] It was 'an attempt to compromise between two conflicting forces which confronted each other in England or perhaps to speak more accurately, in the minds of many Englishmen. To satisfy one of these the Government said: "We will ask at the Hague for measures of disarmament." To satisfy the

---

[1] *Albany Review*, April 1907, p. 5.

[2] The *Daily Mail*, 6 Mar. 1907, reminded the Government that it had no mandate from the nation 'to weaken its Navy for the sole purpose of providing funds for doles to the Socialists'. The *National Review*, April 1907, called the article 'perilous twaddle'. Arthur Lee's comment in the Commons on a debate on the Navy Estimates was more to the point. 'Really it was getting very difficult to know where the Hague Conference and the enthusiasm of the Prime Minister was leading them. It was apparently leading to unfortunate misunderstandings with both friends and acquaintances. . . . The Prime Minister's remarkable manifesto just published in *The Nation* . . . did not seem to have met with the hearty sympathy of foreign countries which, no doubt the right hon. Gentleman anticipated. They had been received with ill-concealed anxiety in France, and open irritation in Germany': *Hansard*, iv: 170: 665.

[3] There were sufficient grounds for German suspicion of Britain's motives. Tweedmouth in the Lords (*Hansard*, iv: 162: 303–4) had given different reasons from those provided by Robertson in the Commons for the reduction of the naval programme. *The Times*, 31 July 1906, commenting on this inconsistency, stated, 'the Government's actions would not deceive any foreign Power'.

[4] See Fitzroy, i, 317–18: 'Whilst most of the European Powers regard the attitude of the English Government as a somewhat transparent hypocrisy, Germany entertains the conviction that it is directed against her and forms part of the Machiavellian designs which she had discerned behind the naval policy of Sir J. Fisher. . . . Every move in the game which can be attributed to English intrigue is held to be a step towards . . . the destruction of the German Navy'; see also, *B.D.*, VI: 2–3.

other it added immediately: "But they must not endanger the nation's safety or sea power".'[1] It was asking too much to suppose that other nations would accept without any qualms assurances that Britain's sea power was of a non-aggressive character and was exclusively a weapon of defence.[2]

The article was a mistake. But the honesty of the author's intentions was unfairly impugned and grossly misrepresented. It had been a political blunder of considerable magnitude for the repercussions it caused both at home as well as abroad. By choosing to place the article in *The Nation*, Campbell-Bannerman exaggerated the impression at home that his views were those of a section only of the Liberal party, and immediately increased the suspicion that Radical influence could endanger the country's security. This suspicion was reciprocated by the Radicals who supposed, and not without cause,[3] that the Prime Minister was being left in the lurch by his ministerial colleagues. In fact, when the article appeared there was already a strong impression among leading members of the Government that any attempt to secure a general limitation of armaments at the Hague would prove fruitless. This view was shared by the King. It was doubly unfortunate that Campbell-Bannerman's 'best and bravest act of a good and brave career'[4] should raise Radical hopes of success at the Hague to their highest when the chances of their being realised diminished.

On 30 April Campbell-Bannerman's worst fears were realised when Prince von Bülow announced in the Reichstag to laughter and cheers that Germany declined to discuss the question of disarmament at the Hague. 'We confine ourselves to allowing those Powers which look forward to some result from that discussion to conduct the discussion alone.'[5]

English Radicals were not so much surprised by Bülow's words[6] as

---

[1] Halévy, *The Rule of Democracy*, 223–4.

[2] This argument had first been mooted by Balfour in May 1906, *Hansard*, iv:156:410ff, and adopted by the Liberal leaders. However, its worthlessness is apparent from Grey's instructions to Sir Edward Fry, chief British delegate at the Hague Conference: 'The Government cannot agree to any resolution which would diminish the effective means which the Navy has of bringing pressure to bear upon the enemy.'

[3] When Balfour made a strong attack upon the Government's naval policy in general and Campbell-Bannerman's article in particular (*Hansard*, iv:170:675–684), there was much comment in the lobby of the House that Campbell-Bannerman had been left alone upon the Government front bench. It was particularly unfortunate that of all his colleagues, Grey 'should have missed so fitting an opportunity of reaffirming his adhesion to the Prime Minister's proposals', *Manchester Guardian*, 6 Mar. 1907.

[4] *Concord*, xxiii, no. 3, Mar. 1907, p. 25.

[5] Report of speech, *Manchester Guardian*, 1 May 1907.

[6] The Russian *communiqué* which summed up the attitude of the Powers

by 'the solidity and determination of the speech uttered as it was to the unanimous chorus of German opinion'. This unanimity 'could not fail to make a deep and painful impression'.[1] Radicals could no longer console themselves that the German nation was any more enlightened than its Government. If anything, the Chancellor had 'contrived to appear more moderate and more neighbourly than most of the party leaders who supported him'. *The Nation* concluded:

> We have to face the fact that the Radicals . . . are quite as decidedly opposed to the English policy as any of the Conservative groups . . . it would be folly to minimise the profound differences which separate us. They are neither accidental nor temporary, and for many years to come they are likely to be the decisive factor in European history.[2]

Not all organs of Radical opinion were as pessimistic in their appraisal of this latest move by Germany as was *The Nation*, but only Stead in his *Review of Reviews* could be so blind as to consider Bülow's 'genial and pacific utterances' reassuring, on the ground that Germany might well have declined even attendance at the Conference.[3] A more typical and realistic Radical appraisal was made by G. H. Perris: 'The Hague Conference is robbed in advance of much of its interest and importance, for it is evident that, as regards the question of armaments, the most we can now hope for is a good advertisement for a practical scheme.'[4]

Though bitterly disappointed, Campbell-Bannerman put the best face on the matter he could in the circumstances. When asked by the Tories if he would now authorise the construction of the third Dreadnought which had been contingent upon the result of the Hague Conference, he flatly rejected their proposal.[5] In a speech at Manchester later that week he made a civil reply to Bülow.

> We have not been without hope, although the hope may have been faint at times, that all the great Powers, including Germany, might see their way to join in a discussion (on the

---

towards the programme of the Hague Conference, had already destroyed the hope that Germany might after all consent to discuss the English proposals for limitation of armaments.

[1] *The Nation*, 4 May 1907.
[2] *Ibid.*
[3] *Review of Reviews*, May 1907.
[4] *Concord*, xxiii, no. 5, May 1907, p. 54. Francis Hirst in the *Albany Review*, June 1907, p. 255, anticipated the line to be taken later by most Radical critics: 'We must not be surprised or unduly alarmed because at first sight Germany shrinks from the proposal and refuses to take part in the discussion. It is disappointing no doubt, but the cause is intelligible. Nay, *the cause lies in our own policy, and is removable at our pleasure*' (my italics).
[5] *Hansard*, iv:173:1356.

reduction of armaments); and, now that we know that the discussion must be conducted without Germany participating, I will not pretend that we are not greatly disappointed. . . . I do not despair of something yet being done, though it will be far more difficult to accomplish without the general concurrence of all the great Powers in the preliminary proposition that such a reduction is a thing to be desired and sought for . . . Prince Bülow and the German Government appear to believe that such a method is delusive, and so they recognise that they can have no share in it. I recognise the candour with which Prince Bülow has said they must stand away from it altogether, and though the Government deeply regret it, they appreciate the candour with which it has been stated and the friendly tone of the Chancellor's speech.[1]

Now that the reduction of armaments had been effectively ruled out as a topic of worthwhile discussion at the Hague Conference, Campbell-Bannerman, with the best will in the world, was put in an impossible situation. Britain alone could not hope effectively to promote the Radical case for disarmament at the Hague. So the Conference was doomed to meet without any real Radical impetus or inspiration, even if it did escape the public outburst of scepticism that had greeted its predecessor. Most Radicals were resigned, even before the Conference began, not to expect too much, and in this they were not to be disappointed.[2]

H. W. Nevinson, who had been retained by the *Chronicle* to report on any war that might occur, now found himself together with Brailsford and his wife covering the great peace conference. The delegates, he noted, were not exactly the sort of men one would have chosen to usher in a new era for mankind. 'Frock coated, top hatted, portentous . . . the great majority elderly diplomatists, ambassadors, long inured to the stifling atmosphere of Courts, Foreign Ministers who have served their time of intrigue, professors who worship tradition and laws . . . though no doubt, all worthy and honourable gentlemen.' There too were the international propagandists of the pacifist creed, and most prominent among them W. T. Stead, 'bouncing with vitality and running over with human kindness towards Emperors, Kings, peoples and a bevy of girls alike; exuberant for peace, and in the end calling for as many battleships as we could

---

[1] Quoted Spender, *Campbell-Bannerman*, ii, 331–2.
[2] 'We must not expect too much from the Hague Conference though he who is at the Head of Government wishes that the utmost be accomplished which is possible, and he has plenty of stalwart supporters. . . . We are not content with the present expenditure on armaments . . . and we are trying to stiffen the backs of those who desire a more reasonable state of things.' A. G. C. Harvey, 13 June 1907 to Arbitration Association at their annual meeting.

possibly build'.[1] Though the sessions were to be held in secret, this did not deter Stead from publishing his *Courier de la Conférence*, a 'daily chronicle of the debates of the first Parliament of the world'.

By a dramatic coincidence, the formal opening of the Conference coincided with the dissolution of the Russian duma.[2] The tone of the Conference was set by the President, M. Nelidoff, in his opening address when he conjured the delegates' passions for peace and justice for mankind with the less than inspiring message: 'Let us not be too ambitious.' Any fears he may have had on this score were rapidly dispelled by the programme of discussions, for the greatest portion of time was absorbed with talk of war. The *Albany Review* noted that 'the great objects for which the people care are lost in a maze of diplomatic technicalities'.[3] More bitterly, *The Nation* complained: 'There is no danger of the ambitions of peace. War has its victories no less renowned.'[4] To call it a peace conference, declared Nevinson, was

> an amusing instance of ironic mockery, for nothing was further from the thoughts of all than peace. Are neutral ships to be sunk at sight in war? Are defenceless cities to be destroyed by bombs in war? Is poison gas a decent way of killing people in war? These questions were discussed and the ultimate result was as though two farmers long accustomed to confirm their neighbourliness by burning each other's ricks, had met for a conference upon their future behaviour and had parted amicably with the agreement in future to use safety matches only.[5]

But what of the British delegation led by Sir Edward Fry? Stead constantly complained about the British delegates,[6] and even less exuberant commentators were disappointed. But Radical dissatis-

[1] Nevison, 219.

[2] See *New Age*, 20 June 1907: 'We cannot conceive the nature of the mind that fails to be moved by the spectacle of a world gradually formulating in its blundering fashion the terms of a humaner peace side by side with a bureaucracy blundering to bloody doom. . . . The genius of Aeschylus could not have created a more poignant missive nor have invented a more tragic chorus.' In fact the more practical irony, as far as the success of the Conference and the future of Anglo-German relations were concerned, was that while the delegates wrangled at the Hague, 'Anglo-German naval rivalry reached a new and hitherto unequalled stage of mutual suspicion and bitterness', S. B. Fay, *The Origins of the World War* (2nd rev. edn. 1930), 234.

[3] *Albany Review*, Aug. 1907, p. 482.

[4] *The Nation*, 20 July 1907.

[5] Nevison, 219–20. G. H. Perris writing in February 1907, had sadly anticipated that 'the international assembly on which we count so much may degenerate into a Grand Committee on the rules of warfare': *Concord* xxiii, no 2, Feb. 1907, p. 14.

[6] See for example, *Courier de la Conférence*, 18 July 1907; see also, Bertha von Suttner, *Der Kampf um Vermeidung des Weltkrieges*, ii, 42, and Count Max Montgelas, *British Foreign Policy under Sir Edward Grey* (1928), 18.

faction was a direct result of their own unrealistic assessment of the possibilities. Therefore they had only themselves to blame when their exaggerated hopes were not realised. Once Bülow's speech had made it obvious that there could not be a realistic debate on the limitation of armaments, Radicals turned their hopes to the question of private property carried by sea during war time. They considered that such cargo should be immune from capture or destruction by belligerents. The Russians had made a proposal to this end and the case was espoused by the United States. In May *The Nation* was saying: 'The sincerity of our professions, the whole character of our naval power as a defensive and unaggressive force will be judged by the attitude we assume on that question.'[1] By this time a Radical campaign on the 'Rights of Capture' had been fairly launched.

In the Cabinet, Loreburn and Edmund Robertson were declared supporters of the idea; and Francis Hirst was only the most ardent of a number of protagonists outside Parliament.[2] They argued that such a reform would safeguard British supplies of food and materials in war time, deprive the German navalists of their best argument for expansion, and at the same time demonstrate to the world the pacific intent of Britain's Navy. But, the Admiralty was unanimously opposed to the idea. *The Nation* commented querulously: 'We don't seem to believe in peace and we are not prepared to give up a possible advantage in war.'[3] Lord Reay, one of Britain's delegates to the Conference, in a letter to Campbell-Bannerman bemoaned the sad fate of the representatives of a Liberal Government reduced to impotence by the obduracy of Admiralty 'experts' who were prepared to argue that even a small marine collier of one hundred tons might be classed as an auxiliary man o'war.[4] Bannerman sent on this *cri de*

---

[1] *The Nation*, 4 May 1907.

[2] See *Report of Royal Commission on Supply of Food and Raw Material in Time of War*, Parliamentary Papers, 1905, vol. 39—Reservation of E. Robertson at p. 116; also, *Commerce and Property in Naval Warfare: A Letter of the Lord Chancellor* (1906), Ed. Francis Hirst. This was a reprint of a letter by the then Sir Robert Reid, which appeared in *The Times*, 14 Oct. 1905. It argued for the immunity of private property at sea being brought before the Hague Conference with a view to an extension of the Declaration of Paris, 1856. The argument had a very respectable Radical lineage going back via Cobden to Brougham. Asquith supported Loreburn and Robertson, but Grey was firmly opposed. Sydenham, who had submitted a memorandum in May 1906 urging 'that we have nothing to gain and much to lose by abandoning the right', was assured by Hardinge in June 1907 that the Foreign Office would be 'quite firm': Lord Sydenham of Combe, *My Working Life* (1927), 203–4.

[3] *The Nation*, 20 July 1907; see also its attacks on Grey on the same subject, 15 and 22 Feb. 1908.

[4] For an explanation of the Admiralty attitude to the question of armament limitation, see A. J. Marder, *From the Dreadnought to Scapa Flow: the road to war 1904–14* (1961), 132–3 and 158. The Admiralty had sound allies in the Foreign Office. Of the seven foolscap pages of instruction given to the British

cœur to the Foreign Office, but all was in vain. Lord Reay's estimate of the situation was correct. The *beau rôle* at the Conference was not Britain's but had passed to Germany and America.[1] Discussions were vague and incoherent; Britain's intentions were presented in the worst possible light, and many delegates used the opportunity cynically to parade their contempt for what they considered were the illusions of pacifism.

In the Commons the Radicals made clear their discontent and their disillusionment. Reports they received from the Conference were without exception depressing. *New Age* laughed at the discomfort of the Radicals:

> We have found it difficult to take the Hague's philanthropic ambitions seriously and the event has fully justified our scepticism. . . . We have never expected universal peace as the result of the Hague Conference. Neither the Tsar, who initiated the scheme, nor the various capitalist Governments which have fallen in with it, want universal peace on the only conditions upon which it is desirable or permanently possible: the condition of universal justice.[2]

Radicals appealed to Campbell-Bannerman as the only person who might offer them some comfort. Percy Alden, Byles and Ramsay MacDonald pressed at Question Time in the House for information.[3] Finally, stung by the jeers and contempt of their opponents, at the end of July they moved for a reduction in the estimates for naval construction. Their motion was defeated by 263 votes to 86. But it was no insignificant demonstration of frustration and discontent that some fifty votes could be mustered in their support from the Government side of the House.

Now was the winter of their discontent. However, as so often in the past when matters seemed to be at their worst, the Radicals' perennial optimism broke through the seeming unrelieved pattern of gloom. Anglo-German agreement on the establishment of an International Prize Court was heralded by the *Manchester Guardian* as 'The First Achievement of the Conference'.[4] *The Nation* also seized upon this welcome crumb of comfort under the headline, 'Surprise at the Hague'. Perhaps 'the more ideal presentment of the case for peace had so far failed', but the Prime Minister could at least console

---

delegates and signed by Grey on 12 June 1907, barely half a sheet was concerned with matters other than regulations for the conduct of war. Most significantly, there was not even a mention of arbitration.
[1] See Spender, *Campbell-Bannerman*, ii, 333ff.
[2] *New Age*, 25 July 1907, p. 193.
[3] See *Hansard*, iv:178:46; and 179:131.
[4] *Manchester Guardian*, 30 July 1907.

himself 'with the thought that it has pushed on the most material form of European statesmanship to a point that brings it fairly into line with ideal progress'.[1]

A day was even secured for the discussion of the limitation of armaments at the very end of the Conference, but when the resolution was presented by Sir Edward Fry it proved to be a pious nothing that declared it 'highly desirable' for there to be discussions among the Powers on the means of limitation. In the absence of the German delegation, this was passed unanimously. Stead in desperation poured scorn on this empty gesture. Throughout the whole Conference, in public and private, he had ridiculed and reviled the British delegation unmercifully. Grey had been moved to remonstrate with him but to no avail. Of Britain's conduct at the Conference Stead avowed he had 'seldom seen a more miserable and scandalous débâcle'.[2] However, the majority of Radicals, inured to frustration and failure, were always ready to find something to cheer. Together with its resolution on the limitation of armaments, Britain had proposed an exchange of information on programmes of naval construction between the Powers. *The Nation* grasped eagerly at this straw. Here was an attempt to check the alarm engendered by naval armaments competition. What was more, 'if this declaration be sincerely translated into diplomacy, it may open the way to the creation of a definite and powerful League of Peace'. This was, to say the least, a somewhat abridged and translated version of Campbell-Bannerman's earlier glorious vision. A month earlier the *Albany Review* had considered that 'the conception of a "League of Peace" had been relegated to a decent obscurity'. The *Manchester Guardian* made a more sober assessment of the proposal but thought that despite its limitations it might yet prove the most practical move. 'The Government is to be congratulated on a proposal which for all its seeming modesty may contain within it the germ of a wholesome revolution in international relations.'[3] All then was not black for the Radicals. Yet in their hearts they had to admit that 'the Conference that met under such happy auspices, and on which high hopes were set . . . [had] in the main been a failure'. It was better frankly to admit as

---

[1] *The Nation*, 3 Aug. 1907.
[2] Quoted Whyte, ii, 291. Later when he wrote his history of the Conference, Stead somewhat modified these earlier views; see also his 'Impressions from the Hague', *Contemporary Review*, xcii, 730, where he described the Conference as 'a conspicuous landmark in the history of mankind'. Stead at this stage was probably more interested in undermining the critics of the Conference than in giving a sober assessment of the facts; see his biographer's comments, ii, 287.
[3] *Manchester Guardian*, 19 Aug. 1907.

much 'than to attempt to prove as had been done in some quarters, that important results had been achieved'.[1]

Why had the Hague Conference been such a failure? The Radicals found their target in

> the wretched policy of national selfishness which wrecked some of the best projects presented to the Conference. If we analyse the voluminous reports of its proceedings, we everywhere find evidence of that policy. The old mandate to diplomats seemed to have found its way into the new gathering: 'Take as much as you can and only give as much as you must.' Suspect your colleagues, dissect their motives and watch their moves. If they propose an arrest of armaments, perhaps they want to steal a march on you.[2]

Nor was Great Britain guiltless. It had been hoped, and not without reason, that on the important question of immunity of capture of private property at sea during any naval war, the situation would be reformed and placed upon the same footing as property upon land. Despite support for this view from within the Cabinet, they had 'reckoned without the naval experts, and the result was that Great Britain opposed the change and nothing was done'.[3]

Though the record of the Conference from a Radical point of view was a sorry one, they saw no reason why they need be pessimistic about the peace movement as a whole.[4] At the very least, conferences like the one at The Hague marked the beginning, no matter how faltering, of international organisation; the first expressions of a trend towards the international government which was bound to come. They must never abandon the hope that such a movement could avert the cataclysm which the otherwise unbridled forces of destruction were intent upon preparing.[5] Now was not a time for

---

[1] J. F. Green in *Concord*, xxiii, no. 11, Nov. 1907, 110–12; cf. *Albany Review*, Oct. 1907, p. 6. *New Age*, 22 Aug. 1907, p. 257, unlike the Radical journals was 'inspired at the prospect of turning from the futilities of the Hague to a genuine expression of international solidarity given by the Socialist Congress at Stuttgart'. However, a British delegate at the Stuttgart Congress, Harry Quelch, was expelled for calling the Hague Conference 'a thieves' supper party', thus calling down upon his head the opprobrium of the Radical Press. See, for example, *Daily News*, 24 Aug. 1907. The elements of farce were often present, not only in the actions of the delegates to the International, but also in the reports of their activities by a less than objective Press.

[2] *Concord*, xxiii, no. 11, Nov. 1907, 112.

[3] *Ibid*; see also *Albany Review*, Sept. 1907, p. 604: 'The pathetic failure of our representatives at the Hague must we fear be ascribed to the Foreign Office.'

[4] See, for example, A. Beesly, 'Pacifism' in *Positivist Review*, Nov. 1907.

[5] See Baker and Baker, 149–50. See also J. Macdonell, 'The Hague Conference: the gains and losses', *Albany Review*, Sept. 1907, pp. 608–17: 'It is an easy task to find shortcomings and imperfections. . . . All the same it is a beginning of an organisation such as the world has not known; the first realising of the hopes of far-reaching and seeing spirits.'

relaxation of effort. Even if the frontal assault upon the armaments problem had failed, limitation could still be achieved by indirect means.[1] One champion of disarmament could not, however, blink at the Hague failure. Speaking at the Guildhall on 9 November Campbell-Bannerman confessed to having been 'over-sanguine' in his hopes that the Hague might have stopped 'the self-defeating race of armaments'. However, he pleaded it was impossible for one nation to exceed the general standard of goodwill, though he assured his audience with fine Liberal instinct and rare political tact 'no foreign Power was less anxious in the cause of peace than ourselves'.[2]

Unfortunately, the Foreign Office was convinced that there was little evidence to support Campbell-Bannerman's case.[3] Eyre Crowe writing to Dilke claimed that disarmament was 'a thing no sane man believes in or cares about'. The only achievement of the Hague Conference was

> to accentuate the fact that the Powers are divided by serious differences. Our disarmament crusade has been the best advertisement of the German Navy League and every German has by now been persuaded that England is exhausted, has reached the end of her tether, and must speedily collapse, if the pressure is kept up. You will find that this impression now prevails all over Germany.[4]

The sad truth was that the gap between the reductionists and their opponents was wider than ever after the Hague Conference, and even Fisher's statement that Britain's fleet was *'nulli secundus'* and that Britons 'might sleep quiet in their beds' undisturbed by the bogies of invasion conjured up by the febrile imagination of Leo Maxse in his *National Review*,[5] could not close the ever widening divide. Naval arrangements held in suspense for the period of the Conference could not be deferred indefinitely. The advantage of building the first Dreadnought would not remain unchallenged. For the moment both parties looked to their strength. The time for fresh blows would come in the spring with the Naval Estimate debates.

[1] See *Manchester Guardian*, 19 Nov. 1907.
[2] Reported, *ibid.*, 11 Nov. 1907.
[3] However, if Campbell-Bannerman could not upbraid Germany, German Radicals were outspoken in their condemnation of their country's attitude and regarded Germany responsible for the failure of the Conference; see, *inter alia*, Alfred Fried, *Die zweite Haager Conferenz. Ihre Arbeitan, ihre Ergegnisse, ihre Bedeutung* (1908), *passim*.
[4] Eyre Crowe to Dilke, 15 Oct. 1907, quoted Steiner, 115.
[5] Fisher in speech at Guildhall, 9 Nov. 1907. The reason for Fisher's confidence is apparent in the letter that he wrote to the King a month earlier, 4 Oct. 1907: his correspondence, *Fear God and Dread Nought*, ed. A. J. Marder (1952–59), ii, 141. For Maxse's reaction to Fisher's speech, see his letter to the *Daily Express*, 12 Nov. 1907.

Chapter 4   The Naval Crisis: 1908–10

Prelude, 1908

On 3 October 1907 Dumas, the British naval attaché in Berlin, reported that a number of German newspapers were forecasting that there would be either a new German Navy Law, or that an amendment of the 1900 Navy Law would be introduced in the forthcoming session of the Reichstag.[1] On 18 November the actual proposals were published in the *North German Gazette*. Provision was to be made to shorten the life of battleships and to replace outdated vessels with Dreadnoughts. There was to be a new programme of construction spread over a period of ten years, with three Dreadnoughts to be laid down in 1908 and 1909, four in 1910, two in 1911, and one annually thereafter up to 1917.[2] This supplementary law was accepted by the budget committee of the Reichstag in January 1908, and became law in February. The only opposition to the proposal in the Reichstag came from the Socialists. Bebel warned that it would be the cause of an anti-German reaction in Britain, but von Tirpitz denied that England was uneasy about the supplementary law, and he quoted British journalists to prove his point. At the same time he strongly disclaimed any intention of Germany either building against the British navy or ever disputing Britain's naval supremacy.

The Radicals were not unduly surprised by the news from Germany. To them it seemed the natural result of the failure of Campbell-Bannerman's proposals for the international reduction of armaments at The Hague.[3] The *Daily Mail* boldly claimed that Germany's dominant idea was 'to build a fleet which shall fulfil the hopes and desires of the Pan Germans and be mightier than the mightiest navy

---

[1] See *B.D.* VI: 60–1. The *Berliner Neueste Nachrichten* went as far as to suggest the German Government acted as it had because it had been sent an ultimatum by the armour plate manufacturers.
[2] For an analysis of the German proposals, see, *B.D.* VI, 68–76 and 118–21.
[3] See, *inter alia*, *The Nation*, 'Diary of the Week', 23 Nov. 1907.

in the world.'[1] W. T. Stead, as a diversion from preaching his peace crusade, launched a campaign for two British Dreadnought keels to be laid to every one by Germany. These proposals received the headline approbation of the *Daily Mail*, and the *Navy League Journal* for January informed members that they were to keep their eyes steadily fixed upon the naval programme for 1908. If it should not come up to Mr Stead's minimum, then they must prepare to exert themselves to the utmost. The Navy League threw a sport fathered by H. F. Wyatt and L. G. Horton-Smith, the Imperial Maritime League. Its declared purpose, according to the parent body, was 'to use the Navy as a stick for the present Government's back'.[2]

The Liberal Press was unhappy about the revised German pro-gramme but they saw no reason to consider the move in itself alarming. The British margin of naval superiority was after all over-whelming. There would be no need for a scare programme of naval construction. The German supplementary law was 'a gift from Mars to the Jingo coteries and members of the "Blue Funk School"', who could be expected to keep a shrewd eye upon those Departments at work on the Estimates.[3] But it should be remembered, the German programme was 'not an act but a project', and that the 'Germans were merely following the lead of British naval policy'.[4] Meanwhile, the Radicals contented themselves by producing their own articles as 'an antidote to Navy League vapourings'.[5]

A series of speeches by prominent statesmen in December 1907 and January 1908, brought little comfort to those who looked forward to reductions in the Naval Estimates. Tweedmouth, the First Lord of the Admiralty, speaking at Chelmsford on 3 December outlined a scheme for a naval basin at Rosyth large enough to accommodate

[1] *Daily Mail*, 25 Nov. 1907.
[2] The Imperial Maritime League, known as the 'Navier League', was founded by Navy League dissidents with the prime objective of removing Jackie Fisher. At that time there was considerable dissension within the ranks of the German Navy League. 'Perhaps', claimed *Concord*, 'if this process extends to both countries, there may be hope that the naval alarmists, like the Kilkenny cats, will end by exterminating each other.' This hope was further encouraged by the split between supporters of Beresford and Fisher within the higher ranks of the navy itself. The only deduction to be drawn was that 'Naval Jingoism is a kind of rabies; having united to bite the public, these gentlemen are now breaking up into droves and rending one another': *Concord*, xxiv, no. 2, Feb. 1908, p. 20.
[3] *Ibid.*, Jan. 1908, p. 11.
[4] *The Nation*, 8 Feb. 1908 and 23 Nov. 1907.
[5] *Concord, ante. The Economist*, 22 Feb. 1908, claimed that because of Ger-many's financial position, the prospect of their naval programme being realised was 'extremely doubtful, in fact so improbable that it ought not to be regarded seriously'.

one hundred and twelve ships of war. This was to be part of the new 'watching basis' against the German fleet. He admitted that it would cost a great deal of money, and *The Nation* observed: 'This does not point to the expected reductions in the Naval Estimates. . . . The situation is serious for the large body of Liberal members who are deeply pledged to a substantial reduction of warlike expenditure.'[1]

Lord Lansdowne, in a speech at Edinburgh on 11 December, approved of Grey's foreign policy as 'non-partisan', but sneered at the 'shattering of Campbell-Bannerman's cloud-built castles of peace' and his policy of 'fewer Dreadnoughts and more canal boats'. Of course, the Radicals could expect such sentiments from a Tory peer, but two reserved speeches by Grey clearly indicated that any hope for a substantial cut in the forthcoming Navy Estimates was now not likely. Grey saw no reason for the German programme impelling Britain to rush into further naval expenditure. However, 'if the new foreign programme was carried out it would render continued reductions impossible, our interest in the maintenance of the fleet being not merely the protection of our commerce but the national life and independence'.[2]

The Radicals remained not unduly alarmed. G. P. Gooch, writing on the prospects of the new parliamentary session in the *Albany Review*, claimed that

> The rapid increase in the German Navy is due more to the example set by Britain between 1895 and 1905 than to any other cause, and the fortifications of Rosyth may perhaps be regarded as the latest move in this game of ruinous rivalry. There is, however, no reason why the latest extravagances of German Imperialism should divert us from our duty of bringing our Budget of national defence within more reasonable limits.

Gooch suggested two reasons for this. First, it had been 'the declared policy of the Liberal leaders in Opposition'. Second, it was 'essential to the success of the Government's social policy'.[3] At the same time, Radicals could not ignore the fact that leaks of information from the Cabinet were very disquieting. *The Nation* was not prepared to accept any excuse for an increase in the Naval Estimates.

> We say that the Liberal Government is under a pledge of loyalty to itself and to the Party that brought it into being to disregard the unthinking movement for a fresh start in naval expenditure, itself following on the great Dreadnought development. Who

[1] *The Nation*, 7 Dec. 1907.
[2] Speeches of Grey on 19 Dec. 1907 and 15 Jan. 1908, reported in *The Nation*, 21 Dec. 1907, p. 418 and 18 Jan. 1908, p. 553.
[3] *Albany Review*, Feb. 1908, pp. 458–86.

will take the responsibility for such a departure? ... Not a progressive and peaceful administration, pledged to economy to the very hilt.[1]

In December 1907, the Sea Lords had presented a revised ship building programme which envisaged an increase of one and a quarter million pounds over the previous year's Estimates. This they considered 'most moderate', as their original proposal for an increase of £2,150,000 had been trimmed to appease a shocked Asquith.[2] This contretemps had brought Tweedmouth almost to the point of resigning from the Admiralty. Esher commented, 'It is only natural that the Government should resent putting up the Naval Estimates by £2,000,000. Their *decision* is that the Estimates are not to exceed last year's figures.'[3] The new claim for an increase of more than a million pounds caused a Cabinet crisis which was exacerbated by Radical action.

In November 1907, before the official announcement of the German programme, the Radical Reduction of Armaments Committee had presented Campbell-Bannerman with a strongly worded memorial insisting on the need for retrenchment in armament expenditure. This had been signed by 136 Liberal and Radical M.P.s.[4] In January, the Executive Committee of the Liberal Members of Parliament issued a statement on the Estimates moving for a reduction of expenditure upon armaments,[5] and in that same month the National Liberal Federation, meeting in conference at Leicester, petitioned the Prime Minister urging on him the advisability of curbing expenditure on naval armaments.[6] However, the real threat of Radical rebellion was made clear to the Government on the opening day of the new parliamentary session, when the leading spirits of the November memorandum declared that they had decided to move an amendment to the Address signifying their regret at the absence of Government proposals for reducing armaments.

[1] *The Nation*, 18 Jan. 1908.
[2] Asquith's position was difficult. He was a Liberal Chancellor of the Exchequer with all that traditionally implied in retrenchment of armament expenditure. At the same time, he was the acknowledged leader of the Imperialists in the Cabinet. While he was prepared to oppose military or naval expenditure, he never went to the same lengths as his successor, Lloyd George. On this, see Roy Jenkins, *Asquith* (1964), 167–8.   [3] *E.P.*, ii, 268.
[4] The memorial sent 4 Nov. 1907 had been drafted by Murray Macdonald and Brunner. They were convinced that they could have had more than 136 signatures had they 'prosecute[d] a personal canvass among all the supporters of the Government'. Fisher described the facts as set out in the paper as 'quite true' when writing to the King. For a full account of this, see Stephen Koss, *Sir John Brunner* (1970), 217 and Appendix I. Also, Tilney Bassett, *Life of J. E. Ellis*, 237.
[5] See *Concord*, xxiv, no. 2, Feb. 1908, p. 16.
[6] See Francis Hirst, *A. G. C. Harvey: a memoir*, 66.

The Cabinet had every reason to be alarmed. It was calculated that if the amendment, which was due to be debated on 5 February, went to a division, the Government would be in a minority of a hundred.[1] Asquith was deputed to interview representatives of the Radicals who informed him that they would vote against the Government. An attempt by Whiteley, the Liberal Chief Whip, to check the rebels, was of no avail. Asquith informed Campbell-Bannerman of the situation and the Prime Minister gave his pledge that the Reductionists would be given a day for the discussion of their motion. The Radical Press was overjoyed at this triumph. The Radicals 'had taken up a firm stand on a matter of high principle and shown that they were not to be set aside by a few blasts from the Jingo war trumpet'.[2] The *Daily Mail* might bray that the era of economy was over and finished and that the nation must be prepared to see the Estimates rise annually, or else make ready to surrender the command of the sea and abandon the Empire;[3] but, *The Nation* chose to ignore this pessimistic forecast.

> . . . The dramatic intervention of the Liberal party in Parliament has, we hope, secured an arrest of the policy of a heavy and permanent increase in armaments. . . . It is freely stated that both the Prime Minister and the Chancellor of the Exchequer regard the action of the majority with not unfriendly eyes, and that they may have before them no harder task than the forcing of a half open door.[4]

The facts were otherwise than *The Nation's* cheerful surmise.

An emergency meeting of the Cabinet had been held on the afternoon of 4 February. It had been concluded that the Government was facing defeat on the Murray Macdonald amendment. Therefore, it was unanimously decided that the Naval Estimates were to be reduced by £1,340,000 to bring them below the figures for the previous year. A subcommittee of the Cabinet—Harcourt, Lloyd George and McKenna—had been appointed to effect this resolution.

That day, Harcourt summoned Fisher to his room in the Commons and informed him of the Cabinet's decision. When Fisher pointed out that the Estimates had already been signed and approved by the Cabinet and that in any event they were at their irreducible minimum, Harcourt adopted an arrogant tone with him. Either five Cabinet members would resign or the Board of Admiralty. Harcourt made plain that the latter alternative was the more likely, and when

[1] See *E.P.*, ii, 281.
[3] *Daily Mail*, 7 Feb. 1908.
[2] *Concord*, xxiv, no. 2, Feb. 1908, p. 20.
[4] *The Nation*, 8 Feb. 1908.

Fisher pointed out that it would be difficult to replace the Board, he was told that Beresford was only too ready to accept the office of First Sea Lord. Fisher accepted this most unwelcome news, noted that the matter seemed to be settled already, and left.

No sooner had Fisher arrived at the Admiralty than he received a note from Churchill asking him to dine that evening so that urgent business could be discussed with Lloyd George. At their meeting Lloyd George, though adopting a more conciliatory style than had Harcourt earlier, still insisted that the Naval Estimates had to be cut. Fisher offered a possible solution—to deduct a sum from the Estimates and present them to Parliament with a note stating that the Board of Admiralty consented on the understanding that the efficiency of the Fleet would be maintained and that any deficit would be met out of supplementary Estimates. Fisher's proposition was laughed out of court by Churchill. Lloyd George persisted, maintaining that Beresford was not only ready to take over, but was prepared to cut the Estimates by two million pounds. Fisher was not impressed. They might go ahead with Beresford but they would be sold out within three months as the irreducible minimum had been reached. The dinner party broke up without any further progress.

The next day, 5 February, Lloyd George asked Fisher to meet him at the Board of Trade. There he urged the First Sea Lord to agree to a reduction for the year on the understanding that the following year he might have any sum he pleased. Fisher asked for time to explain this extraordinary proposal to the Admiralty Board which was due to meet at midday. Lloyd George attended the meeting, and heard Fisher advise the Board that it would not be wise to appear to be forcing the Government's hand. But having gone through the votes yet again, the Board concluded that they must stick to their original figures as they represented the absolute minimum.

The next move was for Fisher to ask Robertson, a great friend of the Prime Minister, to see Campbell-Bannerman, explain the situation, and to go through each vote separately, showing the impossibility of making any cuts. This Robertson did, Campbell-Bannerman listening carefully the while. Next, Asquith was sent for; Campbell-Bannerman repeated to the Chancellor the gist of what Robertson had said, and then declared, 'I have decided that the Naval Estimates are to stand. Haldane will take £300,000 off his instead. Nothing need be said at present to any other member of the Cabinet.'[1]

The matter could not rest there. The Cabinet remained divided, and Tweedmouth, hounded by his Admiralty advisers and unhappy

[1] See *E.P.*, ii, 281–2.

because he felt that his opinion was neither sought nor valued, threatened resignation.[1] It was another week before a compromise was finally achieved. Lloyd George favoured a similar scheme to that proposed by Fisher on 4 February which Churchill then had laughed at. This was the compromise accepted, the sum involved being £400,000. In effect, the Cabinet would present its Naval Estimates on an instalment basis—a foretaste of the 'contingency' programme device that was to be employed in 1909. The move had been designed to placate the Radicals, and Robertson was forced to admit as much when he was challenged by Lee in the Commons.[2]

While the Cabinet wrestled with the Naval Estimates, the *Daily News* published a list of Liberal Imperialist members of Parliament who had declared their determination to oppose the Liberal pacifists.[3] *Concord* lightly dismissed the group as 'the young bloods of Liberalism', and at the same time encouraged the *Daily News* and *The Nation* to 'keep up the counterblast to the lukewarm leanings to Imperialism of the *Westminster Gazette* and the *Daily Chronicle*'.[4] But the tide of fortune was swinging away from the Radicals. Despite the comfortable assertions of the Radical Press,[5] it was suspected that the reductionists had suffered a defeat in the Cabinet. However, the most depressing thought was that 'any increase in Naval Estimates would bring Britain perceptibly nearer a conflict with Germany'. *The Nation* reiterated this theme throughout February and March 1908. 'A huge British programme, rapidly produced in answer to the German instrument will make not for peace but for war. That war will never be waged by Liberal statesmen. But its inevitability may, in a fatal hour, be decreed by them.'[6]

On 19 February eighty-two members of the centre section of the Liberal party memorialised the Prime Minister calling for 'complete efficiency' in Imperial defence and deprecating any pressure upon the Government to modify the Naval Estimates. *The Nation* warned: 'If on Monday week the Liberal Party is committed to a great new naval programme, the Party unity is gravely qualified, while the period both of economy and social reform is practically

[1] See Tweedmouth to Campbell-Bannerman, 12 Feb. 1908, *Asquith MSS*, vol. 21. 'I unfortunately am the person primarily responsible for the Admiralty, and feel very keenly that important matters can be treated without my knowledge and concurrence.'
[2] See *Hansard*, iv:185:586.
[3] *Daily News*, 11 Feb. 1908.
[4] *Concord*, xxiv, no. 2, Feb. 1908, p. 21.
[5] See, *inter alia*, 'National expenditure and social reform', *Albany Review*, March 1908, pp. 712ff.; 'The German Fleet', *Contemporary Review*, March 1908, xciii, pp. 336ff.
[6] See *The Nation*, 1 Feb. 1908, p. 624, and 8 Feb. 1908, p. 661.

closed. We look confidently to the Prime Minister and Mr Asquith to avert such a disaster.'[1]

The Peace Day meeting for 1908 held at Caxton Hall on 27 February had a somewhat strained atmosphere. The President, Leonard Courtney, spoke with his usual courage and determination. 'If we would make our Government and the nation sincere and active in the prosecution of peace, we must press upon them the necessity of setting the tune of peace instead of war and mistrust.' As the time for debating the Murray Macdonald amendment approached, the burden on the reductionist Liberal members increased. They were torn between their loyalty to the Government and their determination to hold, if they could, the hands of those who demanded an instant British *riposte* to the revised German shipbuilding programme. They considered the wording of their amendment to be moderate, and that the alternative wording proposed by the Government missed the point.[2] They believed the question was not one of national safety being in peril, but 'the wise accord of civilised and Christian nations'.[3] But it was never easy to vote against the Government. Some idea of the pressures they suffered can be gained from the diary entries of John Ellis, a prominent backbench Radical, who had recently retired from the Government because of his age and ill health. His biographer records:

> It was no less than the keenest pain to vote against the Government which he had served so long. Yet he did it. The Quaker ethos was sufficient still. He was confident that the example of England in reducing armaments would be followed throughout Europe. Other countries would be so utterly beaten in the commercial race by the handicap of war expenditure that they would be compelled to spend in their turn as little as possible on armies and navies.[4]

This neat combination of moral and economic arguments still did not make the decision an easy one for Ellis, and he recorded there was 'much mental perturbation among supporters of the Govern-

---

[1] See, *ibid.*, 22 Feb. 1908.
[2] Terms of the Radical amendment—'That in view of the continued friendly relations with foreign powers announced in the gracious Speech from the Throne, this House trusts that further reductions may be made in expenditure on armaments, and effect be given to the policy of retrenchment and reform to which the Government is pledged', *Hansard*, iv: 185:369. The terms of the Government's amendment were—'That in view of the continued friendly relations with foreign Powers announced in the gracious Speech from the Throne, this House will support His Majesty's Ministers in such economies of naval and military expenditure as are consistent with the adequate defence of His Majesty's dominions.' *Hansard*, iv: 185:382-3.
[3] *The Nation*, 29 Feb. 1908.
[4] Tilney Bassett, 239-40; and Diary entry of John Ellis for 2 Mar. 1908.

ment'; 2 March, when the amendment would be debated, promised for many Radicals to be a 'rather painful evening'.[1]

Murray Macdonald moved his amendment in solemn if somewhat sullen manner. The Liberal benches below the gangway seethed with revolt, but it was Sir John Brunner seconding the amendment who lit Radicals' hearts with a short speech frequently punctuated with cheers especially when he referred to the question of 'experts'.

> I have employed experts for over thirty-three years, in matters of all sorts, and paid for their opinion, but I have never allowed them to dictate my policy. . . . I am one of those who think the men in the Government should be strong enough to decide their policy for themselves and bear the responsibility. They certainly should be strong enough to keep the experts quite out of sight and prevent them from dropping confidential documents about and popping in and out of newspaper offices. I want strong men at the head of the Government.[2]

Asquith replied for the Government in a long, moderate and dexterously balanced speech, but his defence of the Estimates fell coldly upon Radical ears.[3] Balfour chose to play the part of villain, and particularly offended with his assertion that a pacific policy and skilful diplomacy were not to be regarded as governing factors in relation to the size of armaments.[4] *Concord*, commenting bitterly upon Balfour's 'heresy', wondered, 'Has it never occurred to him and his supporters that the best form of national defence consists in a friendly and just dealing with other nations, and in avoidance of the acerbities and provocations upon which armaments really flourish?' They concluded that the trouble with Balfour was that he, like so many others, had no belief in the efficacy of moral values.[5]

Socialists, in the period before the debate, had not been deeply stirred by the question. Their Press, as on most issues, held contradictory views. *New Age* canvassed for the strongest possible Navy at almost any price.[6] Keir Hardie's *Labour Leader* was too engrossed

[1] Regret at having to censure their leaders and avowals of loyalty, were a constant preface to letters of complaint sent by Radicals. See, for example, H. J. Wilson to Asquith 9 Feb. 1909, quoted Mosa Anderson, *H. J. Wilson: fighter for freedom* (1953), 80. Also, Brunner's letter to *Chester Chronicle*, 30 Jan. 1909, 'It affords me no pleasure . . . to act the part of "candid friend",' quoted Koss, *Brunner*, 219.

[2] *Hansard*, iv:185:365–6.

[3] Asquith's attempts at conciliating the rival sections of his party—a very natural action for the heir to the Liberal leadership—caused him to be accused by *The Times* of playing 'the not very enviable part of Mr Facing-both-Ways'.

[4] *Hansard*, iv:185:456–7.

[5] *Concord*, xxiv, n. 3, Mar. 1908, p. 35.

[6] *New Age*, 15 Feb. 1908, p. 302; and 29 Feb. 1908, pp. 340–1; cf. the report of the debate in *Labour Leader*, 6 Mar. 1908, p. 154.

in the new Licensing Bill to pay any heed to the armaments question. Clynes was the only Labour contributor to the debate. He criticised the moderation of the Radical amendment, and silenced Tory truculence by reminding them that, 'the great cries of the victors have never yet counterbalanced the groans and agony of those who were slain in war'.[1] When it came to the division, all the Labour members in the House, save one, voted against the Government. Even so the Radical amendment was defeated by 320 votes to 73.

Sir John Brunner in the course of his speech had said, 'if every member who sympathises with this resolution were to vote against the Government, they [the Government] would be in a minority'. The fact that a discrepancy existed between the strength of general sympathy for their cause and strength in the division lobby, afforded a challenge to pacifists to begin a much more thorough and extensive organisation of peace sentiment in the constituencies than before had been attempted.

> Is the strength of Pacifism in the constituencies as formidable as the influence of the Services, the clamour of the contractors and the rage of the Jingo Press? As practical politicians we must take this lesson to heart and begin to marshal our forces in the constituencies in the same way that the Temperance, Trade Union and other movements have learned to do. Then we shall see the gulf between faith and practice narrowed—at least on the more progressive side of the House.[2]

Undoubtedly the Radicals had enjoyed considerable sympathy among Liberals both in the Commons and outside. The lesson *The Nation* drew from this was that the Government would do well 'to follow the historical lines of British defensive policy, which, when they were moderate, produced moderation in others, and since they have become extravagant, are, by force of imitation, upsetting half the budgets of Europe'.[3]

The public had anticipated, with more than usual interest, the appearance of the year's Naval Estimates. When they were published on 24 February the extreme Tory Press was outright in its condemnation of the projected construction programme. The *Daily Mail* in banner headlines crudely adumbrated the Radical dilemma of conscience and priority. 'Is Britain going to surrender her maritime supremacy to provide old age pensions?'[4] The Liberal Press was divided. The more Radical journals felt less inclined than either the *Daily News* or the *Manchester Guardian* to hail the increase in the

[1] *Hansard*, iv:185:430–34.   [2] See *Concord*, xxiv, no. 3, Mar. 1908, p. 35.
[3] *The Nation*, 7 Mar. 1908, p. 816.   [4] *Daily Mail*, 25 Feb. 1908.

Estimates as 'nominal' and as a victory over alarmist opinion. The *Albany Review* in its survey of current events noted with concern:

> The mere fact that a Liberal Government in a time of profound peace should be spending about sixty millions a year upon the Army and Navy is startling enough. It becomes graver still when the fact is realised that the Imperialist Government of Lord Salisbury and Mr Chamberlain thought it perfectly safe before the South African War to spend twenty millions less.[1]

The most reassuring feature of the Estimates was that the explanatory memorandum accompanying them suggested that there might be no need to increase the building programme for 1909. But, this was a direct contradiction of the Admiralty memorandum issued in December 1907 which had stated unequivocally that it was an 'absolute certainty' there would have to be a larger battleship programme in 1909.[2]

In the drawn-out debates in the Commons on the Naval Estimates, Tory spokesmen pointed out that it was misleading to view Britain's naval superiority in 1908 in isolation. Their major concern was Britain's 'capacity for output' compared with that of Germany. Could British shipyards and munition contractors build and equip warships with the necessary armour plate and calibre of guns, quicker than the Germans? Robertson had admitted there was the possibility that Germany might accelerate her building programme, but in that eventuality Britain would also accelerate to maintain a sufficient margin of superiority. On 9 March Balfour inquired whether Germany would enjoy a lead in capital ships by the Autumn of 1911, given that the existing programme and building rates of the two countries were maintained. Asquith promptly repudiated the unspoken implication of Balfour's question.

> I will say without the faintest hesitation, that if . . . there is a probability . . . of the German programme being carried out in the way the paper figures suggest . . . we should provide not only for a sufficient number of ships, but for such a date for laying down those ships that at the end of 1911 the superiority of Germany . . . would not be an actual fact. I hope that is quite explicit. That is the policy of His Majesty's Government. It remains on record, and I think I ought to reassure the House that we do not intend in this matter to be left behind.[3]

Asquith's statement of intention was received with relief by the Tory Press and passive acceptance by most Liberal newspapers, but

---

[1] *Albany Review*, Mar. 1908, p. 712. See also *The Nation*, 29 Feb. 1908, pp. 778 and 782–3.
[2] Cf. Admiralty Memorandum, Dec. 1907, cited Marder, 137; and *Hansard*, iv:185: Appendix III.   [3] *Hansard*, iv:185:1372.

not *The Nation*. It expressed deep regret that Asquith should have allowed himself to be drawn into Balfour's 'hypothetical scare-mongering'. The perils of the situation were not material but moral, residing 'in the manner in which the Conservative Party under Mr Balfour's direction, is heading straight for war with Germany'.[1]

Esher was delighted with Asquith's statement but believed 'it would never have been obtained but for the Kaiser's letter. The net result of that famous epistle has been to force the Government to give a pledge that in the next three years they will lay down ships enough to ensure our superiority. So good has come out of evil, if evil it was.'[2] The incident of the Kaiser's letter to Tweedmouth afforded one of the more bizarre moments in the struggle for the 1908–09 Naval Estimates.

The German Ambassador in London, Count Metternich, had pressed the Kaiser in a number of letters, that the assurances von Tirpitz had offered to the Reichstag simply were not true. Britain was concerned about the new German Naval Law. Von Stumm, then temporary chargé d'affaires, had informed William in November 1907 that 'even the strongest supporters of a policy friendly to Germany accept the view that two English ships must be built for every German ship'. Metternich believed that it was 'better in the interests of good Anglo-German relations that there should be no illusions on this matter in Germany'.[3] William dismissed this uncomfortable and inconvenient advice and information out of hand. But he did not choose to ignore a letter of Esher's which was published in *The Times* on 6 February 1908.[4]

The Kaiser was moved to write on his own initiative and without the knowledge of either his Chancellor or the German Foreign Office, to refute this 'piece of unmitigated balderdash' written by the 'supervisor of the foundations and drains of the Royal Palaces. . . . If England built 60, 90 or 100 battleships there would be no change in the German plans.' Germans noted with displeasure that whenever the British programme of naval construction was discussed, invariably there was reference to the German Navy. They would be grate-

---

[1] *The Nation*, 14 Mar. 1908.
[2] *E.P.*, ii, 295.
[3] Letters of Von Stumm and Metternich, quoted, E. L. Woodward, *Great Britain and the German Navy* (1964), 157–8.
[4] A month later, reviewing the whole incident in a letter to Fisher, 25 Mar. 1908, Esher had no regrets concerning his letter which had sparked off the whole business. 'It was well worth all the bother . . . to have done anything, however little, for the Navy. *I shall always believe that we were at the parting of the ways.* The Nation was on its trial. The struggle is far from over yet. . . . Next year there will be a bitter fight.' *E.P.*, ii, 298 (my italics).

ful if 'Germany were left out of the discussion'.[1] This letter, couched in the Kaiser's least diplomatic style, was addressed to Tweedmouth. The First Lord, flattered at receiving a personal letter from the Kaiser, treated it as a compliment. With extraordinary lack of sense he talked of little else, reading it to friends and acquaintances alike. He had shown the letter to Sir Edward Grey, but instead of channelling his reply through the Foreign Office, he compounded his earlier indiscretion by replying privately to the Kaiser enclosing details of the Naval Estimates which then had not been published in Parliament.

It was hardly surprising, after such monumentally indiscreet behaviour, that a journalist should have learned all about it. That part fell to *The Times's* military correspondent, Repington. It seemed to him to have been 'an insidious attempt to influence in German interests a British First Lord, and at a most critical moment, namely, just before the Estimates were coming on in Parliament'.[2] Repington determined to publish his information, and did so in a letter to his editor. *The Times* supported him with a strongly worded editorial.

> If there was any doubt before about the meaning of German naval expansion none can remain after an attempt of this kind to influence the Minister responsible for our Navy in a direction favourable to German interests; an attempt, in other words, to make it more easy for German preparations to overtake our own.[3]

Rather surprisingly, almost without exception,[4] the Press denounced *The Times* for attempting to create a scare. An intended bombshell proved a rather wretched squib. *The Times*, hoping to provide an *exposé*, had merely revealed a mare's nest.

Asquith knew nothing of the Tweedmouth–Kaiser correspondence until he read about it in *The Times* for 6 March. A Cabinet meeting was held that day, and it was decided to gloss over the matter. Asquith informed the Commons that the Kaiser's letter had been treated as a private communication.[5] But nothing was said about Tweedmouth's disclosure of the Estimates to the Kaiser. In this deception, Asquith enjoyed the invaluable support of the Tory leaders whom he had taken into his confidence.[6] They agreed to maintain a neutral position, accepting that to publish Tweedmouth's

[1] There is a copy of the Kaiser's letter in *Asquith MSS*, vol. 19, f. 249, and a copy of Tweedmouth's reply, 20 Feb. 1908, vol. 19, f. 251.
[2] Repington, 284.   [3] *The Times*, 6 Mar. 1908.
[4] The *Daily Express* was the only paper to join wholeheartedly with *The Times*. See the comments in *New Age*, 14 Mar. 1908, p. 381.
[5] *Hansard*, iv: 185: 1067–8.
[6] See Magnus, *Edward VII*, 375.

indiscreet reply would cause alarm in the Commons and aggravate Anglo-German relations.

The Germans appeared to be pleased by the 'calm and dignified manner' with which the incident had been treated by the majority of the British Press and by Parliament.[1] However, the affair had served to intensify bad feeling in official circles towards Germany for what was considered to have been an uncalled for interference in Britain's affairs. Typically, the Radicals sought comfort in the incident. They thought that the Tweedmouth episode could be turned to good account by opening formal and official communications with Germany on the subject of armaments in the spirit of their declaration at the Hague Conference. 'England as the predominant naval power could well afford to take the initiative in such negotiations, and the present Government will not fulfil the expectations of its supporters if it fails to do so.'[2]

Tweedmouth had offered an explanation of his conduct in the Lords on 9 March, but it had not proved satisfactory.[3] The First Lord's career had been damaged beyond repair by Repington's disclosure. The only other incident of note was Rosebery's public congratulation of his own foresight in predicting the dangerous consequences of the *entente cordiale*.[4] As if his position and authority were not already sufficiently undermined, Tweedmouth made a weak response to Cawdor's interpretation of the 'Two Power Standard'. This was in a Naval Armaments debate in the Lords on 19 March. Tweedmouth had but a few more weeks to serve at the Admiralty before his banishment to relative anonymity as President of the Council.

Campbell-Bannerman had taken no part in the Commons debates on the Naval Estimates. He had suffered a severe heart attack on 13 November, and it was not until 20 January that he had again undertaken any business. In the following three weeks he 'seemed to have recovered all his old buoyancy and energy'.[5] He presided over the meetings of the Cabinet that prepared the King's Speech for the

[1] See report of Berlin correspondent in *Daily Telegraph*, 10 Mar. 1908.
[2] *Concord*, xxiv, no. 3, Mar. 1908, p. 35; cf. *Daily Chronicle*, 9 Mar. 1908. See also the recommendations of the Committee of International Arbitration and Peace Association in a letter to Grey, 23 Mar. 1908. In his reply Grey referred the Committee to the answer that he had given Bellairs in the Commons on 13 Mar. 1908, i.e. that Britain was prepared to communicate naval information annually with any other Power prepared to adopt the same course, as had been indicated earlier by the Senior British Plenipotentiary at the Hague Conference. The letters are printed in *Concord* for April 1908, pp. 41–2.
[3] *Hansard*, iv:185:1135–6.
[4] *Ibid.*, iv:185: 1075–7.
[5] Spender, *Campbell-Bannerman*, ii, 377. Cf. the comments of King Edward in *E.P.*, ii, 280.

opening of the new Parliamentary Session. On 12 February he made his last speech in the Commons, suffered another severe heart attack that night, and thereafter never left his room at 10 Downing Street. Though at first he gave the appearance of rallying, his condition continued to deteriorate. He was forced to resign on 3 April, and on 22 April, Britain's first Radical Prime Minister died.

Campbell-Bannerman on his retirement enjoyed the satisfaction of the plaudits of many of those who had vilified him but three years before. 'He was', said Esher, 'an amiable man.'[1] For the Radicals, the Prime Minister's death was a bitter and unique tragedy. 'The Peace Party in Europe', said *Concord*, 'has lost its most powerful and convinced statesman.' It was to Campbell-Bannerman they owed it that Rosebery,

> The lordly decadent and his Liberal League disappeared after the Duke of Cambridge and his umbrella; that Chamberlain was worn out, Balfour discredited; and once again there was a clear issue between reform and reaction, peace and provocation, with a solid majority on the right side in command of the Commons and Whitehall.[2]

Radicals always tended to exaggerate Campbell-Bannerman's contribution and influence in politics. Even a contemporary Radical critic was bound to admit that 'they took a too personal view of political life'.[3] In later years, Radicals were to look back upon the death of Campbell-Bannerman as the decisive turning-point in Britain's conduct of foreign policy; the time when the Liberal imperialists, at last relieved of the incubus of a Radical Prime Minister, pursued policies that Campbell-Bannerman would never have tolerated.

Asquith's tribute to Campbell-Bannerman in the Commons was, for Radicals, the 'absolutely perfect' expression of the man's idealism.[4] 'Great causes appealed to him. He was not ashamed, even on the verge of old age, to see visions and to dream dreams. He had no misgivings as to the future of democracy. He had a single-minded and unquenchable faith in the unceasing progress and the growing unity of mankind.'[5] This was the man the Radicals wished to remember; the Opposition leader who had stirred Liberal ranks with his 'methods of Barbarism' speech; the Prime Minister who had proclaimed the vision of a 'League of Peace'. The world would 'surely remember his record with gratitude, and think of him with

---

[1] *E.P.*, ii, 301.   [2] *Concord*, xxiv, no. 4, Apr. 1908, p. 37.
[3] *Albany Review*, May 1908, pp. 237–8.
[4] John Ellis, quoted Bassett, p. 243.   [5] *Hansard*, iv:187:1043.

loving remembrance as one of the true reconcilers and peace-makers'.[1]

Asquith had spoken too of Campbell-Bannerman as a man of 'practical shrewdness', of his 'selection of means in the daily work of tilling the political field'. It was Sir Henry's 'shrewdness' that the Radicals had counted upon to control the imperialist members of his Cabinet. Radicals trusted him to keep a watchful eye upon Grey, yet that minister had enjoyed more independence in his exercise of policy than had his Tory predecessor. The Foreign Secretary virtually excluded the Prime Minister from the conduct of foreign policy, which adds point to Hardinge's remark that 'C-B was the best Prime Minister there had been from a Foreign Office point of view and supports us in everything.'[2] Twice Campbell-Bannerman had indicated his concern about the implications of the military conversations with France, and twice he had acquiesced in their continuance. Once he had been convinced of their efficacy, he had firmly supported Haldane's Army reforms. He rejected any reduction of the Naval Estimates for 1908–09, despite the opposition of the reductionists in the Cabinet, on the strength of a single interview with his friend Robertson. These decisions may or may not have been correct. What is certain is they were not the decisions of a doctrinaire Radical. When it came to paper work, Campbell-Bannerman had never been noted for his diligence. In any event, for the greater part of the time he was Prime Minister he was plagued by ill health, advancing years and private grief. His undoubted contribution to his party was that he appeared to give some homogeneity of purpose to an otherwise unwieldy and divided majority. A shrewd blend of idealism and experience allowed him to effect a union between groups that in Opposition had been overtly hostile to one another. He taught the Liberals once again to think and act as the party of Government. The emotional idealism of the Radical backbencher, which to a certain extent he always retained, inspired his principles. But it was experience and practicality that tempered his decision-making. As with many another Radical, Campbell-Bannerman's attachment to the ideals of arbitration and disarmament were more a matter of sentimental preference than of absolute conviction.

At the time of Campbell-Bannerman's resignation, the Liberal

[1] Speech by H. S. Perris, Secretary of the National Peace Council. It was the element of heroic idealism in Campbell-Bannerman that the Radicals always stressed. Hence, they did not approve of Spender's official life of Campbell-Bannerman, which emphasises the man's practical wisdom. See Francis Hirst, *In the Golden Days* (1947), 251ff.
[2] Quoted, José F. Harris and Cameron Hazlehurst, 'Campbell-Bannerman as Prime Minister', *History*, lv (1970), 380.

party 'presented the anomalous spectacle of a radical, peace-loving, nonconformist body with a Liberal League head'.[1] Asquith's succession as leader was assured.[2] For weeks, speculation had been rife as to the composition of the new Cabinet.[3] Though there was little doubt who would lead the Cabinet, there were those who saw Grey or Haldane as Prime Minister. Morley, being the man he was, even considered the possibility of his own candidature for that post, but was to achieve his apotheosis in the Lords as Viscount Morley of Blackburn. A fitting reward, noted the *Labour Leader*, for one whose policies in India had been thoroughly reactionary.[4] The Radical Press did not question Asquith's right to the succession, but there were reservations and doubts about his 'essential Liberalism'.

> His association with Imperialism of the type of Lord Rosebery does not encourage the hope that he will advance the positive aspects of pacifist statesmanship. . . . With Sir Edward Grey and Mr Haldane as his intimate counsellors, it is to be feared that positive progress in the direction of peace ideals will be slow and cautious.[5]

The Nation, least inclined of all the Radical journals to whistling in the dark to keep up its spirits, strangely presumed that of late Asquith had been showing 'an increasing inclination to the Left' of his party. This, by their calculation, was just as well, for 'only by and with the Left' would 'Asquith be able to govern. Five-sixths of the Liberal Parliamentary Party are Left wing.' This last was perhaps a pardonable exaggeration in the circumstances. But a week later *The Nation* was asserting that 'Liberal Imperialism' had been 'only a passing phase' which had declined 'when the normal tendencies of . . . [Liberal] policy regained their accustomed strength'.[6] The *Labour Leader* poured scorn on the suggestion that the left wing of the Liberal Party could expect to be strengthened in a Cabinet led by the 'inscrutable' Asquith. When the Cabinet list was announced, its damning verdict was 'different yet the same'.[7] Others were not so sure.

Esher had considered Asquith's Cabinet-making would be a

[1] Stephen McKenna, *While I Remember* (1921), 99.
[2] See A. Gollin, 'Asquith: a new view', in *A Century of Conflict* (1966), ed. Martin Gilbert, 112ff.
[3] See *E.P.*, ii, 278, 284 and 290. For a comparison of the merits of the rival candidates for the leadership, see *New Age*, 30 Nov. 1907, p. 81; 8 Feb. 1908, p. 281; and 11 Apr. 1908, p. 461. *New Age* supported Haldane, describing him as 'the only successful Minister in Bannerman's Cabinet'.
[4] *Labour Leader*, 17 Apr. 1908, p. 246.
[5] 'A Pacifist Diary', *Concord*, xxiv, no. 4, Apr. 1908, p. 44.
[6] *The Nation*, 11 and 18 Apr. 1908.
[7] *Labour Leader*, 10 Apr. 1908, p. 230; and 17 Apr. 1908, p. 248.

'cumbrous task of putting patches in . . . after tearing out the frayed pieces'.[1] Rejecting the idea of being his own Chancellor of the Exchequer, and gratefully accepting Morley's assurance that he had 'no special aptitude for that post under present prospects',[2] Asquith gave the job to Lloyd George. This was a pleasing appointment to the Radicals, for the Welshman could confidently be expected to 'speak plain words about extravagance and uneconomic expenditure to the Heads of the Spending Services'.[3] They also noted with pleasure the elevation to Cabinet rank of Lloyd George's Radical twin, Churchill. Thus, a powerful combination for economy was effected. It was a bonus to have Tweedmouth replaced at the Admiralty by the Treasury-trained McKenna.[4] The other pleasing feature was the elevation of Charles Masterman, an 'advanced' thinker on questions of social reform and a member of the Radical Balkans Committee. The *Labour Leader* noted wistfully that this 'avowed Socialist' was 'not likely to vote against the Government any longer'.[5]

A straw in the wind ought to have caused the Radicals to reflect that not all might be as promising as it seemed. Lewis Harcourt, who had been a strenuous proponent of economy in military and naval expenditure, was not given the preferment in Cabinet rank that could have been expected. 'Harcourt', Asquith coldly informed Esher, 'must wait his turn'.[6] Soon the Radicals would have cause to regret also the retirement of Robertson from the Admiralty where he had displayed a 'true Scottish tenacity for arithmetical calculations'.[7]

At a meeting of Liberal M.P.s and representatives of the party organisation at the Reform Club on 29 April, Asquith's leadership of the party was endorsed. Though a purely formal proceeding, the chairman, Sir John Brunner, urged on Asquith the need to conduct Britain's foreign policy in the same spirit as had inspired Campbell-Bannerman's speech at the Albert Hall in 1905. It was made apparent to the new Prime Minister that the Radicals in his party were determined there should be no more talk of increases in naval and military expenditure.[8]

---

[1] *E.P.*, ii, 301.   [2] Jenkins, 183.   [3] *Concord*, xxiv, no. 4, p. 44.
[4] McKenna's support of economy while at the Treasury was more a reflection of his stubborn departmentalism than any deep-rooted conviction. Once his allegiance was transferred to the Admiralty he became an equally stubborn supporter of their case. However, at the time the King was concerned that McKenna might prove too much the economist at the Admiralty and therefore insisted as a safeguard that Fisher remain as First Sea Lord. See Jenkins, 183.
[5] *Labour Leader*, 17 Apr. 1908, p. 248.
[6] *E.P.*, ii, 303   [7] Marder, 142.
[8] Report of meeting and Brunner's speech in *The Times*, 1 May 1908.

Panic and collapse, 1909–10

Asquith's new Cabinet settled to its tasks. McKenna, whose appointment had afforded the Radicals so much pleasure, within weeks of assuming his new office gave every indication of capitulating to the demands of the Sea Lords. Fisher wrote joyously of this to Esher.

> Yesterday [4 May 1908] with all Sea Lords present McKenna formally agreed to 4 Dreadnoughts and *if necessary* 6 Dreadnoughts next year—perhaps the greatest triumph ever known.
> As he says, he has to eat every word he has said at the Treasury and Cabinet, but I am giving him some jam.[1]

McKenna was certain that Harcourt would resign from the Cabinet when told of the decision. However, his greatest concern was what Lloyd George's reaction would be to the news. There was little love lost between the Chancellor and the First Lord. Fisher was anxious lest having inveigled McKenna so swiftly and surely into his net, he now might '*funk* standing up to Lloyd George'.[2] Esher was convinced that there need be no concern upon that particular score. In July he noted that Lloyd George in conversation with Metternich had stated that he was determined to maintain Britain's relative naval strength *vis-à-vis* Germany, even if it meant borrowing a hundred millions for the fleet.[3] These were hardly the sentiments one would expect to be expressed by an avowed Radical and supposedly stalwart economist. Again, at the height of the Cabinet dissensions over the Naval Estimates in February 1909, after a conversation with Lloyd George, Esher wrote, 'Ll. G. in his heart does not care a bit for economy, and is quite ready to face Parliament with any amount of deficit, and to "go" for a big navy. He is plucky and an Imperialist at heart, if he is anything. Besides, he despises the "stalwarts" of his own side.'[4] Though his analysis of Lloyd George reveals more of Esher's desires than George's true character, he had discerned more clearly than most the essential aggression, the combative streak in the Chancellor.

For political debate, the summer and autumn of 1908 was a period of relative calm. The Opposition had striven, without much success, to suggest that the Liberal Government was not fit to be entrusted with the nation's security. The charge was old and well worn; the ministerial response was equally predictable. The usual platitudes were repeated about Britain having an adequate margin of superiority in naval forces to combat any possible enemies. What

---

[1] Fisher to Esher, 5 May 1908, *E.P.*, ii, 309.
[2] *Ibid.*   [3] *E.P.*, ii, 329–30.   [4] *E.P.*, ii, 370.

could be meant by an 'adequate margin' became *the* matter for speculation. However, when Arthur Lee in the Commons gloomily contrasted Germany's 'relentless' naval policy with Britain's 'hand-to-mouth' methods, he was sharply rebuked by McKenna.[1]

Depression in the shipbuilding and engineering industries was used by the Tories to make political capital at the expense of the Government, and to exert pressure for an increase in the naval building programme. The *Daily Mail*, which had become almost an adjunct of the Service Press, was not slow to take up the case. 'If the Government is not composed of Stoney-hearted pedants, the shipbuilding vote should be given out now . . . 80 per cent of the cost of a battleship goes in wages to the British worker. A large shipbuilding programme is the best preventive of distress.'[2] The Navy League pursued the hare of unemployment to the particular embarrassment of the Radicals. Those who were members for constituencies intimately concerned with shipbuilding or the manufacture of armaments, were loath to preach the unadulterated doctrine: 'If you wish for peace, prepare for peace.' It was comparatively easy to combat the cruder products of Conservative propaganda. But it was not easy to convince unemployed, or depressed workers threatened with unemployment, that it was better not to build warships when their very lives depended upon the wages they earned from the construction of those engines of war. Homilies delivered on the wickedness of militarism and the benefits of peace were better appreciated by middle-class consciences than by working-class stomachs.

> I could easily show you, *The Arbiter* had said, that if it were content to leave taxes as they are and revert to the expenditure of 1898, our own Government could in ten years' time provide every working class family in England, Scotland and Ireland with a home twice as large, at half the rent it pays at present, and that the State would then be left with a handsome annual rental of several millions to apply to the reduction of taxes or of the national debt.[3]

These worthy arguments, by the Editor of the *Economist*, of future Utopian prospects, were not convincing propaganda in the short term. Ten years was an unimaginably long time to expect unemployed men to wait when their families were already in dire need. In

[1] Hansard, iv: 192: 424 (Lee) and 435ff. (McKenna).
[2] *Daily Mail*, 18 Apr. 1908, quoted Marder, 156.
[3] *The Arbiter in Council* (1906), 467. See also *Concord*, xxv, nos. 1/2, Jan. and Feb. 1909, *passim*; and in particular the speech of W. A. Appleton, Secretary of the General Federation of Trade Unions to the National Council of Peace Societies, 22 Feb. 1909.

the autumn of 1908, Lloyd George and Churchill, the two ministers who within months were to urge the most stringent economies in shipbuilding, appealed unavailingly to McKenna to combat unemployment in the shipbuilding and engineering industries by building in excess of the year's Estimates.[1]

The Tories in Parliament, and their Press outside, sedulously maintained their insistence that an enormous increase in naval expenditure was necessary to insure the nation's safety. *The Times's* suggestion that the increase should be of the order of £5 million, was a conservative demand compared with Stead and the Navy League, who were intent that their policy of two keels to one should be implemented whatever the cost. The Radicals answered these demands as best they could, repeating the well-worn arguments, presenting memorials to the Government,[2] and passing the inevitable pious resolutions.[3] Eversley produced two of his comforting articles in *The Nation* on the *matériel* and *personnel* of the Navy designed to 'dispel any lingering belief' that it would be either necessary or desirable to make any large additions to the shipbuilding vote. Though the Opposition and the Service Press were the main targets of his censures, he did not spare the Government.

> It is clear that a great error was committed by the present Government when it came into power . . . in not at once reducing its naval and military expenditure to a peace footing. Had this been done it is improbable that Germany would have propounded its recent naval programme. The opportunity was lost and what we are now reduced to hope for is that there will be no further increase.[4]

The *Manchester Guardian* added its voice to the Radical pleas for moderation. Let no more ships be built than were absolutely neces-

---

[1] See Telegram of Lloyd George to McKenna, 11 Sept. 1908 and McKenna's reply 12 Sept. 1908. Copies in *Asquith MSS.* vol 20, fol. 83 and 85. Lloyd George urged that 'the question requires serious and immediate attention'. McKenna in his reply pointed out that the solution Lloyd George had suggested would involve 'staggering increases in expenditure'. He assumed that both Churchill and Lloyd George were 'prepared for the consequences'. No more was heard of the matter. See also Stephen McKenna, *Reginald McKenna 1863–1943: a memoir* (1948), 79. There is a very interesting comment on McKenna's attitude to unemployment in *New Age*, 25 July 1908, p. 242.

[2] A memorial signed by 144 members was presented to the Government urging the necessity for reduction in defence expenditure because of improved relations with other countries. This was on 24 July. A further memorial was sent to Asquith by the Reduction of Armaments Committee on 26 November, insisting upon economies in the Naval Estimates.

[3] There were two from the National Council of Peace Societies alone in November 1908, demanding resumption of discussions for a naval understanding with Germany.

[4] *The Nation*, 1 and 5 Aug. 1908. Eversley's arguments for reductions were the antithesis of those made by the Government's Admiralty advisers.

sary, for if the Government were to show moderation now, by 1912 when Germany was due to reduce her naval programme, Britain's 'naval difficulties' with Germany would be 'as good as solved'.[1]

The Radicals had every reason to repose trust in McKenna, judging by the manner in which he had rebuffed Arthur Lee for his alarmist talk in the Commons. But as the months passed, the First Lord seemed to show an increasing ambivalence in his attitude to retrenchment when he made public pronouncements concerning the Navy. In October he had argued that Britain ought not to show alarm at the 'paper programmes' of other Powers. Yet in November, speaking in the City, he 'made no apology for saying that the cost of maintaining Britain's naval supremacy would inevitably be high'.[2] Asquith chose to make a similar observation when speaking at the Lord Mayor's Banquet. Lee, accepting this proferred cue, inquired at Question Time on 12 November whether the Government accepted 'the Two Power Standard of naval strength as meaning a predominance of ten per cent over the combined strengths in capital ships of the two next strongest Powers'. Asquith replied that he did, and repeated this assurance to the same questioner eleven days later.[3] The Times declared its pleasure at the Prime Minister's avowal, for if Britain should not define her policy then 'some other Power might hope by persistent effort to tire us out in the race'.[4]

The Tory member Lee, for once in concert with a Radical, Murray Macdonald, questioned Asquith frequently in the Commons on the interpretation of the Two Power Standard. But Asquith was too experienced a Parliamentarian to be drawn into making indiscreet disclosures. He merely said that the Government would, 'continue to follow the policy which had now been followed for a number of years. . . . The dominating consideration with us is that we should maintain our superiority at sea. As has often been explained . . . we regard the Two Power standard as a workable formula to give effect to that.'[5] Such statements by the Prime Minister were difficult for the Radicals to fault. No question inspired a greater ambivalence of attitude and sentiment among Radical and Labour members—with the exception of a few determined pacifists—than that of the size and capability of the Navy. Most of them accepted Britain's need to maintain her maritime supremacy over other nations. It was part of the Radical

---

[1] *Manchester Guardian*, 15 Sept. 1908, see also comment 14 July, 30 Sept. 1908 and 29 Jan. 1909.
[2] Speeches made by McKenna at Pontypool, Glasgow, Sheffield and the City of London, reported in *The Times*, 2, 17 and 30 Oct. and 10 Nov. 1908.
[3] *Hansard*, iv:196:560 and 1768.
[4] *The Times*, 13 Nov. 1908.
[5] *Hansard*, iv:196:1768–9 and 198:2113–14.

tradition that they should subscribe to this doctrine. Had not the *Westminster Gazette* in 1893 proclaimed: 'From Cromwell to Cobden good Radicals have ever insisted on an all-powerful Navy'?[1] Most Radicals wished Britain to maintain the strongest and best fleet in the world. What they would not believe was that this necessarily meant any steep increase in naval expenditure. They could not accept the argument that, for an accurate comparison of the relative strengths of the navies of the Powers, Dreadnought-type vessels alone should be considered. They were not prepared to ignore Britain's massive superiority in every other type of warship. It was apparent to them that their opponents were maintaining a pernicious thesis with the sole purpose of extracting money from the pockets of the people to enlarge the patronage of the great spending departments at the expense of much-needed social improvements. The advice of the so-called 'experts' was worthless, for no official could ever be expected to admit that economy would yield the necessary funds to satisfy these new demands. No contractor had ever complained that his contracts with the Admiralty or the War Office were too lucrative. Prodigality and inefficiency always went hand in hand.[2]

While the Jingo Press increased the violence of its demands for astronomical rises in naval expenditure, the Radicals found their champion and the keeper of the Liberal conscience in the young President of the Board of Trade, Winston Churchill. In a series of public speeches he poured ridicule upon the 'Dreadnought fear all school'. He denounced 'the braggart call for sensational expenditure upon armaments' as the result of 'a false lying panic started in the party interests of the Conservatives'. Churchill promised his constituents that he at least, as had his father before him, would not be driven by the

> windy agitations of ignorant, interested and excited hotheads into wasting the public money upon armaments upon a scale clearly not designed merely for purposes of material defence, but being a part of a showy, sensational, aggressive and Jingo policy, which is supposed to gain popularity from certain unthinking sections of the community. We take our stand against that.

According to Churchill, a Liberal

> ought to stand as a restraining force against an extravagant policy. He is a man who ought to keep cool in the presence of

[1] Quoted Taylor, *The Trouble Makers*, 105. For an analysis of the ambivalence of attitude displayed by Radicals and Socialists, largely because of their pride in the Navy, and the surprising paradoxes that it could produce, see Halévy, *The Rule of Democracy*, 411–12.

[2] See, *inter alia*, Francis Hirst, *The Six Panics and other essays* (1913), 51ff.

Jingo clamour. He is a man who believes that confidence between nations begets confidence, and that the spirit of goodwill makes the safety it seeks. And above all, I think a Liberal is a man who should keep a sour look for scaremongers of every kind and size, however distinguished, however ridiculous.[1]

The Radical Press took comfort from Churchill's bold assessment of the 'realities' of the situation. Warnings, even those by well-placed Ministers, that suggested that anyone expecting reductions in the forthcoming estimates was living in cloud-cuckoo-land, were ignored.[2] When it was rumoured that the Naval Estimates might well rise by more than £6 million, the *Manchester Guardian* ridiculed the idea. Such a massive increase could only be justified by national danger.[3] *The Nation* in February 1909 was still asserting there could be no reason for a naval scare when 'judged by modern criteria of fighting strength' the British Navy was 'not less than four times as strong as Germany's'.

> We conclude . . . that a broad margin of complete naval security remains with us on a more reasonable programme to which we hope the Government and the Admiralty will finally assent. What more can, or should or will a party do whose prime concern lies with the building up of . . . the moral causes of European peace and social reform? To what authority in its past could it appeal for a different policy? . . . In spirit, how fatal would be a breach with the masters and founders of Liberalism?[4]

But the true measure of the mounting anxiety of the months preceding the 1909-10 Naval Estimates cannot be traced in the designedly complacent assertions of Radical journalists.

By the middle of October 1908 it was widely rumoured that Germany was accelerating her naval building programme, and reports to that effect appeared in the British Press.[5] When the Government was questioned, however, they maintained that they had 'no official information on the subject'.[6] On 20 November the German Naval Estimates were published. Four days later in the House of Lords, Cawdor complained of the 'dangerous delay' in the laying down of British ships, and urged the Government to combat this by the laying down of six or seven capital ships in the next two years.[7] The Reduction of Armaments Committee responded by sending Asquith

---

[1] Quoted Hirst, *The Six Panics*, 91-2.
[2] See the increasing note of urgency in McKenna's public statements culminating with a speech in January 1909, reported in *The Times*, 29 Jan. 1909.
[3] *Manchester Guardian*, 29 Jan. 1909.
[4] *The Nation*, 27 Feb. 1909; see also 6 Feb. 1909.
[5] *The Times*, 15 Oct. and 30 Nov. 1908.
[6] *Hansard*, iv:196:35.   [7] *Hansard*, iv:197:28-9.

on 26 November, a memorial insisting that there should be further economies in the 1909 Naval Estimates. They followed this with a personal interview of Asquith by Brunner and Murray Macdonald on 2 December. They conveyed the 'profound dissatisfaction' of their Committee's members with the Prime Minister's apparent acceptance of the Tory interpretation of the Two-Power Standard when he had replied to Lee at Question Time in the Commons on 12 November.[1]

The German Naval Estimates could be interpreted as implying an increase either in the speed of construction or the size of warships being built. There were knowledgeable advocates of both views. The Admiralty favoured the first alternative, an increase in the speed of construction. They based their belief in an accelerated German building programme on the evidence available in the German Press in October 1908, information received from the new naval attaché in Berlin, the British consul in Danzig, and from other sources, both official and unofficial. During the course of 1908 the climate of opinion at the Admiralty had changed completely from one of complacency to exaggerated concern at Germany's naval capability. The Director of Naval Intelligence, on the strength of reports by the naval and military attachés in Berlin, who appear to have relied unduly on the German Press for their intelligence, considered by September 1908 that the situation was 'most serious' and that Britain would ultimately 'bitterly regret' any diminution of will to maintain superiority over Germany's navy. The Second Sea Lord was convinced that 'the best way to keep peace' was 'an overwhelmingly strong and superior Navy to Germany's'. The Admiralty exaggerated Germany's naval efficiency and power and underestimated Britain's. It must be remembered that the diplomatic scene in the autumn and winter of 1908-09, with the successive Casablanca and Bosnian crises, was not one to encourage optimism.[2] By January 1909, the Sea Lords considered that it was 'a practical certainty' that Germany would have seventeen Dreadnoughts and battle cruisers by the spring of 1912, not thirteen as in the official building schedule for that period. There was even the possibility that Germany might have twenty-one such warships if her full shipbuilding capacity was employed and no financial restrictions were imposed. In the light of this truly terrifying prospect conjured up by their own interpretation of the supposed facts, the Sea Lords amended

---

[1] For a detailed account, see Koss, *Brunner*, 223. Asquith's statement on the Two Power Standard went much further than had Campbell-Bannerman's on the same subject, which had always been qualified as 'a rough guide only'.
[2] See Marder, 146-9. Some of the reports of the naval attaché in Berlin are printed in Woodward, Appendix VI.

their recommendations for the 1909 building programme. They required eight Dreadnoughts to be completed by the Spring of 1912, the last two to be laid down by the end of March 1910.[1] In effect, the Admiralty were demanding the maximum building programme for Dreadnoughts that British shipyards could produce.

Early in December, McKenna had received a request from Grey for a general report upon German shipbuilding. The report was sent on 30 December and McKenna enclosed with it a doleful letter. 'Speaking for myself I have no doubt whatever that Germany means to build up to the full extent of her capacity . . . If by any spurt Germany can once catch us up we have no longer any such superior building capacity as would ensure our supremacy.'[2] Four days later on 3 January, McKenna wrote in equally pessimistic terms to Asquith:

> I am anxious to avoid alarmist language, but I cannot resist the following conclusions which it is my duty to submit to you.
> (1) Germany is anticipating the shipbuilding programme laid down by the Law of 1907.
> (2) She is doing so secretly.
> (3) She will certainly have 13 big ships in commission in the spring of 1912.
> (4) She will probably have 21 big ships in commission in the spring of 1912.
> (5) German capacity to build Dreadnoughts is at this moment equal to ours.
> The last conclusion is the most alarming, and if justified would give the public a rude awakening should it become known.[3]

For some time the question of whether Germany had the capability substantially to accelerate her shipbuilding programme had been a source of concern to certain ministers, and in particular Grey. On 18 December he had informed Metternich that Great Britain might have to lay down additional Dreadnoughts in 1909 because 'British plans depended upon the pace at which the German naval programme was carried out'.[4] The Foreign Secretary, as did the First Lord, received a mass of intelligence from a variety of sources that suggested the Germans were covertly breaking the Fleet Laws and building much in advance of their advertised programme. Both men believed that in the interests of national safety, Britain ought to retain a margin of superiority over her rival. As responsible ministers, it was their duty to draw their own conclusions as to what course

[1] See, Memorandum of Sea Lords to First Lord, 15(?) Jan. 1909, quoted Marder, 155–6.
[2] McKenna, *Reginald McKenna*, 71–2.
[3] *Ibid.*, 72–3.   [4] *B.D.* VI, 173.

ought to be adopted in the light of the evidence provided by their agents and expert advisers concerning Germany's intentions. Their subsequent decisions, they stoutly maintained, were their own, but from the beginning the predilection of both men was for a 'big navy' solution. It would have taken a man of unusual character and determination to withstand the pressures of professional experts all pointing to the one conclusion.

One of these sources of private information on German naval acceleration was a Mr H. H. Mulliner, who at that time was the managing director of the Coventry Ordnance Works. The Mulliner Affair was to become part of Radical mythology. The unfortunate man became a symbol for all the other 'merchants of death', the armour-plate manufacturers; and many Radicals were convinced that he, more than any other, was responsible for the eventual acceptance of the eight Dreadnought programme by the Liberal Government.[1]

Mulliner, in the course of his frequent business trips to the Continent, discovered that German machine-tool manufacturers were engaged on large orders for Krupp, the leading German armaments manufacturer. He concluded that this must be an extension of Krupp's productive capacity providing Germany with vastly increased facilities for the speedier construction of armour plate, guns and gun mountings. He first passed on this information to the War Office on 11 May 1906. They in their turn informed the Admiralty, where Mulliner's statements appear to have been ignored, as was

---

[1] Mulliner himself was to a large extent responsible for the subsequent unfortunate publicity that he suffered at the hands of Radical writers. He had insisted upon making the story of his actions public, because he considered that, as a result of the information that he had supplied, the Admiralty had victimised his firm. See the letters of Mulliner to the *Standard*, 26 June 1909 (anonymous), and to *The Times*, 2 and 6 Aug., 21 Sept. and 17 Dec. 1909, and 1, 3, 6 and 18 Jan. 1910; see also *Hansard*, v:15:418; 420–8 and 456.

Whether Mulliner's influence was as marginal in the 1909 naval scare as Woodward (pp. 481–4) and Marder (pp. 156–9) claim, is open to doubt. What is certain is that his disclosures to the Opposition leaders allowed them to stoke the fires of panic and agitation. The armament manufacturers were a powerful and influential lobby and enjoyed a number of advantages when exerting pressure upon any Government. See Marder, 157–8. For detailed criticisms of the armament manufacturers written by Radicals, see, *inter alia*, G. H. Perris, *The War Traders* (1914); F. Hirst, *The Six Panics*, 59–102, and *Armaments: the race and the crisis* (1937); Walton Newbold, *How Europe Armed for War* (n.d.); and a host of other contemporary pamphlets and papers. They all make common cause upon the 'armour plate ring' who are held primarily responsible for the escalation in armaments in the prewar period, and the subsequent war. The best recent comment on this subject is contained in Clive Trebilcock's article, 'Legends of the British armament industry, 1890–1914', *Journal of Contemporary History* (1970), 3–19. I am indebted to Dr Trebilcock and Prof. A. J. Marder, for the advice and information they have given out on this subject.

the further intelligence that he supplied in the period down to April 1908. But in the autumn of 1908 information from their own sources persuaded the Admiralty that Mulliner's earlier disclosures ought to be treated seriously. Mulliner always maintained that the Admiralty ignored his earlier information as they suspected his motives.[1] In February 1909 Mulliner was asked to lay his information before the Committee of Imperial Defence. There he was told that the evidence he supplied corroborated that already obtained by the Committee.

The all-important factor that controlled the speed with which a Dreadnought was completed, was the production of the guns and gun mountings to arm the warships. On 19 February Asquith met representatives of British armaments firms to discuss the production of gun turrets.[2] The evidence they supplied the Prime Minister was disquieting. The best output of gun turrets that they could promise was unimpressive when compared with the supposed German production. Mulliner asserted that Krupp could produce fifty-four turrets in a year—a statement heavily underlined in the notes Asquith made of the meeting. Undoubtedly the Prime Minister was impressed by what he had been told, as is apparent from the discussion held in his room at the Commons four days later attended by Lloyd George, McKenna, Grey, Fisher and Jellicoe. Several times Asquith referred anxiously to Mulliner's evidence, and Fisher and McKenna encouraged his agitation and concern.[3] Asquith was even anxious that Admiralty orders should immediately be given to Mulliner's works for the construction of gun turrets, as at the time the firm was not producing any. The tone of the whole meeting was one of extravagant concern at Germany's shipbuilding capacity and speed of construction, and the Admiralty representatives did what they could to intensify this mood.

[1] Mulliner's company was operating in debt. Since establishment in 1904, it had received no substantial Admiralty orders. Thoughts of producing gun mountings as the result of an increased Dreadnought construction programme by the Admiralty could not have been other than a pleasing prospect. Patriotic motives might well have actuated Mulliner's 'pestering' of the Government, but the advantages to be gained by his company were not inconsiderable.

[2] In Asquith's personal notes of the 19 February meeting, the name of Mulliner is underlined. However, in the official minutes of the meeting of 23 February, Mulliner's name is left out when reference is made to the meeting of the 19th, and the name of Molineux substituted in handwriting. This is obviously a clerical error. See *Asquith MSS.*, vol 21.

[3] ASQUITH: I was very much struck by the evidence of the Coventry man Mr (Mulliner).
and again—I confess I was very much alarmed by the evidence that Krupp can turn out 54 turrets in a year—enough for 11 battleships.
FISHER: That is so.
MCKENNA: We know they can do it, because they are doing it.
From the typewritten verbatim report of the meeting, 23 Feb. 1909, in *Asquith MSS.*, vol 21.

R A W—F

LLOYD GEORGE: It seems to me to be an imperative necessity on our part that we should have the necessary manufacturing capacity in this country to beat the Germans if they make up their minds to go on.

ASQUITH: Whether you beat them or not, you must leave yourself open to do something more approaching to a level with them.

MCKENNA: Yes; we are hopelessly behind them now.

ASQUITH: We are at present in a parlous condition.

LLOYD GEORGE: I think Mr Molineux (*Mulliner*) exaggerated—not deliberately, I think, because he had information.

ASQUITH: And it is the only information we have, really.

LLOYD GEORGE: Except Dawson.

MCKENNA: And Dawson said he did not know.[1]

If the information they had been supplied was correct, then the implications were alarming for a Government which ever since it had come into office had assured the public that Britain possessed a wide and unassailable margin of superiority in naval strength over any potential enemies. With many of their own supporters demanding retrenchment in naval expenditure, the Opposition howling for increases, the Government was in an extremely embarrassing position as they guiltily husbanded their frightening intelligence.

When the 'big navy' supporters had responded to the supposed acceleration in the German naval building programme by demanding six capital ships in the 1909–10 Estimates, the 'economists' in the Cabinet violently resisted. As far as they were concerned, a programme of four capital ships was quite enough for one year. Of the merits of their case, the five leading 'economists'—Lloyd George, Churchill, Harcourt, Morley and Burns—had no doubt. But for personal reasons, the three last named ministers were disinclined to make common cause with the other two.

Lloyd George's credentials as a Radical economist were unimpeachable. But Churchill's Radical advocacy was viewed by many with an understandable ill-ease and suspicion. Pacific propaganda sounded strange in the mouth of a man who had sought martial glory on the battlefields of two continents and who had abandoned the profession of arms because of monotony and the need to gratify an insatiable appetite for adventure. Churchill was hated by the Tories with that vindictive hostility reserved only for apostates. In concert with Lloyd George, he seemed determined on flouting Asquith's authority, making McKenna's position in the Cabinet untenable, and showing complete indifference to those ideals in

[1] *Asquith MSS*, vol. 21.

foreign policy of which Grey had declared himself the guardian.[1]

During December 1908 and January 1909 the division hardened between the 'little navy' men in the Cabinet, who declared they would resign if more than four Dreadnoughts were contemplated; and the 'big navy' men—Grey, Crewe, Haldane, Runciman and McKenna—who were equally determined upon a programme of six Dreadnoughts.[2] Asquith was disposed towards the 'big navy' school of thought, but he was anxious to do nothing that might precipitate the crisis. He waited for a favourable opportunity to present itself to effect a compromise between the seemingly irreconcilable halves of his Cabinet. Never was his policy of 'wait and see' put to a sterner test.

The Radicals in the Cabinet were not impressed by the Admiralty evidence. They did not believe that it pointed to Germany secretly building in excess of the Navy Law. The explanation that Lloyd George favoured was that the German Government was attempting to relieve unemployment by starting the construction of battleships a few months in advance of the statutory period. The Radicals were more concerned with the menace that increased naval spending implied to the social programme for the next parliamentary session than any thoughts of German aggression. Nor was this their only consideration. Lloyd George pointed out in a long letter he wrote to Asquith on 2 February:

> The discussion of the Naval Estimates threatens to re-open all the old controversies which rent the party for years and brought it to impotence and contempt. You alone can save us from this prospect of sterile and squalid disruption. . . . I will not dwell upon the emphatic pledges given by all of us before and at the last general election to reduce the gigantic expenditure on armaments built up by the recklessness of our predecessors.[3] Scores of our most loyal supporters in the House of Commons take these pledges seriously and even a £3,000,000 increase will chill their zeal for the Govt. and an assured increase of 5 to £6,000,000 for next year will stagger them . . . [They] will hardly think it worthwhile to make an effort to keep in office a Liberal Ministry.[4]

[1] See Fitzroy, i, 377.
[2] McKenna, in fact, was conspiring with Fisher throughout this period for a programme of eight Dreadnoughts, though they thought that six would be sufficient.
[3] Grey had a neat answer to this argument. He wrote to Asquith, 5 Feb. 1909, 'I, like others, advocated retrenchment at the last election, but I always excepted the Navy from my promises and in any case, promises must be subordinated to national safety', *Asquith MSS*, vol. 21.
[4] Lloyd George to Asquith, 2 Feb. 1909, *Asquith MSS*, vol. 21.

By the last week in January, Cabinet dissension over the Naval Estimates was public property.[1]

Churchill, impetuous as ever, made the pace in the Cabinet for the reductionist cause with a Memorandum on 2 February. He expressed considerable scepticism about the dangers of a German naval challenge to Britain's supremacy. Provided with technical arguments by Admiral Custance and Sir William White, both leading members of the anti-Fisher lobby,[2] Churchill listed eleven arguments for rejecting the Admiralty plea for more Dreadnoughts, concluding: 'It cannot, therefore, be argued that national safety is involved in the question of whether four or six Dreadnoughts should be laid down this financial year. No justification has in my view been shown for six. My conclusion is four Dreadnoughts should be announced to Parliament as the programme for 1909–10.'[3] McKenna replied with a Memorandum to the Cabinet on 5 February and Churchill returned to the attack with another two days later.

The Cabinet appeared divided beyond hope of ever achieving compromise. When Cabinets were held, they proved wrangling and abortive affairs. After one such meeting on 15 February, Asquith reported to the King that the members of the opposed camps were; for four Dreadnoughts, Churchill, Harcourt, Burns and Morley; for six Dreadnoughts, Grey, Runciman, Crewe and Buxton. When Lloyd George proposed a flexible long term British naval building programme the speed of which was to vary according to what the Germans built, this suggestion had been received favourably by Asquith, Grey and Crewe.[4] A Cabinet sub-committee was set up to examine the possibilities of this scheme but did not make much headway.

In the King's speech opening the new Parliamentary Session on 16 February, there was mention of 'an increase which has become necessary in the cost of my Navy'.[5] This, according to Charles Masterman, was a *ballon d'essai* sent up by a divided Cabinet to seek out and test opinion within the Liberal party. 'The crisis', Lucy Masterman wrote in her diary, 'is still on and getting more serious.

---

[1] See *The Times*, 22 Jan. 1909.
[2] Fisher maintained the two men only helped Churchill because they knew that Fisher would resign if the four Dreadnought programme was accepted. See Marder, 160.
[3] Cabinet Memorandum, 2 Feb. 1909.
[4] This proposal had been contained in Lloyd George's letter to Asquith of 2 February. Lloyd George had then pointed out that the Admiralty's plans were either too excessive, given their estimate of Germany's construction capacity was incorrect, as seemed likely to Lloyd George, but given their estimate was correct, then it followed their demands were insufficient.
[5] *Hansard*, v:1:13.

... Morley has not been "squared" but is still firm. ... Winston and Ll. G. are fighting for all they are worth, certain that the party is behind them, as the Liberal Press certainly is.'[1]

With his Cabinet, like his party, divided, the Tories intensifying their attacks in Parliament and the Press, and the Liberals having suffered a series of by-election defeats, Asquith knew that he could ill-afford to dispense with support from any quarter. Nevertheless, he admitted there were times when he was sorely tempted to summarily cashier both Churchill and Lloyd George who were proving such an unmitigated nuisance. In moments of despair, Asquith found Grey his greatest stand-by, 'always sound, temperate and strong'.[2]

Asquith had to move cautiously. Not so the ebullient Fisher who loudly exclaimed to all and sundry that 'The P.M. was behaving "abominably" ... the much maligned McKenna was the only good man—he and Grey. Grey was a rock. McK. came to fire me out. "I had better be frank Sir John", he said, "we will have three or four new battleships but no more." I let him talk and now by Jove it's Fisher, we'll have eight!'[3]

When Austen Chamberlain had suggested to Admiral May that all the Sea Lords needed to do to get their way, as they had over the Spencer Programme, was to sit tight, within the hour he received a note from Fisher—'My beloved Austen, I am sitting tight! Yours till Hell freezes!'[4] Fisher, with most of the Establishment on his side, still did not despise the propaganda value of Garvin's *Observer* which he assiduously supplied with indiscreet revelations. Fisher assured Garvin that they had nothing to fear either from Asquith or McKenna. Asquith might talk of holding naval increases down to £6 million, but this was no more 'than an artful dodge to conciliate the ... [Radicals] and let them suppose the Admiralty demands had been reduced'. Fisher was convinced that Asquith was merely playing the Radical reductionists along.[5]

At a meeting of the Cabinet on 24 February, the day following the conference in the Prime Minister's room when the awful implications of the armament manufacturers' evidence had been discussed, 'a sudden curve developed'[6] in the arguments. Asquith, who until that moment had allowed his ministers to make the pace, immediately

[1] Lucy Masterman, *C.F.G. Masterman* (1939), 124.
[2] Asquith to his wife, 20 Feb. 1909, quoted Spender and Asquith, i, 254.
[3] Record of conversation with Fisher, 23 Feb. 1909, Chamberlain, *Politics from Inside* (1936), 150-1.
[4] *Ibid.*, 150.
[5] See Fisher to Garvin, 3, 11 Feb. and 11 Mar. 1909, quoted A. M. Gollin, *The Observer and J. L. Garvin*, 68-73.
[6] Spender and Asquith, i, 254.

took advantage of the opportunity afforded to offer a solution which, strangely, was found acceptable to all sides. In essence Asquith's proposal was the same as that made earlier by Lloyd George[1]—four ships to be laid down immediately and another four if and when required.[2] It was not the end of all the wrangling, but it did provide a formula for immediate purposes. Effectively, the result of accepting the formula was defeat for the 'economists' in the Cabinet. As Asquith himself wrote more than a decade later: 'Estimates presented upon the authority of a Cabinet in which the advocates of peace and economy and the enemies of militarism were known to have a predominant voice . . . could not, in principle and as a whole, be opposed by the Liberal Party'.[3] For Asquith it was a considerable triumph. He had created compromise where there had been hopeless antagonism, and that without a single resignation.

The Radical Reduction of Armaments Committee had decided to oppose the Naval Estimates for 1909, but a series of accidents and misfortunes dogged them from the start. Their eventual protest was ineffectual. J. Allen Baker, who had been successful in the sessional ballot, decided with his friends to move a formal amendment proposing a reduction in the new naval construction programme. Though

[1] Lloyd George had made his proposal known to Spender and had invited comment. Spender rejected Lloyd George's scheme on the grounds, *inter alia*, that: (1) It was unconstitutional; and (2) 'A *Liberal* party, which respected the House of Commons would surely dislike this much more than having the bigger programme all at once. Honestly, I can't conceive you as a Liberal Chancellor of the Exchequer making yourself party to this proposal. Common sense and statesmanship seem to me equally at war with it. Surely it would proclaim itself at once as a transparent shuffle which would convict the Government openly of disingenuousness and lack of courage. I don't believe the Radicals would say thank you for it, and a large number of the rest would greatly resent it. . . . Honestly . . . I cannot imagine any Government committing itself to this course.' Spender to Lloyd George, 18 Feb. 1909, quoted Wilson Harris, *J. A. Spender*, 93–4.
[2] The exact terms of the compromise were described by Asquith in his Cabinet letter to the King, 24 Feb. 1909.

'(1) 4 new Dreadnoughts to be in any event laid down in the ensuing financial year; (2) an Act of Parliament to be passed this Session providing for a programme of naval construction so calculated as to keep us always ahead of the German programme; (3) power to be given in the Act to make forward contracts for the ships of next year—so that the Government will be able (if so advised), next autumn, to place orders for 4 additional Dreadnoughts, to be laid down not later than 1st April 1910. This will ensure our having a very substantial preponderance over Germany at the critical time—viz March–June 1912.' This arrangement was subsequently altered, the Navy Act being dropped and provision for the second four Dreadnoughts made in a footnote to the Estimates. The important point to note in the terms of this 'concordat' as Asquith described it, is that reference is made to 'the ships of *next* year', that is to those of the *1910* Estimates. This point was to become a major bone of contention between the reductionists and the 'big navy' supporters in the following months.
[3] Asquith, *The Genesis of the War*, 109.

it may seem paradoxical, no members of Parliament had a more highly developed sense of loyalty and duty towards the Government than
that group of Radicals who sought year by year to diminish the armaments burden. It was always a struggle of conscience for them to
overcome the persistent subterranean efforts of the Government to
persuade them to withdraw their amendment. They had to lay the
spectre of the Opposition, for tactical reasons, voting with them and
defeating the Government.

The Radical Press showered advice and encouragement on those
members who were opposed to any increase in the Naval Estimates.
'We observe that an Amendment is to be moved to the Address and
we hope that its supporters will have the pluck to go to a division
despite the crack of the Party Whip.'[1] An irate 'pacifist' correspondent to Concord even suggested that the Radical members would
do better to abandon their gentlemanly reproaches of the Government
by resolution and copy the methods of the Suffragettes. 'Why don't
you take that anti-scare resolution of yours and force it down the
Ministerialists throats? . . . terrorise Asquith, Grey and Co., and raid
their strongholds, official and private. Oh, that I could rouse you,
Christabelise you to desperate action.'[2]

Though the Radicals were disheartened by the apparent collapse
of their supporters within the Cabinet, they refused to be intimidated
by the Whip's office. They now knew there was little hope of them
succeeding in any vote in the Commons. Nevertheless, they determined not to capitulate. The General Committee of the National Liberal
Federation met on 26 February, and unanimously resolved that on the
available evidence they could not accept that a case had been made for
the proposed increases in naval expenditure. The meeting revealed
a determined and militant mood among Liberal backbenchers, and
W. P. Byles insisted that upon no account would the Federation
allow itself to become 'a wing of the Whip's room'.[3] The imminence
of the moment of crisis brought with it a stiffening of attitude, and
exaggerated the Radicals' sense of responsibility and destiny.[4] But
the Radicals suffered as always from an unrealistic assessment of their
influence and support within the Liberal party. Strangely, their sworn
enemies were their unwitting allies in this self-deception. 'Tory
spokesmen . . . insidiously exaggerated the influence of the Little
Navyites within the Liberal Party in order to tar the party as a whole
with the brush of defeatism.'[5]

[1] Concord, xxv, no. 2, Feb. 1909, p. 14.
[2] Ibid., no. 4, April 1909, pp. 45–6.
[3] Report of meeting in Manchester Guardian, 27 Feb. 1909.
[4] See Nation, 6 Mar. 1909, p. 845.   [5] Koss, Brunner, 228.

The Estimates were published on 12 March. They showed an increase of £3 million over those of the previous year. The Radicals had feared and expected worse. The four Dreadnoughts that were to be laid down in 1909 could be viewed as a normal building programme. As for the 'contingent four', even the *Manchester Guardian* had recognised that in certain circumstances work would have to start in advance upon the 1910 programme.[1] What none of the Radicals could realise was that the publication of the Estimates was the calm before the storm. The figures, with their cold assertion of alternatives and possible contingencies, hid the almost hysterical urgency to implement the full programme that had overtaken several leading members of the Government.

McKenna presented his Estimates to a packed and expectant Commons on 16 March. Despite Radical accounts to the contrary, his speech was a lucid statement of the facts as he knew them, and was free of any party rancour. He emphasised that Britain had tried everything without success to check the naval arms race. He concluded that no one could claim that Britain was setting the pace in naval armaments. The Government was merely responding responsibly to new uncertainties. The speed with which Germany could construct and arm her Dreadnoughts was unknown. Britain could no longer be sure of retaining her superiority at sea if they ever allowed themselves to fall behind in the construction of 'this newest and best class of ship'.[2]

Balfour followed McKenna and immediately claimed that the Government's proposed programme of Dreadnought construction was 'utterly insufficient'. He challenged McKenna's figures concerning the potential capacity of Germany to construct Dreadnoughts as compared with Britain. According to his calculations, unless the Government immediately rectified its mistake by employing all the country's available manufacturing power to the task of providing Dreadnoughts then, by 1912 Britain would be hard pressed to maintain a one Power standard.[3]

Such alarmist sentiments were to be expected from the Tory leader. But Asquith, when he replied, far from taking his opponent to task, stated that he had no complaints to make, either with the tone or the substance of Balfour's speech. While he questioned the accuracy of Balfour's figures, Asquith confessed that he himself had been mistaken on two important matters in the previous year. The

---

[1] *Manchester Guardian*, 29 Jan. and 9 Feb. 1909.
[2] *Hansard*, v:2:930ff.
[3] *Ibid.*, v:2: 944ff.

essential consideration remained—Britain could no longer rely on building warships at a faster rate than Germany. This was 'the fatal and most serious fact'.[1]

Such was the effect of Asquith's revelation, when he sat down the House remained in stunned silence for several minutes. Members were shocked by the Prime Minister's admission of what amounted to a grave crisis of national safety. In the moment that Asquith revealed the apparent seriousness of the situation, any lingering hope of success for their amendment that the Radical reductionists might still have cherished was abandoned. The heart of their case was destroyed. The overwhelming, unassailable, naval superiority Britain enjoyed over all other Powers which they so often had stressed, apparently no longer existed. An entry in John Ellis's diary vividly portrays the effect of Asquith's speech upon the supporters of the Amendment.

> Asquith's . . . admissions as to German accelerations, and our want of knowledge of them, produce[d] the most profound effect. Our men scattered like sheep. I do not think at that moment five Liberals would have voted against increase. Harvey[2] collapsed. The only thing to do was to tide it over.[3]

When the debate continued the following day, most of the Radicals remained stunned by Asquith's information. Harvey was so fearful that he decided not to move the amendment. His speech was weak and unconvincing. Most reductionists were relieved, thinking the issue would not now be forced to a decision. A few Radical stalwarts were not to be denied and they determined that the House should be divided upon the main question 'that the Speaker leave the chair'. Brunner in a rather pale speech intended to rally the forces, countered Ryland Atkins's assertion that the Government had now proved its case for increases up to the hilt. Only weeks before Atkins had moved the resolution at a meeting of the National Liberal Federation that there should be no increase in the Naval Estimates. The reductionists were most cheered by speeches from Labour's Arthur Henderson and a spirited assault upon Asquith by the Irish leader, John Dillon. Henderson pointed out that the Government's case did not rest upon irrefutable evidence but assumption and suspicion. There was no need for Radicals to be panicked by the scarifying opinions promoted by their own front bench. Dillon boldly claimed

[1] *Ibid.*, v:2:955ff.
[2] A. G. C. Harvey, the Radical member for Rochdale, had been deputed to move the reductionist amendment when his friend Allen Baker, who for weeks had been assiduously preparing a general statement of the case for moderation in Britain's naval programme, was struck down by influenza and on the day of the debate was too ill to attend the House.
[3] 16 Mar. 1909, quoted Bassett, 253.

it was his opinion that the Government's proposed increases were unnecessary. They had created a panic by ignoring Britain's enormous strength in pre-Dreadnought ships. When the House was divided, 83 members voted for reduction. Of the 143 signatories of the February protest, only 28 Liberals voted against the Government. The comparative respectability of the final total in the reductionist lobby was due to the support of Irish and Labour members. Ellis recorded in his diary: 'The Jingoes rampant and overdoing it altogether, surely we shall see more truth and soberness in a few days.'[1]

Now that the Government had revealed its concern, the 'big navy' supporters did not find it difficult to produce widespread panic among the people. Esher, a keen supporter of the eight Dreadnought programme, had no illusions about the political realities of the situation. 'The Government', he wrote, 'will have to be smitten hard. . . . Well engineered [the naval scare] will bring us our eight Dreadnoughts.' The Cabinet was still divided and uncertain. McKenna was 'bitter against Lloyd George and Churchill', and Haldane, for his attempts to patch the quarrels between his colleagues, was abused by everyone.[2]

The Labour Press was not slow in making capital out of Liberal discomfiture. 'It is obvious', said the *Labour Leader*, 'that the Liberal Party is passing into a moribund condition. . . . Liberalism for the Asquiths, the Greys, the Haldanes and the McKennas means a shilling to the poor, a crown to the rich, a paltry pension to the old broken workers, and enormous contracts to the financiers.'[3] But there was as much dissension within the Labour as the Liberal camp. Politicians bickered one with the other. John Ward was censured for proclaiming his faith in 'the wisest and most progressive Government with which this country has hitherto been blessed'. Militant Socialists were even displeased with Henderson who had led the attack upon the Government. They wanted to turn mild 'Uncle Arthur' into another Jaurès who would proclaim that at the first sign of war the workers would revolt. If Henderson had shown courage, it was but the courage of Liberal ideas. At a time when they needed to be most articulate, Labour members like the Radicals were 'for the most part inarticulate'. They had behaved pusillanimously. They could not have offered a more flattering tribute to Germany's power. They had 'given in to the Directors of the Blue Funk Co . . . the fraudulent contractor, the vampirical financier, the adulterator

---

[1] Quoted Bassett, 254.   [2] *E.P.*, ii, 377–8.
[3] *Labour Leader*, 19 Mar. 1909, p. 184.

of food, the army clothing sweater, the astute shipbuilder, the pantaloon in putties and the champagne Admiral'.[1] However, on one issue all were agreed. The people were not the miscreants responsible for perpetrating this wickedness. It was the war contractors who chose to waste Britain's substance for their own profit. It was they who would sacrifice old age pensions for 'eight monstrous steel obsolescences'.[2]

The admissions of national danger by Asquith and McKenna, which had so effectively spiked the opposition of the Radical reductionists and drawn the majority scampering back to the Liberal fold, provided so much ammunition to the Tories with which to censure the Government for not having done enough. Austen Chamberlain thought the Cabinet 'had altogether miscalculated the forces at work'. There was 'very considerable discomfort and uneasiness about their position', and Asquith in particular was showing 'a restlessness and irritation which are perhaps the best possible evidence of his consciousness of the weakness of his case'.[3]

Adopting the slogan coined by George Wyndham—'We want eight, and we won't wait'—the 'Patriotic' Press seized on the conditional clauses in the Estimates concerning the contingent four Dreadnoughts. Primed by Fisher, Garvin in his *Observer* demanded: 'Englishmen must insist on "the Eight, the whole Eight, and nothing but the Eight", with more to follow, and break any man or faction that now stands in the way.'[4] The Radicals in their turn sharpened their polemic. 'L'audace, l'audace, toujours l'audace ', G. H. Perris was moved to cry in the *Labour Leader* at Garvin's 'Impressive impudence'. How dare the *Observer* claim that unless the eight Dreadnoughts were immediately laid down, Sir Edward Grey together with the whole Board of Admiralty, civil and professional, would resign? How dare Garvin suggest the Lords would force a dissolution by rejecting the Budget? 'The lies of this kind of Jingoism that prefers poverty, war, any kind of anarchy to social reform . . . must be choked in its throat.'[5] But, the Jingo Press was in full cry. 'Panic', said the *Daily News*, 'always infectious is spreading like the plague.'[6] Even the normally reserved Esher was all for hanging the Board of Admiralty if they did not stick out for the eight ships. *Hysteria navalis* gripped the nation.

In the Commons, the Opposition, capitalising on the country's

[1] *New Age*, 25 Mar. 1909, p. 433-7.
[2] *Labour Leader*, 26 Mar. 1909, p. 203.
[3] Austen Chamberlain, *Politics from the Inside*, 160-1.
[4] *Observer*, 21 Mar. 1909.   [5] *Labour Leader*, 26 Mar. 1909, p. 198.
[6] *Daily News*, 23 Mar. 1909.

anxiety, was intemperate in its comments about Germany, and virulent in its criticism of the Government's 'parsimony and procrastination'. While the Government had indulged in 'dreams of universal disarmament' they had put the country in grave peril. It was doubtful, 'even with heroic exertions', whether it would ever again catch up with warship production.[1] In vain Government leaders attempted to retrieve a situation for which they were in part responsible.

'What have we got to fear?' asked McKenna. Asquith persistently refused to pledge the Government to the certain building of the four contingent Dreadnoughts. 'Henry', said Mrs Asquith to Arthur Lyttelton, 'is very worried by all this naval business, but he is going to make a great speech on Monday as soon as the debate is renewed which will put everything right and be a great triumph for him.'[2] The speech was made on 22 March. *The Nation* described it as 'admirable', but unfortunately it had been delivered a week too late.[3] Denouncing the 'unpatriotic, unscrupulous misrepresentation' of Britain's naval unpreparedness as so many 'mischievous legends', Asquith claimed, 'It was absurd to attempt to suggest that Britain was in a condition which ought to excite alarm and disquietude'.[4] Balfour riposted that the Government no longer seemed alive to the dangers of the situation as they had been on 16 March. He angrily insisted that the eight Dreadnoughts should be laid down immediately, and announced that a motion of censure would be brought against the Government. According to the *Daily Telegraph*, the only explanation for the Government's apparent climb down from the position adopted on 16 March, which could 'imperil the whole priceless heritage of centuries', was, 'to balance a party budget'.[5]

The *Daily Telegraph*, as was fitting for the mouthpiece of City opinion, in its editorials clearly reveals that much of the Dreadnought agitation was not primarily actuated by anxieties for national security. At its best, they and other Tory agencies engineered the panic for ideological reasons; at its worst it was promoted for reasons of financial gain. Many Tories welcomed the naval scare as the ideal means of distracting the public's attention from pressing and costly questions of social reform. As an irate correspondent to *The Times* charged Lloyd George: he was intent upon robbing the national hen roost 'to pay for the Socialist eggs he has hatched'. The whole issue was baldly summarised by a Tory member Samuel Roberts, speaking in the Commons on 16 March. 'If we are not safe as a nation what is

[1] *Hansard*, v:2:1084.   [2] Chamberlain, p. 164.
[3] *The Nation*, 27 Mar. 1909.   [4] *Hansard*, v:2:1503ff.
[5] *Daily Telegraph*, 24 Mar. 1909.

the use of our spending time in talking about social reform?' Roberts it may be noted was a director of both Cammel Laird and the Coventry Ordnance Works. The most commendable zeal to succour the country in its 'moment of need' was shown in the public pronouncements of the boards of the armament manufacturing companies. 'All else should wait while we provide eight' was a slogan happily designed to serve the country and at the same time enhance their profits.[1]

In the circumstances there was no alternative for the Radicals but to rally to the Government's support. Statements now made by ministers intended to allay the panic, caused Radicals to suspect that the admissions made in debate on 16 March were both unwise and unnecessary. Sir Charles Dilke, though a Radical, had always been a strong supporter of a big navy and he claimed there was no cause for alarm. The evidence elicited to suggest there was cause for anxiety had been fully acknowledged a year earlier.[2]

Had an unnecessary panic been promoted simply to frighten the Radical reductionists into supporting their front bench? The evidence seemed to the Radicals to point in that direction. On 17 March, Tirpitz had made a statement to the Budget Committee of the Reichstag, that Metternich had that day provided Grey with the information that by the autumn of 1912 Germany would have only thirteen Dreadnoughts, and that included three battle cruisers or Invincibles, and not seventeen as McKenna had said, or twenty-one as Balfour had claimed. Germany was not building faster than the Naval Laws provided. When, in the censure debate on 29 March, Grey, making the principal speech for the Government, confirmed Tirpitz's claim and said that the Government accepted the German statement entirely, the Radicals not unreasonably concluded that this amounted to an admission that the statements made on 16 March were based upon incorrect evidence. Therefore, the four contingent Dreadnoughts could only be regarded as an anticipation of the 1910–11 programme, and the Government would in time make the necessary adjustments.

On the basis of Tirpitz's statement, and the fuller semi-official explanation in the *Kölnische Zeitung*, the *Manchester Guardian* criticised the Government for miscalculation and abuse of the term acceleration. The Government should admit that it had made a mistake based upon wrong information. However, most of the Liberal Press followed Spender's lead in the *Westminster Gazette* where he

---

[1] See, *inter alia, Hansard*, v:2:972; *The Times*, 23 Mar. 1909; *Daily Telegraph* 19 Mar. 1909; *Pall Mall Gazette*, 22 Mar. 1909; and Buxton, i, 505ff.
[2] *Hansard*, v:2:1495.

claimed that although Tirpitz's assurances were all to the good, 'we have necessarily to take into account Mr Asquith's qualification that no charge of bad faith will lie against the German Government if different circumstances arise to alter this intention'. Though politely expressed, Spender's conclusion amounted to calling Tirpitz a liar.[1]

Grey's speech was important to the Radicals from another point of view. The Foreign Secretary had declared that if the expenditure upon armaments went 'on at the rate at which it has recently increased, sooner of later . . . it will submerge civilisation'. Here was a solemn and significant warning of the perils of the armaments race. Yet Grey had stressed earlier in his speech the 'peaceful progression and improved relations' between Germany and Britain since the conclusion of the Algeciras Conference. His forecast of the future relations between Germany and Britain was that they would 'walk together in peace and amity'.[2] So far as the Radicals were concerned, there could not have been clearer proof that there was an absurd and dangerous gap between policy and armaments.

The Tory vote of censure was lost by 353 votes to 135, but no one was converted by the debate. Each side remained convinced that they had made their case. The reason was simple. Churchill was to write, when he was First Lord of the Admiralty, 'in the technical discussion of naval details there is such a wealth of facts that the point of the argument turns rather upon their selection than upon their substance'.[3]

The final wording of the footnote to the Estimates, concerning the contingency programme, was not finally settled until 5 March.[4] Prior to this, there had been considerable wrangling between Asquith and McKenna as to the form of words to be used. Urged on by his Sea Lords, McKenna wanted the Government expressly committed to a programme of eight Dreadnoughts in the one year. The 'economists' who had been sticking out for four against the demand for six, could hardly be expected to accept eight as a satisfactory compromise. McKenna and Fisher employed Grey as a lever to persuade Asquith of the imperative need to meet their case. The Foreign Secretary wrote to the Prime Minister on 4 March:

> Fisher came to see me this afternoon by desire of McKenna. He was in much anxiety as to the Cabinet decision about Navy

---

[1] See and compare, *Manchester Guardian*, 19, 23, 24, 27, 30, 31 Mar. and 19 Apr. 1909 and *Westminster Gazette*, 19 Apr. 1909.
[2] *Hansard*, v: 3: 61ff.
[3] Cabinet paper, 10 Jan. 1914, quoted Marder, 169.
[4] The footnote appeared on p. 226 of the Naval Estimates; it is printed in Marder, 162.

Estimates. He detailed to me definite information as to German building of guns at Krupps and states that in his opinion orders should be given for eight battleships. . . . To add to his anxiety Winston Churchill has told him definitely that the Cabinet would allow four ships this year, four and no more for next year. I told him I had been growing more and more uncomfortable about the progress of German shipbuilding and what he told me now only confirmed the personal opinion at which I had arrived already.[1]

Grey need not have been concerned. Asquith was already convinced. But, his problem as party leader was to devise a stratagem which gave the First Lord what he wanted without making as much apparent to the reductionists. McKenna, when writing to Asquith, made it clear that he stood by the Sea Lords who considered that it would be 'a gross violation of their duty' to accept less than eight Dreadnoughts for 1909. Asquith wrote to McKenna: 'I do not see how it is possible for me to say more than I regard my personal and public honour pledged to secure that before Parliament separates adequate authority shall be given *in that sense.*'[2]

It was this assurance by Asquith, from which the First Lord could imply that the Admiralty would get their eight Dreadnoughts, that persuaded the Sea Lords to accept the wording of the footnote which Asquith suggested. To cover himself, when McKenna replied to Asquith on 4 March, he enclosed a Memorandum from the Sea Lords which said: 'We accept your assurance that the Prime Minister regards the situation with the same anxiety as yourself and that he has no doubt that the additional ships will be ordered.'

Fisher wrote to McKenna: 'There is a certain sweet certainty about "six in the estimates" which is lacking in the Bill with possibly evading phrases capable of being twisted against us, but I've no doubt of your seeing to it.'[3] It was not McKenna who had seen to it, but Asquith. The final form of the footnote covering the contingent four Dreadnoughts, left open the question of whether they were to be considered as part of the 1909 or 1910 building programme. 'Churchill and Lloyd George smelling a rat were now willing that there should be six Dreadnoughts in the Estimates. It was too late. The Admiralty would not hear of it.'[4]

Because of the footnote's ambiguity, debates as to its exact implication continued both within the Cabinet and outside. The agitation for eight Dreadnoughts was maintained, though soon to be cut short

[1] Grey to Asquith, 4 Mar. 1909, *Asquith MSS*, vol. 21.
[2] McKenna, *Reginald McKenna*, 82, my italics.
[3] *Ibid.*, p. 83.   [4] Marder, 163.

by the publication of Lloyd George's controversial Budget proposals on 29 April. Meanwhile, the Admiralty merrily assumed that it would have its way. Grey and McKenna promoted the case for eight in the Cabinet, and Fisher, singularly free of any doubts in the matter, wrote cheerfully to Esher after the debate in the Commons on 29 March: 'Grey rubbed in . . . yesterday . . . The *8* this year won't affect next year.'[1] Lloyd George and Churchill remained convinced that no definite promises had been made concerning the second four Dreadnoughts. There the matter remained temporarily. Grey and McKenna were, however, not only angry with the adamantine opposition of Churchill and Lloyd George, but were increasingly concerned with Asquith. He seemed to be lending his support to the reductionist case when in a speech at Glasgow on 17 April, he stressed Britain's strength in pre-Dreadnoughts and suggested that it might be unwise to lay down eight Dreadnoughts in one year when an improved battleship might soon be forthcoming. Grey was distressed and offended by these signs of 'weakness' in the Prime Minister.[2]

The announcement, in April 1909, of the Italian and Austrian Dreadnought programmes changed everything. This new factor, combined with the mounting Budget crisis and the possibility that an early general election would have to be called, allowed the implementation of the contingent Dreadnought programme to be approved by the Cabinet on 21 July without any apparent difficulty. Thoughts were more sharply attracted to the pressing problems on the domestic front, and in any event, the decision did not affect the question of whether the four new ships were an extension of the 1909 building programme or an anticipation of the 1910 programme.

The Cabinet's decision was announced to the Commons by McKenna on 26 July. When the First Lord attempted to justify this latest move by reference to Austria's Dreadnought programme, he was given a roasting by Murray Macdonald and Dillon. McKenna sought to evade the barbs of their criticism by relying on vague and shifty platitudes. Macdonald claimed that Grey in the 29 March debate had accepted German assurances concerning their building plans. McKenna had said nothing to indicate that the Government thought these assurances were now false. Therefore, it was clear that the Government had not established their case for putting the contingency plan into operation. What is more, they had admitted that the particular

[1] Admiral Fisher, *Memories and Records* (1920), i, 190. Though Grey had said that if the ships were ordered it would be 'without prejudice to next year's programme', he had added the *caveat* that, 'if we find we have got . . . the situation fully in hand . . . we might dispense with ships next year.'
[2] See Marder, 170.

threat, for which the plan had been devised, had not materialised. Wriggle as he might, McKenna knew that he was hooked, and changing the grounds of his argument from moment to moment did not make for a convincing defence of the Government's action.

The Radical Press found McKenna's explanation quite unsatisfactory. Clearly the only conclusion to be drawn was that the House and the country had been tricked in March. The *Labour Leader* reminded its readers that it had warned at the time, the statement McKenna had given the Commons could only mean that eight Dreadnoughts would be built or begun in 1909. The contingency plan was 'a fake, too thin and transparent to impose upon any sane or ordinarily observant person'. It had been designed 'to placate a section of the Liberal party who were uneasy about wanton armaments competition'. Now, 'that same precious pair, Asquith and McKenna, with solemn and measured eloquence' revealed their 'confidence trick' to their benighted supporters.[1] It was vain to inquire what circumstances had arisen between March and July to persuade the First Lord that the contingency programme should be implemented. The Austrian Dreadnought programme was merely a convenient excuse. McKenna and the Admiralty Board had been convinced of the need for eight Dreadnoughts in March.

In a division, most notable for the number of absentees, the contingent programme was approved by 280 votes to 98. The minority vote was for the greatest part made up of Irish members. Thirty-seven Radicals voted against the Government together with eleven Labour members. Five Labour members actually supported the Government.

But the division had still not resolved the ambiguity of the extra Dreadnoughts. To which year's building programme, 1909 or 1910, did they belong? Arthur Lee, who led the Tory assault on the Government's naval programme, in July questioned whether any member of the House knew the answer. If the four Dreadnoughts were part of the 1910 programme, as the Radical Press seemed to assume, then, Lee maintained, the Government's programme was inadequate. Asquith, whenever he was questioned by members on the subject, did nothing to make the situation any clearer. The *Manchester Guardian*, which in March had taken *The Times* to task for suggesting the eight Dreadnoughts were all part of the 1909 programme, in August objected to Lee's 'Phantom four' being 'suspended in mid-air between this year and next'.[2] The question was not resolved until the

---

[1] *Labour Leader*, 30 July 1909, p. 491.
[2] *Manchester Guardian*, 15 Mar. and 4 Aug. 1909.

publication in March 1910 of the Naval Estimates for 1910–11. Then it was finally apparent that the four contingent Dreadnoughts were part of the 1909 programme. Together with the five provided by the 1910–11 Estimates, thirteen Dreadnoughts were to be laid down for the two years.

The 1910 Estimates demanded the unprecedented total of £40 million. However, this time there was no widespread threat of revolt by the Radicals. Their strength and their spirit had been sapped by the previous year's struggle. The Reduction of Armaments Committee, which only two years before had threatened the life of the Government over a comparatively nominal increase, weakly acquiesced in this gigantic step. They expressed merely their 'profound regret' at the increased expenditure, but considered that the House of Lords question made it advisable they should not dissipate their energies upon other matters. The staunch pacifists in the Commons forced a division on 15 March 1910, but could muster only a handful of supporters in their lobby. 'Was there ever such a betrayal?', asked *Concord*. The Liberal Government was guilty of

> an act of treachery which must be resented by every man to whom peace, democracy and the betterment of social conditions are dear. A betrayal . . . of the traditional principles of the Liberal and Labour parties. . . . There would have been no chance of the acceptance of . . . [the Navy Estimates] by the Government majority in the Commons were it not for the constitutional crisis.[1]

Without doubt, the villain had been Asquith. The *Labour Leader* was not alone in wondering whether Philip Snowden had modified his earlier opinion that the Prime Minister was 'the most honest person' in the House.

When the forecasts of Germany's naval strength in the spring of 1912 were overtaken by reality, they proved to have been grossly exaggerated. There were not twenty-one Dreadnoughts, or even seventeen, but nine. In later years, Radical critics were to make much capital out of this, insisting that Asquith and McKenna had wilfully employed false statements to extract monstrously swollen Estimates from an unwilling and unwitting Commons. The Prime Minister and the First Lord of the Admiralty had 'engineered' a crisis, thus 'perpetrating an offence against the Commons . . ., the taxpayer . . ., the Colonies and Germany.'[2] The facts were otherwise. Asquith and McKenna in the spring of 1909 were convinced that Germany was

[1] *Concord*, xxvi, no. 3, Mar. 1910, p. 31.
[2] Hirst, *The Six Panics*, 98.

outbuilding Britain and that Britain's margin of superiority in Dreadnoughts was seriously imperilled. If anything, they were more concerned than their statements in the House indicated. McKenna's rôle was obvious, but Asquith as leader of the Liberal party was put in an extremely difficult position. By means of what can only be described as a lawyer's ploy, he used an ambiguously worded footnote to the 1909 Naval Estimates to maintain an undivided Cabinet and deceive the reductionists in his party long enough to make their eventual protest ineffectual.

The passage of time and an ambiguously worded clause were not the only aids Asquith enjoyed in weakening Radical opposition. Most Radicals were eager to forget the divisive problems of foreign policy and armaments, and to unite with the Government in a crusade on domestic issues against the old enemy, the Tories. They welcomed Lloyd George's budget and the subsequent crisis with the Lords. Such battles 're-heated the forces out of which all Liberal triumphs . . . [grew] . . ., the enthusiasm of the main body of the Party'.[1]

There remained that handful of Radicals for whom attachment to the ideals of peace and universal disarmament was more than sentiment to be easily set aside. Peace and progress was their deeply engrained faith. They refused to ignore, they could not ignore, what was for them the central issue of politics. They believed that the Liberal Government had fallen into fundamental error. Moral power was the force that really commanded predominance in the world. It only required a courageous lead by Britain in the matter of disarmament for a response surely to be evoked from the rest of the world. The maintenance of European peace was incomparably the most important question with which the Government had to deal. Peace would only be maintained when the competitive increase in armaments was stopped.

These Radicals did not see themselves as vague idealists promoting Utopian policies. They were as aware as their critics of the powerful forces in Europe intent upon war. It was for this reason they desired Britain to take a bold initiative, to be unequivocal, to be persistent in support of disarmament by international agreement.[2] They refused to rush along with their fellow Radicals and cheerfully beat their ploughshares into spears with which to attack the Tories. Though they should be defeated again and again by massive majorities in the division lobbies of the Commons, they relentlessly pursued

[1] *The Nation*, 8 May 1909; see also the same, 31 July 1909.
[2] See Baker and Baker, 163–5.

their policy, insisting that the voice of conscience would never be stilled. For the moment they relied on the support of the parliamentary Labour party. The two halves of the Radical group in the Commons were not to join in the effective condemnation of armament increases until the shock of the Agadir Crisis in 1911 once more renewed old loyalties.

Chapter 5

The Rise and Fall of the Triple Entente, 1908–11

Dubious partners

If Prince von Bülow rejected as fanciful the idea that Britain was intent on isolating Germany in Europe, the bulk of German opinion was not so readily convinced.[1] Most Germans believed that Grey, abetted by King Edward, was intent upon the military and diplomatic encirclement of the Fatherland. 'England,' said Besserman, leader of the National Liberal Party, when speaking in the Reichstag in April 1907, 'England is everywhere.' He was expressing the universal fear of his countrymen. That fear increased in intensity as the grand design of British diplomacy seemed complete when, in September 1907 with the signing of the Anglo-Russian Convention, Russia was drawn securely within the Anglo-French embrace. Germany's diplomacy appeared to be impotent when faced by the cunning of the British Foreign Office. Thus unease fed upon suspicion in the German mind and in May 1908, when M. Fallières, the President of France, paid a state visit to Britain, fears of a policy of encirclement were confirmed. Germans could not forget that even in the comparatively expansive and generous atmosphere generated by the Kaiser's visit to England at the end of 1907, it had been made clear that no diplomatic moves could be contemplated without England's entente partners first being apprised and consulted.

On 25 May 1908 President Fallières was welcomed to England by smiling weather and wildly enthusiastic crowds. At a banquet given in his honour at Buckingham Palace, the French President and the English King exchanged toasts to the *entente resserrée* and the *entente permanente*. Tardieu in *Temps*, a newspaper known to be privy to the wishes of the Quai d'Orsay, claimed that there should be a formal alliance between France and Britain with the necessary military and naval arrangements. He stipulated that the essential condition for

[1] See, *inter alia*, E. M. Carroll, *Germany and the Great Powers 1866–1914* (1938), 575ff.; and Hale, 310–11.

such an alliance was Britain's adoption of universal military service. *The Nation* chided Tardieu for showing 'little of the Liberal spirit of his predecessor, de Pressensé'. However, his 'outrageous request for conscription', that caused many Liberals anxiously to examine more closely 'la Belle Alliance', was no more than the repetition of that same request Clemenceau had made a year earlier to King Edward when they had met at Marienbad.[1] Tardieu's bold suggestion was treated coldly by the English Press, including *The Times*.[2] Aside from the question of conscription, Radical opinion was particularly concerned that there should be so much as the suggestion of a formal alliance between France and Great Britain. 'The day for alliances is over. Alliances imply military and naval cooperation of an offensive as well as a defensive character . . . they add to the ferment of pugnacity still working in all the reactionaries of Europe.'[3] Talk of an alliance only served to 'awake distrust among the Powers and evoke the war spirit. They increase the desire for armaments.'[4]

The principle of the entente, which the Radicals had initially welcomed with enthusiasm, now seemed to be developing unwanted and sinister overtones. Perhaps an understanding that was based upon a bargain concerning French rights in Morocco and British rights in Egypt smacked too much of honour among thieves. 'The trouble with special understandings', wrote C. E. Maurice, 'is that they begin with enthusiasm for peace but too frequently end in equally keen enthusiasm for a new war.'[5] It was all very well for idealists in France and England to suppose that a league between the two great Liberal democracies must be a force for good in the world. The whole concept of the entente had been sullied by Britain developing her relations with Japan and Russia. That would seem to give the lie to her Liberal intentions. 'Popular sympathy' for the entente might still survive among Radicals and Socialists, but it was no good denying that France had 'done little if anything to aid Liberal purposes'.[6] There were good reasons for Radicals to be both

---

[1] See Lee, *King Edward VII*, ii, 628–9; and J. A. Spender, *Fifty Years of Europe* (1933), 290 and 306.

[2] The *Manchester Guardian*, 29 May 1908, noted suspiciously that it was 'certainly singular that so many French journalists . . . should all agree to think that . . . [an exchange of compliments] . . . contemplated a change which, so far as we know, has not occurred to any Englishman on reading them.'

[3] *New Age*, 6 June 1908, p. 102; cf. *The Nation*, 20 June 1908: 'If our understandings were frankly alliances we should at least be able to add the naval resources of France to our own in our competitive reckonings. But at present we have all the risks of an alliance and none of the securities.'

[4] *Labour Leader*, 5 June 1908, p. 360.

[5] *Concord*, xxiv, no. 6, June 1908, p. 68.

[6] *The Nation*, 30 May 1908.

dissatisfied with and suspicious of France as a suitable partner with Britain to insure the peace of Europe.

A French Government under Clemenceau's leadership was very properly a matter of concern to Radicals. Few French statesmen had done more than he to keep alive a feeling of hostility towards Germany. Clemenceau was convinced that 'an implacable fatality from which we cannot escape will force some day the military weapon forged by the founding of the German Empire upon the battlefield'. War with Germany, he believed, was inevitable. 'We must do nothing to provoke it, but we must be ready to wage it . . . it will be a life and death struggle.'[1] Clemenceau was no opportunist who, for the sake of peace, would acquiesce in maintaining the European *status quo*. To British Radicals it was patent that Clemenceau was dedicated to giving an anti-German emphasis to France's policies. Why else should he have been the darling of French chauvinists?

In March 1907 an anti-European riot at Marrakesh resulted in the death of a French subject, Dr Mauchamp. On the pretext of insuring the safety of their other subjects in Morocco, the French Government ordered the occupation of Oudjda, a town near the Algerian frontier. At first English Radical opinion was sympathetic, but it was soon discerned that France was using the death of Mauchamp as an excuse to settle accounts in Morocco in direct contravention of the Algeciras Settlement. This suspicion was subsequently confirmed by French action that summer in Casablanca. After a series of provocations, a native mob killed some European workmen. The French Government totally mismanaged the affair and there were further disorders and rioting. As a reprisal, a French cruiser bombarded several defenceless Moorish coastal villages. To Radicals, French policy was yet another illustration of the evils of imperialism—grab and violence by a European Power at the expense of a hapless native population. To make matters worse, the British Government was prepared to support 'ces messieurs de l'entente cordiale', presumably because the perception of cruelty was blunted when the sufferers were mere infidels. Cunninghame Graham, in a letter to *The Nation*, pointed out the parallel with the British bombardment of Alexandria.[2] To add insult to injury, delegates of the French Government at the Hague were at that very moment about to sign a convention prohibiting the bombardment of undefended coastal towns.[3] One had to be very

---

[1] See *Aurore*, 18 June 1905; and *Les Carnets de Georges Louis* (Paris, 1926), i, 21, quoted E. M. Carroll, *French Public Opinion and Foreign Affairs 1870–1914* (1931), 224–5.
[2] *The Nation*, 31 Aug. 1907.
[3] See *Albany Review*, Sept. 1907, pp. 605–6.

simpleminded indeed to suppose that French action in Morocco was in any way concerned with questions of morality or civilisation.

France's status as a 'lending Power' had always been cause for concern among Radicals and Socialists.

> Piles of shares and bonds are waiting in the shade of certain bank safes till such time as French blood shall have fructified their value and made them marketable commodities. . . . Consider the long list of French financial undertakings in Morocco. La Banque d'Etat du Maroc, 15½ million francs; La Compagnie Marocaine, 3½ million francs; La Compagnie Immobiliers du Maroc, 2 million francs; and a host of others.

Given such facts, it was 'not difficult to understand why it became indispensable that the roar of French cannon should be heard at Casablanca'.[1] Here was the true logic of imperialism in practice—the masquerade of 'pacific penetration' in the name of civilisation, and the reality of bloodshed, conquest and exploitation. And all this, as Hobson had clearly pointed out, for the benefit of the investor.[2]

The parallel, to which Cunninghame Graham had drawn attention in his letter to *The Nation*, was enhanced when Mulai Hafid, playing the part of Arabi Pasha, rebelled against his brother the French client Sultan, Abdul Aziz. Within a year, despite the support of the French, Abdul Aziz was put to flight by Mulai Hafid. The English Radical Press was jubilant. That large fund of sympathy felt when the entente was born had already been exhausted by France's policy in Morocco. Many Radicals now took pleasure in France's humiliation. *The Nation* rejoiced at Mulai Hafid's triumph gained at the expense of 'the tool of a foreign invasion'. Not only had the fortunes of Abdul Aziz been ruined, but also 'the dreams of the French Colonial Party'. France had not acted in Morocco as a great or a wise Power. Where the French should have led, they had 'conquered, enslaved and sent a punitive expedition'. France's mistaken policies had arisen 'from a single root, the dominance at the Foreign Office of a group of powerful financiers whose only concern was to push their monetary interests in Morocco'.[3] This pleasure at Mulai Hafid's triumph marked the temporary disenchantment of Radical opinion with France. Her blatant imperialism disqualified France as a fit partner for Liberal England in international affairs.

---

[1] *Concord*, xxiii, no 9/10, Sept./Oct., 1907, p. 106. 'The object of the policy of *pénétration pacifique* was . . . to rob the Moors of their country. . . . The pace was forced at the behest of the Colonial Party headed by Étienne of Oran and the international financiers . . . anxious to float Moorish mining, town development, agricultural and other companies on the Paris Bourse': *New Age*, 12 Sept. 1908, p. 384.
[2] See *The Nation*, 14 Sept. 1907, and *Albany Review*, Oct. 1907, pp. 7–8.
[3] *The Nation*, 29 Aug. 1908.

It was not the Radicals alone who were concerned by French policy in Morocco. England waited to see what action Germany would take. 'Germany cannot be expected to consent to France's adventures', *The Nation* claimed, 'without exacting a heavy price.'[1] But even when the French bombarded Casablanca, much to everyone's surprise and none more than the British Foreign office, Germany assured France of her goodwill.[2] When the Germans proved somewhat hasty in their desire to recognise Mulai Hafid's successful revolt, Pichon, the French Foreign Minister, showed extreme intransigence towards the Germans. Eyre Crowe wrote darkly of Germany being about 'to resort to another bullying campaign intended to frighten and cow France into a yielding mood'.[3] However, in the event it was the Germans who gave way.

The particular concern of Radicals was that the British Government was being more French than the French. A Liberal Government was seemingly accepting the lead of its 'patriotic' Press and giving support to a Power whose enterprises in Morocco were 'morally the equivalent of buccaneering'.[4] Anglo-German relations were difficult enough without the added complications provided by France pursuing her imperialist ventures in Morocco. These fears were bluntly articulated by *Concord*. 'What demands might the French make and Britain acquiesce in as an ally in relation to her Moroccan policy?'[5] The *Manchester Guardian* had anticipated this 'dilemma of conscience' when it categorically asserted in September 1907 that under the terms of the entente Great Britain was not bound to support France.[6] Least of all should Britain be involved at the possible price of a European war in countenancing 'a policy of crime and bloodshed merely to save the faces of French politicians'.[7] The only sane and moral policy was for the French to quit Morocco. It was 'illogical that those who claimed Alsace Lorraine should be willing to take the Fatherland of other people'. French policy in Morrocco was 'a pretext, and Britain should recognise the sordid reality . . . fine words were merely the cover for *les coups de Bourse*'.[8]

On 25 September 1908 events took another turn for the worse, when the French 'raised an obscure incident to the level of an inter-

---

[1] *The Nation*, 14 Sept. 1907.
[2] See *D.G.P.* xxiv, 217, 218 and 221; *B.D.* vii, 69.   [3] *B.D.* vii, 90.
[4] *New Age*, 5 Sept. 1908, p. 363.
[5] *Concord*, xxiv, no. 6, June 1908, p. 67.
[6] *Manchester Guardian*, 9 Sept. 1907; cf. *New Age*, 12 Sept. 1908, p. 384. 'England's hands are tied. She in a moment of aberration gave France a free hand in Morocco in order to get her own way in Egypt.'
[7] Letter of Cunninghame Graham to *The Nation*, 29 Aug. 1908.
[8] *Concord*, xxiv, no. 11, Nov. 1908, p. 140.

national crisis' by 'giving Prussian formalism the appearance of a wanton and maliciously-timed attack'.[1] Three Germans, who were among a party of deserters from the French Foreign Legion, were arrested by the French military police. During the ensuing mêlée, the dragoman of the German consulate was struck while escorting the deserters on board a ship. At first both France and Germany showed restraint. There appeared to be no desire on either side to magnify the incident. The Kaiser, in particular, was anxious that there should be a prompt settlement. He considered that the fate of three German deserters was not something for which it was worth damaging improved relations with France. Yet it was the Kaiser who was unwittingly responsible for the next stage in the incident. On 28 October an indiscreet interview he had given months earlier was published in the *Daily Telegraph*. Reaction in England followed the usual pattern. The Radical and Socialist Press greeted 'this latest and astounding exhibition of royal eccentricity'[2] with amused toleration. The 'patriotic' Press made capital out of the Kaiser's foolish remarks in order to strengthen their demand for an increased Dreadnought programme. In Germany the publication of the interview roused a storm of protest and an unprecedented attack on the Government was threatened for the forthcoming session of the Reichstag. The interview had unfortunate repercussions in France as well. In emphasising his personal love of England, the Kaiser had attempted to discredit France in British eyes by claiming that the French had initiated negotiations for a Continental league to interfere in the Boer War. Of a sudden the stage was set for an international crisis.

In an attempt to distract German opinion, Bülow instructed Radolin to demand satisfaction of the French for the maltreatment of a German consular official and the immediate and unconditional release of the three German deserters. The French refused. Once more Eyre Crowe at the Foreign Office circulated gloomy minutes about his forebodings concerning Germany's evil intent, and Grey warned McKenna that it would be as well if the British Fleet was placed on the alert.[3] But while the chauvinist elements of the French and German Press clamoured loudly for war and Grey anxiously awaited developments, the Germans had already modified their demands.

[1] *The Nation*, 14 Nov. 1908.
[2] *Labour Leader*, 6 Nov. 1908, p. 705. Much of the content of the Kaiser's article should have already been familiar to English readers. The interventionist episode had been discussed in an article by 'Ignotus' in the *National Review*, Dec. 1907; and in the same journal in an article by André Mévil, July 1908; and by J. L. Bashford in the *Strand Magazine*, 1 Jan. 1908, p. 22. The sensation caused by the article was due to its timing rather than its content. See Hale, 313–22.   [3] *B.D.* VII, 126, 132.

Bülow agreed to Cambon's suggestion that there should be a statement of reciprocal regret and that the whole matter should go to
arbitration. The formula was publicly announced on 10 November.
The Nation claimed that it was 'quite superfluous' to comment upon
the settlement of a 'trivial controversy'. Certain newspapers, 'con-
fessedly in touch with official sources of information', had talked 'as
though it might have led to a European war'. If Europe had been
brought to 'this sombre situation', then it was because of the 'pursuit
of Imperialism, secretive and anti-democratic diplomacy and the
refusal to secure peace by the limitation of armaments'.[1] Here again
was the all too familiar rehearsal of Radical complaints concerning
the conduct of Britain's foreign policy. Nothing, it seemed, had
changed for the better.

Then less than three months after this incident, much to the surprise of most Englishmen, who had been conditioned by their Press
to believe that France and Germany were irreconcilably at odds over
Morocco, the two Governments announced that they had reached
accord. No group was more delighted by this news than Britain's
Socialists and Radicals. Had they not applauded when Jaurès
had made his eloquent appeal for Franco-German rapprochement in January? 'Such a move', Keir Hardie had said, 'would be
supported by the democracy of all countries.'[2] Radical opinion
immediately performed a smart about face in its attitude towards
France. The real reason for this, however, was that the ending
of the 'Moroccan squabble made the task of bringing England and
Germany together much easier'. The dispute between Germany and
France over Morocco had 'given a recurring anti-German edge
to the Anglo-French understanding'.[3] Now there was no longer any
reason to suppose that the entente was directed against Germany.

If France, as Britain's partner in international affairs, was sufficient
cause of concern to the Radicals, Russia proved an even graver
source of anxiety.[4] At the best Radicals had greeted the Anglo-
Russian Convention with suspicion. Though many had not openly

---

[1] *The Nation*, 14 Nov. 1908.
[2] *Labour Leader*, 22 Jan. 1909, p. 56.
[3] *The Nation*, 13 Feb. 1909, p. 734.
[4] See Brailsford's letter to *The Times*, 10 Sept. 1907. 'The explanation [of the
Anglo-Russian Convention] is . . . that we have made sacrifices in Asia in
order to win Russian support elsewhere. The plain fact is that the Agreement
has been concluded to restore the European balance of power or, as some would
put it, to isolate Germany . . . Had peace been our object we should have sought
it rather at Berlin than at St Petersburg.'

said as much, they had been deeply offended by a closer union between Liberal England and autocratic Russia. They were to regret
this alliance—and none more than the parliamentary Labour party—
when Balfour chose to make sport of them for accepting without
protest the Anglo-Russian Agreement. They could only reply that
though they might have unwisely swallowed the gnat of an agreement between the two countries, 'the Government and its Tory
supporters' should not be surprised when they strained 'at the thought
of that agreement becoming a rapprochement and then by degrees an
alliance'.[1] Labour and Radical dissatisfaction at Britain consorting
with Russia was sharply highlighted when, in May 1908, the public
were told that King Edward attended by Charles Hardinge intended
to pay a visit to the Tsar at Reval.

'Nothing will convince us', said *New Age*, 'that there is the smallest
desire in England for any closer rapprochement with Russia.'[2] However, most of the British Press received the announcement of King
Edward's forthcoming visit to the Tsar with equanimity. The *Daily
News* alone sounded a note of alarm.[3] *The Nation* went no further
than to express 'mixed feelings' at the news, though it did enter the
caveat that people seemed singularly less sensitive in matters of
national liberty than they would have been but a few years earlier.[4]
Roused from its normal somnolence when commenting on foreign
affairs, the *Labour Leader* drew a grim contrast between the visit of
President Fallières and the proposed meeting of the two monarchs
at Reval. Ramsay MacDonald roundly condemned the royal meeting
as 'an insult to Britain'. At public meetings held throughout the
country, Labour speakers, following the lead given them by Keir
Hardie, condemned 'England consorting with murderers'.[5] In the
Commons the Labour party challenged the Government's decision.
They were readily repelled on points of procedure by a less than
sympathetic Speaker, and, in substance, by an avuncular Asquith
who appeared to be determined to minimise the significance of the
state visit. The Prime Minister's comfortable assurances that the
meeting of the Tsar and the King bore no relation whatsoever to the
internal affairs of either monarch's country, did nothing to convince
Radical opinion or palliate its criticisms. Radicals hoped against
hope that, as with the Cronstadt visit in 1906, if they maintained
sufficient pressure the Government would eventually be forced to
abandon the project. To this end they employed Question Time in

[1] *New Age*, 13 June 1908, p. 122.   [2] *New Age*, 30 May 1908, p. 81.
[3] *Daily News*, 27 May 1908.   [4] *The Nation*, 25 May 1908.
[5] See *Labour Leader*, 29 May 1908, pp. 344-5, 350; and 12 June 1908, p. 372.

the Commons to present in the form of interrogatories as many damaging statements and reflections upon the Russian Government as fact and ingenuity allowed.[1] It was intolerable to think that 'a barbarous régime with its Humpty Dumpty upon his tottering throne' should be provided with fresh credit in the world money market to perpetuate its crimes against humanity because a Liberal Government had decided the King should visit the Tsar.[2]

At last, the sniping campaign at Question Time was rewarded by a full scale debate when, on 4 June, the Labour Party moved a reduction in the Foreign Office vote.[3] Grey faced his critics flanked upon the Treasury Bench by Haldane and Asquith—'the most reactionary trio in the whole Cabinet'.[4] Labour and Radical speeches were neither closely reasoned nor showy; indeed, most showed evidence of rather hasty composition. There was nothing new in the repeated rehearsal of the crimes of the Russian Government though members on the Liberal benches listened to the speeches with considerable sympathy. One speaker, the Labour member, O'Grady, made a palpable hit which was greeted with the applause of Government back-benchers when he claimed: 'We heard nothing of this when the late Premier was in his place.'

Grey, when it was his turn to reply, far from adopting a defensive attitude, challenged his critics. He argued that the Government's Russian policy was based on agreement and cordial understanding and was directed towards peace, whereas the policy advocated by his critics would lead to war. 'I say that as between these two policies I am and I always have been for a fair and loyal understanding between the two countries working together in matters where their interests touch. I stand by that, and if the House rejects it or makes it impossible I fall with it.' Grey's impassioned plea, and the threat of resignation if his policies were not accepted, was sufficient to win over many of his Radical critics.[5] G. H. Perris, who as a result of the

[1] The culmination of this particular mode of attack on the Government was a monster question put down by Keir Hardie which was not accepted at the table of the House; see *Hansard*, iv: 190:60–2.
[2] The 1905 Franco-British loan was already exhausted. In three years the Russian National Debt had risen from 460 to 665 million sterling. The current year's Budget had a deficit of £20 million. As a direct result of the Reval visit the price quoted for the Russian loan on the British Stock Market rose 7½ points. Concern about the possibility of increased credit for the Russian Government led to a spate of antisemitic comment in some of the Radical and Socialist journals: see *New Age*, 20 June 1908, p. 141 and compare *Albany Review*, July 1908, p. 476. See also *Daily News*, 17 May 1907 and 18 Feb. 1908.
[3] For Reval Debate, see *Hansard*, iv: 190:211ff.
[4] *Labour Leader*, 13 June 1908, p. 379.
[5] See, for example, *Manchester Guardian*, 5 June 1908. Though only fifty-nine members—a handful of Radicals, most of the Labour members, and a few

debate left the Liberal and joined the Labour party, upbraided these 'weaker brethren'. Grey's 'cold, detached, gracefully arrogant manner was exactly calculated to impress weak minds. . . . The way he threw the Labour men on the defensive when he should have been defending his own actions was . . . undeniably bold and clever.'[1] But Grey's critics virtually ignored the most singular feature of his speech—the Foreign Secretary's identification of the 1907 Convention, the Reval visit and the concept of a full entente. Early in his speech Grey stated that the Reval visit was not intended to initiate any new negotiations with the Russian Government and was desired for its political effect alone. However, he then claimed that if Edward's visit was cancelled, 'you might as well tear up the Anglo-Russian Convention'. Grey could not have indicated more clearly that it was his intention to force the pace of Anglo-Russian rapprochement.

It was too easy to dub, as Grey did, the Labour critics of his Russian policy, as 'extreme and violent men' who by their intransigence made it 'impossible for the Government . . . to bring out the merits of the question'.[2] To think thus was entirely to misunderstand Labour's case. Labour members believed the only interpretation that could be put on the Reval visit was that it was part of a general policy of the Government to engage in a European alliance system. Labour was bound to oppose such a policy as it was 'not only dangerous to international peace . . . but a challenge to Labour's internationalism'. If Grey was pursuing a peace policy, then it should be a matter of discrimination and not dictated by expediency. He was 'violating the general Liberal spirit of Western enlightenment . . . by associating with the Czar'. To insist upon the King going to Reval was to injure the very spirit to which Grey claimed he paid homage. When examined, the principles that underlay the visit revealed

the folly of believing that the Liberal Party knew any better than it did during the South African War what its own prin-

---

Irish Nationalists—voted against Grey, that in no way represented the sum total of resentment against Grey's policy. See P. W. Wilson in *Daily News*, 5 July 1908. See also Fred Maddison, *Hansard*, iv:190:261–3. Any Radical Liberal who chose to vote against the Government had to overcome considerable social as well as political pressures. This fact is well illustrated by the notorious treatment of Arthur Ponsonby who, because he supported the Radicals in the vote, had his name omitted from the list of invitations to the King's garden party. See Magnus, 405–6. It is of interest to note that when Ponsonby was censured for his actions by the Liberal Whip, J. A. Pease, the 'rebel' professed, tongue in cheek, that he had no intention of being troublesome, and would 'probably get [his] conscience completely under control before long'. See, H. S. Weinroth, 'Radicals and balance of power 1902–1914,' *The Historical Journal* xiii, 4 (1970), 668.
[1] *Concord*, xxiv, no. 6, June 1908, p. 64.
[2] Grey to Knollys, 25 July 1909, quoted Trevelyan, 192.

ciples were or how they intended to carry them out. . . . The implication of Grey's speech was that the House of Commons was the echo of the Foreign Office. Every Liberal Member who voted for Grey voted in favour of national policy being settled by the whims of an individual Minister. Liberalism when it supported Grey flouted itself.[1]

To add to the confusion, Grey would consider a frank statement of the policy he was fashioning at the behest of his Foreign Office officials as 'indecorous in the highest degree; and he is nothing if not decorous'.

There is something in the wind which he dares not name . . . the question is one of principle, not detail. England is prepared to trust a Liberal Cabinet so long as a Liberal Cabinet trusts England. Surely we can be informed whether the present plan in foreign affairs is one of general amicability or one of offensive and defensive alliances. Ententes we can understand and support . . . but alliances are a horse of another colour; their day is gone by.[2]

Radical members of the Liberal Party were more moderate in their opposition to Grey's Russian policy than Labour members, and more guarded in their criticisms. Many were impressed that the moderate constitutionalist party in Russia favoured the visit taking place.[3] When Nevinson censured Grey in a letter to the *Manchester Guardian*, he was sharply reprimanded. Was it reasonable to expect Grey to be the servant of an English view of Russian interests which was not held by the Russians themselves? According to the *Guardian* there was no middle way to pursue. The only available alternatives were 'the odious European policy of Palmerston', or Grey's policy 'as he explained it last night'.[4] As well as reprimanding Nevinson, the *Guardian* was expressly rejecting the course which the *Daily News* had supported. No one, that paper had maintained, wished to return to the old days of Anglo-Russian friction, but this did not imply that 'correctitude should be exaggerated into affection'.[5] *The Nation*, in tracing the historical evolution of Liberal foreign policy, took a more charitable view of Palmerston than had the *Guardian*. It noted

---

[1] Ramsay MacDonald in *Labour Leader*, 12 June 1908, p. 377.
[2] *New Age*, 20 June 1908, pp. 141–2.
[3] Socialists rejected this claim, pointing to the decree promulgated in June that dismissed Constitutional Democrats from all zemstvos and municipal bodies. Also, the most conservative elements of the Russian Press, *Novoe Vremya* and even a chauvinistic 'rag' like *Sviet*, warmly commended the visit. Surely this was sufficient cause to have doubts? See *New Age*, 4 July 1908, p. 181.
[4] *Manchester Guardian*, 5 and 6 June 1908.
[5] *Daily News*, 5 June 1908.

that Grey appeared indifferent to liberty and was thus separated sharply from the Liberal tradition in foreign policy that Palmerston, Russell and Gladstone had maintained. Only a mind which had failed to grasp the elements of Liberalism 'would dispute the right to allow sympathy for the victims of Russian autocracy to govern the degree of cordiality to be shown in relations with the Russian Government'.[1]

Attitudes towards Russia exacerbated differences of outlook within the Radical camp. On the one hand there were those who subscribed to the old Cobdenite Radicalism. At the time, this particular theme in Radical thinking was best represented by the *Manchester Guardian*. On the other hand, *The Nation* represented a more impatient Radicalism prepared to sever its ties with a tradition it found increasingly irksome, embarrassing and outmoded. In May, when *The Nation* had discussed the possibility of Britain's involvement in a new Triple Alliance, it had pointed out with evident satisfaction that 'of the three cardinal points of the Manchester doctrine—free trade, non-intervention in the affairs of Europe, and laisser-faire in internal politics—only the first remains. It is an evolution which the modern Liberal welcomes in principle. . . . Non-intervention was a sterile and impracticable ideal.'[2]

Despite intense Labour and Radical pressure, the two monarchs met at Reval. From that moment the expression Triple Entente, signifying the network of understandings between England, France and Russia, enjoyed common currency. Leo Maxse was happy to assert that now it was the duty of patriotic Englishmen to form as firm and faithful a friendship with Russia as with France.[3] *The Times* pointed out that understandings readily became the parents of alliances should unjustifiable aggression by others ever render alliances necessary.[4] Radicals and Socialists alike shrank from this project. Though they differed in matters of detail, most Radical journals now reverted to supporting a policy of isolationism. Regardless of those principles which had hitherto guided Britain's foreign policy, Grey had adopted 'an ignoble policy of alliance and intrigue . . . to forestall German ambitions'.[5] It was *The Nation* that gave the

---

[1] *The Nation*, 6 and 13 June 1908.
[2] *The Nation*, 30 May 1908.
[3] *National Review*, June 1908, p. 506.
[4] *The Times*, 11 June 1908.
[5] *New Age*, 18 July 1908, p. 224. The presence of Fisher and Sir John French in Edward's suite meant only one thing to continental observers—military and naval conversations between Russia and Britain. Here was proof of the true European significance of the Anglo-Russian convention. There was widespread alarm in Germany that there might be war. The Kaiser remarked at a military review at Döberitz: 'Yes, it now appears as though they want to

lead to the other Radical journals in discerning exactly what lay behind Britain's foreign policy. It was not that Grey had aggressive designs towards Germany, but he seemed to believe that war with Germany was inevitable and it was this that governed and explained the man's whole strategy.

> He sees the risk to European Peace from German ambitions and he raises against that danger barrier behind barrier, and after insurance, reinsurance . . . he seems to be nervously seeking for allies on the Continent. . . . A more dangerous policy than his of isolating a formidable and alert Power, it would be hard to conceive. . . . Such preparations against the 'inevitable' war . . . tend to realise the fear that has become an obsession.[1]

With talk of a Triple Entente having become general,[2] even the *Manchester Guardian* showed signs of being prepared to abandon its former, so-called 'responsible', approach to questions of foreign policy that had manifested itself in the piecemeal examination of world events and a distrust of general theories. Now it declared its concern that the Anglo-Russian Convention appeared to have been the prelude to a general understanding with Russia in Europe. There was also concern that Parliament had not been offered a frank and simple explanation of the general tendencies of Britain's foreign policy.[3]

Radical opposition to the Liberal Government's Russian policy was ineffectual because, unlike the Labour party, they enjoyed no simple unanimity of approach on this subject.[4] The interests of several groups pulled disconcertingly in opposite directions. Thus those Radicals whose major concern was the problem of subject races struggling to be rid of the yoke of Turkish oppression saw in the Anglo-Russian Convention an opportunity to breathe more life into the moribund Liberal policy of friendship towards Russia. This could be employed to bring pressure upon the Turks for reform and at the same time control Austro-German meddling in Balkan affairs.

For years peace in the East had been maintained on the basis of an understanding between Austria and Russia. When, in January 1908, the Porte conceded the Sandjak Railway to Austria, the Balkan

---

encircle us. We will know how to bear that. The German has never fought better than when he has had to defend himself on all sides. Just let them attack. We are ready.' See Carroll, 578 and n.28.
[1] *The Nation*, 13 June 1908, pp. 369–70.
[2] See, for example, Ellis Barker, 'The Triple Entente and the Triple Alliance', *Nineteenth Century*, lvix, July 1908, pp. 1ff.
[3] *Manchester Guardian*, July 1908.
[4] For the more 'veteran' Radicals like Loreburn and Courtney who supported

Radicals considered that in a move to realise the old Pan-German dream of Salonika being made a great Austro-German port, the Austrians had violated not merely the spirit of the agreement between them and Russia but had betrayed the cause of Macedonian reform. Given these circumstances, the Balkan Radicals were not slow in realising the advantages that might flow from Anglo-Russian alignment.[1] Thus, while most Radicals were highly indignant that King Edward should visit the Tsar at Reval, the Balkan Radicals supported the move enthusiastically. W. A. Moore, Secretary of the Balkan Committee, wrote in the *Albany Review* for August 1908 that the Anglo-Russian entente merited the 'warmest approbation of all lovers of peace in Great Britain'.[2]

When G. P. Gooch in the Commons demanded that Grey should speak out on Britain taking Russia as a partner in Macedonian reform,[3] Grey responded with a defence of his policy which included a rebuke for Austria.[4] This speech won a warm response from Radicals of all shades of opinion and interest. Then events gave yet another twist to the situation. In July 1908, the Young Turk revolution broke out in Constantinople. It was Grey who, in debate in the Commons, gave a lead to Radical opinion which they were glad to accept. The Foreign Secretary welcomed the new development in Turkey and while he counselled caution declared that his sympathy was with those who at long last were trying to introduce much needed reform.[5] *The Nation* recanted its earlier criticism of the Foreign Secretary. He had 'never made a better speech'. Those who in the past had been his critics would be 'the first to thank him for the utterances which were the expression of the best impulses of English public opinion'.[6] Radical enthusiasm for the Young Turk movement was unbounded. Their revolution saved the embarrassment of those who, while they deplored the association of Liberal England with autocratic Russia,

---

the Convention with Russia, it was largely a question of priorities. As the *Manchester Guardian* put it, while cautioning Grey not to bring Russia and Britain any closer together: 'the policy of Agreement with Russia is valuable because its effect . . . is to diminish very sensibly the risks of a European war': 2 Sept. 1907. This group of Radicals who formed a new Russian Committee which vied for Radical support with the more extreme 'Friends of Russian Freedom', was well disposed to the Russian moderates. As to the Tsar, they pitied rather than hated him. See Kate Courtney to Mrs Byles, 17 May 1909, *Courtney Collection*, vol x, fol. 34; Diary entry 14 July 1909, Vol. xxxiii, p. 154. For a variety of views on policy towards Russia, see Symposium of Dilke, Brailsford and Nevinson, 'The King and the Tsar', *Socialist Review* July 1908.
[1] See *Albany Review*, Mar. 1908, pp. 718-19; *Daily News*, 27 May 1908.
[2] *Albany Review*, Aug. 1908, p. 560.
[3] *Hansard*, iv:184:1663ff.   [4] *Hansard*, iv:184:1992ff.
[5] *Ibid.*, iv:193:965.   [6] *The Nation*, 1 Aug. 1908, p. 627.

nevertheless realised the value of that relationship to achieve reforms in Macedonia. Now that desired end could be realised without any need for cooperation with Russia. The Young Turk revolution meant that Macedonia would at last be afforded relief from the cruelty and disorder imposed by Turkish rule. The succeeding months served to confirm for the Radicals their wisdom in supporting the Young Turks. They appeared to be pursuing a policy that was both wise and moderate. Then, suddenly, in October 1908, Austria annexed Bosnia Herzegovina and Bulgaria chose that moment to declare her independence of Turkey.

In the name of the sanctity of treaties, Grey strongly protested at Austria's action. For the moment all parties in Britain were united in their denunciation of Austria and their support for Grey. *New Age* went so far as to claim that there had not been a single event 'in the last hundred years which has called forth so unanimous condemnation from every section of the British community' as had these 'various *coups de mains* in the Balkans'.[1] *The Nation* wholeheartedly approved 'the directness and manliness of Sir Edward Grey's attitude'. He had saved Europe from the danger of acquiescence in the Austrian coup. If England was to help the Young Turks, then it would depend upon Grey's 'ability to keep Russia within the Liberal camp'. The crisis had served to 'consolidate the Triple Entente of England, Russia and France'. *The Nation* accepted that it would be 'a mistake to suppose that either public or official opinion in Russia share the disinterested and sympathetic attitude of England towards the Young Turk movement', and Grey's task remained 'at best one of the utmost delicacy'. However, so far Grey had done well, and he should be given 'every encouragement to pursue the policy that he so bravely and opportunely began'.[2] Grey's Labour critics were not so ready to abandon their reservations about the wisdom or the good faith of the Foreign Secretary. They made it no secret that they were more concerned about the problems of unemployment in England than a double *coup d'état* in the Balkans. If England had managed to come through the immediate crisis cleanhanded then one could depend upon it that the result had been due more to good luck than sound judgment. The incident had served once more to reveal 'the nefarious complicity of Russia and Germany, the hypocrisy of the Concert of Europe, and was a grievous reminder of Europe's unhealed sores and the possibility of perils and surprises still in store'.[3]

The Nation had declared its doubts as to the possibility of any

---

[1] *New Age*, 17 Oct. 1908, p. 485.   [2] *The Nation*, 17 and 24 Oct. 1908.
[3] *Labour Leader*, 9 Oct. 1908, p. 648.

intimate rapprochement between Russia and Britain, but for the moment the diplomacy of the Central Powers was thoroughly discredited in Radical eyes. It was enough that Russia had been 'detached from Austrian intrigue', and the Radicals were not immediately concerned with the effect that this might have upon Anglo-German relations. Meanwhile, the Balkan Committee maintained its fervid support of the Young Turks, sending them messages of congratulation, delegates to the opening session of newly democratic Turkey's first Parliament, and producing propaganda full of extravagant praise for the new régime.[1]

While Radical applause for Grey's initial stand against Austria's action had been loud, it was not long-lasting. Instead of the crisis coming to a head, it continued to drag on and was a constant reminder of the uneasy state of relations between the great Powers. It was for this reason, rather than the intrinsic rights or wrongs of the Balkan problem, that many Radicals had to reassess the attitude they had adopted. At the beginning of the crisis they had been obtuse in not recognising Grey's actions would inevitably widen the divide between the Triple Entente and the Central Powers. At a time when they should have concerned themselves with the wider implications of the situation, they concentrated on the infraction of international law. Thus, ignoring the obvious uneasiness of the German Foreign Office, they praised Grey as 'the guardian spirit of international law'. By 1910, when Radical efforts were concentrated on the problem of rapprochement between Germany and Britain, they were anxious to state that Grey's legalistic attitude over Bosnia Herzegovina had almost driven Europe into war. Yet when Britain's entente partner, Russia, crushed Finland, nothing was said. Could it be that Grey demanded higher standards of Germany than of France or Russia?[2] Surely, they argued, if Grey really had been determined to act briskly and firmly, the problem would not have dragged on interminably, poisoning relations between Britain and Germany. Immediate anger at Germany's actions had been justified. It had been nothing less than the just course to support the concept of the sanctity of treaties and to protect nascent democracy in Turkey in the form of the Young Turk movement. But it became increasingly difficult for Radicals to continue condemning Austria week in week out when the Jingo Press was doing just that in an attempt to justify a massive increase in naval armaments and to arouse fear and hatred of Germany

---

[1] See *inter alia*, C. R. Buxton, *Turkey in Revolution* (1909), *passim;* Victoria de Bunsen, *Charles Roden Buxton* (1948), 54ff; *The Times*, 9 and 28 Oct. 1908.
[2] See *Manchester Guardian*, 6 and 8 Oct. 1908 and *The Nation*, 'Our ally', 23 April, 1910; and 'The Duma and Finland', 11 June 1910.

to fever pitch. From the beginning of the crisis some Radicals had believed that Austria's action ought to have been accepted as a *fait accompli*. After all, a case could be stated justifying Austria's action. The so-called coup was no more than the establishment of a *de jure* claim for what had been Austria's *de facto* sovereignty in Bosnia. Even those Radicals who had been most uncompromising in their criticism of Austria, as the crisis continued, tempered their comments. The *Manchester Guardian* so changed the tone of its editorial comment on the Bosnian crisis that by December it was claiming that to lecture Austria on her wickedness was 'a form of cant being very much overdone'.[1]

At first, Radicals had lent their tacit if not enthusiastic support for Foreign Office cooperation with Russia against Austria. As the months passed, they grew increasingly concerned that Grey's policy was putting Austria into quarantine. This would effectively obstruct the restoration of the Concert of Europe, an ideal dear to the hearts of all Radicals. By January 1909 even *The Nation* was prepared to admit that Austria's actions were understandable if one took into account 'the pronounced anti-German flavour of our foreign policy'. That there had been no direct encounter between Berlin and London did not reflect credit on Edward Grey but was due largely to 'the reticence and self-suppression of German diplomacy'. The 'most deplorable feature' of the whole crisis had been 'the marked isolation of Germany'.[2]

In a letter to *The Times*,[3] Leonard Courtney questioned whether even Grey's initial action had been correct. This was to do no more than echo the sentiments bluntly professed by Dilke in the Commons. Grey had made altogether too much fuss over the actions of Austria and Bulgaria. Dissension was rife in the Radical camp. While Courtney and his friend, Sir Edward Fry, took one another to task over questions of law and morality in the letter columns of *The Times*, that newspaper took pleasure in pointing out Radical dissension, and admonished 'the school that never weary of exhorting the unregenerate to put not their trust in armies and fleets but in international law and arbitration tribunals'.[4] In February, with the accelerating naval armaments crisis causing more immediate concern to the Radicals than the fate of Bosnia Herzegovina, *The Nation*, reviewing the whole episode, claimed that the cause of the trouble in the Balkans had been the inability of the British Government to even

---

[1] Cf. *Manchester Guardian*, 6 Oct., 10 and 17 Nov. and 3 Dec. 1908.
[2] *The Nation*, 9 Jan. and 6 Feb. 1909.   [3] *The Times*, Jan 1909.
[4] Quoted Gooch, *Courtney*, 555.

attempt to secure German cooperation in European affairs. A stable equilibrium in Europe was impossible so long as Britain pursued a policy of boycott and isolation towards Germany and Austria. Germany had a leading place in Europe's affairs and it was fatuous to attempt to settle a question like the Balkans without consulting her interests. Grey may have been satisfied because somehow he had managed to keep the peace, but this had been achieved at a price. He was 'leaving for his successor a heritage of problems and temptations which it should have been the first object of Liberal policy to remove'.[1]

It was not in the Balkans alone that Britain's new-found partnership with Russia caused anxiety to Radical and Labour critics. By the terms of the Anglo-Russian Convention, both signatories had pledged that they would respect Persia's integrity and independence. The Radicals constituted themselves the guarantors of that pledge. To have done less, they would have maintained, was to ignore both their right and duty. A Persian Committee was set up with H. F. B. Lynch as its chairman and Edward Granville Browne, an authority on Persia and an avowed opponent of the Anglo-Russian Convention, as vice chairman. In the Commons, Lynch enjoyed the support of among others John Dillon, Vickerman Rutherford, Philip Morrell and Arthur Ponsonby.

Shortly after the Reval meeting of King Edward and the Tsar, the Shah of Persia, Mohammed Ali, who since his succession in January 1907 had been conducting a campaign against a constitutionalist movement in his country, with the aid of a Russian Colonel, Liakhoff, and his band of Cossacks, arrested some members of the Persian Parliament and destroyed the palace where Parliament met. English Radical opinion was incensed by this outrage. The *Manchester Guardian*, which had given its support to Grey at the time of the Reval visit, now urged on the Foreign Secretary the importance of insisting that the Russian Government recall their troops in Persia. For Russia to retain her troops in Persia any longer was to endanger

---

[1] *The Nation*, 6 Feb. 1909; see also unfinished letter by Courtney intended for publication in *The Times* but not sent. *Courtney Collection*, vol. 10, fol. 32. 'What has been the outcome of the excited language and diplomatic gesticulation of Ministers, of politicians and of the Press? After months of heated feeling we find ourselves landed in a far less guarded acceptance of the annexation of Bosnia and Herzegovina than was open to us at the outset. We have excited the animosity . . . of almost every section of opinion in Austria Hungary, we are regarded with no gratitude in Servia and . . . we seem to have developed some additional and quite unnecessary roughness of friction between ourselves and Germany. . . . Why could we not have seen this at once—that overpowering logic of events that we recognise today, and have been a pacificator working with that other pacificator, Germany, from the beginning instead of being dragged into acquiescence . . .?'

not only the Persian constitution but also the Anglo-Russian Convention.[1] *The Nation*, when reviewing Grey's Asiatic policy, had concluded more in anger than in sorrow that he had abandoned 'the old Liberal policy of supporting struggling nationalities' for 'a series of deals between expanding Empires'.[2]

The situation in Persia continued to deteriorate and Grey was given a torrid time in the Commons by his Radical, Labour and Irish critics. By January 1909 the Shah's enemies had considerably strengthened their position in the provinces. The Shah was now isolated both from north and south Persia. *Novoe Vremya* claimed that there should be intervention to prevent a 'palace tragedy and wholesale uprisings'. Foreign councillors should be appointed to all the departments of state. The Radicals were outraged that Russia should even contemplate such measures. They were determined that Persia should not be turned into another Egypt under a condominium.[3] The *Manchester Guardian* maintained all that was required to settle Persia's affairs was for the British and Russian Governments to leave well alone. The Persians were quite capable of settling their own dispute.[4] *The Times* might assert that complete confidence could be placed in Grey's and Isvolsky's intentions as they 'did not desire to interfere with Persia's internal affairs to a greater degree than could be helped', but no Radical was prepared to accept the prospect of intervention with equanimity. *The Nation* warned Grey that there would be tragic consequences for Britain's credit in the East if she was seen to comply with Isvolsky's policy in Persia.[5]

When, in February, Grey firmly rejected Russian proposals for a joint Anglo-Russian loan to the Shah, the Radicals assumed that the Foreign Secretary's action had been dictated by their campaign. Grey outlined the contents of the memorandum he had sent the Russians when replying in the Commons to a question put to him by Dillon.[6] Grey stated that he had determined the best course to be followed was that Britain should stand entirely aloof from the internal affairs of Persia. Naturally, *The Nation* found this answer 'very reassuring'.[7] However, within a month Grey's fortunes with the critics of his Persian policy had slumped again. Russian columns intervened in the relief of Tabriz. Despite this temporary reversal, fortune favoured the nationalist cause. Under the inspired leadership of Sardar Assad they determined to push on to the capital, Tehran.

[1] *Manchester Guardian*, 1 July 1908.
[2] *The Nation*, 27 June 1908.   [3] *Ibid.*, 16 Jan. 1909.
[4] See *Manchester Guardian*, 2, 13, 20, 22 and 25 Jan. 1909.
[5] *The Nation*, 23 Jan. 1909.   [6] *Hansard*, v:1:709.
[7] *The Nation*, 27 Feb. 1909.

Russian intervention was inevitable, and protest though they might, there was nothing that the Radicals could do. As Grey was committed to the larger issues involved in the entente principle, he was hardly in a position to exercise influence or urge restraint upon the Russians. In the Commons, Grey eventually was forced to deny that the Anglo-Russian Convention in any way made Britain responsible for Russian behaviour in Persia.[1] The Radicals were not convinced. Granville Browne in a letter to the *Manchester Guardian* assured its readers that there were no limits to Grey's compliance to the Tsar's Government.[2]

The Persian Nationalists were successful in forcing an entry to Tehran. They deposed the Shah who fled to exile in Odessa, all this before the Russian forces, who were encamped many miles to the north of Tehran, could even be mobilised. That the crisis finally had been resolved as the Radicals would have wished was in no part due to Grey. The whole episode had done nothing to increase the Foreign Secretary's credit with the Radicals. On the contrary, it had done much to increase their suspicion that his behaviour could only be accounted for by some design that he had explained neither to his Party nor the country.

> All true friends of Persia will rejoice that the desperate struggle
> . . . has culminated in a Nationalist victory . . . Sir Edward
> Grey's excuse [for Russian intervention] was a diplomatic one
> and too transparent to deceive anyone. . . . Grey is a diplomat
> of the type characteristic of the old régime—a man incapable of
> generous sentiment on behalf of struggling nationalities. . . .
> As a statesmen he is shortsighted and morally deficient.[3]

But as far as the Labour party was concerned, the apparent conclusion of the Persian episode was not the nadir of Grey's fortunes in 1909. They were never as quick to forgive or forget Grey's actions as were the Radicals.

It was unfortunate enough that Britain's diplomacy had been tarnished by Edward's visit to the Tsar at Reval. At no price was the Labour Party prepared to accept a return visit by the Tsar to England. They would have nothing to do with 'the hanging Tsar . . . a callous autocrat whose rule is branded with infamy'.[4] In June the Independent Labour party had issued a manifesto that had declared roundly 'the Russian régime is blacker and bloodier than ever'. On Sunday, 25 July, the whole spectrum of English Socialist opinion was represented at a meeting in Trafalgar Square where the speakers

---

[1] *Hansard*, v:7:1829.   [2] *Manchester Guardian*, 12 July 1909.
[3] *Labour Leader*, 16 July 1909, p. 456.   [4] *Ibid*.

joined in condemning, not only the visit of the Tsar and 'his infernal régime', but also Grey, whom Shaw pronounced, 'the worst Foreign Minister England ever had'.[1] *New Age* responded to this claim.

> From Denshawai to Cowes it is difficult to recall a single act of Sir Edward Grey's that has been characterised, we will not say by liberality, but even by Liberalism . . . If England is to resume her place and lead the Liberal van, then Grey must be called upon to abdicate his dishonourable pre-eminence. Down, we say, with the Tsar! Down with Sir Edward Grey![2]

In the month of the Tsar's visit to Cowes, *New Age* developed a comprehensive estimate of Grey's policy that was inspired by twin themes—the intimate relationship between foreign and domestic policy;[3] and Britain's declining status as a leading nation in the world's affairs. *New Age* declared that the conduct of foreign policy was not an abstract science disassociated from everyday life. On the contrary it was 'the nation writ large in action'. Inevitably, the visit of the Tsar could only be followed by 'an impetus to reaction no less severe than in his own unhappy country'. Foreign policy was being dictated by 'payment for the uncertain neutrality of Russia'. Grey was 'conniving' at Russian control of Persia while assuring the Commons to the contrary. Everything followed as a result of the 'unholy alliance between Britain and Russia' that had so sapped Britain's pride and honour that 'we tremble in our shoes when we hear that the Tsar has said "Good morning" to the Kaiser'. England had 'nothing to gain and much to lose' from association with Russia. Britain's leaders were being 'reckless of the nation's good name, prestige . . . and self respect'.[4] For a journal designed to attract an intelligent, *avant-garde* readership, *New Age* showed a surprising lack of stamina when pursuing general theories, and too easily abandoned ideas to score polemical points. Thus, after the Tsar's visit, instead of developing their thesis about Grey, they lapsed once more into offence. Grey was 'merely a blank in the English mind; a nothing, a gaping hollow, a misunderstanding'. His foreign policy supposedly subtle was 'in reality incomprehensible. He does not understand it himself

---

[1] Reports of meeting in *Labour Leader*, 30 July 1909, p. 494; *New Age*, 5 Aug. 1909, p. 271.
[2] *New Age*, 5 Aug. 1909, p. 278.
[3] This particular theme was later most explicitly spelled out by G. H. Perris. 'These things depend upon each other and involve each other; it is inevitable as soon as the logic of social life becomes explicit, that the men who wish to retain their own feudal powers and privileges should resort to mischief-making on international relations, and appeals for ruinous expenditure upon unnecessary armaments.' *Concord*, xxvi, no. 1, Jan. 1910, p. 1.
[4] *New Age*, 1 July 1909, p. 190; 8 July, p. 210; 15 July, p. 231; and 29 July, p. 263.

and nobody can understand it for the simple reason there is nothing to understand. The *Daily Mail* is more competent than Sir Edward Grey to pursue a foreign policy and that is the most offensive remark we can make.'[1]

Some Radicals were loath to criticise the Tsar's visit. Yet, even in those quarters where normally there was hesitation felt in censuring Grey, the Tsar's visit prompted a new more vigorous criticism of the Foreign Secretary. Felix Moscheles, addressing the annual meeting of the International Arbitration and Peace Association, claimed that the only possible explanation for Britain finding it 'very desirable, in fact of paramount importance to be on good terms with the Russian Government' was that 'we are indulging in the costly luxury of preparing for war with Germany'. He upbraided those Radicals like MacCallum Scott, secretary of the Radical Parliamentary Russian Committee, who had resigned from that body because he was convinced that the Russian Liberals desired the Tsar's visit. 'No policy', avowed Moscheles, 'excuses consorting with murderers.'

> The Peace Movement has no higher duty than to tell the truth about these affairs—the truth cannot insult or injure any honest man. All virtue will be gone from the cause if we water down truth to a canting compliance or put it in chains to some superstitious 'reason of State'. . . . It is a question of conscience, and Britain ought to summon the courage to denounce criminal misrule when and wherever it is practised.[2]

Labour and Radical protests were ineffectual. The Tsar paid his visit to Cowes. However, *The Nation* claimed that not all had been lost. 'England . . . despite the decay of the old traditions', had acted 'as a sort of Euripidean chorus in front of the continental stage. The nation's mind had been expressed elsewhere' than in

> The hole and corner homage we have crawled like slaves to pay
> Where the Tsar had found shelter in the steel encircled bay.
> Judge then how Britons love thee, when her moneybags give voice
> To acclaim thy gracious visit to the land of Freedom's choice.[3]

The salute of naval guns at Cowes had not been a national welcome; and the freedom of the City of London that had been given the Tsar, enshrined 'no more than the hopes of the financiers'. As to an *entente cordiale* with Russia, that 'was not yet in sight'.[4] G. H. Perris,

---

[1] *New Age*, 12 Aug. 1909, p. 294.
[2] Reported in *Concord*, xxv, no. 7/8, July/Aug. 1909, p. 78.
[3] A reader's 'poem' published in *Labour Leader*, 23 July 1909, p. 470.
[4] *The Nation*, 7 Aug. 1909.

in an open letter to Grey published in the *Labour Leader*, poured scorn on Grey's 'policy of the Triple Entente against the Triple Alliance'. It was a 'miserable failure', for 'Pichon, Bülow, Aehrenthal, and even that poor rogue Isvolsky, all bettered you. . . . When I am told you have kept the peace I cannot but recall the costs and risks of your great game of Encirclement. Failure, Sir, is the lot of the best; but the friendship of the Tsar is a distinction odious beyond all mere failures.'[1]

What purpose lay behind Grey's policy of friendship towards Russia? What claim had he to pursuing a Liberal foreign policy when 'from Algeciras to Casablanca and from Reval to Cowes', he 'followed in Lord Lansdowne's footsteps', and 'nowhere bettered his precept and example'?[2] *The Nation* believed it knew the answer. Grey's sole concern was to find continental allies for Britain. If this hypothesis was correct then it helped to make sense of a number of otherwise unusual and unexplained features of recent British diplomacy. Why, for example, had Grey refused to press more urgently for reforms in the Congo? Could it be that he was reluctant to exert pressure on French financiers who had considerable interests in the Congo and were known to be influential in the counsels of the French Government? The Triple Entente had insured 'the penetration of Morocco and the virtual partition of Persia, but it fails when our purpose is to employ an influence in any humane service'. Russia's offences were condoned 'for the simple reason that our whole policy abroad is now subordinated to the one object of consolidating the Triple Entente against the German Alliance'. Grey in the name of Britain was subscribing to a 'policy of groups', the balance of power theory that was 'in flat contradiction of the idea of a European concert'.[3]

If *The Nation* was correct in its analysis of the principles that guided Grey's policy, then it was hardly surprising that Radicals and Socialists would not support the Foreign Secretary. They were determinedly opposed to the theory of a balance of power in Europe. For them it remained, as it had been for Bright, a 'false idol' and a 'foul fetish'. Such a policy could have 'neither finality nor rest . . . only an endless vista of shifting forces and a hopeless prospect of increasing armaments'. If such a policy were pursued it 'could never lead to a "League of Peace" '. Above all other considerations, it 'negated the idea of a Concert of Europe'.[4] On all grounds, moral

[1] *Labour Leader*, 30 July, 1909 p. 489.
[2] *Ibid.*; cf. *The Nation*, 15 and 22 Jan. 1910.
[3] *The Nation*, 26 June 1909.
[4] *Ibid.*, 25 May 1909.

and practical, the concept of a balance of power was totally unacceptable. To hold fast to that theory was 'to condemn Britain in
advance to a succession of wars, for an artificial equilibrium' would
'always be upset in obedience to natural laws of growth'.[1] Even if
for a moment it could be supposed that such a policy was practicable,
the price demanded was far too high. There was not merely the
question of constantly escalating armament costs, but the liberty of
peoples rightly struggling to be free in Persia and North Africa, in
the Congo and in Russia. Britain would be bound to less scrupulous
Powers where otherwise she might have spoken freely and acted in-
dependently, and thus given the lead to all men who loved liberty
and peace. What advantage could be counted from such a policy?
In Russia, Grey had given 'another lease of life to foul tyranny',
and in Europe 'enhanced those jealousies which divided . . . [it]
into two armed camps'.[2] In the diplomatic world of give and take,
Britain was following a policy 'which at the present seems to be
mostly giving'.[3] What possible case could be made for a defensive
alignment between a sea Power like Britain, and France and Russia
which were pre-eminently land Powers? Russia was too distant for
Britain to afford her effective military aid. To be of any practical
use to France, Britain would have to adopt conscription, and that
was unthinkable. If any event, the entente with France had been
designed for 'the advancement of the liberal ideals of peace and
social reform'.[4] Certainly, it had not been prompted by military
considerations. What possible reason could Grey have for his obsessive concern with Germany's intentions? The Kaiser had frequently avowed his love for England. Nor was there any valid
economic reason why Britain should beware of Germany. If one
only ignored the unreasoned braying of both countries' Jingo Press,
it was patent that the democracies ardently wished for peace. In
short, the Radicals were in no way convinced of the reality of a
'German menace' which apparently was the mainspring of Grey's
whole policy.

Temporarily, Radical optimism had been shaken by the display
of Teutonic strength at the time of the Bosnian crisis. But even then
their talk had been not of the insurance afforded by the Triple
Entente but of the advantages of a policy of isolation.[5] A Triple
Entente offered more to France and Russia than to Britain. The

---

[1] *U.D.C. Pamphlet* (1916), no. 14a, p. 22.
[2] *Concord*, xxvi, no. 1, Jan. 1910, p. 2.
[3] *Manchester Guardian*, 24 Sept. 1910.   [4] *Ibid.*, 27 Jan. 1908.
[5] See, for example, *The Nation*, 3 Apr. and 17 July 1909; *Manchester Guardian*,
17 May 1909.

general consensus of Radical opinion was that Britain had chosen
unwisely. From the beginning the bargain had been a poor one. It
would be better to recognise that Germany was the leading Power in
Europe and have her as a friend than 'to coquet with the idea . . . of
forming European combinations against [her]'.[1] The significance
of the Bosnian crisis was that it marked the first important diplomatic victory the Central Powers had won since the formation of the
ententes between Britain, Russia and France. When Isvolsky unconditionally surrendered to Germany's demands, Grey had been
put in an embarrassing position. It was he who had been responsible
for creating the apparent solidarity of the Triple Entente. Now, as
Bülow had foreseen, it had collapsed, and the futility of Grey's
diplomatic stratagems seemed revealed to all. With France accepting Germany's terms, England had no choice but to abandon her
efforts to secure satisfaction for Serbia. 'A sad ending', Nicolson
noted. But the most significant fact remained that France dragged
her feet from the beginning and had chosen to settle her Moroccan
difficulties with Germany in the middle of the crisis. Nicolson could
not have been more pessimistic in his overall assessment of the
diplomatic situation. The hegemony of the Central Powers in Europe
seemed assured and England once more stood isolated. 'The Franco-
Russian alliance had not borne the test: and the Anglo-Russian
entente [was] not sufficiently deep-rooted to have any appreciable
influence.'[2]

E. J. Dillon, who had always been a sympathetic critic of Grey's
policy, claimed that the Bosnian crisis heralded a new epoch in
European affairs. The notion that a union of Slav, Anglo-Saxon and
Gaul was strong had been exploded. The conduct during the crisis
of the member Powers of the Triple Entente, suggested that a

---

[1] *Manchester Guardian*, 7 July 1909.
[2] Nicolson, *Lord Carnock*, 305. Nicolson strongly supported the idea that the
ententes should be turned into alliances. He constantly urged this on his
master. He had been checked by the Foreign Office for using the term 'Triple
Entente' in his official correspondence. Neither Hardinge nor Grey thought it
desirable that the ententes should be turned into alliances; there were too
many practical difficulties as Hardinge pointed out. 'There is no hope of this
while the present government is in office in this country. I am almost certain
that certain members of the Cabinet assiduously spread a report that in the
event of a general conflagration, England should stand aside. I mention this
to show how impossible it is to hope for a step forward by the government to
a closer entente or even alliance with Russia. . . . When Balfour comes into
office it may be different, but we must hope that it may not be too late':
Hardinge to Nicolson, 12 Apr. 1909; quoted Steiner, 97. Nicolson's extreme
pro-Russian orientation was to undermine his influence at the Foreign Office
when he became Permanent Under Secretary, a post for which he was unsuited
and had accepted with reluctance. See Nicolson, *Lord Carnock*, 334; and Lord
Vansittart, *The Mist Procession* (1958), 99.

prodigious and perilous mistake had been made.[1] Rosebery, whose heart, according to Churchill, responded 'instinctively to any re-adjustment or disturbance of the balance of power',[2] roused himself from retirement long enough to pronounce that Europe was heading for catastrophe and that men were living in the calm before the storm.[3] But the months passed and the storm did not break. The former sharp divisions between entente partners and the Central Powers seemed to blur and merge. Some Radicals, who in the heat of the crisis had trembled on the edge of apostasy,[4] once more strengthened their resolve. Rejecting the incessant cries of the Tories that Germany was a menace to Europe's peace and order, they once more adopted an optimistic view assuming that as the threatened blow had not materialised then international affairs must have taken a turn for the better. Though 'there had been plenty of explosive material always at hand', and though large issues had been 'mis-handled by decorated ephemeral personages', when Radicals looked back at 1909 they found that 'its most comforting distinction' was that despite the efforts of the Jingoes 'there had been no great war'.[5]

In 1910 all the indications were that the international situation was perceptibly improving. In the Congo there was reason to sup-pose at last that there would be a settlement. The Foreign Office was prepared to support new reform plans and was afforded the cordial encouragement of the United States of America and to a certain extent that of Germany. With the death of Leopold II and the accession of a new King of the Belgians who was popularly credited with having liberal tendencies, the worst obstacles to a more humane régime seemed to have been removed. In the course of but a few months the problem of Congo reform had undergone a dramatic change and E. D. Morel's agitation seemed to be bearing fruit.[6] In Turkey there were still elements in the situation that were cause for anxiety, but it would have been foolish and unjust to entertain any-thing other than the highest expectations. 'If we cannot settle our own feudal magnates in a single session of Parliament, it is absurd to look for a sudden transformation of the varied communities that stretch from the Balkans to Baghdad, and from Mount Ararat to

[1] *Contemporary Review*, xcv, May 1909, p. 619.
[2] W. S. Churchill, *Great Contemporaries* (reprint edn, 1941), 17.
[3] For accounts of this extraordinary speech, see J. A. Spender, *Life, Journalism and Politics*, i, 227; Rhodes James, 471–2.
[4] *The Nation*, for example, at one point (3 April 1909), talked of 'policy having outrun armaments'.
[5] *Concord*, xxvi, no. 1, 1910, p. 1.
[6] See S. J. S. Cookey, *Britain and the Congo Question* (1968), 208ff.

the Red Sea.'[1] At the very least, Turkey now had a centre of regular government, and discussion between parties was open.

In Persia, 'though viciously handicapped by our alliance with the Russian land grabbers', the Nationalists had won a dramatic and complete success. In Morocco, matters at last seemed to be settled by the Franco-German agreement. The replacement of Prince von Bülow as Chancellor by Bethmann-Hollweg, as far as the Radicals were concerned, could hardly have been bettered, and in Bethmann's early diplomatic actions they discerned 'encouraging evidence that the new Chancellor intend[ed] to improve upon the record of his predecessor'.[2]

In Russia, Isvolsky, dispirited by his personal humiliation in the Bosnian crisis, welcomed the opportunity of retiring as Foreign Minister to become ambassador in Paris. In September 1910 he was replaced by Sazonov, a man who was under no illusions as to why the British Government had been keen to maintain its Convention with Russia. Sazonov, together with the Tsar, hastened to meet the Kaiser at Potsdam. The German Emperor was accompanied by Kiderlen. The Germans, in return for a written assurance that Germany was neither obligated nor prepared to side with Austria, asked Russia to pledge in writing that she did not favour England's anti-German policy. This request Sazonov steadfastly refused. However, this refusal did not confound the resources of German diplomacy. With the active aid of Tardieu and possibly Isvolsky,[3] news of a 'Potsdam Agreement' was 'leaked' to the Press. The lie was given official confirmation by Bethmann-Hollweg when on 10 December he assured the Reichstag that a definite agreement had been reached between Russian and Germany. In future neither Power would enter a hostile combination against the other. The *Daily News* concluded that Bethmann-Hollweg's statement meant that the Triple Entente once and for all had been repudiated. The *Manchester Guardian* was not prepared to go quite so far in its estimate of the implications of the German Chancellor's speech. They welcomed the agreement between Russia and Germany which implied for them no disloyalty to the entente but proof that the two Power blocs were interpenetrable. As such there was no danger that the entente system would ever be converted into a military alliance.[4]

---

[1] *Concord*, xxvi, no. 1, Jan. 1910, pp. 2–3.   [2] *Ibid.*
[3] See Taylor, *The Struggle for Mastery in Europe*, 464.
[4] Cf. *Daily News* and *Manchester Guardian*, 11 Jan. 1911. Weinroth, *op. cit.*, p. 673, n. 87, points out that the deduction drawn by the *Daily News* from Hollweg's speech, serves 'as an excellent example of how Radical journals tended to be carried away by declarations of statesmen'.

Radical opinion, which had always been most critical of Grey's policy towards Russia, seized upon the Potsdam agreement as proof of Russia's perfidy. Surely no one any longer could believe that by allowing Russia a free hand in Persia she would provide a reliable ally against Germany? To believe as much was to reveal a monumental ignorance of the very elements of European politics.[1]

With France and Germany composing their differences in Morocco, and Russia having made an agreement with Germany, no one could doubt the European system of ententes and alliances that during the past years had bedevilled international relationships was now in a complete state of flux. Any objective appraisal of the solidarity of the Triple Entente revealed that it had been no more than a myth which had been encouraged by Tories and Jingoes as the means of increasing Anglo-German discord. *The Nation* was almost truculent in its disavowal of Deschanel's canard, published in *Temps*, which claimed that Britain was bound to a definite concerted scheme with France and Russia that excluded any freedom of action with regard to any other Powers. The Liberal Party would never countenance such a policy.[2] The *Daily News* declared that it was ridiculous to suppose that Britain was involved in group rivalry with the Central Powers.[3] And if this was not enough, a month later the official voice of Liberalism in the shape of Spender's *Westminster Gazette*, ridiculed the idea that Britain for a moment had been diverted from her true aim in international politics to engage in rivalries and policies that only could add greatly to her liabilities while undermining her strength.[4] Conservative opinion was incensed by this Radical interpretation of the European diplomatic scene. Leo Maxse in particular raged against 'our Cocoa contemporaries who are intent upon throwing the whole of Europe into the arms of Germany'.[5] What better confirmation could there have been for the Radicals that their estimate of the international situation and of Britain's commitments was the correct one? The Radicals would have had even greater cause for good humour than Maxse's ill-tempered outburst had afforded if they had been able to read the instructions sent by Nicolson, now permanent head of the Foreign Office, to the British Ambassador at St Petersburg. Buchanan, given the opportunity, was to deny to Sazanov that the opinions expressed in *The Nation* and the *Daily News*, in any wise represented the views of the Government. The Ambassador might suggest that the inspiration for this journa-

---

[1] See *Manchester Guardian*, 12 and 13 Dec. 1910.
[2] *The Nation*, 31 Dec. 1910.   [3] *Daily News*, 29 Dec. 1910.
[4] *Westminster Gazette*, 19 Jan. 1911.   [5] *National Review*, Feb. 1911, p. 886

listic *jeu d'esprit* was none other than the German embassy in London![1]

There remained one matter that occasioned momentary concern, when a chance retort made by Pichon in the French Chamber was reported in the English Press. Pichon avowed that it would be singular for anyone to assert that the Anglo-French entente was unproductive and that the military conversations between the two countries had ceased.[2] There were a few cautionary, half-sceptical comments in the Radical Press,[3] and in March Fred Jowett asked in the Commons whether there was an undertaking, promise or understanding with France that in certain eventualities British troops would be sent to assist the French Army. He received a negative reply. When Jowett returned to the subject three weeks later, Grey informed him that the extent of Britain's obligation to France was contained in the Anglo-French Convention which had been laid before Parliament. There was no other agreement bearing upon the subject.[4] This assurance by Grey was enough to allay any lingering doubts the Radicals still might have had. Any ideas about the military understanding with France could be safely dropped. 'The idea that a military understanding is in force may now, we think, be dropped. . . . If the promise was ever given. . . . The Algeciras Convention and the Morocco Treaty between France and Germany may surely be said to have closed that chapter . . . once and for all.'[5]

[1] *D.D.* x i:637 and 640.   [2] *The Times*, Feb. 1911.
[3] See *Daily News*, 4 Feb. 1911; *The Nation*, 11 Feb. 1911.
[4] *Hansard*, v:22:1190; and v:23:1490.
[5] *Manchester Guardian*, 8 Apr. 1911. Considering the importance that the Radicals themselves were later to attach to the military conversations between the French and British Staffs, it has to be remembered that rumours of some sort of military convention were commonplace during the period 1905–11. Pichon's chance remark was therefore only the latest instalment in a continuing story. Radical attitudes to the rumour were conditioned by their immediate outlook on the diplomatic scene. Thus, when talk of the Triple Entente was general, *The Nation*, 13 June 1908, admitted 'few competent authorities doubt that we already have some military convention with France'. At times when the diplomatic outlook was bright, Radicals were only too happy to pour ridicule upon the idea. Their questions in the House of Commons, e.g. *Hansard*, v:8:705 (Dillon); v:15:769 (Byles); were never successful in eliciting the truth from ministers because they were too specific. They were looking for a 'convention' rather than 'conversations'.

New Age refused to believe the assurances of ministers, and when the subject arose again in July after a statement in the Commons by Asquith referring to 'our treaty obligations with France', Verdad, who wrote the Foreign Affairs column in the *New Age*, took the Radicals to task for their naïvety. 'As readers to this column are aware there is a military agreement drawn up practically in the form of a treaty, whereby we are bound to assist our French neighbours in the event of a war with Germany. We supply this assistance by sending from 100,000 men upwards to the German borders, via Belgium in the event of serious trouble . . . While the general Press, by Mr Asquith's reference to "treaty obligations" understands the Anglo-French Agreement of 1904, I understand this military agreement . . . about which Mr Jowett

The last ghost of Grey's Triple Entente policy seemed to have been safely laid.

Friendship with Germany

The Radical and Labour opponents of the Liberal Government's foreign policy were convinced that the first practical step that had to be taken to create amity between the divided nations of Europe was the development of sound and friendly relations between Great Britain and Germany. Somehow a way had to be found of reconciling the two nations. They were equally convinced that the prospects of reconciliation were not as bleak as the Yellow Press of both countries would have had men believe. Even at the darkest moments of Anglo-German hostility, continuing if fitful publicity had supported the idea of an Anglo-German entente. After all, the concept of an Anglo-French entente was much more of a psychological paradox than one between the two 'Anglo-Saxon' nations. 'Close connections are but natural: for we are of the same blood, and in the main of the same religion, while in fundamental characteristics no two nations resemble one another more closely than the English and the Germans.'[1] The International Arbitration and Peace Association was but one of many similar bodies that urged the Government to recognise its *duty*, 'to bring about an understanding with Germany . . . and thereby remove the danger of war and make possible some mutual arrangement for a limitation of those armaments which are such a heavy burden on the population of both countries'.[2]

No group spoke louder or longer for reconciliation with Germany than the various pacifist[3] organisations. In their attitude towards

---

vainly questioned Sir Edward Grey in the House of Commons several weeks ago. The agreement exists, but it is the duty of the Foreign Secretary to deny its existence, otherwise diplomatic complications would ensue, and such complications might result in the agreement going into effect sooner than was intended by those who drew it up.' 13 July 1911, p. 243.

[1] *Edinburgh Review*, Oct. 1909, p. 447; cf. *Manchester Guardian*, 7 June 1909. 'If our statesmen had the wit to make friendship with France and even with Russia with both of whom our political quarrels were far older and more difficult of adjustment, then why not have Germany as a friend rather than an enemy?'

[2] Executive Committee Resolution, 1 Sept. 1908.

[3] The term 'pacifist' presents enormous difficulties. The word did not become current until 1907, and its use up to 1914 was often ambiguous and lax. See Halévy, *The Rule of Democracy*, 222, n. 1. Pacifism must not be confused with the assertion that the technical condition of peace is better than war. The most ardent Jingo would frequently declare as much while urging massive increases in armament expenditure and an aggressive, forward foreign policy. The essential condition of the committed pacifist is that he should be above party. Yet manifestly, most of the effective pacifist advocates were members either of the Radical wing of the Liberal Party or the I.L.P. Therefore it is

Germany they were not the deluded innocents that their detractors made them out to be.[1] They were under no illusions as to the untrustworthiness of the German Government, and in particular the Kaiser. His character apart, he was an arbitrary monarch and therefore could never be a reliable friend of peace.[2] But, when they analysed the international situation, pacifists were always quick to draw a distinction between Governments and the people. The organisation

---

not surprising that they suffered pangs of conscience and were often confused. Edward G. Smith, writing in February 1912 about 'The complete pacifist' had this to say about the pacifist and foreign policy and party.

'Questions of Peace and War very often depend upon foreign policy, and foreign policy is, to a great extent, the affair of the party in power or the Cabinet in power, or even the Minister in power. The pacifist must regard that party, the Cabinet or that Minister without prejudice and without pity. There must be no question of "party loyalty". Party loyalty means too often a surrender of judgment or conscience, or both. The Pacifist is for no party; he is for peace. There can be for him no consideration of Toryism, Liberalism or Socialism. The Party Pacifist is a dangerous absurdity.' (See *Concord*, Feb. 1912, p. 15.) By Smith's definition, most of the recognised pacifist agencies and agents were not pacifist!

Smith was censured in subsequent issues of *Concord* for his 'too exclusive' view of pacifism. Arthur Ponsonby in *Democracy and Diplomacy* (1915), 28, made a number of pertinent observations on what he called 'pacifist advocacy'. 'Of late years the pacifists who formerly based their advocacy of peace on humanitarian and sentimental grounds have been reinforced by a very much larger section who lay more stress on the futility than on the cruelty of war, and support their contention with arguments which appeal to the financier, the economist, the sociologist, and the merchant. The result has been that an increasing number of people have become convinced that peace is the most vital and practical interest of the people, whose real enemy is no foreign nation, whatever its views may be, but the social evils which have to be continually combated at home. . . . Although this more enlightened opinion gained ground . . . it proved powerless and utterly negligible when the recent crisis (1914 war) came.'

Cf. 'description' of pacifism in *New Age*, 23 March 1911, pp. 481–2: 'There are those who yearn for universal peace and warm at its name solely because peace is cheap. Precisely the same mental phenomenon can be induced in them by the prospect of suddenly reducing the cost of any industrial article. Then there are those who advocate peace because they imagine peace is good for trade. These dwell upon Imports and Exports as the ledger accounts of human salvation, and incidentally of wordly wealth. Thirdly, the ministers of cheap religions are to be found among the glowing mass of pacifism. Finally, there are the untutored socialists who regard peace as an indispensable condition of Social Reform.'

[1] Pacifists asserted that it was not they who were the deluded party but the *Bellumists*. 'Not we are the dreamers, the utopians, but those who set their alarm clocks to signal the hour that threatens the Island with invasion and the Empire with destruction. They are hibernating in a fool's paradise and dreaming wild dreams of unopposed grab and grind. They are the ones who want awakening to the fact that half their day is past. . . . A revolt has broken out . . . against those who have taken possession of the nation's resources and are using them in defence of their own privileges. . . . The hungry want bread, not Dreadnoughts, and they mean to get it.' *Concord*, xxvi, no. 11, mid-Dec. 1910, p. 134.

[2] See, for example, diary entry of Kate Courtney as early as Dec. 1905. 'Although I hope most improbable, no one can say the irresponsible personality of the German Kaiser might not produce a world convulsion', *Courtney Collection*, xxii, p. 83.

and preparation for war was in all countries a professional business reserved into the hands of a distinct military caste whose instincts and interests were conspicuously different from and generally opposed to those of the community. The pacific professions of such men were never to be trusted as 'they are hedged about with a thousand and one reservations'. The animosity, even hatred, that had been created between Germany and England was 'a valuable asset to be placed to the credit of unscrupulous warmongers'.[1] The normal state of 'the man in the street' in both countries concerning the causes of national embroilment, was nescience or quiescence. In Germany, in particular, there would never be any hope for the friends of peace between nations until the Government had been brought to reflect much more closely the mind of the masses of the people.[2] Always there was the unspoken assumption that the barbarous instinct of pugnacity was not the vice of the people but of their leaders. Pacifists concluded, if pacifism was to succeed they would have to work upon prophylactic lines. The social body had to be strengthened so that disputes would become rarer and when they did occur would assume a less threatening character.

> We have to aim at a healthier and sounder condition of the international body politic. It is the fresh air of open speech, the sunshine of civilisation and of true human fellowship that will destroy the germs that spur us on to international jealousies and internecine strife. We must travel much, exchange visits, whether between students, teachers, journalists, burgomasters or rulers.[3]

An informal movement for the exchange of visits between German and British delegations had been launched shortly after the formation of the Anglo-German Friendship Committee in November 1905. While Sir Thomas Barclay, a Manchester businessman, was can-

[1] Felix Moscheles, in *Concord*, xxiv, no. 10, Oct. 1908, p. 119.
[2] After the reverses in the 1907 elections, the fortunes of the Social Democratic party in Germany improved. Many Radicals took this to be a hopeful sign that in the struggle between the 'Two Germanies', the antiwar element would finally succeed. Although the Social Democrats might not be strong enough to control the Reichstag, their presence in increasing numbers would help to control the tide of German aggression. Cf. S. Verdad in *New Age*, 25 May 1911, p. 76: 'To think that, merely because a few extra Socialist Deputies are returned, the policy of the Government will be altered accordingly, is nonsense. The Government of the German Empire, and even more especially of Prussia, is autocratic, and it will take more than two or three general elections to change this practice. I am not expressing an opinion; I am recording a fact.'
[3] Alfred Fried, reported, *Concord xxiv*, no. 2, Feb. 1908, p. 23. The practical measures suggested clearly indicate the difference of meaning attached to the phrase 'strengthening the social body' between men like Fried and the Social Democratic Federation. The point is neatly illustrated by a letter of H. M. Hyndman's to Buxton, 4 Mar. 1905, quoted H. N. Fieldhouse, 'Noel Buxton and A. J. P. Taylor's "The Troublemakers" ', in *A Century of Conflict 1850–1950*, ed. Martin Gilbert (1966), 181.

vassing support for Anglo-German friendship among German chambers of commerce, George Cadbury played host to a group of German burgomasters. These initial moves in 1906 were viewed with suspicion and hostility by the Foreign Office. Eyre Crowe in particular was irritated and concerned lest the exchange of visits should create an unfavourable impression in France.[1] But the floodtide of exchanges came during the time when the 1909 Naval Estimates crisis was at its height. Kautsky and Ledebour lectured on the folly of war and Bernstein hastened to add his ministrations to those of the leading theoreticians of German Social Democracy. Groups of German working men were entertained by Radical and Labour members of Parliament, and Ramsay MacDonald led a reciprocal British Labour delegation to Germany. Nor were the Churches backward in lending their support to this peace agitation,[2] due mainly to the efforts of the Quaker M.P., J. Allen Baker, who had won the support of Germany's religious leaders for the establishment of an Associated Council of Churches of the British and German Empires. The visible crowning achievement of the movement for Anglo-German Friendship during this period, was the World Peace Congress held in London, and the meeting of the Inter-Parliamentary Union held in Berlin. Both gatherings were 'endorsed, supported and directed by Liberal and Radical forces from both countries'.[3]

There was an anachronistic flavour about these attempts to forge closer links between Germany and Britain by the meeting and entertainment of delegations from the two countries. They were too much imbued with a cosy, middle-class gentility. This 'tea-party' approach was far removed from the devious and calculated stratagems of the conduct of international politics.[4] It was not that the

---

[1] See B.D. III: 359.

[2] Cf. comments of Kate Courtney, 4 Apr. 1909: 'Hardly a wise word to stem the tide of folly from Cabinet policies, and still less from ministers of religion.' *Courtney Collection*, xxxiii, 121.

[3] There is a summary of these activities in Howard Weinroth's perceptive article, *loc. cit.*, pp. 661-2. Contemporary reports of the meetings of delegates from Germany and Britain, and all the activities of the Anglo-German friendship movement, can be read in the Radical Press. Particularly full treatment is given in *Concord*, and the *Arbitrator*. For Allen Baker's contribution, see. Baker and Baker, 173-9. On limitations of these activities, see *ibid.*, 169ff.

Halévy's implication, that there were a disproportionate number of Germans and German Jews in the leadership of the Anglo-German friendship movement, is unfair and untrue. Among the seven names he lists is that of Sir John Brunner, who was not a Jew but a Unitarian, and not a German but the son of a Swiss schoolmaster who settled in England ten years before Brunner was born. None of the other six names he lists played any important part in the organisation of the Anglo-German Friendship Society. The impetus for that movement came from Radical and nonconformist roots. See Halévy, *The Rule of Democracy*, 409.

[4] See editorial comment in *New Age*, 8 Aug. 1908, p. 282. 'The organisers of

pacifists were unaware of the serious limitations of their method of tackling the problem. But what practicable alternatives were available to them?[1] It was obvious to them that their activities could never hope to bear fruit unless the German and British Governments were brought into accord. There had to be an agreement between the two Governments. This would be the complement of the *entente cordiale* with France. Achieve this, and not only would Anglo-German friendship be placed upon a sure basis, but new life would be breathed into the Concert of Europe. To this end pacifists could only protest, suggest, agitate. The practical means for implementing their ideals were limited. In Parliament, even their well organised rebellion against the increased Naval Estimates in 1909 had ended in total failure.

Then, in November 1909, the pacifist case was suddenly and considerably strengthened by the publication of a book written by an English businessman, Norman Angell. It was entitled *Europe's Optical Illusion*. The book enjoyed enormous and immediate success, and within a year an enlarged and revised edition had been produced: *The Great Illusion: a study of the relation of military power in nations to their economic and social advantages*. Angell's analysis challenged the posture hitherto assumed by Jingoes and every European Government as axiomatic and unassailable. He argued that such was the degree of economic interdependence that had developed between the leading Powers in the preceding two or three generations, to damage an enemy was effectively to inflict damage on oneself. Therefore, why should nations ruin themselves by a monstrous growth in armament expenditure when the benefits of conquest were purely illusory and when annexation provided no advantage to the annexing country? On the contrary, it acted as a stimulus to the defeated country. To avoid war, Angell concluded, was a matter of common sense and self-interest. To believe that war could ever again be a source of profit to the victor was Europe's illusion.

---

the Universal Peace Congress, with whose ultimate object all Socialists are most heartily in sympathy, are to be congratulated upon the number of pacific utterances which they managed to elicit from leading statesmen in this country. We doubt, however, whether such utterances count for much.' H. M. Hyndman was meanwhile busily engaged in defeating ideas of Anglo-German rapprochement with a strident article in the *Clarion* on 'The coming German war'. The only way to universal peace was 'to replace the rule of Kings and princes in Europe by the rule of the people. . . . As long as there is a German Kaiser and a Russian Tsar, each with an army and navy ready to fight at his whim, the friends of peace will be able to achieve little.'

[1] See Felix Moscheles's appeal, *Concord*, xxvi, no. 11, mid-Dec. 1910, p. 134. 'Help us, then, with your advice, how best to conduct the campaign, guide us where we want guidance, lead us where we want leadership.'

A new school of thought grew up around Angell's book. His thesis was welcomed by academics and hardheaded businessmen alike. Centres were established where Angell's writings were examined, dissected and approved. Here was a philosophy that was particularly congenial to pacifist and Radical thought. Ever since their electoral triumph in 1906, the Radicals had been hard pressed to repel the attacks of militarists and tariff reformers. Now in one book they were provided with arguments that justified their belief in Free Trade and their policy of disarmament. It was true that some of their number were concerned that while Angell clearly demonstrated the economic fallacies of Jingoism he did not appear to appreciate the force of moral protest against war. C. E. Maurice, reviewing Angell's book for *Concord*, suggested that this rather injured the force of his economic arguments: 'Moral protest, though it works more slowly works more surely in the end, for it strikes at that fundamental evil of human nature which St James showed long since to be the real source of war.'[1]

However, such highminded reservations were soon set aside in the heat of debate with the common Jingo foe. 'Once convince men that war does not pay, and the sentiment in favour of war which we find so hard to overcome must needs give way before economic facts. Men will then be prepared to see war as they now see slavery and religious persecution, as not only wrong but useless.' Was this perhaps making a great moral question merely one of self interest? That dilemma was capable of resolution. If one looked deep enough morality and expediency were one. 'It was one of our weak points in our case against war that our opponents could always retort that our ideals were impracticable and impossible of realisation. . . . Now the last link in our chain of argument has been forged and we can meet them on their own ground.'[2]

It was better and easier to embrace Angell's arguments than to quibble about them. Angell attributed the disappointing results of pacifist propaganda to its advocates founding their appeal on the grounds of morality rather than interest. By December 1910, when Angell's book had appeared in its new guise as *The Great Illusion*, J. A. Farrer was prepared to make the claim that the plea of interest had always been 'the main underlying argument of pacifists against war. Mr Angell can hardly claim that he has discovered that argument.'[3]

[1] *Concord*, xxvi, no. 1, Jan. 1910, pp. 14–15.
[2] A. Honora Enfield, in an 'Address on the Educational Aspect of the Peace Movement', Outer Temple, 23 Feb. 1910.
[3] *Concord*, xxvi, no. 12, Dec. 1910, pp. 140–1.

The greatest difficulties that members of the peace movement faced were first, how far should the doctrine of non-resistance be carried? Second, what were the best means available for them to remove the impression that the peace movement was purely negative? Third, what would constitute a suitable practical field for the activities which pacifists were anxious to promote? It was no good their denying the fact that there was a rift in the pacifist lute.[1] Members of the Society of Friends, for example, could be an embarrassment. In their writings all too often they seemed to do more justice and even feel more toleration towards those who were diametrically opposed to them than towards those who, while sharing many of their aims and admiring their ideals, could not accept their absolute attitude on questions of war and peace. Quakers seemed constitutionally incapable of recognising the possibility that men could feel moral indignation against a war because it was unjust, aggressive and involved with oppression and cruelty, quite apart from the question of whether killing in any circumstances was unjustifiable. Nor were Quakers prepared to recognise appeals made to legal tribunals as a half-way measure towards the goal of universal peace. Many so-called pacifists, whose pacifism was more a matter of sentiment than anything else, must have concurred with C. E. Maurice's judgment, that the ends of the peace movement would be attained more quickly if there was more understanding and effective union 'between those whom we heartily recognise as the advance guard of the movement, and those who find temporary rest in half-way houses and who recognise a gain in achievements which fall short of the highest ideal'.[2]

The frequent claim made by the Labour party in Parliament and Socialists outside the Commons, that Socialism offered a unique anodyne to soothe away the hatred and suspicion of nation for nation, does not bear close examination. British Socialists on the issue of peace spoke with a multiplicity of voices that made play with the economic determinism of Marx. Capitalism was the immoral yet legalised system that enabled the owners of land and money to take an annual toll from the labour of the workers. The rich, receiving annually more than they could spend on themselves, looked for profitable investment. This surplus wealth seeking investment was

[1] See Felix Moscheles, 'A Scheme' in *Concord*, xxvi, no. 11, Nov. 1910, pp. 122–3: 'We lack cohesion. If we could only combine in our efforts to push that wheel, to dig up that root, to proclaim and to preach, we should advance more rapidly; but we are not strong because we are not united.'
[2] Review of Stephen Hobhouse's *The Pathway or the Practice of Peace*, in *Concord*, xxvi, no. 1, Jan. 1910, pp. 15–16.

the first great cause of huge armaments, war scares and wars. It was the loan mongers, the gambling stockbroker and the cheating contractor allied with a venal Press that forced men into war. The poor were gulled to pay with their labour and their lives because of the predominance of a small and privileged rich class. There was no natural enmity between this nation or that. The only enemy to be fought was the evil of capitalism.

An ideology that explained war as the inevitable result of the economic structure of capitalism was both too pessimistic and too revolutionary to appeal to a wide public. If war was inherent in society as it existed, then the logical resolution was that the existing system should be overthrown by revolution. Such a conclusion conflicted with deep-seated tradition. Nor, apparently, were many Socialists aware of the logic of the arguments that they so forcibly propounded. Thus, a Fabian like J. A. Fallows, lecturing on 'Socialism and peace' to a Free Church audience at Hampstead, could condemn capitalism in the most intransigent Marxist terms, and in the same speech avow his conviction that Socialism had to be brought to the people by instalments.[1] This confusion of thought is manifest in the writings and speeches of men like Thorne, Quelch, Hyndman and Blatchford, who when faced by German militarism, reacted with talk of citizen armies recruited by universal service for national defence. Given the opportunity they were as insular, as exuberantly patriotic, as the most jingoistic Tory. They were strangely parochial for men who professed to be internationalists. Their approach and response to problems of international relationships was essentially emotional. Labour's leaders in Parliament were quick to rap the knuckles of those Socialists who indulged in such emotional junketing.[2]

Keir Hardie and Ramsay MacDonald were wise enough to keep their Marxist speeches for meetings of the Socialist International. On the floor of the House of Commons and in the columns of their newspapers, they spoke of familiar Radical measures in Radical tones.[3] They proposed no new initiative to solve the ills of the international situation; they offered no revolutionary panacea, nor did they even hint that such was needed.[4] So far as the conduct and

---

[1] Reported, *Concord*, xxv, no. 4, Apr. 1909, p. 50
[2] See, for example, *Labour Leader*, 14 Aug. 1908, p. 521.
[3] Even noted 'firebrands' like Quelch, in the most sympathetic of atmospheres, could still talk very much like a Gladstonian Radical. Addressing the Annual Congress of the German Social Democratic party at Nuremberg, 14 Sept. 1908, Quelch's most 'revolutionary' statement was that although England was a democratic country her diplomatists acted without reference to the people.   [4] Cf. Halévy, *The Rule of Democracy*, 408-9.

criticism of Britain's foreign affairs were concerned, they did not effectively distinguish either themselves or their policies from the Radical members of the Liberal Party. In truth, they could not. H. W. Massingham, when he wrote in 1909 of there being 'two organised political forces opposed to militarism . . . the British Liberal and Labour parties and Continental Socialism',[1] was recording an accomplished fact. Labour in Parliament had no distinctive voice on foreign affairs and no unique contribution to make in providing a possible solution to the problem of Anglo-German hostility. However, this did not stop Labour's leaders from claiming that there was a fundamental difference between their proposals and the older style 'pacifism' of the Radicals.

In October 1910 the Independent Labour party organised a national campaign against the increasing burden of armaments. More than two hundred and fifty meetings were held up and down the country, each addressed by a Labour M.P. Each time, a common resolution was moved protesting against the growing burden of armaments and urging the workers in every country to adopt common action 'to advance the case for social justice and international peace and defeat the purposes of the scare mongers and the war makers'. This ideal was to be achieved, not by militant workers rising in revolution against their wicked exploiters, but by arbitration. The International Peace and Arbitration Association, with its genteel, middle class, Lib-Lab, Radical membership, had been advocating the same measure for years. It was all very well for Ramsay MacDonald, when addressing the faithful at the Manchester Free Trade Hall, to claim that 'we are going to make Europe sheathe the sword. . . . That is what the Labour party is going to do. It is the only party that can do it.'[2] But neither MacDonald nor any other Labour leader indicated exactly what were Labour's special qualifications to undertake such a bold and grave mission.

In January 1911 the Labour party preceded its annual conference with a Special Conference on Disarmament and the Present International Situation. A resolution on arbitration was adopted without any difficulties, but when it was suggested that the recommendations of the International Socialist Congress, which had been held at Copenhagen in 1910, should be adopted, and in particular the use of the general strike as a means of preventing war, a lively debate ensued. Keir Hardie, somewhat halfheartedly, supported the *investigation* of the possibilities of a general strike as an antiwar weapon. Arthur Henderson led the opposition to this revolutionary idea. He

[1] *The Nation*, 6 Mar. 1909.   [2] *Peace Year Book* (*1911*), 69–70.

was opposed 'to the advocacy of a general strike . . . [as this] would divert attention from parliamentary action'. Henderson and his supporters were successful in their opposition. *Concord* censured Henderson for his lack of spirit.

> Let every legitimate weapon—political or other—be used in carrying on the war against war. We are inclined to think that the rank and file workmen are getting a little tired of the ineffectiveness of the 'elected Person' on this subject and will soon be ready to take the matter into their own hands.[1]

It is true that by 1912 the Labour Party Conference had grown sufficiently bold to authorise an inquiry into the use of strike action to halt wars, but nothing ever came of it.

As far as practical measures were concerned, Labour's 'pacifism' was no different from the old-style Radical pacifism. There were the same pious avowals of good faith in the brotherhood of men, the internationalism of workmen and the desire for the peaceful settlement of disputes by arbitration. The constant addition of the rider that war was 'not the doing of working people but of political and economic interests which are antagonistic to the people', was merely genuflection to a tribal god that Radicals and Socialists alike mindlessly honoured. 'The Labour party', declared Philip Snowden, 'is unitedly and unanimously opposed to war for economic and humanitarian reasons.'[2] Any Liberal Radical would have said as much. When Labour spoke of war and peace in Parliament or the country, it broadcast abroad the voice of orthodox Radicalism: no more secret diplomacy, remove the burden of taxation for militarism, more pensions, fewer Dreadnoughts; just a little more reason, a little more enlightenment in the conduct of foreign affairs and the mutual goodwill of workmen for one another throughout the world would flourish and ensure everlasting peace.

By strange irony, an official German estimate of the European scene to a certain extent would have complemented the Radical belief that there were good grounds for supposing that relations between Germany and Britain were ready for improvement. The Triple Entente, of France, Britain and Russia, had proved a flimsier construction under stress than might have been supposed. Patently, the ties between the members were too weak to justify serious alarm in Germany.[3] France had proved very lukewarm in her support of

---

[1] *Concord*, xxvii, no. 2, Feb. 1911, p. 17. [2] *Peace Year Book* (*1913*), 35–45.
[3] The Potsdam agreement certainly caused alarm to the French, and Cambon was quick to preach to the British the virtues of 'keeping in close touch and acting in accord'. See *B.D.* x, i, 654.

Russia's Balkan ambitions. Germany had appeared to enjoy a diplomatic triumph over Bosnia Herzegovina. The British naval scare undoubtedly had been officially inspired. Yet, when carefully analysed, it revealed, not a spirit of aggression directed against Germany, but an obsessive defensive psychology. The death of King Edward convinced many Germans that the policy of encircling Germany was finished, for the King of England they believed had been the inspiration and leader of that conspiracy.[1] The implications of the meeting between the Tsar and the Kaiser at Potsdam and the subsequent agreement were obvious. Russia was detached from the Triple Entente. Now the time was ripe to seek friendship with Britain. Any war scare could only be to Germany's disadvantage as its most probable effect would be to arouse the spirit of patriotic resistance among Englishmen and so strengthen once more the ties of the Triple Entente.

For British Radicals a fortuitous combination of factors convinced them that the times were favourable to effect an improvement in Anglo-German relations. The replacement of Bülow as Germany's Chancellor by Bethmann-Hollweg in July 1909, was seen by *New Age* as 'an opportunity to come to an understanding with Germany. Prince Bülow did not understand England.'[2] Others, initially, were much cooler in their reception. Bernstein, writing in *The Nation*, saw no political significance in the replacement of 'a versatile diplomatist' by 'a cultured bureaucrat'.[3] But, as the months passed, there was an increasing enthusiasm and friendliness shown for Bethmann-Hollweg, and the feeling grew among Radicals that his appointment had marked the moment when Anglo-German relations took a turn for the better. The discovery, from the tardy admissions of ministers, that the estimates of Germany's Dreadnought production during the Naval Estimate debates of 1909 had been grossly inaccurate, encouraged the belief among supporters of disarmament that any talk of a German peril was similarly exaggerated. There was real hope for a lessening of Anglo-German naval rivalry. The German Naval Law provided that in 1912 Germany's Dreadnought construction would be halved. Not only this, all the indications from

---

[1] The Germans were not alone in their belief that Edward was a force in British diplomacy. The belief was shared by a number of Socialists, especially Hyndman's supporters. There was a frequent and hectic correspondence on the subject in *New Age*. Grey ridiculed the notion and gives his estimate of Edward's contribution in *Twenty-Five Years*, i, 202–17. See also Esher *The Influence of King Edward and Essays on Other Subjects* (1915), 50. In his essay, which appeared first as an article in *Deutsche Revue*, June 1910, Esher expressed the wish that the Anglo-French entente be transformed into a Triple Entente of France, England and Germany.

[2] *New Age*, 22 July 1909, p. 246.

[3] *The Nation*, 24 July 1909. See also *Contemporary Review*, xcvi, p. 246.

Germany pointed to an increasing opposition to the big navy policy. Therefore, what possible reason was there to fear that the provision of the German Naval Law would be increased? Even Bernstein, never the most optimistic of writers on German affairs, in July 1910 was prepared to admit that German Jingoism was in a backwater and claimed that their stock had fallen very low.[1] It appeared that there was such a desire for peace in Germany that the only factor remaining as an obstacle to a political settlement between the two nations was the group of perverse and ill-favoured men in England who were determined upon promoting strife between the two countries.[2] Therefore the strategy to be employed by those who supported rapprochement between Germany and Britain was clear. It was their task to combat and repudiate the lies, panics and insinuations of scaremongers and Jingoes who for their own selfish reasons were bent upon 'inevitable' war between Germany and England.

The exigencies of domestic politics kept the question of Anglo-German relations in the forefront of the public's attention. The general election of January 1910 had been precipitated by the House of Lords rejecting Lloyd George's budget proposals. However, at the hustings, it was not so much on the constitutional issue that Tory candidates concentrated their efforts, but tariff reform and national defence. Their action, claimed G. H. Perris, was 'a perfectly natural part of the attempt of a class whose privileges are threatened to cajole or frighten the people back from the path of domestic reform'.[3] It was Balfour who gave the lead to his party faithful. He was too experienced a campaigner to fail to recognise that a Liberal Government was always open to the suspicion that it would not make adequate appropriations for national defence. The Dreadnought scare was still fresh in men's minds. To the British public, complex diplomatic manœuvrings between the nations of Europe merely concentrated attention upon one issue that clearly concerned them—the fortunes of the Navy. The Navy was not a problem fit only for discussion by 'experts'. History, together with a general disposition bolstered by a series of outrageous fictional fantasies that popularised theories about German plans for an imminent descent on England's shores, meant that the fortunes of the Navy engaged the interest of the nation. The Navy was the chief symbol and agency of the power of the state. There were very few Englishmen who doubted the validity of the prescription that Britannia should always rule the waves. 'Patriotic' publicists, like Maxse and

[1] *The Nation*, 30 July 1910.   [2] *Ibid.*, 1 Oct. 1910.
[3] *Concord*, xxvi, no. 1, Jan. 1910, p. 1.

Chirol, Repington and Garvin, all assiduously primed from official sources about the German 'menace', prepared the public mind to accept a reduction of the complex pattern of international relationships and rivalries, with its thousand cross currents and divergences, to a single, simple thesis—Germany's political aims and ambitions were incompatible with the future security of the British Empire. Britain's Navy alone stood between Germany and the realisation of its designs for world hegemony. Whatever the cost, the Navy, as Britain's sole guarantee of security, must never be placed in jeopardy. Balfour encouraged his lieutenants to make capital out of this tide of emotional, simplistic, prejudice. The Tory leader instructed his audience at Henley: 'Go about at this moment if you will and consult the statesmen and diplomats of the lesser Powers and I am perfectly confident that you will find among them an absolute unanimity of opinion that a struggle sooner or later between this country and Germany is inevitable.'[1] Grey, a few days later, sharply denounced Balfour's speech. According to the Foreign Secretary, there had never been less reason to talk of an Anglo-German war.[2]

The *Manchester Guardian* was not impressed by the Tory attempt to drum up popular alarm. It was a typically sordid, pre-election, party manœuvre. 'Last April they were all anti-Germans and patriots, presently Dukes; then . . . beer as being more popular, then Protection, and now it is patriotism again . . .' This 'deliberate raking of the fires of hell for votes' by the Tories was 'an act of political depravity' and 'no party extremity could excuse such behaviour'.[3] The Tories had an ally in the Socialist, Robert Blatchford. He had been commissioned by Kennedy Jones to write up his impressions of the German threat for the *Daily Mail*. The first of his series of ten articles, entitled 'The Menace', appeared on 13 December. Blatchford was not the kind of publicist who suffered qualms about the accuracy of his information. He had a message to give the people, and the people eagerly read what he had to offer.[4] He did not mince his words.

> I write these articles because I believe that Germany is deliberately preparing to destroy the British Empire; and because I know that we are not ready or able to defend ourselves against a sudden and formidable attack. . . . At the present moment the

[1] *Daily News*, 6 Jan. 1910.
[2] *Manchester Guardian*, 8 and 11 Jan. 1910.
[3] *Manchester Guardian*, 20 Dec. 1909.
[4] See Kennedy Jones, *Fleet Street and Downing Street*, 253. For contemporary corrections of Blatchford's facts, see, *inter alia*, J. F. Green, 'Mr Blatchford's inaccuracies', *Concord*, xxvi, no. 1, Jan. 1910, p. 9. See also Hale, 376-7, n. 13.

whole country is in a ferment about the Budget and the Peers, and the Election. It seems sheer criminal lunacy to waste time and strength in chasing such political bubbles when the existence of the Empire is threatened.[1]

Blatchford's contribution to the German scare caused concern in official circles. The King 'lamented Blatchford's violence'.[2] Bethmann-Hollweg made no secret of his anger at the anti-German tone of so much of the election publicity. Grey excused the articles as 'not really anti-German but alarmist'. He declared that he was 'not going to be driven out of [his] course by the *Daily Mail* and the Peers . . . but for any one of us to attempt to moderate their writing and speeches would only lead to the redoubling of their efforts'.[3] However, Liberal ministers recognised that they had to counter Tory propaganda. Consequently, their statements about Britain's preparedness for war often bordered on the provocative. Lloyd George boasted to an audience at Grimsby: 'There is not a German who does not know that if the German fleet, in a moment of madness, ever attempted to take us, that German fleet would be at the bottom of the German Ocean in a very few hours.'[4] While the Tories insisted that the German and British fleets were dangerously near equality, the Liberals stoutly maintained the superiority of the British fleet.

The National Peace Council in January 1910 issued a manifesto, signed by, amongst others, Leonard Courtney and Spence-Watson, claiming the Tory election campaign was 'a base attempt to confuse judgment by exciting fear and jealousy of a friendly Power . . . an appeal to ignoble prejudice by an odious agitation'. *The Nation*, in an article entitled 'The price of Mr Balfour', maintained that Germany recognised if the Tory party was to form the next Government then 'honourable and peaceful relationships between the two

---

[1] *Daily Mail*, 12 Dec. 1909. The ten articles appeared between 13 and 23 Dec. 1909.
[2] *E.P.*, ii, 422. Esher, writing to his son, enclosed a copy of the *Daily Mail*, 'to show you the unscrupulousness of those people. They would be quite ready to get up a war with Germany in order to cover up their probable defeat on the Budget. I don't think political crime can go much lower than that. Blatchford—whom they are exploiting—is a Socialist and a self-advertising fellow. I suppose the country and the Germans will see through the dodge', *E.P.*, ii, 426.
[3] *B.D.*, vi, 319; cf. Hale, 377. 'Blatchford stated shrilly and impolitely in the language of the common people . . . what diplomats had been whispering to one another and what had been said a thousand times in the service magazines and the half-crown monthlies. The German striving for political hegemony, which threatened the general peace and independence of Europe, and the identification of the defence of the Empire with the defence of France, were all assumptions that were implicit in the British policy of the ententes.'
[4] Reported *Daily News*, 15 Jan. 1910.

countries would rest on an entirely different footing from that which obtains under Mr Asquith and Sir Edward Grey'.[1] Fortunately, the German Press did not rise to the bait offered by Blatchford and Balfour. Expressions of Anglo-German hostility and of the inevitability of war between the two Powers were no more than 'the sickly scream of a desperately pressed politician'.[2] Pacifist groups in the two countries laboured to allay the distrust promoted by the election campaign. Dr Adolf Richter, President of the German Peace Society, wrote to the Committee of the International Peace and Arbitration Association:

> Dear Colleagues and Friends—. . . our hearty thanks for the energetic manner with which you have replied to . . . [those] who have been trying by misrepresentation and distrust to disturb the steadily growing agreement between our two countries. We can assure you that not only the German Peace Society, but also the larger part of the German people, reciprocates your friendly dispositions, and that the German pacifists are always on the look-out ready to oppose the incitements of certain well-known small factions.[3]

Nor was the official voice of Germany silent. The German Ambassador, at a banquet in honour of his Emperor's birthday, administered an effective rebuke to the scaremongers:

> There are people who assert that we are only waiting the opportunity to fall upon any weaker Power. To such hallucinations of timorous souls it is not easy to reply. The mind that can conceive them is not open to reasonable argument. Our conscience, however, is clear. We can point to the fact that Germany has kept the peace for nearly forty years.

Count Metternich skilfully deployed the arguments of Norman Angell to rebut Balfour's aspersions concerning Germany's *Welt-*

---

[1] *The Nation*, 15 Jan. 1910. A week later, 22 Jan. 1910, *The Nation*, in a mild attack upon Grey, inconsistently stated that 'Sir Edward Grey has introduced no innovations in the policy laid down by Lord Lansdowne. If Lord Lansdowne were to return to Downing Street, the main lines of our diplomacy would remain unchanged.'

[2] *Neue Freie Presse*, quoted *The Nation*, 8 Jan. 1910. Fried's editorial assessment in the *Neue Freie Presse* echoed the sentiments of Lloyd George in a speech he made at Peckham, where he had reproved Balfour for 'plucking the feathers of the German eagle's tail with his war alarms . . . the last resort of a desperate man who sees that his game is lost'; see Owen, 186–7. In a survey of European reactions to the general election, 22 Jan. 1910, *The Nation* noted the difference of attitude shown by the German Press, and the 'Government-inspired' *Temps* and *Novoe Vremya* of Britain's entente partners that had hoped for the return of a Tory Government.

[3] 1 Jan. 1910 quoted *Concord*, xxvi, no. 1, Jan. 1910, p. 14. On the same page is recorded the initial protest of the Executive Committee on the British Arbitration and Peace Association, 21 Dec. 1909 which, *inter alia*, pressed the British and German Governments to negotiate an agreement for the limitation of armaments.

politik. 'I have never believed that among the commercial and industrial nations . . . [today] . . . the destruction of one or two rivals could mean advantage to the other.' Germany's *Weltpolitik* had no sinister intent but was 'a policy aiming at the peaceful acquisition of new markets'. Germany had 'no pretensions to becoming the strongest Power on the sea'. Her fleet, 'fixed by Act of Parliament', was designed to 'protect our commercial and colonial interests'. *The Times* questioned Count Metternich's facts and sincerity.[1] The *Manchester Guardian* demolished their case:

> The only answer that *The Times* can think of to the Ambassador's declaration is to put forward an interpretation of words from the Act of 1900 (Germany's Naval Law) which is not only garbled and demonstrably false, but historically impossible. But why answer? Why not simply accept the word of a man of honour.[2]

This was to be the last shot in the general election campaign of January 1910. G. H. Perris claimed with satisfaction that 'The German Government and people, so far from being tempted into a perilous controversy with our reactionaries, have shown themselves more and more sensible of the peril of armed rivalry and increasingly desirous of an agreement on the subject.'[3] The Liberals were once more in power, and though their massive majority of 1906 had been considerably eroded, 'the Balfour Gang' with their dangerous delusions were still condemned to the political wilderness.

The alarums and excursions of the election campaign seemed to have a cathartic effect. Most Radical energies were concentrated upon the great constitutional question of the future status of the House of Lords.[4] Though one of the first items dealt with by the new Parliament was an increase in the Naval Estimates, the disarmament lobby did not put up a convincing fight. They seemed resigned if regretful that they could do nothing. There was no panic as in 1909: only 'the pale wraith of the Spring scare and its successors remained after the election vanished.'[5] The Tories went through the accustomed

---

[1] *The Times*, 29 Jan. 1910.   [2] *Manchester Guardian*, 31 Jan. 1910.
[3] *Concord*, xxvi, no. 1, Jan. 1910, p. 2.
[4] See Churchill to King Edward, 11 Mar. 1910, quoted Marder, 215. 'In ordinary circumstances these Estimates would have led to vehement debates in the House of Commons [but] . . . no difficulty will arise. [The House of Lords] issue dominates the situation. The resistance to expenditure of all kinds was never at a more feeble ebb.'
[5] *The Nation*, 5 Mar. 1910, cf. *Daily Mail*, 10 Mar. 1910, 'The Estimates are as much as we can expect from a Radical Government though far from ideal'; and *Daily News*, 10 Mar. 1910, 'the appetite of this monster of armaments grows by what it feeds on. . . . It is the creation of irrational hates and craven fears.'

motions; the exaggerated forecasts, the condemnation of the Government's proposals. Five new Dreadnoughts and five cruisers were a betrayal of the two Power standard. Even their Press showed little spirit, and only those papers owned by Northcliffe, which now included *The Times*, conducted the debate with anything like the fervour of 1909.[1]

The death of King Edward in May 1910 was a circumstance that favoured a further relaxation of the tension between Germany and England. Radicals, like the rest of Edward's subjects, mourned their sovereign's death. They paid tribute, though not without some reservations,[2] to his diplomatic ability. They recalled the words with which he had greeted the deputies from the Universal Peace Congress at Buckingham Palace less than two years earlier.

> Rulers and statesmen can set before themselves no higher aim than the promotion of national good understanding and cordial friendship among the nations of the world. It is the surest and the most direct means whereby humanity may be enabled to realise its noblest ideals, and its attainment will ever be the object of my own constant endeavours.

Now Edward the Peacemaker was dead. He had begun to lay the foundations of Anglo-German friendship by his visit to Berlin in 1909. That visit, six months after Cronberg and only three months after the unfortunate *Daily Telegraph* interview, had been an advance to the German nation as much as to their Kaiser. If only Edward had lived, undoubtedly he would have finished his great task of reconciliation, the crowning diplomatic achievement of his career.

But Edward's death had relieved the Kaiser's vanity. William had created the monarch's part of progresses to other European countries, yet his uncle had bested him at his own invention. Now that his competitor was dead, the sorrow William felt was real. 'My firm belief', wrote Esher to Fisher, 'is that of all the royal visitors the only mourner was this extraordinary Kaiser.'[3] The crowds who watched Edward's cortège pass, noted the Kaiser's obvious sorrow.

---

[1] For their claim that British preparations were insufficient to meet Germany's massive preparations, see articles listed by Hale, 378, n. 19. When Balfour attempted to stir up the naval problem in Oct. 1910 by a speech in Glasgow indicting the Government's conduct of naval affairs and in particular the 'most lamentable and dangerous' margin in Dreadnought superiority over Germany, his efforts came to nothing and his scaremongering was effectively dealt with by McKenna in the Commons. Balfour had been under considerable pressure for some time to make an 'aggressive' speech. It was Esher who suggested he might try 'rubbing in the Navy', see *E.P.*, iii, 25.
[2] See for example *Concord*, xxvi, no. 5, May 1910, p. 53.
[3] Esher to Fisher, 24 May 1910, in *E.P.* iii:4.

'Before he left England something not unlike reconciliation had been effected between the British people and the German Emperor'.[1] The 'traces of tears' in the Emperor's eyes were evidence of the 'sincerity of his goodwill towards us', declared the *Manchester Guardian*. This 'should once and for all convince even the most nervously distrustful of our politicians of the baselessness of the fears which they have sought to implant in our minds. . . . This league of princes will be a nucleus round which a close bond of international amity and mutual confidence should quickly grow'.[2]

During the second general election of 1910, questions of defence and foreign policy did not figure anything like as prominently in the Press and on the platform as they had in January.[3] The brilliant invective, the lies and counter-lies that the politicians and publicists scattered abroad, concentrated upon domestic issues; Home Rule and the fate of the House of Lords. The true rhythm of British politics seemed to be restored.

> After all our patriotic palaverings, a man's foes are still those of his own household—the employer who starves him in a lockout; . . . the infatuated believers in the Big Loaf; . . . the political self-seekers who believe they have a divine right to do wrong . . . It is quite amusing to reflect that the imperial fire-eaters who

[1] Halévy, *The Rule of Democracy*, 419.

[2] *Manchester Guardian*, 20 May 1910. The *Guardian*'s 'league of princes' was not an idea guaranteed to appeal to Socialist opinion that stoutly maintained the best hope for peace lay in 'the solidarity of the democracies of Europe . . . united under the Socialist Flag'. See motion at Albert Hall meeting of the Independent Labour Party, Dec. 1910.

[3] William Stewart, who worked on the *Labour Leader*, in his biography of Keir Hardie published in 1921, claimed: 'During the whole of this General Election the subject of war was never mentioned. Foreign policy was never mentioned. Armaments were never mentioned. . . . As a decoy-duck Lloyd George was a success. He attracted the fire that should have been directed against Grey and Haldane and the British war-lords. Only the Socialists were alive to the impending danger. . . . But the people never heard them. . . . They were listening to Lloyd George and "waiting and seeing" . . . what Mr Asquith was going to give them' (pp. 294–307).

Stewart's claim is not accurate. He was at pains to emphasise the importance of the I.L.P.'s anti-armaments campaign. Oct.–Dec. 1910. The I.L.P. was more inclined than any other Radical group to ignore international issues and to be preoccupied with domestic problems. Stewart's writing is, as Maccoby says (p. 69), 'dominated by overtones from the trench-massacres of 1914–18'. The claim that Labour in 1910 was concerned about the possibility of war is correct. They were afraid that Britain would be involved in a continental engagement because she would be dragged in as the Tsar's ally. It was 'disgust with the Tsar' and his 'foul tyranny' that coloured Labour's assessment of Grey's policy. As to the causes of war generally, they shared the same assumptions as the Radical Liberals.

The major concern of the I.L.P., during this period was neither the international weather, nor the 'political comedy' or 'farce' as they variously dubbed the constitutional struggle between the Commons and the Lords, but their future as parliamentary party. Their fortunes seemed seriously undermined by the Osborne Judgment.

have been thinking in Dreadnoughts and pining for Conscription in order to defend the United Kingdom against a phantom foe from without, have latterly superceded their German war scare by an English Civil War scare.[1]

The arsenal of party political ill will and strife was replete with domestic concerns.

Early in November 1910 Asquith at the Guildhall had made a most encouraging speech deploring the arms race. *The Nation* responded enthusiastically: 'We believe that it expressed a definite purpose which now guides our policy.' The Prime Minister had outlined 'a slower, but in the end . . ., a more hopeful method of attacking the problem than that which Sir Henry Campbell-Bannerman sketched with his splendid courage and directness of mind.'[2] This apparent initiative by Asquith, seemingly was accepted by the German Chancellor. Bethmann-Hollweg urged that there should be Anglo-German discussions of their mutual economic and political interests. Grey and Metternich joined their voices to the chorus. All the indications were that at last the time was ripe for an agreement between Germany and Britain. A year earlier the *Manchester Guardian* had warned that Britain could not afford to stand apart from the 'new circle of ententes'.[3] These warnings now became a demand.

Why are we more insistent in other people's quarrels, whether Russia's with Persia or France's in Morocco, than they are in their own? . . . Though Germany invites us and our own interests second the invitation, other Powers which have really serious causes of disagreement forestall us and conclude agreements with Germany which we might have made betimes.[4]

Noel Buxton in the Commons, urged upon the Government the *need* for an agreement with Germany. If ordinary diplomatic channels were inadequate, then why shouldn't a special mission be undertaken led either by Grey or perhaps Haldane, 'the Minister so renowned for his intimacy with German life and German people'?[5]

[1] William Heaford in *Concord*, xxvi, no. 11, Dec. 1910, p. 135. He was referring in particular to the warning by Curzon about the Belfast Unionists raising funds for civil conflict. See *The Times*, 4 Dec. 1910.
[2] *The Nation*, 12 Nov. 1910. In its way, this statement by *The Nation* was an extraordinary one because it implied the abandonment of support for a policy of direct assault upon the question of armaments upon which premiss *The Nation* had been launched with Campbell-Bannerman's article on the Hague Conference and Disarmament. The *Manchester Guardian* had argued for more than a year that if there was to be an agreement between Germany and Britain rather than a mere *détente*, then it followed that there should be a political agreement to precede or accompany any agreement governing reduction of armaments. *The Nation* was only slowly weaned to this view.
[3] *Manchester Guardian*, 20 Dec. 1909.   [4] *Ibid.*, 11 Nov. 1911.
[5] *Hansard*, v:22:1335.

The Radicals had been at a loss to establish the specific cause of estrangement between Germany and Britain. Whatever it was it seemed singulary elusive. What they sought was an issue, like that of Egypt and Morocco, which had led to the Anglo-French entente of 1904; that is, an area which was both a source of potential conflict between the nations and yet at the same time was an issue of common interest. In 1907 the *Daily News* had suggested that rapprochement between Germany and Britain might begin with the Powers devising a treaty that would guarantee the *status quo* of Belgium and Holland. This had proved a non-starter.[1] Later there had been talk of combined Anglo-German pressure upon Leopold, to force the Belgian king to introduce reforms in his Congo territories. This would have the merit of not only contributing to Anglo-German friendship but also would be a humanitarian action in the best Radical tradition. The scheme foundered in the face of the intransigence of the British Foreign Office.[2]

If not the Congo, then what about the question of Germany's 'place in the sun'? Professor Delbrück of Berlin University, writing in the *Contemporary Review*, flatly rejected the suggestion that Germany wished to acquire vast colonial territories. But, he admitted, there was an area where 'German influence, German capital, German commerce, German engineering and German intelligence [could] compete on equal terms with other nations', and 'that without the necessity of a disastrous war of rivalry between Germany and England'.[3] Delbrück was alluding to Turkey and the Baghdad Railway project. Here was the issue that the Radicals sought. It satisfied all their necessary conditions. 'An understanding', declared *The Nation*, 'would react at once upon all our relations and pave the way to the true goal of Anglo-German policy—an agreement over armaments.'[4] The *Manchester Guardian* was equally enthusiastic.

---

[1] *Daily News*, 20 Dec. 1907.
[2] E. D. Morel, the leading Radical protagonist for reform in the Congo, doubted the possibility of this move from the beginning. He doubted the honesty of Grey's expressed fears that a decisive step taken by the British Government might lead to unwanted European complications. He suspected the truth of the matter was a secret treaty between France and Britain which committed Britain to actions of which the public neither knew nor would have approved. Thus was born Morel's campaign for open diplomacy and the significant rôle he was subsequently to play in the U.D.C. See *Bulletin of the Institute of Historical Research*, xxxvi: 94 (1963), 168–80; Cookey, 250; and W. S. Adams, *Edwardian Portraits* (1957), 198.
[3] *Contemporary Review*, xcvi, Oct. 1909, p. 405.
[4] *The Nation*, 25 Dec. 1909; see also 1 Jan. 1910: 'It is possible to find in the Baghdad Railway a ground for common action, and to use it to demonstrate our drive for cooperation in a way which ought, if we are careful, to respect Turkish susceptibilities and interests, to advance the trade of both countries, while conferring great benefits upon a derelict but potentially wealthy area.'

'The first revolution in our foreign policy was the popular outcry in England against the proposed schemes of cooperation with Germany in the Baghdad Railway project. Perhaps now it could serve to mitigate the rivalry.'[1] The omens for success appeared particularly favourable. Sir Ernest Cassel resumed his talks with German bankers about finance for the Baghdad Railway, and the obvious if tentative peace feelers put out by Bethmann-Hollweg in a speech to the Reichstag, suggested that the diplomatic climate was conducive to agreement.[2] A year later *The Nation* was still very hopeful of an agreement arising out of collaboration over the railway. 'The key to the whole European situation is in our hands, and the door which waits to be unlocked in . . . Baghdad. . . . To succeed is probably to end the dread of war for ever in Europe.'[3] But the French effectively frustrated Cassel's plans of British finance for Germany's schemes, and the Agadir crisis rudely interrupted the talks between British and German negotiators while they were still searching for the means to resolve their countries' conflicting interests in Turkey.

Two other issues were canvassed by the Radicals as a possible means of effecting a political agreement between Germany and Britain. The *Manchester Guardian*, as was fitting for the voice of Northern manufacturing interests, favoured a policy of 'open markets'. This, it was claimed, 'is a natural basis of understanding'. The disadvantage with this scheme was that 'unfortunately the Foreign Office [was] not in close touch with commerce'.[4] There remained that hoary favourite of Radical championship; 'The right of capture'. If only merchantmen were made immune from capture, claimed *The Nation*, 'we should counter the only serious argument which makes a great navy a necessity. The political financiers of the commerce destroyers are the worse enemies of peace for they alone provide an adequate motive for the resort to force.'[5] Lord Weardale, in his presidential address to the sixth National Peace Congress, 14 June 1910, claimed:

> There is no question more urgent than that of the immunity of private property at sea, and none more likely, if happily solved to tend to the establishment of peace . . . Last year, at an international Conference at London, the good work was accomplished of codifying the law of commercial blockade and it is now possible to maintain a commercial blockade and at the

[1] *Manchester Guardian*, 12 May 1910.   [2] *The Nation*, 18 Dec. 1909.
[3] *The Nation*, 17 Dec. 1910.   [4] *Manchester Guardian*, 11 Apr. 1910.
[5] *The Nation*, 1 Jan. 1910.

same time surrender the right of capture of private property at sea . . . [Germany] has established a great maritime trade, and so long as we maintain the right of capture of private property at sea is it surprising that Germany should have a great fleet to protect herself, is it not wrong to deny the same right to Germany? Take away the necessity for that protection, guarantee to them the security of their trade and commerce and the necessity for that expensive fleet will disappear.[1]

An international naval conference, meeting in London from December 1908 to February 1909, had issued a Declaration which, though it constituted a notable improvement upon the Declaration of Paris, 1856, still remained to be ratified. Though Sir Edward Grey had promised the Commons liberty to discuss the Declaration, an entire parliamentary session passed too crowded with more pressing business for time to be given for debating the issue. In 1910, the ratification of the Declaration of London was quietly dropped. *The Nation* censured the Government for its 'lack of moral courage to take the golden key'.[2] Radical hopes had again been blighted and 'the party opposed to internationalising the code of naval warfare and granting greater freedom to neutral commerce finally won the day'.[3]

If English Radical opinion was frustrated in its search for an issue out of which might grow the longed for agreement between Britain and Germany, they had not been mistaken in their estimate that there was the desire to negotiate an understanding between the two nations. Unknown to them, Bethmann-Hollweg, on becoming Germany's Chancellor, had wasted little time in making an approach to the British Government about a possible agreement. To the Germans, the circumstances for such an approach seemed particularly favourable. Sufficient time had elapsed to allow for the tension over the Bosnian incident to subside. Perhaps for the first time in many

---

[1] Reported *Concord*, xxvi, no. 6, June 1910, p. 70–1. See also Fred Maddison's speech seconding motion on abolition of right to capture. 'The European situation at the present time is largely a question between England and Germany, and if the object of the resolution can be attained it will do more than anything else to bring about a reduction in our armaments and secure harmony and good feeling among warlike nations. The abolition of the capture of private property will be good for England. It will also be good for the world.'

[2] See *The Nation*, 25 Feb. 1911; also 10 Apr. 1909.

[3] Halévy, *The Rule of Democracy*, 399–400. For attitude of Radicals to Declaration see, *inter alia*, F. E. Bray, *British Rights at Sea under the Declaration of London* (1911), especially the introduction by J. M. Robertson. Not all Radical opinion accepted the Declaration without reservation. See, for example, *Concord*, xxvii, no. 4, Apr. 1911, pp. 42–3. Disputes about the Declaration of London continued for three years. See *Annual Register*, 1909, p. 58: 1910, p. 255; 1911, pp. 152, 137, 275 and 279; see also *E.P.*, iii: 45.

years, they felt that Germany could approach England on equal diplomatic terms. Undoubtedly, a rapprochement would be in the interests of both Governments. The Germans did not believe that the 1909 naval panic could be counted as an obstacle, and some diplomatists were even prepared to believe that popular fantasies about Germany's intention to invade England would make Britain's diplomatists more ready to consider an arrangement. Bülow, when he had been Chancellor, had maintained hope of an agreement by constantly stressing in his speeches to the Reichstag the community of interests shared by the British and the Germans in all parts of the world. The Kaiser supported moves for an understanding with Britain. German military opinion after the Bosnian crisis wanted more emphasis to be placed upon the army and less upon the navy. In the face of this opposition, the German Minister of Marine, Tirpitz, became far less intransigent in his demands.

Bethmann-Hollweg was very much under the influence of Kiderlen-Wächter, a man with long experience of foreign affairs. Kiderlen was able to impress his views upon Bethmann and he, like Tirpitz, insisted that before the naval experts should be involved in discussions there had to be a political rapprochement of some kind.[1] The price that Germany sought for a naval agreement was a high one: that Britain's ties with Russia and France should be weakened so that if the Central Powers should ever engage in hostilities with the Dual Alliance, Britain would stand aside as a neutral. From time to time Germany varied the price she asked, from Britain's neutrality to loose arrangements between the two countries for consultation on questions of mutual concern. But it soon became clear that political accord was impossible and Germany showed little interest in the talks for a naval understanding which dragged on interminably without achieving much.

Germany had overestimated her bargaining power and underestimated the vitality of the Triple Entente. Bethmann was too inflexible in his attitude. Kiderlen, who effectively dictated Bethmann's views on foreign policy, too long had been out of touch with the current diplomatic scene,[2] and was too unimaginative to understand the mentality of the British Foreign Office concerning the Anglo-French and Anglo-Russian ententes. It was of no value for the Germans, in negotiations with Grey, to stress that German public opinion could only be persuaded to accept a naval agreement after a

---

[1] See Carroll, 637.
[2] Kiderlen had been virtually banished from active participation in foreign affairs for ten years because Bülow had shown the Kaiser some of Kiderlen's letters which made indiscreet jokes about William's ill-mannered behaviour.

political agreement. Grey didn't care a fig for German public opinion, and neither did his most intimate advisers.[1]

Though Grey was finally responsible for decisions, from the beginning his Foreign Office advisers were adamant in their opposition to any settlement with Germany. Eyre Crowe, to whose opinion of Germany's policy Grey and Hardinge always paid the greatest attention, did not believe that Germany's terms were worth serious consideration. Their offers were either insincere or minimal. In any event, a political agreement between Britain and Germany would only serve to endanger the French entente and England's security.[2] Grey's private secretary, Louis Mallet, until he became assistant under secretary at the Foreign Office, persistently whispered in Grey's ear that he should beware of 'falling into the trap' the Germans were setting and thus allow 'the policy of the last few years . . . [to] go by the board'.[3] As to talk of finding a neutrality formula between the two Powers, Hardinge, in a memorandum he had drafted in April 1909, had declared unreservedly this could only be a trap designed to tie England's hands while Germany consolidated her hold upon the continent of Europe. Eventually Britain would be forced to become 'a satellite of the German constellation'.[4]

Grey informed the Cabinet on 1 September 1909 that Bethmann-Hollweg desired an Anglo-German understanding. His colleagues responded to this news with caution rather than enthusiasm. Grey was to tell Goschen, the British ambassador in Berlin, to inform Bethmann that Britain would listen sympathetically to any proposals for an understanding the German Chancellor might make. But these proposals should not be inconsistent with the preservation of 'existing relations and friendships with other Powers'.[5] The question of an understanding with Germany was not discussed again in the Cabinet until the following July. Then it was Loreburn who raised the possibility of a closer understanding between the two Powers. Grey indicated the course that negotiations had followed since the previous autumn, and told ministers that it would be inexpedient to enter into an engagement with Germany that might lead to misunderstanding and possibly the loss of French or Russian friendship. The Cabinet seem to have concurred in this judgment without dissent. Grey then promised he would circulate a draft of the memorandum for Goschen.[6]

Ten days later, when Grey submitted his draft memorandum, the

[1] See *B.D.* vi, 290, 293.   [2] See Steiner, 116–17.
[3] *Ibid.*, 104.   [4] *B.D.* v, 823–6.
[5] Cabinet Letter, 1 Sept. 1909 and *B.D.* vi, 194.
[6] *Ibid.*, 20 July 1910.

Cabinet chose to amend it. This in its way was an extraordinary move. At a time when a host of difficult domestic issues more than occupied ministers' time, they chose to take sufficient interest in foreign affairs actually to alter the words of a memorandum drafted by the Foreign Secretary. It was as though, after five years in government, they had suddenly realised the importance of foreign affairs. Not least the strangest factor in this episode was that the initiative to discuss an understanding with Germany came from Lord Chancellor Loreburn.

This new interest by ministers in foreign affairs, and in particular relations between Germany and Britain, led on 20 January 1911 to a unique development. A Cabinet Committee,[1] comprising Asquith, Lloyd George, Morley, Crewe and Runciman, was set up to consider a memorandum to be submitted to Bethmann. This move caused great fluttering in the Foreign Office dovecote. Arthur Nicolson intensely disliked the development. Grey was 'perfectly sound', but Nicolson was afraid of 'several members in the Cabinet who desire to come to what they term a "friendly understanding" with Germany at almost any cost'.[2] Nicolson viewed with great suspicion any activities designed to promote Anglo-German friendship. His particular concern was that Grey, in attempting to steer a middle course between the Germanophiles in the Cabinet who were pressing for an agreement, and his own loyalty to the existing ententes with France and Russia, would 'move too far from our original position. . . . Personally, I do not see how it is possible that we should ever arrive at a satisfactory agreement.'[3] So intense was Nicolson's fear of the situation, that he positively welcomed the Agadir troubles as he thought it would 'open the eyes of all those who have been so clamorous of late for an understanding with Germany'.[4]

On 8 March 1911 the Cabinet considered the draft memorandum prepared by the five-man committee. In the discussion that preceded revision, the most interesting point that emerged was that ministers recognised the difficulty with which in the end they would have to deal: to find a suitable formula acceptable to all the Powers 'in view of the impossibility of France openly abandoning, as against Germany, the policy of *revanche*'.[5] Here was the Radical complaint about France and about the entente policy generally, articulated

---

[1] See Steiner, 124–5; J. P. Mackintosh, *The British Cabinet* (2nd edn., 1968), 334–5.
[2] *B.D.* VI, 440.
[3] Nicolson to Hardinge, 2 Mar. 1911, quoted Steiner, 124.
[4] *B.D.* VII, 359; and VI, 461.
[5] Cabinet Letter, 9 Mar. 1911.

without any reservation in open Cabinet. Yet not one Radical Minister chose to protest. When one considers the angry complaints initiated by Loreburn and Morley later in that year, about the lack of information on the military conversations with France, one cannot help but wonder whether the explanation for their inconsistency was simple pique. The draft memorandum was revised and sent off the same day. It stated boldly: 'His Majesty's Government believe that the special interests which have led to the present grouping of Powers, do not involve anything in the nature of opposition and still less of hostile purpose among them.' There was to be no political agreement without a simultaneous naval one.[1]

The German reply was received on 9 May 1911. What Bethmann wanted was a general political agreement that would make the idea of a purely naval agreement superfluous. The Germans requested 'a general understanding which would preclude all possibility of an attack by one party on the other'. British comment on the Chancellor's insistence that a neutrality formula should be worked out, was not very hopeful. As the Cabinet did nothing about Bethmann's request, effectively the German terms were rejected. Thus, after two years of negotiations, the virtual result was deadlock. Negotiations still continued upon limited plans for an exchange of information between Germany and Britain on work in hand or projected for the dockyards, but even these were interrupted by the flare-up of trouble at Agadir.

A false dawn

Sir Arthur Nicolson had gloomily noted the growth in popularity of the Society for Anglo-German Friendship under the vigorous patronage of Lascelles. Throughout 1910, the Radical Press earnestly continued to advocate the conclusion of a political agreement with Germany. Time wore on, and the public neither heard nor saw any real evidence of fruitful negotiations for an agreement. However, there was plenty of evidence of the British and German Governments maintaining a warlike scale of armaments. In the search for peace perhaps men of good will would do well to reconsider their priorities?

> Calumnies, libels and lies are breeding hatred, and pin-pricks harmless at first, are gradually making way for sword thrusts. The petty fiction of mutual trust and amity is belied by the stern reality of gigantic armaments, and we may well ask: is it not a farce to toast one another and swear eternal friendship

[1] *B.D.* VI, 444.

whilst we are openly sharpening our swords on every political grindstone and proclaiming the vital importance of keeping our powder dry? . . . we know that the most genuine Entente or Verständigung does not suffice to regulate *international* any more than it has sufficed to regulate *National* relations.[1]

There was a rising groundswell of opposition to increasing armaments from Radical and Labour ranks. The reductionist lobby in Parliament, so conclusively defeated in 1909 and quiescent in 1910, rallied its forces, and once more took up the cry for retrenchment in armament expenditure.

The Government could not afford to ignore the restlessness of its Radical supporters. There was certainly sufficient cause for Radical impatience and concern. They supported a Liberal Government that in its turn claimed it supported economy in armaments. Yet every year the cost of the Navy increased. There had been a programme of eight Dreadnoughts, then the next year five more of the monsters. Was there never to be an end to this competition in shipbuilding? Would the naval architects go on forever designing bigger, more expensive battleships and the factories turn out ever bigger ordnance with which to equip them? With the increasing importance of the submarine as a warship, and the obvious military potential of the aeroplane and airship,[2] there seemed no end to the engines of destruction Governments would willingly finance and with which mankind, in a moment of folly, might wreak terrible and irremediable harm. Surely, if not conscience, then common sense dictated that expenditure upon armaments must be drastically curtailed.

In the Cabinet Lloyd George led the 'economist' faction. He was determined to achieve a cut in the forthcoming Naval Estimates. However, such a move was fraught with political difficulties. C. F. G. Masterman, who supported Lloyd George's desire to lower the estimates, was concerned that the time was not opportune for a move that would involve the Chancellor threatening resignation. If Lloyd George resigned and carried his fight to the country, as he said he would, then the Government would not be able to pass the Parliament Bill. Lloyd George asked Masterman, 'When is the time opportune for breaking up a Government? If there are strong reasons this session there will be strong reasons also next session and the session after.' The power and the demands of the Sea Lords were growing. They were dictating the policy and expenditure of the country. If a tolerable state of affairs was to be restored they had to be

---

[1] *Concord*, xxvii, no. 1, Jan. 1911, p. 15.
[2] See letter of John Galsworthy in *The Times*, 8 Apr. 1911.

met and defeated. A stand would have to be made if the Government was to be true to its Liberal principles. Lloyd George was sanguine of his chances of success when he talked to C. P. Scott on 17 February.[1] But the Chancellor was effectively outmanœuvred by the First Lord. McKenna would only pledge himself to a cut in the 1913 Estimates, and even that would depend upon Germany reducing her building programme and Haldane agreeing to the Army sharing the proposed reduction of £4,400,000.[2]

The Naval Estimates for 1911–12, published on 9 March, totalled £44,392,500, and made provision for five new capital ships. A month earlier, when answering a question in the Commons, McKenna had frankly admitted that his predictions in March 1909, of Germany's potential Dreadnought programme, had been inaccurate. If the First Lord admitted his mistake and consequently Britain had been overbuilding Dreadnoughts, was it not sensible that the Estimates should be reduced to at the very least £40 million, and provision be made for four new Dreadnoughts?[3] Instead of this, at a time of 'profound peace' the Estimates were at their highest level ever. Such estimates were not merely 'enormous' and 'exaggerated', they were 'provocative' and could not be justified.[4]

Ever optimistic, the reductionists looked for portents that world opinion supported their plea. They noted with satisfaction that on 24 February, in a vote on the construction of two new cruisers in the French Chamber, the Socialist Marcel Sembat had tabled a motion that the Foreign Minister should immediately propose to other Governments a concerted limitation of armaments. Though strongly opposed by the Government, Sembat's motion had been supported by 115 Republican votes as well as the votes of 75 Socialist Deputies. A resolution that the subject should be discussed at the Third Hague Conference received a majority of almost 400 votes. In the Reichstag, National Liberal, Progressist and Centre Deputies, as well as the Socialists, had insisted that the idea of an international agreement on armaments was not Utopian and that the question of a reduction in armaments could no longer be simply put aside with contempt.

[1] See for this incident, *The Political Diaries of C. P. Scott* (1970), edited by Trevor Wilson, 38–41.
[2] See Marder, 218. It has to be remembered that Lloyd George was a very sick man during this period. There were widespread rumours that he was dying from cancer of the throat. He did not fully recover his strength until May 1911. Other leading 'economists' in the Cabinet were also far from well, particularly Churchill and Harcourt. This had been brought on by strain and overwork. See Austen Chamberlain, 330–2.
[3] The current rumour was that the Admiralty was pressing for six new Dreadnoughts and the Cabinet wanted five.
[4] See *Daily News, Manchester Guardian*, 10 Mar. 1911.

In Italy and Austria as well, the reductionist movement seemed to be gathering strength.

On 13 March the reductionist lobby gained a day for debate in the Commons, when Murray Macdonald moved and Arthur Ponsonby seconded the motion that 'this House views with alarm the enormous increase during recent years in the expenditure on the army and the navy and is of the opinion that it ought to be diminished'.[1] It was 1908 all over again, and the Radical arguments were, as then, mostly based on the Cobden Club pamphlet of 1905. Macdonald's speech was able and close-reasoned. The Liberal Government had been returned in 1906 pledged to reduce expenditure on arms. Since then armaments had continued to increase enormously. What possible danger could explain the Government's repudiation of its pledge? 'That is the question to which we have never had any reply, good, bad or indifferent, from any member of the Government since they came into office . . .' Macdonald went so far as to declare that even if Britain was sure that foreign Powers would not follow her example, it would still be as well for Britain to reduce. Ponsonby, seconding Murray Macdonald, caustically noted that a policy for huge expenditure upon armaments was only accepted by Liberalism when Liberals were in office.

Joseph King, introducing an amendment, showed by his attack upon Murray Macdonald the confusion in the Lib-Lab Radical ranks on any question that affected the Navy.

> The hon. member for Stirling Burghs referred to our great ships of war as engines of death, and nothing more. To every citizen who views the great Naval Review to which we look forward . . . there will come, I venture to say, not only the feeling that they are great instruments of death, but that they are great emblems of the defence and power of our country. The point of view of the average man, whether he be Conservative or Liberal, is this— that so long as other countries maintain emblems, such as armies and navies, to give expression to their power and force, so long must we also maintain armies and navies in some way, at any rate, to a proportionate extent.

J. F. Green in *Concord* upbraided King for his 'singularly fatuous remarks' designed to suggest that he represented 'a more fully democratic point of view' more in line with the feelings of 'the man in the street' than 'the old type of intellectual Radical'. Green claimed 'the fact that the Labour Party is wholeheartedly on the anti-armaments side is surely a sufficient answer to this absurd idea,

[1] For debate, see *Hansard*, v: 22: 1877ff.

that Mr King's neo-Radicalism is more democratic than Mr Macdonald's or Mr Ponsonby's'. However, Green gave the lie to his own
argument by posing the rhetorical question: 'But is the "man in the
street" democratic?'[1] The 'pacific intent of the democracies' was
merely an argument of convenience for pacifists like Green. As to
the Labour Party in Parliament, Keir Hardie's speech clearly
showed that on the issue of armaments, Labour members were
Radical sheep who did not even pretend to put on the wolf's clothes
of Marxism. Hardie advocated Angellism and open diplomacy. His
hint, that if Lloyd George was the strong anti-armaments man he
professed to be he would do well to follow the example of Randolph
Churchill, was, in the circumstances, not merited.

Reginald McKenna discharged his difficult task of defending the
naval programme, representing it to the Tories as adequate to
maintain absolute supremacy, while making the same evidence seem
palatable to the 'little Navy' section of his own party. It was
apparent that 'he was a good deal more uneasy over the opposition
of his nominal friends than over the regular Opposition'.[2] He did
hold out the faint hope that Britain had reached the 'high tide' in
its naval estimates, but if there was to be any decrease in subsequent
years this depended upon there being no changes in the German
Navy Law. The First Lord's speech was heard in chilling silence by
his own back-benchers. 'The absence of applause during the speech
was almost as much as a vote of censure upon a Minister who has
shown himself to be nothing but a tool of the experts at the
Admiralty.'[3]

Asquith was absent from the House during the debate because his
daughter had suddenly fallen seriously ill. Therefore, the task of
replying for the Government to the malcontents of its own side fell
to Sir Edward Grey's unhappy lot. Grey seized the opportunity, and
in a speech that combined 'anguish and optimism exactly suited to
Radical feeling'[4] soothed away the fears of most of the Government's
Radical critics.

Grey stressed that although Europe might be divided into two
groups, during the last five years there had been a progressive removal

[1] *Concord*, xxvii, no. 3, Mid-March 1911, p. 25.   [2] Marder, 219.
[3] *Concord*, xxvii, no. 3, p. 26.
[4] Dorey, 237. See comments in *New Age*, 23 Mar. 1911, p. 481. 'It was not
necessary . . . to reduce Fleet Street and Nonconformity to a quivering jelly
of sentiment to ensure their acceptance of the current Navy Bill . . . We are
disposed to laugh somewhat cynically at the spectacle of England submitting
to have its leg pulled by Sir Edward Grey. . . . Sir Edward, who pursues
fishing as an occupation, should know better than to fish for sprats with
mackerel.'

of the possible causes of dispute between them. He spoke with an unaccustomed warmth of the excellent relations between the British and German Governments. 'Yet the armaments increase . . . It does not follow . . . that one nation can put a stop to the rivalry by dropping out of the race . . . On the contrary, it might very well be that if one nation dropped out of the competition it might momentarily give a spurt in expenditure in some other.' If not unilateral disarmament, what solution did Grey have to offer to remedy the race in armaments?

> What we have to look for is any beneficent movement which will go to the root of the matter, and so affect public opinion, not in one country but in all. That may lead to first of all the tide ceasing to flow, then turning, then, I hope, ebbing. I can conceive of but one thing that will really affect this Military and Naval expenditure of the world on the wholesale scale in which it must be affected if there is to be a real and sure relief. You will not get it till nations do what individuals have done, come to regard an appeal to law as the natural course for nations, instead of an appeal to force. Public opinion has been moving. Arbitration has been increasing. But you must take a large step further before the increase of arbitration will really affect this expenditure on armaments.

With the Government's Radical critics visibly responding to the sentiments he expressed, Grey reached the *dénouement*. He quoted two speeches of the President of the United States that proposed extending the principles of arbitration to all international disputes, including 'questions of honour'. The Government would be delighted to take up the President's proposals.

> I know that to bring about changes of this kind public opinion has to rise to a high plane, higher than it can rise in ordinary times . . . but the times are not ordinary. . . . The great nations of the world are in bondage, in increasing bondage, at the present moment, to their armies and navies, and it does not seem to me impossible that in some future years they may discover, as individuals have discovered, that law is a better remedy than force, and that all the time they have been in bondage to this tremendous expenditure, the prison door has been locked on the inside.[1]

The reductionists responded wholeheartedly to Grey's words. Never, declared the saintly Allen Baker, had the House been more deeply moved.[2] Nevertheless, the Radical motion was not withdrawn.

[1] Grey's speech, *Hansard*, v:22:1977–91.
[2] *Hansard*, v:22:1996.

In the division Murray Macdonald and Ponsonby had only 56 supporters, as against 276 who voted for the Government.

Had Grey been entirely sincere in his speech? It had been made at short notice and he had allowed himself an unaccustomed freedom in declaring his hopes for the future of Europe. The speech had been designed for the moment and the audience. When shortly he spoke to the Dominion delegates in the Committee of Imperial Defence, he allowed himself no flights of fancy; his conception of Britain's relations with Germany was hardheaded and pessimistic.[1]

Reactions in the Radical Press to Grey's speech were mixed. Those who had not been exposed personally to Grey's eloquence were less ready to be swept off their feet by his Utopian vision of future international relations. It was agreed generally that as a speech it was probably the best Grey had ever made. However, if his arguments in opposition to the reductionist motion were examined carefully, they did not appear convincing. Granted there was the old general sympathy with opposition to armaments, a candid admission of their danger to civilisation; but as to doing anything in the way of reduction, Grey had declared an absolute *non possumus*, and that in spite of his insistence that Britain's foreign relations were not strained. Much had been made of Grey's support of the hope, expressed by McKenna, that the Naval Estimates had now reached their high tide, but this when examined was balanced by all sorts of vague limitations —'*If* the programmes of other powers follow their nominal and intended course', and so on. All Radical and pacifist opinion welcomed Grey's endorsement of Taft's suggested Treaty of Arbitration, but even here there lurked hidden dangers.

> There may not merely be an Anglo-American Arbitration Treaty, but an Anglo-American naval and military alliance. In fact, this was hinted at by Sir Edward Grey, and has been endorsed by a section of the reactionary Press. And there is only too much reason to fear that this may be the outcome of negotiations. The Foreign Secretary has unfortunately always been a Balance of Power rather than a Concert of Europe man. Now this will not do. We do not want the Roosevelt 'big stick' policy. Emphatically we do not want an Anglo-American alliance to boss the world, or as a rival to other combinations. Moreover, there are questions that cannot be settled by arbitration, still less by the balance of hostile Powers, but which might and should be settled by a Concert of Powers.[2]

[1] See *B.D.* vi, 781.

[2] *Concord*, xxvii, no. 3, mid-Mar. 1911, p. 26. Sir Edward's 'hint' came near the end of his speech. 'It is true that the two nations who did that [i.e. make an arbitration treaty] might still be exposed to attack from a third nation who

John Dillon was not the only man that was convinced Grey's speech was no more than a 'red herring of gigantic proportions'.[1]

But it was Massingham, writing in *The Nation*, who reflected the hopes of most Radicals. He claimed:

> There are two Sir Edward Greys—a Grey that takes no step that the intelligent official cannot take with him, and Grey who does not disdain the dreams of mankind, and is even visibly touched by them . . . the second personality emerged in an almost impassioned sketch of a warless world. . . . For the first time on this melancholy evening the Liberals broke into loud acclamations. A new and wider horizon had been opened, with a prospect of escape from the encircling vision of Dreadnoughts.[2]

Intoxicated by the wine of their own hopes, the Radicals abandoned caution, despite the strictures of the *Manchester Guardian*. The *Guardian* did not want Radicals to ignore either McKenna's 'confession' or to pin too much faith upon Grey's vague visions of future world peace, about which it was frankly sceptical.[3] The critic, with the advantage of hindsight, can recognise that the significant feature of Grey's speech was not what he had said but what he had left unsaid. The implication of his contention that it was not England that was forcing the pace of armaments, was that the responsibility was entirely Germany's. And Germany's naval building was dictated by a schedule which could not be changed. He did not tell the Commons that in the naval negotiations that had been going on between the two countries for two years, the Germans had expressed their willingness to consider naval limitation provided Britain met Germany's desire for a political agreement. If Grey had published the German terms, there would have been immediate and violent objections from imperialist and balance of power supporters. What is more, Grey would have had to declare publicly where his own loyalties lay. So Parliament, and indeed the nation, were told nothing. They were never afforded the opportunity to choose between the policy that Grey advocated, supported by the Cabinet and the officials of the Foreign Office, and the alternative of a political and naval agreement with Germany.

The projected Treaty between the United States and Britain had no direct connection with the European divide between Entente and

---

had not entered into such agreement. I think it would probably lead to their following it up by an agreement that they would join with each other in any case in which one only had a quarrel with a third Power by which arbitration was refused.'

[1] *Hansard*, v:22:2530.   [2] *The Nation*, 18 Mar. 1911.
Manchester Guardian, 14 and 15 Mar. 1911.

Alliance Powers. Nevertheless, it was argued, if two major Powers could reach such a high degree of accord so as to be prepared to sign a compact of this nature, then surely this augured well for similar arrangements between other Powers. The *Manchester Guardian* admitted that 'the first unlimited treaty of arbitration will be the longest step to universal peace . . . for once you can prove that arbitration in all subjects is compatible with sovereign rights, you are within sight of a true federation of European nations'.[1] Philip Snowden avowed the promise held out by Grey's speech had renewed his hope and faith in humanity and his belief in the ultimate triumph of love and righteousness.[2] The *Daily News* discerned the steady rise 'to full flood' of public enthusiasm.[3] The Churches, nonconformist and established, gave thanks for Taft's declaration and expressed their gratitude to God 'for the noble response of Sir Edward Grey'.[4] The culmination of this unprecedented ecumenical enthusiasm was a meeting at the Guildhall, where Asquith moved and Balfour seconded a resolution that pledged their 'support to the principles of . . . [an Anglo-American arbitration] treaty as serving the highest interests of the two nations and as tending to promote the peace of the world'. Felix Moscheles writing in *Concord* of 'the day the Lion and the Lamb lay down together' claimed:

> That manifestation of unity in the service of a great cause made every pioneer of the movement, every true Pacifist, glow with pleasure, and even the most unimaginative of them could not but look confidently into the future, whilst the stoniest diplomat must have felt his officially regulated pulses considerably quickened.[5]

Asquith, in a speech frequently interrupted by cheers, declared

> I do not think I am using language of exaggeration when I say we are here . . . today to record the most signal victory in our time in the international sphere of the power of reason and the sense of brotherhood. . . . Our eirenicon contains and implies no message of menace to the rest or any part of mankind. It is not even an alliance, aggressive or defensive.[6] It simply means that within the vast area for which, as States, we are severally responsible, war is ruled out as the possible arbiter of conceivable differences. Other things, we may hope and believe will follow.[7]

[1] *Manchester Guardian*, 29 Apr. 1911.
[2] *Christian Commonwealth*, 22 Feb. 1911.   [3] *Daily News*, 18 Mar. 1911.
[4] Resolution of the Baptist Union, reported *Manchester Guardian*, 23 Mar. 1911.
[5] *Concord*, xxvii, no. 5, mid-May 1911, p. 49.
[6] A response to the criticism of some Radicals. Grey had emphasised the same point in a speech he made at the annual banquet of the International Arbitration League, 17 Mar. 1911.   [7] *The Times*, 29 Mar. 1911.

Nor were any other of the principal speakers, Balfour for the Opposition, the Archbishop of Canterbury, the Roman Catholic Archbishop Bourne, the Rev. F. B. Meyer for the Free Churches, Sir Joseph Ward for the Empire and Dr Adler the Chief Rabbi, less fulsome in their declarations of pleasure and support for the treaty.

Amid all this enthusiasm and high spirits, a slight chill was injected by Bethmann's speech to the Reichstag on 30 March. The German Chancellor claimed in his opinion the Anglo-American Arbitration Treaty created nothing new; it merely put the seal on an existing *de facto* state of affairs. It had caught the minds of America and Britain at their best and fixed them there. Anglo-German relations had not reached that state of maturation. Indeed, as long as 'men were men and states were states', talk of disarmament and a string of arbitration treaties was impractical and Utopian. In principle there was no difference between Bethmann's speech and Grey's. The difference was in their choice of words and tone of address; Grey had wanted to disarm possible critics, Bethmann could afford to be stiff and uncompromising towards the Social Democrats in the Reichstag. Hirst in the *Economist* wrote of his offence at the 'undisguised brutality' of Bethmann's speech.[1] But the *Manchester Guardian* declared that the German Chancellor's 'cold douche of Bismarckian realism' was the required antidote 'to take after an emotional hot bath'.[2]

The leaders of the Anglo-German friendship movement emphasised the happier elements in Bethmann's speech. Lord Weardale was convinced that it was the harbinger of a treaty with Germany in the not too distant future.[3] Ramsay MacDonald meanwhile had predicted that France and Germany would soon join Britain. All that was required was that a 'few political changes' should take place in Germany.[4] The Kaiser's Government had rejected the initiative of the American Government to conclude a general treaty of arbitration. But lest England claim this showed Germany's bad faith, the Germans could point the finger of censure at Britain. After years of procrastination, the House of Lords was in the process of rejecting the Declaration of London, thus effectively nullifying the greater part of the work accomplished at the Second Hague Conference. Nor was the Anglo-American Arbitration Treaty to enjoy a happier fate than the Declaration. The Senate struck out Article III of the Treaty,

[1] *Economist*, 5 Apr. 1911.
[2] *Manchester Guardian*, 3 Apr. 1911; cf. *The Nation*, 8 Apr. 1911, that took an exactly opposite point of view.
[3] *Manchester Guardian*, 19 May 1911.
[4] *Manchester Guardian*, 22 Apr. 1911.

reducing its effect to that of the Convention already existing between the two countries. The ironic feature was that the Senate's opposition was primarily motivated by a jealous concern for its control over foreign affairs.[1]

But all this lay in the future. For the moment, the friends of peace, and in particular the supporters of closer relations between Germany and Britain, saw nothing but promise in the international situation. If their morale was high, there was a corresponding despondency in Jingo hearts. Grey, Leo Maxse grumbled, had 'opened the floodgates of fatuity' with his speech. Now 'every flatulent fool' was 'on the peace path'.[2] The Anglo-German Friendship Society was reorganised and an inaugural meeting was held at the Mansion House on 1 May, where an enthusiastic audience was addressed by Lascelles, Weardale and other 'great leaders of thought'.[3] Lord Chancellor Loreburn publicly declared his hope that the Government would inaugurate a policy to place Britain in the same relation towards Germany as was hoped would be attained with the United States of America.[4]

In May the Kaiser, accompanied by his wife and two of his sons, paid a private visit to England to attend the unveiling of a memorial to his grandmother, Queen Victoria. William hoped that the occasion would serve to improve relations between Germany and Britain. A reserved policy by Germany had already contributed to an appreciable *détente*. Indeed, the attitude of Germany's allies argued in favour of maintaining reserve.[5] It had been a long time since Germany's leaders had been so lavish with peaceful assurances. The Kaiser had hoped to engage in political conversations during his stay, but had been disappointed in this by Grey's insistence that the visit be regarded merely as a family gathering.[6] Nevertheless, the visit was a splendid success. The crowds in the streets warmly welcomed the Emperor. He responded with equal enthusiasm. The Radicals were complacent and apparently with good reason. 'We doubt', noted the *Manchester Guardian*, 'whether the poison of the Jingo newspapers for the last five or six years can really have done as much mischief

[1] See *Concord*, 26 Mar. 1912, p. 30.
[2] *National Review*, Apr. 1911.
[3] *Concord*, xxvii, no. 5, mid-May 1911, p. 54.
[4] *Concord*, xxvii, no. 5, mid-May 1911, p. 54.
[5] Italy's obvious eagerness for Tripoli threatened either the weakening of the Triple Alliance or the alienation of Turkey. Austria had no desire to be involved in a Franco-German quarrel, and Germany had been prepared to promise Sazonov at Potsdam that she would refuse to support any Austrian attack upon Russia or any policy that was even indirectly hostile to Russia in the Balkans. See Carroll, 634 and 644.
[6] See Nicolson, *George the Fifth*, 182.

among the people as is commonly supposed.'[1] The chief aim in foreign affairs now, should be the pursuit of friendship with Germany along with the old policy of friendship towards France. The *Guardian* was convinced that 'everything seems to be in good train to that end'.[2] The Kaiser left England shortly after the National Peace Council celebrated its Peace Day with a reception in London. Delegates to that meeting pledged themselves 'unremittingly to combat the rule of force and injustice by the introduction of the reign of justice and equity'.[3]

As the Kaiser was preparing to leave for the railway station, he asked his cousin whether he thought the French were acting in accordance with the Algeciras Agreement. King George remarked it was best to forget the Agreement. Fundamentally there was no difference between what France was doing in Morocco and what England had done earlier in Egypt. Therefore, England was not going to place obstacles in France's path and Germany would do well to recognise the *fait accompli*. William assured George that he would never wage a war for the sake of Morocco. King George said nothing.[4]

---

[1] Leonard Courtney in a speech at Church House, 28 Apr. 1911 had forcibly pointed out to the Radicals and the pacifists generally, who were always prone to blame most things on the Jingo Press, that the true origin of estrangement lay in the mistrusts and jealousies of the ordinary man.
[2] *Manchester Guardian*, 17 May 1911.
[3] See *Concord*, xxviii, no. 6, mid-June 1911, pp. 70–1.
[4] See Nicolson, *King Geoge*, 185–6.

Chapter 6   The Foreign Secretary is Censured for his Pains

The *Panther*'s leap

Only chauvinist opinion in France had been openly hostile to the Accord made with Germany in 1909 over Morocco. From the beginning, however, the prospects for its success had been doubtful. Every attempt to provide for economic cooperation between the two countries had been unsuccessful. The French considered that their supremacy in Morocco was part of the natural order of things, and therefore believed that any concessions made to Germany were a matter of France's goodwill rather than any claim of right by Germany. Perhaps, *Patrie* all along had been correct in its estimate of the Franco-German arrangement? 'Frenchmen and Germans cannot be in "accord" so long as the question of Alsace-Lorraine is not solved. The recognition of France's rights in Morocco do not return Metz and Strassburg to us.'[1]

In December 1910 a French cruiser landed troops at the open port of Agadir. The French Government were quick to explain to Germany that this was intended to stop gun running, and reiterated assurances of their loyalty to the Act of Algeciras. Not surprisingly, in the circumstances, these assurances inspired little confidence with the Germans. By the spring of 1911 it was apparent that all attempts to revive the policy of colonial cooperation between the Germans and the French had failed.

The native population in Morocco was restless. They believed that France was more interested in the subjugation than the pacification of their country. Their discontent was brought to a head when two Moroccan deserters were executed upon the authority of the French military mission at Fez. The native population rioted, and the French Cabinet decided that a military expedition had to be sent to relieve the French forces in the Moroccan capital. Though the French

[1] *Patrie*, 12 Feb. 1909, quoted Carroll, *French Public Opinion*, 234.

Government maintained that the riots were serious, the claim was questioned by the greater part of the French Press. It was obvious that the actions contemplated by the French would have an immediate impact on relations with Germany. Before the French Cabinet even authorized the sending of the expedition, Kiderlen had indicated Germany's willingness to dispose of the entire question, provided Germany was compensated. Meanwhile, Bethmann-Hollweg had strongly advised against sending the expedition. It would certainly upset public opinion in Germany and might lead to a holy war in Morocco. Nevertheless, the expedition was despatched. The French Government represented their decision to the Press as a desire to protect foreign interests in Fez. Their action, they claimed, was justified by international practice and had nothing to do with the Algeciras Act. Germany, therefore, could neither complain nor claim compensation.

Albert de Mun, the French Catholic leader who supported a forward policy in Morocco, declared: 'Let no one speak this time of foreign complications, let no one make use of the German spectre. . . . Neither Germany nor Europe will say anything because they can say nothing.' André Mévil at the same time assured his readers that France was 'acting in perfect harmony with Russia and England who are ready to support our efforts with all necessary energy'. Jaurès for his part refused to admit that Fez was in any danger. The real danger, he protested, was that France's policy could lead to war. Support for this point of view came from the dark hints of the extreme Nationalist, Charles Maurras. 'The solution of the Morocco crisis is not to be found at Fez but among the pines of the Vosges. What is afoot in Morocco makes sense only if we are prepared to fight in the Vosges.'[1]

The German plan was to await events. Once the French expedition was in Fez they would send warships to one or two Moroccan ports on the pretext of protecting the interests of German nationals. If, meanwhile, France was prepared to make concessions, the situation would be altered. However, neither from the Monis Cabinet nor that of Caillaux which had replaced it in June, came any mention of compensation for Germany. On I July von Schoen informed the Quai d'Orsay that his Government had despatched the gunboat *Panther* to Agadir for the protection of German merchants there. The ship would be withdrawn as soon as there was no further danger to German merchants.

---

[1] *Echo de Paris, Gaulois, Humanité, Action Française*, 21, 22 April and 5 May 1911 respectively: all quoted by Carroll, *French Public Opinion*, 237–8.

The British Foreign Office had not looked with any favour upon France's activities in Morocco. What particularly concerned Eyre Crowe was that the French Government, relying upon the good faith of England, would make political bargains with Germany at Britain's expense. However, when Germany interfered, Crowe immediately changed his tune and became an active partisan of the French cause. He believed that the Germans had sent the *Panther* to Agadir because the improvement in Anglo-German relations had encouraged the Germans to suppose that Britain would stand aside from any Franco-German dispute. The Foreign Office was particularly worried and puzzled because of Britain's exclusion from the whole affair. Could it be that the Germans were striking a bargain with the French over Morocco at Britain's expense? When he learned of Germany's request for compensation in the French Congo, Crowe in a minute claimed: 'This is a trial of strength if anything. Concession means not loss of interests or loss of prestige. It means defeat, with all its inevitable consequences.'[1] Above all else, Crowe was distressed by the manner in which the Cabinet was handling the crisis. 'It seems to me', Crowe wrote to Bertie, 'our Cabinet are all on the run and the strong hints we are giving to France that she must let Germany into Morocco make me ashamed as well as angry.'[2]

A special meeting of the Cabinet had been convened on 4 July to consider Germany's action in sending the *Panther* to Agadir. It was agreed that Grey should inform Metternich that Britain could not allow the future of Morocco to be settled behind her back. Nicolson had wanted a warship to be sent to Agadir, but the Cabinet would have nothing of this. Grey spoke to Metternich and at a meeting of the Cabinet on 11 July gave a 'very reassuring report' to his colleagues.[3] Meanwhile Goschen, in conversation with Kiderlen, reminded the German Minister that Britain could not accept any resettlement of Morocco to which she was not a party. However, he did not make any further remarks that 'might disturb . . . [Kiderlen's] equanimity.' Nicolson on 12 July told Metternich that the British Government intended to adopt a reserved attitude until such time as Germany's aims were clarified. On 18 July Bertie telegraphed from Paris the news that Germany was demanding compensation in the French Congo.[4]

At a meeting of the Cabinet the next day, after 'long and animated discussion', it was decided that whatever should be said to Germany

[1] *B.D.* VII, 179, 352, 383, 392.
[2] Crowe to Bertie, 20 July 1911, quoted Steiner, 142.
[3] Cabinet Letter, 12 July 1911.   [4] *B.D.* VII, 373, 388, 392.

about her request was best delayed until another meeting had been held. Grey had wanted Germany to be told immediately that a new Moroccan conference should be called and that if this proposal was rejected, Britain would act to protect her interests. The Cabinet did decide to tell the French that, provided the conditions were reasonable, Germany's gaining a foothold in Morocco would not be regarded as fatal to British interests and could not be treated as a *casus belli*.[1] After the Cabinet Grey wrote to Asquith in despairing tones that Germany would see that though she made excessive demands of France Britain apparently remained unmoved.[2]

The next day, C. P. Scott breakfasted with Loreburn. The Lord Chancellor was in a grim mood. He warned Scott, 'Take care we don't get into war with Germany. Always remember that this is a Liberal League Government.'[3] Loreburn's estimate of the strength of the Radicals within the Cabinet was not reassuring. He considered Harcourt to be the most reliable friend of peace. Morley was of little use—'weak and very captious'; Burns was well-meaning but counted for little. He pointed out to Scott

> the great weakening of the real Radical Liberal element in the Cabinet since Campbell-Bannerman's death. Besides the substitution of Asquith for Campbell-Bannerman there had been the loss of Bryce, Elgin, . . . Ripon and Gladstone (weak but well-meaning). In their places Churchill (unstable), Pease (a nobody), Runciman and Samuel (men owing promotion to and dependent on Asquith, and Runciman at least[,] an avowed Liberal Leaguer)—altogether an almost purely Liberal League Cabinet.[4]

The Cabinet met again on 21 July, and this time authorised Grey to point out that Germany had for seventeen days taken no notice of the Foreign Secretary's statement of the British position. While Britain wished Germany well in any negotiations for compensation elsewhere, they were not prepared to recognise any resettlement of Morocco in the making of which they had no voice.[5] Plainly, this statement strengthened Grey's hand. It was more in line with what he would have desired. Even so his position remained difficult. He still had not made clear his policy to his colleagues, nor did he believe the time was yet ripe for disclosure. Up to 18 July the diplomatic situation had been temperate. Then, when Germany made it

[1] Cabinet Letter, 20 July 1911.   [2] *B.D.* VII, 399.
[3] Scott, *Political Diaries*, 20 July 1911, p. 42; cf. Lloyd George's comment, *ibid.*, p. 39.
[4] Scott, *Diaries*, 6/8 Sept. 1911, pp. 52–3.
[5] Cabinet Letter, 22 July 1911.

obvious that she was prepared to push France hard, the situation became acute. All Grey could do was to try to draw ministers in the direction he desired. At the same time, his better judgment dictated that what was required was not an ambiguous conversation with Metternich,[1] but a stiff note to the German Government.

It was at this moment of quandary and indecision that Lloyd George paid a visit to Grey and read to him a passage he wished to use in a speech he was to make that evening. Here was the opportunity Grey had been vainly seeking. He 'cordially agreed' to Lloyd George's suggestion. Though the words suggested were vague, Germany would recognise the implied warning. The message would be even more effective coming from the 'Radical' Chancellor. Above all else, while serving Grey's purpose it would avoid the inconveniences and embarrassment of any Cabinet wrangles.

How is Lloyd George's intervention to be explained? He enjoyed taking the initiative with his Mansion House speech, and in later years did not regret his action. On the contrary, he was prepared to claim in his *War Memoirs* that if a similar stroke had been made in 1914, war might have been averted[2]—to say the least, a bold assertion. In conversation with Scott the day after his speech he maintained that he had not wished Germany 'through ignorance of

[1] See *B.D.* VII, 411.

[2] See Lloyd George, i, 26–7. Churchill's comments seem the most pertinent explanation. 'How could [Metternich] know what Mr Lloyd George was going to do? Until a few hours before, his colleagues did not know. Working with him in close association, I did not know. No one knew. Until his mind was definitely made up, he did not know himself.' *The World Crisis*, 47.

Lloyd George's penchant for the dramatic is well catalogued. Therefore it is of significance that when a messenger was sent to Lloyd George to attend on Grey, the Chancellor turned to Churchill with whom he was walking and announced: 'That's my speech. The Germans may demand my resignation as they did Delcassé's.' Churchill replied, 'That will make you the most popular man in England' (see *World Crisis*, 45).

If my conjecture about the reasons why Grey welcomed Lloyd George's speech is correct, then it throws a strange light on Grey's assessment of diplomacy in a time of crisis. He had sanctioned a public statement which had no point unless it was intended to produce a strong reaction in the Press. But the timing of this move was of the essence. Diplomatic resources had by no means been exhausted. Metternich had not had time to reply to Grey's grave words on 21 July. Everyone knew that the French and Germans were engaged only in the preliminary bargaining over Morocco and the French Congo. Britain had not been insulted, humbled, her prestige trammelled, nor her interests interfered with. Yet at this juncture, Grey seized the opportunity of employing what amounted to a publicity technique. He deliberately invoked an instrument which previously he had condemned. He could not but have foreseen the consequences of his crass action. Grey was soon to deplore any consorting with the Press when he had unhappily to extricate the Foreign Office with some remaining shreds of dignity after the reported indiscretions of Sir Fairfax Cartwright, Britain's Ambassador in Vienna, who for four years poisoned Anglo-German relations by his lying intelligence, 'inspired' by Germanophobia. See *Hansard*, v:30:1450 and *B.D.* VII, 656. On the Cartwright farrago, see Hale, 399–403.

our real intentions to commit herself so far that she could not withdraw, as happened with Russia before the Crimean war'. Lloyd
George did not deny that Germany had as much right to claim
compensation for giving France a free hand politically in Morocco as
Britain had claimed and received. When Scott questioned Lloyd
George about the general underlying reason for British foreign
policy the Chancellor admitted it was

> to give to France such support as would prevent her from falling
> under the virtual control of Germany and estrangement from
> us. This would mean the break up of the Triple Entente, as if
> France retired Russia would at once do the same and we should
> again be faced with the old troubles about the frontier of India.
> It would mean also the complete ascendancy of Germany in
> Europe and some fine day we might have the First Lord of the
> Admiralty coming to us and saying that instead of building
> against two powers we had to build against six. . . . But the
> history of the Napoleonic wars showed that any power which
> achieved European dominance in the last resort came to check
> against England, which so long as she retained her sea-power
> could not be coerced, and that would be the inevitable sequel to
> a German as to a French supremacy.[1]

A. C. Murray, a Liberal M.P., and brother of the Liberal Chief Whip
who was present throughout the conversation, listened with interest
to the Chancellor's 'endeavour to inculcate a little common-sense and
patriotism into the head of Scott . . . in respect of the Morocco
situation'.[2] Lloyd George's explanation must have been quite a shock
to Scott. To Massingham the only explanation for the Chancellor's
unfortunate outburst was that he had been put up to it by Grey and
the Foreign Office.[3]

The report from the British Minister in Tangier, that the tribes
around Fez were in rebellion against the Sultan, was made on the
same day that the Commons began the Committee stage of the
Parliament Bill. A week later it was apparent to everyone that
France intended to intervene in Morocco, and the military expedition was dispatched to Fez. If ever there had been any hope of
settling the Moroccan disturbances without the whole question of the
Algeciras Settlement being raised, this was effectively scuppered by
Spain's occupation in June of key positions in her sphere of influence

---

[1] Scott, *Diaries* (22 July 1911), 46–7.
[2] Murray's Diary, quoted *ibid*.
[3] *The Nation*, 6 Jan. 1912. Lloyd George during this period was very much
persona grata as far as the Foreign Office was concerned. Nicolson told Sir
Almeric Fitzroy in November 1911, 'there was no member of the Cabinet he
had found such a stand-by throughout recent difficulties . . . no one . . . could
do better if he would only observe sufficient reticence' (*Memoirs*, ii, 471).

in Morocco. The *Panther* anchored off Agadir on 1 July. On 19 July it was reported in the British Press that the deposed Shah of Persia was making a bid to regain his throne. The next day, *Matin* revealed Germany's demand for the French Congo as recompense for her acquiescence in France's activities in Morocco. On 21 July Lloyd George made his Mansion House speech.

> If a situation were to be forced upon us in which peace could only be preserved by the surrender of the great and beneficent position Britain has won by centuries of heroism and achievement by allowing Britain to be treated where her interests were vitally affected as if she were of no account in the Cabinet of Nations, then I say emphatically that peace at that price could be a humiliation, intolerable for a great country like ours to endure. National honour is no party question.

Three days later in a debate in the Commons on the Lords' amendments to the Parliament Bill, there were scenes of extraordinary political passion and the sitting had to be abandoned. Asquith had been howled down by a pack of Tory M.P.s led by F. E. Smith and Lord Hugh Cecil, while Balfour sat seemingly unruffled by this extraordinary behaviour. Churchill described the affair as a 'squalid, frigid, organised attempt to insult the Prime Minister'.

On 27 July, Asquith made a statement in the House about the Moroccan situation. The problem of the powers of the House of Lords was finally settled after the high drama of the debate in the Lords of the 9/10 July when the Die-hards had been narrowly defeated by the defection of 'the Gaiters and the Rats'. 'Society was split, and at the Carlton Club members checked up *Hansard* before they spoke to one another.'[1] The attention of the general public, however, was focused on a series of strikes which, after a temporary interruption at the beginning of July, broke out afresh with unexampled violence, first at the Port of London and then Liverpool. There were riots; troops were called in; there were shootings and deaths. The strike spread to the railwaymen. 'War has begun', declared the Secretary of the Railwaymen's Union. It was not war between Germany and Britain to which he referred but the class war.

Meanwhile, the situation in Persia had deteriorated considerably. Once more the Parliamentary Persia Committee was revived. On 19 August the morning newspapers warned their readers that the rupture of Franco-German negotiations was imminent. That same day, contrary to established usage, at the request of the Army General Staff, the Commons passed without any debate an Official

1 See Owen, 206.

Secrets Act designed to reinforce the powers of censorship enjoyed by the Government in time of war. The next day the Russians published the terms of the agreement that they had made with Germany the previous year. Then as suddenly as this rash of troubles had arisen, they subsided. The Cabinet, in the person of Lloyd George, made a supreme effort to prevent a general strike by the railway workers. The Chancellor pleaded with the railway directors and the trade union officials to come to an agreement in the national interest as the country trembled on the edge of war. The plea was successful. The strike was not called. As suddenly, the menace of war vanished, and Parliament was prorogued for its summer recess on 22 August.

Ramsay MacDonald's attitude, as leader of the Parliamentary Labour party, is of considerable interest, as it reveals the impotence of Labour as it tussled with uncomfortable dogmas and competing priorities. MacDonald was suffering the intolerable personal burden of the approaching death, after a harrowing illness, of his beloved wife. He rejected the contagion of *syndicalisme révolutionnaire*, as propounded with some philosophical rigour by Georges Sorel in his *Réflexions sur la Violence*, and by a few hotheads in the trade union movement. He did not favour strikes. Like Snowden, MacDonald thought them 'a confession of lost faith in democracy'. They were a weapon to be employed as a last resort. He supported compromise, even at the price of the enmity of the bulk of the I.L.P., who thought he had sold the pass. MacDonald was committed to Parliament, and he exhorted the labouring masses and his own parliamentary supporters to patience and discipline. MacDonald was an aesthete and a puritan. He supported the Government's action over Agadir, though he did criticise Lloyd George's speech. That would better have been made by Asquith than by the leader of the pacifist wing of the Liberals. Lloyd George had 'discouraged the activities of peace organisations and peace forces in Germany' by his words. Even so, in the same speech MacDonald made at Edinburgh to his Socialist critics who had censured his actions in July 1911, he asserted: 'If there was any sort of feeling in the mind of, say, the German Foreign Minister that he could play with fire and be safe because there would be hampering influences in this country, he [MacDonald] had to say something which did not encourage the Minister in that particular game.'[1]

The reason for the delayed Radical reaction to events in Morocco is largely explained by developments in the domestic political scene. Since their success in the 1906 election, the Liberal Govern-

[1] See Elton, *Life of Ramsay MacDonald* (1939.), 201–31

ment had been thwarted time and time again by the opposition of the House of Lords. The Tories in the Lords had allied their strength with that of their much weakened colleagues in the Commons in a determined effort, in Balfour's words, to 'still control the destinies of this great Empire'. Tory philosophy suggested that it was inconceivable that a House of Commons sporting so many Radical members was fitted to lead the nation. What is more, Tories believed that, provided they exercised caution, there was no reason why the Lords should not become a 'theatre of compromise' where Government measures could be 'modified'. This would not only frustrate Radical measures, but by stealth the Upper House might emerge from the conflict greatly strengthened. The Lords had begun their campaign by mutilating the Government's Education Bill. Though warned by Campbell-Bannerman that 'The resources of the House of Commons are not exhausted and I say with conviction that a way must be found by which the will of the people, expressed through their elected representatives in this House, will be made to prevail', the Lords continued to axe other important Government measures. How long the unsatisfactory relations between the two Houses of Parliament would have been tolerated by the Government is a matter of conjecture. But in 1909 the Lords were engineered into defending difficult ground when they rejected Lloyd George's budget. Their action brought such a storm about their ears that did not cease to rage until their powers had been emasculated by the Parliament Act 1911.

The Radicals were all agreed that the status and powers of the Lords was *the* dominating political issue. They had always been quick to grumble when the subject seemed to fall into the background. Therefore, when the Government chose to take issue with the Lords in 1911, it was no time for the Radicals to criticise or attack the Liberal leaders. If they had any doubts on this score, the violence of the Tories convinced them that their first priority was loyalty. Party passions rose to frightening heights. The Commons was frequently in uproar. Through all the squalid scenes, the jeers, the counter jeers, the lies, the insults, the Liberal leaders held firm, piloting their measure of reform to its final triumphant acceptance. The Radicals were proud of the manner in which ministers had behaved.

When evaluating the opposition of the Radicals to the Liberal Government's foreign policy, one has to consider their strength in the Commons. The two elections of 1910 had reduced the size of the Liberal Party in the Commons by about a third. The Government no longer enjoyed a majority over all the other parties combined. The Radical group in the Commons had lost a number of stalwarts through death, retirement and defeat at the polls, but their position had not been weakened in relation to other factions in the Liberal party.[1] Though the Liberals and Tories had almost the same number of members, this did not add to the influence of minority groups attached by alliance to the Government. On the contrary, the Radicals, Irish and Labour were even more securely shackled to the Government than before. The sad experience of the Radicals was that when the Liberal Government had enjoyed a massive majority they had protested on a number of issues but without avail. Now they could not even afford the luxury of ineffectual protest. The Irish members, though they might occasionally grumble, were strictly whipped and irretrievably committed to the Liberal alliance. Labour members, for all their bold independent talk in the constituencies, recognised which side their bread was buttered and supported the Government. The alternative of a Tory Government was always the best guarantee of loyalty from dissident opinion.[2]

One further example may be adduced to explain the apparent reluctance of Radicals to take up the Agadir issue. Lloyd George's Mansion House speech had something of the same effect in producing a feeling of national crisis as had Asquith's damaging admission

---

[1] Cremer was dead, Brunner retired for health reasons, Gooch, Lynch and Cotton amongst others had been defeated at the polls. Useful gains included Harvey, King, Noel Buxton, Mason, Rowntree and Whitehouse.

[2] For the Irish, see F. S. L. Lyons, *The Irish Parliamentary Party* (1951), 252–3; 257–9. The parliamentary Labour party could not afford another election with its funds already dissipated and the Osborne Judgment still hanging over them. Therefore Labour had to be circumspect in its conduct. The dreaded possibility was that if Labour moved an amendment and were supported in the lobbies by the Conservatives, then the only hope for the Liberal Government would be if the Irish chose to save them. In March 1910 this awful possibility almost occurred. MacDonald had moved an official Party resolution on the wages of Government employees. It suddenly became apparent that the Conservatives were supporting them in the lobby, with the result that sixteen of the nineteen Labour members who were voting had hurriedly to retrace their steps from the Aye lobby and vote against their own amendment.

When at the next Annual Labour Conference, MacDonald had to defend these men against the charge that they had defeated the amendment to protect a Liberal Government, he emphasised that to defeat the Government was not in Labour's interest: see Elton, 181–2. The loyalty of the Irish and Labour members to the Government was purchased during negotiations at the end of 1910. Labour was promised a reversal of the effects of the Osborne Judgment; the Irish, Home Rule after the House of Lords had been made impotent. There is undoubtedly a case in constitutional law that the Government was manipulating the constitution to its own ends as the price for eighty grossly over-valued Irish votes. See the Tory Manual produced for the first 1910 election—*The Case Against Radicalism: a fighting brief for Unionist candidates, agents and speakers.*

about Germany's capacity to build Dreadnoughts in the naval debate in 1909. Less than a week after the Chancellor made his speech, the Radicals had been afforded an excellent opportunity to question the Government about its foreign policy and to attack Lloyd George for his provocative words. But when the Foreign Office vote was debated on 27 July, comment upon Morocco was limited to a few remarks by front bench spokesmen. The House rose early, the only criticism having been voiced by Ramsay MacDonald. Even he had seen fit to hope that no European Power would suppose that the spirit of national unity was weakened by party divisions.[1] Lloyd George had spoken for the nation, declared the *Daily News*.[2] Nicolson, writing to Buchanan on 1 August, could scarce contain his satisfaction that there was a perfect unanimity of British opinion, and that even the extreme Liberal sections were determined to stand by France.[3] Criticism would only be voiced when the immediate threat of danger had disappeared.

Radical opinion had not been unduly alarmed, either by the sending of the French expedition to Fez, or the German riposte of dispatching the *Panther* to Agadir. The French might claim their move was dictated by a desire to protect Europeans from danger, but this was no more than 'passionate excuses for war';[4] a pretext 'as mendacious as the legends by which Dr Jameson sought to excuse his rush to Johannesburg'.[5] Events were following the accustomed pattern of any sordid imperialistic venture. The Spaniards and the French were acting as two bands of *conquistadores* who couldn't agree about the limits of their rifling operations.

> Europe has no right on the strength of admitted Moorish defects and barbarities, to carve slices out of Morocco and to throw the Moors to the wolves. If the wild tribes of North Africa resent the 'peaceful penetration' of European industrialism, they have every precedent in history to justify their suspicions and arouse their enmity. Up to the present we have been more successful in debasing our own ideals in Africa than in uplifting the ideals of the native. The sooner we discard the pretence of being the

[1] Debate in *Hansard*, v:28:1827ff. MacDonald's speech, cols. 1829–31.
[2] *Daily News*, 24 July 1911.   [3] *B.D.* vii, 493.
[4] *Manchester Guardian*, 26 Apr. 1911.
[5] *The Nation*, 6 May, 1911. As far as *New Age* was concerned, the reopening of the Moroccan question had been inevitable as soon as Delcassé took office in the Monis Government. 'The whole French Cabinet is dominated by Delcassé. He has determined upon a bold, forward policy as the best means of reaffirming the prestige of France in Europe. . . . M. Delcassé feels sure that Germany won't think it worthwhile to fight over Morocco, and if she does . . . why, let Germany fight and be damned to her says the French Government. Who would have expected this? It is all due to the personality of one man.' *New Age*, 4 May 1911, p. 3.

harbingers of a lofty civilisation in the lands where we despoil and enslave the native, the less will the surrounding air be polluted by the miasma of our conceited self-righteousness.[1]

Nor was there much sympathy felt for the Germans. Their accord with France had made it all the easier for that country to carry on with its piratical policies in Morocco. When the *Panther* arrived at Agadir, *The Nation* declared that this was a 'highly provocative act'. There was no fear, however, that this move might lead to international complications. It was 'a conversational opening'[2] which was to be expected. Germany merely wished for compensation from France. This resigned and somewhat complacent attitude to the Morocco situation among Radicals, was shattered by Lloyd George's speech.

The German Press initially dismissed the Chancellor's statement as of no particular importance. As there had been no specific reference to Germany there was no reason to take offence. Any German statesman might have said as much. But in London, the British Press was intent upon spelling out the implication of Lloyd George's words. The *Westminster Gazette* might have described them as 'studiously conciliatory';[3] the *Morning Post, The Times* and even the *Daily News* claimed the speech had been an official announcement of the Government's support for France.[4] The *Daily Chronicle*, supposed by the Germans to have official connections, claimed that Lloyd George had been expressing 'the considered judgment of the Cabinet' and the speech had been intended as 'a word in season'.[5] There was a violent reaction in the German Press. For the moment there was more ill-feeling towards Britain than France. All joined in condemning Britain's meddling in an affair that did not concern her. Here was evidence that England systematically obstructed Germany's expansion. Her intervention could never be justified as an act of self-defence. It was inspired by the desire to make sure she was given something in Morocco. One thing was certain, Germany would not be intimidated by threats from England.[6]

The day before Lloyd George's speech, C. P. Scott had taken tea with Courtney at the House of Lords. They had discussed Germany's demand for compensation in the French Congo and for a port on the African coast. While they considered this serious, Courtney was more concerned about Grey's probable attitude to the situation.

---

[1] *Concord*, xxviii, no. 6, mid-June 1911, p. 69.
[2] *The Nation*, July 1911.   [3] *Westminster Gazette*, 21 July 1911.
[4] *Post*, 22 July 1911: others, 24 July 1911.
[5] *Daily Chronicle* 22 July 1911.
[6] See, E. M. Carroll, *Germany and the Great Powers* (1938), 668–70.

Both men agreed that talk of a German naval station in West Africa 'cutting Britain's two great trade routes' was a mockery. Britain could not expect to keep all the naval stations in the world to herself. The argument that there would be a consequent rapid increase in the naval estimates, would only materialise if Britain had the folly to invite it. Scott had hoped to have an interview with Asquith but this had been impossible. He therefore wrote the Prime Minister a strong letter concerning the Morocco crisis.

> That we should go to war in order to prevent Germany from acquiring a naval station on the West African coast has I believe not occurred to most Liberals as even a possibility, but what I have no doubt of is that if such a thing were to happen it would pulverise the Party. There is no feeling among Liberals here [Manchester] against Germany—it is generally recognised that her policy of the open-door in Morocco has even been of material service to us—and that there would be any deadly danger to our interests in her acquiring a West African port would be wholly disbelieved. I can imagine no more foolish war and none more fatal alike to Party and to national interests than one with Germany on this matter.[1]

After the outburst in the German Press at Lloyd George's speech, the Radical Press in their turn gave sympathetic consideration to the German case in law for sending the *Panther* to Agadir. It was manifest that from the beginning France had been determined to destroy the Algeciras Settlement. Only a fool would believe the declaration in the preamble to Algeciras Act that the independence and integrity of Morocco was a reality. France was dominant in that country, and Germany had recognised as much by the accord of 1909. France had not honoured her commitments under that accord. Hence, the voyage of the *Panther* was 'merely a more noisy and dramatic continuation of the bargain of 1909 when France herself bought a recognition of her political position in Morocco in return for economic concessions to Germany which she had not yet paid'.[2] No British strategic or commercial interests were involved, so what could Asquith have meant by his alarming statement to the Commons on 6 July when he said that though he was confident that a solution would be found by diplomatic means, Britain's part would be determined by her interests and her obligations towards France?[3] Britain had no obligations towards France. Any she might

---

[1] Scott, *Diaries*, 43–4.
[2] *The Nation*, 5 Aug. 1911; see also E. D. Morel, *Morocco in Diplomacy* (1912), *passim*.
[3] *Hansard*, v:27:1341.

have had under the Anglo-French entente of 1904 surely had been cancelled by the Algeciras Settlement?[1]

To the *Manchester Guardian* it seemed that the voyage of the *Panther* could be equated with the Kaiser's visit to Tangier in 1905; both were designed to secure the 'open door'.[2] *The Nation* argued that as France and Spain were intent on carving up Morocco what possible difference could it make to Britain if Germany had a share in the spoils as well?[3] The *Manchester Guardian* was not prepared to accept this argument. Britain should not be content to watch France and Germany negotiate without Britain being involved. The question was one that ought to be thrashed out between the three Powers.[4] This explains why the *Guardian's* criticism of Lloyd George's speech was directed to the looseness of the words. No excuse had to be offered for Britain needing to defend her vital interests. In a leader the *Manchester Guardian* declared: 'We have a right to protect our interests in any resettlement of the Morocco question. If that be all that our Government is contending for, it will have the unanimous support of the country, and we cannot think that Germany would be so ill-advised as to dispute it.'[5] But what evidence was there of Germany threatening Britain's commercial interests? The *Guardian* admitted, when the settlement was published in November, that Germany, far from infringing Britain's interests, had secured better terms for the commerce of all Powers than the British Foreign Office had achieved by the 1904 entente.[6]

Radical criticism concentrated upon the Mansion House speech. In the circumstances this was understandable, for the speech had been the only overt British intervention in the whole affair. There was no diplomatic crisis before the speech. Afterwards, relations between Germany and England were strained for several days.

---

[1] C. P. Scott wrote that he discovered Grey was unaware that all treaties inconsistent with the Algeciras Act were cancelled by it. See J. L. Hammond, *C. P. Scott of the 'Manchester Guardian'* (1934), 160. In point of fact this was not so. The cancellation applied to only those treaties to which Morocco was a party. E. D. Morel chose to gloss over this point (*Morocco in Diplomacy*, 76–7).

The fascinating points about the two conversations between Grey and Scott (25 July and 3 Nov. 1911) recorded by Hammond are (i) Grey's admission that his present policy was conditioned by his reading of the events of the previous century and his experience as Under Secretary at the Foreign Office; and (ii) Grey's claim that diplomatic support for France in Morocco implied, if it was to be of any value, the possibility of military support. This surely amounts to an admission by Grey that options were no longer open. Britain was committed to France come what may (see pp. 161–4).

[2] *Manchester Guardian*, 7 July 1911.   [3] *The Nation*, 8 July 1911.
[4] *Manchester Guardian*, 18 July 1911.
[5] *Ibid.*, 26 July 1911.   [6] *Ibid.*, 6 Nov. 1911.

Metternich and Grey had met to the background of a steadily rising tide of public excitement. The German Ambassador had appealed to Grey to make some effort to allay this dangerous animosity, and it was in response to this appeal that Asquith made his reassuring statement to the Commons that very afternoon.[1] When, in November, Grey recounted to the Commons the events of July, he claimed that after Asquith's speech there were 'no further difficulties between the German Government and ourselves about the Moroccan negotiations'.[2]

The feature of the Mansion House speech that most upset the Radicals, was that it had been made by the key Radical representative in the Cabinet, the very man they looked to as leader of the peace party. F. W. Hirst expressed their sense of bewilderment. It was too 'extravagant' to believe that 'Lloyd George or any other responsible person is thinking of asking millions of his innocent . . . countrymen to give up their lives for a continental squabble about which they know nothing and care less'.[3] It simply was not good enough for Grey to suggest that Lloyd George's words were no more than a platitude on the lips of a minister of a great Power.[4]

This explanation would not wash with the *Daily News*, nor with Morley. He wrote to Asquith: 'It is all very well to say that the speech was nothing but *bona verba*. You cannot detach a speech from all the consequences.'[5] No one could suppose that Grey was so naïve as not to have realised the importance and possible consequences that might flow from the speech when Lloyd George had shown him the draft of what he intended to say to the bankers. All that had been achieved, according to *The Nation*, was that if war had been declared, the chief fault would have lain at Britain's door. Britain had needlessly complicated the whole issue by introducing balance of power notions.[6]

What of official explanations of Britain's part in the Moroccan crisis? Was Britain motivated by the fact that for more than three weeks the Germans had not replied to a communication concerning Morocco? Strangely, it was Ramsay MacDonald who gave this story currency in an article in the *Socialist Review*. When Bernstein asked him for confirmation of the story, MacDonald elaborated his theme by claiming when eventually the German reply was received it was insulting. This had precipitated Lloyd George's speech. Bernstein then repeated the story in the German Press, hoping

[1] *Hansard*, v:28:1827–8.   [2] *Ibid.*, v:32:54.
[3] *Manchester Guardian*, 24 July 1911.   [4] *Hansard*, v:32:50.
[5] Morley to Asquith, 27 July 1911, Asquith MSS.
[6] *The Nation*, 16 Sept. 1911.

thereby to make Germans appreciate the British point of view.[1] When Grey volunteered the excuse of Germany's delay as the reason for the Agadır crisis, Bethmann-Hollweg told the Reichstag that Germany's intentions had been fully explained on 1 July. What Germany had looked for was some evidence of Britain's goodwill.[2] *The Nation* concluded that if Grey could not offer a more convincing explanation then he would stand convicted of something very like 'wanton provocation'.[3]

'Public speeches', A. J. P. Taylor has said, 'are a dangerous diplomatic weapon.'[4] The Radicals were correct in their estimate that the Mansion House speech was a blunder. Members of the parliamentary Labour party were not as confused by the moves made at Agadir as the Radicals. They were neither as emotionally nor as intellectually committed to the Government as were the Liberal Radicals. Their estimate of the situation was that in all essentials it was no more than the continuation of a Great Power struggle over a disputed colonial territory. Britain had become involved because obviously there was some secret commitment to France which had been embodied in the 1904 entente. Ramsay MacDonald was not satisfied with this estimate. He did not believe that the Government harboured any ill intentions towards Germany or that Britain could have sat idly by watching two other Powers carving up Morocco. The speech by Lloyd George had undoubtedly been a political blunder, but this was not the nub of the situation. If one was to allocate blame for the crisis, then the prime responsibility lay with the German bureaucracy. It was they who had led their people into a difficult and dangerous situation involving the fortunes of other nations.[5]

---

[1] The episode is related in *Manchester Guardian*, 17 Nov. 1911.
[2] See Carroll, *Germany and the Great Powers*, 696.
[3] *The Nation*, 25 Nov. 1911.   [4] *The Struggle for Mastery in Europe*, 471.
[5] See *Labour Leader*, 11 Aug. 1911. One of the fascinating features of the Press response to Lloyd George's speech is the way that without the institutional aid of a Press bureau the Government was able to bring all the significant agencies of opinion and communication together. In the face of a supposed foreign threat the Press closed its ranks. The only significant deserter was the *Manchester Guardian*. This caused concern to a Government that had little support from the major newspapers, and it is ironic that Scott had been pressed by Lloyd George to remain faithful to the cause (see Scott, *Diaries*, 46–7). Though Scott, in accordance with Lloyd George's expressed wish, did not offer editorial comment in the *Guardian* on the Mansion House speech, Grey's attitude at a breakfast conversation he had with Scott on 25 July decided the *Guardian's* editor that he must at least express mild disagreement with Britain's interpretation of her obligations and interests. All Grey had spoken of was the importance of Germany moderating her demands so that France would not be compelled to reject them. He did not suggest France should make concessions to Germany to pay her off, as she had already paid off Britain (see Hammond, 153–63).

Why did Socialists and many Radicals vacillate on questions of peace and intervention? First, the overall political situation made them loath to criticise the Government. Second, strategically they could not afford to endanger the life of the Government to which their own fortunes were so intimately bound. Third, there was confusion in their own minds concerning loyalty and priorities. The attachment of many of them to the ideals of peace was sentimental and emotional. In the final analysis most of them would choose to stand by the Government in times of national peril. Only for those Radicals who were thoroughgoing peace men—Quakers like Allen Baker—was there no conflict of interest and priority. Howard Weinroth has put the matter pertinently. 'In considering . . . [Radical] reactions in 1911 towards the near-war situation, it may be asked whether a "Belgium" was really necessary to bring them into line should the Government opt for involvement in a continental struggle so as to preserve the balance of power.'[1] The answer must be no.

One thing remained when the crisis receded and men could once more safely parade their ideals. The Agadir crisis, and more particularly, Grey's handling of it, revealed and exaggerated a division in Liberal thinking on foreign policy somewhat akin to that division inspired by the Boer War. When Lloyd George lined up with Asquith and Grey over Agadir, Radical opposition to a broad interpretation of Britain's obligation to France and the entente system effectively had collapsed. The Government was committed to the Foreign Office view that the Agadir crisis was not a sordid deal over real estate in Africa but a manifestation of the European balance. England was committed to protect France from Germany, whatever the cost. All else was peripheral. Grey in time would be censured for his attachment to the theory of the balance of power. Meanwhile, the division on foreign affairs was hardened by developments in Tripoli and Persia.

Persia and Tripoli

Delegates to the Nineteenth International Peace Congress in Rome were forced to meet at Berne because of the threat of a cholera outbreak. Felix Moscheles, who was attending as the representative of the International Peace and Arbitration Association, was

> pleased that the farce in which we were to take our part was not enacted. For death-dealing purposes the cholera scourge was

[1] Howard Weinroth, 'Radicals and balance of power, 1902–14', *Historical Journal*, xiii, no. 4 (1970), p. 676.

considered slow and insufficient, and the war decimator was summoned. That was an unexpected *coup d'état*, a new departure, an ultimatum before the overture to the drama. No time for 'conversations', no opportunity for bluff, no blank cartridge, but fire and sword to enforce—nobody quite knows what. It is monstrous![1]

The reason for his outburst was the sudden invasion of Tripoli by the Italians.

From the beginning there was a gnawing suspicion in Radical minds that the Foreign Office had, if not encouraged the Italians in their adventure, at least willingly consented to it. Presumably the expected reward for this perfidy would be the detachment of the Italians from the Triple Alliance. What value now talk of high moral principles? It was greed that motivated international relations.

> I grabbed, thou grabbest, he grabbed;
> We, you, they grabbed and will grab;
> I grab if I can, he would grab if he could;
> If I may grab this, thou mayst grab that;
> Combined we can grab our neighbour's brother's land;
> and so on.

There is a good deal written and said about intervention. Kaisers or Kings are being pathetically appealed to for their good offices, but they decline to interfere. They feel that they might be interfered with when their turn comes to raid and to annex. So they form a ring to see fair play, which means what, in their opinion is fair and favourable to their respective rights and interests, and they deliberately trample underfoot the Convention they as deliberately discussed and signed at the Hague.[2]

According to the *Guardian*, public opinion had been more nearly unanimous in its condemnation of Italy than it had been over any other issue of the time. Surely, Grey could find some way of voicing the nation's protest? Had he not interfered when Austria had annexed Bosnia Herzegovina? Though Austria's action then had been no more than a recognition of the *de facto* situation, Grey had been quick to assert that Austria had flouted the public law of Europe. Every argument the Foreign Secretary had advanced on that occasion applied to this, only more so. If England failed to act this time it would be an overt repudiation of those very principles she had formerly maintained. It would reveal Britain's fine sentiments were merely sticks with which to beat Germany.[3]

[1] Moscheles's Diary, 30 Sept. 1911, in *Concord*, xxviii, no. 8, Oct. 1911, p. 86.
[2] Moscheles's Diary in *Concord*, 3 Oct. 1911.
[3] See *Manchester Guardian*, 26 Sept. to 3 Oct. 1911. The Italian Press claimed that Britain had foreknowledge of their country's intention to invade Tripoli. At first the *Manchester Guardian* was not prepared to accept this intelligence,

One of the reasons for Radical concern with Italy's invasion of Tripoli was that it endangered the whole stability of the Turkish Empire. All the Balkan nations were impatiently waiting for the opportunity to break up the ramshackle Empire and, as everyone knew, such a move might well be the prelude to a major European war. For all their shortcomings the Young Turks still seemed to be the best hope for the future of the Turkish Empire. They in their turn looked to that Radical opinion in England which had supported them at the time of their *coup d'état*, in the hope that they would again receive succour now they had been attacked by the Italians.[1] Once again unlikely protagonists in the Radical camp were united in their criticism of the Foreign Office. W. T. Stead, recently returned from a visit to Turkey and as usual bubbling over with enthusiasm for his latest cause, bitterly lamented in his *Review of Reviews* that Britain no longer had a Gladstone who would cry out against this injustice. Joshua Rowntree asked, could not Great Britain rise to greatness in this crisis which afflicted Turkey?[2] But the only official reaction to these and like passionate appeals was for Britain to declare her neutrality.

The Radicals mounted a campaign in the Commons led by Mason, a very independent Radical who had been returned for Coventry in the 1910 election. Questions were asked in the House, but the questioners achieved nothing for their pains. The Government stonewalled with every reply. A new note of urgency developed when alarming reports were received concerning atrocities committed by the Italian troops in Tripoli.

Making . . . every concession to the inhuman doctrine of 'military necessity', it can scarcely be denied that the Italian repression of what, after all, was only a movement in favour of national independence, sinned and sins on the side of merciless ferocity. The official reticences or denials in high places will not avail to satisfy the conscience of Europe, or stifle the voice of international indignation. The damning proofs of guilt are too

---

but on 3 Oct. it reported that 'Mr Lucien Wolf, writing in the *Daily Graphic* says that our Foreign Office was aware a month ago that Italy intended to take steps in Tripoli'. When Sir Edward Grey refused to see a deputation from the Peace Society, who brought with them a protest memorandum on the Italian action, suspicions must have been confirmed. Grey's comment on Italy's action in his Memoirs is simply, 'Italy's conquest of Tripoli was a shock to [the *status quo* of Turkey]' (i, 260). He has nothing else to say of the incident.
[1] See letter of Ahmed Riza, President of the Turkish Chamber of Deputies, in *Daily News*, 13 Oct. 1911: 'I am persuaded that our noble and loyal friends in Great Britain will not abandon us in this crisis and that if steps are now taken they will not be ineffective or unfruitful.'
[2] *Review of Reviews,* November 1911; *Manchester Guardian,* 5 Oct. 1911.

many to be hidden away; indeed they are, unfortunately, too well authenticated for effective denial. Perhaps the most serious thing about these ugly episodes is this; that the complicity of the Powers that will not dare, or do not care, to intervene in the name of humanity, for the prevention of a renewal of these horrors, will set a new and dangerous precedent in favour of adopting equally merciless methods of warfare during the rest of the twentieth century. The guilt is presently that of Italy, but prospectively it becomes the joint and separate responsibility of staid official Europe. . . . For that reason the protest against these barbarities becomes a necessary measure of national and international defence.[1]

When, in the Commons, the Radicals pressed Asquith and Grey to explain the diplomatic antecedents of the Tripoli campaign and to comment on the barbaric manner in which the war was being fought, neither man appeared to be moved. Britain was neutral. Therefore they could neither interfere in the situation nor volunteer any information.[2] In vain Mason pressed for an adjournment debate. McCallum Scott was censured by the Speaker for expressing too plainly his sentiments on Italy's actions in Tripoli. Even procedure would seem to have been intended to thwart the Radical appeals.[3]

Throughout November, Mason feverishly attempted behind the scenes to rally a protest in the Commons upon a non-party basis, but to little avail. The usual meetings of protest were held; the usual protesters attended and said their pieces. Grey meanwhile confirmed in the House that the Italians had annexed Tripoli.[4] Though Dillon, McCallum Scott and the redoubtable Silvester Horne addressed well designed questions to the Foreign Secretary asking for information, all were blunted by an impassive Grey. In the circumstances the only possible conclusion was that the Government deliberately chose not to recognise the evils perpetrated by the Italians, even less to censure them. Nor were the Government's critics wrong in this conjecture. The atrocities were true, no matter what Bertie might have thought.[5] The whole episode had been a brutal exercise in

---

[1] William Heaford, *Concord*, xxviii, no. 9, Nov. 1911, p. 102.

[2] The National Peace Council representing the Peace Associations and numerous other bodies, requested that the British Government should offer mediation, either by itself or in cooperation with other Powers under the terms of the Hague Conventions of 1899 and 1907. The request was ignored. Pacifists noted that while Governments proclaimed their neutrality, they nevertheless continued to allow loans to be raised in their countries for the purpose of carrying on the war. This was a virtual breach of neutrality. To stop the loans could stop the fighting. See *Concord*, xxviii, no. 8, Oct. 1911, p. 96.

[3] See *Hansard*, v:30:5 and 271; also, David Mason, *Six Years of Politics* (1917), *passim*.

[4] *Hansard*, v:30:1453.   [5] *B.D.* xi, i, 299.

greed. Grey knew as much, but a theory of Germany's determination to secure the hegemony of Europe stifled his better impulses. It is difficult to justify his rejection of humanity in the hope of Italy's neutrality in 1914. It says much for Grey's obsession with the German 'menace' that this man of undoubted sensibility could be so unmoved as to describe the barbarous campaign of Italy in Tripoli as 'tiresome'.[1]

At such times it was difficult to be an optimist. The situation in Persia that had once seemed resolved in the name of good sense, nationalism and parliamentary democracy, with the Shah banished to his deserved exile in Odessa, suddenly became a live issue. Only the day after Lloyd George's Mansion House speech, *The Nation* dolefully informed its readers, 'There is once more a Persian question'.[2] The ex-Shah, far from being in safe keeping in Russia, was again on the warpath, financed by Russia and supported by Russian troops. Civil strife broke out in Persia, and Grey bewailed his lot. On top of all his other cares and duties he would again have to face his Persian critics in the Commons. What could he say to them? They rejected his assurances that Russia had remained loyal to the policy of non-intervention agreed in the Anglo-Russian Convention. He tried to show that the Shah had eluded his Russian captors. A likely story, thought Grey's critics. The Russians had merely waited for a favourable moment to release him. Reinsured by their agreement with Germany at Potsdam, and with Britain embroiled in Morocco, the Russians had judged their time and their opportunity well. Imagine then the Radicals' delight when the Shah's expedition foundered. But the troubles in Persia were only beginning.

In Grey's own words, 'Persian finance was hopeless without Western advice'. He added, unnecessarily considering the perilous state of Russia's exchequer, that 'finance was not the strong point of the Russians'.[3] As the idea of a British financial adviser in Teheran, which was in the Russian sphere of influence, was unacceptable, and as any European adviser would be suspected of using influence either in favour of Russia or Britain, an American, Morgan Shuster, was invited to fill the rôle early in 1911. Shuster was an amiable and able man. He quickly won the respect of the British representative in Persia, Sir George Barclay, as well as that of the Persians. But he suffered from the sin of wishing to indulge his own initiative and ability. Afforded wide powers by the Persians to regenerate their economy, he set out to do just that. At the same time Shuster indicated to the British and Russian Governments that they should

---

[1] See Grey, i, 260.   [2] *The Nation*, 22 July 1911.   [3] Grey, i, 168.

keep their hands out of his particular pie. His attitude could not have been more pleasing to the Radicals. They had argued ceaselessly that a regenerate Persia was in Britain's interests. However, the necessary corollary of Shuster's activities would be a weakening of Russian influence in the north of Persia. Inevitably this would lead to friction between the two great Powers. From the beginning Shuster's eventual fate was sealed.

With the sympathetic aid of Russia, M. Mornard, a Belgian customs official, attempted to frustrate Shuster's work. This ill-conceived ploy failed, but the future of Shuster in Persia was decided when he offered the command of the Treasury Gendarmerie to Major Stokes, who at the time was military attaché in Teheran. The Russians protested, and Grey acceded to the pressure. When Stokes attempted to resign his post as attaché in order to take up his new appointment, his resignation was refused. Next, the Russians indicated that they could not much longer delay 'measures of extreme vigour'. Grey blustered but to no avail. He even vaguely hinted at a revision of his attitude to Russia, a threat which caused Nicolson to desire fervently a Persian capitulation in face of Russian demands. Nicolson's wish was satisfied when, on 22 December, Barclay reported that the Persians had given in, and Shuster, the innocent victim of European high diplomatic politics, left Persia in January 1912. Grey's conclusions on Shuster's fortune are sufficient commentary upon the issue.

> His departure was a loss, but it was the lesser of two evils. His aims were admirable and just, but he had not realised that Russian interference in the north of Persia could only be ousted by force; that Britain was not prepared to embark on a great European war for that purpose and that Britain was the only country that had any interest in seeing Russia restrained. He attempted what was good, but what could only be done by force; and there was no force available for the purpose.[1]

This is neat comment on Grey's deviousness or impotence, depending on where one's sympathies lie. The Persian question, on Grey's own

---

[1] Grey, i, 169. The Persian story can be read in *B.D.* x, i, 801, 815, 820, 828, 831, 847, 851, 887, 890, 907, and 908. See also on the Stokes issue, *Hansard* v: 30:980. On Barclay's sympathy towards Shuster, see Nicolson, *Lord Carnock*, 356. George Buchanan's comments on the situation in Persia made to Almeric Fitzroy in November, are particularly interesting. He said that 'the action of Russia in Persia was creating a very difficult situation, and one that disturbed Sir Edward Grey most seriously. Somewhat like Italy in Tripoli, she had precipitately seized an indifferent pretext for presenting an ultimatum, when a little patience would have given her a much better opportunity. *The feeling being so strained, the Foreign Office cannot risk giving umbrage to Russia, though the steps she has taken are quite inconsistent with our mutual engagements, and in the end we shall probably have to acquiesce in proceedings we altogether condemn. Such is the risky game of European combinations.*' (My italics.)

admission, tried his patience more than any other subject. But from the beginning the Foreign Secretary was committed to supporting Russia as a counterweight to the Central Powers. Though Russia might act in such a manner as to make friendly relations with Britain almost impossible, Grey could do nothing except resign. When he had threatened to resign, this had been enough to make most of the dissident Radicals return like sheep to the fold of the Liberal party. Grey's policy was a powerful aid to Tsarist Russia. It is sufficient comment on Russia's diplomatic incompetence that she did not make more of her willing accomplice. If there was little skill in the diplomatic stratagems of the great Powers, there was even less of morality, conscience and humanity.

Needless to say, Grey's Radical and Labour critics were indignant with the manner in which he conducted affairs in Persia. In 1911–12 Persia was the subject of more comment in the national Press than in 1907–09. This was because Shuster contributed to the debate by his long letter to *The Times*, published on 9 and 10 November; and Professor E. G. Browne, in constant touch with affairs in Persia, wrote a number of angry letters which were published in the *Manchester Guardian*. As to debate in the Commons, the lack of Blue Books did not deter the Radicals from criticising Grey. If anything, on occasion they appeared to be better informed of the facts of the situation, by intelligence supplied by their friends in Persia, than did the Foreign Secretary.[1] Indignation at Grey's amoral attitude

[1] The trouble with Blue Books was that they were carefully edited before publication. They were always published more with an eye to possible foreign response than to provide information for domestic critics. Grey was always careful to omit or alter despatches that might reveal differences between Britain and her entente partners. This was true in particular of the Persian Blue Books which were designed to quieten Grey's Radical critics. Hardinge's advice to Barclay on the Armenian Blue Book, in May 1908, clearly indicates the Foreign Office view on the subject. 'As regards the Armenian Blue Book, we have to publish these things at certain times; there are several members of Parliament who take a very keen interest in Armenian affairs prompted, no doubt, by some of the Armenian Societies in London. We do not mind how much you bowdlerize the Blue Book as long as we are able to publish something; with us it is really the quantity and not the quality that are wanted for the House of Commons.' Though there was an increase in the number of pressure groups and in the demand for information during the period 1906–14, Grey remained less generous in his treatment of Parliament than had his predecessors in that office. As Temperley and Penson observe: 'Judged by the Blue-book test, Sir Edward Grey took the public into his confidence very much less than did Palmerston . . . While Blue-books on domestic affairs expanded and multiplied at the end of the century, those on foreign affairs lessened both in number and interest.' See, *inter alia*, on this subject, Steiner, 194–6; Temperley and Penson, 'British secret diplomacy from Canning to Grey', *Cambridge Historical Journal*, vi (1938), 1–32; L. Penson, 'Obligations by treaty: their place in British foreign policy 1898–1914', in A. Sarkissian, ed., *Studies in Diplomatic History and Historiography in honour of G. P. Gooch* (1961), 76–89.

towards the fate of the Persian nation reached unprecedented heights when, in January 1912, the Radical Press prominently advertised the massacres which had taken place in Tabriz. The Persian Committee called a meeting at the Opera House in London for 15 January, which was heavily oversubscribed. Their campaign against the Government was given a further boost by Shuster's presence in the country on his way back to the United States. On 24 January he addressed a public meeting in Manchester in response to a petition from the citizens of that city. The *Manchester Guardian* afforded his speech massive coverage, as they did the banquet in Shuster's honour given by the Persian Committee in London on 29 January.[1] Thus, the Radicals were afforded the considerable advantage of talking to the man who had been most intimately involved in the recent crisis in Persian affairs. Little wonder that, when Parliament reopened in February, the Radicals made sure that there was an Amendment to the Address on the Persian question.[2]

By the strangest of political alliances, the Radicals found influential support for their campaign, criticising the Government's handling of the Persian situation, from certain elements in the Tory party. Lord Curzon lent his powerful vice-regal voice in support of independence for Persia. There was little offence, and there should have been even less surprise in Radical hearts, that at this particular juncture Lord Curzon should have chosen to come to their rescue. Curzon's intervention was not motivated by the same highminded idealism as the Radicals, but his belief that British interests were not being safeguarded by the Foreign Office. By happy coincidence, notions of *imperium* and idealism were joined by economics—a seemingly irresistible trio. The disorders in Persia caused dislocation to British trade there and a subsequent diminution of profits. The possible collapse of the Persian buffer zone and the prospect of defending the long Anglo-Russian frontier filled strategists, both amateur and professional alike, with alarm. The *Manchester Guardian* noted the combination of forces, selfless and selfish, that were

[1] See *Manchester Guardian*, 25 Jan. and 1 Feb. 1912. The low estate to which Grey's handling of Persian affairs had reduced even his supporters, is reflected in Spender's comments in the *Westminster Gazette*, 31 Jan. 1912. January 1912 produced a deluge of articles and pamphlets full of unbridled criticism of Grey: see, *inter alia*, Contemporary Review, ci, 642–51; *Nineteenth Century*, lxxi, 40–7; *Fortnightly Review*, xcl, 1–10.

[2] The Radical case was made by Morrell, Ponsonby, Dillon, Mason, O'Grady and Buxton: see *Hansard*, v: 34:628ff. This parliamentary activity was accompanied by a flood of letters and resolutions from the usual quarters. Copies of the letter sent Grey by the Persia Committee, and resolutions by the International Arbitration and Peace Association and by the Council of the Union of Ethical Societies are printed in *Concord*, mid-February 1912, pp. 19–22.

concerned for Persia's welfare: 'Manchester merchants and Persian scholars, enthusiasts for freedom and for our good name as its friend, and men like Lord Curzon, who are most deeply concerned with Persia as part of a great Imperial problem.'[1] If one asked how this combination had come about, the answer was patent. 'By the plain paths of practical commonsense they reach conclusions substantially the same as others have reached through love of Persia or the cause of freedom and nationalism or of international justice.'[2] As if this combination of idealism and interest was not enough, the Government strengthened the 'unholy alliance' by favouring a Russian sponsored scheme for a Trans-Persian railway. The Radicals, not to be outdone by the Tories in matters martial, were quick to voice their protest at Grey's apparent disregard of Britain's strategic interests. The Foreign Secretary had 'reversed the traditions and annulled the labours of a century'. Radicals made fine play with talk of abandoning the bulwarks of Empire, and *The Nation* offended the logic of its tradition with the *non sequitur*: 'Where does the British Empire come in?'[3]

The gathering of Grey's critics

In July, when the Agadir Crisis had been at its height, the Government's Radical critics in the Commons had been quiescent. Undoubtedly many had adopted silence out of a mistaken sense of their duty to be loyal to the Government at a time of apparent danger to the nation's fortunes. An opportunity had been afforded to ventilate their grievances because 27 July had some weeks previously been set aside for a Foreign Office debate. But Grey's critics, for the most part, had been content on that occasion to limit their remarks to Persian affairs. They made no attempt to disavow Lloyd George's Mansion House speech or to counteract what they believed to have been its evil influence upon relations between Germany and Britain. For those members who claimed that they could read the portents of the times, their action in remaining silent reflects upon them little credit. Like Hamlet, conscience seemed to have made cowards of them all.

During the summer recess, Buxton and Whitehouse, two Radical

---

[1] See *Manchester Guardian*, 1 Dec. 1911. Curzon's involvement was embarrassing for the Tory Press, who ignored his contribution. *The Morning Post*, 21 Nov. 1911, did allow itself the laconic comment: 'Refrain from all gossip on foreign policy. The impression should not be let abroad that Grey does not enjoy the support of the nation as a whole.'
[2] *Manchester Guardian*, 24 Dec. 1911; cf. *The Nation*, 23 Dec. 1911.
[3] *The Nation*, 8 June 1912, p. 350.

backbenchers who were particularly concerned with the deteriorating relations between Germany and Britain, paid a visit to Berlin. Their fears that Lloyd George's speech had been a major blunder were all too readily confirmed by their conversations with the British Ambassador. In a spirit of despair Goschen informed Buxton that the Chancellor's speech 'had undone all our work'.[1] From the friends of an Anglo-German understanding in Berlin, Buxton and Whitehouse were left in no doubt that relations had been soured, and there was an uncomfortable heritage of offence felt by the Germans at what seemed to them to have been England's unwonted and unnecessary interference in a matter which had not been her concern.

On his return to England, Buxton determined that he would give all his energies to diminishing the ill-feeling and misunderstanding between Germany and Britain. He canvassed the opinions of other M.P.s, and they signed a memorial which he presented to Asquith, urging the Government 'to remove the mischievous impression now prevailing in Germany as to the attitude of this country towards her', and, 'to reassure the German Government and people that no responsible body in the United Kingdom wishes to deny to Germany her share in the settlement of great international questions, or to view with hostility her legitimate aspirations as a Great Power.' Above all else, the signatories urged Asquith to ensure that the Anglo-French entente 'will not be allowed to stand in the way of cordial rapprochement with Germany'. Asquith was neither surprised nor unduly impressed by this impassioned plea from the pacific wing of his own party. He was more than a mite undiplomatic when, on receiving the memorial, he inquired, 'Are there any Conservatives among the signatures?' The expected reply was forthcoming, 'Only Bentinck'.[2] Buxton's biographer claims the incident revealed very clearly how 'the robust representatives of the Liberal Imperialist School—Grey, Haldane and Asquith' believed that now they could ignore with impunity the progressive pacifist element in their party.[3]

During the late summer of 1911 Grey also received pleas from the Radicals concerning the estrangement between Germany and Britain. Courtney, apologising that he should interrupt the Foreign Secretary's holiday, pressed Grey to accept the logic of Germany's

---

[1] Conwell-Evans, 58.   [2] Lord Henry Bentinck.
[3] Conwell-Evans, 58–9. The wording of the memorial had been agreed by the Political Committee of the National Peace Council in October 1911 but was not presented until November. It was signed by eighty M.P.s. Conwell-Evans's chronology of events is not to be trusted. The bound *Monthly Circular, 1911–15* of the N.P.C., is the most trustworthy guide. See also, reports in the *Manchester Guardian.*

place in Europe. She was a strong and growing Power. It was inevitable that she should demand recognition of her status. The United States of America had done as much, and Britain had acquiesced. Why then did Britain have to be jealous of 'an inevitable fact' when it concerned Germany? Grey replied that he *hoped* Courtney's desire for better relations with Germany would be realised; he *hoped* that a settlement would be made between France and Germany that would make things easier, and he *hoped* there would be no more misunderstandings.[1] If hope was the strong suit of the Foreign Secretary, where were the practical manifestations of his sublime optimism? As far as Grey's radical critics were concerned, the sad story of inept and immoral diplomatic chicanery which had been revealed, not only in the crisis over Agadir but in the sad fortunes of Persia and Tripoli, was merely the gloomy backdrop to the chilling military preparations of the autumn of 1911. Arthur Ponsonby, in November 1911, leaked the alarming information that in September Germany and England had stood upon the verge of war. The *Daily Chronicle* headlined Ponsonby's 'alarming statement',[2] and in the *Contemporary Review* Noel Buxton gave a vivid description of how 'In the month of September both sides were prepared to attack. Horses were bought. English officers were recalled from leave. In Germany even the reservist got his equipment ready. . . . In England the secret was well kept; in Germany the rumours were sufficient to produce a panic on the Berlin Bourse.'[3] This disturbing intelligence of how near Britain and Germany had been to war in

---

[1] For both letters see, Gooch, *Courtney*, 567–8 (my italics).
[2] *Daily Chronicle*, 15 Nov. 1911. The further significance of the treatment of Ponsonby's information by the *Chronicle* was that at no time had that newspaper been anti-Grey in its editorials.
[3] *Contemporary Review*, Nov. 1911, p. 605. During September in *New Age*, the Foreign Affairs column spelled out the dangers of war and the measures taken in preparation: 'Leave was stopped at the instigation of the War Office. . . . Coal was got in readiness, simply because the Army authorities were making arrangements to send 60,000 men to the Continent within thirty-six hours after the outbreak of hostilities. They were to be shipped to Flushing . . . and they were to be followed within forty-eight hours by a further contingent of 50,000 men—horse, foot, artillery, commissariat, Ambulance corps and so on, complete. . . . This information may seem strange to those who have constantly denied that we are under any agreement or compulsion to aid France. I am, nevertheless, prepared to stand by it in spite of all official technical denials. It is absolutely accurate.' S. Verdad in *New Age*, 28 Sept. 1911, p. 509. Verdad believed the reason why his information was not openly accepted was because 'of the cowardice of the English Nonconformists' and their press. Verdad had a particularly low opinion of *The Nation*. From Tory sources there had been a number of 'inspired' leaks designed to bring censure upon the head of the Admiralty. See speech of W. V. Faber at Andover, 9 Nov. 1911, reprinted *Daily Telegraph*, 20 Nov. 1911; and A.W.A. Pollock, 'Some strategical questions' in *Nineteenth Century and After*, Oct. 1911, pp. 796–804. See further, Williamson, 201.

September 1911, merely confirmed the gloomy forebodings most Radicals harboured. Since August, the National Peace Council in a plethora of meetings and memorials, repeatedly had declared its concern. In October Sir Frank Lascelles, until 1908 British Ambassador in Berlin and now Chairman of the Anglo-German Friendship Society, warned a meeting of the Church Congress that

> A war between England and Germany would be one of the greatest calamities which could befall the world. Each country would certainly suffer incalculable loss, and it was difficult to understand what advantage either would obtain from a successful war. England if successful, might destroy the German fleet and thus secure her undisputed predominance at sea. Germany, if successful, might curtail the power of England and perhaps obtain some of her colonial possessions. But, it was inconceivable that either Power should annihilate the other, or obtain more than a temporary advantage. There was no ground of quarrel between England and Germany, and there was no question pending between the two countries which would not be susceptible of arrangement by negotiation. There was certainly none that would justify a war.[1]

Though Lascelles attempted to cover up his gloomy forebodings with a facile optimism, the *Manchester Guardian* would have none of it. 'Let no one think that there is nothing to fear. If the present tendencies continue unchecked the disaster to European civilisation of war between England and Germany will certainly come.'[2] The Radicals and their allies were very much aware of the imminent dangers of war that threatened Germany and Britain since that ill-fated day when, in Dillon's words, 'Pandora's box had been opened' by the French marching on Fez. Never had the Radical and Socialist Press been so occupied as now with analysis and comment upon foreign affairs. In the moment of crisis, Radicals, in their new found unity and strength of purpose, recalled the warmth of their mutual support in 'Pre-Boer times'.[3]

In October, Dr Clifford and H. G. Chancellor, a Radical M.P., formed a 'New League of Universal Brotherhood', and launched an appeal for a 'People's Peace Propaganda' to protest against war, militarism and increased armaments.[4] The National Peace Council called a special meeting in November to develop a campaign for an understanding with Germany. They determined to employ 'every

---

[1] *N.P.C. Bound Minutes 1911–15*, no. 2, 15 Oct. 1911.
[2] See *Manchester Guardian*, 5 Oct. 1911.
[3] *Courtney Diary*, 1 Nov. 1911.
[4] See *Manchester Guardian*, 21 Oct. 1911.

means of pressing this question of a friendly policy'.[1] The Anglo-German Friendship Society held a meeting at the Mansion House on 2 November. Lascelles, abandoning his former optimism, told his audience that 'Never in my experience has there been a greater feeling of ill will towards England in Germany than that which has arisen during the last few months.' A resolution was passed expressing the desire 'to remove all existing misunderstandings with Germany and to emphatically reassure the German nation that no responsible body in the United Kingdom wishes to deny to Germany her title to a share in the settlement of international questions, or to view with unjustifiable hostility her colonial ambitions.' As a first practical step towards establishing friendly relations between the two Powers they suggested holding an Anglo-German Exhibition in 1913.[2]

Determined that the 'science' of economics should be heard supporting the moral and sentimental arguments of those who deprecated the possibility of war between Germany and Britain, Francis Hirst in a powerful editorial in the *Economist* asserted: 'There is no getting away from the fact that before the colonial policy of Mr. Chamberlain and the foreign policy of Sir Edward Grey Consols stood at 113, the income tax was 8d, the death duties were comparatively moderate and there was no sugar duty.'[3] If this catalogue of economic woes was not guaranteed to stir working-class concern, Joseph Finn in an article contributed to *Concord*, with plangent tones manipulated the gamut of available economic arguments to prove that the foundation of peace between Germany and Britain would follow as the logical consequence of the federation of world industry.[4] If the conception of a speaker to the Oldham Chamber of Commerce was somewhat less sophisticated and disinterested, his warning was that much clearer. If Britain went to war with Germany then a half of Oldham's cotton spindles would be stopped.[5]

Nor would the Labour party be denied its contribution to the debate. Labour M.P.s earnestly condemned Grey's policy towards Germany. The man was cold and secret; his policies were an offence to the Liberal tradition.[6] The Foreign Office needed to be curbed by

[1] *N.P.C.*, no. 5, 15 Nov. 1911; cf. *New Age*, 30 Nov. 1911, p. 101.
[2] *N.P.C.*, no. 5, 15 Nov. 1911.
[3] *The Economist*, 11 Nov. 1911. The joining of Grey's name with that of Chamberlain is significant comment on how leading Radicals viewed the Imperialist sympathies of Grey and by implication, his leader Asquith.
[4] *Concord*, xxviii, no. 9, Nov. 1911, pp. 99–100.
[5] Reported, *Oldham Daily Standard*, 28 Nov. 1911, quoted Dorey, p. 351.
[6] See Keir Hardie, reported *Manchester Guardian*, 4 Dec. 1912; also Henderson, *ibid*. During November and December 1911, the Labour party attempted, in some measure, to claim the leadership of the anti-Grey faction. Most of

fear of the public. The public ought to be informed about the responsibilities ministers were incurring on their behalf.[1] All the members of the parliamentary Labour party, in an unusual display of unity, signed a letter of fraternal greetings to their 'comrades', the Social Democratic members of the Reichstag.

> The present unfortunate estrangement between our two countries is not the doing of the working people of the countries, but of political and economic interests which are antagonistic to these people, and which are powerful only when they work in secret as they do now.
>
> It is all the more necessary that those who represent the popular mind and the common well-being should demonstrate in an unmistakable way their international solidarity and goodwill; and we ask you to convey to the classes you represent in Germany assurances of the friendship of those whom we represent in Great Britain and to believe that the desire of our country—as we are sure is the desire of yours—is that we should dwell in peace together, and that all our differences, both political and economic, should be settled by the rational means of arbitration and not by the barbaric means of war.[2]

The signatories made sure that a copy of their letter was received by the Foreign Secretary.

Out of the confusion of doubts, fears and remedies, Grey's Radical opponents forged a more convincing intellectual theory to explain what was wrong with Britain's foreign policy. It was Arthur Ponsonby who provided the lead which others followed. The problem as Ponsonby saw it was

> how the pacific, progressive and moderating opinion of democracy may be introduced into international as well as national affairs, and as to how a democratic state can discover the proper means of expressing itself in the Council of nations. . . . In the realm of foreign affairs . . . the concentration of power in the executive, or, rather in the hands of one individual, has now begun to present itself in the light of a serious danger.[3]

Ponsonby concentrated his attacks on the general underlying principles of the conduct of foreign policy, but even in this restricted

---

their efforts concentrated upon implying that the Radicals in the Liberal party were a spent force. See, for example, *Labour Leader*, 15 Nov. 1911, p. 785. 'What is the attitude of English Radicals towards Sir Edward Grey? The Radical element in Liberalism has practically ceased to count since the death of Sir Charles Dilke. He was the last of the great Radicals, and though the Dilke tradition remains, no one has arisen to take his place. A Radical group still meets from time to time, but they are leaderless, timid and ineffective. Were it otherwise, the Grey policy would be boldly challenged.'

[1] Ramsay MacDonald, reported *ibid.*, 20 and 23 Dec. 1911.

[2] *N.P.C.*, no. 6, 15 Dec. 1911.

[3] Arthur Ponsonby, *Democracy and the Control of Foreign Affairs* (1912), 5–7; cf. *New Age*, 30 Nov. 1911, p. 101 and 29 Feb. 1912, pp. 412–13.

area he was not able to escape the question of personalities, and his identification of the nature of the problem only reveals how ill-equipped the Radicals were to tackle it. Their political naïvety constantly limited their effectiveness as critics. They might vilify Grey, but he had only to threaten resignation and this was enough for most of them to support the Foreign Secretary. Could it be that the very nature of diplomacy poisoned a man's rational faculties? The traditional world of politics was full of artificial values. In domestic policy there were signs that the atmosphere of this false world was waning, but what a different picture when one considered foreign policy.

> In considering Mr Lloyd George as a domestic politician one has to admit that he is directly dealing with real things . . . he can see things, and as far as he with his normal limitations can know what anything is, he knows what they are. But when we consider Mr Lloyd George dealing with foreign politics we have quite another state of things. The atmosphere has changed. The human men and women and children, concerning whom the Chancellor of the Exchequer enjoys being pathetic, have disappeared. When he takes a hand in the game of Anglo-German snarling, he talks the usual twaddle about national honour and dignity. He forgot all about the real men, women and children, and remembered the false shibboleths and catchwords . . . Germans . . . Moors and Persians are our fellow men. Our enemies are the diplomatists and foreign ministers. National dignity! In the street, outside my window, there is a starving man.[1]

In the autumn of 1911, the Radicals determined that they would focus the attention of the nation both on the broad question of principle that underlay the conduct of foreign affairs, and the more specific question of Anglo-German estrangement and hostility.

A number of 'interested parties', including Courtney, Scott, Massingham and Mackarness, had combined with Buxton and Ponsonby in the production of a memorial to Asquith questioning Britain's policy towards Germany. On 14 November the group met at the New Reform Club under the chairmanship of Courtney, and Ponsonby read a paper to them on democratic control of foreign policy. There followed a lively discussion. They agreed that some means of effecting parliamentary control was imperative, but they could not agree about the best method of achieving this desired end. Ponsonby was not in favour of the proposal to set up a non-party foreign affairs committee. On the other hand, he thought that an officially

[1] E. G. Smith, 'A plea for common sense', *Concord*, xxviii, no. 10, mid-Dec. 1911, p. 115.

recognised Liberal committee might be set up which could act both as a source of information and to explain policy, thus providing the means of two-way communication between back-bench members and the Government. Others doubted whether any sort of committee was required. Official committees were not favoured, as this would have involved a change in the constitution of Parliament producing as it would something analogous to the existing Foreign Affairs Committee of the French Chamber. Therefore, no real attempt was made to give this particular proposal serious consideration. The *Manchester Guardian* argued that foreign policy was most effectively controlled by the whole of the Commons, and not by committees. 'Foreign policy, unlike finance, is not an accumulation of details that cannot be handled satisfactorily by the whole House. Its success or failure depends on the application of a few simple principles to facts which as a rule are not very numerous nor very complicated.'[1] In this fashion the *Guardian* announced its contempt for the supposed intricacies of the conduct of foreign affairs. Unofficial party committees could be set up without the complications of institutional innovation, and when Ponsonby and Buxton circularised back benchers, more than eighty of them agreed to join a 'Liberal Foreign Affairs Committee'. The members held their first meeting on 6 December, and Buxton and Ponsonby, for their energies and enterprise, were respectively elected Chairman and Vice-Chairman. That their fellow members should not be left in doubt as to their purpose and intention, the Committee issued a statement.

> A group has been formed to organize opinion on foreign questions representing the whole Liberal Party.[2] The idea is prevalent that Parliament has abrogated its function in regard to foreign things and that this is not in accord with the doctrine of democracy . . . The movement is not an attempt to get diplomatic negotiations made public[3] . . . it is a protest against the obscurantist doctrine of diplomacy[4]. . . .

[1] *Manchester Guardian*, 15 Nov. 1911.
[2] This claim was not correct. The Committee was popularly referred to as the 'Radical Foreign Affairs Group.' Its chairmen were successively Buxton, Morell and then Ponsonby. The membership of its executive committee was almost exclusively made up of men who were in the parliamentary vanguard of those who opposed increases in armament expenditure and held Radical views on foreign policy. All the well-known Radical champions were there, from the Quakers, Allen-Baker, Harvey and Rowntree, to Gordon Harvey, King, Wedgwood, M'Callum Scott, Whitehouse, Mason and Silvester Horne.
[3] See *The Times*, 16 Nov. 1911. 'The suggestion . . . is made in some Radical quarters that at a critical time diplomatic negotiations should be conducted in public . . .' The charge was an old one made against the Radicals. The seconder of Richards's motion in 1886 had anticipated Gladstone's attack upon this point by categorically denying it: see *Hansard*, iii:33:1397. The Radicals had continued to suffer this charge and in a way they were themselves responsible

In this country Parliament has none of the control exercised even in autocratic states by official Foreign Affairs Committees.[1] Therefore all the more need exists for some organization of Parliamentary opinion. This applies to policy, as, for instance, in regard to Germany and Persia, but also to the question of system, as, for example, the plutocratic qualifications for posts in the foreign service and the relations of the diplomatic and consular services. With regard to Parliament it is felt that there should be more discussion, no discouragement of questions, and fewer appeals for silence. Sir Edward Grey has expressed his readiness for further debates when a desire is indicated; it is for party groups to give such indication.

The statement ended with a pious affirmation that could have been interpreted in some quarters as an implied threat. They would be 'keeping in touch with members of the Cabinet'.[2] One member at least of that august body, John Morley, had expressed his strong approval of the formation of the group. Apart from setting up an executive committee, the group divided into a number of subgroups each of two members charged with a special responsibility to study particular questions. These were: Anglo-German relations, Persia, Russia, the Near East, the Far East, the Congo and Arbitration. The groups were to meet frequently until in 1914 their organisation was brought to an abrupt end by the outbreak of war.

Conwell-Evans has criticised the ineffectiveness of the Liberal Foreign Affairs Committee on the grounds that after showing alarm

for this because they would insist upon talking of 'secret diplomacy'. When Sir Henry Norman, though obviously sympathetic towards some of the aims of the Radicals, declared that 'diplomacy could not be conducted in the full blaze of daily publicity', Wedgwood answered him, borrowing a phrase from the Foreign Secretary. 'We do not want to be interfering in petty details, in tapping the barometer on every particular question to see whether the Foreign Office is moving upon Liberal lines. . . . We think we have a genuine right to say to Liberal ministers, we expect broad Liberal principles to be followed.' See *Hansard*, v:32:2543 (Norman) and 2621 (Wedgwood).

Ponsonby made it quite clear in his book that: 'There can be no question of asking the Foreign Secretary to lay his cards on the table so that while we see them others against whom he is playing see them too.' At the same time he asked was it unreasonable that the people who in the end paid with their money and their lives should be told what game the Foreign Secretary was playing? See *Democracy and the Control of Foreign Affairs*, 12. Cf. Halévy's unfair claim that Ponsonby was 'demanding that foreign policy should be subject at every step to popular control', *op. cit.*, 436–7. Ponsonby's actual proposals were: more debates on foreign affairs in the Commons; fair answers to parliamentary questions; more Blue Books; more frequent statements by the Foreign Secretary on policy to be made outside the Commons.

[4] A further note of confusion was introduced by the Radicals in that when they talked of diplomacy they meant usually foreign policy. They retained the word diplomacy, as in 'secret diplomacy', because of its propaganda overtones, being associated in the popular mind with intrigue and vested aristocratic interest.

[1] See Koss, *Brunner*, 241.

[2] The statement is quoted in full in Conwell-Evans, 81–2.

in times of crisis they 'always relapsed into a placid calm, and remained blissfully ignorant that only the obvious symptom had for the moment disappeared'. Few members exerted themselves with vigour, he charges, and they were in general 'too easily satisfied and lulled into tranquillity by the soothing speeches of the Foreign Secretary and by the misleading assurances of the Prime Minister.'[1] The criticisms are true in substance, but Conwell-Evans is not altogether fair in not indicating the amount of interest and activity the Committee engendered by its actions. The members, at least, were successful in their initial aim of stimulating dissatisfaction at the conduct of foreign affairs, and of harnessing that discontent so that the voice of dissent in Parliament was both more coherent and less ambiguous. They were divided among themselves about the efficacy of promoting institutional changes, and in any event knew that Asquith did not look upon such suggestions with any favour.[2] One cannot question the effectiveness of the Radical Committee in making its voice heard. They contributed two thirds of the speeches to the Foreign Office debate of 14 December[3] and the debate of 27 November arose mainly as a result of their activities, and the public anxiety fostered by their insistent propaganda.

Beside the Liberal Foreign Affairs Committee, another Radical

[1] See Conwell-Evans, 83-4.
[2] When a meeting of Liberal, Labour and Irish M.P.s was called under the chairmanship of Ramsay MacDonald in March 1912, the majority opposed the establishment of an official committee. See F. W. Hirst, ed., *Harvey*, 84-6. The choice of Ramsay MacDonald as Chairman of this inter-party meeting is in itself interesting. Already there were indications among the Radical members of the Liberal party that they were more attracted towards MacDonald's leadership than they were by their own. Buxton has recorded in the draft of his autobiography that: 'We were all sympathetic with Ramsay MacDonald who had just become Labour Leader, and we were naturally disapproved of by the mass of Liberal members, many of whom appeared to us little distinguishable from the Tories' (quoted Fieldhouse in Gilbert, *A Century of Conflict*, 177.) Given, as Professor Fieldhouse has said, their particular conception of Liberalism, the later transition of most of them in 1919 to the Labour party is easily understandable.
MacDonald was of the opinion that the control of foreign policy was a matter for the House of Commons as a whole and no fit concern for a committee. It was he who requested Asquith to set up an official inquiry into the problems of keeping the Commons informed of foreign affairs. Whitehouse requested a return showing the methods adopted by other countries to deal with this problem. See, *Hansard*, v:32:1401, (MacDonald); v:31:673, and Parliamentary Papers, lxviii:297ff. (Whitehouse). The *Manchester Guardian* 6 Apr. 1912, thought that a new committee, far from throwing more light upon the conduct of foreign affairs, 'might even increase the mystery-mongering which is the bane of foreign politics'. All that was required, the [Guardian believed, was forty or so determined members who were prepared to establish parliamentary control by their criticism. The growth of the Foreign Office's independence was the result of there having been no strong body of critics in the House united in their opposition. With the informal Radical Committee they now had all the organisation they required.
[3] *Hansard*, v:32:2543ff.

committee to consider foreign affairs was formed at about the same time. The initiative for forming Lord Courtney's Committee—named after its president—was primarily L. T. Hobhouse's. He was aided by J. A. Hobson, and had the active support of the leading spirits of the other Radical Foreign Affairs Committee. Courtney had been offered the Presidency after he had addressed a swingeing attack upon Grey in the Lords on 28 November. The Committee, despite its high hopes and the bravado of its early days, within a year 'was forced to close down from sheer lack of membership and funds'.[1] It organised one successful conference on foreign policy on 27 November 1912. During the year of its existence

> funds were raised by subscription, and R. C. K. Ensor, at this time out of employment as a result of the amalgamation of the *Daily News* and the *Morning Leader*, was secured as paid secretary. An office was opened, where a collection of relevant books, periodicals, foreign newspapers and the like was assembled and the secretary was on duty, with all available information on foreign affairs at his fingertips, [*sic*] to brief M.P.s.[2]

The statement of aims to which the Committee subscribed, indicated three areas of priority other than publicity for foreign affairs and greater parliamentary control. It amounted to a Radical catechism, a reassertion of faith. They opposed the policy of entangling alliances so that Britain might have a 'free hand in dealing with international questions in accordance with its own interests and sympathies'; they reasserted 'the traditional sympathy' of Britain 'with the causes of national freedom and constitutional government abroad'; they advocated 'a friendly approach to the German Government' that would 'serve to discover a basis of practical agreement'.[3]

Among the vice-Presidents of the Courtney Committee was Sir John Brunner. Events during and after the Agadir crisis convinced Brunner that, although he still suffered from the failing health that had necessitated his withdrawal from Parliament in 1910, and though denied the comfort of his wife who had died in April, he could no longer afford a life of leisure away from politics. On 23 November, Brunner was elected President of the National Liberal Federation.

[1] Hobson and Ginsberg, *Hobhouse, his Life and Work* (1931), 48.
[2] Information given to A. J. Dorey by Ensor and quoted in Dr Dorey's D.Phil. thesis (1964), p. 296.
[3] See Gooch, *Courtney*, 572–3. Cf. *New Age*, 30 Nov. 1911, p. 101. 'When I think of the tension existing in European diplomacy at the present time, it is, I confess, with some irritation that I learn of the stale platitudes of the Radicals regarding friendship with this country and with that one, brotherly love, the abolition of war, march of humanity, Hague Tribunal (who ever hears of the Hague Tribunal nowadays?), and all the rest of the idealistic stock-in-trade.'

At the time of Brunner's succession to office, the Federation's powers had been so emasculated that Liberal party leaders discounted its influence, indeed ignored its existence. Because of the dominance of the Liberal whips, its compliance with Government wishes could be taken for granted. Brunner determined that under his stewardship the Federation would enjoy a new lease of life and be inspired by his purpose, strategy and disposition.[1]

At the meeting of the N.L.F., when Brunner accepted the Presidency, the occasion was not allowed to pass without mention of the international crisis of the summer and the subsequent resentment and suspicion felt both in Germany and Britain. Brunner moved a formal vote of thanks to the Kaiser for 'using his influence in the direction of peace'. This was a reference to Bethmann-Hollweg's rebuke to the hotter spirits in the Reichstag who had fulminated against Britain's perfidy. Brunner trusted that the British Government in their turn would be moved (shamed?) to take similar steps to mute the anti-German sentiments that had emanated primarily from the Conservative benches in the Commons. The Radical Press, recognising that they enjoyed a new ally, were fulsome in their praise of the N.L.F. meeting. *The Nation* declared that the meeting had provided 'a powerful and enthusiastic demonstration in favour of an understanding with Germany' that gave 'direct marching orders to the Government'. Even Spender, who in no way shared Massingham's suspicion about the purposes of the Foreign Office, was prepared to admit in the *Westminster Gazette* that the spirit of the proceedings provided a 'message for Germany' and 'an instruction to the Cabinet and Parliament'. Brunner was well pleased with his first meeting as President of the National Liberal Federation. He would breathe more purpose into that too long moribund body. If he had any regret, it was that he had not confounded those enemies of the poor who chose to dissipate the nation's fortunes upon Dreadnoughts rather than social reforms, with an apposite quotation from Isaiah: 'It is ye who have eaten up the vineyard. The spoil of the poor is in your houses. What mean ye that ye crush My people and grind the face of the poor?' Rightly, Koss claims, here is testimony that the religious conviction, less pronounced in Brunner's case than in many other Radical leaders, provided the peace campaign and the campaign for Anglo-German understanding with both impulse and justification. The National Liberal Federation,

---

[1] For this section on Brunner and the National Liberal Federation, I am indebted to Professor S. E. Koss; quotations unless otherwise stated are taken from his book *Sir John Brunner: radical plutocrat* (1970), chap. II.

under Brunner's Presidency, was to prove another stick with which to beat the conscience of the Foreign Secretary and the rest of the Cabinet.

It would be as well at this point in the story to examine probably the most crippling handicap that Radical opinion suffered during the period up to the first world war. The emasculation of the political influence of the National Liberal Federation is a classic example of the incubus of provincialism.[1] As late as 1912, writers talked of the virility of the North and the lethargy of the South',[2] and could even suppose that the seat of Government would be moved from London to the provinces. The opening of offices in Manchester by the national Press was instanced as both portent and manifestation of this change. In fact, the result was the encouragement of metropolitan rather than Mancunian influence. The decline in the influence of the provincial Press illustrates the point. During late Victorian times there had been a happy balance between London and provincial journalism—each allotted their area, and each a powerful influence within those environs. The staple of papers before the revolution wrought by the *Daily Mail* was politics; column after column of verbatim reportage of speeches by major and minor politicians, and editorials dissecting and commenting upon the latest political controversy. The *Daily Mail* changed all this, and while it was not explicitly anti-provincial, its influence inevitably undermined the variety of provincial attitudes, and encouraged a uniformity of approach to politics as much as it revolutionised the make-up of newspapers and their orientation to serve a wider, less discriminating, less articulate, less well-educated, leisured and politically conscious readership. Stories of 'human interest'—murder, divorce, social scandal, sport—reinforced the growing apathy of the public towards politics. Rosebery's horses were of more interest than Rosebery's politics. Working men did not stand at street corners earnestly discussing reform politics as in the Chartist days; they whiled away their leisure hours with idle talk of pigeons, horses and greyhounds.[3]

A major factor in undermining the influence of the great provincial cities of the North and the Midlands had been the Redistribution Act of 1885. At the time, the leading provincial newspapers had been highly critical of the move. They recognised the one-time unity of the provincial cities, when they had spoken with weight and authority in the legislature and the country, was gone.[4] Thus, though the

[1] See R. Spence Watson, *The National Liberal Federation from its Commencement to the General Election of 1906* (1907), 59–60.
[2] Quoted Denald Read, *The English Provinces* (1964), 272, n.1.
[3] See Read, 230.   [4] See *Annual Register*, 1884, p. 255.

Manchester Guardian under Scott's long editorship established itself as the leading provincial newspaper, its influence was less than was apparent. And when *The Nation* in 1910 recognised the *Guardian's* key rôle as the voice of Radicalism and 'the natural rallying ground of British democracy', it was only confirming the dwindling authority of a spirit that belonged to an area whose influence was declining rapidly and inevitably.[1]

The parliamentary Labour party did not escape this handicap. Labour members in the 1906–14 Parliaments, though they dignified themselves with the name party, were in effect a provincial interest group. Labour exerted more influence in the country than in Parliament. Of the twenty-nine Labour members elected in 1906, five only came from London and the south-east. The Labour party, despite the brave words and calculations of its leaders, remained, to the outbreak of war in 1914, a pressure group that drew its inspiration and sustenance from the industrial towns of northern England and the scarred towns in the narrow valleys of South Wales.

Grey disarms some of his critics

The Radicals were obviously spoiling for a 'showdown' with the Foreign Secretary, and that devoutly to be desired confrontation could not much longer be delayed. Bethmann-Hollweg had talked of 'a clean slate', a wiping clear of all the sad incidents that had bedevilled Anglo-German relations in the past so that the two Powers could face the future in amity with their dignity intact. Grey, tired by his exertions and anxious because, though the crisis was past the Radicals now seemed intent on stirring up trouble, deprecated their assertions and surmises. Why did they choose this moment when danger had vanished to excite themselves? Why were they every five minutes tapping the barometer of international relations to see whether or not it was rising? Wouldn't their time be better employed in preparing for the usual Christmas pleasures?[2] But the Radicals would not be denied by 'the soft answer that turneth away wrath'. Edward Browne, in a letter to the *Manchester Guardian*, catalogued the infamies, both of British foreign policy and the Foreign Secretary. Sir Edward had shown

> a cynical indifference to the fate of the weak nations and the human suffering involved in their conquest; while even those sacred 'British interests' about which alone he professes concern

[1] *The Nation*, 24 Sept. 1910.
[2] See Grey's speeches in *Hansard*, v:32:54–55 and at Plymouth, reported *Manchester Guardian*, 6 Dec. 1911.

seem to be readily sacrificed to please France or Russia or to propitiate that modern Moloch 'the Balance of Power'. No statesman, I suppose, ever entered upon the responsibilities of office with a more general approval or a more universal sympathy, and few, I should think, have given rise to such deep disappointment. What has been the net result of his policy? The destruction of Morocco (including . . . the destruction of British commercial interests in that country) to please France; the threatened destruction of Persia to please Russia; the alienation of Mahometan sympathies throughout the world; the lowering of British prestige; the lowering of international morality; an unceasing feud with Germany, giving rise to perpetual war scares and ever-increasing expenditure on armaments; a reputation for tortuous and secret diplomacy without parallel, I believe, in the history of this country; and an undisguised impatience of Parliamentary criticism and contempt for public opinion which can scarcely be matched outside Russia, whence the present ideals of the British Foreign Office seem to be derived.

This was only the beginning of Browne's criticisms. It says much for the feeling of desperation and frustration among thinking Radicals, that Browne could avow: 'If the Conservatives had an alternative foreign policy of a saner, safer, and more generous and chivalrous character, I think that many convinced Liberals would be inclined to sacrifice all other considerations to this.'[1] But, unfortunately, the Conservatives did not offer an acceptable alternative policy.

Sir Edward Grey, in spite of his waning reputation, can count on the support of the official Liberals and a great majority of the Unionists; and even if the opinion of Parliament on foreign policy could be taken, it is doubtful if thirty members would support a vote of censure. . . . Does the Foreign Office care one straw for all the protests and indignation meetings which are held in this country? . . . The theory that the foreign policy of this country is in any way affected by popular sentiment is in these days, I fear, one of Max Nordau's 'Conventional Lies of Modern Civilization'.[2]

Browne's passionate letter to the *Guardian* is important, not so much for the depths of his dissatisfaction with Grey's conduct of foreign policy, or the length of his catalogue of woes, but because of the

[1] Cf. *Labour Leader*, 24 Nov. 1911, p. 744. 'The official Liberal party has lost the old vision and the old faith. It picks up armaments. It lends itself to the international intrigues of financiers. It degrades the country and blunts the sense of national freedom by entangling alliances. . . . It is impossible to imagine how the foreign policy of Tory jingoes could be worse than that of the present Government. Better a hundred times the "splendid isolation" boasted by Lord Salisbury than the crippling and compromising alliances of Sir Edward Grey.'
[2] Letter to *Manchester Guardian*, 12 Nov. 1911.

helplessness he felt, even before Grey answered his criticisms, that like all Radicals he could do nothing really effective to change the situation. The institutional framework hampered and hindered criticism. The only response Radicals seemed capable of producing was to be listened to with benign tolerance, and then ignored.[1] The 'mysteries' of diplomacy were not for men of common clay. They were condemned 'to walk by faith and not by sight amidst confusing intricacies and reticences . . . the consciousness of the nations would remain affrighted so long as the realms of diplomacy, the subterranean regions of the chancelleries of Europe, remained a dark and unexplored continent of traps, tricks and pitfalls'.[2] A number of Radicals like Browne believed that their lot was not only hapless but hopeless. Could they in conscience any longer believe the entente with France had been a force for good? Was it not the harbinger, the source of *La Guerre qui vient* that Delaisi had prophesied in May 1911?[3]

Why, asked the Radicals, if Britain was joined to France by an entente, had Grey behaved in July and August as though it was an alliance? Would a secret treaty explain Britain's apparent commitment to France, a commitment that dictated 'we would have to go to war over a few miserable miles of African desert'?[4] On 21 November Grey announced to the Commons that the secret articles annexed to the 1904 entente would soon be published.[5] But when, a few days later, the articles were published, with surprise and relief the Radicals discovered they were innocuous.[6] When the *Daily News* was ingenuous enough to suppose there were doubtless 'big secrets' concerning engagements made by the Liberal Government since it had come into office, Grey, with a fine show of indignation, knocked their artless suggestion on the head.[7] Perhaps all the time the sinister import of the entente had been contained in the public articles? Grey

[1] See *New Age*, 2 Mar. 1911, p. 400. 'The game is as innocuous as bridge for love, at which all that can be lost is honour or temper—things that do not matter. It is not war and it is not discussion. It is Parliamentary Debate. The reports should be published, not by *Hansard*, but by de la Rue.'
[2] William Heaford in *Concord*, xxviii, no. 10, mid-Dec., 1911, p. 117. See also evidence of Balfour, Asquith and Mr Speaker to Select Committee of House of Commons Procedure (1914), particularly questions 1704–06; 2284–86; and 3002–03; also Arthur Ponsonby, *Democracy and Diplomacy* (1915), 48–54.
[3] Francis Delaisi, *La Guerre Qui Vient* (edn de la Guerre Sociale, Paris, 1911); reviewed in *Concord*, July 1911, pp. 76–7.
[4] See Koss, *Brunner*, 245.   [5] *Hansard*, v:31:1006.
[6] See, *inter alia*, *Manchester Guardian*, 25 Nov. 1911. The publication of the secret articles went a long way to spiking the Radical guns that were being trained upon Grey for the debate in three days upon foreign policy. It was a neat move by Grey that cost him nothing, and gained for him an important initiative.
[7] *Daily News*, 25 Nov. 1911; *Hansard*, v:32:57–8.

in April had talked of 'obligations . . . expressed or implied in the Anglo-French Convention laid before Parliament'.[1] However, when the Tory member, Kinloch-Cooke, asked what exactly was implied in the terms, he was informed that diplomatic support neither pledged nor withheld armed support.[2] The matter was no clearer; the Government was past master at hiding its tergiversation in a cloud of sophist platitudes and circumlocution.

The Radicals sought one overriding thesis that would explain Grey's conduct of Britain's foreign policy. When they considered apparently unrelated episodes—Persia, Morocco, the Congo, Tripoli—one unifying factor was shared by all these aberrations of the Liberal spirit; one explanation afforded the key to understanding—a dread, an obsessive fear of Germany. Why else should Britain have purchased Russian friendship at the price of Persia's integrity? It could only be Britain's 'continued dread' of Germany.[3] When 'sentiment, honour, justice, expediency, commerce, strategy and . . . prestige' would dictate one policy in Persia, Grey had chosen the opposite because Britain's relations with Germany lay at the root of this as of so many other problems.[4] Germany and Britain acting together, might well have forestalled Italy's barbarous campaign in Tripoli, but Britain had played Pilate in the hope of thereby detaching Italy from the Triple Alliance.[5] German pressure in the Congo had been enough for Britain to come rushing in shining armour to support France, and no matter how one construed the 1904 entente it had certainly not pledged Britain's support to France in such a contingency. Yet Britain had been brought to the verge of war because Germany was 'Grey's great bogey' and he was prepared to pay any price, to crush, invade or abandon nationalities, tear up treaties, support violence, aggression and intrigue, in order that he might thwart the supposed German danger.[6] Talk of treaty obligations, secret or open, was vain. The *Manchester Guardian* maintained the source of danger was the entente—not the entente of 1904, but its perversion due to the unauthorised revival of the pernicious doctrine of the balance of power in Europe. It was no longer an entente but an alliance, an alliance directed against Germany.[7] How could Grey any longer deny that this and this alone explained his policy?

Grey did not shirk the task allotted him when he rose to reply to his critics in a crowded and expectant Commons on 27 November.

---

[1] *Hansard*, v:23–1490.   [2] *Ibid.*, v:32:5.   [3] *The Nation*, 5 Aug. 1911.
[4] *Hansard*, v:34:638, Ponsonby.   [5] *Ibid.*, v:149:50, Mason.
[6] *The Nation*, 2 Dec. 1911.   [7] *Manchester Guardian*, 27 Nov. 1911.

That task had been made more formidable by a significant shift of opinion towards Germany in the Conservative-Unionist camp. Certain elements of that party, alarmed by the spread of labour unrest and burdened by increased taxation, questioned whether in the circumstances Grey's conduct of foreign policy was as prudent as they had formerly supposed. In Parliament, Bonar Law in the Commons and Lansdowne in the Lords, while generally approving the Liberal Government's conduct of foreign affairs, nevertheless criticised the interference of Lloyd George with his Mansion House speech. The recruitment of a demagogue to purvey Government policy was prejudicial to the cause of peace. Some elements of the Tory Press, less inhibited by their reversal of attitude than politicians, changed almost overnight from open hostility towards Germany to supporting a rapprochement with that country.[1]

When Grey spoke in general terms of foreign policy, admittedly there were features that were appealing to his Radical critics. Britain, he declared, was sated as far as expansion for herself was concerned, and it was not her desire to adopt a dog in the manger policy towards the aspirations of other Powers in that particular direction. But his words on the balance of power and splendid isolation filled many Radical hearts with foreboding.

> The ideal of splendid isolation contemplated a balance of power in Europe to which we were not to be a party, and from which we were to be able to stand aside in the happy position of having no obligations and being able to take advantage of any difficulties which arose in Europe between opposing Powers. That policy is not a possible one now—It is the negation of policy . . . the disastrous consequences of such an attitude of mingled interference and drift would soon become apparent in expenditure on armaments . . . and sooner or later the very peace that people desired to preserve would topple over. Such an attitude would not even gain us the friendship of Germany.[2]

Grey did his job as well as he alone could. Reading his speech in cold print, it is impossible to begin to imagine the extraordinary powers of persuasiveness the man enjoyed in the Commons. Once again he employed those same tactics that had been so successful against the critics of his Russian policy. He did not defend his own position so much as attack his enemies, pouring scorn upon their ideas,

---

[1] *Hansard*, v 32 : 70 and Lords, v : 10 : 392. For examples of change in attitude of Tory Press, see Halévy, *The Rule of Democracy*, 437, and n. 2. *Labour Leader*, 1 Dec. 1911, p. 761, drew a comparison between Bonar Law's 'infinitely warmer feeling and sincerity of purpose' towards Germany, and Grey's 'chilly and frost-bitten cordiality'.

[2] *Hansard*, v : 32 : 60–1.

suggesting that his policy was best suited to gain those ends the Radicals most desired. Undoubtedly, it had been, as Asquith wrote to Crewe, 'a great performance and in every way characteristic; and it had the effect, which he alone is capable of producing in the House of Commons, of "torpedoing" the whole debate'.[1] Asquith, as the Liberal party's leader, had every reason to be pleased with the Foreign Secretary. He had sharpened Grey's argument in the face of Radical criticism by avowing: 'We are influenced in our conduct outside the strict letter of Treaty obligations by the desire to maintain in their full strength the friendships we have formed, and the understandings we have entered into.'[2] The *Daily News* did not miss the point. It boldy headlined next day: 'No secret agreements but must support France.'[3]

If Grey had drawn his critics' sting even before they made their contribution, at least they were able to advertise their discontent. Ramsay MacDonald castigated the notion, to which Bonar Law had gratuitously paid homage, that continuity in foreign policy was desirable. Why, he asked, retain the policies of one's predecessors if they were bad? The entente policy was evil, and nowhere was this more patent than in Persia, where for Russian friendship the basic principles of Liberalism has been offended. Labour suspected that Grey would make alliances of his ententes and thus drag the ignorant nations to war at the behest of a small faction of the Government. Asquith hotly denied MacDonald's assertions. Then Dillon condemned Grey for his penchant for secrecy, and Keir Hardie,

---

[1] Asquith to Crewe, 30 Nov. 1911. Asquith MSS. See also Morley's comments upon Grey retailed to Almeric Fitzroy, *Memoirs*, ii, 4711. Morley declared that 'he knew no one so capable upon a critical occasion of choosing his words with precision and felicity . . . for judgement, temper and lucidity on a matter which required the most delicate handling, nothing could have exceeded . . . [Grey's] speech.' Esher claimed Grey's speech 'made one proud of the House of Commons, of one's country and of him [Grey]'. *E.P.*, iii, 75. In the Commons, Keir Hardie and Ramsay MacDonald chided the Radicals for giving in too easily to the Foreign Secretary. However, if contemporary analyses of Socialist foreign policy are examined, so-called Socialist measures did not differ from those measures being advocated by the Radicals. See, for example, William Anderson (Chairman of the I.L.P.) 'Socialism and foreign-affairs: Labour's policy in the international field', *Labour Leader*, 8 Dec. 1911, p. 770.
[2] *Hansard*, v:32:110.
[3] *Daily News*, 28 Nov. 1911. By January 1912 Gardiner's *Daily News* was boldly placed in the Radical vanguard demanding 'The time has come to state with a clearness which cannot be mistaken that Sir Edward Grey as Foreign Secretary is impossible' (10 Jan. 1912). Tory critics, writing during and immediately after the war, were convinced that the attack upon Grey had been 'fomented by German misrepresentation and intrigue, skilfully acting upon the peculiar susceptibilities of radical fantacism'; see F. S. Oliver, *Ordeal by Battle* (1915), 299. This book though not published until 1915 had been completed in 1914, and had been written as a propaganda work in support of Lord Roberts's campaign for National Service.

Henderson and Noel Buxton declared their disappointment with Grey's obvious coolness towards Germany.

Kate Courtney's claim that the Liberal Press greeted Grey's speech with a chorus of regret[1] simply was not true. Many Radicals believed that Grey had totally vindicated his handling of affairs. If the whole-hearted support of Spender's *Westminster Gazette* was to be anticipated, the *Daily Chronicle* also declared its unquestioning conviction that Grey was correct, and what criticism there was in the *Economist* was mild and muted. The *Manchester Guardian* was not persuaded to change its tune, nor was *The Nation*. But for the moment Grey had spilled much of the wind out of Radical sails. The *Guardian* had demanded Grey once and for all should repudiate the balance of power doctrine,[2] but he had refused. What is more, he had charged his critics with being behind the times.

The Radicals recognised that Germany was an expansionist Power. They believed the expansion she sought was economic and extra-European. Both prize and struggle were outside Europe.

> The struggle for a balance of power in Europe is, in truth, a mere mirage. Nothing in Europe is at stake. We delude ourselves into the contrary belief only because diplomatists, seated round the European chessboard, are playing with ships in the North Sea and armies on the Rhine for railways and harbours at the ends of the earth.[3]

On this view, the rôle of armies and navies was not as engines of war but pawns in the game of diplomacy. Grey totally misunderstood the nature of the game he was playing. He seemed to cast the Kaiser in the role of a Napoleon, or a Louis XIV, and Britain as the threatened custodian of European liberties. Nothing could be further from the truth. Where was the evidence for the singular parallel the Foreign Secretary was intent upon drawing? What nations was Germany supposed to have dominated, what thrones had she toppled, what peoples had she dispossessed? Of all the Great Powers in the last generation, Germany alone had not substantially increased her territories. Grey insisted upon playing Don Quixote, tilting at phantasmagoric windmills created by the Foreign Office. Britain sacrificed honour, interest and good sense in the pursuit of delusions.[4] Germany simply was not the aggressive Power that Grey had made her out to be. In any event, was not Britain the most powerful nation in the world? Was not her navy supreme upon the seven seas? It behoved Britain in the interests of her citizens as well as the rest of

[1] *Courtney Diary*, 1 Dec. 1911.   [2] *Manchester Guardian*, 3 Nov. 1911.
[3] *The Nation*, 30 Dec. 1911.   [4] *The Nation*, 7 Oct. and 23 Dec. 1911.

the world to be 'a courteous giant' and 'live on good terms with his neighbours'.[1] Then Britain's policy might be one of 'predominance of power without provocation; strength . . . combined with friendship'.[2]

To all these assertions, Grey would have replied if he could, and had he dared,[3] that it was not he, but his critics who were deluded about England's rôle and Germany's intentions. For years, a constant theme in his letters to intimate colleagues and friends had been Germany's aggressive intentions. To keep the peace was a difficult, almost a hopeless task. In 1908 he wrote to Ella Pease: 'It is 38 years since Germany had her last war, and she is very strong and very restless, like a person whose boots are too small for him. I don't think there will be a war at present, but it will be difficult to keep the peace of Europe for another five years.'[4] Should his critics charge him with applying one standard to Germany and another to France, Grey would only remind them that 'Germany is an aggressive power, France is not'.[5] J. A. Hobson, to whom Grey made this remark, was not much impressed. In a pamphlet he produced a year later, *The German Panic*, Hobson stated that political and military 'experts' based their fears and suspicions upon the slenderest of evidence. This was the material out of which panic was created.[6]

The day after Grey's speech in the Commons, Courtney in the Lords delivered a withering attack upon the Foreign Secretary and the Liberal Government's stewardship of Britain's foreign policy. Britain had made friends with France, with Russia, with the United States of America. Why had not the same happy result been achieved with Germany? The whole Agadir incident had been handled inefficiently and discourteously. The language Grey had employed to the German Ambassador was France's not England's.

> I have never shared the extreme anxiety of those who thought we might be at war next day; but we were in a very bad situation because we had forgotten our proper position, and instead of being, with the other Powers, protectors of Morocco under the Act of Algeciras, we had become partisans of France.

It was well that Bethmann-Hollweg had talked of a clean slate, but

---

[1] *Ibid.*, 17 Feb. 1912.   [2] *Hansard*, v:32:126—Noel Buxton.
[3] In later years Radical critics were to make much of Grey's inability to express the true nature of the policies that he was following and his interpretation of the German 'menace'. Among the many passages on this subject, see, in particular: Loreburn, *How the War Came* (1919), 19–20; and Hammond, *C. P. Scott*, 173–4.
[4] Nov. 1908, quoted Trevelyan, 155.   [5] See Dorey, 317.
[6] See J. A. Hobson, *The German Panic* (1913), 29–30.

that was impossible to secure because Grey had chosen to make
Britain's friendship with France exclusive. The man seemed to be-
lieve that it was impossible to establish a cordial friendship with
Germany.

> Why does he not make the offer? His conception is a divided
> Europe. He seems to regard as impossible the notion of a unity
> of Christendom, a family of nations, a concert of Europe. The
> lesson of the last few months is that our foreign policy should
> no longer be inspired by that notion of the balance of power
> which has been the bane of successive generations. We want a
> new conception of international duty, a foreign policy based on
> the federation of the Powers in one body not two camps. . . . I
> am sorry I have to speak so firmly but . . . The greater our
> respect for his [Grey's] character, the more we are bound to
> express our dissent from the policy which we trace not only in
> his words but in every deed of his official career, and we are
> bound to express a hope that that false conception of foreign
> policy may disappear from the councils of the nation.[1]

It had been Courtney's greatest speech since entering the Lords, and
if Morley, in repudiating the accuracy of Courtney's description of
Grey's policy, had proved a doughty champion of the Foreign
Secretary, to judge from remarks made to Haldane a few days later,
the President of the Council, in private at least, had agreed with
much Courtney had said.[2]

If Grey had succeeded in 'torpedoing' some of his critics, there still
remained that hard Radical core who were not convinced. G. H.
Perris charged Grey with wanting to treat the House of Commons
like Sazonov treated the Duma.

> Thus evil communications corrupt good manners. But the
> British Parliament is as old in centuries as the Duma in years.
> It has lived down stronger bureaucrats than the present Foreign
> Minister and it will yet insist on controlling foreign as fully as it
> controls domestic policy . . . Sir Edward Grey stands alone; but
> so long as the Foreign Office is unreformed the unrelaxing
> vigilance of the friends of peace will be needed to prevent the
> recurrence of the danger.[3]

If G. M. Trevelyan was correct in his estimate when he wrote to
Courtney that 'You seem to have been the only one of our politicians who thought fit to say what I believe half or more than half

---

[1] See, Gooch, *Courtney*, 568–70.
[2] 'I could have seconded Courtney myself', Morley was overheard to say to
Haldane, see *Courtney Diary*, 1 Dec. 1911.
[3] G. H. Perris, 'Why we ran the Risk of War', *Concord*, xxviii, no. 10, p. 111.

the nation thinks at heart',[1] then there was cause indeed for rejoicing in the Radical camp. But why then had Snowden, writing in the *Christian Commonwealth*, appeared so grim and woeful as he scanned 'the dark and dismal' international outlook? The truth was that what the Radicals were pleased to call the Concert of Europe was capable only of producing jarring notes of discord. Grey's speech had not provided relief from anxiety. It had merely produced in the Tory Press grossly injurious assertions of self-will and arrogance that had brought the consummation of Anglo-German conflict perceptibly nearer. The Radicals had more cause for consternation than confidence, despair than hope. Felix Moscheles, posing the question 'Is it Peace or War?', claimed:

> We cannot but realise to the fullest extent the dangers connected with the present régime. What with equivocations and perversions, intrigues and revelations and what with skulking informers and double-faced spies, one must be in daily expectation of some new raid, invasion or annexation, and none can foretell when and where the ever threatening universal conflagration may break out.

Yet the same writer in the space of a few paragraphs, by hope could confound his own logic.

> War will go simply because the dispossessed will no longer sacrifice their lives for the possessed, and will not allow themselves to be perennially sweated at home and periodically dismembered abroad. Anti-militarism and anti-patriotism will triumph over those two insidious enemies of mankind, Caesarism and national egotism, and the patriotism which today we crown with laurels, will cease to be a standing menace to the peace of the world and pass away. . . . You may deplore and disbelieve; I have faith and rejoice.[2]

Optimism was the mainspring of the Radical spirit in its appreciation of the conduct of the world's affairs. The Radicals' tragedy was that the source of their greatest strength was paradoxically the source of their vulnerability in politics. Their hope was always proof against experience.

[1] Letter to Courtney, quoted Gooch, 571.
[2] *Concord*, xxviii, no. 10. Dec. 1911, pp. 112–13.

Chapter 7   A Cabinet Interlude—the Die is Cast

A packed Defence Committee

From the moment of his appointment as Director of Military Operations in August 1910, General Henry Wilson was the one constant and most important figure in Anglo-French military relations. His character was marked by two important traits—he had an arrogant conviction of the wisdom of his own opinions, and a penchant for intrigue. He was a most competent staff officer, and devoted his energies with a singular preoccupation to the problems of England's involvement in a continental war with Germany. At the Staff College at Camberley he discoursed on the subject day and night.[1] He was convinced beyond any shadow of doubt that Germany intended to attack France through Belgium, and as Britain was the guarantor of Belgium's neutrality, inevitably the British Army would be involved.[2] There was one other significant feature of Wilson's thinking. He was not given to charitable opinions about his fellow men, but when it came to politicians and their involvement in military matters, his contempt was absolute. He had no patience with amateur strategists.

In January 1911 Wilson was particularly concerned with the arrangements, or rather the lack of them, for the mobilisation of British divisions in the event of a German invasion of France. Nicholson, Chief of the Imperial General Staff, was apparently indifferent to the problem. Much to Wilson's frustration, his chief seemed to have little thought of war. Nevertheless, Wilson badgered both his fellow officers and the Minister for War. Through his incessant efforts, and with the help of Grey, by March Wilson had effected tentative arrangements for the embarkation of an expeditionary force from Southampton by the ninth day of mobilisation.

[1] See Fisher to Spender, 27 Feb. 1911, Fisher Correspondence, *Fear God and Dread Nought*, ii, 359.
[2] Williamson, 169.

However, the location of an adequate supply of horses proved so intractable a problem that in July and August, when the Agadir crisis was at its height, there were still insufficient to meet all requirements.[1] What was more, because of the First Sea Lord's stubborn opposition to any idea of cooperation or coordination of planning with the War Office, in August 1911 there were still no settled arrangements for the transportation of British troops to the Continent.

Henry Wilson did not limit his efforts exclusively to the question of mobilisation. He determined that the size of the expeditionary force should be increased from four to six divisions, and to that end, by March 1911, had devised a plan that would force the hand of the Committee of Imperial Defence. Wilson's new arrangements meant that there would have to be changes in the plans previously drawn up by the British and French General Staff. Wilson brought a new sense of purpose and urgency to the Anglo-French military conversations. Abandoning the cautious circumspection that until then had characterised contacts between the two sides, Wilson emphasised that close relations were 'vital for both countries'. His obvious sympathy for the French, and his apparent desire for British intervention, buttressed the importance he attached to the conversations. He promised Huguet that the Staff talks were a guarantee of British assistance. Wilson's attitude more than offset the scrupulous lip service he continued to pay the proposition that the conversations were noncommittal.[2]

The former leisurely pace of the military talks was interrupted by the arrival of the *Panther* at Agadir. With Haldane's knowledge, but without Cabinet sanction, Wilson set out for Paris on 19 July. The next day he met his French counterparts and also conversed with Messiny, the French Minister for War. Wilson, while he was careful to declare that his presence in Paris could not be taken to imply committal on the part of his Government, nevertheless pointed out that advance cooperation between the French and British Staffs 'could singularly influence that definitive decision'.[3] Before returning to England, Wilson signed an accord with the French Chief of Staff, Dubail, that included the declaration that the British expeditionary force would consist of six divisions of infantry and one of cavalry.

Wilson was back in England by 21 July. There followed a month of comparative quiescence for the Anglo-French talks, but in Sep-

[1] C. E. Callwell, *Field Marshal Sir Henry Wilson* (1927) i, 91–2; 97–8.
[2] Williamson, 172–3.
[3] See Callwell, i, 96; B.D. vii, 640; and A. M. Messiny, *Mes Souvenirs* (Paris, 1937), 267–8.

tember Wilson was alarmed by intelligence he had received that Joffre, who had replaced Dubail as Chief of the French Staff, seemed to be contemplating the possibility of an immediate war with Germany. In haste Wilson sought out Huguet and impressed on him that if there was to be a war, then it was vital that Germany should appear the responsible party. Should France be the aggressor, opinion in Britain would be divided and 'English intervention would find itself greatly retarded'.[1] This meeting was on 9 September, and the rest of the month was a period of considerable Anglo-French military activity. In October military clamour was stilled by the progress made in diplomatic negotiations over the fate of Morocco. However, the essential consideration, so far as General Wilson was concerned, was his conviction that Anglo-French military preparation had now reached a point where it could withstand a practical test. With the relaxation of international tension, Wilson felt free to take a holiday in France and Belgium. At Mars-la-Tour on the Franco-German frontier he laid at the base of a war memorial a fragment of a 'map I have been carrying showing the areas of concentration of the British forces on her [France's] territory'.[2] It was as if by his symbolic act Wilson wished to affirm that as long as he remained Director of Military Operations he would employ 'all his considerable energies and persuasive powers to promote the cause of British military intervention on the Continent'.[3]

When the Agadir crisis had been at its height, General Wilson had not confined his demonic energy to the preparation of the expeditionary force and the military conversations. He had also bent the full force of his considerable personality and the weight of his arguments on Grey and Haldane to convince them of the imperative need to employ British military intervention on the Continent in the event of war between France and Germany. On 9 August he attended a luncheon at Haldane's invitation. The two other guests were the Foreign Secretary and Eyre Crowe. Wilson recorded in his diary:

> After lunch we discussed the present German-Morocco state of affairs. Grey began by asking me if I thought Germany was going to war with France and us. This was a question I ought to have asked him. However, I replied in the negative. He advanced the theory that Russia was a governing factor, which I shattered rather rudely. . . . After a long and, I believe, ineffectual talk, the chief points I made were three: First, that we *must* join the French. Second that we *must* mobilise the same day as the

---

[1] Williamson, 177-8.   [2] Callwell, i, 105.   [3] Williamson, 182.

French. Third, that we *must* send all six divisions. These were agreed to, but with no great heartiness. . . . I was profoundly dissatisfied with the grasp of the situation possessed by Grey and Haldane.[1]

Wilson had a particularly poor opinion of Grey. He thought of the Foreign Secretary as 'an ignorant, vain and weak man'. Henry Wilson was ill-equipped by nature and by lack of information to judge the capabilities and disposition of Grey. His personal portrait of the Foreign Secretary reveals more of the author than the subject. Yet, there was much truth in the General's estimate that Grey knew 'nothing of policy and strategy going hand in hand'.[2]

On 11 August Wilson circulated two papers designed to prove both the necessity and value of British military intervention on the Continent. These papers evoked an almost immediate response from Winston Churchill. To that moment the young Home Secretary had been the brilliant protagonist for the Radical 'economist' group in the Cabinet. Now, indulging a hereditary disposition, and asserting the prerogative of youth to change its mind, he joined the martial van. This was to be no sudden infatuation as soon rejected as embraced. Churchill, though not tied to London by official claims, had kept the company of Edward Grey throughout the month of August 'for love of the crisis'. According to Grey, Winston

> followed the anxieties of the Foreign Office with intense interest. . . . Let me not be supposed to imply that Churchill was working for war, or desired it: he followed all the diplomacy closely, but never either in Council or in conversation with me did he urge an aggressive line. It was only that his high-metalled spirit was exhilarated by the air of crisis and high events.[3]

The Home Secretary, once so scathing in his denunciation of Haldane's expeditionary force, in the moment of national crisis changed his attitude not only to the Army but to the reality of the German 'menace'.

Henry Wilson had argued in his papers that the *immediate* intervention of British troops would have a decisive influence upon the fortunes of the Kaiser's army. Churchill, while accepting Wilson's premise that there would be an extensive violation of Belgian territory by the German army, believed that the D.M.O. was much too sanguine in his estimate of the French army's capabilities. Churchill argued that the decisive question was not whether Britain should

[1] Callwell, i. 98–9.
[2] Wilson's Diary, 9 Aug. 1911, quoted Williamson, 184.
[3] Grey, i, 238.

intervene, but when and with what force. Personally he favoured four divisions assembling at the outbreak of hostilities, but they should not be engaged in action until forty days after the outbreak of war. The remaining two divisions Churchill wished to be kept in Britain until such time as the Navy had established a blockade of the Continent.[1] Wilson rejected Churchill's memorandum as 'a ridiculous and fantastic paper'. However, from that moment was forged an important bond between the two men that was to grow in respect and amity throughout the coming months. Winston was drawn within that privileged group who were given access to Wilson's detailed plans and computations of troop movements, and frequent memoranda were exchanged between the two men.

Throughout July and August, when all had been a fever of excitement and preparation at the War Office, the Admiralty had appeared nonchalant and lacking in concern. This manifestation of disdain for the Army's war fever was not affected. The First Sea Lord simply refused to believe that there was any danger of war, and to indicate his indifference, spent a weekend in July shooting in Scotland.[2] Churchill, in a lather of excitement, was extremely apprehensive about the Admiralty's lack of concern. He told Lloyd George: 'They are so cocksure, *insouciant* and apathetic, so far as one can judge from all that one sees and hears.'[3] Churchill's anxiety was shared by his Radical 'twin' at the Exchequer who wrote to Winston in August:

> I have been reading the Foreign Office papers. They are full of menace. The thunderclouds are gathering. I am not at all satisfied that we are prepared, or that we are preparing. When the terrible character of the issue is considered, we seem to me to take it all much too carelessly. . . . I am inclined to think the chances of war are multiplying . . . 'Be ye therefore ready'![4]

This solicitude evinced by the Chancellor and the Home Secretary for Britain's preparations for war, was not shared by the First Lord of the Admiralty. It was not until 25 July, when urgently prompted by Grey after Metternich's hostile response to the Mansion House speech, that McKenna was moved to issue a warning order to the Fleet. At a time when Grey judged the Fleet might be attacked immediately,[5] Britain's naval forces were scattered abroad. The Admiralty had even lost touch with the German High Seas Fleet who were sailing as a single unit in the North Sea. Those British

[1] See Winston Churchill, *World Crisis*, 55–7.
[2] See Marder, 243.   [3] See Owen, 213.
[4] Lloyd George to Churchill, 27 Aug. 1911, quoted *ibid.*, 212.
[5] See Churchill, *World Crisis*, 46.

ships that had returned from manœuvres could not be refuelled, since the necessary colliers were held up by a strike at Cardiff. Then it was discovered that the Navy's cordite reserves were insufficiently protected—an easy target for any saboteur. 'The whole thing', wrote Henry Wilson, for once without exaggeration, 'is like a pantomime.'[1] Churchill reminded Grey, 'Our margins of naval strength are so big if only we are ready: but are we ready? Are you absolutely sure we are ready?'[2]

The Admiralty was too busily engaged in upholding its independence from the unwelcome pretensions of the War Office to concern itself overmuch with what it considered were merely administrative niceties. They confidently asserted that when the time came the senior service would, as always, match the moment with its endeavours. Meanwhile energy was best reserved to combat the upstart suggestion that their primary function would be to ferry the British expeditionary force to France in the event of continental conflict. The First Lords, Sea and Civil, were as one in their unyielding opposition to the idea, and Fisher lent them his moral support. From Lucerne where he was holidaying, Fisher wrote to McKenna admonishing him never to give way to Haldane. Once entertain plans for landing British troops in France and this would be enough to cast the Government out of office! The object of such an exercise, Fisher was convinced, would only be to increase military influence, enlarge the Army Estimates and to impose compulsory service. Fisher's particular concern was that Haldane might 'nobble' Asquith.[3] As the Admiralty supported a view of strategy quite different from that of the War Office, a clash between the two Service Departments could not long be delayed.

On 10 August Henry Wilson had written in his Diary: 'Haldane sent for me early this morning. . . . He said he had had a useful dinner last night of Asquith, McKenna, Grey and Churchill. He had told those ignorant men something of war with the result that Asquith arranged for a small meeting of the C.I.D., for tomorrow week.'[4] In fact, the meeting Wilson mentions was held on 23 August. It was a remarkable meeting in a number of ways, but most particularly in that the all day session was the first designed to review the whole of British strategy. Until now, the Committee of Imperial Defence had been a failure as a coordinating institution. This was no

[1] Callwell, i, 97–8; also Marder, 244–6.
[2] Churchill to Grey, 30 July 1911, quoted Williamson, 182.
[3] Fisher to McKenna, 20 Aug. 1944, in Correspondence, *Fear God and Dread Nought*, ii, 380.
[4] Callwell, i, 99.

more than a reflection of its chairman's inclinations. Asquith, whenever and wherever possible, postponed difficult problems to the very last moment. As the head of the C.I.D., it was the Prime Minister's responsibility to reconcile the differing strategical concepts of the Admiralty and the War Office. But until the summer of 1911, British strategic policy remained both uncoordinated and contradictory. The report of a subcommittee of the C.I.D., had pointed out in July 1909 that 'the expediency of sending a military force abroad, or of relying on naval means only, is a matter which can only be determined when the occasion arises by the Government of the day'.[1] Thus, it was acknowledged that the choice between competing strategical concepts was for the politicans to make, and more particularly for the Prime Minister.[2]

The meeting was called at a time when Parliament had recessed after the most stormy session of its recent history. Members of the Cabinet, exhausted by their exertions, were about to disperse for their holidays. Asquith took the chair at the meeting and the other members present were: Lloyd George, Churchill, Grey, McKenna and Haldane as interested ministers; Generals Nicholson, French and Wilson for the Army; and Ottley, Bethell and A. K. Wilson for the Navy. In some ways the absentees from that meeting are of more significance than those who attended. Esher, who would normally have been there, was not present because he was convalescing after an operation. Kitchener had declined an invitation because, as he told Haldane, 'he was sure the Germans would beat the French and he would have no part in any decisions which the Ministers might think fit to take'.[3] Of the leading Radicals in the Cabinet, Morley was already absent from London on holiday in Scotland. Loreburn, Harcourt and Crewe did not receive an invitation to attend. Esher was convinced that to call a very secret meeting to discuss the action to be taken by Britain if she joined France in a war against Germany was 'not a very wise proceeding'.[4]

The meeting was divided into two sessions. At the first, Wilson, as Director of Military Operations, stated the views of the Army

[1] Sub-Committee Report on the Military needs of the Empire, 24 July 1909 quoted Williamson, 111.
[2] See J. P. Mackintosh, 'The role of the Committee of Imperial Defence before 1914', *English Historical Review*, 77 (1962), pp. 490–503; and Johnson, *Defence by Committee*, 95–101.
[3] *E.P.*, iii, 58. Kitchener had already informed Lloyd George that the Germans would walk through the French Army like a covey of partridges. However, he told Churchill that he had a fairly good opinion of the French Army's quality. At least there was general agreement that the Belgian Army would be of little value. See Owen, 213.
[4] *E.P.*, iii, 58.

General Staff. Marshalling his arguments with great aplomb, Wilson produced overwhelming and detailed evidence to indicate the probable German plan of campaign. Then he outlined intended British moves.

> [Wilson] asserted that if six British divisions[1] were sent to take position on the extreme French left, immediately war was declared, the chances of repulsing the Germans in the first great shock of battle were favourable. Every French soldier would fight with double confidence if he knew he was not fighting alone. Upon the strength of Russia General Wilson spoke with great foresight, and the account which he gave of the slow mobilisation of the Russian Army swept away many illusions.[2]

Churchill continued his description of the meeting. 'There was of course considerable discussion and much questioning before we adjourned at 2 o'clock.'[3] When the meeting was resumed it was the turn of the Admiralty, and A. K. Wilson expounded their views of the strategy involved in a war with Germany. 'He did not', says Churchill, 'reveal the Admiralty war plans. Those he kept locked away in his own brain, but he indicated that they embodied the principle of a close blockade of the enemy's ports.'

> In the main the Admiralty thought that we should confine our efforts to the sea; that if our small Army were sent to the Continent it would be swallowed up among the immense hosts conflicting there, whereas if kept in ships or ready to embark for counter-strokes upon the German coast, it would draw off more than its own weight of numbers from the German fighting line. This view, which was violently combated by the Generals, did not commend itself to the bulk of those present.[4]

The meeting had proved to be a triumph for War Office opinion in general, and Henry Wilson's view of strategy in particular. In the face of the General's masterly exposition, the Admiralty's case, presented in halting fashion by the First Sea Lord, had appeared even to a sympathetic listener 'to have been cooked up at the last minute'.[5] In any event, given 'that particular audience', the Admiralty's plan 'ran no chance'.[6] Later that same evening, Wilson received a note from Haldane: 'You did admirably today. Lucid and real grip. Your exposition made a real impression.' There was

[1] Henry Wilson at no time made mention of the accord he had signed with Dubail in July concerning the number of divisions to be dispatched.
[2] Wilson was always scathing of minister's hopes based upon the Russian Army. He made no secret of his contempt for these views, but ministers stuck to them with considerable obstinacy. See, for instance, the letters of Lloyd George and Churchill, quoted Owen, 212.
[3] W. S. Churchill, *World Crisis*, 53.   [4] *Ibid.*, 54.
[5] Lord Hankey, *The Supreme Command* (1961), i, 81.   [6] Callwell, i, 99.

every reason for Wilson to believe that he had done his work well and that he had 'convinced the Ministers of the necessity of instant action'.[1] Certainly, matters could no longer be allowed to drift along as they had for the past years. 'The profound difference', as Churchill described it, 'between the military and naval staffs in such critical times upon such fundamental issues', was clear to all who had attended the fateful meeting.[2]

Hankey wrote to Fisher that it was his belief that as no decision had been arrived at during the meeting as between the two competing strategic views, this meant in effect defeat for the War Office's case.[3] However, on mature reflection the same author claimed: 'From that time onward there was never any doubt what would be the grand strategy in the event of our being drawn into a continental war in support of France.'[4] There was no further meeting of the Committee of Imperial Defence to discuss overall strategic coordination before the outbreak of war in 1914. Nor did anyone ever question Wilson's arguments, or examine thoroughly the implications of intervention by the British Army.[5]

It has been claimed that 'the key person in the dramatic changes of October 1911' that followed as a direct result of the C.I.D., meeting in August 'was Haldane, the brilliant Secretary of State for War'.[6] This judgment is incorrect for, as in the naval crisis of 1909, the key rôle once again was assigned to Asquith. To understand Asquith's point of view, one must consider the vexed question of the military conversations between France and Britain that had been instituted in the first month of the Liberal Government's period of office.

In April 1911 Grey, because of pressure of circumstances, was obliged to send Asquith an informal account of the arrangements that had been made in 1906 for conversations between the French and British military staffs. The manner in which Grey wrote strongly suggests that the Prime Minister was being given this information for the first time.[7] Asquith, perhaps as his biographer suggests,[8] because he was informed of the conversations so late in the day, adopted a cool attitude towards them. Thus, in early September 1911, Asquith informed Grey that in his opinion the conversations seemed 'rather dangerous; especially the part which refers to possible British assistance. The French ought not to be encouraged to make their plans on any assumption of this kind.' Grey replied with extra-

[1] Callwell, i, 100.   [2] Churchill, 54.
[3] Hankey to Fisher, 24 Aug. 1911, quoted Marder, 393.
[4] Hankey, i. 82.   [5] See Mackintosh, 501–3.
[6] Marder, 246.   [7] Grey, i, 94.   [8] Jenkins, *Asquith*, 243.

ordinary ingenuousness that though the conversations, like minister's speeches, encouraged the French to expect support, he did not see how this could be helped. If the conversations were now cancelled it would only cause consternation.[1]

During the course of the C.I.D., meeting on 23 August, Asquith had on several occasions interrupted the arguments in an attempt to reconcile the Admiralty and War Office positions. By his questioning of Nicholson, the Prime Minister also made it clear that if an Expeditionary force were to be dispatched to the Continent then he favoured sending no more than four divisions. Two divisions should be retained in Britain to repel any German raids. The Prime Minister reminded the meeting that this had been the recommendation of the 1908 subcommittee on invasion.[2] The meeting had broken up with the Admiralty and the War Office representatives at loggerheads. The next day Haldane wrote a sharp letter to Asquith clearly indicating that he would resign unless the Admiralty worked in complete harmony with the wishes of the Army General Staff. 'Our problems of defence [being] numerous and complex . . . they can only be solved correctly by a properly organized and scientifically trained War Staff, working in the closest cooperation with the military General Staff under the general direction of the War Office.'[3] Asquith replied a week later: 'Sir A. Wilson's "plan" can only be described as puerile, and I have dismissed it at once as wholly impracticable. The impression left on me after consideration of the whole discussion is . . . that in principle, the General Staff scheme is the only alternative.' Then, ten days later, Asquith wrote again to Haldane. 'The arguments as put in the W.O. letter are, of course, conclusive as against Sir A.W.'s scheme.' He then added significantly: 'I hope, however, that we may not have again to consider the contingency.'[4] Like most senior members of his Government, Asquith passed through moments of nervousness when he examined the international scene, but always his natural inclination was to avert his eyes as quickly as possible from any prospect of war. It was not that war was considered an unlikely contingency but that the very idea was distasteful.

During the succeeding weeks of late summer 1911, Asquith's dislike for the notion of intervention on the Continent by a British Army appeared to strengthen. As a guest of the King at Balmoral, the Prime Minister on 4 October spent an hour with Esher discussing strategy. According to Esher, Asquith's views on the subject would

[1] Grey, i, 95.   [2] See Williamson, 190.
[3] Sir Frederick Maurice, *Haldane* (1937), i, 283.   [4] Williamson, 193.

have astonished Haldane and the General Staff. The Prime Minister accepted the need for reform at the Admiralty. While Asquith admitted he favoured the idea of a staff, nothing could be done until Admiral Wilson was replaced as First Sea Lord. Nor would the changes cease there, for Asquith proposed 'to make a change in the supreme head of the Admiralty'. The Prime Minister was quick to add that such changes would have to wait until the following April. So much on the credit side of the ledger for the War Office. But the Prime Minister went on to declare his opposition to the General Staff scheme of landing a British Army in France—at least, he would not hear of the dispatch of more than four divisions. At this point Esher reminded Asquith of the uncomfortable fact that, as the War Office had already worked out detailed plans with the French General Staff, Britain was committed to fight, and that 'whether the Cabinet likes it or not'. Recording their conversation in his *Journal*, Esher added: 'It is certainly an extraordinary thing that our officers should have been permitted to arrange all details, trains, landing concentration, etc., when the Cabinet has never been consulted.'[1]

Asquith could not but be aware of the paradoxical situation into which he had been engineered. The prerogative of decision, in all but name, had been usurped from his hands by the plans, promises and hints of General Wilson. That the usurpation should not become apparent he had either to accept the Admiralty's case, or implement certain ministerial changes that would ensure success for the War Office's plans, even though he did not approve of all the particulars. McKenna would have to go from the Admiralty. That much was certain. He was too faithful a servant of the Sea Lords to allow easy surrender to the War Office. But when, and by whom, should McKenna be replaced?

Asquith had already resolved these problems when, two weeks after his conversation with Esher, he had a confrontation with McKenna. Despite the Prime Minister's honeyed words of praise, consolation and hope, the lavish expressions of goodwill and gratitude, the interview must have been painful for McKenna. The First Lord carried the argument to his chief declaring in no uncertain terms that the Admiralty were adamantly opposed to the War Office's suggestion that British troops be employed in France. Asquith responded by assuring McKenna there was no cause for concern as he was equally opposed to such schemes. When McKenna boldly suggested that the War Office might exert pressure on

[1] *E.P.*, iii, 60–1.

Asquith, the Prime Minister answered what was in effect a true bill of indictment, with the hot assertion that he was no mere figurehead to be 'pushed along against his will and without his knowledge'. As long as he remained Prime Minister there would be no cause for anxiety. He was opposed to War Office schemes. Nor did he believe in war. Had he thought war probable, he would not have contemplated taking the Admiralty away from McKenna. McKenna pleaded for a temporary stay of execution, but Asquith rejected it.[1] The die was cast. Whatever reservations Asquith might have entertained, the ministerial changes upon which he had determined guaranteed the triumph of War Office strategy. When France and Germany came to blows, British troops would stand in the French lines.

Throughout September Haldane had constantly pressed Asquith to make changes in the naval leadership. Towards the end of the month he intensified his campaign and was joined in his efforts by the youthful Home Secretary. What uncomfortable apprehensions the Minister of War must have entertained about his new ally. Haldane coveted the Admiralty for himself. He felt that he had discharged the greatest part of his burden as War Minister. Now it was his anxious ambition to coordinate the work of the two great Service Departments. He had no reservations concerning his fitness to be First Lord. It was true that by his own admission he had 'but little experience of the Navy'. Yet, 'I felt I was almost the only person available who was equipped to cope with the problem of the Naval War Staff.[2] I think the Prime Minister held much the same view but we had to be careful to say nothing of impending changes.'[3] Unfortunately for Haldane's calculations, there was now a Minister just as eager a suppliant for the post of First Lord, and equally convinced of his unique fitness to undertake the task of devising a naval war staff.

Asquith, on holiday in Scotland, was preoccupied with the problem of the changes at the Admiralty. There were a number of weighty reasons that militated against Haldane's appointment as First Lord. There was the fact that he was now in the Lords—but this was more an argument of convenience than substance.[4] It was not that

---

[1] McKenna's notes of conversation, 20 Oct. 1911, quoted Marder, 250ff.
[2] During McKenna's conversation with Asquith no mention was made of the institution of a Naval Staff at the Admiralty, the basic issue which required the Cabinet reshuffle.
[3] R. B. Haldane, *Autobiography*, 230.
[4] This was the reason that Asquith was to give Haldane for his not receiving the Admiralty. With an uncustomary lack of charity, Haldane suggests in his *Autobiography* that the argument was provided for Asquith by Churchill.

Asquith doubted Haldane's capacity for the post, but the Prime Minister considered that 'it would be wounding to the *amour propre* of the Admiralty to send it the same new broom which had already cleaned up the War Office'.[1] There was another and more compelling political reason why Asquith should favour Churchill for the Admiralty rather than 'Pussy' Haldane. If Churchill went to the Admiralty, then he would be permanently detached from the 'economists' in the Cabinet. Asquith could not be certain, but the move might have the considerable bonus of bringing Lloyd George over with his 'lieutenant'. So far as the balance of factions within the Government was concerned, and as leader Asquith had constantly to bear this factor in mind, the Prime Minister could not ignore the possibility that a disgruntled McKenna might return to his first loyalty and be a powerful ally to the Radical economist group in the Cabinet. If Churchill was not wooed out of the Radical camp by a suitable *pourboire*, then the balance of forces in the Administration would be heavily weighted in their favour. There were sufficient rumblings of discontent from that quarter already for Asquith to know that there would be uncomfortable confrontations in the Cabinet in the very near future.

Churchill joined the Asquiths as a house guest on 27 September. Haldane, anxious to apprise the Premier of the case for his being given the Admiralty, drove over from Cloan to Archerfield only to be welcomed at the doorway by Winston. During the succeeding days the two aspirants advertised their claims for precedence to one another and to Asquith. Neither man was hindered by modesty in judging his own abilities. In the event Haldane was disappointed. By his appointment Churchill's whole life was invested with a new significance. He told Asquith's daughter: 'This is the big thing—the biggest thing that has ever come my way—the chance I should have chosen before all others. I shall pour into it everything I've got.'[2] Haldane bore his disappointment without any resentment towards his brilliant young colleague. Within a short while he was writing to his mother:

> Winston and L.G. dined with me last night and we had a very useful talk. This is now a very harmonious Cabinet. It is odd to think that three years ago I had to fight those two for every penny for my army reforms. Winston is full of enthusiasm

---

There is no reason to suppose that Asquith concerned himself with the question of Haldane getting the Woolsack which he had been denied in 1905. See Haldane, *Autobiography*, 230–1.

[1] Violet Bonham Carter, *Churchill as I Knew Him*, 247.

[2] Bonham Carter, 249.

about the Admiralty. . . . It is delightful to work with him.
L.G. too has quite changed his attitude.[1]

Asquith's ministerial shuffle was already bringing about one of its
desired results.

McKenna exchanged offices with Churchill on 25 October. The Admiralty did not require telling that they had lost a loyal and staunch
supporter. In the three and a half years since he had replaced the
unfortunate Tweedmouth as First Lord, McKenna had stoutly
promoted, in Cabinet and Commons, the views of his professional
advisers. The Sea Lords and the civil servants apprehensively
awaited Churchill. He might not be loyal, or dignified, or steadfast;[2]
he might very well be 'a wind bag' and 'a self-advertising mounte-
bank'.[3] He would certainly be master of his own domain.

Confrontation

Radical members of the Cabinet who interested themselves in the
conduct of foreign affairs had reason for feelings of apprehension
and displeasure at the way in which their Government was dealing
with the Franco-German quarrel in Morocco. But, the bitterness of
the resentment they felt for Grey was more a reflection of their
sense of political impotence than distaste for the measures that the
Foreign Secretary propounded. In a word, their pride had been injured. Two days after the momentous meeting of the Committee of
Imperial Defence, of which Loreburn at that time had no knowledge,
the Lord Chancellor wrote a sharp note of rebuke and warning to
Edward Grey.

> I greatly fear that France expects our military and naval
> support . . . I believe that you could not give it if you wished,
> in this which is a purely French quarrel. I believe you could not
> carry it in the present House of Commons except by a majority
> very largely composed of Conservatives and with a very large
> number of [the] Ministerial side against you and this would
> mean that the present government would not carry on. . . .
> [France] ought to be told we cannot go beyond diplomatic
> support in this quarrel.

Grey was not impressed by Loreburn's strictures, or the barely
veiled threats. He replied that the Cabinet alone could authorise a

---

[1] Sommer, 248–9.
[2] *The Spectator*, 28 Oct. 1911.
[3] These are two of the more charitable descriptions Leo Maxse allowed himself
when commenting upon the new First Lord in his *National Review*. Maxse
had a poor opinion of Liberal First Lords and had thought Tweedmouth better
fitted to be Astronomer Royal than go to the Admiralty!

statement of the kind Loreburn had suggested, and he refused to alter his policy.[1]

Loreburn was never the easiest of colleagues to get along with in Cabinet—he wore his 'pro-Boer' mantle too self-consciously for Grey, Haldane or even Asquith to find him comfortable company. Yet the manner in which he learned of the secret events of August was guaranteed to injure his vanity and stoke the fires of his indignation and wrath against the 'Liberal Leaguers'. Alfred Lyttelton, a former Conservative Colonial Secretary, during the course of a conversation with Loreburn, casually remarked that Unionist leaders had been approached and asked whether their support could be relied upon in the event of war with Germany. Lyttelton assumed that Loreburn (as a Cabinet member) must have known of this. The startled Lord Chancellor hid his ignorance and learned further that

> everything had been arranged for the landing of a force of 150,000 men on the French coast down to the minutest detail of the time of departure and arrival of the trains and the stations at which they should get refreshments. This had all been arranged by members of the Committee of Imperial Defence.[2]

Consumed with righteous indignation, Loreburn consulted Morley and Harcourt about this baleful intelligence, only to find they knew already. To all three men it was patent that their exclusion from the meeting on 23 August had been deliberate. Certainly, there appeared to be no legitimate excuse for Morley's proscription, as he was a member of the Committee of Imperial Defence.

There had been ample opportunity to inform ministers of the meeting. There were four Cabinets held between the time that Asquith arranged for the calling of the Committee of Imperial Defence and its assembling.[3] A meeting on 14 August of Asquith, Grey, Lloyd George, Churchill and their host, Haldane, had decided 'the present course of German diplomacy rendered every possible precaution necessary'. The knot of negotiations might be cut at any moment and 'a pistol presented at the head of France'. Therefore, anything to facilitate a quick 'counter-stroke' to thwart Germany's plans had

[1] Loreburn to Grey, 25 Aug. 1911 and Grey to Loreburn, 30 Aug. 1911, quoted Williamson, 157.
[2] Scott, *Diaries*, edited Wilson, 62. There is an account of the incident based on the same source in Hammond's *C. P. Scott*, 143ff, but Loreburn's dates have not been corrected as they have by Trevor Wilson, 61, n. 35.
[3] Cabinets were held on 11, 16, 17 and 22 Aug. 1911. Morocco is only mentioned in the Cabinet letter for one of these meetings, 17 Aug. 1911, when Grey reported that the situation had improved and the Cabinet decided there was no need to send a warship to Agadir as Nicolson had wanted. The Cabinet was preoccupied at this time with labour troubles.

to be considered. The Clerk to the Privy Council, his 'curiosity not unmixed with misgiving inspired by the mutual relations of members of the Cabinet', was assured that Lord Morley, who had heard the week before what was brewing, would 'leave the Government' should they act in such manner as would suggest that Britain would support France in her quarrel. However, Fitzroy now recorded: 'Lord Morley having gone to Scotland, it was considered unnecessary to trouble him, and I agreed that, if the course proposed had the sanction of the Prime Minister, nothing further was required.'[1] There is no doubt that Morley's exclusion from the extraordinary[2] meeting of the C.I.D., was deliberate. Morley may have been a 'senile wreck', as his 'friend' the Lord Chancellor described him, but as an accomplished political gossip he did not lack for unofficial sources of information. Within a fortnight of the meeting, Asquith was writing in a secret note to Haldane that evidently someone had informed Morley who was 'quite the most impossible colleague that ever entered a Cabinet'.[3]

Morley did not resign as he threatened he would some weeks previously. Threats of resignation had become almost a way of life for the Lord President at this stage of his career. As the senior Cabinet member of the discontented Radical trio, it was Morley who was chosen to raise the issue in Cabinet. The prospect of Radical censures and wrangles in the Cabinet must have been more distressing for Grey than for Asquith. The Prime Minister had his own reservations about the military conversations with France.[4] Now the matter could be fully ventilated in Cabinet without any abstentions, real or contrived.

When all the Ministers had returned to London from their vacations, Morley drew attention to the military conversations in the Cabinet of 1 November. Asquith reported to the King:

> Lord Morley raised the question of the inexpediency of communications being held or allowed between the General Staff of the War Office and the General Staff of foreign states, such as France, in regard to possible military cooperation, without the previous knowledge and directions of the Cabinet. Lord Haldane explained what had actually been done, the communications in question having been initiated as far back as 1906 with Sir H. Campbell-Bannerman's sanction, and resumed in more detail during the spring and summer of the present year. The

---

[1] See Fitzroy, ii, 461.
[2] The covering letter sent by Ottley to Asquith with the minutes for the meeting did not bear the usual number, but the legend, 'Secret'.
[3] Asquith to Haldane, 9 Sept. 1911, quoted Williamson, 197.
[4] See *ante*.

Prime Minister pointed out that all questions of policy have been and must be reserved for the decision of the Cabinet, and that it is quite outside the function of military or naval officers to prejudge such questions. . . . Considerable discussion ensued.[1]

Asquith's account to the King reveals the strategy of excuse employed by Grey, Haldane and Asquith; the reason why the Radicals could not possibly find the 'explanation' satisfactory; and more, Asquith's inability to recognise that the military conversations committed Britain to a particular military strategy that must, and indeed did, shape policy. The reference to Campbell-Bannerman, whose death had put his Radicalism beyond reproach, was patently a device to disarm the suspicions of the malcontents. Both Grey and Asquith insisted that the French Government knew Britain was not committed by the talks. The Radicals were not impressed. They believed that no worthy defence had been made to their charges—efforts had been confined to diverting the discussion to the merits of the action taken and away from the fact of its concealment. The matter could not be allowed to rest there. When Loreburn said that he took it for granted that in future nothing of the sort would occur again, Churchill in some passion rashly demurred. The Lord Chancellor declared if such was the case, then clearly they must meet again and have the matter out.[2]

The second meeting took place on 15 November. While Balfour struggled to retain the leadership of the Tories, Asquith was furiously employed in keeping his Government intact. Loreburn, never a man of guile, informed Asquith's secretary that if the Prime Minister did not comply with the requests of the Radical ministers then there would be eight resignations[3]—a hollow threat. Asquith in his letter to the King wrote of 'a prolonged and animated discussion'. In truth the debate was acrimonious. The dissidents had prepared two resolutions for discussion, but the nub of the issue between the parties was in Loreburn's repeated plaint, 'Why were we not told?' No satisfactory answer was forthcoming.

Grey defended the conversations. He insisted that neither the conversations nor any diplomatic engagements had compromised Britain's 'freedom of decision of action in the event of a war between France and Germany'. To prove his assertion, Grey quoted a dispatch sent by Cambon in September to Caillaux which observed that if France appeared in the rôle of aggressor in any war with Germany, 'the result would be that France would not be able to count on

---

[1] Cabinet letter, 2 Nov. 1911, quoted Jenkins, 244.
[2] Scott, *Diaries*, 62.   [3] *Ibid.*, 61.

British support'.[1] The Radicals seemed no happier after this explanation, and Asquith intervened to suggest two propositions which, after some debate, were agreed to unanimously. They were:

(i) That no communications should take place between the General Staff here and the Staffs of other countries which can, directly or indirectly, commit this country to military or naval intervention.

(ii) That such communications, if they relate to concerted action by land or sea, should not be entered into without the previous approval of the Cabinet.[2]

The wording of the second proposition had been the subject of an altercation between Asquith and Loreburn. The Lord Chancellor insisted on the word 'previous' being inserted. 'You are very suspicious,' said Asquith. 'We have reason to be,' retorted Loreburn.[3] The Prime Minister did not require to be a lawyer to appreciate the import of the additional word. Grey had not liked the second proposition. Though he subsequently crossed out the remark, he wrote on Asquith's original draft: 'I think the last paragraph is a little tight.' It was intended to be restrictive, and Grey must have realised the implied rebuke was designed for him.

One thing remained. The Radicals had drafted 'a statement of facts'—a rehearsal of the events that had led them to draw up their propositions. Asquith, Grey, Lloyd George, Churchill and possibly Haldane, duly signed it.[4] After his contribution at the beginning of the meeting, Grey had remained silent. Now as he rose with other ministers to leave the Cabinet he declared in abstract manner, 'I always said we ought to be fair to the Cabinet.' Grey would always enjoy the last word.

With the Cabinet ended, Loreburn suggested to Morley and Harcourt that all three of them should resign as a protest. But his two companions did not agree, and Loreburn reluctantly acquiesced in their decision. The Cabinet had not followed the path that the Lord Chancellor would have wished. He had intended to bring forward resolutions that would have laid down certain guidelines for the future conduct of foreign policy. But he was old and tired, and illness was soon to force him to retire. The Radical campaign within the Cabinet had been prosecuted with little effect. Tactically, it would

---

[1] The words were taken from a minute by Nicolson, 2 Nov. 1911, *B.D.*, VI, 617.
[2] Cabinet Letter, 16 Nov. 1911, quoted Jenkins, 244–5.
[3] Scott, *Diaries*, 63.
[4] *Ibid.* Scott's account is based on a conversation with Loreburn in October 1914, three years *after* the Cabinet meeting.

have been better for Loreburn to have led the challenge, but Morley, sunk in a dotage that exaggerated his vanity, 'would do nothing unless put in the front and given all the credit'. Morley had been chosen to move the resolution in November because his friends feared he would otherwise oppose it.[1] Harcourt lacked the presence to cut any figure in the Cabinet, no matter his courage and wisdom. To compensate for the loss of Lloyd George and Churchill from the Radical fold, there had been the doubtful acquisition of McKenna. But the new Home Secretary's change of heart was more a case of pique at the manner in which he had been dismissed from the Admiralty by Asquith—his sympathies had been too long engaged with Grey's entente plans to make him an effective critic of foreign policy.[2] It was Loreburn's opinion that the Cabinet was 'rotten'. He charged Asquith with being nerveless, but the Prime Minister had successfully ridden out another difficult Cabinet crisis. His ploy of detaching Churchill and Lloyd George had succeeded better than he might have expected.[3]

The one man who could certainly feel well pleased with the eventual result of the two Cabinet meetings was Wilson. The Radicals had not been slow in identifying him as one of the villains of the piece. Wilson knew that 'the dirty ignorant curs' and 'wasters', as in his singular fashion he identified the peace party in the Cabinet, were calling for his head. The Minister for War comforted Wilson on this score as the General recorded in his Diary:

> Haldane sent for me this morning. I found old Nick [Nicholson, the C.I.G.S.] in his room. Haldane told me there was no question of my being asked to leave the W.O. On the contrary he twice told me how 'amazingly' well I had done, and how I impressed his colleagues at the meeting of August 23. The fact was, he told me, that there was a serious difference in the Cabinet. Asquith, Haldane, Lloyd George, Grey and Winston on one side

[1] Scott, *Diaries*, 62.
[2] See McKenna's 'admission' to Scott in Feb. 1914, Scott, *Diaries*, 81.
[3] The metamorphosis of Lloyd George's attitude can be traced in letters. Austen Chamberlain wrote to his wife during the period:
19 Aug. 1911: 'A talk with George . . . [He] at least has learned something since he got into office, and does not like that ass *** affect indifference to foreign affairs.'
23 Sept. 1911: 'It is an unmixed blessing that the Government Liberals . . . should have learned what manner of men they [the Germans] are and what dangers we have to confront. I don't think that Lloyd George will forget his lesson.'
23 Oct. 1911: '[Balfour] told me . . . that at Balmoral he had seen Grey, George and, I think, Asquith. They had talked freely about Foreign Affairs. Grey serious but moderate. Ll. George very bellicose—and so on. Balfour was rather shocked by his violence': see *Politics from Inside* (1936), 346, 353, and 363.

agreeing with my lecture of August 23, whilst Morley, Crewe, Harcourt, McKenna, and some of the small fry were mad that they were not present on August 23 . . . and were opposed to all idea of war, and especially angry with me, Morley and others quoting my teaching at the S[taff] C[ollege] and so forth. The Government fear that there may be a split, but Haldane told me he had informed Asquith that if there was a change of policy he would go.[1]

Before the Cabinet on 15 November, Asquith and Haldane met to concert plans on the best way to frustrate the Radicals.[2] The formula Asquith offered in his two propositions, which had been accepted by the Cabinet, staved off any further debate on the subject of staff talks until mid-1912 and the start of the naval conversations. Haldane recognised their value when he reported to his mother that, though the meeting had not been a pleasant experience, he had left it 'unhampered in any material point'.[3] It was true the formula restricted future exchanges, but those conversations already in progress were not halted. The proviso that the talks were noncommittal in no way presented a new restriction, for Wilson had always formally acknowledged that fact, while assiduously undermining its effect by frequent unofficial assurances to the French Staff and to the French Minister for War. The measure of Wilson's truculence may be gauged by the fact that less than a fortnight after the Cabinet he was rejoicing at Grey's speech to the Commons because it would 'annoy the Germans and the Radicals which is *good*'; approving Churchill's 'comprehensive and clean sweep' of the Admiralty;[4] and annoyed by 'the somnolence in the office' was 'preparing another bomb to see if I can wake things up'.[5] The vagueness of Asquith's propositions meant that Wilson had no need to inform the Cabinet of his regular discussions with the French. However, most important, 'the continuance of the staff talks ensured the primacy of the strategy of continental intervention. By his formula, as with the shift of Churchill to the Admiralty, Asquith had supported the War Office's strategic preferences.'[6]

To what extent had the Radicals been 'deceived' as later they were to maintain?[7] When Grey read Cambon's report to Caillaux, all

---

[1] Callwell, i, 106–7.   [2] See Mackintosh, 338, n. 40.
[3] *Ibid.*, 339, n. 41.
[4] Wilson was very much in Churchill's confidence, see *Diary*, 21 Nov. 1911: 'I had an hour with Winston Churchill this afternoon. He was most nice. Told me many things, and, in fact, was most open. *He will play in with us all he can*, and I feel sure will do a great deal of good in the Admiralty'. (My italics.)
[5] Callwell, i. 107.   [6] Williamson, 200.
[7] See, for example, Loreburn, *How the War Came*, 71ff.

the ministers present must have realised that, in the event of a German attack on the French, British troops would go to the aid of France. All ministers knew that since 1906 the French and British Staffs had been discussing this possibility. It did not require too great a feat of imagination on the part of the Radicals to read between the lines of these 'revelations' the direction to which British policy was committed. They had not been told everything, but had they the will, there was no reason why they should not have discovered the whole truth for themselves.

Chapter 8   Hopes of Peace: Designs for War

'Pourparlers'

Grey had put a brave face upon his defence of foreign policy in the Commons in November 1911. Temporarily his critics were gagged. But the groundswell of Radical discontent was too strong to be resisted for long by one speech, no matter how skilful. Perhaps the best measure of Grey's concern with the continued strength of criticism against him was that he made a number of public speeches. On 19 January 1912 he was telling his constituents in Northumberland he was so busy he knew little about the criticisms that were being made of him—but nevertheless he discussed them at length! On 15 February at Manchester, the very centre of his opponents, he made two speeches on foreign policy, both containing warm references to Germany and optimistic assurances about Persia. Grey, throughout his tenure of the Foreign Office, was never lightly tempted to emerge from the darkness and secrecy of Whitehall into the glare afforded by the public stage. To Leo Maxse it seemed that the Radicals were getting the upper hand. He was particularly wary of the efforts of the 'Potsdam Party' who sought a better understanding with Germany. They were, he claimed, a

> miscellaneous assortment . . . of ex-Ambassadors on the stump, Cocoa Quakers, Hebrew journalists at the beck and call of German diplomats, soft-headed Sentimentalists, snobs hypnotised by Hohenzollern blandishments, cranks convinced that their own country is always in the wrong, cosmopolitan financiers domiciled in London in order to do 'good work' for the Fatherland.[1]

There was a new belligerence, a determination in the Radical camp to 'smash Grey'.[2] In Hirst's opinion, such a task would not have been

---

[1] Quoted Koss, *Brunner*, 252–3.
[2] There is an account of the 'Grey must go' campaign conducted by the Radi-

difficult had the Commons contained a Cobden or a Bright. Yet, failing that possibility, it still remained that if pressure was steadily applied to the Foreign Secretary, in the end they would get what they wanted. It was all a matter of priorities. As a journalist, Hirst believed that the prevailing tensions between Germany and Britain could in large part be ascribed to the deliberate efforts of both countries' yellow journalists. The first step to counteract this evil was to send a correspondent to Berlin who could be relied upon to remit objective reports of German events and opinions. The man chosen for the task was Dudley Ward. Ernest Schuster and John Brunner agreed to finance the project for a year. Ward was introduced to the editors of some of the Liberal newspapers at a luncheon in the National Liberal Club on 18 December. The editors were informed that Ward would 'act as Press correspondent with the object of promoting friendly relations between Germany and England'.[1]

Francis Hirst was also the instigator of the move to exert pressure on the Government through the component associations of the National Liberal Federation. Initial efforts were frustrated by the unwillingness of the Whips to supply Brunner with a list of the names and addresses of chairmen and secretaries. 'Fancy refusing the request of the President,' expostulated Hirst. 'It is a regular caucus for the pulling of wires and not for the translation of principles into practice.'[2] Not easily thwarted, Hirst, in concert with Massingham, published a letter in *The Nation* instructing the Liberal Associations to do their duty, and that promptly. 'The Liberal Press and the opinion of the rank and file are powerful agencies.'[3] Among other associations, the Manchester Liberal Federation sent a sharp letter to Grey expressing their deep concern at recent developments in the Government's foreign policy.

> They would urge the Government to make it plain to the French Government that the 'entente' or friendly understanding with France concluded seven years ago is not to be understood as an alliance involving any of the obligations of an alliance, and that it leaves us perfectly free to enter into similar close and cordial relations with other European powers and notably with Germany.[4]

---

cals and Labour in John Murray's 'Foreign policy debated: Sir Edward Grey and his critics, 1911–12', in *Power, Public Opinion and Diplomacy* (1959), ed. L. P. Wallace and W. C. Askew.
[1] Hirst to Brunner, 5 and 19 Dec. 1911, quoted Koss, *Brunner*, 246–7 and n. 2
[2] Hirst to Brunner, 29 Dec. 1911, quoted Koss, *Brunner*, 248.
[3] Letter in *The Nation*, 30 Dec. 1911, signed 'Public Economy'.
[4] Manchester Lib. Fed. to Grey, 12 Jan. 1912, quoted Hammond, *C. P. Scott*, 164–5.

The message to Grey was reinforced by Scott the next day in a leader in the *Manchester Guardian*. Loreburn, who had been in frequent contact with Scott during the period, favoured the action taken. He urged as imperative the need to remove from the entente any appearance or possible implication that it was a defensive alliance. On 17 January, at Brunner's invitation, the executive of the National Liberal Federation met in London. They unanimously passed a resolution declaring their support for 'an earnest effort at friendly understanding with Germany, a country with which we have no real ground of quarrel, but, on the contrary, many powerful ties of race, commerce and historic association'.[1] Loreburn was particularly pleased with the resolution, and told Hirst that 'with the help of support from outside, the change we desire can be accomplished'.[2] Radicals agreed that what was now required was 'something to strike the imagination of the German people'. Psychologically there could not have been a better moment to choose. A new navy law, the *Novelle*, was soon to be presented to the Reichstag. William Fox, a pacifist, had 'a satisfactory interview' with Grey at the Foreign Office on 8 January. He wrote to inform Courtney that the Foreign Secretary had assured him that during the Christmas season he had given the problem considerable thought and was 'favourably disposed to the suggestion that Lord Haldane should be sent to Berlin, . . . on a special mission to open up negotiations'.[3] Four months earlier Kate Courtney had recorded in her diary her husband's opinion that a sweeping change could be effected in Anglo-German relations, if only 'the right man could go and meet the Kaiser in real keen talks'. There were several candidates Courtney considered as suitable for such a task—Bryce, Morley or Haldane. Any of these men was equipped to strike a favourable response.[4] Since October *The Nation* had been canvassing opinion to demand an 'Ambassador of Peace'. Given 'a capable and unprejudiced negotiator' then Anglo-German difficulties would be solved by 'a few months of patient work'.[5]

[1] See *The Nation*, 20 Jan. 1912.
[2] Hirst to Brunner, 18 Jan. 1912, quoted Koss, *Brunner*, 250–1. This was an extraordinary estimate for Loreburn to make. He had already acknowledged to Scott the weakness of the Radical group in the Cabinet. A change of policy would have to mean at least the dismissal of Grey, and this would assuredly mean the dissolution of the Liberal Government. Any competent political commentator, leave alone a Cabinet Minister, would have realised the fatuity of the hope Loreburn expressed. Yet such opinions were constantly exchanged by the Radicals. At their best these opinions can be viewed as 'whistling in the dark' to maintain false hopes.
[3] Fox to Courtney, 9 Jan. 1912. Courtney Collection, vol. x.
[4] Courtney Diary, 21 Oct. 1911.
[5] See *The Nation*, 14 Oct., 25 Nov. and 30 Dec. 1911.

J. Allen Baker, the Quaker M.P., who had been responsible for setting up The Associated Councils of Churches in the British and German Empires for Fostering Friendly Relations between the Two Peoples, after the Agadir troubles had been visited in London by Herr Spiecker, representative of the German Committee. Spiecker suggested that a visit to Berlin by a leading British statesman, who could discuss unsettled questions between the two Governments, might help to remove any outstanding difficulties. Baker went to Berlin and talked with the Chancellor who seemed to favour such a move. Baker reported his conversations to Grey.[1] The Labour party added its voice to the swelling chorus that favoured active steps to hasten Anglo-German rapprochement. Meeting at Birmingham in January 1912, the party reaffirmed its dedication to friendship between the German and British peoples. They added: 'Labour has been much heartened by Socialist successes in the recent Reichstag elections.'[2] *The Nation* did not ignore the opportunity to prick the official Liberal conscience. On issues of peace and militarism, of foreign and Imperial policy, Labour had shown a more consistent and enlightened Liberalism than some of the official representatives of the Liberal Party. The *Manchester Guardian* also took a hand in the act and recommended that cities should follow the example of Glasgow where, at a town meeting, it had been resolved there should be better official relations between Britain and Germany. The chief organ of the provinces demanded 'that the capitals of the industrial north . . . speak to the Foreign Office with a single voice'.[3]

For the Prime Minister and the Foreign Secretary, the problem was to satisfy this mounting pressure for action and appease the hurt pride of Germany without endangering the Anglo-French entente or undermining British naval supremacy. From Germany came indications that in official circles the will for rapprochement was not lacking. Bethmann-Hollweg, under constant pressure from the Army who protested that a disproportionate expenditure on the Navy was interfering with their plans, persuaded the Kaiser that

[1] See Baker and Baker, 199–200.
[2] The Socialists received four million votes and with 110 seats became the strongest party in the Reichstag. The power of the Conservative and Clerical groups seemed to have been broken. However, the key factor remained that the German Government was responsible to the Kaiser and not the Reichstag. *New Age*, 22 Feb. 1912, p. 389, scoffed at the supposed benefits the election results would bring. 'In four million Socialist voters the peace mongers hardly count at all. Like our own Nonconformists, they make their voices heard in a manner out of all proportion to their numbers and weight. . . . The whole nation is unanimous in the desire to secure for Germany a place in the sun. . . . There are no parties but all for the State.'
[3] *Manchester Guardian*, 30 Jan. 1912.

there should be negotiations with Britain for some sort of pact. Neither man was sanguine of the eventual success of such a project—the Kaiser believed that to reconcile the Anglo-French entente with an understanding between Germany and England was to try to square the circle. However, an attempt at reconciliation would cost nothing, and failure could always be laid at England's door as an example of her bad faith.[1] So Ambassador Metternich was given a free hand by Bethmann-Hollweg to raise the matter with Grey, which he did on 20 December 1911.

Grey did not show much enthusiasm for the project. Nevertheless, desultory negotiations continued throughout the Christmas period, due to the efforts of two amateur diplomats, Albert Ballin the ship-builder and Ernest Cassel the banker. When it was suggested that Churchill should have a meeting with Tirpitz, Winston jibbed at the idea. It might be supposed that he had gone to Berlin to act as an apologist for Lloyd George's July speech. In any event, he was too busily engaged with his affairs at the Admiralty to enter into negotiations that, while they might have their uses, could never hope to be successful. However, as Lloyd George would inevitably be calling for economies in his next Budget, it might be an idea to discover Germany's future naval plans. If Germany was obliging, then it might be possible to call a halt in the naval arms race. Churchill, together with Lloyd George, approached Grey and after an informal meeting with Asquith it was agreed to send Cassel to the Kaiser with a three point memorandum proposing as the subject of negotiations, a diplomatic agreement, a colonial agreement, and a reduction in the German naval construction programme. The German reply was not unfavourable. The Kaiser still entertained certain reservations of principle and said he wished to discuss these with Grey. The Emperor's note was accompanied by one from Bethmann-Hollweg. Obligingly it outlined in comprehensive manner the new German Naval Law.[2]

The arrival of the German response coincided with the outbreak of a great coal strike. Grey, at Asquith's request, was put in charge of the negotiations between the coal owners and the miners. Here was the formal excuse for Grey not accepting the Kaiser's invitation to visit Berlin. Both Grey and Asquith agreed that, should Sir Edward go to Berlin, then the discussions would be given an undesirable air of authority that might cause offence to the French. Haldane was then approached by Grey as 'the best person' to go to Germany and,

[1] See Halévy, *The Rule of Democracy*, 568.
[2] Churchill, *World Crisis*, 76–7.

after some discussion, the Minister for War agreed. Grey's attitude to the Berlin mission needs explaining. His advisers were united in their antagonism towards even the idea of talks with the Germans. None was more adamant in his opposition than Arthur Nicolson.

> I do not see why we should abandon the excellent position in which we have been placed, and step down to be involved in endeavours to entangle us in some so-called 'understandings' which would undoubtedly, if not actually impair our relations with France and Russia, in any case render the latter countries somewhat suspicious of us.[1]

Nicolson's hostility guaranteed the subsequent failure of the negotiations. Grey, in his memoirs, claimed that he 'had no great hope that anything would come of the mission'. It was desirable, therefore, that the visit of a British Minister should be private and informal. Then, 'if nothing came of it, there should be no sensation and little disappointment to the public'.[2] The tone of Grey's account of the antecedents to the Haldane Mission and its outcome, is characteristic. The excuses he lists to explain the smallness of his vision, his shuffling, casuistic scepticism, are not convincing.[3] Grey knew that he was evading his responsibilities. His and Churchill's refusal to go to Berlin, represented a considerable and calculated snub to the Germans who were always inordinately sensitive about such actions and whose *amour propre* was still dented by the rebuff their diplomacy had suffered over Agadir. If Grey thought so little could be achieved by the mission and the talks, why did he allow them to continue?

The final responsibility for that decision lay with Asquith. He more than any other man was sensible of the delicate equipoise upon which the Liberal party and his Government stood. Within the Cabinet the balance between competing factions was tremulous. For the moment the strategy of Grey's foreign policy was guaranteed by the uncertain loyalties of Churchill and Lloyd George, both volatile and ambitious men. If nothing more, Radicals like Harcourt and Loreburn were a constant source of nuisance and irritation. This pro-German cabal might present a sterner challenge to authority should they be joined once more by the mercurial 'twins' who now blew hot for war where earlier they had extolled peace and economy.

---

[1] Nicolson to Bertie, 8 Feb. 1912, quoted Steiner, 127.
[2] Grey, i, 252.
[3] Repeated by his biographer, Trevelyan, 228. As far as Grey was concerned 'the gesture' of the Haldane Mission was the best means available to satisfy the Radicals who wanted him out of office. See Bertie's comments: *B.D.* VI, 687.

In Parliament and in the country the Liberal party was beset by problems—unparalleled social unrest accompanied by violence and the unmistakable and uncomfortable rumblings of revolt in Ireland. A small parliamentary majority bolstered by uncertain political bargainings, put a premium on the loyalty of the Liberal party's radical tail. The interference of amateurs—the business friends of princes and the Radical friends of peace—had pushed arrangements to that point where the Government could no longer ignore intervention in mysteries which it was their prerogative alone to exercise. It was at this point in the negotiations that the Cabinet at last was consulted.

The Cabinet met on 2 February. The decisions had already been made; their function was merely to fix the imprimatur of their agreement. There was little enthusiasm shown for the mission. After some discussion it was agreed that to send Grey would be 'premature'. The task should be performed by Haldane.[1] Morley, supposed by Esher to be 'all for capturing German sentiment',[2] told Courtney that he was pessimistic about the possibility of success and he did not favour the scheme.[3] Among those men who distrusted Germany there was little concern. With Cambon and the Russians informed of every move, Esher reasoned there was little danger so long as Haldane was 'not too clever in this matter'.[4] Repington wrote to the editor of *The Times* that Haldane's visit had been agreed as the best way of humouring the Government's followers. He did not anticipate any result other than 'some increased reasonableness among the Radical Left, whom Haldane will purr to sleep when he returns'.[5] The visit was finally approved by the Cabinet on 6 February. The next day Haldane set out for Berlin.

The moment had come to strike a bargain with Germany. *The Nation* had confidently declared as much but a week earlier in an article entitled 'The testing of Sir Edward Grey'.[6] Though the Minister of War should go to Berlin, it was the Foreign Secretary who attracted Radical attention. The Radicals were not unaware of the rumours concerning the *Novelle*, but they refused to be cast down in spirit. Socialist successes in the Reichstag would hinder any proposals for increased naval expenditure. In any event, Haldane's task was to discuss Germany's 'place in the sun'. They did not wish, they did not expect there to be a direct assault on the vexed problem of naval armaments. That subject could wait. The immediate

[1] Cabinet Letter, 3 Feb. 1912.   [2] See *E.P.*, iii, 74.
[3] *Courtney Diary*, 12 Feb. 1912.   [4] *E.P.*, iii, 79–80.
[5] Repington to Buckle, 8 Feb. 1912, quoted Koss, *Haldane*, 250.
[6] *The Nation*, 27 Jan. 1912.

requirement was a settlement, if needs be piecemeal, of the outstanding political questions between England and Germany. This was the only way to resolve Anglo-German doubts and hostility. The priorities were patent.

Since his Mansion House speech, in public at least Lloyd George had given the Radicals no cause for concern. The passing of the months made his wicked July rhetoric seem more like a product of mid-summer madness, an aberration which the Chancellor now regretted. But young Churchill at the Admiralty was never cast for the rôle of penitent. It was not in his nature to hide his refound martial passions under a pall, nor quell the lust of his latest enthusiasm. The Radicals were angered beyond measure when Churchill chose the time of Haldane's visit to Berlin to make a combative public speech on the subject of British naval supremacy. What possessed the First Lord to deliver a philippic on the Navy when that subject was best relegated to the background?[1] The impious Minister declared:

> The British Navy is to us a necessity and, from some points of view, the German Navy is to them more in the nature of a luxury. Our naval power involves British existence. It is existence to us; it is expansion to them. . . . Whatever may happen abroad there will be no whining here, no signals of distress will be hoisted, no cries for help or succour will go up. We will face the future as our ancestors would have faced it, without disquiet, without arrogance, but in stolid and inflexible determination.[2]

The expression *luxus flotte*, brought angry denunciation in the German Press. Churchill returned to London and the reproaches of some of his Cabinet colleagues.[3] Haldane was soon to affirm that Churchill's speech had been no hindrance to negotiations, but Asquith decided Churchill should be admonished, and Morley was delegated as a suitably patrician figure to perform that task.

Haldane returned in triumph from his short visit to Berlin. He confided to his mother,

> I did not go to Berlin with power to make a treaty. These affairs are too vast for that. But I went to investigate and discuss whether one could be made. What may be possible with

---

[1] See *Daily News* and *Manchester Guardian*, 10 Feb. 1912.
[2] Speech at Glasgow, 9 Feb. 1912, quoted Churchill, 77.
[3] For Lloyd George's disapproval see Riddell, *More Pages from My Diary 1908–14* (1934), 37. On the other hand, Churchill's speech was warmly approved by Fisher, leading Tories and *The Times*, *Daily Mail* and *Pall Mall Gazette*. The latter declared it had been 'a very useful corrective to Lord Haldane's . . . demeanour among German statesmen.' For the reactions of Morley, Loreburn and Haldane, see Fitzroy, ii, 477.

English public opinion in the view of the Cabinet remains to be seen. But my work up to this point has been attended with a measure of success that was neither foreseen nor expected . . . The strain has been heavy but I am not tired. It is a solemn call this, and come what may I shall feel that the effort has been to do God's work.[1]

Asquith delightedly informed the Commons that Haldane's mission had 'completely realised' the anticipations it had aroused.[2] Bethmann-Hollweg also made comforting noises in public. Thus, all the omens seemed favourable. The Radicals waited upon an expected announcement—the text of an agreement between the two Powers.

Weeks passed and nothing materialised. Impatient of this unexplained and unexpected delay, eventually Mason asked what were the prospects of an amicable understanding as the outcome of the negotiations. Hope was stilled by the Prime Minister's reply. 'The relations between the two Governments are on a footing that enables them to discuss in a frank and friendly way matters of mutual interest. If this is what is meant by an amicable understanding it has already been achieved and will, I trust and believe, continue.'[3] Mason had asked his question on 30 April. Three weeks earlier Metternich had informed the Foreign Office that since agreement between the Governments had proved impossible the negotiations were closed. In effect, any hopes of a satisfactory conclusion had been abandoned by the third week in March.

Because Grey had been preoccupied with the coal strike, the task of preparing material for the Haldane mission and the subsequent negotiations had fallen upon the unwilling Nicolson. The Germans had been prepared to temporarily suspend the *Novelle*, or at least modify it, provided that Britain in her turn gave a promise of neutrality. Harcourt, McKenna and Loreburn pressed Grey for such an undertaking. Grey had refused. The formula that was presented to the Germans, drawn by Nicolson and approved by Cambon, was designed to be as meaningless as possible. The Kaiser grew exasperated by Britain's patent prevarication, and the German decision to introduce a supplementary naval bill concluded the abortive attempt at reconciliation. Nicolson basked in the sunshine of his friends' approval. They recognised that the Under Secretary had 'been foremost in this good work'. Nicolson, while his fears that there might

---

[1] Quoted Sommer, 264.
[2] *Hansard*, v: 34:33. Morley abandoned his earlier reservations about the wisdom of the mission after a suitably enthusiastic description by Haldane of all that he had accomplished.
[3] *Ibid.*, v:37:1679.

be a possible political arrangement in the future were still not abandoned, allowed himself the satisfaction of self-congratulation. He
had extricated Britain from a quagmire 'into which . . . [we were]
plunged and into which we have been led by our unscrupulous
adversaries and our singularly naïve and feeble negotiators'.[1]

For the Radicals, there was no denying that the Haldane mission,
upon which they had placed so much store and hope, had been a
failure. Had Haldane been the 'capable and unprejudiced negotiator'
that *The Nation* demanded?[2] 'The fault lies with us not with the
Germans', cried the *Manchester Guardian*. Haldane had 'laid hold
of the problem at the wrong end' by attempting to tackle the naval
question head on.[3] *The Nation* was better informed of what had been
the true bargaining counter in Berlin. It did not, however, answer
the question whether Britain ought to offer her neutrality in a
future European war as the price of immediate reduction in Germany's naval construction. *The Nation* merely stated: 'If we refused
to exchange reciprocal guarantees of neutrality with Germany, the
inference is clear that without the knowledge and, we believe, against
the will of public opinion on which this Government relies for its
existence, a continental—virtually a military—engagement has
been contracted.'[4] Whether the Germans had proposed a neutrality
agreement or not, it was surely obvious that the heart of the difficulties between Germany and Britain was the nature of the engagement between Britain and France. If there was to be any
progress towards a détente between Germany and England, then
the first step would have to be for Grey to reverse the claims he
had made in the Commons in November 1911. England did not have

[1] Goschen to Nicolson, 20 Apr. 1912. Nicolson to Bertie, 6 Apr. 1912, quoted
Steiner, *op. cit.*, 127.
[2] See on this, Paul Nathan's three articles in *Nord und Süd*, 'England und
Wir', Feb. 1912: 'I believe *The Nation* is right, and success would be certain
under *one* condition: that public opinion insists upon it. The negotiator must
be found, and the Press, platform and Parliament must speak with no uncertain voice. The echo in Germany will not fail to make itself heard.' All Nathan's
conditions seemed to have been satisfied and yet there was failure. In the
circumstances, some Radicals not unnaturally began to cast suspicious glances
in the direction of Haldane. He was, after all, one of the *triumvirs* of Liberal
imperialism in the Cabinet. These speculations were unfair as Haldane had
done all that he could do for peace given the brief he had. Indeed, the evidence
suggests that he was a better ambassador for a détente with Germany on this
occasion than Morley would have been.
  Nord und Süd was edited by Ludwig Stein, a leading pacifist. He made the
journal a forum for the discussion of the international tensions after the
Agadir crisis taking as his motto '*Détente entre entente et Alliance.*' He was
encouraged by Bethmann-Hollweg. See L. Stein, *Aus dem Leben eines Optimis-
ten* (1930); also Hale, 425–6 and n. 12.
[3] *Manchester Guardian*, 19 Apr. 1912.
[4] *The Nation*, 27 Apr. 1912.

to choose to which continental group she belonged. The *Manchester Guardian* declared roundly that Britain 'belong[ed] to neither [group]—that is the first condition of an understanding between us and Germany'.[1]

If the Radicals were concerned that Grey was too much committed to the French, Bertie and Nicolson feared the opposite. For this reason, both men distrusted any negotiations between Germany and Britain. They did everything in their power to reassure Poincaré, the French Prime Minister, that the Anglo-German talks were meaningless. But Poincaré and the French Ambassador in London, Cambon, remained very concerned. The trouble with the Anglo-French entente for them was that it had not been consecrated by any formal act. Unfortunately it depended, as Poincaré wrote to Cambon in April 1912, 'upon opinion and on the conversations of our General Staffs. Anything which would upset public sentiment will thus destroy it'.[2] With the Moroccan difficulties now settled, what guarantee was there that the entente would remain intact? The Franco-British relationship would have to be placed upon a much less ambiguous footing. Ideally what was required was a written guarantee. The story of Anglo-French diplomatic relations in 1912 is, for the large part, the account of how Cambon and Poincaré wrested from Asquith and Grey the written guarantee they required.

On 15 April Cambon told Nicolson that Poincaré had not found recent British assurances 'sufficiently clear and precise'. He then reiterated the old story of Landsowne's alleged offer of an alliance to France in 1905. The British Under Secretary made no secret of where his own sympathies lay. The trouble was that the sort of accommodation the French were seeking was, for the moment, impossible. The public would not favour an alliance, and misguided elements in the Cabinet desired a closer tie with Germany. In the circumstances, 'it would be far wiser to leave matters as they were— and not to strain an understanding which was at present generally popular, and did not by itself afford the slightest reason to any other country to resent or demur to it'.[3] Cambon was disappointed by Nicolson's gentle rebuff: Asquith and Grey approved of the manner in which he had handled the situation. Grey was to say the same to Cambon, but would add a comforting verbal *caveat*—'although we cannot bind ourselves under all circumstances to go to war with France against Germany, we shall also certainly not bind ourselves

[1] *Manchester Guardian*, 23 May 1912.
[2] *D.D.F.* II, 329.　　　[3] *B.D.* VI, 576.

to Germany not to assist France'.[1] So Cambon's opening move had failed, but now the naval issue afforded the French a fresh opportunity to bind England close. 'What Morocco had once been to the entente the Mediterranean now became.'[2]

By midsummer 1912 most of Britain's naval presence had been removed from the Mediterranean and concentrated in the North Sea area. The move had been inevitable with the expansion of German sea power. Churchill, in a letter to Grey in January, had brusquely underlined the political implications of the move. With Britain having to rely upon French sea power in the Mediterranean, 'certainly no exchange of system would be possible, even if desired by you'.[3] Churchill was stating no more than the truth. England still may have appeared to retain a free hand, but the reality was otherwise. The French eagerly seized the opportunity afforded by their strengthened bargaining position. Cambon once more played suitor to Grey.

Cambon began by making the same point as Churchill: definite naval arrangements depended upon a satisfactory political accord. When Grey hedged by pointing out the two nations were actively engaged in discussing common problems, Cambon responded that while this was true, still 'there was no written understanding'. Grey weakened and promised that he would discuss the idea of a written formula with Asquith.[4] Little by little the Foreign Secretary's reserve was being worn down. Armed with a draft formula provided by Poincaré, Cambon once more laid siege to Grey's scruples on 25 September. Nicolson, who passed the formula on to Grey who was staying at Balmoral, observed that he doubted whether the Cabinet would accept the formula, but added, 'We shall have to sign something . . .'.[5] Grey had conversed with Sazonov, the Russian Foreign Minister, while at Balmoral. From hints at new demands from Russia, and the obvious determination of Poincaré's Government, Grey realised that unless something tangible was forthcoming then there was a real possibility that the entente would be disrupted. England might find herself once more isolated, facing a hostile continent dominated by Germany.[6] However, the decision now lay with Asquith.

Unlike Grey, Asquith had no reservations about the formula. As far as he could see it was 'almost a platitude'.[7] However, there was

[1] B.D. vi, 580.   [2] Williamson, 263.
[3] Churchill to Grey, 31 Jan. 1912, quoted Churchill, World Crisis, 96.
[4] B.D. x, ii, 410.
[5] Nicolson to Grey, 25 Sept. 1912, quoted Williamson, 295.
[6] See B.D. ix, 805–7.   [7] B.D. x, ii, 412.

still the difficult hurdle of the Cabinet to be passed. Grey attempted to sidetrack Cambon by suggesting that he saw no reason why verbal assurances needed to be converted into written ones. Cambon then suggested that an exchange of private letters without any need for publication would serve his purpose. Grey said he would consider this proposal. Subsequently Grey agreed, Asquith having consented providing the Cabinet agreed to the wording of the letters. In the circumstances, Cambon was delighted as the British Cabinet's participation would provide the letters with 'un caractère officiel'.[1] Cambon's satisfaction at the involvement of the Cabinet stemmed from the idea, for which Grey himself was in part responsible, that there were considerable differences between the Foreign Secretary and his Cabinet colleagues. Grey, on the evidence of his prevarication, was no more eager to commit himself to France on paper than any Radical in the Cabinet. Had Cambon but known it, the minute Nicolson had prepared after his meeting with the French Ambassador in April, when Cambon had spoken so overtly of his hopes for Britain's support and had dropped the hint of an alliance, had been sent not to Grey but Morley who was temporarily in charge at the Foreign Office. The first question Cambon asked Grey, after a meeting of the Cabinet in October, was whether the Cabinet had seen the draft formula. The next day he wrote to Poincaré that now all the Cabinet knew of the staff conversations between France and Britain. In fact the conversations had been common knowledge since November of the previous year. Nevertheless, it was to this point that Poincaré particularly directed his attention when congratulating Cambon. 'J'ai apprécié la haute valeur de ces documents. Les études stratégiques, auxquelles procèdent secrètement les Etats-majors des deux pays, ont désormais l'approbation explicite du Gouvernement Britannique.'[2]

The Cabinet had discussed Cambon's formula on 30 October. The most surprising feature of their discussions was that they quibbled, not over the exchange of letters, but the wording of the formula which some Ministers thought 'vague and open to a variety of constructions'. The original formula read: 'In case one or other of the two Governments has reason to fear an act of aggression by a third Power, or complications threatening peace, they would join in discussing the situation and would consider how to act together to ensure the maintenance of peace and to remove all attempts at aggression.'[3] Grey now provided an alternative formula promising automatic consultation at a time of crisis, acknowledging the staff

[1] *D.D.F.* IV, 301.　　[2] *D.D.F.* IV, 562.　　[3] *B.D.* x, ii, 410.

talks, but indicating that joint action between the Powers was not considered obligatory. With this draft the Radicals in the Cabinet were satisfied.[1] So was Poincaré, though he sought a minor alteration which would stiffen the intent. He proposed that there should be an assurance that should the two Governments resolve to act, the basis of their cooperation would be the staff talks. Though Poincaré's suggestion was no more than a slight shift of emphasis, it provoked considerable and animated discussion when the Cabinet considered it on 20 and 21 November. The most to which the ministers would agree was a promise that in any emergency the staff talks 'would at once be taken into consideration and the two Governments would then decide what effect should be given to them'.[2] Cambon accepted the Cabinet's wording, and then he and Grey exchanged private letters. The wording of the first paragraph of the British note was somewhat reserved—the price in fact that Poincaré and Cambon had to pay for the Cabinet's acknowledgement of their 'platitude'.

> From time to time in recent years the French and British naval and military experts have consulted together. It has always been understood that such consultation does not restrict the freedom of either Government to decide at any future time whether or not to assist the other by armed force. We have agreed that consultation between experts is not, and ought not to be regarded as an engagement that commits either Government to action in a contingency that has not arisen and may never arise.[3]

Given the conditions, the French were pleased with their bargain. They had sought a written definition of the entente, worried as they were that the Radical element in the Cabinet was a potent and hostile force. The French considered the exchange of letters a definite strengthening of the entente relationship. Poincaré wrote to Delcassé: 'The importance of these documents will not escape you'.[4]

The British view of the exchange of letters was quite different. When Loreburn considered the letters in his book written after the war, he denounced them as 'implicitly recognis[ing] that a duty existed, while agreeing that naval and military conversations and

---

[1] Cabinet Letter, 1 Nov. 1912.   [2] Cabinet Letter, 21 Nov. 1912.
[3] *B.D.* x, ii, 416. On the true significance of the rejection of 'obligation' by Britain, see L. M. Penson, 'Obligations by treaty: their place in British foreign policy', in *Studies in Diplomatic History*, ed. Sarkissian, 89: 'By 1912 the climax of the association had been reached, and the very repudiation of obligations in the Grey–Cambon letters of the 22nd and 23rd of November constituted as effective a bond as any new Treaty of Obligation could have created.'
[4] *D.D.F.* iv, 563.

dispositions had not created it—in a formal way'.[1] Loreburn's indictment is correct. However, at the time the Radicals in the Cabinet believed that, while leaving the Government's discretion unfettered, they had controlled irregular military and naval consultations. They considered the innocuous wording of the letters a considerable improvement in delineating the true relationship between the entente partners. They, the politicians, were drawing the lines of commitment and not the military. They were mistaken. The doubts and wrangles about the wording of the accord was merely 'sound and fury signifying nothing'. Britain's commitment to France was decided, not by an exchange of letters, but by the staff talks which the Radicals, even when afforded the opportunity, had not stopped. S. R. Williamson has succinctly summed up the situation:

> The Entente Cordiale, conceived in part because of Britain's strategic interests in Moroccan ports, had progressively evolved into a friendly partnership with military and naval features directed against Germany. As a result, by early 1913 there existed not only detailed military and naval preparations but also the guarantee of consultation in times of danger. The quasi-alliance was now largely complete. Paul Cambon had not labored in vain.[2]

Though for months before there had been rumours in the Press that changes could be expected in the constitution of Asquith's Cabinet, the exchange of ministries by Churchill and McKenna in October 1911 had taken everyone by surprise. Had Sir Edward Grey left the Foreign Office, then 'Mr Massingham's darling object would have been fulfilled'. Had 'Lord Morley retired or Ramsay MacDonald been given a seat in the Cabinet in return for his distinguished services to the Liberal party', then no one, avowed *New Age*, would in the least have been surprised. But, as it was, 'nobody has a notion why the changes that have been made have been made'.[3] The Press would not have long to wait to perceive that a very vigorous new broom was being employed at the Admiralty. Sweeping and significant changes were soon instituted by an aggressive, truculent Churchill. Fisher, in Churchill's own words 'a veritable volcano of knowledge and inspiration', was soon installed as Winston's 'unofficial adviser and uncrowned First Sea Lord'.[4] For the moment Fisher chose to remain abroad, encouraging, advising, recommending, inspiring his young master by correspondence, supplementing the written word whenever possible by long conversations aboard the Admiralty yacht, *Enchantress*.

[1] Loreburn, *How the War Came*, 101.   [2] Williamson, 263.
[3] *New Age*, 2 Nov. 1911, p. 3.   [4] Marder, 264.

The battle for the appointment of a Naval War Staff was soon won, but already Churchill's restless energies were preoccupied with another problem. Fisher wrote to Churchill: 'What on earth is the use of our risking our existence for France if we get no return? Let the French take care of the Mediterranean, and a hot time they'll have of it with submarines poking about in that lake. We are well out of it.'[1] Churchill had already ordered the War Staff to draw up plans for a partial withdrawal from the Mediterranean. The result he revealed in a speech to the Commons on 18 March 1912, when he presented his first Estimates. The fourth of the reserve squadrons that were to support the First Fleet would 'be formed from the battleships now stationed in the Mediterranean which will step into the place of the Atlantic Fleet and be based on Gibraltar instead of on Malta'.[2] The redistribution of the fleet for the moment did not attract much attention, and those speakers who did criticise the move were assured by Churchill that British interests in the Mediterranean would not be neglected.

Churchill resolutely pushed on with his schemes. In April he persuaded the Prime Minister that a preliminary meeting of the Committee of Imperial Defence be held in Malta while the two men would be there upon a tour of inspection. Asquith instructed the Committee to consider the effects of the new naval dispositions on the strategic situation in the Mediterranean and elsewhere, and also, 'the degree of reliance to be placed on the cooperation of the French fleet'.[3] To Churchill's surprise, the involvement of the C.I.D., meant that he had to justify his earlier decisions, particularly to Haldane who seemed unnecessarily fussed by the new dispositions of the fleet. As far as Churchill was concerned the logic of his decision had long been settled 'by the brute force of facts.' He wrote to Haldane: 'We cannot possibly hold the Mediterranean or guarantee any of our interests there until we have obtained a decision in the North Sea . . . all we are doing is to make peace dispositions wh. approximate to war necessities. It wd be vy foolish to lose England in safeguarding Egypt.'[4] Haldane, not in the least reassured by Churchill's arguments, showed the First Lord's letter to Henry Wilson. The General's immediate reaction was to advocate alliance with France. Haldane was not enamoured of this suggestion. It would probably mean conscription. It was high time that Churchill was curbed. The Admiralty

---

[1] Fisher to Churchill, 5 Mar. 1912, *Correspondence*, ii, 437.
[2] *Hansard*, v:35:1564.
[3] See *B.D.* x:ii, 381.
[4] Churchill to Haldane, 6 May 1912, quoted R. S. Churchill, *Young Statesman* (1967), 570.

were making decisions without the permission of the Foreign Office, the Cabinet and without discussion by the C.I.D.[1]

Churchill's initiative was causing concern at the Foreign Office as well as the War Office. Ever jealous of their prerogatives, Nicolson and Eyre Crowe were busily advertising their opinion to Conservative politicians, to the military and to Grey, that there should be an alliance with France.[2] Grey could not accept the idea of a defensive alliance; it would mean the break up of the Cabinet.[3] However, for the moment the matter was saved by Churchill's inability to control his enthusiasm. He made the mistake of telling Morley about the proposed meeting of the C.I.D., at Malta, and Morley determined to scupper what he considered 'a dangerous and provocative experiment in the present agitated state of European opinion'. Accordingly, at a Cabinet on 10 May which Churchill did not attend, Morley criticised the proposed meeting at Malta, and given the vigorous support of Grey, Haldane and Harcourt, Asquith was forced to 'signify his abandonment of the design'.[4]

The French meanwhile were concerned by recent developments, and despite Nicolson's warning that their cause would be better served by caution than impetuosity, Cambon on 4 May announced that the French naval attaché wished to renew conversations with the Admiralty. Cambon further made it clear that the French would look after the Mediterranean while the British Navy could concentrate on looking after the Channel and the Northern coast of France. The naval conversations had hitherto been secret. Now the Foreign

[1] Wilson Diary, 3, 7 and 8 May 1912, in Callwell, i, 112–13.
[2] See Austen Chamberlain, *Politics from Inside*, 485–6.
[3] See Chamberlain's account of Nicolson's talk with Morley: 'We have abandoned the Far East, we have abandoned the Mediterranean. I don't call it safe. "What then would you do?" Lord Morley asked me only a few days ago, but when I said, "Make an Alliance with France", he threw up his hands and walked out of the room.' Chamberlain then asked Nicolson why the Government wouldn't take up an alliance when it would have the support of the Conservatives. 'Nicolson again said they couldn't hold together if they tried it. "Well, who would be against it? Asquith, Grey, McKenna (he would follow Asquith) Lloyd George and Winston would support it."
' "Lloyd George and Winston, yes, but I know one who wouldn't."
' "I suppose Morley or perhaps the Lord Chancellor." And then he went on to say that the fact was that they were worn out and felt it and couldn't do anything.' See Austen Chamberlain, 485–6.
The last reported remark of Nicolson's is probably the most significant. The Cabinet was entering a period where its life depended more upon the weaknesses of the opposition than its own inherent strengths. As far as the Radical element were concerned, we were given conflicting reports by members of the group about their capabilities. Morley makes a very interesting estimate of Harcourt's influence in the Cabinet suggesting a very considerable talent working subtly upon the counsels of the Government. Other factors would seem to belie this judgment. See Fitzroy, ii, 486.
[4] There is a full account given by Morley and retold by Sir Almeric Fitzroy, ii, 485–6.

Office and the Cabinet would have to be involved.[1] Asquith maintained that Cabinet sanction was required for naval talks; Churchill claimed that further naval talks were imperative; and Grey insisted that the Cabinet already knew of the previous naval conversations, but how or when they had been told he did not make clear. On 16 May the Cabinet were informed that the French naval attaché required an answer to his enquiries for 'possible naval cooperation between the two countries in the event of war'. Immediately Radical members of the Cabinet made it apparent they at least had profound misgivings about the situation. At last the long range effect of Churchill's reorganisation of the fleet was borne in upon them. It was agreed that when Asquith and Churchill had returned from Malta, the 'whole Mediterranean situation' would have to be 'resurveyed from the point of view both of policy and strategy'.[2] The Cabinet would not discuss the problem again until after the Whitsun recess. The French would have to wait for their talks.

On 15 June Churchill assailed his critics with a powerful memorandum defending his redistribution of the naval forces. The Channel and not the Mediterranean was the place to concentrate naval forces, Churchill argued. To secure the Mediterranean he considered it wise that 'a definite naval arrangement should be made with France without delay'. Should his bold suggestion offend the sensibilities of his Radical colleagues, he hastened to add that such an agreement would not decide the question who should be the ally of whom![3] The problems which Churchill now had to solve had been anticipated by Nicolson in conversation with Grey a month earlier. The Under-Secretary then maintained that if the Admiralty persisted in its schemes in the Mediterranean there were three alternatives available; increase the Naval Estimates, ally with France, or come to agreement with Germany.[4] Churchill's view of the situation was pleasing to no section of the Cabinet. He was treading upon too many carefully tended sensibilities. Outside the Cabinet the voice of the Establishment bitterly disavowed Britain's abandonment of her traditional primacy in the Mediterranean; but inside the Cabinet, Churchill's sternest critics were to be the Radicals led by Reginald McKenna.

So vehement were McKenna's protests at a stormy meeting of the Cabinet on 19 June, so pertinent appeared his criticisms of the whole of Churchill's schemes, that the Cabinet approved the former First

---

[1] *B.D.* x, ii, 385 and 384.   [2] Cabinet Letter, 17 May 1912.
[3] Churchill's Memorandum, 'Naval situation in the Mediterranean', 15 June 1912.
[4] *B.D.* x, ii, 385.

Lord drafting an alternative programme for their consideration. Back and forth the Memoranda passed between the two protagonists. Churchill made play with the *Novelle* as having cut Britain's battleship margin over Germany to eight vessels, the same number as were stationed at Gibraltar. What if the Germans were to launch a surprise attack? Even given a massive new building programme this would be of little help before 1916. In the circumstances the only feasible course was for 'an arrangement with France'.[1] McKenna resisted at all points. He particularly addressed his wrath to the suggestion of an alliance with France, born of 'weakness' and 'dependence'. Churchill charged McKenna with promoting a policy which would guarantee naval disaster, but he did not answer McKenna's charges about Britain being dependent upon France.[2] The arguments were resumed in Cabinet on 27 June, but Churchill could not move his Radical critics and after an abortive session it was agreed to postpone any decision until the C.I.D., had an opportunity to review the problem on 4 July.[3] Meanwhile, the rival forces gathered their strength. Morley for one would not change his opinions at the behest of Churchill. His mind was 'quite made up. No alliance, with or without a mask.'[4] The day before the C.I.D., was to meet, McKenna produced another powerful memorandum condemning Churchill's policy. He maintained the major issue remained the idea of 'an alliance with its obligation to fight in a war not of our own making. . . . What terms would France ultimately demand from us as a condition of protecting us in the Mediterranean?'[5]

The meeting of the Committee of Imperial Defence on 4 July was not packed as had been the cabal of August 1911. The Radicals were present in force this time to view their doughty champion cross swords with Churchill. The six-hour session was dominated by the two men 'tearing each other's eyes out the whole time'.[6] Asquith eventually effected some sort of compromise which had been initially suggested by Esher. Churchill protested to the last, but the Committee's decision represented at least a partial victory for McKenna. There was no doubting that, in Esher's words, it had been 'a tough fight'.[7] But, the main consideration was who would be the victor when the final battle was fought? For the moment the pro-Mediterranean, Establishment–Radical axis had reason for satisfaction. Churchill seemed to be bested. Esher was prepared to claim: 'Whatever the cost may be it is cheaper than a conscript army and

---

[1] Churchill Memorandum, 15 June 1912.
[2] Memoranda, 24 and 25 June 1912.
[3] Cabinet Letter, 28 June 1912.
[4] S. McKenna, *Reginald McKenna*, 147.
[5] Memorandum, 3 July 1912.
[6] Fisher, Correspondence, ii, 470–1.
[7] *E.P.*, iii, 100.

entangling alliances.' To Fisher he wrote, 'foreign alliances are now exploded'. Esher, along with others, would have done well to consider the thought he confided to Balfour. 'It is said that nine times out of ten the wisdom of experience really means the prejudice of custom.'[1] Churchill at that moment would have heartily endorsed Esher's observation.

In the Committee of Imperial Defence, McKenna had established the point of principle he wanted, but the Cabinet found it far from easy to translate principle into reality. On 15 and 16 July the struggle was joined yet again. McKenna argued that what was required was a battleship squadron at Malta capable of withstanding any Austrian Dreadnought fleet. It was one thing to state what was required, another to effect the necessary measures to implement the proposal. To the Radicals present it must by now have become unpleasantly obvious that the economies in the Naval Estimates, upon which they had insisted, were in no small part responsible for the adoption by the Admiralty of a strategy that compensated for numerical weakness by closer attachment to France. In effect, the Radicals were hoist by their own petard—the price of economy was dependence. Churchill patiently refuted McKenna's arguments. Debate was furious but unavailing. On 16 July, Asquith in his report of the Cabinets to the King wrote that they had 'unanimously approved the proposal of the Admiralty'. As for the naval conversations which had been the starting point of all the wrangling, it was agreed to continue 'the communications which have taken place in the past between the French naval and military experts and our own'. Then followed a reservation. But, 'it should be plainly intimated to the French Government that such communications were not to be taken as prejudicing the freedom of decision of either Government as to whether they should or should not cooperate in the event of war.'[2]

It cannot be doubted that Churchill's wings had been clipped by the Cabinet and in the Committee of Imperial Defence. But equally it was patent that the Radicals had won no significant battle. The logic of the situation had not changed. All the talk, the compromises, the manœuvres, the altercation, had effected nothing. Call it an entente or an alliance, declare independence as loudly as she might, Britain was securely tied to France. When the sound and fury was done, that remained the single incontrovertible fact.

[1] See *E.P.*, iii, 100–03.   [2] Cabinet Letter, 16 July 1912.

Keeping faith—friendship with Germany and another disarmament campaign

To keep the faith, to talk of the realisation of a New Jerusalem, to speak of God as the captain marching at their head on the world city of mankind, confidently to expect the lion to lie down with the lamb; all this had been part of the apocalyptic vision soon to be revealed truth in the Radical dawn of 1906. Six long years had passed, of trial and tribulation for the faithful. The vision was still clear but harsh reality impinged. Was there never to be a remedy for this consumption? It seemed that only the older generation of Radicals could still continue to preach the gospel of indiviudal effort and responsibility. Courtney, in a letter to Stein in May 1912, embraced their dilemma.

> The painful puzzle of the international position between Germany and Britain is that both sides desire peace and yet both are full of alarms of war. Where does the fault lie? We blame the newspapers, but newspapers are what their readers make them. We blame governments, but governments are as people choose them. It would seem to follow that if newspapers go wrong, we of the people are to blame for their faults. Anyhow I think that this is our safest moral that peace rests upon us and upon each of us. Let us be incessant in vigilance and in activity to clear ourselves of the jealousies which support misunderstandings and breed wars.[1]

Such advice was all very well, but most Radicals sought another source of blame for the world's ills rather than the acknowledgement of their own faults. Churchill should be their Judas.

Churchill, the Radical apostate, was better cast for the rôle of Dryden's Zimri, a parallel that Hirst was quick to draw as chairman of the Committee for Reduction of Expenditure on Armaments.

> A man so various that he seem'd to be
> Not one, but all mankind's epitome.
> Stiff in opinions, always in the wrong;
> Was everything by starts and nothing long:

The pugnacious personality of the First Lord of the Admiralty was evident in the presentation of his first Estimates to the Commons.[2] There was a convention that the name of 'our chief naval rival' should not be spoken, or, if it was, reference should be suitably apologetic. For Churchill there would be none of this flummery. 'The time has come when both nations ought to understand, without

[1] Courtney to Stein, 1 May 1912, quoted Gooch, *Courtney*, 575.
[2] *Hansard*, v: 35:1549ff.

ill-temper or disguise, what will be the conditions under which the naval competition will be carried on during the next few years.' Churchill would not have it supposed that Britain intended to surrender her naval supremacy. Should Germany increase her fleet of Dreadnoughts, then Britain would respond. Whatever the cost, Britain would always retain a 60 per cent superiority in Dreadnoughts. Britain had decided the relative strengths of the fleets, Germany could dictate the outlay. There was no denying the ingenuity of the First Lord. For years the Tories had pressed for a declaration of determination that Britain would maintain her superiority at sea. Now that declaration had been made. However, for the Radicals he held out the prospects, 'immeasurable in their hope and brightness', of the invitation to Germany to reduce her fleet. The speech had been a success, 'not least', reported the *Manchester Guardian,* 'among those Liberals who are most strongly in favour of an agreement reducing armaments'. They had been 'very much gratified'.[1] *The Nation* wrote of 'The Hope of an Accommodation with Germany'.[2] After all, in the circumstances a 60 per cent margin of superiority was not unreasonable. Also, Churchill had cleverly shifted the ground of possible criticism by declaring his responsibility was to make Britain safe; 'the task of mending the times in which we live' was the responsibility of other hands. What criticism arose was directed towards the Foreign Office and not the Admiralty. Murray Macdonald, a stern proponent of retrenchment in armament expenditure, admitted that in the circumstances there was no point in moving a reduction in the naval estimates.[3] There were a few malcontents, like the Committee of the International Arbitration and Peace Association, who regretted Churchill's 'irritating language towards Germany calculated to endanger friendly relations' and 'the enormous expenditure upon the Navy which has now become normal'.[4] But for the most part, Radicals awaited with keen anticipation the results of Churchill's overture for a 'Naval Holiday'.

Disillusionment not hope was to be the unhappy lot of the Radicals. On 15 May Churchill told the Commons that because of the new German naval law he would be forced to bring in a supplementary estimate.[5] The Prime Minister's trip to Malta sparked off speculation in the Tory Press; eyes were turned to the Mediterranean, and amidst the demands for more ships to patrol those waters, an insistent

---

[1] *Manchester Guardian,* 19 Mar. 1912.   [2] *The Nation,* 23 Feb. 1912.
[3] *Hansard,* v:35:1922.   [4] Reported *Concord,* Mar. 1912, p. 33.
[5] *Hansard,* v:38:1109.

chorus declared the entente with France should be converted into an alliance. The Radical Press as one denounced the idea of an alliance—in the *Manchester Guardian's* view, 'an absurdly disproportionate remedy'.[1] But the *Westminster Gazette* pointed out that the alternatives seemed to them, either an alliance with a conscript army, or increased spending upon the fleet which would leave Britain master of her own policy. The *Westminster Gazette* was convinced the latter was the happier alternative.[2] The Radicals ruefully reflected upon their adage that 'armaments depend mainly on policy'. Agadir had underlined that woeful truth. Now it seemed the wasteful and unproductive expenditure on armaments must continue, abetted by the Admiralty but inspired by the Foreign Office. Could there be another source of this never to be resolved dilemma, another target upon which the peace-loving Radicals could train the guns of their invective? When Churchill would demand his extra millions and a declaration of defiance to hurl at Europe, who could doubt that Parliament would again be hoodwinked? It was futile to protest, claimed W. M. J. Williams in *Concord*, for 'it is quite indifferent whether a Liberal or Tory Administration is in office; our expenditure on armaments is driven forward and decided practically by a number of "armour-plate" firms and their friends backed by a Jingoistic Press.'[3] For the moment Williams' lead was ignored. The campaign against the armaments manufacturers was to wait until the revelations of Liebknecht in the Reichstag in April 1913.

The first hint of the Cabinet's attitude to the disposition of the fleet was provided by Grey when, in a Foreign Office debate in the Commons on 10 July, he defended concentration of resources in the North Sea while insisting Britain retained 'some respectable force in the Mediterranean which is available for use any time'.[4] This was not very reassuring: it must mean a virtual naval alliance with France and possibly Russia as a third unwelcome partner; it certainly suggested that Anglo-German rapprochement in the circumstances was impossible, and there would be fresh and indefinite naval building plans. There was hope that there might yet be delays, for Massingham had heard that Lloyd George was on the point of resigning and a break-up of the Cabinet was imminent if Churchill insisted on his proposals. What could be done to avoid another round of increased armament spending? The Radicals met in anxious

[1] *Manchester Guardian*, 27 May 1912.
[2] *Westminster Gazette*, 30 May 1912.　　[3] *Concord*, July 1912, p. 82.
[4] *Hansard*, v:40:1944.

conclave to discuss tactics. Massingham wanted Brunner to call a special meeting of the National Liberal Federation. From information supplied by Spender and Morley, Hirst was convinced that a letter from Brunner to Asquith threatening such a move would be enough. It 'would produce a very good impression, for A. is a party man par excellence'.[1] But Churchill had his way with the Cabinet before any Radical plans could be coordinated, and on 22 July the First Lord told the Commons what the Government had decided.

Churchill's presentation of the supplementary naval estimates was a supremely clever political performance.[2] He concentrated the Commons' attention not on the Mediterranean but on the threat posed by the new German naval law. The Germans now had 'an extremely formidable fleet' of twenty-nine battleships 'instantly and constantly' ready for war. Opposed to this combination were but thirty-three British battleships some of which were stationed at Gibraltar. It was only towards the end of his speech that Churchill mentioned France. Eight of our cruisers together with the French fleet in the Mediterranean would be more than a match for any possible enemy combination. The *Manchester Guardian* labelled this reluctant admission 'the most alarming single passage in the speech'.[3] The Tories, ignoring Balfour's reserved support for Churchill's plans, with Beresford, Arthur Lee and Bonar Law in the van, called for a crash naval construction programme. It was 1909 all over again, 'Panic made permanent' in the words of *The Nation*,[4] and the Commons submerged in 'a welter of war-talk'.[5] Churchill had revealed himself as a wild Jingo, but what could the Radicals do? Their Reduction of Armaments Committee, while deploring this latest rise in armaments expenditure, could only reflect that, given the policy being pursued, the demands of the Admiralty were not excessive.[6] In truth, many Radicals had feared worse from Churchill than a demand for a million pounds extra for the Navy.[7] They prepared

[1] Hirst to Brunner, 12 and 15 July 1912, quoted Koss, *Brunner*, 254.

[2] *Hansard*, v:41:837–64. The most questionable feature of the speech is contained in the opening remarks; 'the direct cause of the Supplementary Estimates which I am now submitting to the House is to be found in the New German Navy Law . . .' In fact, the *Wehrvorlagen* (German defence bills) had given most money to the Army, and the constructional increases for the Navy were merely one extra Dreadnought in 1913 and 1916 and one other, the date of construction for which was not specified. It was because they had feared much worse that the British Press had handled lightly the passage of the *Novelle* through the Reichstag.

[3] *Manchester Guardian*, 24 July 1912.

[4] *The Nation*, 27 July 1912.

[5] *Daily News*, 24 July 1912.

[6] Report of Committee meeting in *Manchester Guardian*, 23 July 1912.

[7] In the budget of 3 Apr. there had been a net decrease of £307,100, but the revenue surplus of £6,545,000 from the previous year, Lloyd George had

their plans to thwart any more increases that the First Lord might be considering.

Hirst and Massingham once more conspired together to use the National Liberal Federation as the spearhead of a Radical attack against increased armaments costs and a foreign policy that seemed determined upon war in the not too distant future between England and Germany. Meanwhile, a special meeting of the National Peace Council had been held on 31 July, under the chairmanship of Gordon Harvey, which passed unanimously a resolution deploring the conduct of foreign affairs and repudiating the policy of increased armaments.

> We repudiate the idea that a lasting peace can be maintained through the means of the forces of destruction. It has always been our belief that large and increasing armaments can never become the basis of friendship or mutual respect. To the stronger Power their existence is a constant temptation to aggression and interference, for the weaker Power there is always the risk of panic and the feeling of humiliation. They burden the State with vast expense, diverting labour and draining the means available for reform.[1]

The arguments were old and well known. The campaign for disarmament that the Radicals were to wage in 1912 and 1913 was equally predictable both in method and outcome.

The National Liberal Federation was due to meet at Nottingham in November. Hirst decided that the best way to reinforce the resolution, which that meeting would pass, was for Brunner to circulate an appeal for their signatures to the Chairman of every Liberal Association. Morley had told Hirst that he would talk to Grey about an understanding with Germany as he thought the time was ripe for such an effort to succeed. Meanwhile, Massingham and Hirst in *The Nation* and *Economist*, poured out favourable propaganda. Both men were convinced that their self-imposed task of changing the Government's foreign policy was the only way to preserve Liberalism: both men found it difficult to contain their evangelism. 'It is . . . for the National Liberal Federation, at its

---

declared, was to be held over for possible contingencies. The Chancellor made it clear that the main contingency was 'that the existing programmes of other naval powers will not be increased'. The Radicals were concerned by this £6½ million for 'undefined purposes' which they considered a dangerous precedent. They had been afraid that Churdhill might appropriate the whole amount for Dreadnought construction. That possibility had been avoided by the promise of three new Dreadnoughts to be built by Canada. See Bound Minutes of the N.P.C., no. 10, 15 Apr. 1912.
[1] See bound minutes of the N.P.C., no. 14, August 1912.

coming meetings, to consider well, not merely how a Liberal
Ministry can be sustained, but how Liberalism itself can be kept
alive.'[1] With Hirst's assistance, Brunner wrote a lengthy letter to
the Chairman of every Liberal Association.

> I am impelled to write this letter to you by a strong feeling of
> responsibility . . . The Morocco crisis of last year, and the
> warlike concentration of fleets in the North Sea which has
> excited so much apprehension, have opened the eyes of the
> sleepiest politicians to a new and pressing danger. Everyone
> now sees that prosperity and progress at home are bound up
> with the cause of International peace. Armaments and war spell
> poverty and ruin. . . . While Sir Henry Campbell-Bannerman
> lived, there was some relaxation in the growth of military and
> naval expenditure. . . . But the false and shameful naval panic
> of 1909 swept away the spirit of prudence and economy. . . .
> Our Foreign Office and Admiralty have yielded to the clamour
> of the Jingo Press in its campaign of mendacity and provocation.
> Parliament has been misled and estimates have been founded
> upon false forecasts of German expenditure. No heed has been
> paid to the protests of the National Liberal Federation, or to the
> constant criticisms of Liberal economists in Parliament and the
> Press. . . . It is the plain duty of the Liberal Party, the inheritor
> of Gladstone's teachings, to express itself now in language which
> the Prime Minister and his colleagues cannot mistake. . . . Lord
> Haldane's mission to Berlin was ruined by Mr Churchill's war-
> like speeches. There have been faults on both sides; but who
> can doubt that the coldness and pessimism of our Foreign
> Office has been a persistent obstacle to that Anglo-German
> entente which the peoples on both sides of the North Sea clearly
> desire? . . . Our National Liberal Federation is the accredited
> organ of Liberalism. It has now a duty to perform to the
> Government and to the country. It has to ask for a change of
> policy which will remove the friction and suspicions by which
> war is generated, and thus lead to a reduction in armaments. . . .
> We demand and require a clear understanding—that English
> Liberalism at any rate shall have no part or lot in military and
> naval projects for an attack on Germany. This is a sane and
> simple policy . . .[2]

The signature appended to the letter was Brunner's, but everywhere
the hand of Hirst is present. The letter is important as a concise
rehearsal of Radical complaints and ideas from 'the perversion' of
entente 'by secret treaties and dubious understandings . . . into a
dangerous entanglement', to the inevitable reference to the exemp-
tion from capture of 'all peaceful shipping and all peaceful property

---

[1] *The Nation*, 28 Sept. 1912.
[2] The full text of the letter is printed in Koss, *Brunner*, Appendix II,
293–5.

on sea in time of war'. The letter was printed prominently by the *Manchester Guardian* and supported with a first leader claiming that Brunner spoke in the name of traditional Liberalism, and that the two resolutions he attached to his letter represented 'the irreducible minimum if we are to abate the danger which threatens to submerge our civilisation'.[1] Not unexpectedly, *The Nation* also gave its unqualified approval,[2] but to Hirst's consternation, other Radical papers were curiously reticent. Hirst concluded that for the moment official policy must be to lie low and say nothing.[3]

The lead afforded by Brunner was welcomed, and an agitation started. But, the number of associations that responded to Brunner's letter was far less than he had hoped. For those with eyes to see, it should have been apparent that the letter had been best received by those whose minds were already fully in sympathy with its plea. A straw in the wind that Brunner might have heeded was the lack of action by the Lancashire, Cheshire and North Western Liberal Federation; they merely 'took note' of his request. If Brunner was dispirited, and apprehensive that his action might be interpreted as disloyal to his party,[4] Hirst refused to be other than wildly optimistic. Quoting historical parallels of doubtful relevance, he was even rash enough to think it not inconceivable that Grey would have been fortified by their action to resist the machinations of the anti-German reactionaries surrounding him at the Foreign Office![5] Somewhat reassured by Hirst's extraordinary ebullience, Brunner turned his attention to the Anglo-German Understanding Conference which he, together with other leading Radicals, had sponsored. It was to be a considerable affair, lasting three days from its opening at the London Guildhall to the final royal reception at Windsor.

Reports of the Conference[6] reveal the usual complacency by the Radicals. All agreed it had been a 'distinct success'. However, an examination, either of the names of those who attended and played a prominent part, or of the subjects debated, reveals how little real progress the Anglo-German Understanding movement had made. They were still condemning the Jingo Press and offering a change in the right to capture at sea as a panacea for all evils. The Conference did achieve one practical measure; Brunner was coopted onto Courtney's ill-fated Foreign Policy Committee and was to be one of the speakers, together with Morrell, Ramsay MacDonald and Arthur

---

[1] *Manchester Guardian*, 15 Oct. 1912.   [2] *The Nation*, 19 Oct. 1912.
[3] Hirst to Brunner, 16 Oct. 1912, quoted Koss, *Brunner*, 257.
[4] See Brunner's letter in *Manchester Guardian*, 21 Oct. 1912.
[5] Hirst to Brunner, 21, 23 and 29 Oct. 1912, quoted Koss, *Brunner*, 257–8.
[6] See *Concord*, Nov. 1912, pp. 122–3; Minutes of N.P.C., Nov. 1912.

Ponsonby, at a conference held at the Caxton Hall on 26 November when the usual resolutions on armaments and inviolability of private property at sea were approved with acclamation. But the real Radical thrust had already taken place with the meeting of the National Liberal Federation at Nottingham on 21 and 22 November.

Brunner in his presidential address, stressed the need for Anglo-German understanding. Religion, race and economics were mixed in equal parts to show that 'the Germans [were] a strong and manly people like the English', and were as deserving of consideration as the French, and more deserving than the Russians immediately engaged in 'destroying the liberties of Finland'. The speech was greeted by the plaudits of the delegates and the not unexpected compliments of *The Nation* and *Economist*: Massingham and Hirst after all could well claim to have been the mainspring behind the meeting of the Federation. When they praised 'the authentic voice of Liberalism', they were merely acknowledging their own sympathies and sentiments.[1] The *Manchester Guardian* having praised Brunner was more reserved in its approval of Asquith's speech made on the second day of the meeting. The weakest, the least convincing part of that oration had been the string of platitudes that had to pass for comment on international affairs. John Redmond, the Irish leader, who had also spoken that day, drew more affectionate response from the delegates than had the Prime Minister.[2]

When the naval estimates were debated in the new year, the disarmament campaign, for all its initial fine fury and promise, fizzled out like a damp squib. This *débâcle* caused much amusement to the Tories, who did not spare the reductionists for their very poor showing in the Commons' division lobby.[3] Mason, undefeated and unrepentant, gathered a few of the faithful to force a division in March, but only twenty-seven members joined him, and to add insult to injury, the normal leaders of the reductionist group, Molteno and Murray Macdonald, voted with the Government. The reasons for this dismal defeat are not difficult to ascertain. First

[1] The impression of a self-centred group, never looking outward with any objectivity or sense of political reality, is most marked during this particular period. There were innumerable committees set up, meetings held, resolutions passed but nothing was new. The resolutions had been passed a hundred times and always ignored. The chairman of one committee was the secretary of another and the vice-president of a third. See, in particular, Minutes of the N.P.C. for this period.
[2] See report of meeting in *Manchester Guardian*, 22 and 23 Nov. 1912.
[3] See the comments of Craig and Pretyman, *Hansard*, v:50:1954 and 2008-11. In the division, 28 Mar. 1913, *Hansard*, v:502056 there were only 28 votes for the reductionists. The voting figures suggest the debate was very poorly attended and the Secretary of the Admiralty was to refer to the 'peaceful passage' of the Estimates. See *Hansard*, v:51:163-4.

and foremost, there was the question of party loyalty and priorities; a Liberal rather than a Unionist Government at any price; domestic issues before international concerns. *The Nation* had unreservedly recognised this in June 1912. 'When the average Liberal member goes reluctantly into the Government lobby to sanction the present conduct of the Foreign Office, he is voting not at all on the partition of Persia or the handling of Anglo-German relations, or the increase of our armaments. He is voting for Free Trade, and Home Rule and Social Reform.'[1] The same point was to be as unequivocally admitted by the Irish Nationalist member, John Dillon, in the Commons in a debate on the naval estimates in 1914.

> On this occasion, as on many previous occasions . . . I shall vote for the Government against my convictions . . . I am an old Parliamentary hand, and I ask myself when I am going to take any action in Parliament what will be the result of that action, and I certainly am not going, either now or at any future time, to defeat the Government, in order to vote in gentlemen whose only complaint is that the Government are only building four ships when they ought to build nine.[2]

Another reason for the collapse of the reductionist campaign was the apparent success of the Anglo-German understanding campaign with which it had run in tandem. All the signs were that Britain and Germany once more were moving closer together, or at the least, viewing more sympathetically one another's particular problems. In February, statements by the German Foreign Secretary and von Tirpitz suggested that the naval situation was at last approaching stability.[3] If the Pro-Conscription group, with Lord Roberts at its head and abetted by the deluded innocents of Baden-Powell's Boy Scouts, was still demanding compulsory service, there was the comfort of the Socialists in France and Germany sternly and fraternally protesting against any further expansion of armaments and declaring they would oppose any war threatened by the Governments of their respective countries.[4] Meanwhile, affairs in the Balkans diverted much of the Radicals' attention.

[1] *The Nation*, 9 June 1912.   [2] *Hansard*, v:59:309.
[3] See *The Times*, 8 Feb. 1913 and N.P.C. Minutes, no. 21, Mar. 1913. Tirpitz in the Reichstag Budget Committee stated the ratios proposed by Churchill covering the German and British fleets were acceptable to him and he was to repeat this statement before the Budget Commission in Feb. 1914. The Radicals were naturally delighted; equally predictable, the British Ambassador in Berlin and officials at the Foreign Office found the whole thing rather suspicious. See *B.D.* x, ii, 669–88 and 734–41.
[4] See *Concord, Arbitrator*, and N.P.C. Minutes, nos. 18–25, for period Dec. 1912 to July 1913. While the National Service League was conducting its meetings and producing propaganda with unabated enthusiasm, the I.L.P. in Nov. 1913 conducted a massive 'No Conscription' Campaign. For full accounts of activities see, *Labour Leader*, particularly issue, 20 Nov. 1913.

There remained one other reason for the reductionists' failure. That reason was incorporated in the unlikely person of the First Lord of the Admiralty. Churchill had hinted at a diminution in ship construction in 1912. In March 1913 in the Commons, and October of that year in a public speech at Manchester, Winston spelled out his idea of a 'naval holiday'. If the Germans would only stop building their Dreadnoughts for a year, then Britain would do the same. The 'Big Navy' Press in both Germany and Britain were not slow to point out the technical difficulties, indeed, the impossibilities of such a scheme. Churchill, as always, took his own idea very seriously, and Bethmann-Hollweg in the Reichstag was kind enough to make complimentary, even flattering noises without actually officially endorsing the idea. There were never to be official negotiations between the two Governments on the idea. Nevertheless, it was a formidable exercise in public relations, and Churchill's expertise in this field is illustrated by the manner in which he was able to placate the sensibilities of the Radicals while offering encouragement to the Jingoes. Even the naval holiday proposal could be viewed as a clever ploy. If it succeeded it would provide the time to clear up the backlog of work in the naval yards caused by the railway strike, overseas orders, and the ever increasing demands of the Government. The *Pall Mall Gazette*, in the forefront of those journals who demanded ever increasing naval power, considered that Churchill's holiday, all things considered, was 'rather a smart proposal on his part'.[1] If Churchill was sincere in his call for a naval standstill, the timing and the method of making the proposal strongly suggest it was designed as a tactical manœuvre to placate the Radical reductionists.[2] Indeed, all Churchill's public pronouncements upon the Navy during this period seem two edged. He would assure the Conservatives and his own party's big navy supporters that the current delivery of warships was the 'greatest . . . ever recorded in the history of the British Navy', and then in his next speech deplore the increases in naval expenditure and point to the naval holiday proposal as an earnest of Britain's good intent. If only other nations would consider the reasonableness of his proposal then they might be a good way towards ending the mad race.

Thus, for a variety of reasons, the Radicals' campaign against

---

[1] See *Pall Mall Gazette*, 27 Mar. 1913. *Labour Leader*, 27 Nov. 1913 declared Churchill's naval holiday proposal to be 'nothing more than a pious preamble to naval estimates which are likely to be sensational . . . a sop to the political conscience of British Radicals'. No one of sense would take the First Lord's offer seriously.

[2] See *B.D.* x, ii, 721–2.

increased armaments failed in 1912–13. However, outside agencies were to insure that the reductionists would make one last great effort in the winter of 1913 and the spring of 1914 to control Britain's ever-increasing naval budget.

The Suicide Club[1]

Between 1912 and the outbreak of war in 1914 there was a fevered and ever accelerating expansion of military establishments on the Continent. Because the Balkan Wars seemed significantly to upset the European political balance, politicians hastened to insure themselves against unknown contingencies by increased expenditure on armaments. In Germany the Army Bill of 1913 instituted the greatest programme of reform and expansion for twenty years. The French replied with a three-year service law, and the Russians poured money into an expanded system of strategic railroads and added to their already massive land forces. This demand for unprecedented increases in military expenditure fed on eager chauvinist publicity that inflamed Jingo passions. The French were frightened of the Germans. The Germans believed that the French preparations showed that the spirit of *revanche* was reawakened, but were most concerned about Russian designs. In the spring of 1914, Ullrich, the St Petersburg correspondent of the *Kölnische Zeitung*, caused a war scare in Berlin with his accounts of Russia's military and naval preparations. Fear of the Slav menace was the most easily conjured *djinn* of any German war scare, and to heighten the terror there was the further fear that in a confrontation between Germany and Russia, England might be involved as Russia's ally.[2]

The Germans were profoundly pessimistic about the failure of their foreign policy—everywhere their diplomatists had suffered rebuff and failure. If, as a Reichstag deputy admitted, Germans lacked diplomatic ability, at least they were acknowledged as supreme in military matters. It would make sense to concentrate their energies on organising an army better than any other force in the world. Such an army would afford insurance against the incompetence and failure of Germany's diplomats. Strategical considerations, combined with political facts, persuaded some and compelled other Germans to recognise that the existence of Germany in an armed Europe depended, not on grandiose dreams of a *Weltpolitik* based on a navy that challenged the world's supreme naval power,

---

[1] The label applied by J. L. Garvin to the Radical economists.
[2] See Spender, *Life, Journalism and Politics*, ii, 6–7.

but on maintaining massive land forces to repel the Russians and the French who stood so menacingly on their borders. To expand the Army would call for considerable sacrifice by the people—to expand the Navy beyond the provisions made by the 1912 law was impossible. So it happened that as Germany increased military pressure on the Continent, naval pressure against Britain slackened.[1]

To men of radical and pacific persuasion, the eighteen-month prelude before the opening of the world war was a period of comparative peace poisoned by what seemed to them a senseless and baseless competition between the major Powers for increased armaments. How far Radicals had changed their strictures from the winter of 1911–12, when they had concentrated their wrath on Grey's conduct of foreign affairs, may be judged by Joshua Rowntree's presidential speech to the ninth National Peace Congress held at Leeds in June 1913. Far from censuring Grey he praised him unstintingly. 'Sir Edward Grey', declared Rowntree, 'is entitled to grateful honour at the hands of Europe for his successful efforts for peace.' The assembled delegates acknowledged their approval of these sentiments.[2] What exercised their consciences was 'the extravagant piling up of armaments' that would soon reduce men of all nations, in the words of Gambetta, to 'be beggars in front of barracks'. What could explain this madness? Admissions in the Reichstag in April 1913 pointed the Radicals towards the 'culprits' who were intent on Europe's penury and destruction for their gain. Krupp was detected trying to get mendacious articles about intended additional armaments in France, published in French newspapers so that Germany might be readier to launch out into similar expenditure and to buy more war material from Krupp.[3]

For those who were ready to cast stones at the German armament manufacturers, the Radicals were quick to point out that this was a sin not confined to one nation. The *Navy Annual* might rejoice that 'including ships building abroad, about 50 per cent of the armoured shipbuilding of the world is at the present moment in British hands'. J. A. Farrer in an article entitled 'Patriotism and mammon' pointed out that this state of affairs 'would be all very nice were it not that

---

[1] See, *B.D.* x, ii, 714; also Hale, 436–7.

[2] See *Manchester Guardian*, 11 June 1913.

[3] See question in Commons by Cowan, *Hansard*, v:52:544; also *Manchester Guardian*, 22 Apr. 1913; *The Economist* and *The Nation*, 26 Apr. 1913; Francis Delaisi, *La Paix par le Droit* (May 1913). P. W. Wilson in a series of articles in the *Daily News*, 20 to 28 May 1913 resurrected Mulliner and his part in the 1909 Naval panic. William Heaford considered the articles gave convincing proof 'that the English nation is not quite in the position to intone Pharisaic thanks to God that it is not as other people'.

these ships . . . may at any time become an argument for extorting more taxes from ourselves for more ships wherewith to defend ourselves against these very ships which our own countrymen have built, or helped to build'.[1] Radical journalists spared no adjectives in the opprobrious language they used to describe the activities of the armament manufacturers.

Too much insistence cannot be made upon the helpless condition of European civilisation in face of the war spectre whose terrors and alarms are, as all the world knows, manipulated and stage-managed by Krupp and their congeners in every land. The recent revelations in the Reichstag point not so much to the turpitudes and corrupt practices of German armour-plated patriots as to the impotence of Governments generally and the sheep-like slaughterability of our twentieth-century democracies. We have to wince now under the hard blow that war 'scares' are 'made' to order by a subsidised Press; that alarmist rumours are cynically edited and put into circulation in order to stimulate public opinion to make a clamour for more ships and more guns—in the interests of patriotic syndicates whose trade is in death, and in the anti-social causes that produce it; and that in normal circumstances the democracies of every nation are helpless during these crises, as against their political overlords and their armour-plated exploiters, to prevent the ugly onrush to Armageddon. An unscrupulous and inscrutable power of evil, richer than fabled Croesus, panoplied in steel and capable of transmuting the generous blood of heroes into the sordid gold of safe and snug *actionnaires* has sprung up in the heart of the nations. . . . The growth of this excrescence on our modern social organisms . . . is one of the most sinister obstacles infesting the path of national peace and international prosperity. The obstruction must either be removed or civilisation will stumble into inglorious ruin.[2]

The 'armour-plate ring', with its contracts and shareholders, its boards of 'interested' directors, proved a fruitful field for the invective of the Radical journalists,[3] and the questions and speeches in the Commons of Radical and Labour members. Ramsay MacDonald insisted that for half the sum spent upon naval armaments in ten years, an Utopia might have been established in Britain.[4] To the echo of G. H. Perris's despairing cry that the

---

[1] *Concord*, June 1913, p. 53.   [2] *Concord*, June 1913, pp. 56–7.
[3] See *Labour Leader*, 24 Apr. 1913, p. 8, 'The Death Trust': 'The Armaments Trust is the most terrible of all Capitalism's evils. It is an international conspiracy trading in deaths. During this year the nations of Europe will spend £400,000,000 on armaments. Is it not time that the workers of these nations slayed the hideous octopus which lives on their blood? The International Labour and Socialist movement calls them to conflict.'
[4] *Hansard*, v: 55:1511.

British Government was 'powerless' before the machinations of the armament manufacturers,[1] the saintly Philip Snowden vilified poor Mr Mulliner as 'a capitalist ogre', a 'commercial traveller and tout . . . constantly writing to the Government and appealing to them . . . to spend more money on armaments'.[2] The country had been hoaxed in 1909. Why should men allow themselves to be fleeced again at the behest of the armament manufacturers and their toadies of the 'patriotic' Press?[3]

The trouble with many Radicals was that they too readily became victims of their own propaganda. They were more than ever inclined to believe that a sufficient draught of their common-sensical attitude would blow away the accretions of a decade or more of hostility and fear. Trust the good sense of the common labouring man; expose the sordid conspiracy of the armament manufacturers; all would be right in the end. The War Office and the Admiralty had called 'wolf' too often. Their insistence on an ever increasing budget for destruction was the symptom of their megalomania. This time the Radical call for disarmament would be heeded.[4] Meanwhile, Philip Snowden in the editorial columns of the *Labour Leader,* was sternly addressing his troops. The burden of opposition to the Government's Naval Estimates would undoubtedly fall upon the Labour party. The Radicals in the Liberal party were simply not equipped to shake the resolve of the Government to increase expenditure on the Navy. His words of advice were mixed with criticism of some of his parliamentary colleagues.

> There is nothing in the record of the Labour Party more regrettable than the fact that some of its members of Parliament have always voted for every increase in the Army and Navy votes. . . . It is no sufficient excuse that these members represent dockyard and arsenal towns . . . Socialist principles must not be abandoned in order to keep seats. . . . Armaments expenditure is intimately connected with the whole social programme. We must not accept Dreadnoughts in place of better housing.[5]

In December 1912 the Canadian Parliament had laid before it an emergency Naval Bill authorising the expenditure of £7 million on three super-Dreadnoughts which it was intended to place at the

[1] See Perris, *The War Traders*, 24.　　[2] *Hansard*, v: 59: 2126ff.
[3] See Hirst, *The Six Panics, passim*.　　[4] *The Nation*, 27 Dec. 1913.
[5] *Labour Leader*, 11 Dec. 1913, p. 6. See also W. C. Anderson's estimate of the Radicals: 'They will murmur and complain, but nothing more. . . . The present group of Parliamentary Radicals are a feeble-folk, singularly well-meaning and singularly futile and ineffective. They have not among them one strong, forceful and fearless personality, and if they developed one, efforts would quickly be made to tame and muzzle him by office.' *Labour Leader*, 27 Nov. 1913, p. 6.

disposal of the Imperial Government for the defence of the Empire. They were intended to plug the gaps in the defence of the Mediterranean. However, the Senate, showing little concern and less respect for the needs of imperial defence in the Mediterranean, rejected the Bill in May 1913. Sir Wilfrid Laurier declared there was no need for such a measure when there was no emergency, no immediate danger, not even prospective danger. There was immediate consternation at the Admiralty, and in June it was announced that contracts for three vessels would have to be speeded up to make good the deficiency.[1] Concern for British security in the Mediterranean increased a hundredfold when the Italian programme of four super-Dreadnoughts became a fact in September 1913. On 18 October the First Lord of the Admiralty told an audience at Manchester that unless there was some general agreement as to disarmament then the taxpayer could expect heavy demands upon his pocket when the next Naval Estimates were presented. Churchill tempered this message for Radical ears with a reference to his Naval Holiday scheme. 'Winston', it was Esher's view, 'was playing to the Radical gallery again.'[2] What is certain is that only the Radical Press took Churchill's proposal seriously. According to the *Morning Post*, Churchill would be better employed taking a holiday from speechmaking for a year than dabbling with disarmament. Within a month Churchill at the Guildhall spelled out his message, and this time without any Radical sweetener. The next Naval Estimates would show a large increase—only an increase could be expected if he remained at the Admiralty. Lloyd George, quite recovered from his Agadir apostasy and determined upon once more leading the pacifist van, derided Churchill's threats as 'madness'. The public would not tolerate such provocative speeches; and even the Prime Minister, less bland than usual about the indiscretions of his Cabinet's *enfant terrible*, was 'furious'.[3]

Churchill had once more challenged the cardinal tenets of Liberalism. Yet, declared *The Nation*, the First Lord would suffer little for his infamy. If he was afforded a wigging, it would be in words and with the usual lack of effect. Why not take a leaf out of the Tory manual of political practice? There should be obstruction in the Commons, and should that fail, then the protest ought to be

[1] See Comment in *Labour Leader*, 12 June 1913, p. 3: 'Churchill is going from bad to worse . . . this is jingoism naked and unashamed. It is a blow in the face of the growing cordiality between Germany and Great Britain and a downright treachery to the professions of many of his recent speeches . . . the worst effect will be to stimulate again the armament manufacturers in Germany.'
[2] *E.P.*, iii, 142.   [3] See Marder, 316.

carried to the country. Gone was belief in the National Liberal
Federation's ability to achieve any restraint of the Government. It
had become 'an empty ritual, an annual protest which goes un-
heeded'. Both Massingham and Hirst seemed to have lost confidence
in the body which only the previous year they had designated as
their chosen instrument of reform.[1]

Delegates to the Leeds conference did not share the doubts of
Hirst and Massingham. Brunner, in the course of his presidential
speech, reviewed the legislative record of the Government and
condemned the 'growing mad expenditure upon armaments' as not
only inimical to the spirit of Liberalism but a fatal drain upon money
that otherwise would be spent upon social reform. The new aggressive spirit among the leaders of the disarmament group was shown
by Allen Baker's vigorous speech, which went some way outside the
terms of the resolution he was proposing. He boldly asserted, to the
obvious satisfaction of his audience, that 'a situation of great
gravity affecting the welfare of the nation has arisen, and if any
increase is proposed beyond that arising from the programme
already sanctioned by the House of Commons, it should be refused'.
A. G. C. Harvey repeated the threat he had made a week earlier at a
meeting in Rochdale, that he would resign his seat and fight a
by-election if his constituents were dissatisfied with his militant
attitude towards the armaments question. Already there had been a
number of protest meetings up and down the country over the
increased expenditure threatened by the First Lord. Asquith, who
attended the conference on its second day, was only too aware that
his Government was now facing the prospect of a substantial revolt
among its Radical backbenchers. When the Prime Minister addressed
the conference, he vehemently affirmed the Government's commitment to Home Rule; but as to the Naval Estimates, he could not
offer them any hope of substantial relief. *The Nation* observed that
while 'the Liberal party had at last awakened to the question of
armaments with zeal and passion', the Prime Minister had 'virtually
accepted . . . the fatalistic formula . . . that while other Powers do
nothing, we can do nothing either'.[2]

[1] Cf. *Labour Leader*, 4 Dec. 1913, pp. 6–7: 'We are surprised that the rank and
file of the Liberal party should have any hope that the Government will do
anything to realise their expectations. . . . The truth is the Government is far
more under the control of the armaments ring than under the control of the
National Liberal Federation . . . so long as armaments lords and their capitalist
colleagues finance the Liberal party they will take very good care to decide
what its policy shall be.'
[2] Official report of the meeting, 26/27 Nov. 1913, Liberal Publications Department. See also *The Nation*, 29 Nov. 1913, *Manchester Guardian*, 27/28 Nov.
1913; Baker and Baker, 166–7; and Koss, *Brunner*, 262–4.

Asquith had enough trouble on his hands with his Cabinet. The lines were firmly drawn between the economists and the navalists. It was not a situation where he could afford to treat lightly the threat of a backbench revolt. Harvey was not alone in his talk of resignation. *The Nation* pressed the rebels' advantage.

> The question is now becoming one of conscience as well as a feeling that if a Liberal Government merely commits itself to the uncritical Imperialist view on the question of armaments, its estimates are bound to be higher (because of the absence of all hostile pressure both on its foreign policy and its war services) than those of a Tory Government, on which pressure is constant.[1]

On 17 December Asquith faced an unwelcome deputation of some forty critical backbenchers led by Ponsonby, Leif Jones, Molteno and J. Annan Bryce. They bore a memorandum with almost a hundred signatories, affirming their determination to oppose Churchill's proposals. With the Home Rule question affording him enough trouble, the Prime Minister, in his reply to the deputation, talked of party loyalty. The Radicals appeared unmoved by this appeal and decided that they would constitute 'a loosely organised group to watch over the armaments question'.[2] The spirit of revolt was abroad, and Liberal Associations, Free Church Councils and various Chambers of Commerce were busily engaged in giving notice to the Prime Minister that they would not tolerate any increase in the Naval Estimates. Francis Hirst was forming yet another committee for 'Reduction of expenditure upon armaments' designed to secure the support of London business men. Meeting at the Cannon Street Hotel on 16 January, the committee declared they were not frightened of Germany but 'of the armament firms who conspired all over the world to induce people to spend money against each other in armaments'.[3] The mounting pressure of the Radical campaign was reflected in the obvious concern of their enemies. Arthur Lee in the Commons sternly informed the Government that they must on no account surrender to the 'uninformed clamour of a section of their own supporters'.[4] The Navy League, their request to hold a meeting in Glasgow refused by the Lord Provost who stoutly maintained that national security rested upon the lessening of tensions and not on increased armaments, announced a nationwide campaign intended to combat 'the aggressive action

---

[1] *The Nation*, 6 Dec. 1913.
[2] See *Manchester Guardian*, 18 Dec. 1913; 5 Jan. 1914.
[3] *Manchester Guardian*, 6 Jan. 1914.
[4] *Hansard*, v: 59: 106.

of the joint factions of peacemongers, anti-Imperialists and Norman Angellites'.[1]

The New Year was greeted with an appeal from Brunner to

> every Liberal Association which believes in the good old Liberal doctrine of peace, retrenchment, and reform, to pass resolutions before the end of January in favour of reductions in our armament expenditure so that the Government may have fresh evidence of the wishes of the party before the Military and Naval Estimates for the next year are finally settled. . . . I for my part trust that in the next session of Parliament we may see a fruitful change of policy, which will send a message of relief to British taxpayers and of our good will to all the nations of the world.

Brunner's words were powerfully backed by the Liberal Press. An unexpected coadjutor was the *Daily Chronicle*. But that paper had an even better tonic for the Radicals than editorial support for Brunner. The Chancellor of the Exchequer had vouchsafed them an interview wherein he reviewed the 'organised insanity' of the 'overwhelming extravagance of our expenditure upon armaments'. This was by no means the first statement by a minister on the armaments situation. Asquith, at the Guildhall in November, had concluded his speech by deploring the increasing expenditure on armaments. Even Winston had told a Dundee audience in October that he thought the time was ripe for an Anglo-German initiative to tackle the armament problem. But Lloyd George's contribution was of an entirely different order—he was intent on bringing public support to the cause for which he stood in a divided Cabinet. *The Times* gave particular point to Lloyd George's interview when it denounced his 'remarkable and reprehensible' statements. Here was the minister, who at the time of the Agadir incident had given confidence to the French and dispelled misunderstanding, talking in a manner guaranteed to cause the French alarm. *The Times* boldly asserted that whatever the Chancellor of the Exchequer might think, the nation was resolved to maintain its naval supremacy. 'We know that this supremacy is vital not only to our greatness, but to our existence and to our liberty.'[2]

The particular target of the Chancellor's observations patently had been the First Lord of the Admiralty. F. E. Smith was quick to

[1] *Manchester Guardian*, 6 Jan. 1914.
[2] *The Times*, 4 Jan. 1914. There was a further leader occasioned by Lloyd George's interview on 7 Jan., when *The Times* pointed out to the French 'that the views of the pacifists are no more those of England than the ideas of M. Jaurès represent the real mind of France'. *Labour Leader*, 8 Jan. 1914, thought the interview no more than a cunning Liberal ploy. Who could believe the sincerity of the minister who had made the Mansion House speech?

defend his friend Churchill from the 'clumsy and maladroit statement of a bungling amateur whose hands are already too full, and who has never lost an opportunity in compromising and injuring this country in attempts to advertise himself'. Smith's crude polemic contained a shrewd conjecture. Lloyd George's ministerial career had been marked by clever anticipations of political lodestones: the evangelical Radical who had erred and strayed into the camp of the Jingoes in 1911 with his Mansion House speech, would now make amends as the leader of the pacifists and economists. Here was the very man they sought; of towering political stature; a proven fighter commanding strong reserves of power, a messianic leader. Haldane wasn't sure, but he thought Lloyd George was bidding for the leadership of a Labour Radical party.[1] Another minister, Charles Hobhouse, addressing his constituents, revealed that like the Chancellor of the Exchequer he too was devoted to the principles of economy and championed Anglo-German conciliation. No matter the sound and fury engendered by the public, informed observers of the political scene knew that final accounts could only be settled within the confines of the Cabinet.

The leading protagonists in the Cabinet quarrel over the 1914 Naval Estimates, the Chancellor and the First Lord, had long given notice of their differing views. The younger man had characteristically proclaimed his faith in more and more battleships in a public speech. Lloyd George had declared his opposition to Churchill's enterprise at a dinner party for the Prime Minister, Haldane, Grey and Crewe given at No. 11 Downing Street in early November. Balancing the appetites of the Navy, Pensions, Health Insurance and Education, the assembled ministers agreed that Churchill's programme would have to be cut by at least a million and a half pounds. Lloyd George had complained of a possible deficit of ten million unless taxation was increased—a solution not to be lightly undertaken in a year when there was the distinct possibility of a general election. Churchill presented his Estimates to the Cabinet on 15 December. There was an increase of £3 million over the amount for the previous year. This was not acceptable, and Churchill was directed to make sizeable reductions. He was accused of having been unnecessarily extravagant and to have wasted resources upon inessentials. But when Churchill presented his revised Estimates after consultation with his Board, they were still found to be unacceptable. His suggested economies effected a reduction of less than £1 million. If real economies were to be made, then the Dreadnought building

[1] E.P., iii, 151. See also Balfour's comments, quoted Marder, op. cit., 319.

programme would have to be reduced. Samuel insisted that Britain's
60 per cent margin of superiority would be guaranteed by building
two of the proposed four Dreadnoughts in the construction programme. Churchill would have none of this. Once more the Cabinet
had reached an impasse over the Navy, and Asquith was obliged to
adjourn any further discussion until after the Christmas recess.

The apparent point at debate in the Cabinet during January and
February 1914 was the number of Dreadnoughts to be sanctioned
for the new construction programme. However, the real issues at
stake were personal and political. The economists were to be bested,
not by the superior technical arguments in the papers that Churchill
mustered in formidable array to support his case, but by Asquith's
patience and infinite capacity to reconcile the irreconcilable, and
their own eventual, if reluctant, recognition that there was no way of
escaping the logic of the total political situation in which the Liberal
Government found itself in the last year of peace.

Argument in the Cabinet was embittered by the personal antipathy
felt for Churchill by most members of the economist faction. They
not only disliked the man, they distrusted him. It was common
political gossip that Churchill regretted ever leaving the Tories, for
when Balfour fell he might well have become their leader.[1] However
apocryphal the stories, many men believed them because they
wanted to. Lloyd George felt no antipathy towards Churchill. The
affectionate bond forged between the two men when they had fought
for economies in the military and naval establishment, was proof
against their present disagreement. In the notes that the two
ministers exchanged over the Cabinet table, in the letters they
wrote one another, the thrust of argument was sharp, but mutual
courtesy, respect and regard were always present.[2]

In the Cabinet Churchill felt that he had his back to the wall.
Asquith's sympathy for the case that Churchill made is patent. He
refused to accept the First Lord's resignation, though pressed to do
as much by Simon.

> The loss of W.C., though regrettable, is *not* by any means a
> splitting of the party—indeed large Admiralty estimates may
> be capable of being carried *only* because W.C., has gone. The
> party would feel itself strengthened in its Radical element and
> among the Economists; the feeling that the Cabinet *fights for
> economy* but preserves Home Rule unflinchingly is just what is
> wanted. A majority of the Cabinet certainly take this view.[3]

[1] See, for example, Scott, *Diaries*, 63–4.
[2] See letters and notes quoted Owen, 256–8.
[3] Quoted Jenkins, 299.

The make-up of Simon's 'majority' is revealed by another letter written to Asquith a few days later, signed by McKenna, Runciman, Beauchamp and Hobhouse as well as Simon. The names of Harcourt, Morley, Burns and Lloyd George may be added, together with those of Pease and Herbert Samuel. The array might seem formidable, but Asquith knew that if only he could effect an accommodation between Lloyd George and Churchill, then the rest of the dissidents could be brought swiftly to heel. Asquith's method of achieving this desired end seems extraordinarily dilatory. The Prime Minister would wait on events rather than seek to influence them. But, his *modus operandi* was tried, and had proved successful on more than one occasion in the past. He knew the strengths and weaknesses of his colleagues; his monumental patience allowed him to outface and outwit the passions and bitterness of the moment. He would temporise and play the argument along as slowly as possible until other events would overtake their present difficulties. Meanwhile the Prime Minister made cautionary noises about the possibility of going to the country, laced with admonitions and appeals for unity.

From the second week in January, the important argument in the letters exchanged amongst the dissidents was not so much the armaments question as the future of the Liberal Party. Consciences were being overtaken by political actualities. Increased naval expenditure was no longer being measured in the scales of morality but by the number of votes it might cost in the constituencies. Though, as Hobhouse wrote to Harcourt, the Chancellor of the Exchequer had been brought out of his tent[1] and afforded them a formidable ally, the battle was already slipping away from the reductionists' grasp. Perhaps Morley was more astute than C. P. Scott supposed when he admitted that, while he deplored the extravagance and the policy that led to Churchill's increased Estimates, he did not propose to do anything to check them. If Lloyd George resigned, a contingency which McKenna thought laughably improbable, then he would have no weighty support. But should Churchill resign, he could count on Grey joining him, a prospect that would surely bring down the Government.[2] The only hope for the reductionists was that Lloyd George would exercise his personal influence on Churchill. However, in their hearts they must have realised that to conjure any reductions in the First Lord's Estimates on the strength of a friendship that had flourished in the days before Winston's apocalyptic appreciation of the reality of the

1 Hobhouse to Harcourt, 15 Jan. 1914, *Harcourt MSS.*
2 Scott, *Diaries*, 74.

German 'menace', was asking too much even of the Welsh Wizard.

Churchill and Lloyd George exchanged a sharp volley of letters. In a Cabinet memorandum of 10 January Churchill had declared his position quite unequivocally. Britain was

> deeply involved in the European situation. . . . The causes which might lead to general war have not been removed and often remind us of their presence. . . . The world is arming as it has never armed before . . . unless our naval strength is solidly, amply and unswervingly maintained, with due and fair regard to the professional advisers of the Government, I could not feel that I was doing my duty if I did not warn the country of its danger.

The passage of time, and Lloyd George's promptings, did not alter this adamantine purpose. On 26 January Churchill wrote to the Chancellor, 'I recognise your friendship but I ask no favours and I shall enter into no irregular obligation. I am now approaching the end of my resources and I can only await the decision of my colleagues and the Prime Minister.' The First Lord had revised his figures upwards. There were to be no reductions. Lloyd George acknowledged his despair in a letter to Churchill[1] and the next day wrote to the Prime Minister. 'I have laboured in vain to effect an arrangement between Churchill and the critics of his Estimates which would save you and the Cabinet the necessity for entering upon an unpleasant and maybe a disastrous controversy. I have utterly failed.'[2] The signs that Lloyd George would collapse before Churchill's determination, had been apparent to the economists for several days.[3] Lloyd George continued to mouth protests in the Cabinet, but all the time the economists were patently losing ground. By the beginning of February, McKenna, as pugnacious as ever in his demands for value for money, informed Scott that the Chancellor had given up the fight and was now 'a Churchill man'. Lloyd George was 'acting as a bell-wether to bring the stalwarts into the Churchill fold'.[4]

More appeals and warnings from Asquith as to the disastrous consequences of a split over the Estimates, expressions of deep concern and uneasiness from the economists, and on 11 February the First Lord's Estimates were finally approved. Churchill would ask the Commons for a little more than £51½ million, an unprecedented total at a time when apparently the international scene was calm. A sop would be added to placate outraged economical consciences among the Government's supporters. The First Lord would

---

[1] See Owen, 257–8.
[2] Quoted Marder, 324.
[3] See Scott, *Diaries*, 78.
[4] *Ibid.*, 80.

announce that the Estimates for next year would show a substantial reduction. Winston had every right to feel pleased with himself. He had overcome formidable opposition and achieved substantially what he desired. Churchill was prepared to admit the primary reason for his success had been the 'unwearying patience of the Prime Minister and his solid silent support'.[1]

Churchill presented his Estimates to the Commons on 17 March.[2] His long and eloquent speech was divided equally between assurances, to the Tories that there was no need to increase the size of the Estimates, and to his own backbenchers that they could not possibly be decreased. In the circumstances it is not surprising that few expressed satisfaction with the First Lord's performance. Radical members impugned Churchill's Liberalism, questioned his statistics, and berated his strategy for the unfortunate influence it would have on international relations. Philip Snowden enjoyed the greatest success of any of Churchill's critics. Radicals outside Parliament had frequently referred to the 'armaments gang'. Now Snowden, after taunting Lloyd George for abandoning the position he had outlined in his Criccieth interview, brought the full force of his invective to bear upon the influence of the armament manufacturers. His charges were cheered by Labour and Radical members, but when the Government was challenged in the lobbies the opposition melted away to a mere handful.[3]

Though many a Radical conscience was undoubtedly pricked by the unprecedented total that Churchill demanded, though they did not doubt the truth of Snowden's charges, all, save those few for whom reduction of armaments lay at the forefront of their political faith and personal philosophy, recognised that the primary task was to retain the Liberal Government in power. They regretted that money, which might otherwise be spent upon much needed social reforms, should be squandered upon the Services. But the only alternative was a Tory Government that would spend even more on armaments. This was the awful truth that Radical members had constantly to live with.[4] Effectively there was nothing they could do save splutter and rage at the cruel fate which made ministers forget in office the essence of their Liberalism, and reduced them to suffering a parliamentary system which was designed to make the Government's critics impotent. In the sad circumstances it was convenient for Radicals to hide their impotence by claiming this

[1] W. S. Churchill, *World Crisis*, 102–3.   [2] See *Hansard*, v:59:1896ff.
[3] On the two occasions the House was divided after the debates of 2 and 23 Mar. 1914, the largest number the reductionists mustered was 35.
[4] See Scott, *Diaries*, 22 Jan. 1914, 77.

time they had acceded because of the troubles in Ulster. But no one was really convinced by this excuse. *Concord* commented:

> We understand well the difficulties of our friends in the House of Commons; yet, we cannot but think that they might have done something more to bring home to the country and the Cabinet the monstrous character of the Admiralty programme . . . Parliamentary control is becoming weaker instead of stronger; and we see the rules of sound finance and old constitutional safeguards, coolly defied in order to serve an inordinately ambitious policy, and the greed of traders and professional men who alone profit by our sluggishness. . . . We say without hesitation that these Naval Votes, in time of complete peace, are exorbitant in wholesale and retail, in policy and administration. It is a very grievous thing that they were not more seriously challenged.[1]

Churchill's Estimates had received grudging approval from the *Manchester Guardian. The Nation, Economist* and *Daily News* did not so readily abandon their campaign against the First Lord. Hirst prefaced his nine-point condemnation of the Estimates with a broadside at the armament manufacturers for engineering the current panic about Russia in Germany and Austria. His criticisms of the Board of Admiralty and Churchill were more comprehensive than convincing. Even so, a week later he tacked on a postscript, this time condemning Churchill for not even mentioning a naval holiday.[2] The *Daily News* had been equally bitter in its charges against Churchill. What was the value of his so called 'fixed standard' when he altered the ratio to suit himself? Sixty per cent advantage over Germany every day looked more like the old 'two Power' standard. If Churchill was 'the font of profligate extravagance and wasteful administration', what of the other Liberal ministers? Where now was the old Liberal maxim of retrenchment? £360 million had been wasted in nine years on the Navy; half that sum would have swept away many of Britain's social diseases. The British taxpayer was lining the pockets of the arms manufacturers for Dreadnoughts which informed opinion believed would not be able to live with the submarine.[3] But the voices that cried 'shame' were heeded by few. Once more a disarmament campaign, born in

---

[1] *Concord*, Apr. 1914, p. 3.   [2] *Economist*, 14 and 21 Mar. 1914.
[3] See *Daily News*, 19 Mar. 1914. In October 1913 *The Times* had printed a series of articles on 'Warship design' which led to a considerable correspondence condemning the whole Dreadnought policy; see, e.g., letter of Admiral Sir Cyprian Bridge, 17 Oct. 1913. The articles pointed to the violent fluctuations in design of Dreadnoughts and maintained that if submarines could accomplish only a part of what was claimed for them, Dreadnoughts would prove a failure.

promise of strength and resolution, had been vanquished. While the Radicals yet bemoaned their fate, the attention of the public had been drawn from naval affairs to the crisis in Ireland.

The crushing failure of their disarmament campaign left the Radicals with an uneasy conundrum to solve. If ministers were prepared to admit the 'insanity' of ever-increasing arms expenditure —even Churchill had referred to it as a 'pitiful folly'—and if they insisted that the international outlook was 'bright' with scarce a cloud upon the horizon, why did the nations continue to arm at such cost to social progress? Could it be that the situation in Europe was not as pacific as they would believe? Had Grey sincerely recanted his former heresies and set his foot once for all upon the path of peace?

Chapter 9   A Last Exercise in Delusion

Two Balkan Wars

On the eve of the outbreak of the Balkan Wars, Radical opinion could not have been more concerned about or critical of Sir Edward Grey and the manner in which he was mishandling Britain's foreign policy. As though the crisis of Agadir had not been sufficient warning of the foolishness of the Liberal Government's ways, there had been the miserable conclusion to Haldane's mission to Germany, the unbridled jingoism of Churchill at the Admiralty, and above all else, the constant concern that the Anglo-French entente, born of the spirit of Liberalism, had somehow been perverted to become a military and naval alliance with wide reaching obligations as yet publicly undefined. It was a doleful task to review Grey's management of Britain's foreign policy. Should the Foreign Secretary maintain that at the least during his tenure of office the general peace of Europe had been maintained, one had only to consider the cost to realise what a miserable achievement this represented. When posterity reviewed this sad period it would pour imprecations on the Liberals, for the party that had boasted Bright and Gladstone had 'utterly failed in the constructive tasks of peace; we have made an inheritance which must issue either in the slavery of conscription or the curses of war'.[1] Grey at the Foreign Office represented a liability. Lacking the capacity to control events, his predilection was to drift along, 'the deluded victim of a fixed idea'.[2] Yet, when Grey's fortunes were at their lowest ebb, deliverance was at hand from the harsh strictures of his Radical critics. War in the Balkans re-established Grey's credit.

The Young Turk revolution had been welcomed by the Radicals. It had been their hope that order would at last be restored in the Turkish dominions and that tolerance would be shown towards

[1] *The Nation*, 29 June 1912.   [2] *Manchester Guardian*, 26 Aug. 1912.

Turkey's Christian subjects. Radical optimism proved ill founded. Nevinson, who like his fellow members of the Balkan Committee had expected so much when Abdul Hamid had been removed, visited Albania in the autumn of 1911. The experience shattered any hopes he still might have entertained, and he was obliged to record his total disillusionment: 'A race may change its form of Government without changing its nature. It had become evident that the policy of the Young Turks was the policy of the Red Sultan enlarged.'[1]

Slowly the Radicals were forced to admit to themselves that their faith in the Young Turks had been misplaced. In contrast with the *Manchester Guardian*'s description of the ruthless crushing of the Albanian revolt as 'a slight set back', *The Nation* in December 1910 had been forthright in its condemnation of 'The failure of the Young Turks'. The 'progress' of Young Turk rule served only to confirm *The Nation*'s judgment.

The Balkan Committee, which had never been representative of more than a small section of the Radicals, suddenly found itself the focus of public attention at a time when its members were unsure and divided about the attitude they should adopt. Noel Buxton, who from the beginning had been the moving spirit of the Committee, was obliged to write a letter to *The Times* urging the British public to be patient.[2] However, matters continued to deteriorate and the Balkan Committee eventually if reluctantly admitted that their hopes in supporting the Young Turk régime had been entirely disappointed. In January 1912 the Committee sent a sharply critical note to the Turkish Government. It was no longer possible for them to excuse the barbaric activities of the Turkish régime on the grounds either of inexperience or the gravity and complexity of the problems it faced. The Committee's patience was exhausted. Conditions of life in the Turkish provinces had to be improved immediately; the concomitant injustices and cruelties of a ruthless policy of Turkification, must be suppressed. The Committee called upon the civilised nations to insist that the Turkish rulers change their attitude forthwith.[3] Before the outbreak of the Young Turk revolution in 1908 Grey had suggested that Turkish rule might best be placed under international control. By June 1912 the Balkan Committee were prepared to admit that unless a better remedy was immediately available, then the Great Powers would have to intervene.[4]

War in the Balkans seemed inevitable. But, in the short summer months that preceded the outbreak of hostilities, the Radicals still

[1] Nevinson, 274.
[2] Letter to *The Times*, 15 Feb. 1911.
[3] *Ibid.*, 12 Jan. 1912.
[4] *Ibid.*, 20 June 1912.

vainly searched for signs that 'the sick man of Europe' might reform his ways. In July Turkey was rent by internal dissension and the so-called Committee of Union and Progress tumbled from power. The Radicals were loath to abandon all hope of internal reform. Yet these last dwindling sparks of optimism were of as little avail as the *Manchester Guardian*'s stern warning to the Balkan League that on no account should they attack Turkey.[1] The Young Turks when they had overthrown Abdul Hamid had appealed to the principle of nationality. Now that same principle was to be turned against them. Former minions, kept weak because of dissension among themselves that had been encouraged by the Turks, buried their enmity towards one another to make common cause against their master. The prize of national independence welded Serb, Bulgar and Greek together. The armies of the Balkan League went to war against their Turkish oppressor, and though the Turkish army enjoyed much prestige, in Thrace at the battle of Kirk-Kilisse, the Bulgars won an overwhelming victory. That engagement was fought in October. By early December Adrianople had been invested and the armies of the League stood before the lines of Chataldja. In three months the Turkish Empire in Europe that had lasted five hundred years almost ceased to exist.

Those remaining reservations the Radicals might have felt at deserting the Turks were swept away in the passions engendered by war. In a few weeks the swift strokes of the rebel armies achieved more than had decades of pained hopes and futile diplomatic negotiations. *The Nation* enthused, 'a new force is born in Europe'. Now let the wicked Turk be damned for his abominations. If Radical and pacifist opinion seemed untowardly enthusiastic about their new found protégés' military triumphs, many 'pacifists' were so far excited by the prospect of the collapse of Turkish rule in Europe that they claimed this was no ordinary war but a Christian crusade of defence and liberation and therefore worthy of their support. This exculpation of their sudden martial enthusiasm in 1912, was a sad intimation of ready moral surrender by so many 'pacifists' in 1914.

The Balkan War was concerned with nationality and liberty—considerations thrust aside as the price to pay for 'peace with honour' at the Congress of Berlin. The shades of older quarrels, of older loyalties, were summoned to the bar of conscience. The spirit of Gladstone was abroad and Radicals rejoiced. If some were more hesitant in their enthusiasm, it was not because their sympathies

[1] *Manchester Guardian*, 3 Oct. 1912.

were not engaged. They could not ignore the wider European implications of this war of liberty. Were they the witnesses of the final portent of Armageddon?

> One can almost hear the death knell tolling the *Dies Irae* for huge armies, the flower of the youth for many nations. . . . Out of the tangle of races and religions which complicate the problem of confusion in the Near East some mighty volcanic erruption of miscellaneous national hatreds would almost seem fated to arise, if not from the unbridled passions of Turk and Christian at any rate from the jealousies and ambitions of the Great Powers.[1]

The Nation advised that if the war threatened to spread, then Britain should offer her neutrality in exchange for Germany's. They believed that without German support Austria would never challenge Russia.[2] Whatever might happen, the *Manchester Guardian* insisted, Britain should remain neutral.[3] Bulgarians, Servians, Montenegrins, Greeks and Macedonians, all had good cause to fall upon their Muslim master. There was every reason and excuse for their frenzied rush to arms. But when the spoils of war were ready to divide, would the Great Powers be able to resist swooping like vultures upon 'the sick man'? Unlike Turkey's former clients, the Great Powers would need to find a *casus belli*. However, this would afford little difficulty 'for those who deck naked plunder with the garlands of civilisation and would declare their task to promote the interests of Commerce and Christianity'. Diplomacy by the Great Powers, or stealing by finding, call it what you will, was enough to turn the sternest moralist into a cynic.[4]

Concern and suspicion among Radicals, that Britain was covertly pursuing a questionable policy in the Balkans, seemed confirmed by rumours that the Foreign Office was actively involved in encouraging the raising of a loan in London to help the Turks. Surely, asked *The Nation*, Britain was not going to back the wrong horse for a third time?[5] The National Peace Council adopted a resolution strongly condemning the raising of any loan. Such action was 'an obvious infringement of professed neutrality' and would 'tend to prolong the war in the interests of speculators in war loans'. The British Government 'should immediately seek agreement between all Sovereign Powers that at the Third Hague Conference all such loans be considered a direct infringement of neutrality'.[6] While most Radicals demanded unswerving attachment to neutrality whatever

---

[1] *Concord*, Oct. 1911, p. 111. [2] *The Nation*, 21 Dec. 1912.
[3] *Manchester Guardian*, 26 Nov. 1912. [4] *Concord*, Oct. 1911, p. 112.
[5] *The Nation*, 19 Oct. 1912. [6] See N.P.C. Minutes, Nov. 1912.

the cost, small groups of 'pacifists', particularly the International Arbitration League, changed their former policy and now insisted that the Great Powers ought to intervene. The responsibility for the war was theirs. For more than thirty years, 'because they could not swallow their own greedy jealousies', they had done nothing 'to heal the festering wounds by timely measures of justice'. 'A holocaust was now the price to be paid for wisdom', an intolerable calamity endured because international relationships were conducted by 'an irresponsible caste of regal and diplomatic dilettanti lacking all sympathy with national freedom, social progress and international solidarity'. Who could doubt the Great Powers' responsibility? They had

> stood aside while the present combatants sharpened the tools of war. We form a ring around the belligerents as round brutal boxers so they may pound themselves to pulp. . . . The war is the outcome of a system, a code which tolerates and sanctions non-intervention. Small long suffering nations only took the law into their own hands because the Great Powers had not dared to stir.[1]

In the Commons, ministers were not slow in dispelling Radical anxieties about their possible attitude. The Cabinet seemed quite prepared to accept the *fait accompli* won with such amazing speed by the armies of the Balkan League. Nor would the Great Powers, according to Grey, be 'slow in adjusting their view to the march of events'.[2] Lloyd George had caught the Radical mood exactly when he talked of the war as 'extending the boundaries of freedom', a motto which *The Nation* had charged public opinion to take as its own.[3] Nor was the Prime Minister, in his speech in November at the Guildhall, slow to assert that the Government looked forward to recasting the map of Eastern Europe.

Meanwhile, Socialists were anxious that their voice should be heard. The peaceful sentiments of the international proletariat and their opposition to war and all manifestations of the plague of militarism should be loudly advertised. In November and December 1912, a series of meetings were held in all the great European capitals. The Opera House in the Kingsway, London, was filled on 17 November with an audience whose enthusiasm for the cause of peace was only slightly dampened by Edouard Anseele and Ludwig Frank addressing them in French and German. It was of little consequence, for one speech was much like another, and Keir Hardie as president had said all there was to say on the subject.

[1] *Concord*, Nov. 1912, pp. 116–19.
[2] *Hansard*, v:43:1000.   [3] *The Nation*, 19 Oct. 1912.

Is it any wonder the Balkan States refused the mediation of the Great Powers? With the example of India, Egypt, Morocco and Persia before them, how could anything else be expected? (Loud cheers.)

We say here that those on whom the burden of war falls shall have the final word as to whether there shall be peace or war. The foreign affairs of the nation must be discussed in the open light of the day. (Great cheering.) If that puts an end to the knavery, chicanery and dishonesty which has been the character of the diplomacy in the past, the life of the world would be sweeter, and the peace of the world more secure. (Loud and prolonged cheering.)[1]

The audience were assured that the watchword of International Socialist would be War against war! Guerre à la Guerre! Krieg dem Kriege! At a later international congress which met at Basel, this message was taken up by speaker after speaker. All who attended affirmed that they were profoundly aware of the unique significance of the occasion. But strangely, the world's Press virtually ignored this International Socialist exercise in 'Peace on Earth and Goodwill toward all men'.

The tide of events continued to flow favourably for the Balkan League. Most Radical opinion was convinced that nothing more was required than that the Great Powers, acting in concert, should stand aside. By December the Balkan allies forced Turkey to sue for an armistice. London was chosen as the meeting place for the delegates of the belligerents. Time elapsed; the Radicals grew impatient of delay. The victors, far from displaying the Christian virtue of charity, were extremely truculent and made plain their intention to force humiliating terms upon the vanquished Turk. In February the *Manchester Guardian* was claiming that the Great Powers should draft a settlement and impose it upon the parties.[2] Sadly it was not the Turk who was causing delay but the victorious allies who were now clearly preparing to fall upon one another. By May, impatient of endless prevarication, Grey insisted that the delegates to the Balkan Conference either sign a treaty forthwith or leave London. The Foreign Secretary's action earned high praise from the Radicals.

If now at last there was peace between Turkey and her enemies, there was little reason for the Radicals to feel satisfied. Turkish rule in Europe might be ended, but the fair hopes that once had been entertained by that prospect seemed doomed unless the Concert of Europe could be mobilised to stop a further war. However, a

[1] Reported in *Concord*, Nov. 1912, pp. 125–6.
[2] *Manchester Guardian*, 24 Feb. 1913.

second Balkan War was inevitable. It had been obvious during the Balkan Conference that the Greeks and the Serbs had been intent upon delaying settlement merely as a ploy to weaken Bulgaria. The war of liberation was over, but now, 'bitterest of tragedies', the 'triumphant arms of the Crusaders are turned into fratricidal weapons of mutual destruction in the hands of the victorious soldiers of the Cross'.[1] Why did not the Great Powers intervene? It was criminally irresponsible for them to shirk their task.[2] In the Commons, Mason turned on Grey and upbraided him for doing nothing. The Foreign Secretary gave his critic short shrift. 'Am I . . . to come down to this House and ask for a vote of credit . . . to impose peace in the Balkan peninsula?' It was better, Grey explained the next day, that the Powers use their influence for peace while avoiding intervention. Any alternative course, he cleverly suggested, would sunder the present happy agreement between the Powers.[3] Nor was the Government to be stirred into action by the Turkish violation of frontiers agreed by the Treaty of London. Adrianople was retaken; the former Balkan allies were too busily engaged in killing one another to care. Only Buxton and a few friends in the House of Commons vainly fumed at Turkey's cheeky territorial resurrection.

Radicals could not ignore the fact that from the beginning they had hopelessly misunderstood the Balkan imbroglio. Cynics, who had scoffed at the claim made by men like Nevinson that freedom after five centuries of tyranny had at least been achieved in the Balkans, now had their judgment fortified by the spectacle of former allies heaping atrocity upon atrocity as they fought one another with unparalleled ferocity. General public opinion was disgusted by this second war, and the Radicals were well advised to recognise their mistake and wash their hands of the whole sad business of the Balkans.[4] In 'the carnival of lust and brutality with its terrible retinue of crimes and abominations',[5] Radical enthusiasts for the Balkan cause, with their traditions going back to Gladstone, fell silent save for occasional appeals for relief to the suffering. They had long desired the expulsion of the Turk from Europe. Now that hope had been realised only for reality to prove a hideous disappointment. They had championed the Bulgarians and now their protégés rewarded their favour with unmitigated savagery, murder and rapine.

[1] *Concord*, July 1913, p. 66.   [2] See *The Nation*, 31 May 1913.
[3] *Hansard* v:55:1026 and 1036.
[4] Cf. Nevinson's article in *Contemporary Review*, Jan. 1913; and 'Public Opinion and the Balkan Peace' in *The Nation*, 9 Aug. 1913.
[5] *Concord*, Oct. 1913, p. 96.

What satisfaction had been felt by the outcome of the First Balkan War, was more than destroyed by the subsequent strife between the former allies of the Balkan League. Yet a time of disillusion had been saved for most Radical opinion by one unlooked for and unexpected consolation. Throughout the period of the wars there had been every reason and sufficient excuse for a general European conflagration to have broken out. However, instead of increased enmity, relations between Germany and England showed a marked improvement. The strange consolation for all 'this horror and suffering' was that 'apparently it had contributed more than all the efforts of the diplomatists to secure peace for the rest of Europe'.[1] The Radicals had long pleaded for the restoration of the Concert of Europe. Now their wish appeared to have been granted, and the visible embodiment of this new Concert was the meeting of the Ambassadors of the Great Powers under Grey's chairmanship in London. What was more, the meeting was the result of an initiative by the British Foreign Secretary.

Where there had been pessimism, suddenly it was dispelled, and from both sides of the North Sea came comfortable assertions that at last all was well between Germany and Britain. The loyal cooperation between Berlin and London during the prolonged Balkan crisis provided both evidence and point for this optimistic assessment. In four weeks *The Nation* moved from a declaration that Anglo-German relations were better than they had been for a decade, to the confident assumption that Europe was no longer divided into two armed and hostile camps. 'The sense of active struggle to preserve the balance of power has given way to the realisation of a parallel effort to maintain peace.' The threat of a European war had been averted, and the credit for that happy fact belonged in equal parts to the Kaiser and Sir Edward Grey.[2] German and British statesmen for their part, did what they could to further this euphoric mood. Bethmann-Hollweg and Jagow, Asquith and Grey, spoke of one another's countries in considerate and conciliatory tones. Confidence was restored, and the Press reflected this friendlier spirit. Now the publicists busied themselves with much talk of Anglo-German rapprochement. Some were rash enough to suppose that Germany and England were moving from détente towards entente.

In March Asquith, extolling to the Commons the cooperative efforts towards peace that had been made by the Great Powers, drew attention to the 'mutual confidence' inspired by Anglo-German

[1] Philip Morrell in *Contemporary Review*, Apr. 1913.
[2] See *The Nation*, 4 Jan. and 8 Feb. 1913.

cooperation. He silenced a Tory critic by categorically asserting that Britain had no military obligations towards France, official or otherwise.[1] If this was not enough, within a fortnight the Prime Minister replying to Radical promptings declared:

> As has been repeatedly stated, this country is not under any obligation not public and known to Parliament which compels it to take part in any war. . . . If war arises between European Powers there are no unpublished agreements which will restrict or hamper the freedom of the Government or of Parliament to decide whether or not Great Britain should participate in a war.[2]

Could there have been a clearer, more unequivocal statement than the Prime Minister's, that Britain enjoyed a free hand? The Radicals asked themselves by what happy chance had Britain in a few short months chosen once more to adopt a policy suitable for an island Power?[3] *The Nation* was not at all sure that the change had been effected in full consciousness. Nevertheless, there was cause for rejoicing, and the Radical Foreign Affairs Committee, meeting for the first time that parliamentary session, shared the feelings of 'deep satisfaction' at the change.[4] Obviously, the time had come for the Radicals to review their estimate of Grey and his policy. In May the *Manchester Guardian* set itself that task.

A new figure emerges—Grey, the Liberal idealist. The crisis in the Balkans had been resolved without general war in Europe because a solution had been offered that hinged upon twin conceptions of Concert and Law. 'A statesman who held by these conceptions unselfishly and with sincere conviction was sure to end up by dominating the counsels of Europe. We rejoice that this statesman has been an Englishman and a Liberal Foreign Secretary.' Sadly, in the past Grey had erred from the Liberal way, but this might well be explained because at times 'he was hardly his own master'. Happily, now he had shrugged off his tutelage to his Foreign Office officials and 'embraced the ideal of the Concert thus banishing those earlier mistaken principles upon which his policy has been based'.[5] Grey, according to Massingham, had undergone a conversion no less sudden than that of Saul on the road to Damascus.[6] Immediately all was forgiven, and the Foreign Secretary's Radical critics now were lavish in the paeans of praise they bestowed upon him. If Britain was pre-eminent in the councils of the world, then it was due

[1] *Hansard*, v:50:31ff. and 42–3. [2] *Ibid.*, v:50:1316.
[3] *The Nation*, 5 Mar. 1913. [4] *Manchester Guardian*, 2 Apr. 1913.
[5] *Ibid.*, 31 May 1913. [6] *The Nation*, 15 Feb. 1913.

to Grey's 'transparent honesty of method and purpose'.[1] That affirmation was made by Ponsonby in the Commons where only months before he had been pleased to censure the Foreign Secretary's deviousness. MacNeill was bold enough to claim that Grey had taken Parliament more into his confidence than any other previous holder of his post![2] As Grey's critics rushed to acknowledge both his and their change of heart, there was much public recantation of former opinions. Such sudden enthusiasm, so much repentance and forgiveness—it was all a little too much like a revivalist meeting. But should the Radicals ever doubt the reality of Grey's sudden metamorphosis, the image the Foreign Secretary projected in the Commons was of a man lightened of an intolerable burden. Where formerly he had been humourless and grave, now he was cheerful and self-confident. He triumphantly brandished in public his commitment to the ideal of the European Concert. Nor did the Second Balkan War dim this bright refurbished image. Grey's prestige with the Radicals seemed assured. With the Treaty of Bucharest but two days old, the Foreign Secretary went down to the Commons to tell the members that in his opinion the Concert of Europe was firmly established. They need not concern themselves at the adjournment of the Ambassadors' Conference; it merely signified that the delegates, after their strenuous efforts on behalf of peace for the world, were now taking a well-earned holiday. Should members have any apprehensions about the relationships between the Great Powers, they could happily forget them. There no longer existed any differences that might persuade the Powers to once more occupy hostile groups.[3]

Grey's conversion seemed complete. However, his Labour critics were less easily convinced than the Radical Liberals that the Foreign Secretary had changed his ways. It was true, *New Age* admitted, that Sir Edward had developed his skill for negotiations in the last eighteen months.

> But his defects . . . still cling to him. His skill does not extend beyond the limits of mediocrity . . . bold strokes of policy . . . . at critical moments are beyond his abilities altogether. . . . All his good qualities as an English gentleman do not compensate for his lack of diplomatic training and his lack of knowledge of foreign affairs.[4]

Such an uncharitable view of Grey was too soon dismissed by the Radicals. If they were unreserved in their approval of Grey, *Labour Leader* suggested some uncomfortable thoughts as to the price

[1] *Hansard*, v:53:373.   [2] *Ibid.*, v:53:402.
[3] *Ibid.*, v:56:2281ff.   [4] *New Age*, 14 Aug. 1913, p. 447.

Britain would have to pay 'for the roses that are strewn about Grey's feet for saving Europe from calamity'. Grey's triumph was bought by doing Russia's will.

> The truth of the matter is that neither France nor England dare say 'Boo' to Russia. On France she is forcing an obnoxious extension of military service. She is compelling England to do her dirty work in Persia and to dispose the Balkan territories to suit Russian views. She offers nothing in return to other countries.[1]

Labour critics always attached undue significance to Britain's relations with Russia. Concerned as they were primarily with the problem of militarism, they could not ignore the ever-increasing burden of armaments. While there was no evidence of slackening in that particular race they were not disposed to believe Grey's easy assurances that all was well with relations between the Great Powers.

The Radicals too easily concluded that Grey had at last adopted their policies; that the concept of the Triple Entente versus the Triple Alliance and the wicked doctrine of the Balance of Power were now things of the past. If the public tone of Britain's diplomacy would seem to have changed, in reality her foreign policy was still committed to those same principles that had operated since the Liberals first came into power in December 1905. Grey had not adjusted the fundamental postulates of his policy. The ties between London, Paris and St Petersburg remained as tight and as exclusive as ever. Despite public avowals, both by the Prime Minister and the Foreign Secretary, advertising Britain's free hand in the event of war—the possibility of engaging or disengaging with any group of Powers—the military and naval obligations shared by France and Britain meant that England's fortunes were bound to be involved in any future European conflict. If the Radicals took Asquith's and Grey's assurances at their face value, Labour critics did not. *New Age* pointed out, with evident satisfaction, that the Radicals were merely deluding themselves if they thought they at last had brought the Foreign Secretary to heel. If one considered the *spirit* as opposed to the language in which statements about Britain's free hand were made, it was patent they did not contain an atom of truth. But, was there any alternative course available? 'In the present state of European tension we have no other means of looking after our interests, no option but to discuss defensive measures in the Triple Entente in the same way as we have entered a definite agreement with France in regard to the Mediterranean.'[2] *Labour Leader*

[1] *Labour Leader*, 5 June 1913.   [2] *New Age*, 18 June 1914, p. 148.

analysing the cause of tension in Europe maintained the only possible solution was to bridge the gulf between the Triple Alliance and Triple Entente. 'As long as we maintain our present close relationship with France, inevitably we are less friendly towards Germany. When is a statesman going to arise who is capable of creating a Triple Federation of Germany, Great Britain and France?'[1] The Radicals believed that Grey, now he had abjured his former heresies, was such a man. Labour critics were not convinced. They believed there had been no significant change and that Germany remained the prime target of the Foreign Office's hostility, concern and suspicion.

Why were the Radicals so readily deluded? Hopes not facts were the currency of much of their political thinking. Rational and moral sensibilities were too soon blunted or soothed by diplomatic language that foreswore the vocabulary of balance of power politics and tended consciences with talk of loyalty and moral obligation rather than alliances and military and naval dispositions. In truth, it was a gigantic exercise in equivocation and mutual self-deception. Nowhere is this better or more clearly illustrated than by the public statements made by informed men on military matters. It was as though men would draw back from the logical conclusion of the course of events which in large part they were responsible for putting in train.

Esher, as well informed as any man about the Committee of Imperial Defence, better able than most to appreciate the strategical significance of that Committee's decisions in 1911 subsequently accepted by the Cabinet and underlined by Asquith's ministerial shuffle at the Admiralty, now busied himself with the attempted resurrection of the Fisher school of strategy. He wrote to Spender:

> We can only act as a European Power by means of our fleet; and that if France expects us to send an army, and if any British Government contemplates doing this, we require 'compulsion' in order to provide the forces necessary . . . we should disclaim publicly all military responsibility for our friend's policy and action.[2]

Esher, adopting the pseudonym 'An Islander', publicised his views, and the Radical Press seized upon them quoting them with approval. Spender also played his part, upbraiding 'The Fog in Whitehall' and declaring: 'We do not want our policy to be deflected to European

[1] *Labour Leader*, 30 Apr. 1914.
[2] *E.P.*, iii, 123–4.

issues. . . . We want to concentrate on our Empire . . . keep our fleet supreme and our hands free'.[1]

When Roberts's conscriptionists beat loud upon their drum, Seely, bolder than his predecessor at the War Office had ever been, instructed the assembled Commons that Britain's army was concerned exclusively with the needs of her Empire. Members could profitably 'leave out of account thoughts of whether England would or would not be engaged in any continental enterprises'.[2] *The Nation* comforted its readers telling them that conscriptionists' delusions about British involvement in a military campaign in Europe were of no importance—that particular aberration had already been discussed by the Cabinet and set aside.[3] In any event, the climate of general opinion was fixedly opposed to the idea of a British army in the continental sense of that word. Britain was a sea Power. The Navy was the proper object of the nation's pride and concern; it would always suffice for Britain's defence. Those who thought otherwise could be ignored. They were but a few mad militarists intent to force conscription upon an unwilling people. Nor need men concern themselves with the *raison d'être* of Britain's puny expeditionary force. How could such a small body ever influence a continental conflict? The evidence of the past forty years clearly indicated that, with technological advance, modern war had become a matter of swift dispatch. Wars were now won or lost in a matter of weeks. The military 'expert' of the *Manchester Guardian*, in the space of two articles published in February 1914, conclusively proved that the British Expeditionary Force would need four and a half months to mobilise and to be transported to fight in any continental theatre of war. By then the fighting would be over. Readers were expected to draw comfort from this conclusion.[4] *New Age*, which took considerable and informed interest in military matters, was equally convinced that 'even a comparatively small force of 100,000 men would be an effective and important element' that 'might well turn the scales'. The French and British staffs had already 'prepared all their plans' for the swift mobilisation of British troops 'to fight in the neighbourhood of Namur and Liège' against 'German troops coming through Belgium'.[5] But such uncomfortable forecasts were to be discounted when they came from a journal that with Hyndman had long advocated the formation of a citizen army.

Apparent deliverance from the dreaded certainty attached to the

[1] *Westminster Gazette*, 12 April 1913.   [2] *Hansard*, v:51:1580.
[3] *The Nation*, 3 May 1913.   [4] *Manchester Guardian*, 13 and 16 Feb, 1914.
[5] *New Age*, 10 Apr. 1913, p. 545.

balance of power theory only seemed to increase men's myopic view of the world. At least the discomforts of confusion could more easily be banished. Radicals loudly asserted the sanctity of the European Concert and demanded peace, retrenchment and reform. They shut their ears to the continued Tory cry for arms; derided the idea that the strength of the Triple Entente and the Balance of Power had been the best security for peace. Pacifists assured themselves that they were a growing force in the modern world and that they could not any longer be ignored. International Socialism spoke of the unity of the proletariat. No more would workers kill their brothers to satisfy the lust for glory of princes and kings. In Britain, the forces gathering for civil strife in Ireland were a more immediate source of concern and potential peril than the enmities engendered by European factions. Against this shifting and confusing background the Liberal Government seemed to drift purposeless declaiming, 'Wait and See' —as though out of tumult, a growing certainty, an awful apprehension that struggled to be recognised, might somehow be stilled. More than confusion filled the minds of men and Governments. There was a dread that they did not wish to apprehend, a fear they could not bring themselves to articulate. The European sky was clouded with ominous portents. In his diary Henry Nevinson found himself repeatedly recording: 'Vague sense of danger all day without any definite reason.' His nights were haunted by a recurring nightmare from which he 'would wake with the cry of "War!" and feel a melancholy cast over all [his] day'.[1]

Balance or concert?

Though there had been a welcome relaxation in Anglo-German relations, there were sufficient uncomfortable signs to indicate to even the most optimistic Radicals that all was still far from well with Europe. The German army had been considerably enlarged. If this might be excused by growing French chauvinism and Russian military preparations, the Zabern incident in the autumn of 1913 and the subsequent acquittal of the miscreants, even after the Reichstag had censured the Government, was lively proof of the strength of the German militarist lobby. Radicals had always been concerned about the 'Prussian' spirit in the conduct of Germany's affairs. But in March 1914 *The Nation* was prepared to admit that with the growing military might of France and Russia gathering upon Germany's borders, 'the Prussian military caste' would have been

[1] Nevinson, 284.

'less than human if they did not dream of anticipating this crushing accumulation of force'.[1] The Radicals uneasily reminded themselves that more than forty years had elapsed since the annexation of Alsace and Lorraine, and still it remained an incendiary and refractory political problem. No matter how much the Alsatians and the Lorrainers might desire to be a bridge rather than a ditch between Germany and France, they were a 'permanent possible cause of war between the two Great Powers'. The only viable solution 'fruitful in blessings for the world at large is an accommodation, a mutual understanding between the French and the Germans, and even the most optimistic commentators would not suppose this a likely contingency in the present atmosphere of mutual suspicion and barely bridled hostility'.[2]

Since the Agadir incident in 1911, an important feature of the European scene had been the significant growth in French national pride and self confidence. The French now showed more impatience and were markedly less tolerant towards German threats and pin pricks. To Radical observers, the political situation in France was one moment cause for hope and the next cause for despair. Though Caillaux and Jaurès were still forces to be reckoned with in French political life, the rising spirit of nationalism and revanchism first questioned, then rejected any idea of pursuing a conciliatory policy towards Germany.

Though the Radicals were anxious about the state of Franco-German relations, and constantly asserted that the best hope for a stable Europe was a Triple Entente embracing Britain, Germany and France, during the last year of peace, most discomfort and concern was shown for Russia, the third partner in Grey's entente policy. The optimism had long been dissipated of those Radicals who at one time had tempered their compatriots' criticisms of the Romanov régime by hopefully pointing to signs of a growing democratic impetus in Russia. Far from nascent democracy growing in strength encouraged by contact with Liberal Britain, Russia seemed more deeply sunk than ever in a slough of reaction. Had they wished to forget Russia and her diplomatic ties with Britain, the Radicals could not. New developments in Persia, and more particularly the Admiralty's scheme to gain control of the Anglo-Persian Oil Company, meant that Britain was becoming increasingly involved in the neutral zone where the richest oil fields were sited. The logical conclusion of this policy seemed to be that Britain would eventually join with Russia in absorbing the buffer zone and dividing Persia into

---

[1] *The Nation*, 21 Mar. 1914.   [2] *Concord*, Dec. 1913, pp. 118–19.

two parts. Britain in Persia daily more closely reflected Russia's policy. Ponsonby bitterly regretted that Britain in conducting her foreign policy should choose to take a leaf out of Russia's book.[1] The tragedy of British policy was that Russian compliance would one day assuredly have to be purchased by a very heavy indemnity. No statesman would ever consider the Russians to be men of their word. They had contravened both the intention and spirit of the 1907 convention. Far from withdrawing from their zone of influence in North Persia, they were intensifying the process of Russification. Why, asked the Radicals, didn't Grey sever his connections with the Russians? What value was there in joining with the Tsar? *New Age* insisted the only explanation was that Grey was terrified that if he did not support Russia and do her will, then the Triple Entente would be sundered and Russia would join Germany.[2] This estimate of the situation was not far from the truth.

Though the primary aim of Lloyd George's interview, published in the *Daily Chronicle* on New Year's Day 1914, undoubtedly had been to embarrass Churchill, it also cast doubt upon the major postulates of Britain's foreign policy. The Chancellor seemed entirely to discount the German 'menace'. As such, his remarks provoked concern, anger and suspicion in the French and Russian Press. Grey also was angered by Lloyd George's essay into his territory. It could so easily be interpreted as the prelude to Britain betraying her continental friends. The Chancellor's suggestion that England should capitalise on a situation where France and Russia had to match Germany's military might while she slackened her naval building commitment, struck at the very roots of the doctrine of the balance of power. If England relaxed her naval efforts, then Germany could be expected to increase military pressure upon France and Russia. So far as Triple Entente enthusiasts were concerned, the balance between the two opposed groups of alliances would only remain so long as Britain maintained her major naval building programme. It followed that for them British naval policy was not the expression of an independent defensive force, but an important part of the equation between the military might of the Triple Alliance and the Dual Entente. By this token, Grey had every reason to be angry with Lloyd George, and the Chancellor deserved the rebuke administered him by the Foreign Secretary in a speech at Manchester on 3 February. At that particular juncture in European affairs, Grey did not welcome any doubts being cast upon Britain's loyalty to her

[1] *Hansard*, v:63:1176.
[2] *New Age*, 5 June, p. 132; 16 Apr. 1914, p. 741.

entente partners. The inevitable sequel to such doubts would be for France or Russia to seek reassurances of Britain's good faith. The possibility was that they might well seek tangible tokens as proof of Britain's reliability.

For the moment, estimates of Russia's intentions, rather than any fear of Germany, occupied the foreground of British diplomatic concern. Cabinet ministers, and not least Grey, had always been unduly impressed with Russia's might—her leadership of the Slav peoples, the overwhelming size of her army and the vast potential of her material resources. Reports from Ambassador Buchanan into London, and the constant and determined efforts of Grey's senior Foreign Office advisers, tended to inflate the vision of Russia's greatness. Russia also benefited from the unspoken but understood threat that if England's support should prove uncertain, she could always join hands with Germany. Nicolson was concerned that Grey did not seem prepared to go far enough to accommodate the Russians. He wrote to Buchanan: 'I am haunted by the same fear as you—lest Russia become tired of us and strike a bargain with Germany.' Nicolson's recurring nightmare was that Russia, which daily grew to be 'a more formidable power in European politics', might desert to the German camp. He believed that almost any price ought to be paid to avoid that contingency.[1] He was concerned that Grey seemed to have been deluded by the part recently played by Germany in the accommodation over the Balkans. It appeared that Grey, while not wishing to weaken the existing ties of the entente, wanted at the same time to conciliate the Germans. To Nicolson, such a policy was not only contradictory but its outcome would in the end prove disastrous for Britain.

The Russians worked away at Grey through Sazonov and Buchanan. They desired the Triple Entente's conversion into a defensive alliance. Russia argued that if only Britain was definitely committed, then Vienna and Berlin would shrink from facing such formidable odds and at last the peace of Europe would be secured. The Russians were anxious that Britain wished only to play the 'fair-weather friend' with them; that if war broke out with Germany, England would stand idly by. Buchanan sympathised with the Russian point of view and passed on their worries to Grey. At the same time, however, he pointed out to the Russians that a Liberal Government was not likely to change its policy. As though to underline this claim, Grey in March talked to the Commons about Britain retaining her attachment to the good understandings that now existed with

[1] See Steiner, 137–8.

Russia and France, but he hastened to assure his audience that this did not imply converting understandings into 'hard and fast alliances with hard and fast obligations'. Grey insisted Great Britain would continue to depend upon her own resources to protect her vital interests.[1] The Russians were undeterred by Grey's statement, and continued to maintain pressure upon him.

On a visit to England in September 1912 Sazonov had sounded out Grey about the possibilities of an Anglo-Russian naval convention. The Russian Foreign Minister's overture had not been successful on that occasion. Nor had Grey given Sazonov any encouragement to suppose that at a later date such a convention would be welcomed. When the Tsar himself suggested, at the beginning of April 1914, that a defensive alliance should be signed between the two Powers, Buchanan had condemned the proposal as impracticable. It was at this stage that a naval arrangement, similar to that between England and France, was again mooted. Despite assurances by his Foreign Office advisers that such an agreement was desirable, Grey hesitated. He would have preferred any discussions to be deferred as long as possible. At the same time he recognised, should he refuse conversations for a naval arrangement with the Russians, they might well get the impression that they were not being treated upon equal terms with the French.[2] It is not to be supposed that Grey's reluctance was in any way a rejection of the broad principles of the policy he had pursued ever since taking up office in December 1905. Though unpopular with much of his own party and a considerable element in the Tory ranks, the Russian understanding was one of the two linchpins of Grey's overall strategy. The Russians had always been difficult partners, awkward and uncompromising people to negotiate with and ready breakers of promises and pledges. Russian conduct in their sphere of influence in Persia had caused Grey nothing but trouble in the Commons. As late as 29 June 1914, Grey admitted to the House his dissatisfaction with the conduct of the Russians in Persia. On that occasion he went so far as to threaten Benckendorff with a revision of the 1907 agreement and Buchanan was instructed to speak sharply to Sazonov. However, more immediate problems then had emerged to engage the attention of the diplomatists.[3] In the international crisis of July 1914 as in the Liman von Sanders incident, Grey was to reiterate, 'We cannot turn our backs upon Russia'.[4] How long Grey would have continued to prevaricate over

[1] *Hansard*, v:59:2186–90.   [2] See Grey, i, 284.
[3] *Hansard*, v:64:53ff., and 1383ff.; and *B.D.*, x,ii, 547 and 552.
[4] *B.D.* x,i, 407.

talks with the Russians is an interesting but otiose question. Due to pressure from the French, when Grey visited Paris with King George in April, the possibility of a naval agreement between England and Russia was the major topic of the Foreign Secretary's talks.

April 1914 marked the tenth anniversary of the entente between France and England. Here was afforded an opportunity, not to be ignored by supporters of the idea of the Triple Entente, to campaign for a tightening of the diplomatic and military bonds between the three Powers. *The Times* was to be the foremost publicity agent for this task. With the approval of the Foreign Office, *The Times* invited Ernest Lavisse, the eminent French historian, to contribute a letter for publication to mark the anniversary and to stress the importance of the Triple Entente and the balance of power as the safeguards of European peace. Entente enthusiasts had some cause for concern because for the last three years relations between France and Britain had not been particularly cordial. It was true that the bonds of the entente remained comparatively unimpaired, but one could not ignore France's disposition at the conclusion of the Balkan Wars to pursue a policy towards Turkey independent of Britain's. It was patent that Britain could not support the policies of both France and Russia in the Near East. Therefore, in the spring of 1914, there was sufficient reason for concern among those, like *The Times*, who had supported and propagandised the view that peace in Europe depended upon an equilibrium of Triple Alliance and Triple Entente. As a prologue to Lavisse's letter, *The Times* prepared a leading article clearly stating their case entitled, 'A Bulwark of Peace'.

> The division of the Great Powers into two well-balanced groups with intimate relations between the members of each . . . is a check upon inordinate ambitions. . . . All . . . know that a war of group against group would be a measureless calamity. That knowledge brings with it a sense of responsibility which chastens and restrains the boldest and the most reckless. . . . They are no longer unfettered judges in their own cause, answerable to none but to themselves.[1]

A week later, Lavisse's letter was published, together with strong supporting editorial comment. Lavisse expressed the anxiety of many Frenchmen that perhaps British public opinion was less firm than formerly it had been in its support of the entente policy. While not overtly mentioning the transformation of the entente into an

[1] *The Times*, 8 Apr. 1914.

alliance, Lavisse made it clear he considered the present arrangements between the two countries dangerously incomplete.[1]

The Radicals naturally were concerned by the pressure being exerted to turn the agreements between France, Britain and Russia into a military alliance. They would have no truck with such ideas and earnestly advised the Government not even to contemplate the suggestion. The *Manchester Guardian* dismissed the whole concept of the Triple Entente as no more than 'a slovenly piece of diplomatic jargon'.[2] Rather than tighten the bonds of a group that embraced autocratic Russia, the Government ought to exert all its efforts to bring Germany in as a partner with France. This would afford the best possible and only guarantee of lasting peace in Europe.[3] G. H. Perris published in *Concord* an open letter in reply to Lavisse's— 'Entente or Alliance? And for What?' It was to be the last major statement of the 'old pacifist' attitude before war engulfed Europe.

> Of the major events of . . . [the last twenty-five years] I will name only these: For good, the old enmity of England and France is buried, and England has turned from imperial conquest to domestic reform; for ill, the Franco-German feud remains, the Armed Peace has become an incredible monstrosity, and the despotism of the Russian Tsars has been saved by French money and British patronage. There is one other change which must be taken into account. . . . Without the pacifists there would have been no Entente Cordiale. Today, we have several Pacifist Governments among the Great Powers; and everywhere the idea of international democratic union has to be reckoned with.

Perris's optimistic and quite unrealistic estimate of the strength of pacifism, was to be expected. The root of the pacifist case, their statement of intentions and hope, had not altered one wit since 1905 when they had welcomed Campbell-Bannerman's Government in the belief that salvation for the world was just around the corner. Perris censured Lavisse:

> We dreamed and still dream of a League of Peace. Enmity towards Germany is most certainly not a 'common sentiment' between England and France. . . . Why do you desire to convert the Entente into an Alliance, the nucleus of a League of Peace into an aggravation of existing military feuds? Why not say plainly, Monsieur, that the Entente has given Morocco to France, has confirmed England's hold upon Egypt, and has strengthened Russia's hold upon Central Asia and Persia?

[1] *The Times*, 16 Apr. 1914.   [2] *Manchester Guardian*, 23 Apr. 1914.
[3] See *The Nation*, 18 Apr. 1914.

Is it just or even business-like to grudge the small 'compensations' which Germany, Austria and Italy have received? Do you think of obtaining other Moroccos without allowing compensation? This prospect does not appeal to us, and still less does a closer association with the men now in power in Russia. . . . To support an Alliance would be a betrayal of the vital principle of British policy. . . . We will endeavour to pursue the aims of the Entente Cordiale as we originally conceived it, not trusting much to the mandarins on either side, but finding in the steady rise of democratic intelligence everywhere the great hope of the future.[1]

If the pacifist view of European affairs was unrealistic, the Labour Press seemed barely aware that anything was happening in foreign affairs. They were too busily engrossed in their own personal fortunes to afford more than an occasional cursory glance at the European scene. The promised diplomatic junketings in Paris with the royal visit aroused little response. Of course Labour wished for good relations between France and Britain, but not at the price of closer ties with Russia. With unintended humour, *Labour Leader* suggested the pattern of European relationships should mirror the unity of international socialism.[2] *New Age* poured scorn on all the talk of 'joy, mutual interests and peace for the world' occasioned by the anniversary of the *entente cordiale*. Readers were assured, this was no more than the Establishment's response to fears that the 'pro-German party in Russia are setting out to break up the Triple Entente'.[3]

The royal visitors to Paris, with their diplomatic entourage, were afforded a warm welcome by the French. At a formal banquet, French President and English King toasted one another and one another's countries. *The Times* applauded the speeches and quoted with approval Poincaré's reference to the entente as 'a pillar of European equilibrium'.[4] The *Daily News* was distressed by this 'questionable phrase'. 'All good Liberals have strenuously resisted this notion of equilibrium; the conception of the entente as designed to guarantee the balance of power contradicts violently the conception of the entente as only the first and the model of a series of understandings to embrace all the other Great Powers.'[5] *New Age* laughed at, 'the flatulent organ of the cocoa trade talking its usual twaddle, the Radicals as usual deluding themselves'. Of course 'the 1904 agreement very naturally gave birth to an entente of more

[1] *Concord*, May 1914, pp. 27–8.   [2] *Labour Leader*, 30 Apr. 1914.
[3] *New Age*, 16 Apr. 1914, p. 741.   [4] *The Times*, 23 Apr. 1914.
[5] *Daily News*, 23 Apr. 1914.

general character which has since become the surest guarantee of the balance of power in Europe'.[1]

On the last morning of that April visit to Paris, Grey was invited to the Quai d'Orsay where he conversed with Doumergue, the French Prime Minister. Cambon and Bertie were also present. The French were obviously anxious that Britain should accommodate the Russian desire for naval talks. The French had more to fear and more to lose than England from Russian duplicity. They were therefore concerned that the ties between London and St Petersburg should be made as secure as possible. Grey, in his memoirs, asked himself the question 'What was the motive of the French Government?'[2] The Foreign Secretary's conclusions show an extraordinary naïvety. He admitted that Russo-British naval conversations were intended as a further provision for a war with Germany, but believed the French 'at the time . . . had no thought of aggression . . . The idea of *revanche*—of retaking Alsace and Lorraine—though not publicly disowned, had been tacitly given up.' The explanation Grey favoured was that the French 'simply desire[d] to reassure Russia and to keep her loyal'. As to the political value of military and naval conversations, Grey admits that the French might have magnified the importance of the Franco-British military conversations to the Russians.[3] However, even Grey could not have been so simple-minded as not to realise that the political implications of military or naval conversations between Powers were immeasurably their most important feature. The Russians certainly stressed the political importance of conversations with Britain. Isvolsky reported his astonishment 'at Sir Edward Grey's clearly and definitely expressed readiness to tread the path of a closer approach to Russia'. Sazonov could barely contain his satisfaction with the conversations, not because of their military value but their 'great importance . . . from a general political point of view'. Benckendorff summed up the situation in a report to St Petersburg: 'I doubt whether any better guarantee for joint military operations in the event of war could be found than the spirit of this Entente, as it now reveals itself, strengthened by the existing military agreements'.[4] Here was the real basis of the Franco-Russian desire for Britain to engage in naval conversations with the Russians, and Grey was not so much the credulous simpleton, as he makes out, not to have recognised as much from the beginning.

Grey, at his meeting with Gaston Doumergue, had agreed to seek

<hr/>

[1] *New Age*, 30 Apr. 1914, p. 806.   [2] Grey, i, 285.   [3] *Iibd.*, i, 286–7.
[4] See H. Lutz, *Lord Grey and the World War* (1928), 180–1.

Asquith's approval for naval conversations with the Russians. On 2 May, members of the Cabinet received a record of Grey's talks in Paris.

> We should communicate to the Russian Government exactly what the state of things was between France and ourselves. We might let them know of the note that I had given to M. Cambon, and of the conversations that had taken place between the Military and Naval Staffs. Russia would thus be able to see exactly how things stood, and what scope was left for any conversations with her. She would understand that both the French and British Governments were left entirely free to decide whether, in case of war, they would support one another or not.[1]

On 12 May the Cabinet discussed the possibility of Anglo-Russian naval conversations. They approved the manner in which Grey had spoken to Doumergue, and expressed their agreement with the idea of naval talks, provided they were covered by the Grey–Cambon letters of November 1912 'which explained . . . the exact extent of our obligations and intentions in the event of a war of provocation or aggression being directed against France'.[2] Subsequently, at a meeting with Cambon and Benckendorff, Grey handed copies of the letters to the Russian Ambassador. At the same time he told Benckendorff that there was no question of military conversations between Russia and Britain. While emphasising Britain's 'free-hand', Grey said that if the British army should ever be involved in a continental engagement then troops would be allocated to the frontiers of France. These observations by Grey were quite unnecessary. The least gifted amateur strategist would have known that there was no possibility of the small British Expeditionary Force being used to reinforce Russia's massive land forces. Grey recognised there was little or no strategic value in naval conversations with the Russians. Reports from the British naval attaché had made plain that the Russian Baltic Fleet was a negligible force.[3] Both Grey and Benckendorff knew that talk of troop or fleet dispositions was mere window dressing. The crucial feature of the conversations was their political implication.

The Cabinet received a full record of Grey's conversations. On this evidence it cannot be claimed that the Radical members of the Cabinet were not informed of the nature of Britain's attachment both to France and Russia. They seem to have assumed that as long as these relationships were limited to Staff talks, and as long as these

---

[1] *B.D.* **x**, ii, 541.   [2] Cabinet Letter, 14 May 1914.
[3] See Marder, 309–10.

in their turn were governed by the 1912 exchange of letters between Cambon and Grey, then Great Britain's options at a time of possible conflict remained open. In effect, their attitude was a complete reversal of that more realistic one they had adopted towards Staff talks in 1911. Then, they 'had regarded the conversations as a grave indeed dangerous innovation; by 1914 they were viewed as a convenient political expedient which could be sanctioned in a single session, even when the suppliant was a Romanov'.[1]

It was not long before news reached the Wilhelmstrasse that Russia and Britain were contemplating naval conversations. Von Stumm, informed of the diplomatic preliminaries by a member of the staff of the Russian embassy in London, gave the secret to Theodor Wolff, editor of the *Berliner Tageblatt*. The Germans hoped that the object of the talks might be thwarted if they were exposed to unwanted publicity. The first article on the Anglo-Russian talks appeared on 22 May. Wolff emphasised that the contemplated arrangement could only be aimed at Germany, that it would nullify the progress that had been made towards better Anglo-German relations, and would afford German chauvinists a powerful argument for demanding further increases in Germany's naval strength. In a further article published on 2 June, Wolff appealed directly to British Liberals. They must thwart the talks if the movement for reconciliation between Germany and Britain was to be preserved and prosper.[2] Wolff's accurate exposé and his appeal did not go unnoticed.

On 11 June Byles and King, those same Radicals who had questioned Asquith in March 1913, and who then had been informed that there were no unpublished military or naval obligations which might hamper the Government's freedom,[3] now asked Grey 'whether any naval agreement has recently been entered into between Russia and Great Britain, and whether any negotiations with a view to a naval agreement, have recently taken place, or are now pending, between Russia and Great Britain?' Grey assured his questioners, what the Prime Minister had said a year earlier was still true.

> No negotiations have since been concluded with any Power that would make the statement less true. No such negotiations are in progress, and none are likely to be entered upon, as far as I can judge. But, if any agreement were to be concluded that made it necessary to withdraw or modify the Prime Minister's statement of last year . . . it ought, in my opinion, to be, and I suppose that it would be, laid before Parliament.[4]

[1] Williamson, 338.   [2] See Hale, 442–3.
[3] *Hansard*, v:50:1316–17.   [4] *Ibid.*, v:63:457–8.

The Foreign Secretary's reply was more than ambiguous; it was not even an answer to the question he had been asked. He deliberately misrepresented the Cabinet's recent decision to sanction talks with the Russians. Grey suggested in his memoirs, as justification for his action, that the engagements between Britain, France and Russia were not political. Yet since 1906 the Liberal Government had used staff talks as a convenient method of satisfying French and now Russian requests for closer political relations. Grey knew that he was misrepresenting the position to the Commons, and all the members of the Cabinet shared the knowledge. Yet not one Radical minister was bold or honest enough to give the lie to the Foreign Secretary's answer.

The rumours of Anglo-Russian conversations had increased the unease with which Radicals viewed Britain's possible entente commitments. 'Why', asked *The Nation*, 'are we always left in doubt to guess the precise nature of the Triple Entente?'[1] The *Manchester Guardian* had already stated that any agreement Britain might come to with Russia in Paris was bound to be mischievous.[2] C. P. Scott, who knew very well the details of the Anglo-French military talks, could not be expected to be satisfied by any ambiguous answer Grey might give to fob off his critics in the Commons. On 12 June the *Guardian*, commenting upon Grey's answer, declared:

> We do not feel satisfied. The natural interpretation of the statement is that there are unpublished agreements, but that they are contingent in their operation either on some future decision of the Executive or of Parliament. . . . These answers do not allay uneasiness. . . . We hope that the questions of yesterday will be followed up by more, in order that we may know exactly where we stand. . . . The secret, in so far as there is one, is a secret from the British Parliament and people, not from any possible enemy.

The next day, Spender in the *Westminster Gazette* repeated the denial that Grey had made in the Commons.[3] However, few Radicals by now could doubt that there was some sort of agreement. *The Nation* said as much, but hopefully added that it would not qualify Britain's freedom in the event of war.[4]

Diplomatic rumblings continued after Grey's statement in the Commons. It would not have been politic for the Germans to call Grey a liar, but Jagow informed Goschen that if the rumours concerning the naval conversations had been true, 'the consequences

[1] *The Nation*, 30 May 1914.   [2] *Manchester Guardian*, 23 May 1914.
[3] *Westminster Gazette*, 13 June 1914.   [4] *The Nation*, 13 June 1914.

would have been most serious'.[1] Jagow was not the sort of man who could allow a matter to rest, and through Lichnowsky he continued to probe Grey on the state of relations between Russia and Britain.[2] Eventually, embarrassed by Lichnowsky's questions, on 9 July, Grey summoned the German Ambassador to the Foreign Office and told him the truth, or at least that version of the truth that best suited his purpose. He admitted the naval and military conversations with France and Russia. However, Grey minimised and obscured their importance by emphatically insisting that they in no way compromised Britain's freedom of action. It had not been the Foreign Secretary's concern what might have passed during these talks. 'The thing which concerned the Government and myself, and which it was necessary for me to keep in our hands, was whether we should or should not participate if a war arose. If we made any Agreement that entailed obligations upon us, it would not be a secret Agreement. I was pledged to Parliament not to make a secret Agreement of this kind'.[3]

Even after Grey's 'admissions' to Lichnowsky, the Germans were still puzzled and uneasy about the true state of Anglo-Russian relations. Both Bethmann-Hollweg and Jagow hoped that Britain would stand aside if Austria interfered with Serbia, and this hope fed upon the expressions of goodwill that Grey continued to extend to the Germans. Grey, wishing to conciliate the Germans, merely buttressed their delusions. The paradox of the situation was that the duality of Grey's statement to Lichnowsky confused the Germans. The Radicals who had been told nothing were not misled, merely bitterly disillusioned and disappointed.

Before Grey had even made his statement to the Commons, *The Nation* had abandoned any idea that there was a Concert operating its benign influence upon affairs in Europe. The present guide of European diplomacy was 'the sinister policy' of the balance of power. Though Russia stood in the van, no one should delude themselves about Britain's rôle. 'Our complicity is evident.'[4] If the Foreign Secretary's statement to the Commons was taken at its face value, one still had to assume

> that the common action of the forces of the entente has been studied, that dispositions have been made on the hypothesis that in certain events there may be common action. . . . These provisions . . . are really as good as most alliances and rather better than some. . . . Our responsibility and our share is direct

[1] *B.D.*, x, ii, 550. [2] *B.D.* xi, 4.
[3] Quoted Williamson, 342. [4] *The Nation*, 6 June 1914.

R A W—N

and heavy in the rivalries which are in progress and in the conflict which they might by mischance unchain.[1]

Only eight days after this pertinent estimate of Britain's obligations had appeared in *The Nation*, Archduke Franz Ferdinand and his wife were assassinated at Sarajevo. In a few short weeks Europe was plunged into the maelstrom of war.

Ambivalent is the only adjective one can choose to describe Radical attitudes to foreign policy in the final year of peace. At the last they were confounded, not by the secret machinations of diplomatists but the contradictions in their own thinking. In the Foreign Office debate in the Commons on 29 June, the temperature was decidedly cool; members were more concerned with Ireland than the problems of the Near East. Almost a month later, Lloyd George was to declare his confidence in the happy state of the relations enjoyed between Germany and Britain. 'The two great Empires begin to realise that they can cooperate for common ends, and that the points of co-operation are greater and more numerous and more important than the points of possible controversy.'[2] A. G. Gardiner had maintained in the *Daily News* that the feud between Britain and Germany alone was responsible for 'the rattle into barbarism'. The security of the world's peace depended upon the ending of that feud and the initiation of a true Triple Alliance of France, Britain and Germany.[3] Were the Chancellor's words a portent that at last the Radical vision would be realised? Was the European alliance system flexible enough to allow the interpenetration of the two blocs of Powers? Radical faith, radical hope, expected, indeed demanded, an affirmative answer. Yet, the Triple Entente not only remained intact but was stronger and more exclusive than ever. Were they in part to blame for this tragic state of affairs? One cannot escape the conclusion that the Radicals at the last count did not wish to search too avidly for the truth lest they discover it. They would criticise Grey, yet in the next instant rush to applaud and defend him. They would censure the idea of the balance of power, yet assent to its practice in the name of the Concert of Europe. In the Cabinet in the last year of peace, Radical members had been reminded in the clearest manner by Grey, of the entente policy's inherent military and naval obligations. They had given Grey their approval, even though he

[1] *The Nation*, 20 June 1914.
[2] *Hansard*, v:65:727.
[3] *Daily News*, 17 Jan. 1914.

acknowledged that Anglo-French military arrangements were concerned with 'hopes of assistance'. Not one minister had asked Grey in what *exact* circumstances would Britain side with France in a war against Germany.

Chapter 10   War: a question of interest or moral obligation?

A minor irritation

Why did Radical members of Parliament, in the summer of 1914, choose to adopt an almost complacent attitude towards questions of foreign policy? This cannot be explained alone in terms of their optimistic political philosophy, their ignorance, or a political naïvety that allowed them readily to accept comfortable assurances made by ministers. It was more a reflection of their desire to be seen to be loyally supporting their Liberal Government at a time when domestic issues dominated politics. Civil war in Ireland was a distinct possibility. British industry was riven by unprecedented discontent. A quarter of a million men under arms in Ireland and an implacable revolutionary ferment which threatened the total disruption of industry, appeared to pose a more direct and immediate threat to Britain's future and the fortunes of the Liberal party than any foreseeable diplomatic contretemps in Europe. Lloyd George, speaking at the Guildhall on 17 July, had assured his audience that should civil strife in Ulster coincide with a strike threatened by the 'Triple Alliance' of railwaymen, miners and transport workers, then 'the situation will be the gravest with which any Government in this country has had to deal for centuries'. Referring to the diplomatic scene, the Chancellor declared that an incident in the Balkans, no matter how regrettable in itself, was no more than a very small cloud upon the horizon, and to be expected, for 'you never get a perfectly blue sky in foreign affairs'. A minor irritation would soon be solved: ' . . . having got out of greater difficulties last year, we feel confident that the common sense, the patience, the goodwill, the forbearance which enabled us to solve greater and more difficult and more urgent problems last year will enable us to pull through these difficulties at the present moment.' Six days later in the Commons, Lloyd George elaborating on his forecast of the temperature in international affairs, assured the House that relations between Germany and Great Britain were better than they had been for years past. The next day Austria delivered her ultimatum to Serbia.

The Radicals endorsed Lloyd George's vision of a peaceful Europe, though in conscience there was reason enough for them still to harbour worries and suspicions about the conduct and content of Britain's foreign policy. But in public at least, they would have it supposed that after the alarums of 1911, the Government, and the Foreign Secretary in particular, had at last heeded their warnings and advice. Grey, they assured themselves, had 'done a great deal towards meeting them', and for the moment they were prepared to accept this as an argument, or at least an indication, that in time the rest of their wishes would be satisfied.[1]

There was little reason for the Radicals to suppose they had exerted any influence on the Foreign Secretary. In the House he remained as loath to answer questions and as uninformative as ever. If there was cause for satisfaction with the manner in which he had handled the successive Balkan crises of 1912 and 1913, the continued growth of Britain's military and naval establishments, under a Government that professed pacific intentions, was a constant reminder that the root causes of friction between the Great Powers had not been removed. Nor had Grey sought to do anything positive to placate or avert Radical and Labour suspicion and dislike of Britain's entente with Tsarist Russia. Rather, Grey had affirmed his attachment to that tyrannous régime. Though he might stress his determination that 'the best possible relations with other countries should be maintained', nevertheless, the friendship of Great Britain with France and Russia remained 'the starting point of any new development in foreign policy'.[2] The Radicals had constantly emphasised their aversion to any notion of 'continuity' in the conduct of foreign affairs; they stressed the differences in moral content and approach between a Liberal and a Tory view of foreign policy. However, Bonar Law and Balfour made a point of frequently informing the Commons that they not only wholeheartedly approved of the manner in which Grey conducted affairs, but also, that they considered he was pursuing no mere party policy but 'the national policy of Great Britain'. The Tory leaders insisted that when they were returned to power they would continue the policies initiated by Grey.[3] The Radicals might choose to discount as 'jingoistic vapour-

[1] See, for example, Hobhouse to C. P. Scott, 4 June 1913, in Scott, *Diaries*, 89.
[2] *Hansard*, v:40:1994.
[3] See, for example, *Hansard*, v:40:2036 and 56:2297 (Bonar Law); 41:1398 (Balfour).

ings' the insistent assertions by a section of the Press that Britain had
'a binding obligation to assist France by arms', or that 'France has
the power to commit Great Britain to war'; but they could not so
lightly ignore Balfour's frequent references to the Triple Entente as
an alliance, or his spelling out of the implication that any member of
the entente could expect to receive the aid of the other members if
they were ever attacked by the Central Powers. Balfour made no
secret of his conviction that the diplomatic situation meant that
war between any two Great Powers must inevitably involve all the
others. All the leading Unionist spokesmen on foreign, military and
naval affairs, subscribed to the same view. The argument had been
repeated too consistently, too often and too confidently for the
Radicals to dismiss it easily as nothing more than a Jingo puff.[1] Cecil
was not overstating the case when, in questioning Asquith, he declared
that it was 'a very general belief' that England was under an
'obligation' to support France in arms.[2]

If it is argued that the Tories had talked like this for years, it
is strange that it was not until the last twelve months before the
outbreak of war that the Radicals chose to believe ministerial
disclaimers of Tory 'interpretations' of the entente policy. Until
then the Radicals had urged that the inevitable result of the course
to which Grey was committed was to divide Europe into two armed
camps. This had been the constant burden of Ponsonby's arguments.[3]
However, this most persistent and knowledgeable critic of Grey's
policy, in 1913 and 1914 abjured his former beliefs and declared to
the Commons his conviction that the idea of a balance of power had
been replaced in Europe by a concert of the Powers. If this estimate
was based on the apparent détente between Germany and Great
Britain, then it was based on slim evidence indeed. However,
Ponsonby was prepared to affirm, in May 1913, that 'the former
pernicious policy of dividing Europe into two camps . . . has been
abandoned, and I hope abandoned for good'. In mid-July 1914, he
reaffirmed this optimistic estimate when comparing the present
state of Europe with the situation at the time of the Agadir incident.
'[In 1911] the policy of the balance of power was being very strongly

---

[1] For Press, see, *inter alia, Candid Quarterly*, May 1914, i, 389; *The Spectator*,
cxi, 344; *Fortnightly Review*, xcviii, 793. See also F. R. Flournoy, *Parliament
and War* (1927), 208–9.

For speeches of Tories on this theme, see, *inter alia, Hansard*, v:41:865–6
(Balfour); 40:1341 and 1935 (Amery and Ronaldshay); 41:1226, 1281 and
1469 (Middlemore, Kinloch-Cooke and Peel); 51:141 (Parker); 59:2165, 2192
and 2197 (Sykes, Beresford and Lee).

[2] *Hansard*, v:50:42.

[3] See, for example, *Hansard*, v:1411–14.

supported. . . . Then came . . . the Balkans and things changed. The
policy of the balance of power was exchanged for concerted action
among the Powers.'[1]

Ponsonby was an informed critic of foreign affairs. The ordinary
backbench member might be excused for thinking of the European
situation and the possibility of war solely in terms of the relationships
of the Western Powers and to ignore Austria. But the well-informed
had long feared a conflict between Austria and Russia in the Near
East, for Austria was as keen to preserve the *status quo* there as
Russia was to change it. The Balkan wars appeared to bring Germany
and Britain closer together, but at the same time it 'kindled the
antagonism between St Petersburg and Vienna'.[2] One cannot escape
the conclusion that Grey's Radical critics, disheartened by their
frequent and resounding defeats whenever they had been bold enough
to challenge the Government, now were obliged to adopt a blinkered,
passive rôle.

Not all Radicals were satisfied with the conduct of 'the friends of
peace and economy in the House of Commons'. A few declared their
dissatisfaction at the tenth National Peace Conference, but the main
burden of their censure was directed against the failing campaign
against militarism.

> The advocates of peace have too often regarded militarism as
> merely stupid, and conquest as an illusion. Conquest—the
> conquest of the people by their exploiters—is going on all the
> time. Militarism is the systematic exploitation of the supersti-
> tion of the many to serve the greed of a few. We must compel
> our MPs to go forward faster. They are too easily pleased.

G. H. Perris, the author of this statement, returned to the same topic
in the last number of *Concord* to appear before the outbreak of war.
Why was it, asked Perris, when pacifism was a growing force in the
country it was 'flickering out on Parliament'? He argued that Radical
members in Parliament were not fighting for the cause of peace as
stoutly as they might because they were 'hampered by party
obligations. The peace of the North Seas and the welfare of the
British poor is being risked to satisfy old superstitions.' However,
Perris significantly admitted that he saw no way immediately to
salve the situation.[3]

Generally, however, among pacifist and Radical groups in the
early summer of 1914, there were few voices that openly declared
discontent, suspicion or concern with the international scene. On

---

[1] *Hansard*, v: 53:374 and 64:1397.   [2] Gooch, *Under Six Reigns*, 169.
[3] See *Concord*, July 1914, p. 76.

the contrary, they emphasised the reasons for their optimistic estimate of Europe's immediate future. From 1911 to 1913 there had been a series of crises, each successfully overcome. The Moroccan question had been settled; the Balkan wars were over and done. Their greatest cause for concern had always been relations between Germany and Great Britain. Now the two Powers enjoyed a better understanding than at any time during the past decade. Agreement at last had been reached over the Baghdad Railway; Lichnowsky, popular and a known admirer of England, as German Ambassador to London emphasised the common interests of Germany and Britain in peace, as did the Anglophil German Chancellor, Bethmann-Hollweg. In July, *The Arbitrator* 'confidently' predicted that 'an agreement of the closest character' would very soon be announced between Germany and Britain.[1] If it had failed and disappointed in many things, at least one could be certain that a Liberal Government would never commit Britain to a major war.

A gala dinner at the Holborn Restaurant in London, had been the main event organised by the National Peace Council to celebrate Peace Day, 1914. The assembled company were assured by the chairman, the Radical M.P., Gordon Harvey, that never had they met amid happier auguries. 'It is', he said 'my conviction that among the Great Powers there has never before been a greater desire for friendly understanding than there is at the present.' Other speakers were happy to confirm this estimate. If there was cause for concern, then most certainly it was not with the actions and attitudes of the diplomatists. The enemies of a peaceful world were undoubtedly the armament manufacturers. Now that the nefarious designs of these 'war traders' had been so effectively exposed by the Radical Press, it was only reasonable to suppose that their influence on affairs would wither. It could not be denied that the establishment of universal brotherhood would require a force of faith as yet unrevealed. But men of all nations were gradually realising the wickedness and the futility of the present prostitution of their energies and the wasting of their substance on engines of destruction that brought profit to a few and sorrow to many.

At the annual meeting of the National Peace Society, the chairman, J. A. Pease, Quaker and member of the Asquith Cabinet, concluded his general remarks on the futility of war with a direct reference to Anglo-German relations. 'As peace has never been broken between Great Britain and Germany I see no reason why it should ever be broken. Any differences that might arise and that

---

[1] *The Arbitrator*, July 1914, p. 81.

cannot be settled by negotiation, there always remains international arbitration.' The meeting agreed there was every reason to suppose that friendly relations between Germany and Great Britain were very firmly established, and it was Grey who was to echo this profound optimism and belief in the efficacy of simple remedies when he told fellow guests at the Foreign Press Association Dinner on 19 May that 'all that is necessary for the peace of Europe is that nations should give each other credit for goodwill and good intentions'.

In June a decade of National Peace Congresses was marked by a three-day meeting in Liverpool. There, the delegates looked forward to the Third Hague Conference, berated the armament manufacturers, expressed concern about the situation in Ireland, and congratulated themselves on the growing unity and strength of the pacifist movement.[1] Later that same month, in a debate on foreign affairs in the Commons, it was a Radical, Noel Buxton, who declared that it was his pleasure 'to congratulate the Foreign Secretary today upon the fact that matters which are likely to be raised are not questions of *haute politique* at all, but they are comparatively minor questions not involving matters of great danger.' It was midsummer. In London it was the height of the Season—not a time for securing speedy political results. Colonel House, recently arrived in London from the Continent, wrote to President Wilson on 17 June: 'I find here everything cluttered up with social affairs, and it is impossible to work quickly. Here they have their thoughts on Ascot, garden parties, etc., etc. In Germany their one thought is to advance industrially and to glorify war.'[2]

Most Englishmen knew little, and if it was possible, cared even less about the fortunes of the Austro-Hungarian Empire. But for that handful of experts who made it their business to be informed about the Habsburg dominions, the majority were sympathetic towards German rather than Slav aims in central and south-eastern Europe. H. N. Brailsford in his book, *The War of Steel and Gold: a study of the armed peace*, censured Grey for encouraging Russia and thus hampering Austrian action in the Balkans. Austria, Brailsford maintained, ought to have been allowed to annex Serbia and the

---

[1] For previous three paragraphs see Bound Minutes of National Peace Council, nos. 35–7, May–July 1914; *Concord*, June 1914, p. 61, and July, pp. 79–90; *Labour Leader*, 16 July 1914; *The Arbitrator*, July 1914, pp. 81ff.; *Manchester Guardian*, 19/20 May and 10–13 June 1914.
[2] Colonel House to President Wilson, 17 June 1914, quoted *The Intimate Papers of Colonel House* (1926), i, 268.

greater part of Macedonia. If Brailsford's views were to be expected from an extreme Radical, a Liberal imperialist like Sir Harry Johnson could share his opinion. Johnson, considering the possibility of a general European war provoked by a struggle between the Yugoslavs and the Austrians, maintained that British sympathies would always support the Germans against the Russians and the French. Wickham Steed, who as head of the foreign news department of *The Times* directed the policy of that newspaper along more markedly anti-German lines, in his study of the Austro-Hungarian monarchy published in 1913, pointed out that Serbian success in arms had weakened Austria and inevitably the two Germanies were being drawn closer together in the face of a common Slavonic peril. Steed warned his readers that there was a distinct possibility the two Central Powers might anticipate events by attacking Russia. But then he was quick to add an optimistic gloss to his 'catastrophic hypothesis'.[1] Englishmen had quite enough with which to concern themselves to care overmuch for the fate of the Dual Monarchy, or to unravel the complicated racial and nationalistic claims of distant provinces when Catholic and Protestant might at any moment be at one another's throats in John Bull's other island.

On the morning of 28 June 1914, a little before noon, at Sarajevo, capital of the Austrian province of Bosnia Herzegovina, Gavrilo Princip, a Bosnian who lived in Serbia, murdered Archduke Franz Ferdinand, the heir to the Austrian throne. It was not until the next day, when they opened their Monday morning papers, that most Englishmen learned of the assassination. There was a natural shock, sympathy, even concern for the Austrian people, and more particularly their aged Emperor whose heir had been killed. There was widespread disgust felt for the Archduke's murderer, and Horatio Bottomley in his journal, *John Bull*, insisted that Serbia, for complicity in the murder, should be annihilated.[2] The Serbs, with their recent history of regicide, were not a popular people with the English. Almost without exception,[3] the British Press claimed that Austria

---

[1] See Henry Wickham Steed, *The Hapsburg Monarchy* (1913), 294–5; H. N. Brailsford, *The War of Steel and Gold* (1914), 33–4; Sir Harry Johnson, *Common Sense in Foreign Policy* (1913), 48–51; also, R. Seton Watson, *The Southern Slav Question and the Habsburg Monarchy* (1911), *passim*.

[2] See Julia Symons, *Horatio Bottomley: a biography* (1955), 162.

[3] For once in strange alliance, the Tory *Morning Post* and Labour's *Daily Citizen* expressed their distrust of Austria. For accounts of Press attitudes in Germany and Britain during the last weeks before the outbreak of war, see, *inter alia*, J. F. Scott, *Five Weeks: the surge of public opinion on the eve of the Great War* (1927); Theodor Wolff, *The Eve of 1914* (1936); Emil Ludwig, *July 1914* (1929); Willis, *How we went into War*; C. E. Playne, *The Pre-War Mind in England: an historical review* (1928); and Hale, *Publicity and Diplo-*

would be perfectly justified in requiring the Serbian Government to take whatever steps were necessary to prevent any recurrence of a similar outrage. A few political commentators who were familiar with the Pan-Servian movement were for the moment apprehensive that there might be an immediate European crisis. But the days passed, and the Austrian Government still took no action. When Tisza addressed the Parliament in Budapest, the language he used was moderate and reassuring. People wondered at Austria's mildness. Perhaps they had formed a wrong impression of Austria by her violent action in 1908, and now that Aehrenthal was removed from the scene there was no reason to suppose that Austria would pursue an aggressive policy towards Serbia? With Austria announcing no special measures, the fears of even the 'experts' were swiftly allayed. When Scott-James claimed in the editorial columns of *News Weekly* that the assassination of the archduke was 'the crime that followed the crime of a ferocious foreign policy which enjoyed the unfailing support of the archduke and of a tyrannical bureaucracy that desired to mutilate the legitimate aspirations of a small people . . .', the argument was swiftly dismissed by *New Age* as 'inaccurate and a falsehood. . . . However much we may dislike Austria we must admit that the half savage denizens of the Balkans have still a long hill to climb before they reach the cultural level of the Hapsburg dominions.'[1]

The Radical Press noted with regret the death of Franz Ferdinand, though they could not conceal altogether their sympathy for the plight of a subject nationality. However, the political implications of the assassination were worthy of no more than cursory attention. While news from Vienna, Budapest, Belgrade and Sarajevo, rumours of Serbian complicity in the murder, filled the main news pages of the German Press; in English newspapers, relations between Austria and Serbia were soon dismissed, tucked away in comparative anonymity on the inside pages. The headlines were occupied with social and sporting stories; the death of Joseph Chamberlain and the continuing crisis in Ireland. In the period immediately preceding Austria's ultimatum to Serbia, headlines in the British Press were shared by the trial of Madame Caillaux for the murder of the editor of *Le Figaro* and accounts of gun-running in Ulster.

On 17 July, J. A. Spender published a long article in his *West-*

---

macy, chap. xv. The best survey of Radical Press comment in the last week before the outbreak of war is contained in the unpublished thesis of Dorey, 411ff.
[1] See *New Age*, 9 July 1914, pp. 220–1.

minster Gazette analysing the tensions between Austria and Serbia. The general tone of the article was significantly pro-Austrian, and Spender maintained that Serbia would be 'well advised, if she realises the reasonableness of her great neighbour's anxiety, and does whatever may be in her power to allay it, without waiting for a pressure which might involve what Count Tisza calls "warlike complications".' The Russian Ambassador in Vienna was immediately concerned that 'this warning to Servia by an organ of the British Government' would encourage Austria to take extreme measures. It was to no avail that Grey repudiated the Russian Ambassador's interpretation that Spender's article had been officially inspired.[1] The Germans made sure that the Spender article had the widest possible circulation in their Press as a semi-official pronouncement by 'one close to Sir Edward Grey', and it was cited as evidence that Britain would support any action that Austria should choose to take against Serbia. Jagow, making the most he could of the situation, within two days published in the *Norddeutsche Allgemeine Zeitung* a communiqué which maintained that all Europe's Press recognised that Austria would have to clarify her relations with Serbia. If a serious crisis was to be avoided and the dispute localised, then Serbia would have to give way to any demands that Austria might make. As to the exact nature of Austria's demands, Europe did not have to wait long for information. On 21 July, the *Neue Freie Presse* was able to give an exact forecast of Austria's ultimatum, and three days later copies of the official text were delivered to the various foreign offices of the Powers in the principal European capitals. The German Government declared its support for Austria, and from St Petersburg it was announced that Russia would not stand idly by should Serbia be invaded. Overnight a crisis of monstrous proportions had erupted and the British Press was rudely shocked into acknowledging in banner headlines that there was now a 'Grave Danger of War'.

It was not only the British Press that was surprised by the crisis. Permanent officials at the Foreign Office had not been unduly concerned by the murder of Franz Ferdinand. Nicolson could write to the Ambassador in Vienna on 6 July, that Albania apart, there were 'no very urgent and pressing questions to preoccupy us in the rest of Europe'.[2] Grey, that same day in conversation with Lichnowsky, was warned of possible German reaction to the murder. The Foreign Secretary did not share the complacency of his officials, but he did not choose to reveal his apprehensions to his advisers. Grey moved alone. He sought neither the aid of his Foreign Office officials

---

[1] See *B.D.* XI, 46.　　　　　　　[2] *B.D.* XI, 33.

nor the approval of the Cabinet for the course he pursued. Only Asquith, Haldane and Churchill were privy to the Foreign Secretary's actions. It was only by degrees that the Foreign Office experts came to share their master's apprehensions.[1]

Grey, in conversation with Lichnowsky, maintained a cheerful front. He told the German Ambassador that he saw no reason to take too tragic a view of the situation. Obviously Grey believed that Germany would urge circumspection upon the Austrians and, as during the earlier Balkan crises, Berlin and London could work together successfully. Grey was not to know that the Germans had given Austria an unconditional promise of support on 5 July. Grey urged Cambon that should Austria act against Serbia then France should demand moderation of her Russian ally. To still any German ears, the Foreign Secretary emphasised to the Russians the importance of their adopting a conciliatory attitude in Berlin. All these promptings proved fruitless, and when Grey urged direct Austro-Russian talks, it was the Russians who rejected the suggestion. The Russians next proposed joint representation by the Triple Entente Powers in Vienna, and it was London's turn to scotch an initiative. Even before the publication of Austria's ultimatum dramatically heightened the diplomatic crisis, it must have been clear to Grey that his hopes of working with Germany to insure the peace of Europe were ill founded. Grey wished Germany to restrain Austria while Britain restrained Russia: Germany wished Britain to hold back Russia while Austria punished Serbia. That the dichotomy was clear to Jagow is apparent from a telegraphic message he sent Lichnowsky on 18 July.

> Grey is always speaking of the balance of power to be maintained by the two groups of Powers. He must clearly understand that this balance would be totally destroyed if we abandoned Austria and left her to be destroyed by Russia and would be very considerably shaken by a world war. If therefore he is logical and his intentions honourable he must support us and localise the conflict.[2]

The publication of the Austrian ultimatum meant that, for the first time since the beginning of the crisis, Grey was obliged to raise the problem in the Cabinet. His Foreign Office advisers sternly insisted that the merit of Austria's case against Serbia was now irrelevant. The real issue was that of 'the Triple Alliance versus the Triple Entente'.[3] Crowe and Nicolson desired a firm avowal of

[1] See Vansittart, *The Mist Procession* (1958), 122.
[2] Jagow to Lichnowsky, 18 July 1914, *Die Deutschen Dokumente*, i, 100, quoted Halévy, *The Rule of Democracy*, 658–9, n. 2.
[3] *B.D.* xi, 101. See also Steiner, 156–7.

British unity with France and Russia. Grey was not convinced the situation was as extreme as his advisers indicated. In any event, before such a declaration could be made, Cabinet approval would have to be given.

A decent reticence

The Cabinet met on the afternoon of 24 July to discuss the continuing problem of Ulster. It was almost the end of the meeting when Grey rose to read to his colleagues the terms of the Austrian ultimatum. It was the first time for a month that ministers had discussed foreign affairs. In Asquith's own words, Grey's statement revealed that 'the European situation [was] about as bad as it [could] possibly be'. It was certain that Serbia could never comply with Austria's 'bullying and humiliating ultimatum'. Austria would march upon Serbia and 'This means almost inevitably that Russia will come on the scene in defence of Servia and if so it is difficult both for Germany and France to refrain from lending a hand. So that we are within measurable distance of a real Armageddon.'[1] This melancholy confidence, the Prime Minister bestowed on Miss Venetia Stanley. Asquith's letter to the King referred to 'the gravest event for many years past in European politics . . . the prelude to a war in which at least 4 of the Great Powers might be involved'.[2] Despite this immediate and pessimistic prognosis by their leader, ministers do not seem to have examined or even considered the possibility of Britain's involvement in war. It must be supposed that so unexpected was the news and the subsequent development of events so rapid that, as Crewe later affirmed, Cabinet members felt they were suddenly living in a dream world more appropriate to a novel by H. G. Wells.[3] In truth, the real problem was that ministers were already exhausted by their efforts to find some solution to the prolonged Irish crisis. Only with great difficulty were they able to shift their attention to foreign affairs—a subject for which, at the best of times, most of them had little enthusiasm. However serious the Austro-Serbian squabble, it was not sufficient to stop Grey from spending the weekend fishing in Hampshire, or most of the other ministers from taking leave of London.[4] Only Churchill, scenting

---

[1] Asquith to Venetia Stanley 27 July 1914, quoted as his 'Contemporary Notes' by Asquith in *Memories and Reflections* (1928), ii, 5.

[2] Cabinet Letter, 25 July 1914.

[3] Crewe to Hardinge, 6 Aug. 1914, quoted James Pope-Hennessy, *Lord Crewe: the likeness of a Liberal* (1955), 144–5.

[4] The weekend habit died hard. On 31 July, both Asquith and Lloyd George confirmed arrangements to spend 1/2 Aug. away from London.

battle, stayed in town. The First and Second Fleets were already concentrated. The Third (Reserve) Fleet was to complete its mobilisation that weekend. The First Lord sent orders that the fleet was to be kept at the point of readiness at Portland.

When the Cabinet reassembled on the Monday, the time for discussion was shared between Ireland and the worsening European problem. Ministers approved Grey's suggestion[1] of a Four Power Conference and also Churchill's order to the fleet. These decisions apart, however, there was no discussion as to possible action Britain might take if the Four Power conference failed. Nor would they discuss 'Britain's obligations in regard to the neutrality of Belgium'. That subject could wait until a further meeting in two days' time.[2]

John Burns, soon to resign from the Cabinet, in a note he wrote that day, makes clear his mind was already made up as to the course he intended to follow.

> The outlook for war rather serious. Why four Great Powers should fight over Servia no fellow can understand. This I know, there is one fellow who will have nothing to do with such a criminal folly the effects of which will be appalling to the weaker nations who will be involved. It must be averted by all the means in our power.
>
> Apart from the merits of the case it is my especial duty to dissociate myself and the principles I hold and the trusteeship of the working classes which I carry from such a universal crime as the contemplated war will be.
>
> My duty is clear and at all costs will be done.[3]

Later that same day, C. P. Scott met Lloyd George at the Treasury. The Chancellor assured Scott that he knew of no minister who would be in favour of taking part in any war in the first instance. A leader in *The Times* promising England's support to the Dual Alliance of France and Russia in time of war, was worthy of nothing but derision.

[1] The initiative for the idea of a Four Power Conference had come from Nicolson. The Under-Secretary, anxious to please the Russians, thought that the conference would be at least a gesture towards Britain's entente partners.
[2] Cabinet Letter, 28 July 1914, quoted Asquith and Spender, ii, 81.
[3] 27 July 1914. B.M.Add.MSS. 46308. No one was ever quite sure what were Burns's reasons for resigning. He refused to make a statement to the House. A diary entry, 23 Sept. 1915, records a meeting in Whitehall with Fisher when Burns gave as his reasons: 'Splendid Isolation. No Balance of Power. No Incorporation in continental system. If you want a war with Germany, the best, cheapest and only certain way [is] on the sea alone . . .' He was to repeat these reasons to other people over a period of years, but, in 1933, in conversation with Sir Ernest Benn he claimed that the real reason was that 'we fought on the wrong side. . . . If you wanted a war you ought to have fought the French and not the Germans'. None of these explanations seems convincing and one is left to suppose that Burns was committed to resignation should Britain fight a war against any adversary. See William Kent, *Labour's Lost Leader* (1950), 238–40.

It did not even represent the views of officials at the Foreign Office. Lloyd George was prepared to admit, however, that should the German fleet attack French towns via the Channel, then this would pose a difficult question. It was evident that Lloyd George was prepared, even at that date, to go a certain way to support France and Russia in putting pressure upon Austria. To Scott he made no secret of his pro-French leanings.[1]

The next day, Tuesday 28 July, despite a conciliatory reply to her ultimatum, Austria declared war on Serbia. Grey's proposed conference in London was rejected by the Germans, and Asquith knew now that 'nothing but a miracle could avert' war. After a dinner party that evening, Asquith joined Grey and Haldane at the Foreign Office where, until I a.m., they 'talk[ed] over the situation and tr[ied] to discover bridges and outlets'.[2] The three men must have known that the prospect could not have been bleaker.[3]

The Cabinet meeting of 29 July was the first that was concerned entirely with the deteriorating European scene. In his diary, Burns described it as 'a critical Cabinet' where the 'situation [was] seriously reviewed from all points of view'. He then added, somewhat inconsequentially: 'It was decided not to decide.'[4] In fact two decisions had been taken. The first was to send warning telegrams to initiate 'a precautionary period'. Largely due to Haldane's efforts when he had been Minister for War, for several years there had existed a 'war book', and at two o'clock on that Wednesday afternoon the order was given to begin turning its pages. The second decision concerned Britain's attitude should Germany violate Belgium's neutrality. Asquith reported to the King:

> The Cabinet consider that this matter, if it arises, will be rather one of policy than of legal obligation . . . it was agreed that Sir E. Grey should be authorised to inform the German and French ambassadors that at this stage we were unable to pledge ourselves in advance, either under all conditions to stand aside or in any conditions to join in.[5]

Asquith's biographer describes this statement as 'a little pusillanimous, but so it was bound to be unless the Cabinet was to be split wide open'. Was the Cabinet's decision at this stage—to deny any obligations to France arising out of the entente relationship—because of the influence of 'a potential peace party comprising no less than ten ministers—of a total of twenty'?[6]

[1] Scott, *Diaries*, 27 July 1914, 91–2.
[2] H. H. Asquith, *Memories*, ii, 6.   [3] See Grey, i, 321.
[4] Burns's Diary, 29 July 1914, B.M.Add.MSS. 46336.
[5] Cabinet Letter, 30 July 1914, quoted Spender and Asquith, ii, 31.
[6] Jenkins, 325.

Morley, in his *Memorandum on Resignation* wrote of 'The Cabinet for the first time bec[oming] seriously uneasy about the danger of these foreign affairs to our own cohesion. For the very first time something of the old cleavage between the Liberal League and the faithful Campbell-Bannerman, Harcourt and myself began to be very sensibly felt.'[1] Morley's memory invested the dichotomy in Cabinet opinion with an ancestry and an identifiable homogeneity that did not exist. There was never within the Cabinet a 'peace party' opposed to another group determined upon war. If Morley and Burns are excluded, then what we are left with is a group of men, none of whom wanted war but were forced by degrees to accept a fortune over which they had no control. As each day brought baleful confirmation that Europe was sliding further over the precipice into war, Asquith still stubbornly clung to the belief that the best hope for peace lay in Britain refusing to commit herself. 'We want to keep out of it', wrote Asquith on 29 July, 'but the worst thing we could do would be to announce to the world at the present time that in *no circumstances* would we intervene.'[2] Ministers now knew they faced 'the most momentous problem', a problem, moreover, that they were uncertain how to resolve. In such circumstances it was natural for politicians to promote necessity as a virtue. As Samuel wrote to his wife: 'Our action is held in suspense for if both sides do not know what we shall do, both will be the less willing to run risks.'[3]

As Morley left the Cabinet on 29 July, Burns caught him by the arm and said, with some emphasis, 'Now mind, we look to you to stand firm.'[4] Morley might have had the capacity 'to run the course and keep faith',[5] but this 'broken man in old age', as Jack Pease described him, was not keen to pose as a leader around whom might gather those ministers who distrusted Asquith and Grey. He would resign, for he would not brook becoming a party to a Slavonic movement against Teuton influence.[6] But, if there was to be a party formed within the Cabinet 'zealous against extension of entente to alliance' and 'in favour of neutrality', then that task was best left to Harcourt who was already busily engaged in organising and sounding opinion among his colleagues while fortifying his own resolution by passing notes across the Cabinet table to Morley with

[1] John Morley, *Memorandum on Resignation: August 1914* (1928), 7.
[2] Asquith to Venetia Stanley, 29 July 1913, quoted Jenkins, 326.
[3] Samuel to Beatrice Samuel, 29 July 1914, quoted Cameron Hazlehurst, *Politicians at War* (1971), 79.
[4] Morley, *Memorandum on Resignation*, 7.
[5] Morley to Spender, 6 Aug. 1914, Spender Papers, B.M.Add.MSS. 46392.
[6] See Fitzroy, ii, 557.

the affirmation that it was 'more and more evident' that he must resign.[1]

Harcourt's undoubted appetite for intrigue, in itself was not sufficient to qualify him for leadership of a group of men whose only certainty was their uncertainty of purpose. He could never provide the necessary intellectual or moral impetus. Nor was Simon, probably the most able and articulate member of the group, of sufficient seniority to make an effective leader. One man was pre-eminently qualified for that rôle, Lloyd George. He was the acknowledged leader of the economists who had pressed for years for reductions in expenditure upon the Army and the Navy. Three times within the month he had publicly declared his belief that relations between Germany and Britain were mended—'there is none of that snarling we used to see'. As Chancellor of the Exchequer, Lloyd George stood second only to Asquith in the hierarchy of the Liberal party. Asquith was sensible of Lloyd George's position and influence, and we may discount Margot Asquith's extravagant suggestion that her husband ever contemplated isolating the 'peace party' by forming a coalition. He was prepared to use that contingency as a threat to promote discipline, but Asquith was determined from the beginning of the crisis to keep his Liberal Cabinet together as long as was possible, and he recognised that Lloyd George's support was the key to that enterprise.[2] Lloyd George was the subject of pleas and finally barely veiled threats from the neutralists who sought to win his support for their cause, but all to no avail.

Had Lloyd George so wished, an early declaration would have placed him in a position where he would have been able to lead a powerful antiwar party. Instead he attended meetings of the dissident ministers and listened sympathetically to their plaints, but never chose to promote himself as their leader. The Chancellor was cognisant of the plans of all factions, but committed to none. Even while Lulu Harcourt was urging Lloyd George in Cabinet to 'speak for us now', the Chancellor was privy to Churchill's scheming with the Tories for a possible coalition. There was no need for Masterman to counsel Lloyd George to *'fight* for unity'.[3] The Welshman had from the beginning chosen to be 'sensible and statesmanlike for keeping the position . . . open'.[4] He in his turn was to advise patience as the better part than belligerence to Churchill so that 'we might come together'.[5] Lloyd George listened to his colleagues' opinions

[1] Morley, 4.   [2] See Margot Asquith, ii, 127 and Jenkins, 326.
[3] Cabinet Notes, 29 July and 1 Aug. 1914, quoted Owen, 264–5.
[4] H. H. Asquith, ii, 7.
[5] Cabinet Note, 1 Aug. 1914, quoted Owen, *supra*.

but never unequivocally declared his own. His mistress, Frances Stevenson, believed that 'L.G.'s mind was really made up from the first, that he knew we would have to go in . . .'[1] The Chancellor temporised, playing a part until such time as 'a *casus belli* which everyone . . . would understand'[2] should appear. For Radical, peace-loving Lloyd George, 'the invasion of Belgium was . . . [the] heaven-sent excuse for supporting a declaration of war'.[3]

With the rapid deterioration of the international situation, there were constant appeals from the Russians and the French, addressed to their entente partner, asking for some tangible proof that they enjoyed Britain's support. In particular, the Russians were anxious that Britain should reject the German belief that Britain would remain neutral. Grey reassured the Russian Ambassador by pointing to the retained mobilisation of the Third Fleet. That ought to have been enough to dispel any wrong impressions the Germans might have entertained. However, Benckendorff in his turn was not to suppose from this that Britain promised Russia anything more than 'diplomatic action'.[4]

After the Cabinet meeting on 29 July, Grey summoned the German and French Ambassadors to the Foreign Office. Lichnowsky again was told that Britain would stay out of the quarrel between Austria and Serbia. However, should British or French interests become endangered, then Great Britain might be forced to intervene. This warning by Grey overstepped the instructions he had been given by the Cabinet and, as though to compensate for his excess, when Grey spoke to Cambon he adopted a blunt manner. He told the French Ambassador what he had said to Lichnowsky, but then stressed that should France become involved with Germany they must remember that Britain was 'free from engagements' and that British interests alone would dictate what course Britain would follow. The 'special agreement' between the two Powers had been concerned with Moroccan difficulties, and Grey took pains to stress the differences between the crises of 1905 and 1911 and the present Balkan imbroglio. The French were not to suppose that the concentration of the Fleet implied British participation.[5] Cambon did not respond to Grey's discouraging explanation of the British attitude to the situation with the concern that might have been expected and could have been excused in the circumstances. 'Probably he regarded the Foreign Secretary's straight talk to Lichnowsky as more significant

---

[1] Frances Lloyd George, *The Years that are Past* (1967), 73–4.
[2] See R. S. Churchill, p. 531.   [3] Frances Lloyd George, *supra*.
[4] *B.D.*, **XI**, 177.   [5] *Ibid.*, 283.

than his distinctions between Morocco and the Balkans.'[1] Meanwhile, events in Berlin dictated a further step by Britain upon the path to war.

On the evening of 29 July, Goschen was summoned to meet the German Chancellor. Bethmann-Hollweg made a determined bid for British neutrality. The Chancellor declared it was his belief that the main principle governing British policy was the determination that France should not be crushed in any conflict. Germany would give every assurance to the British Government that if Britain remained neutral, then she would respect French territorial integrity and Dutch neutrality. This pledge Bethmann could not extend to cover the French colonies, nor, in the event of war, could he guarantee Belgian neutrality. However, as long as the Belgians did not fight against Germany their territorial integrity would be respected. The Chancellor concluded by stressing that it had always been his policy to bring about an understanding with Britain and he hoped that his present assurances might be the basis of a general neutrality agreement between the two countries.[2]

Bethmann's initiative was extraordinarily maladroit. It indicated that Germany clearly contemplated war with France and that imperial strategy was committed to sending troops through Belgium. Further, it presented Grey with the perfect excuse for arguing that British involvement arose, not from any duty expressed or implied by the entente relationship, but because she was a guarantor of Belgium's neutrality. Crowe could not resist the opportunity to emphasise the line of policy he had been urging upon Grey. 'It is clear', he argued in a minute to Goschen's telegram, 'that Germany is practically determined to go to war and that the one restraining influence so far has been the fear of England joining the defence of France and Belgium'. Grey's Foreign Office advisers were convinced that at last Britain would have unequivocally to declare her position.

Grey was already angered and exasperated by Bethmann's and Jagow's response to his call for a conference of the representatives of the Great Powers. The Foreign Secretary could only believe that the German Chancellor was being driven by forces over which he had no control.[3] The new German initiative filled Grey with despair. 'We were henceforth to converse upon how we should conduct ourselves in war, no longer how war could be avoided. But even that was not the worst feature introduced into new negotiations. The proposal made to us meant everlasting dishonour if we accepted it.'[4] Grey straightway prepared an answer.

[1] Williamson, 348.   [2] *B.D.*, xi, 293.   [3] See Grey, i, 321–3.   [4] *Ibid.*, i, 326.

His Majesty's Government cannot for a moment entertain the Chancellor's proposal that they should bind themselves to neutrality on such terms . . . it would be a disgrace for us to make this bargain with Germany at the expense of France—a disgrace from which the good name of this country would never recover. The Chancellor also, in effect, asks us to bargain away whatever obligation or interest we have as regards the neutrality of Belgium. We could not entertain that bargain either.[1]

Asquith approved of Grey's draft, and it was sent without receiving Cabinet agreement. 'It was certain', Grey writes in his memoirs, 'that the Cabinet would agree that this bid for neutrality could not be accepted. . . . In the afternoon both Goschen's telegram and mine were read to the Cabinet, and they approved what had been done.'[2] In fact, the Cabinet did not meet until the next day.

With *The Times* mounting a strong campaign in its columns claiming that it was not any longer merely a matter of moral obligation that Britain support France but a question of self interest,[3] and the French pressing determinedly for British support, the Cabinet still refused to make up its mind. Though news had arrived that Russia had mobilised, when Grey had another 'rather painful'[4] interview with Cambon on 30 July, at which the French Ambassador reminded the Foreign Secretary of the exchange of letters in November 1912, Grey would only reiterate that British public opinion would not support intervention and that he would raise the entire question with the Cabinet when it met next day.[5] If Cambon hoped for better news after that Cabinet, he was to be sorely disappointed.

Though within a week Asquith was to brand in the Commons the German initiative for neutrality as a document 'we might have thrown aside without consideration and almost without answer', the Cabinet at that Friday meeting were prepared to conclude only that 'British opinion would not enable us to support France—a violation of Belgium might alter public opinion, but we could say nothing to commit ourselves'.[6] Thus, the 'rather shameless' German offer, as Asquith described it, which had provoked Grey to 'a white heat of passion',[7] had little effect on the Cabinet. For the most part their sole intent seemed to be to avoid making any decision. 'Of course,

[1] *B.D.*, XI, 303.   [2] Grey, i, 329.
[3] See *The Times*, 30 July 1914. By 1 Aug. the argument of self interest had been advanced even further. 'We dare not stand aside; our strongest interest is in the law of self-preservation.'
[4] H. H. Asquith, ii, 7.
[5] *B.D.* XI, 319.
[6] Pease Diary, 31 July 1914, quoted Hazlehurst, 84.
[7] See Hazlehurst, 81 and n. 2.

everybody longs to stand aside', noted Asquith.[1] The Prime Minister must have felt that most of his colleagues had abandoned thought for hope, and would have substituted wishes for policie.

When the Cabinet met again next day, if anything the balance seemed to be moving in favour of the neutralists. Though Churchill, pugnacious as ever, occupied more than half the time of the meeting with his arguments, the Cabinet eventually refused to sanction his request that the Fleet reserves should be called out and that final naval preparations for war be made. Churchill recorded that his colleagues were disinclined to believe that such moves were 'necessary to our safety'.[2] Morley and Simon argued that the Government should make an immediate declaration that in *no circumstances* would Great Britain be involved in war. They pleaded that their view was shared by a large and important body of opinion—'the great industrial centres of the North of England . . . the banking and commercial authorities in London, including the heads of the Bank of England . . .'—all were 'adverse to any steps which might be construed into a resolve to take sides in the present dispute'. So far as Morley was concerned, the only part Britain ought to play was 'to press France to exercise restraint upon Russia'. Any other action 'would be more likely to precipitate than avert war'.[3] Grey had responded to these pleas with the flat affirmation that if the Cabinet adopted an uncompromising policy of non-intervention, then he would have to resign. Lloyd George played intermediary between the two sides, urging the while that the question should remain open. Asquith's sympathies were with Grey. He could contemplate the loss of Morley and even Simon with a degree of equanimity, but should Grey go, then he would go also and 'the whole thing would break up'.[4]

At this meeting of the Cabinet it was decided that the expeditionary force should not be sent to the Continent. As Grey later informed a startled and angry Cambon, 'such a step has always been regarded here as very dangerous and doubtful. It was one that we could not propose and Parliament would not authorise unless our interests were deeply and desperately involved.' In vain Cambon pleaded that Britain had an obligation to help France.[5] The decision bore all the appearance of a last minute triumph for that group within the Cabinet, of whom the leading figure was Reginald McKenna, that had always rejected General Wilson's concept of Britain's strategic rôle in a continental war. Though Asquith had

[1] H. H. Asquith, *Memories.*   [2] W. S. Churchill, *The World Crisis*, 216.
[3] Fitzroy, ii, 338.   [4] H. H. Asquith, *Memories*, ii, 7–8.
[5] *B.D.*, xi, 426.

replaced McKenna with Churchill at the Admiralty in 1912, a substantial element in the Cabinet had never been reconciled to the
idea that Britain should play any part upon the Continent with her
Army.[1] When Grey informed Nicolson of the Cabinet's decision,
the Under-Secretary was dumbfounded. 'This is impossible', he
expostulated. 'You have over and over again promised M. Cambon
that if Germany was the aggressor you would stand by France.'
Grey replied lamely, 'Yes, but he has nothing in writing.'[2] It seemed
that a crucial and crippling blow had been struck at the entente
relationship, and Runciman for one, could scarce conceal his pride
and satisfaction when he told Charles Trevelyan of the Cabinet's
decision.[3]

It is impossible to suppose that Asquith and Grey did not recognise that the decision made nonsense of all the designs and preparations that had followed from the contacts between the British and
French Staffs since the military conversations had first started. Both
men were sympathetic towards French claims on British support.
However, for Asquith, as Prime Minister and Liberal leader, his
first priority was to insure, if at all possible, a united Government.
On the Sunday, Asquith was to write to Miss Stanley: 'The despatch of the expeditionary force to help France is *at this moment*
out of the question and would serve no object.'[4] Asquith's attitude
to the despatch of the B.E.F., makes no sense in terms of military
strategy, but if all other considerations are divorced save the question
of political priorities, then the move may be seen as a *temporary* ploy
concerned only with the immediate fate of the Cabinet. A short
hold-up in the mobilisation of the expeditionary force was a comparatively small price to pay for a united Cabinet. The pressure of
circumstances would soon insure the reversal of that decision. Meanwhile, the decision had the further advantage of encouraging the belief among the dissidents that, should Britain eventually be forced
to take offensive action, the Navy alone would be concerned. Naval
commitment best fitted Britain's tradition; it would be relatively
inexpensive—not more than £25 million a year was Churchill's
estimate[5]—and there was always the possibility that Germany
would hesitate to challenge Britain's sea power. Thus, the erroneous belief that their decision not to send the expeditionary force

[1] See W. S. Churchill, *World Crisis*, 231.
[2] See Williamson, 353, n. 34.
[3] See 'Charles Trevelyan's personal record of the days that led up to War of
1914 and to his resignation', p. 1, Trevelyan MSS.
[4] Asquith to Venetia Stanley, 2 Aug. 1914, quoted Hazlehurst, 90 (my italics).
[5] Cabinet Note, Churchill to Lloyd George, quoted R. S. Churchill, *Young
Statesman*, 718.

delineated Britain's rôle in any possible conflict, encouraged the 'hesitants', as Fitzroy called them,[1] to be firmer than otherwise they would have been concerning the question of Belgium's neutrality.

The ministers parted in 'fairly amicable mood'. The main question remained Belgium and its neutrality. Grey had been authorised to warn the German Ambassador that if any combatant violated Belgium then it would be 'extremely difficult to restrain public feeling'. This, together with a refusal to promise absolute British neutrality, even if Germany respected Belgian territory, was intended to have a sobering effect in Berlin.[2] For Cambon, Grey could only suggest, as some recompense for his bitter news about the expeditionary force, that should the German navy make a move towards the Channel, or the German army attack Belgium, then this might alter the balance of British opinion. There was no question of Grey giving Cambon a pledge about the German fleet, but he promised the Ambassador that he would remind his Cabinet colleagues about France's undefended North coastline. Though the Cabinet might remain united, Cambon at that moment must have had the gravest doubts about the unity and value of the entente. Burns recorded in his diary that in all his colleagues' minds there still 'rested the belief and hope for agreement'. After lunch that day he had urged Grey 'to press for the triumphs of peace rather than the laurels of war, the one everlasting, the other withers and fades'.[3] Asquith was 'still not quite hopeless about peace, though far from hopeful'.[4] But for Grey there remained no hope that there would be a happy issue out of their present difficulties. The morrow only offered the prospect of another 'tussle' with the Cabinet.[5]

Three-quarters of an hour before the Cabinet was due to meet on Sunday morning, Harcourt, Beauchamp, Pease, Simon and Runciman joined in anxious conclave with Lloyd George at the Chancellor's house. If the purpose of that meeting was to concert some plan of action, that intention was frustrated, as the only thing they could all agree upon after their short discussion was that none of them was 'prepared to go to war *now*'. Yet even this hesitant conclusion they qualified, for they admitted that 'in certain circumstances'—they instanced 'the invasion wholesale of Belgium'—they might have to 'reconsider' their attitude.[6]

Since last the Cabinet had met, there had been a number of significant events. Germany had declared war on Russia. Even though

[1] H. H. Asquith, *Memories*, ii, 8.   [2] *B.D.* XI, 448.
[3] Burns's Diary, 1 Aug. 1914.   [4] H. H. Asquith, *Memories*, ii, 8.
[5] See Hazlehurst, 91.
[6] Pease Diary, 2 Aug. 1914 (My italics), quoted Hazlehurst, 66.

the Cabinet had decided otherwise, Churchill, given Asquith's approval,[1] had finalised British naval mobilisation. Then early that Sunday morning, the news had reached London that German troops had occupied Luxembourg. Strategically, this move made sense only if Germany's next step was the invasion of Belgium. This event in itself was enough to invest the meeting of the Cabinet with a heightened sense of urgency. They could not continue to prevaricate much longer. Then just before the meeting was to start, Asquith was handed a letter signed by the Tory leader, Bonar Law, stating that 'it would be fatal to the honour and security of the United Kingdom to hesitate in supporting France and Russia at the present juncture; and we offer our unhesitating support to the Government in any measures they may consider necessary for that object'. Asquith read the letter to the assembled ministers but apparently it had little effect on their deliberations.[2] However, the interesting feature of the letter is that there is no mention of Belgian neutrality.[3] The Tory leadership sought action on the basis of the informal understanding between France and Great Britain. They at least were determined to support France and not see Britain stand alone in dangerous isolation. The letter had been designed to bring pressure to bear upon 'Squiff and his Cabinet',[4] but what hope was there for this upon the terms the Tories dictated when Harcourt had assured Morley, before the Cabinet deliberations began, that he believed he could count on no less than ten or eleven men against the view that there was an obligation in honour or policy to take sides with France?

The 'fair discussion', begun at eleven in the morning, did not end until two in the afternoon. Grey faced his colleagues with the proposal that an announcement should be made to both France and Germany that if German ships entered the Channel then Britain would regard that as a hostile act. Crewe was foremost in asserting there should be no hesitation to go to war over the Channel. When McKenna suggested the Channel should be neutralised to both France and Germany, Grey insisted that he was not prepared to quibble any longer. We were either neutral or we were not. If the Cabinet

---

[1] See W. S. Churchill, *Great Contemporaries*, 122.
[2] See Grey, i, 336–7.
[3] Less than a week before the declaration of war, Bonar Law said to Grey that the Tory party would not be united in their support of war unless Belgium was invaded by Germany. That assessment of rank and file Tory opinion was still true at the time the Tory leadership drew up their letter.
[4] For full text of letter see Robert Blake, *The Unknown Prime Minister* (1955), 220–5. See also Callwell, i, 153–6 and Austen Chamberlain, *Down the Years* (1935), 92–102.

chose for neutrality then he would go. Grey was plainly angry with Germany, but he could not carry enough ministers with him for his out and out proposal. After 'much difficulty', the Foreign Secretary was authorised to promise the French and warn the Germans that Great Britain would not tolerate German action in the Channel. At last, Grey had received instructions from the Cabinet as to the conditions upon which they were prepared to go to war. The price of this decision was the resignation, to be briefly postponed at Asquith's request, of John Burns. Burns declared that he could not be a party to what was no less than a challenge to Germany tantamount to a declaration of war. Though Morley cautioned Burns that he would be unwise to resign on that particular issue, his counsel was of no avail.[1] Morley would stay awhile, yet he was conscious that 'step by step' Grey was 'drawing the Cabinet on' to support armed intervention instead of neutrality. British interests— 'the door-step argument'—might dictate the expediency of the Cabinet's decision, but it could not be denied that it also represented a victory for the entente as well. The French had appealed for assistance and the British Government had appeared disinterested. That morning's decision meant that Britain had adopted a course that might well end with her going to war alongside France against Germany. The first significant breach had been made in the neutralist case.

Having successfully negotiated the first session of that Sunday with the Cabinet, Asquith wrote to Miss Stanley giving her a résumé of the morning's meeting. His letter concluded with a six-point summary of the situation designed to indicate that the Prime Minister was 'quite clear' in his own mind 'as to what [was] right and wrong'. However, it merely illustrates how confused Asquith's thinking was at this stage on the question of any liability England might have towards France. While denying any obligation to give military or naval help to Britain's entente partners, Asquith could then add: 'We must not forget the ties created by our long-standing and intimate friendship with France.'[2]

Meanwhile Morley, together with Simon and Lloyd George, had driven to Beauchamp's house for lunch. In their carriage the three ministers talked of their determination to resign, and indeed, throughout the luncheon, which was also attended by Harcourt, Samuel, McKinnon, Wood and Pease, from what was said it might

---

[1] This paragraph on the first meeting of the Cabinet on 2 Aug. is based upon Morley's *Memorandum*; and a Memorandum of Runciman, 2 Aug. 1914, and a letter by Samuel to his wife, 2 Aug. 1914, both quoted by Hazlehurst, 92–4.
[2] H. H. Asquith, *Memories*, ii, 9.

have been supposed that all present were determined that on no account should England be involved in a central European quarrel on the grounds of a mistaken sense of obligation arising out of the entente relationship. Burns had been right in his action, and they should never have approved the message Grey had given Cambon. Yet for all this bold talk, Morley was not convinced of the ministers' resolution. In truth, the meeting was 'a very shallow affair'. Morley was determined on his own resignation, but he would not play leader to this group. Nor did he see any 'standard-bearer' who might play that part. Lloyd George obviously did not seek the rôle, nor was it clear why 'the passing computations for the hour inside his lively brain' had brought the Chancellor among the group. Asquith did not seem overconcerned about these gatherings of ministers anxiously discussing what they should or should not decide. He was kept well informed of their deliberations, and had charged Pease, with whom he had lunched, 'to keep the *conciliabule* to which he was going "out of mischief" '.[1] One man's decision alone could disturb the Prime Minister's equanimity. 'What is Lloyd George going to do?', he inquired of Samuel, who had recounted the afternoon's discussion to Asquith. As to that question, Samuel was no more certain of the answer than Morley, but he declared that it was his belief that for most of the Cabinet the Belgium issue would decide the path they chose. Whatever his colleagues should decide, Asquith made clear his determination to stand by Grey.[2] Before the evening Cabinet, there was another brief discussion between ministers at Lloyd George's house, after which, according to Samuel, the situation was 'easier'[3] There had obviously been a distinct shift in opinion among ministers since the morning when Asquith recognised the Cabniet had stood upon 'the brink of a split'.[4]

Despite the move towards unity, that evening's meeting of the Cabinet was no easy one. Grey insisted that a strong stand should be made on the question of Belgium's neutrality. The Belgians had already declared their own determination to safeguard their neutral position: the only drawback about their attitude, as far as Grey's argument was concerned, was that they had made clear they had no reason to suspect German intentions to violate their territory, nor would they appeal for aid to the guaranteeing Powers should Germany violate their neutrality. The Belgians intended to rely on their own forces to resist aggression from whatever quarter it might

[1] Morley, *Memorandum*, 14–20.
[2] Viscount Samuel, *Memoirs*, 104.
[3] Samuel to Beatrice Samuel, 2 Aug. 1914, quoted Hazlehurst, 97.
[4] Asquith, *Memories*, ii, 8.

come.[1] After much discussion, the Cabinet finally agreed 'without any attempt to state a formula, that . . . a substantial violation of the neutrality of [Belgium] . . . would place us in the situation contemplated as possible by Mr Gladstone in 1870, when interference with Belgian independence was held to compel us to take action'.[2] Though this collective expression of Cabinet opinion was guarded and reserved, nevertheless, it marked the complete abdication by the neutralists of their case. The only conceivable hope that now remained of Great Britain not being involved in the war was that the condition—'substantial violation'—would not be satisfied. Once again, as in 1912, the Radicals in the Cabinet had salved their tender consciences by resting principle upon a verbal nuance.

That evening after dinner, a despatch was received that Belgium was likely to be invaded by the German armies. Already in Brussels, the Belgian Government had been handed the German ultimatum. Grey and Haldane went post-haste to Downing Street to confer with the Prime Minister, and there the three men agreed that the British Army should be mobilised. Asquith also agreed that the information should be communicated to Cambon, and the Prime Minister transferred the Seals of the War Office from his own keeping to Haldane's.[3]

Before the Cabinet next morning, which met to discuss the outlines of Grey's speech to the Commons, Morley informed Lloyd George that he had handed in his resignation. The Chancellor seemed astonished by the news. 'But if you go, it will put us who don't go in a great hole', was his singular comment. Lloyd George inquired whether Morley had considered the news of Germany bullying Belgium, for that had quite changed his and Runciman's attitude. Morley replied that though the news might be bad, that did not alter his aversion to 'the French entente policy and its extended application'. The Cabinet was an indeterminate affair, notable mainly for Asquith's firm avowal that nothing would induce him to separate from Grey, and Simon's blubbering assertion that he, like Morley, Burns and Beauchamp, must resign.[4] The Cabinet was now committed to go to war and whatever effect the news that four ministers had baulked at that decision would be more than offset by the Chancellor of the Exchequer remaining. Whether, because of the emotional atmosphere, exhaustion, or simple relief that at last the Government was committed to a definite course of action, the Cabinet did not discuss any of the contingent arrangements that followed

[1] See *B.D.*, XI, 476, and Trevelyan, 255.
[2] Crewe to George V, Cabinet letter, 2 Aug. 1914, quoted Spender and Asquith, ii, 82.
[3] Haldane, *Autobiography*, 275.   [4]Morley, *Memorandum*, 26.

upon their decision. As Churchill recorded: 'No decision had been taken to send an ultimatum to Germany or to declare war upon Germany, still less to send an army to France. These decisions were never taken at any Cabinet. They were compelled by the force of events, and rest on the authority of the Prime Minister.'[1] All now waited upon Grey's statement in the Commons.

Why had the neutralist case collapsed with scarce a whimper when Asquith admitted that the majority of his colleagues shared the view of the ministers that had resigned, and more, that a majority of Liberals in the Commons were inclined 'pretty strongly in the same direction'?[2] Undoubtedly, the main reason for their weakness was that they lacked a leader. Once Lloyd George eschewed that part the Radical cause in the Cabinet was lost. Nor can one discount ministers' desire to retain a share in power and influence. Simon's scruples, despite his disingenuous assertion to the contrary in his autobiography,[3] were to be overborne by Asquith's hints of preferment. If Burns and Morley are excluded, no minister was keen to surrender his seals of office. Nor was any of them a pacifist save Pease, and for the Quaker President of the Peace Society, Belgian neutrality presented a moral imperative that he could not deny—'to repudiate our undertaking to preserve Belgium's neutrality would be dishonourable and discreditable'.

> I have come to the conclusion that Friend as I am by conviction it would be a cowardly and selfish act on my part to seek my own rest of mind and leave to my colleagues the distasteful and hateful work. . . . I know I cannot expect all Friends to share my views, but there are some things in which one is obliged to come to a decision for one's self under such Guidance as one is given.[4]

Charles Trevelyan dismissed Pease's letter of explanation and justification as but 'sticking plaster for a broken leg'.[5]

One cannot escape the conclusion that the Radical members of the Cabinet were more anxious to find reasons why they might support war than insist upon peace. 'Harcourt', it was Trevelyan's estimate, 'is of the opportunist type in the long run',[6] and sadly, that judgment would seem to fit most of the Radicals in the Cabinet. Conscience demanded a decent reticence, but no practical politician should be so immoderate as to embrace martyrdom and the loss of

---

[1] W. S. Churchill, *World Crisis*, 220.   [2] Morley, *Memorandum*, 25.
[3] Viscount Simon, *Retrospect* (1952), 95.
[4] Pease to J. B. Hodgkin, 4 Aug. 1914, *Elspeth Hodgkin MSS.*, Temp. Box III.
[5] Charles Trevelyan, 'Personal Record' (typescript), p. 6. *Trev. MSS.*
[6] Charles Trevelyan, *ibid.*, p. 5.

office for the sake of an ideal. In those final days of indecision one consideration grew to certainty—if Britain was to go to war, then it was better the country should be led in that enterprise by the Liberals, 'the party which by training and tradition regarded war with the deepest aversion and . . . regarded itself as specially charged with the promotion of peace'.[1] It was a very short step from this argument to buttress intention by the claim that it was nothing less than their *duty* to ensure that, as far as possible, the effects of war should be mitigated for the working classes whose welfare was their particular charge. The alternative was to surrender power to the Tories and 'nothing would justify them in this'.[2]

In the end, the German invasion of Belgium, dictated by the dead hand of General Schlieffen, provided the public 'justification' that Radical ministers sought. They would consent to war, not for any obligation owed to France, but because British interests dictated they could do no less.

> I have acted not from any obligation of Treaty or of honour, for neither existed, and it has been part of my work for the last four years to make it perfectly plain that such was the fact, but there were three overwhelming British interests which I could not abandon:
> 1. That the German fleet should not occupy, under our neutrality, the North Sea and English Channel.
> 2. That they should not seize and occupy the north-western part of France opposite our shores.
> 3. That they should not violate the ultimate independence of Belgium and thereafter occupy Antwerp as a standing menace to us.[3]

Thus, in his newly discovered rôle as strategist, Harcourt abandoned the cause of neutrality and peace. It was only right that one who had been foremost in advertising his concern that Britain ought not go to war, should have abandoned his scruples, not for the sake of entente or even 'Poor Little Belgium', but for 'British interests'. The siren call of patriotism could scarce be resisted in the Cabinet room when outside the crowds thronging the streets declared their resolution with cheering and by singing the *Marseillaise* and *God Save the King*. Ministers that Monday afternoon could hardly make their way through the crowds down Downing Street to Westminster to hear Grey make his statement in the Commons.

[1] Lloyd George, i, 220.
[2] Runciman to Trevelyan, 4 Aug. 1914, *Trev. MSS.*
[3] Harcourt to F. G. Thomas, 5 Aug. 1914, *Harcourt Papers.*

'Fight . . . against this incipient madness'[1]

Few Englishmen on Monday, 27 July 1914, could have supposed, let alone have expected, that in a week, war with Germany would become a practical certainty. Though, save Saturday and Sunday, Parliament met each day throughout that week of crisis, on no occasion was there a general discussion of the international situation. On 27 July, Grey made a brief statement to the Commons recounting the major steps that he had taken up to that time, but no general debate followed. Later that same day, when an opportunity was afforded the House on a Naval Estimate vote to debate the European situation, members allowed themselves to be dissuaded from such action by the blandishments of Beresford and Long.[2] The statement made by Grey on 27 July, together with his speech on 3 August, were to be the only major sources of official information given to the Commons before the outbreak of war. No diplomatic correspondence was made available to members—the White Paper, parts of which were to be the source of angry comment by the Radicals[3]—was not published until 5 August.

Before 3 August, there was little opportunity for members to express any opinion on the Government's policy in the House. The meagre information the House was vouchsafed came in reply to questions from the Leader of the Opposition. On 28 July Asquith told the Commons that he had nothing to communicate but that members should not draw any unfavourable inference from this. Next day the Prime Minister pronounced the situation extremely grave, since Austria had declared war upon Serbia. On 30 July Grey declared that Russia had begun partial mobilisation; and on 31 July, as the House was about to adjourn for the weekend, members were informed that German mobilisation was a distinct probability.[4] Thus, members were obliged to formulate their opinions without any information from the Government, and to communicate those opinions to the Government and the public by conversation or correspondence. From the evidence available, it is apparent that in the early stages of the crisis a substantial majority of members

[1] See J. P. E. Wedgwood to J. C. Wedgwood, 31 July 1914, *Wedgwood MSS.*, 'Fight now as you never fought in your life against this incipient madness which would drag England into war for the benefit of the bloody Czar. If this conspiracy succeeds the Government will fall and a wave of jingoism will sweep away every democratic movement. . . . Truly, patriotism is one of the most loathsome of the vices.'
[2] See *Hansard*, v:65:955–6.
[3] Documents 85, 101 and 102 were to cause particular concern. See E. D. Morel to Charles Trevelyan, 6 Aug. 1914, *Morel Papers*, F.6, File 1.
[4] *Hansard*, v:65:1123, 1324, 1574 and 1787–8.

from both sides of the House did not favour the Government taking active steps for intervention. It was Churchill's opinion that had Grey told Germany that should she attack France or Belgium Great Britain would intervene, then the Commons would have repudiated his action. Indeed Churchill maintained that until the weekend adjournment, the attitude of the House of Commons remained 'most uncertain'.[1] On 1 August, the *Daily Chronicle* declared that not only were 'the vast majority of Government supporters very decidedly against British participation in any European war', but also that 'many Conservatives share the same view'. In a letter published that same day in the *Westminster Gazette*, T. C. Taylor, a back-bench Liberal M.P., wrote, 'For once the democracy and the City are united against war. The Government may rely upon the bitterest opposition of their own supporters should they by any conceivable mischance take sides in a contest in which Mr Asquith says "this country has no interests of its own directly at stake".' *The Nation* claimed: 'There has been no crisis in which the public opinion of the English people has been so definitely opposed to war.'[2]

Radical members in the Commons reacted slowly to the European crisis. They seem to have been genuinely bewildered by the sudden turn in affairs. Their attention had been concentrated upon other matters, particularly the festering problem of Ireland. Nor were they well-equipped to make a rapid reassessment or adjustment to face this sudden new emergency. They had their certain fixed notions which they could not easily abandon. Above all else, they supposed that no Liberal Government would ever be involved in a European war. It would be a disavowal of all that Liberalism stood for. Despite the evidence afforded by domestic politics, despite the concern they had long felt about the manner in which Grey had conducted foreign affairs, they still believed that if Britain should become involved in an international quarrel it would be resolved, not by resorting to violence, but by an exercise of reason and arbitration. They *must* trust their Government. 'I believe that the great majority of the Cabinet are absolutely sound on keeping England out of the war',[3] wrote the Quaker M.P. Edmund Harvey to his father. In his diary another Liberal M.P., Richard Holt, recorded: 'What England will do seems uncertain tho' it is almost impossible to believe that a Liberal Government can be guilty of the crime of dragging us into this conflict in which we are no way interested.'[4] On Sunday, 2

---

[1] W. S. Churchill, *World Crisis*, 229.   [2] *The Nation*, 1 Aug. 1914.
[3] T. E. Harvey to W. Harvey, 30 July 1914, *Harvey MSS*.
[4] Holt Diary, 2 Aug. 1914, *Holt MSS*.

August, though he had already had two uncomfortable meetings with Grey, and had received enough information from Runciman to know that the Cabinet was divided on Britain's neutrality, Charles Trevelyan 'did not believe that we were going to war. I still *trusted* the Government'.[1]

There was every reason to suppose that the Government would not become involved in Europe. On two occasions, Asquith had made explicit assurances to the Commons repudiating the suggestion that Great Britain was under an obligation to take part in any war; and Grey had reinforced these statements by one of his own but a few weeks ago.[2] Should Radicals now openly question the veracity of the Prime Minister and the Foreign Secretary? Should they cast doubt on the *bona fides* of the Government; openly advertise their worry, distrust and suspicion? 'We ought so far, to credit [the Government] with desiring to keep the country out of the mêlée', wrote Bryce to Spender.[3] Radicals would best serve the cause of peace if they trusted the Government and did not choose this moment, of all times, to advertise differences within the Liberal party. Enjoined to be silent, they confined their concern to their private conversations, letters and diaries.

> Sir E. Grey most promptly tried to get the other European Powers to join us in offering mediation but without complete success. What neither he nor Asquith have said is whether we will remain neutral. Leonard is perturbed by this omission, especially as *The Times* is dwelling on our 'alliance' and the balance as binding us to action under possible circumstances— the circumstances being France joining in the war.[4]

Courtney may well have been concerned, yet when A. G. Gardiner invited him to declare that concern in the columns of the *Daily News* the veteran Radical declined. 'Many things have to be taken into account. I have been moving among men saying a word here and there; . . . but I must choose the moment for speech or writing even at the risk of being too late.'[5] If the politicians hesitated to speak openly, the newspapers were obliged to proffer an opinion.

The greater part of editorial opinion in the British Press had inclined to condemn Serbia and justify the action taken by Austria. They had hoped that the dispute would be settled by mediation,

[1] Charles Trevelyan, p. 3, my italics.
[2] Statements made in Commons; 10 Mar. 1912, 24 Mar. 1913 and 11 June 1914.
[3] Bryce to Spender, 31 July 1914, quoted Hazlehurst, 39; see also Wilson Harris, 37–8.
[4] Kate Courtney Diary, 30 July 1914.
[5] Courtney to A. G. Gardiner, 30 July 1914, *Gardiner Papers*.

and when that possibility was thwarted by Austria's declaration of war, that the conflict would be localised. It was only after Russian mobilisation and the resultant German ultimatum, that most newspapers seriously began to consider Britain's rôle in the struggle. The Tory Press, almost without exception, demanded that the Government should proclaim its determination to support Britain's entente partners. The Liberal Press was divided. There were those, like the *Westminster Gazette* and the *Daily Chronicle*, who, while they condemned the violent campaign for intervention being conducted by the Tory Press, were not prepared to take a positive stand either for or against neutrality. They waited on the Government to provide a lead. 'At this stage it is best for those who are troubled by no official responsibility not to start dictating to Sir Edward Grey. There are times, and this is one, when the crew of the ship had better be prepared to carry out, in any event, the orders of their appointed captain . . .'[1] In Spender's opinion, the situation was 'beyond journalism, and all that journalists could hope to do was not to do mischief'.[2] But, Scott's *Manchester Guardian*, A. G. Gardiner's *Daily News*, Massingham's *Nation* and the *Liverpool Post*, did not choose to affect Spender's reserve, and wholeheartedly supported the case for neutrality. These newspapers were not loath to give advice to the Government as a counterblast to 'the Harmsworth Press . . . shrieking for war'.[3] Though it was A. G. Gardiner who best met the arguments of the interventionists with 'masterpieces of polemical journalism',[4] the case for neutrality was presented in most detail in the columns of the *Manchester Guardian*. While in the background Scott exerted what pressure he could on Radical members of the Cabinet, his paper advertised the Radical cause, never wavering in its opposition to 'the participation of this country in the greatest crime of our time.'[5]

After Grey's statement to the Commons on 27 July, the *Guardian*'s leader next day asserted:

> The best hope of our success in the part of mediators, which we have very properly assumed, is that our impartiality should be above suspicion. . . . We have no . . . commitments. Not only are we neutral now, but we could and ought to remain neutral throughout the whole course of the war. It is strange that Sir E. Grey should not have referred to this fact, which is the chief source of our moral authority in Europe . . . the whole future of

---

[1] *Daily Chronicle*, 1 Aug. 1914.
[2] Spender, *Life, Journalism and Politics*, ii, 12.
[3] C. Trevelyan, p. 1; see also Burns, Diary, 2 Aug. 1914, B.M.Add.MSS. 46336, and Holt, Diary, 2 Aug. 1914.
[4] Hale, 463.   [5] *Manchester Guardian*, 4 Aug. 1914.

England depends on the suppression of the spirit that if Russia, Germany and France start fighting we must start too. It is war to the knife between it and Liberalism. Either it kills us or we kill it.[1]

When Asquith pronounced to the Commons a situation of 'extreme gravity', the *Guardian* responded:

The first duty [of Englishmen] is to England and the peace of England . . . though our neutrality ought to be assured, it is not . . . Sir E. Grey walks deliberately past opportunities of saying that we are and will be neutral in the quarrels of Europe . . . We are friends with every Power in Europe. Why give a preference to one friend over another?[2]

The *Manchester Guardian*'s leader for 1 August revealed an almost hysterical note. 'There is in our midst an organised conspiracy to drag us into war should the attempts of the peace-makers fail.' The object of these 'conspirators' was to involve Britain in war for balance of power notions, to protect Belgium's neutrality, and for the sake of her honour. Each of these claims for intervention the *Guardian* denied. If England believed in the balance of power doctrine, then this was an argument to intervene on the side of Germany, not Russia. There was 'no entanglement in Belgium . . . we are . . . absolutely free'. As to the third claim: 'for honour's sake we must keep the peace . . . if we decide differently then we violate dozens of promises made to our own people. If those promises are broken, then England's honour will be tarnished.'[3] Even when Germany had declared war on Russia and France, the *Manchester Guardian* insisted the Germans had struck the first blow because they were 'uncertain of the neutrality of England'.

We deeply regret it but we understand. . . . We are, if possible, more convinced than ever that duty and interest alike demand that this country should not make itself an accessory to the crime against reason and human happiness that is now beginning. . . . England alone among the Great Powers stood quite outside the entanglements of the European system which is now breaking up . . . by neutrality we may be in the best possible position to restrain the victor from a wrong or brutal use of his triumph.[4]

The *Manchester Guardian* did not confine itself to giving advice to the Government and the nation. Its letter columns were filled with the pleas of prominent Radicals demanding that Britain preserve her neutrality. It reported the activities of the neutralists, paying

[1] *Ibid.*, 28 July 1914. [2] *Ibid.*, 31 July 1914.
[3] *Ibid.*, 1 Aug. 1914.
[4] *Ibid.*, 3 Aug. 1914.

particular attention to meetings of the Liberal backbenchers'
foreign policy committee. On 1 August the *Guardian* reported:

> Two meetings of the Liberal foreign policy group were held
> today. It is understood that about thirty to forty members
> attend these meetings, but the support which they are receiving
> in the party far exceeds that number. I estimate that four-fifths
> of the Government's supporters associate themselves informally
> with the position of Mr Ponsonby and his colleagues.[1]

Support for Ponsonby's committee was nothing like as general as
the *Guardian* supposed. Indeed, members of the committee were
divided among themselves as to what policy they should counsel
the Government to follow.

The Foreign Affairs Committee, formed in December 1911, by
1914 had lost much of its original sharp critical impetus. In its hey-
day it had never had a bigger membership than about eighty who
shared a unanimity of opinion in nothing save their common interest and concern in the conduct of foreign affairs. In so far as one
could associate a particular line of policy with the Committee, this
would be no more than a reflection of the tireless energy and influence of three men who were the leaders of the group—Philip
Morrell, Noel Buxton and Arthur Ponsonby. The members were often
as uncertain about the tactics they should pursue as they were
divided about what exactly was wrong with the manner in which
Britain's foreign affairs was being conducted. However, for all its
failings, the Committee was the principal forum for Radical discussion of foreign policy and therefore it was the natural, ready-made
nucleus for Liberal backbench debate in a time of crisis.

On 29 July, eleven Radicals[2]—'a small representative meeting of
members of the Liberal Foreign Affairs group', was how Ponsonby
described them—after discussing the European situation, instructed
Ponsonby to forward to Grey a resolution which they had passed
unanimously. Together with the resolution was a letter signed by
Ponsonby relating what had passed at the meeting.

> The most complete confidence was expressed by the meeting in
> yourself and there was a keen desire to support you in your
> efforts to restrict the area of warfare to the two powers immedi-
> ately concerned. We are most anxious to take no action which
> would embarrass you in the delicate negotiations which you
> are now conducting and it was decided that our proceedings

---

[1] *Ibid.*, 1 Aug. 1914, p. 5.
[2] Arthur Ponsonby, W. H. Dickinson, Thomas Lough, C. N. Nicolson, P. Molteno, P. Morrell, N. Buxton, Arnold Rowntree, H. Nuttall, D. M. Mason and
G. J. Bentham.

should not be reported to the Press . . . it was the feeling of the meeting that we could not support the Government in any military or naval operations which would carry this country beyond its existing treaty obligations. It was felt that if both France and Russia were informed that on no account would we be drawn into war even though they and other European powers were involved it would have a moderating effect on their policy . . .

The attached resolution urged that 'Great Britain in no conceivable circumstances should depart from a position of strict neutrality'.[1]

On receiving this letter, Grey immediately sent for Ponsonby. The Foreign Secretary promised that he would pass on the resolution to the Prime Minister, asked that the committee should not publicise its activities, and assured Ponsonby that Britain was 'absolutely free and working for peace'. Nevertheless, Grey would not make any open statement that Britain would not be drawn into the conflict, as he maintained that doubt upon this score was a useful counter for his deployment in negotiation.[2] Grey, under considerable strain, was not always as polite or as forthcoming in his conversations with backbench members of his party as he had been with Ponsonby. He admits that on one occasion he spoke 'pretty roughly' to a Liberal member who addressed him in the lobby of the Commons on the subject of Britain's neutrality.[3] Charles Trevelyan recalled the first time he became anxious about the situation was after a casual meeting with Grey.

> I went up to him [Grey] and asked him for news. I said something quite politely about the matter concerning us not at all, and that I presumed we should be strictly neutral. He replied in an extraordinarily hard, unsympathetic way. He seemed to be coldly angry with me. . . . So obvious was it that he disliked the idea of neutrality, that I got extraordinarily uncomfortable, without knowing what it all meant. It created a profound distrust in my mind.[4]

On 30 July the Foreign Affairs Committee met again, and Ponsonby reported to the twenty-two members present his conversation with Grey. After some discussion, Ponsonby was once more instructed to write, but this time to the Prime Minister. The letter was sharp and to the point. If the Cabinet should decide to take part in the European conflict, then they must withdraw their support from the Government. This view, Ponsonby assured Asquith, was shared

---

[1] Full text of letter and resolution quoted Hazlehurst, 35–7.
[2] Ponsonby's Notes of Grey's statement to him, 29 July 1914, quoted Hazlehurst, 37.   [3] Grey, i, 338.   [4] Charles Trevelyan, p. 1.

by nine-tenths of the party. Asquith does not seem to have been unduly perturbed by this threatening note from his backbenchers. He had never concerned himself overmuch with what the rank and file of the parliamentary Liberal party were thinking. His tactics had always been to capture the Cabinet for any measure he supported. Thereafter, success was assured.[1] What is more, if Ponsonby's 'threat' is carefully examined, there appear a number of grave weaknesses. He wrote of nine-tenths of the party, but then admits, and that with exaggeration, that as yet he was not 'able to speak actually for more than 30 members'. The letters to both Grey and Asquith contained significant qualifications of the neutralist case. Great Britain was not to be committed to a war 'in which neither treaty obligations, British interests, British honour nor even sentiments of friendship are *at present* in the remotest degree involved'.[2] Here was the vulnerable part of the Radical case. For the moment Britain may have been free of any treaty obligations, but what if Belgium was invaded? Grey recounts how the Liberal member who spoke of neutrality reacted when the Foreign Secretary asked ' "Suppose Germany violates the neutrality of Belgium?" For a moment he paused, like one who, running at speed, finds himself confronted by an obstacle, unexpected and unforeseen. Then he said with emphasis, "She won't do it." "I don't say she will, but supposing she does?" "She won't do it", he repeated confidently, ...'[3] Kate Courtney admitted in her diary that 'German violation of Belgium neutrality was the rock on which all the anti-war feeling was shipwrecked'. It was not that the Radicals had not considered the possibility, they just *hoped* it would never materialise. 'I shared that feeling that we could not stand by—but hoped no German soldier would get in Belgium.'[4] And Richard Holt recorded in his diary: 'I had thought we might and should have kept out of the war but when Germany decided on an unprovoked attack upon Belgium . . . it seemed impossible for us to stand by.'[5] Asquith, then, could discount Ponsonby's threat because it was apparent that even the hard Radical core of the party was divided about the Belgian contingency. From the account of these days in the diary of Christopher Addison, who attended most of the Foreign Affairs Committee meetings, we know of the rebels' abject misery and the confusion in their minds. They were 'as helpless as rats in a trap'.[6]

---

[1] See Asquith and Spender, ii, 95.
[2] Ponsonby to Asquith, 30 July 1914, quoted Hazlehurst, 38 (my italics).
[3] Grey, i, 338.   [4] Courtney Diary, 9 Aug. 1914.
[5] Holt Diary, 9 Aug. 1914.
[6] Christopher Addison, *Politics From Within* (1924), i, 32.

In their helplessness the Radicals were forced to trust in the good faith of the Government. Edmund Harvey, reporting events in a letter to his father, wrote that he dreaded the influence of Churchill in the Cabinet.[1] Yet it was Winston that Ponsonby sought as an ally for the neutralist cause. He counselled Churchill to 'use all your influence towards moderation'. While the young minister was prepared to agree that 'Balkan quarrels are no vital concern of ours', he asked Ponsonby what if France and Belgium were drawn into the conflict. 'It would be wrong at this moment to pronounce finally one way or another as to our duty or our interests.'[2] The Foreign Affairs Committee met twice on Friday, 31 July. At the morning session they agreed that they would not press the awkward private-notice question which Ponsonby had informed the Prime Minister they would ask Grey. When they met again that evening it was decided that they would do nothing definite until after the weekend. By then, it would be too late. Their procrastination was in fact no more than the tacit recognition that they were confused. Divided among themselves, they did not know what to do for the best. On a motion that Britain should remain neutral no matter what happened to Belgium, twenty-three only of those present voted. Even the nineteen who supported the resolution confessed that it was little more than the expression of a pious hope.[3]

While the Radicals hesitated, undecided about the best strategy to pursue, one man acted with certainty and promptitude. Norman Angell returned to London from the Old Jordans conference—'so encouraging in all the evidence that it gave of the ferment of new and more hopeful ideas in the minds of the youngsters there gathered' —to find his desk littered with telegrams and letters all demanding 'Where are you going to stand if war breaks out?'[4] Angell determined that the best course he could advise was to delay the entry of Great Britain into war for as long as was possible. 'As a neutral, Britain could exert pressure upon both combatants. . . . This sort of power . . . would disappear the moment she entered the war.' To that end, on 28 July, Angell and his friends formed a Neutrality League. Kate Courtney noted: 'It looks as if the Liberal rank and file will at last mobilise and put pressure upon the Government.'[5]

[1] T. E. Harvey to W. Harvey, 30 July 1914, Harvey MSS.
[2] Ponsonby to Churchill and Churchill to Ponsonby, 31 July 1914, quoted in R. S. Churchill, *Winston Churchill Companion Volume* (1969), ii:3, 1190–1 and *Young Statesman*, 715–16.
[3] See Addison, i, 37.
[4] This and subsequent quotations in this section, unless otherwise cited, from Norman Angell, *After All* (1951), 180–3.
[5] Courtney Diary, 1 Aug. 1914.

A manifesto was issued that was concerned mainly with the problem of increasing Russian influence in Europe because of war.

> It is urged that we must ensure the Victory of France and Russia in order to maintain the Balance of Power. If we are successful in securing the victory of Russia in this war, we shall upset the balance enormously by making her the dominant military power of Europe, possibly the dictator both in this Continent and in Asia. . . . Germany, on the other hand, is a nation of 65 millions, wedged in between hostile States, highly civilised, with a culture that has contributed greatly in the past to western civilisation, racially allied to ourselves and with moral ideals largely resembling our own. . . . Our two peoples have maintained unbroken peace since their earliest history. The last war that we fought upon the Continent was for the purpose of checking the growth of Russia. We are now asked to go to war to promote it.

The League also printed half a million leaflets—'Shall We Fight for a Russian Europe?'—which voluntary workers distributed in London and the provinces.

Angell's part, as the man of action in the cause of peace, was recorded by Charles Trevelyan, whose own activities were circumscribed by his membership of the Government. Morning, 31 July:

> I found him [Angell] preparing for a Press demonstration next week in favour of neutrality. He had become rigidly practical. He was buying up whole sheets of newspapers for advertising neutrality . . . August 1: Angell was hard at work for next week, the only man indeed who seemed to have much initiative. The Neutrality Committee with Hobson and Graham Wallas was getting names but did not know how to act furiously in an emergency.[1]

But even Angell's energy and purpose were of no avail. Events overwhelmed intention. C. P. Scott wrote to Angell on 5 August: 'With all your promptitude you were too late, as we all were. It is a monstrous thing that the country should find itself at war to all intents and purposes without being consulted.'[2]

Meanwhile the Labour party had not been idle in its efforts to keep Britain out of war, but all along there was a sense of disbelief that the conflagration they had so long dreaded should materialise so suddenly and from a seemingly insignificant and certainly remote source. 'The war must be stopped and we must stop it,' wrote W. C. Anderson in the *Labour Leader*, but then added, 'I am not certain, even now, that the Big Powers of Europe and the

[1] Charles Trevelyan, pp. 1–3.
[2] Scott to Angell, 5 Aug. 1914, quoted Angell, 185.

financial interests behind them will allow the struggle to be carried very far.'[1] In 1907 the International had issued a declaration, re-affirmed at Copenhagen in 1910, that

> If war threatens to break out, it is the duty of the working class in the countries concerned and of their parliamentary representatives, with the help of the International Socialist Bureau as a means of coordinating their action, to use every effort to prevent war by all the means which seem to them most appropriate, having regard to the sharpness of the class war and to the general political situation.
>
> Should war none the less break out, their duty is to intervene to bring it promptly to an end, and with all their energies to use the political and economic crisis created by the war to rouse the populace from its slumbers, and to hasten the fall of capitalist domination.[2]

A compromise verbal formula riddled with dubious assumptions was to prove a worthless banner behind which the forces of European Socialism might march to wage their war against war.

The International Socialist Bureau met at Brussels on 29 July. The meeting had been summoned in some haste to consider the effect of Austria's declaration of war upon Serbia. So little apprehensive were the delegates of a general European war, that they decided the meeting of the International should go ahead, merely promoting the date of meeting from 23 to the 9 August, and changing the venue from Vienna to Paris. That evening, after their deliberations, there was held a great public meeting in Brussels, and the crowds were addressed by Hugo Haase, Jaurès, Emile Vandervelde and Keir Hardie. They still did not comprehend, they would not believe, that general war was imminent. The next day the delegates parted to return to their homes.[3]

On 30 July the parliamentary Labour party unanimously adopted a resolution that though war might not be altogether prevented, Britain would stay out. 'All labour organisations in the country' were charged 'to watch events vigilantly so as to oppose, if need be, in the most effective way, any action which might involve Great Britain in war'.[4] The assassination of Jaurès brought an awful sense of immediacy and actuality to socialists who still could not believe that Britain would be involved in war. On 1 August, the British section of the International issued a manifesto against war signed

[1] *Labour Leader*, 30 July 1914.
[2] Quoted G. D. H. Cole, *A History of the Labour Party from 1914* (1948), 5.
[3] See William Stewart, *J. Keir Hardie* (1921), 342-3 and Agnes Hamilton, *Arthur Henderson* (1938), 93-4.
[4] *Manchester Guardian*, 31 July 1914.

by the chairman, Keir Hardie, and the secretary, Arthur Henderson. The manifesto was titled, *An Appeal to the British Working Class.*

> It is for you to take full account of the desperate situation and to act promptly and vigorously in the interests of peace. You have never been consulted about the war . . . everywhere vehement protests are made against the greed and intrigues of militarists and armament-mongers. We call upon you to do the same here in Great Britain . . . compel the governing class and their Press who are eager to commit you to cooperate with Russian despotism to keep silence and respect the decision of the overwhelming majority of the people, who will have neither part nor lot in such infamy. The success of Russia at the present day would be a curse on the world . . . workers stand together therefore for peace. Combine and conquer the militarist enemy and the self-seeking imperialist . . . proclaim that for you the days of plunder and butchery have gone by. . . . Down with class rule! Down with the rule of brute force! Down with war! Up with the peaceful rule of the people![1]

The *Manchester Guardian* insisted that 'what is wanted is an open demonstration which can serve as a rallying point for public opinion'.[2] Telegrams were despatched, arrangements were feverishly made, and on Sunday, 2 August, public meetings were held in all parts of the country. The most important of these meetings, held in Trafalgar Square, London, was a monster rally organised by the British section of the International Socialist Bureau. Beneath lowering skies, an anxious crowd was addressed by a dozen speakers uniting in passionate protest against being dragged into an alliance with Tsarist Russia, denouncing the needless horror of war, and counting its cost in unemployment and the suffering of the innocent. The enthusiasm of the audience was intense, the cheers for international solidarity were loud and long, the singing of the *Red Flag* and the *Internationale* passionate. A violent downpour of rain did not check the 'comrades . . . who stood gallantly to their umbrellas and cheered for "the war against war" ' while a group of 'feeble-hearted jingoes' who had 'attempted a war demonstration on the edge of the gathering' scattered before the fury of the storm.[3] The inevitable resolution was carried by acclamation.

> We protest against any step being taken by the Government of this country to support Russia, either directly or in consequence of an undertaking with France, as being not only offensive to the political traditions of the country but disastrous to Europe,

---

[1] *Labour Leader*, 6 Aug. 1914.   [2] *Manchester Guardian*, 1 Aug. 1914.
[3] *Labour Leader*, 6 Aug. 1914. The I.L.P. weekly also gives details of the other meetings held throughout the country.

and declare that as we have no interest, direct or indirect, in the threatened quarrels which may result from the action of Servia, the Government of Great Britain should rigidly decline to engage in war, but should confine itself to efforts to bring about peace as speedily as possible.

The meeting over, the crowd dispersed, wandering unhappily, and for the most part in silence, about the streets; exchanging rumours, harbouring hopes that shrank while fears grew. Most of the speakers had made their way to Ramsay MacDonald's flat in Lincoln's Inn Fields. He had not attended the meeting because he had been previously summoned for consultation to Downing Street. When he returned, he brought no cheerful news to his anxious friends. Mac-Donald had told Morley, whom he had encountered in the street, that he would have nothing to do with the war; but he had grimly reassured other ministers, who were still doubtful whether there would be popular support for the war, that it 'would be the most popular war the country had ever fought'. MacDonald could no longer doubt that Britain would be involved in battle. That evening, dining at Lord Riddell's house with Masterman, Simon and Lloyd George, Labour's leader avowed, 'In three months there will be bread riots, and we shall come in.'[1]

'Let every man look into his own heart, his own feelings and construe the extent of the obligation for himself'[2]

Monday afternoon, 3 August, and the Commons was suffocatingly crowded; the gangways obstructed, Liberal, Labour and Conservative members unaccustomedly seated together, the galleries full; everyone eager, expectant, waiting upon the words of the Foreign Secretary. A little after three o'clock, Sir Edward Grey rose in his place to make the speech that, for most men, was to be the decisive moment in the crisis. He did not feel nervous. 'At such a moment there could be neither hope of personal success nor fear of personal failure. In a great crisis a man who has to act or speak stands bare and stripped of choice. He has to do what is in him to do: just this is what he will and must do, and he can do no other.'[3] The speech, as remarkable for its lack of preparation[4] as the rapture of its reception,[5] was presented in Grey's usual style, fumbling and hesitant. He did not argue his case, he appealed 'to the individual conscience,

---

1 Elton, 242–4.
2 From Grey's speech, *Hansard*, v: 65: 1809–27.
3 Grey, ii, 14.
4 See Grey's own comments and A. C. Murray, *Master and Brother* (1945), 123.
5 See G. M. Trevelyan, 265.

thereby disarming criticism', and all with an apparent and 'perfect sincerity' so that the listener was drawn 'on to the irresistible conclusion that war was inevitable for us'.[1]

Grey began his speech by attempting to establish the correct tone to which the House might respond. He need not have concerned himself—every struggling, stumbling sentence, promoted the potency of his sincerity and advertised the honesty of his purpose. He cautioned his audience to approach the crisis 'from the point of British interests, British honour and British obligations, free from all passion as to why peace has not been preserved'. The fears that Britain had a secret engagement to France, he dismissed. Britain's hands were free:

> What the Prime Minister and I said to the House of Commons was perfectly justified, and that as regards our freedom to decide in a crisis what our line should be, whether we should intervene or whether we should abstain, the Government remained perfectly free, and *a fortiori*, the House of Commons remains perfectly free.

Of course, the entente had created mutual friendship between the two nations, but did that imply obligation? Grey asked the members to search their hearts to supply the answer, and to help them in their search reminded them that France had bared her Northern seaboard because of that confidence in, and friendship she felt for Britain. Could Britain stand idly by 'if a foreign fleet engaged in a war which France had not sought . . . came down the English Channel and bombarded and battered the undefended coasts of France'? And should France withdraw her fleet from the Mediterranean, then would not British interests be in jeopardy? The Government, therefore, in honour and for the sake of Britain's interests, had told the French that should the German fleet enter the Channel then Britain would afford France naval assistance.

With Britain's relationship to France disposed of, Grey now turned his attention to the question of Belgium. The House was led gently from the terms of the 1839 treaty, via the opinions of Gladstone in 1870, to the appeal of Albert, King of the Belgians, to King George for diplomatic intervention. 'Diplomatic intervention took place last week on our part. What can diplomatic intervention do now? We have great and vital interests in the independence—and integrity is the least part—of Belgium.' Could Britain stand aside—

---

[1] See Cecil's comment, quoted Trevelyan, 265; and George, Baron Riddell, *War Diary* (n.d.), 31.

saving questions of treaty obligation—while Belgium, and possibly France and probably Holland, lost their independence?

> If, in a crisis like this, we run away . . . , I doubt whether, whatever material force we might have at the end, it would be of very much value in face of the respect that we should have lost. And do not believe, whether a Great Power stands outside this war or not, it is going to be in a position at the end of it to exert its superior strength. For us, with a powerful fleet, which we believe able to protect our commerce, to protect our shores, and to protect our interests, if we are engaged in war, we shall suffer but little more than we shall suffer even if we stand aside.

Grey made plain the Government had determined that action by Britain could not long be delayed. Last week they had striven persistently and earnestly for peace. 'But that is over . . .'

> I have put the vital facts before the House, and if, as seems not improbable, we are forced, and rapidly forced, to take our stand upon those issues, then I believe, when the country realises what is at stake, what the real issues are, . . . we shall be supported throughout, not only by the House of Commons, but by the determination, the resolution, the courage, and the endurance of the whole country.

Grey's immediate prediction was confirmed by the loud applause of the members as he concluded his speech. The news that Grey had been cheered brought 'inexpressible relief' to the Foreign Office.[1] In Addison's opinion, Grey's speech had 'crushed out all hope of peace and of our being able to keep clear'.[2] The Foreign Secretary, who avowed he hated war,[3] had insured that Britain should have her part in Armageddon. Charles Trevelyan would record in sorrow, amazement and anger:

> I was prepared for bad news, but in no way for the bare-faced appeal to passion. He gave not a single argument why we should support France. But he showed he had all along been leading her to expect our support and appealed to us as bound in honour. . . . The Liberals, very few of them, cheered at all, whatever they did later, while the Tories shouted with delight.[4]

When Grey concluded his speech he knew that 'he was possessed in overwhelming measure of the support of the assembly'.[5] After the Foreign Secretary, Bonar Law pledged the Unionist party, and then Redmond, amidst great enthusiasm, promised Irish support for war. Describing the scene, the parliamentary correspondent of

---

[1] G. M. Trevelyan, 265.
[2] Addison, i, 32.
[3] See Nicolson, *Lord Carnock*, 422.
[4] Charles Trevelyan, p. 5.
[5] W. S. Churchill, *World Crisis*, 235.

R A W—P

the *Manchester Guardian* wrote, 'To convince doubters of the soundness of the Government's decision only one thing more was needed—a declaration from Mr Ramsay MacDonald that the Government was doing wrong. This was given at once.'[1]

Even as MacDonald rose to speak, there were murmurs of hostility and some members ostentatiously left the Commons. He knew what he had to say would not be welcome to a House, the greater part of which was already intoxicated with patriotic passion.

> I think he [Grey] is wrong. I think the Government which he represents and for which he speaks is wrong. . . . There has been no crime committed by statesmen of this character without those statesmen appealing to their nation's honour. We fought the Crimean War because of our honour. We rushed to South Africa because of our honour. The right hon. Gentleman is appealing to us today because of our honour. . . . So far as we are concerned, whatever may happen, whatever may be said about us, whatever attacks may be made upon us, we will say that this country ought to have remained neutral, because in the deepest part of our hearts we believe that is right, and that that alone is consistent with the honour of the country.

MacDonald had spoken as leader of his party. Within two days, wavering, then bending before the blast of popular opinion, all save four members of the parliamentary Labour party rejected the resolution of its Executive that Britain should have remained neutral, and MacDonald resigned the leadership to Henderson.

The voice of dissent within the Liberal ranks was not to be heard until the evening, when the House reassembled with scarce a minister present. There had been a short meeting of the Cabinet meanwhile, when it had been decided to postpone consideration of what to reply to Germany's ultimatum to Belgium. Grey was to take it on himself to draft and send the ultimatum to Germany, insisting she should withdraw her demands on Belgium. Unless a satisfactory reply was received in London by 11.00 p.m. on 4 August—and no such reply was expected—then the British Government would be obliged to 'take all steps in their power to uphold the neutrality of Belgium'.[2] The Commons could scarce contain their impatience and anger in the short adjournment debate that ended that momentous day, as speaker after speaker rose from the Liberal benches not to affirm but to denounce the Government's policy. Of the fifteen Liberal members that spoke, four only supported Grey, and two of these in qualified fashion.[3] Eventually Balfour, outraged by a series of

---

[1] *Manchester Guardian*, 4 Aug. 1914.   [2] *B.D.* XI, 594.
[3] Complete debate, see *Hansard*, v:65:1810–84. Markham and Pringle were the only Liberal speakers to give unqualified support to Grey.

speeches that had extolled the cause of neutrality, demanded the debate be adjourned. 'What we have been having tonight', he declared, 'are the very dregs and lees of the Debate, in no sense representing the various views of the Members of this House.'

There was no reason for the Radicals to suppose that their appeals would be heeded in the last hours of peace. How could they expect success when their every hope and wish had been always cruelly disappointed? They insisted that the people demanded peace, yet this affirmation was scarcely audible in the din of martial enthusiasm. The nation, for the most part, willingly embraced war, thrilled with the excitement and the panoply of arms. Germany had broken the peace. Her ally Austria had tried to humiliate Serbia even as Germany now bullied brave little Belgium. 'I pictured France and Russia as the victims of aggression. . . . I felt the Jingo spirit rising within me. I sympathized with the Frenchmen who muttered, *Nous en avons assez*. We all had had enough of it. If they asked for it, they should have it. Let the wager of battle decide.'[1] Hamilton Fyfe's recollection of his mood as Britain went to war, was more typical of the general attitude than that voiced by a Harvey or a Rowntree. The Radicals were helpless to stem the tide, as Arthur Ponsonby had been forced to admit. 'The war fever had already begun . . . I saw bands of half drunken youths waving flags, and I saw a group outside a great club in St James's Street being encouraged by members of the club from the balcony. . . . And that is what is called patriotism.'

The Nation, so long the leading voice of Radicalism, in an article published four days after the beginning of war, admitted defeat. 'We have no criticism to offer.'[2] Who would respect or listen to the voice of Radicalism now?

> Who in the future will pay attention to the *Daily News* . . . the *Manchester Guardian* and other journals of the same stamp? These idealists . . . who refuse to look reality in the face and prefer to be deceived and to deceive their followers. . . . Who will heed when the Lord Courtneys and Wedgwoods and the Trevelyans presume to air their baby views on so complicated a subject as foreign politics and our duties towards our friends and allies? I venture to say, after what has happened, no one.[3]

What of Socialism, in which *The Nation* had declared its trust, as capable of 'checking any war for any end save the defence so legitimate and inevitable that even a Socialist conscience would regret-

---

[1] Hamilton Fyfe, *The Making of an Optimist* (1921), 27–8.
[2] *The Nation*, 'The War of Fear', 8 Aug. 1914.
[3] *New Age*, 13 Aug. 1914.

fully approve it'?[1] The Independent Labour party had advertised that claim boldly but a few days before war began.[2] Now Keir Hardie admitted

> the great outstanding fact is the impotence of the moral and Labour forces of Europe . . . the working-class movement, Trade-Unionist and Socialist alike, is contemptuously passed over. Ten million Socialist and Labour votes in Europe, without a trace or vestige of power to prevent war! Our demonstrations and speeches and resolutions are all alike futile. We simply do not count.[3]

Though all would have seemed lost, and many, like Kate Courtney, must have felt that 'further action for peace [was] hopeless for a season',[4] yet in this darkest hour of their fortunes some Radicals still refused to abandon hope. The day after war was declared, Charles Trevelyan wrote to E. D. Morel: 'There is a body of Liberal members united for common action on the war question, trying to establish connection with the Labour party. Ponsonby, Morrell and Rowntree inspire it. I think it more than likely that it may be an organisation which could connect with outside efforts and groups.'[5]

Already the spirit of dissent in foreign affairs was being reorganised, soon to emerge as the influential Union of Democratic Control. The genius of Radicalism was the capacity of some of its finer spirits always to harbour and support a brighter vision of the future.

> Democracy may rise stronger out of this terrible refining fire. And I hope, my friend, that both the passionate, impatient ones like you, and the slower ones like me . . . may be less critical of each other than we have been—For this fearful common enemy has overwhelmed all we care about.
>
> But the seed grows in this wonderful earth, and perhaps what we now laboriously sow, watered with the tears of millions, may grow to a great harvest. . . . It is the right *spirit* that gives life, as now it is the wrong spirit that killeth.[6]

---

[1] *The Nation*, 17 May 1914.   [2] See *Labour Leader*, 30 July 1914.
[3] *Ibid.*, 6 Aug. 1914.   [4] Courtney Diary, 9 Aug. 1914.
[5] Trevelyan to E. D. Morel, 5 Aug. 1914, E. D. Morel Papers, F.6, File 1, U.D.C. Early Documents.
[6] Charles Trevelyan to Lansbury, 7 Aug. 1914, Lansbury Collection, vol. vii, f. 170.

Select Bibliography of Printed Sources

A. Biographies (Arranged by subject)

Christopher Addison
ADDISON, CHRISTOPHER. *Politics from Within*, 2 vols, Herbert Jenkins, 1924

L. S. Amery
AMERY, L. S. *My Political Life*, 3 vols, Hutchinson, 1953–55

Norman Angell
ANGELL, NORMAN. *After All: The autobiography of Norman Angell*, Hamish Hamilton, 1951

H. H. Asquith, 1st Earl of Oxford and Asquith
ASQUITH, HERBERT HENRY. *The Genesis of the War*, Cassell, 1923
ASQUITH, HERBERT HENRY. *Fifty Years of Parliament*, Cassell, 2 vols, 1926
ASQUITH, HERBERT HENRY. *Memories and Reflections; 1852–1927*, 2 vols, Cassell, 1928
JENKINS, ROY. *Asquith*, Collins, 1964
SPENDER, J. A., and ASQUITH, CYRIL. *Life of Lord Oxford and Asquith*, 2 vols, Hutchinson, 1932

Lady Asquith
ASQUITH, MARGOT. *Autobiography* (Butterworth 1920), Penguin Books, 2 vols, 1936

J. Allen Baker
BAKER, E. B., and BAKER, P. J. NOEL. *J. Allen Baker, M.P.: a memoir*, The Swathmore Press, 1927

Arthur James Balfour, 1st Earl of Balfour
DUGDALE, BLANCHE. *Arthur James Balfour*, 2 vols, Hutchinson, 1936

Augustine Birrell
BIRRELL, AUGUSTINE. *Things Past Redress*, Faber, 1937

Wilfrid Scawen Blunt
BLUNT, WILFRID SCAWEN. *My Diaries: being a personal narrative of events, 1888–1914*, 2 vols, Martin Secker, 1919–20

Horatio Bottomley
SYMONS, JULIAN. *Horatio Bottomley: a biography*, Cresset Press, 1955

Sir John Brunner
KOSS, STEPHEN E. *Sir John Brunner: Radical Plutocrat 1842–1919*, Cambridge University Press, 1970
James Bryce
FISHER, H. A. L. *James Bryce*, 2 vols, Macmillan, 1927
John Buchan, 1st Baron Tweedsmuir
BUCHAN, JOHN. *Memory-Hold-the-Door*, Hodder & Stoughton, 1940
John Burns
KENT, WILLIAM. *John Burns: Labour's Lost Leader*, Williams & Norgate, 1950
C. R. Buxton
BUNSEN, VICTORIA DE. *Charles Roden Buxton: a memoir*, Allen & Unwin, 1948
Noel Buxton
ANDERSON, MOSA. *Noel Buxton: a life*, Allen & Unwin, 1952
CONWELL-EVANS, T. P. *Foreign Policy from a Back-Bench, 1904–18: a study based on the papers of Lord Noel Buxton*, Oxford University Press, 1932
George Cadbury
GARDINER, A. G. *Life of George Cadbury*, Cassell, 1923
Edward Cadogan
CADOGAN, EDWARD. *Before the Deluge: memories and reflections*, Murray, 1961
Sir Henry Campbell-Bannerman
SPENDER, J. A. *Life of the Rt. Hon. Sir Henry Campbell-Bannerman*, 2 vols, Hodder & Stoughton, 1924
Austen Chamberlain
CHAMBERLAIN, AUSTEN. *Down the Years*, Cassell, 1935
CHAMBERLAIN, AUSTEN. *Politics from Inside: an epistolary chronicle, 1906–1914*, Cassell, 1936
Joseph Chamberlain
FRASER, PETER. *Joseph Chamberlain*, Cassell, 1966
GARVIN, J. L. *Chamberlain*, Macmillan 2 vols, 1932–33
Winston Spencer Churchill
CHURCHILL, WINSTON S. *The World Crisis, 1911–1914*, Butterworth, 1923
CHURCHILL, W. S. *Great Contemporaries* (Butterworth, 1937), reprint Macmillan, 1942
BONHAM CARTER, VIOLET. *Winston Churchill As I Knew Him* (Eyre & Spottiswoode and Collins, 1965), Pan Books, 1967
CHURCHILL, RANDOLPH S. *Young Statesman, 1901–14*, Heinemann, 1967
Leonard Courtney, 1st Baron Courtney of Penwith
GOOCH, G. P. *Life of Lord Courtney*, Macmillan, 1920
Sir Randal Cremer
EVANS, HOWARD. *Sir Randal Cremer: his life and work*, Fisher Unwin, 1909
Lord Crewe
POPE-HENNESSY, JAMES. *Lord Crewe 1858–1945: the likeness of a Liberal*, Constable, 1955

Sir Charles Dilke
GWYNNE, STEPHEN, and TUCKWELL, G. M. *The Life of the Rt. Hon. Charles W. Dilke*, 2 vols, Murray, 1917

King Edward VII
LEE, SIR SIDNEY. *King Edward VII*, 2 vols, Macmillan, 1925–27
MAGNUS, PHILIP. *King Edward the Seventh*, Murray, 1964

Viscount Elibank
MURRAY, A. C. *Master and Brother: the Murrays of Elibank*, Murray, 1945

John Edward Ellis
BASSETT, A. TILNEY. *The Life of the Rt. Hon. John Edward Ellis, M.P.*, Macmillan, 1914

Lord Esher
ESHER, REGINALD, VISCOUNT. *Journals and Letters of Reginald Viscount Esher 1860–1915*, ed. Oliver Esher and M. V. Brett, 3 vols, Nicholson and Watson, 1934–38 (abbr. as *E.P.*)

John Fisher, 1st Baron Fisher of Kilverstone
FISHER, JOHN. *Memories and Records*, New York, Doran, 1920
FISHER, JOHN ARBUTHNOT, 1st Baron Fisher of Kilverstone. *Fear God and Dread Nought: the Correspondence of Admiral of the Fleet Lord Fisher of Kilverstone*, ed. A. J. Marder, 3 vols, Cape 1952–59
BACON, ADMIRAL R. H. The *Life of Lord Fisher of Kilverstone*, 2 vols, Doubleday, 1929
HOUGH, RICHARD. *First Sea Lord: an authorised biography of Admiral Lord Fisher*, Allen & Unwin, 1970

Sir Almeric Fitzroy
FITZROY, SIR ALMERIC. *Memoirs*, 2 vols, Hutchinson, 1927

Hamilton Fyfe
FYFE, HAMILTON. *The Making of an Optimist*, Leonard Parsons, 1921
FYFE, HAMILTON. *Sixty Years of Fleet Street*, W. H. Allen, 1949

J. L. Garvin
GARVIN, KATHARINE. *J. L. Garvin: a memoir*, Heinemann, 1948
GOLLIN, A. M. *The Observer and J. L. Garvin, 1908–14: a study in great editorship*, Oxford University Press, 1960

King George V
NICOLSON, SIR HAROLD. *King George V: his life and reign*, Constable, 1952

G. P. Gooch
GOOCH, G. P. *Under Six Reigns*, Longmans, 1958

Edward Grey, 1st Viscount Grey of Fallodon
GREY, EDWARD. *Twenty-five Years: 1892–1916*, 2 vols, Hodder & Stoughton, 1925
TREVELYAN, G. M. *Grey of Fallodon*, Longmans, 1937
ROBBINS, KEITH. *Sir Edward Grey: a biography of Lord Grey of Fallodon*, Cassell, 1971

R. B. Haldane, 1st Viscount Haldane
HALDANE, RICHARD. *Richard Burdon Haldane: an autobiography*, Hodder & Stoughton, 1929
HALDANE, R. B. *Before the War*, Cassell, 1920

MAURICE, SIR FREDERICK. *Haldane 1856–1915*, 2 vols, Faber, 1937

KOSS, STEPHEN E. *Lord Haldane: scapegoat for Liberalism*, Columbia University Press, 1969

SOMMER, DUDLEY. *Haldane of Cloan: his life and times 1856–1928*, Allen & Unwin, 1960

Sir Maurice Hankey

ROSKILL, S. W. *Hankey, Man of Secrets 1877–1918*, Collins, 1970

J. Keir Hardie

STEWART, WILLIAM. *J. Keir Hardie: a biography*, Waverley, 1921

Charles, 1st Baron Hardinge of Penshurst

HARDINGE, CHARLES. *Old Diplomacy*, Murray, 1947

A. G. C. Harvey

HIRST, F. W., ed. *A. G. C. Harvey: a memoir*, Cobden Sanderson, 1926

Arthur Henderson

HAMILTON, MARY AGNES. *Arthur Henderson*, Heinemann, 1938

F. W. Hirst

HIRST, F. W. *In the Golden Days*, Muller, 1947

L. T. Hobhouse

HOBSON, J. A. and GINSBERG, M. *L. T. Hobhouse; his life and work*, Allen & Unwin, 1931

Stephen Hobhouse

HOBHOUSE, STEPHEN. *Forty Years and an Epilogue: an autobiography*, James Clarke, 1951

Colonel E. M. House

SEYMOUR, CHARLES, ed. *The Intimate Papers of Colonel House*, 2 vols, Benn, 1926

H. M. Hyndman

HYNDMAN, H. M. *The Record of an Adventurous Life*, Macmillan, 1911

Lord Kitchener

MAGNUS, PHILIP. *Kitchener: portrait of an Imperialist*, Murray, 1958

Andrew Bonar Law

BLAKE, ROBERT. *The Unknown Prime Minister: the life and times of Alfred Bonar Law 1858–1923*, Eyre & Spottiswoode, 1955

David Lloyd George

LLOYD GEORGE, DAVID. *War Memoirs*, 2 vols, Odhams, 1934

JONES, THOMAS. *Lloyd George*, Oxford University Press, 1951

OWEN, FRANK. *Tempestuous Journey: Lloyd George, his life and times*, Hutchinson, 1954

J. Ramsay MacDonald

ELTON, LORD. *Life of James Ramsay MacDonald*, Collins, 1939

Reginald McKenna

MCKENNA, STEPHEN. *Reginald McKenna 1863–1943: a memoir*, Eyre & Spottiswoode, 1948

Stephen McKenna

MCKENNA, STEPHEN. *While I Remember*, Thornton Butterworth, 1921

David M. Mason

MASON, DAVID M. *Six Years of Politics*, Murray, 1917

C. F. G. Masterman
MASTERMAN, LUCY. *C. F. G. Masterman: a biography*, Nicholson & Watson, 1939

A. M. Messiny
MESSINY, A. M. *Mes Souvenirs*, Paris, 1937

Alfred, 1st Viscount Milner
GOLLIN, A. M. *Proconsul in Politics: Lord Milner*, Blond, 1964

John Morley, 1st Viscount Morley
MORLEY, JOHN. *Recollections*, 2 vols, Macmillan, 1917

MORLEY, JOHN. *Memorandum on Resignation: August 1914*, Macmillan, 1928

MORGAN, J. H. *John Viscount Morley: an appreciation and some reminiscences*, Murray, 1924

HAMMER, D. A. *John Morley: Liberal intellectual in politics*, Oxford, Clarendon Press, 1968

KOSS, STEPHEN E. *John Morley at the India Office, 1905–10*, Yale University Press, 1969

H. W. Nevinson
NEVINSON, H. W. *Fire of Life*, Gollancz, 1935

Sir Arthur Nicolson, Bt, 1st Baron Carnock
NICOLSON, SIR HAROLD. *Sir Arthur Nicolson, Bart., First Lord Carnock: a study in the old diplomacy*, Constable, 1930

Walter H. Page
HENDRICK, B. J. *The Life and Letters of Walter H. Page*, Heinemann, 1930

Charles à Court Repington
REPINGTON, CHARLES. *Vestigia*, Constable, 1919

Ripon, 1st Marquess of
WOLF, LUCIEN. *Life of Lord Ripon*, Murray, 2 vols, 1921

George Allardyce Riddell, 1st Baron Riddell
RIDDELL, LORD. *War Diary*, Nicholson & Watson, 1933

RIDDELL, LORD. *More Pages from my Diary 1908–14*, Country Life, 1934

James Rennell Rodd, 1st Baron Rennell of Rodd
RODD, JAMES RENNELL. *Social and Diplomatic Memories 1902–1919*, Edward Arnold, 1925

Lord Rosebery, 5th Earl
JAMES, ROBERT RHODES. *Rosebery*, Weidenfeld & Nicolson, 1964

CREWE, MARQUESS OF. *Life of Rosebery*, Murray, 1930

Bertrand Russell, 3rd Earl Russell
RUSSELL, BERTRAND. *The Autobiography of Bertrand Russell*, 3 vols, Allen & Unwin, 1967–69

Herbert Louis Samuel, 1st Viscount Samuel
SAMUEL, HERBERT. *Memoirs*, Cresset Press, 1945

C. P. Scott
SCOTT, C. P. *The Political Diaries of C. P. Scott, 1911–1928*, ed. Trevor Wilson, Collins, 1970

HAMMOND, J. L. *C. P. Scott of the Manchester Guardian*, Bell, 1934

MONTAGUE, C. E. and others. *C. P. Scott 1846–1932: the making of the 'Manchester Guardian'*, Muller, 1946

Sir John Simon, 1st Viscount Simon
SIMON, LORD. *Retrospect*, Hutchinson, 1953

Philip Snowden
SNOWDEN, PHILIP. *An Autobiography*, 2 vols, Nicholson & Watson, 1934

J. A. Spender
SPENDER, J. A. *Life, Journalism and Politics*, 2 vols, Cassell, 1927
HARRIS, WILSON. *J. A. Spender*, Cassell, 1946

Sir Cecil Spring Rice
GWYNN, STEPHEN, ed. *The Letters and Friendships of Sir Cecil Spring Rice: a record*, 2 vols, Constable, 1929

W. T. Stead
WHYTE, FREDERICK. *The Life of W. T. Stead*, 2 vols, Cape, 1925

Lord Sydenham [George Clarke]
SYDENHAM, LORD. *My Working Life*, Murray, 1927

Beatrice and Sidney Webb
WEBB, BEATRICE. *Our Partnership*, Longmans, 1948

Josiah Wedgwood
WEDGWOOD, JOSIAH. *Memoirs of a Fighting Life*, Hutchinson, 1941
WEDGWOOD, C. V. *The Last of the Radicals: Josiah Wedgwood, M.P.*, Cape 1951

Sir Henry Wilson
CALLWELL, C. E. *Field Marshal Sir Henry Wilson: his life and diaries*, 2 vols, Cassell, 1927
COLLIER, BASIL. *Brasshat: a biography of F.M. Sir Henry Wilson*, Secker & Warburg, 1961

Henry J. Wilson
ANDERSON, MOSA. *Henry Joseph Wilson: fighter for freedom 1833–1914*, James Clarke, 1953

B. Contemporary Comment

AMERY, L. S. *The Problem of the Army*, E. Arnold, 1903
ANGELL, NORMAN. *The Policy Behind Armaments*, National Peace Council, 1911
ANGELL, NORMAN. *Europe's Optical Illusion*, Simpkin, Marshall, 1909
ANGELL, NORMAN. *The Great Illusion*, Heinemann, 1912
ANGELL, NORMAN. *War and the Workers*, National Labour Press, 1914
BALLOU, ADIN. *Christian Non Resistance in all its Important Bearings Illustrated and Defended*, Universal Peace Union, 1910
BLATCHFORD, ROBERT. *Germany and England*, Associated Newspapers, 1909
BRAILSFORD, H. N. *The War of Steel and Gold*, G. Bell, 1914
BRAILSFORD, H. N. *The Origins of the Great War*, no. IVa, U.D.C. pamphlet (reprint from *Contemporary Review*, Sept. 1914)
BRAY, F. E. *British Rights at Sea under the Declaration of London*, P. S. King & Son, 1911
BUXTON, C. R. *Turkey in Revolution*, Unwin, 1909

COBDEN CLUB. *The Burden of Armaments: a plea for retrenchment*, Fisher Unwin, 1905

COTTERILL, C. C. *The Victory of Love*, A. C. Fifield, 1910

COURTNEY, LORD. *Peace or War?* International Arbitration and Peace Assocn, 1911

CRAMB, J. A. *Germany and England*, Murray, 1914

DICKINSON, G. LOWES. *The International Anarchy, 1904–14*, Century Co, 1926

EDMONSON, ROBERT. *No Conscription*, International Arbitration and Peace Assocn, 1911

FARRER, J. A. *The Moral Cant About Conscription*, International Arbitration and Peace Assocn, 1908

FARRER, J. A. *Invasion and Conscription: some letters from a mere civilian to a famous general*, Fisher Unwin, 1909

GRANE, W. L. *The Passing of War: a study in things making for peace*, Macmillan, 1912

HAMILTON, SIR IAN. *Compulsory Service, a study of the question in the light of experience*, Murray, 1910

HANNA, H. B. *Can Germany Invade England?* Methuen, 1913

HIRST, F. W. *The Arbiter in Council*, Macmillan, 1906

HIRST, F. W. *Plain Words on Military and Naval Retrenchment*, Political Committee of the New Reform Club, Leaflet no. 8, 1906

HIRST, F. W. *The Policy and Finance of Modern Armaments with special reference to Anglo-German Rivalry*, International Arbitration League, 1912

HIRST, F. W. *The Six Panics and other essays*, Methuen, 1913

HIRST, F. W., ed. *Commerce and Property in Naval Warfare*, see Loreburn.

HOBHOUSE, STEPHEN. *The Pathway, or the practice of peace*, Headley Bros, 1909

HOBSON, J. A. *The German Panic*, The Cobden Club, 1913

HODGKIN, H. T. *A Quaker View of the War*, Northern Friends Peace Board, 1914

JOHNSON, SIR HARRY. *Common Sense in Foreign Policy*, 1913

LINDSAY, A. D. *War Against War*, Oxford Pamphlets, 1914

LOREBURN, LORD. *Commerce and Property in Naval Warfare*, ed. F. W. Hirst, Macmillan, 1906

LOREBURN, LORD. *How the War Came*, Methuen, 1919

LYNCH, FREDERICK. *The Peace Problem*, Revell & Co, 1911

MCCLURE, S. S. *Obstacles to Peace*, Houghton Mifflin, 1917

MOREL, E. D. *Morocco in Diplomacy*, Smith Elder & Co, 1912

MOREL, E. D. *Truth and the War*, National Labour Press, 1914

MUIR, RAMSAY. *The National Principle and the War*, Oxford Pamphlets, 1914

MURRAY, GILBERT. *The Foreign Policy of Sir Edward Grey 1906–15*, Oxford, Clarendon Press, 1915

NEVINSON, H. W. *Peace and War in the Balance*, Watts, 1911

NEWBIGIN, E. R. *War and Trade*, Andrew Dickson, 1908

NEWBOLD, J. T. WALTON. *How Europe Armed for War 1871–1914*, Blackfriars Press, n.d.

NORMAN, C. *Britain and the War*, National Labour Press, 1914

OLIVER, F. SCOTT. *Ordeal by Battle*, Macmillan, 1915

PERRIS, G. H. *For an Arrest of Armaments: a Note for the Second Hague Conference*, International Peace and Arbitration Assocn, 1906

PERRIS, G. H. *Hands Across the Sea: Labour's plea for international peace*, National Labour Press, 1910

PERRIS, G. H. *Our Foreign Policy and Sir Edward Grey's Failure*, Melrose, 1912

PERRIS, G. H. *The War Traders*, Chancery Lane Press, 1914

PONSONBY, ARTHUR. *Democracy and the Control of Foreign Affairs*, A. C. Fifield, 1912

PONSONBY, ARTHUR. *Democracy and Diplomacy*, Methuen, 1915

PONSONBY, ARTHUR. *Parliament and Foreign Policy*, U.D.C. Pamphlet, no. 5a, 1914

ROWNTREE, JOSEPH. *The Principles of Peace*, Delittle, Fenwick & Co, 1914

ROWNTREE, JOSHUA. *Justice Not Force*, National Peace Council, 1913

RUSSELL, BERTRAND. *The Policy of the Entente 1904–14: a reply to Professor Gilbert Murray*, National Labour Press, 1915

RUSSELL, BERTRAND. *War: the Offspring of Fear*, U.D.C. Pamphlet, no. 3a, 1916

STEAD, W. T. *The Liberal Ministry of 1906*, pamphlet, W. T. Stead, 1906

U.D.C. *The Balance of Power*, Pamphlet, no. 14a, 1916

U.D.C. *The Morrow of the War*, Pamphlet, no. 1a, 1916

WEHBERG, HANS. *Capture in War on Land and Sea*, P. S. King & Son, 1911

WILKINSON, SPENSER. *Britain at Bay*, Constable, 1910

WILLIS, IRENE COOPER. *How We Went into the War: a study of Liberal idealism*, National Labour Press, n.d.

WILLIS, IRENE COOPER. *How We Got on with the War: a further study of Liberal idealism*, National Labour Press, n.d.

WITHERS, HARTLEY. *Stocks and Shares*, Smith, Elder, 1910

C. General Works

ADAMS, W. S. *Edwardian Heritage*, Muller, 1949

ADAMS, W. S. *Edwardian Portraits*, Secker & Warburg, 1957

ADDISON, CHRISTOPHER. *Politics from Within, 1911–1918*, 2 vols, Herbert Jenkins, 1924

ALBERTINI, LUIGI. *The Origins of the War of 1914*, trans. and ed. I. M. Massey, 3 vols, Oxford University Press, 1952

ANDERSON, EUGENE N. *The First Moroccan Crisis 1904–06*, University of Chicago Press, 1940

ATTLEE, C. R. *The Labour Party in Perspective*, Gollancz, 1937

AYERST, DAVID. *Guardian: Biography of a Paper*, Collins, 1971

BARLOW, I. C. *The Agadir Crisis*, University of North Carolina Press, 1940

BISHOP, D. G. *The Administration of British Foreign Relations*, Syracuse University Press, 1961

BLOCH, CAMILLE. *The Causes of the World War*, trans. Jane Soames, Allen & Unwin, 1935

BULLOCK, ALAN and SHOCK, M., eds. *The Liberal Tradition: from Fox to Keynes*, Oxford University Press, paperback edn, 1967

BYRD, R. O. *Quaker Ways in Foreign Policy*, University of Toronto Press, 1960

CARROLL, E. M. *French Public Opinion and Foreign Affairs 1870–1914*, Century Co, 1931

CARROLL, E. M. *Germany and the Great Powers 1866–1914: a study in public opinion and foreign policy*, Prentice-Hall, 1938

CHILSTON, 3rd VISCOUNT. *Chief Whip*, Routledge & Kegan Paul, 1961

CHURCHILL, ROGERS PLATT. *The Anglo-Russian Convention of 1907*, Torch Press, 1939

CLARKE, I. F. *Voices Prophesying War 1763–1984*, Oxford University Press, 1966

CLARKE, P. F. *Lancashire and the New Liberalism*, Cambridge University Press, 1971

COCKS, H. F. LOVELL. *The Nonconformist Conscience*, Independent Press, 1943

COLE, G. D. H. *A History of the Labour Party from 1914*, Routledge & Kegan Paul, 1948

COLLINS, DOREEN. *Aspects of British Politics: 1904–19*, Pergamon Press, 1965

COOKEY, S. J. S. *Britain and the Congo Question: 1885–1913*, Longmans, 1968

DANGERFIELD, GEORGE. *The Strange Death of Liberal England*, Constable, 1936

DERRY, J. W. *The Radical Tradition*, Macmillan, 1967

DUNLOP, J. K. *The Development of the British Army 1899–1914*, Methuen, 1938

EHRMAN, JOHN. *Cabinet Government and War 1890–1940*, Cambridge University Press, 1958

ENSOR, R. C. K. *England 1870–1914*, Oxford, Clarendon Press, 1936

ESHER, VISCOUNT. *The Influence of King Edward and essays on other subjects*, Murray, 1915

FAY, S. B. *The Origins of the World War*, 2nd rev. edn, Macmillan, 1930

FLOURNOY, F. R. *Parliament and War: the relation of the British Parliament to the administration of foreign policy in connection with the initiation of war*, P. S. King & Son, 1927

FYFE, HAMILTON. *The British Liberal Party: an historical sketch*, Allen & Unwin, 1928

GARDINER, A. G. *Prophets, Priests and Kings*, Dent, 1913

GARDNER, LESLIE. *The British Admiralty*, Blackwood, 1968

GOOCH, G. P. *History of Our Time 1885–1913*, rev. edn, Williams & Norgate, 1914

GOOCH, G. P. *Recent Revelations of European Diplomacy*, 4th rev. edn, Longmans, 1940

GOOCH, G. P. *Studies in Diplomacy and Statecraft*, Longmans, 1942

GOSSES, F. *The Management of British Foreign Policy before the First World War*, trans. E. C. van der Gaaf, Sijthoff, 1948

GOUDSWAARD, J. M. *Some Aspects of the End of Britain's Splendid Isolation 1898–1914*, Brussels, 1952

HALE, O. J. *Publicity and Diplomacy, with special reference to England and Germany*, Appleton Century, 1940

HALÉVY, ELIE. *Imperialism and the Rise of Labour 1895–1905*, Benn, paperback, 1961

HALÉVY, ELIE. *The Rule of Democracy 1905–1914*, Benn, paperback, 1961

HANKEY, LORD. *Government Control in War*, Cambridge University Press, 1945

HANKEY, LORD. *The Supreme Command 1914–18*, 2 vols, Allen & Unwin, 1961

HAZLEHURST, CAMERON. *Politicians at War, July 1914 to May 1915*, Cape, 1971

HIRST, F. W. *Armaments, the Race and the Crisis*, Cobden Sanderson, 1937

HIRST, MARGARET E. *The Quakers in Peace and War: an account of their peace principles and practice*, Swathmore Press, 1923

INGRAM, KENNETH. *Fifty Years of the National Peace Council*, National Peace Council, 1958

JOHNSON, F. A. *Defence by Committee: the British Committee of Imperial Defence 1885–1959*, Oxford University Press, 1960

JONES, KENNEDY. *Fleet Street and Downing Street*, W. H. Allen, 1927

KING, C. T. *The Asquith Parliament (1906–09): a popular history of its men and its measures*, Hutchinson, 1910

KOEBNER, R. and SCHMIDT, H. D. *Imperialism: the story and significance of a political word 1840–1960*, Cambridge University Press, 1964

LUDWIG, EMIL. *July 1914*, Putnam, 1929

LUTZ, HERMANN. *Lord Grey and the World War*, trans. E. W. Dickes, Allen & Unwin, 1928

LUVAAS, JAY. *The Education of an Army: British military thought, 1815–1940*, Cassell, 1965

LYONS, F. S. L. *The Irish Parliamentary Party*, Faber, 1951

MCCALLUM, R. B. *The Liberal Party from Earl Grey to Asquith*, Gollancz 1963

MACCOBY, S. *English Radicalism 1886–1914*, Allen & Unwin, 1953

MACCOBY, S. *English Radicalism: the End?* Allen & Unwin, 1961

MACDONALD, J. RAMSAY. *The Socialist Movement*, Williams & Norgate, 1911

MACKINTOSH, J. P. *The British Cabinet*, 2nd edn, Stevens, 1968

MARDER, A. J. *From the Dreadnought to Scapa Flow: the road to war 1904–14*, Oxford University Press, 1961

MONTGELAS, MAX. *British Foreign Policy under Sir Edward Grey*, trans. W. C. Dreher, ed. H. E. Barnes, Knopf, 1928

MONGER, G. *The End of Isolation*, Nelson, 1963

PLAYNE, CAROLINE E. *Society at War 1914–16*, Allen & Unwin, 1931

PLAYNE, CAROLINE E. *The Pre-war Mind in Britain: an historical review*, Allen & Unwin, 1928

PORTER, BERNARD. *Critics of Empire: British Radical attitudes to colonialism in Africa 1895–1914*, Macmillan, 1968

RATTIGAN, W. F. A. *Diversions of a Diplomat*, Chapman & Hall, 1924

READ, DONALD. *The English Provinces, c. 1760–1960*, E. Arnold, 1964

RICHARDS, PETER G. *Parliament and Foreign Affairs*, Allen & Unwin, 1967

ROLLO, P. J. V. *Entente Cordiale: the origins and negotiations of the Anglo-French agreements of 8 April 1904*, Macmillan, 1969

ROWLAND, PETER. *The Last Liberal Governments: the promised land 1905–10*, Cresset Press, 1968

SARKISSIAN, A. O., ed. *Studies in Diplomatic History and Historiography in honour of G. P. Gooch*, Longmans, 1961.

SCHURMAN, D. M. *The Education of a Navy*, Cassell, 1965

SCOTT, J. F. *Five Weeks: the surge of public opinion on the eve of the Great War*, 1927

SHAW, GEORGE BERNARD. *Fabianism and the Empire*, Grant Richards, 1900

SPENDER, J. A. *The Public Life*, Cassell, 1925

STANSKY, PETER, ed. *The Left and War: the British Labour Party and World War I*, Oxford University Press, 1969

STEED, HENRY WICKHAM. *The Hapsburg Monarchy*, Constable, 1913

STEINER, ZARA S. *The Foreign Office and Foreign Policy 1898–1914*, Cambridge University Press, 1969

TAYLOR, A. J. P. *The Struggle for Mastery in Europe 1848–1918*, Oxford, Clarendon Press, 1954

TAYLOR, A. J. P. *The Trouble Makers: dissent over foreign policy, 1792–1939* (Hamish Hamilton, 1957), paperback edn, Panther, 1969

TEMPERLEY, H. and PENSON, L. A. *A Century of Diplomatic Blue Books 1814–1914*, Cambridge University Press, 1938

TILLEY, J. and GASELEE, S. *The Foreign Office*, Putnam, 1933

THE TIMES. *History of The Times*, vols. iii and iv, pt. 1, The Times, 1952

TURNER, L. C. F. *Origin of the First World War*, Edward Arnold, 1970

TYLER, J. E. *The British Army and the Continent: 1904–14*, Edward Arnold, 1938

VANSITTART, LORD. *The Mist Procession*, Hutchinson, 1958

WALLACE, L. P. and ASKEW, W. C. *Power, Public Opinion and Diplomacy*, Duke University Press, 1959

WATSON, R. SPENCE, *The National Liberal Federation from its Commencement to the general election of 1906*, 1907

WILLIAMSON, S. R., jr. *The Politics of Grand Strategy: Britain and France prepare for war, 1904–14*, Harvard University Press, 1969

WILSON, TREVOR. *The Downfall of the Liberal Party: 1914–35*, Collins, 1936

WOLFF, THEODOR. *The Eve of 1914*, trs. E. W. Dickes, Gollancz, 1935; Knopf, 1936

WOODWARD, E. L. *Great Britain and the German Navy*, Cass, 1964

D. Articles, essays etc.

ADAMS, W. S. 'E. D. Morel and his friends', in the author's *Edwardian Portraits*, Secker & Warburg, 1957

ASTON, SIR GEORGE. 'The Entente Cordiale and the "Military conversations" ', *Quarterly Review*, 1932, pp. 363–83

BAKER, H. T. 'Lord Haldane', *Army Quarterly*, October 1928

BRIGGS, ASA. 'The political scene', in Simon Nowell Smith, ed. *Edwardian England 1901–14*, Oxford University Press, 1964; also, essays in same volume by P. K. KEMP, 'The Royal Navy'; and CYRIL FALLS, 'The Army'

BUTTERFIELD, H. 'Sir Edward Grey in July 1914', *Historical Studies*, 1965, vol. v, pp. 1–25

CLINE, C. A. 'E. D. Morel and the crusade against the Foreign Office', *Journal of Modern History*, June 1967, vol. xxxix, pp. 126–31

COLE, MARGARET. 'In the past', *The Political Quarterly*, 1969, vol. xl, no. 4, pp. 363–73

COOPER, H. B. 'British policy in the Balkans 1908–09', *Historical Journal*, 1964, vol. vii, no. 2, pp. 258–79

DOREY, A. J. 'Radical Liberal criticism of British foreign policy 1906–14', Unpublished D. Phil Thesis, Oxford, 1964

DEXTER, BYRON. 'Lord Grey and the problem of an alliance', *Foreign Affairs*, January 1952, vol. xxx, pp. 298–309

EDWARDS, E. W. 'The Franco-German Agreement in Morocco 1909', *English Historical Review*, July 1963, vol. lxxviii, pp. 483–513

FIELDHOUSE, H. N. 'Noel Buxton and A. J. P. Taylor's "The Trouble Makers" ', in Martin Gilbert (ed.), *A Century of Conflict*, Hamish Hamilton, 1966

GREY, EDWARD and others. 'Viscount Haldane of Cloan: The Man and his Work', reprinted from *Public Administration*, October 1928

HARGREAVES, J. D. 'The Origins of the Anglo-French military conversations in 1905', in *History*, 1954, vol. xxxvi, no. 128, pp. 244–8

HARRIS, JOSÉ F. and HAZLEHURST, CAMERON, 'Campbell-Bannerman as Prime Minister', *History*, vol. lv, 1970, pp. 360–83

HELMREIGH, J. E. 'Belgian concern over neutrality and British intentions 1906–14', *Journal of Modern History*, 1964, vol. xxxvi, pp. 416–27

HANAK, H. 'The Union of Democratic Control during the First World War', *Bulletin of the Institute of Historical Research*, 1963, vol. xxxvi, no. 94, pp. 168–80

MACKINTOSH, J. P. 'The rôle of the Committee of Imperial Defence before 1914', *English Historical Review*, 1962, vol. lxxvii, pp. 490–503

MORRIS, A. J. A. 'Haldane's Army reforms 1906–08: the deception of the Radicals', *History*, vol. lvi, 1971, pp. 17–34. 'The English Radicals and the Second Hague Conference 1907', *Journal of Modern History*, 1971, vol. xliii

MURRAY, JOHN A. 'Foreign policy debated: Sir Edward Grey and his critics, 1911–12', in L. P. Wallace and W. C. Askew, eds, *Power, Public Opinion and Diplomacy*, Duke University Press, 1959

PENSON, LILLIAN M. 'Obligations by treaty: their place in British foreign policy, 1898–1914', in A. O. Sarkissian, ed., *Studies in Diplomatic History and Historiography*, Longmans, 1961

ROBBINS, K. G. 'The abolition of war: a study in the organisation and ideology of the Peace Movement, 1914–19', unpublished D. Phil. thesis, Oxford, 1964

STEINER, ZARA S. 'Grey, Hardinge and the Foreign Office 1906–10', *The Historical Journal*, 1965, vol. xv, pp. 415–39

TAYLOR, A. J. P. 'British policy in Morocco 1886–1908', *English Historical Review*, 1951, vol. lxvi, pp. 342–74

TAYLOR, A. J. P. '1914: Events in Britain' in *The Listener*, 16 July, 1964

TEMPERLEY, H. W. V. 'British secret diplomacy from Canning to Grey', *Cambridge Historical Journal*, 1938, vol. vi, pp. 16–32

THOMAS, J. A. 'The House of Commons 1906–11: an analysis of its economic and social character', University of Wales Press, 1958

TREBILCOCK, CLIVE. 'Legends of the British armament industry 1890–1914: a revision', *Journal of Contemporary History*, 1970 pp. 3–19

WALSH, WALTER. 'Lord Morley's "Memorandum of Resignation" ', Free Religious Movement, 1928

WEINROTH, HOWARD S. 'The British Radicals and the balance of power 1902–14', *The Historical Journal*, 1970, vol. xiii, pp. 653–82

WILLIAMS, B. J. 'The strategic background to the Anglo-Russian Entente', *The Historical Journal*, 1966 vol. ix, pp. 360–73

E. Miscellaneous

i. Diplomatic documents—

B.D.   *British Documents on the Origins of the War 1898–1914*, London, 1926–38

D.D.F.   *Documents Diplomatiques Français 1871–1914*, series ii and iii, Paris, 1930–53

D.G.P.   *Die Grosse Politik der Europäischen Kabinette 1871–1914*, ed. J. Lepsius, A. Mendelssohn-Bartholdy and F. Thimme, Berlin, 1922–27

ii. Serial publications

Daily Express, Daily Mail, Daily Telegraph, The Times, Daily Herald, Daily News, Manchester Guardian, The Tribune, Westminster Gazette, Observer, Reynolds News, Birmingham Daily Post, Yorkshire Post, Liverpool Daily Post, Labour Leader

Journals

The Speaker, The Nation, Labour Record and Review, The New Age, The Arbitrator, Concord, Albany Review, Contemporary Review, The Economist, Christian Commonwealth, National Review, Review of Reviews, War & Peace, Ploughshare, The Spectator, The Herald of Peace, Peace & Goodwill, The Peacemaker, Rationalist Peace Quarterly, Socialist Review

iii. Others—

Annual Register

BUTLER, DAVID and FREEMAN, JENNIE. *British Political Facts, 1900–1967*, 2nd edn, Macmillan, 1968

Hansard, Parliamentary Debates, 4th and 5th series

Peace Year Book, 1910–14

Reformers' Year Book

Whitaker's Almanack

Who Was Who

Index

Abdul Aziz, 172
Abdul Hamid, 349–50, 369
Acland, Arthur, 20
Addison, Christopher, 410, 417
Admiralty, Board of, 107 and n., 108,
   111 and n., 125–8, 132, 144, 146–
   149, 163, 224, 286–7, 291–2,
   294–5, 300n., 317, 337, 346, 359
Aehrenthal, Baron von, 191, 383
Agadir crisis, 1911, 168, 218, 222–3,
   235–51, 259, 261, 269, 279, 283–6,
   295, 325, 337, 348, 362, 378
Ahmed Riza, 253n.
Akaba incident, 40
Alden, Percy, 100, 118
Algeciras Conference, 1906, 35, 39n.,
   40, 43n., 47–8, 162, 234
Alsace Lorraine, 173, 235, 362
Anderson, W. C. 277n., 336n., 412
Angell, Norman, 202–3, 411–12
Angellism, 227
Anglo-American Arbitration Treaty,
   1911, 228–33
Anglo-French Entente, 1904, 10–11,
   25–5, 34–9, 41, 45–6, 50–1, 53,
   65, 75, 169–71, 173, 197 and n.,
   198, 202, 203n., 217, 220, 248 and
   n., 250, 274–5, 277, 305–7, 312,
   317, 325, 328, 348, 366–8, 416–17
Anglo-French Naval Conversations,
   1912, 318–20, 322
Anglo-German Conciliation Committee, 45–6
Anglo-German friendship,
   and Nat. Lib. Fed. resolution, 305
   and the Labour Party, 306
   (Mentioned), 198–223, 270
Anglo-German Friendship Society,
   223, 232–3, 262–3
Anglo-German Understanding Conference, 1912, 329, 331
Anglo-Japanese Treaty, 1905, 55, 57
   and n.
Anglo-Persian Oil Company, 362
Anglo-Russian Convention, 1907, 33n.,
   67–70, 75, 80, 88, 90–1, 169, 170

and n., 176, 178, 180n., 186–8,
   193, 220, 255, 363, 365, 377–8
Anglo-Russian Naval Conversations
   negotiations for, 364–71
Anseele, Edouard, 352
Appleton, W. A., 104, 141n.
Arbiter in Council, 141
Armaments (including, disarmament
   retrenchment and armament
   manufacturers), 2, 7–9, 25–6, 45
   and n., 47, 52, 72, 81–2, 85, 97–8,
   99 and n., 100–1, 111–15, 119,
   122, 124–6, 128, 129 and n., 130–
   132, 135, 139, 155, 158, 160, 165,
   170, 175, 184, 192, 203, 205–6,
   212n., 215n., 216 and n., 217, 223–
   226, 228–30, 270, 309, 323–47, 380
Army,
   Estimates 1906, 85–6, 88
   1908, 82, 89–90
   Haldane's 'Hegelian' Army, 73n.
   need for reform, 72
   pre-1906 strategic rôle, 75–6 and n.
   army reform and social reform, 84–5,
   92
Asquith, H. H.,
   and Relugas Compact, 14–16, 20
   problems with arms retrenchment
   as Chancellor, 125 and n.
   and Kaiser–Tweedmouth Correspondence, 134–35
   succession as Prime Minister, 138
   forms first Cabinet, 138–9
   on 'Two Power Standard', 143, 146
   disposed to support 'Big Navy'
   school, 151
   tempted to cashier Churchill and
   Ll. George, 153
   impressed by Mulliner's evidence,
   149, 150 and n.
   admits shipbuilding deficiency,
   1909, 160–4
   and footnote to 1909 naval estimates, 162–4, 166–7
   and Edward's Reval visit, 176
   deplores arms' race, 1910, 216

Asquith, H. H.—*contd.*
and Anglo-American Arbitration Treaty, 231
statement on Agadir crisis, July 1911, 241, 247, 249
weaknesses as chairman of C.I.D., 287–8
on military conversations with France, 290–1, 297
attempts to reconcile W.O. and Admiralty thinking, 291
agrees to principle of war staff, 291–292
concept of war as 'distasteful', 291
dislikes idea of British intervention on Continent, 292
meeting with McKenna, 1911, 292–293
reasons for changes at Admiralty, 293–4
maintains Cabinet unity, Nov. 1911, 298–9
decisions support W.O. strategic preferences, 301
and Haldane's Berlin Mission, 1912, 306–8, 311
and Grey–Cambon letters, 313–17
and ministerial reshuffle, Oct. 1911, 317
speech to Nat. Lib. Fed., Nov. 1912, 330
anger with Churchill, 1913, 337
and 1914 naval estimates in Cabinet, 339–45
statement on military 'obligation', 1913, 356–8
on Austrian ultimatum to Serbia, 386
on rejection of Four Power conference, 388
concerned with possible action of Ll. George, 390, 399
decision not to mobilise Expeditionary Force, 394–5
confusion of ideas in final crisis, 398
statements to Commons in final crisis, 403–4, 407
explicit assurances on 'free hand', 405
and relations with Radical Foreign Affairs Ctte., 409–10
(Mentioned), 4, 13, 17–19, 54, 78, 80–4, 107n., 126–7, 130, 132–3, 140, 152, 197n., 212, 215n., 222, 227, 238, 244, 251, 254, 260, 265, 274n., 277, 295–6, 310, 318–19 and n., 320–1, 326, 338, 352, 365, 370, 389, 397
Asquith, Margot, 13, 23n., 160, 390
Associated Council of Churches, 201, 306
Atkins, Ryland, 157

Avebury, Lord, 46, 103

Bagdad Railway project, 217–18, 380
Baker, J. Allen, 154, 157 and n., 201, 228, 251, 266n., 306, 338
Balance of Power, doctrine of, 41, 44, 191–2, 194, 229, 251, 276, 278, 280, 358, 361, 366, 369, 373, 378–9, 387n., 405–7
Balfour, A. J.,
resignation as Prime Minister, 17
on significance of 1906 election, 21, 27n.
on Churchill as an 'economist', 83
as a critic of Haldane, 89–90
on 'policy and armaments', 130
and 1909 naval estimates, 156
demands eight Dreadnoughts, 160
and Jan. 1910 election campaign, 209–10
attempts to renew naval panic, Dec. 1910, 214n.
and Anglo-American Arbitration Treaty, 231–2
insists Triple Entente is an alliance, 378
(Mentioned), 35, 101, 106, 108, 113n., 132–3, 136, 193n., 212n., 241, 243, 274n., 298, 300n., 322, 326, 342, 418–19
Balkan Committee, 349
Balkan League, 350, 352–3
Balkan Wars, 331, 333, 348–61, 377–380
Ballin, Albert, 307
Baptist Union, 231 and n.
Barclay, Sir Thomas, 200
Bashford, J. L., 174n.
Beauchamp, Earl, 343, 396, 398, 400
Bebel, F. A., 122
Belgium, neutrality of, 282, 387–8, 396–402, 404, 407, 410–11, 416–417
Bellairs, Capt. Carlyon, 101, 109n., 135n.
Benckendorff, Count, 53–4, 62, 365, 369–70, 391
Benn, Sir Ernest, 387n.
Bentham, G. J., 408n.
Bentinck, Lord Henry, 260
Beresford, Adm. Lord Charles, 127, 326, 403
Bernstein, Edouard, 208, 249
Bertie, Francis, 23n., 237, 254, 313, 369
Bethel, Adm. Sir A., 288
Bethmann-Hollweg, Count Theobald von, 195, 208, 216, 219, 223, 232, 236, 250, 270, 272, 279, 306–7, 311, 312n., 332, 373, 380, 390
Birrell, Augustine, 20, 90n.
Bismarck, Prince Otto von, 11

chford, Robert,
  Daily Mail 'scare' articles, 210–11
  (Mentioned), 205, 211n., 212
Blue Books, 257 and n., 267n.
Blue Funk School, 123
Blunt, Wilfrid Scawen, 21n., 28n.
Boer War, 1–3, 6–7, 13–14, 19, 71,
  132, 174, 178, 251
Bosnian Crisis, 1908–09, 94, 146, 183–
  184, 193, 195, 208, 252
Bottomley, Horatio, 382
Bourgeois, Léon, 41
Brailsford, H. N., 12, 60, 63,175n., 381
Bright, John, 4, 6, 110, 191, 304, 348
Brodrick, St. John W., 71
Brougham, Lord, 117n.
Browne, Professor E. G., 186, 188,
  257, 272–4
Brunner, Sir John, 88, 105n., 130–1,
  139, 157, 201n., 244n., 269–70
  and n., 271, 304–5, 326–30, 340
Bryce, J. Annan, 339
Bryce, Lord, 5, 20, 46n., 238, 305, 405
Buchanan, George, 196, 245, 256n.,
  364–5
Bülow, Prince von, 43, 49–50, 113–14,
  169, 174–5, 191, 193, 195, 208,
  220 and n.
Burns, John, 4, 20, 80–1, 150, 152,
  238, 343, 387 and n., 388–9, 396,
  398–401
Burritt, Elihu, 110
Buxton, C. R., 68
Buxton, Noel, 200n., 216, 244n., 255n.,
  259–61, 265–6 and n., 268n., 278,
  349, 354, 381, 408 and n.
Buxton, Sydney, 20, 152
Byles, Sir William P., 90, 98, 101, 118,
  155, 371

Cabinet Committee on Foreign Policy,
  1911, 222 and n.
Cabinet Committee on Haldane's reforms, 79–80, 82
Cadbury, George, 64, 201
Caillaux, Joseph, 236, 298, 301, 362
Caillaux, Madame, 383
Cambon, Paul, 23, 35–9, 42, 72, 175,
  207n., 298, 301, 309, 311, 313–15,
  319, 369–70, 385, 391, 393–4,
  396, 400
Campbell-Bannerman, Sir Henry,
  on Imperialism, 3
  'methods of barbarism', 7, 22, 136
  anticipation of office, 13
  claim to leadership of Liberals, 7, 13
  views on Germany, 1905, 15
  concern with Rosebery, 17
  and Relugas Compact, 14–16
  and construction of Cabinet, 18–20
  'League of Peace' speech, 24–5, 97,
    101–2, 139
  relationship with Grey, 32, 43–4
  and military conversations, 37–9,
    42–3
  as chairman of Cabinet, 32
  'Vive la Douma' speech, 62
  on Army reform in Opposition, 71–
    72
  understanding of Haldane's re-
    forms, 78, 91,
  as Haldane's guarantor with Radi-
    cals, 71, 81, 95–6
  illness and retirement, 81, 135–6
  and pleads for disarmament, 100–5,
    107
  The Nation article, 111–13, 216n.
  Reply to Bülow on disarmament,
    114–15.
  agrees to reductionist amendment,
    1908, 126
  and 1908 naval estimates, 126–8,
    137
  estimates of
    by Asquith, 136–7
    the Radicals, 135–7
    the Foreign Office, 137
  (Mentioned, 36, 49n., 50, 55, 58,
    103–4, 108, 117, 119, 121–2, 125,
    146n., 216, 238, 243, 297–8, 328,
    367, 389
Canadian Emergency Navy Bill,
  1913, 336–7
Cardwell, Viscount, 75, 79–80
Carrington, Earl, 20
Carter, Violet Bonham, 294
Cartwright, Sir Fairfax, 239n.
Casablanca, 171, 173
Cassel, Sir Ernest, 218, 307
Cawdor, Earl, 135, 145
Cawdor Programme, 107 and n.
Cecil, Lord Hugh, 241
Chamberlain, Austen, 153, 159, 300n.,
  319n.
Chamberlain, Joseph, 1, 5, 13, 19, 34,
  103, 132, 136, 263 and n., 383
Chancellor, H. G., 262
Chirol, Valentine, 210
Church Congress, 1911 meeting, 262
Churchill, Lord Randolph, 8, 227
Churchill, Winston, S.,
  appointed President Board of
    Trade, 81, 139
  friendship with Ll. George, 81, 342–
    344
  as Army 'economist', 81–4
  and 1908 naval estimates, 127–8
  as keeper of Liberal conscience,
    144–5
  and unemployment in shipbuilding,
    142 and n.
  and 1909 naval estimates, 150, 152–4
  on ambiguity of naval evidence,
    162

Churchill, Winston, S.—*contd.*
suspects tricked over four Dreadnoughts, 163
on Ll. George's Mansion House speech, 239n.
and Agadir crisis, 285
replies to Gen. Wilson on Expeditionary Force, 285–6
friendship with Gen. Wilson, 286, 301n.
concern with Admiralty's nonchalance, July 1911, 286–7
covets post of First Lord, 293
appointed First Lord, 294–5, 301
'Luxusflotte' speech, Feb. 1912, 310
presents first naval estimates in Commons, 318
and abortive Malta C.I.D. meeting, 318–20
quarrels over disposition of Med. Fleet, 1912, 320–2
as a Radical apostate, 323
1912 naval estimates in Commons, 323–4
and supplementary estimates, 1912, 326 and n.
and 'Naval Holiday' proposal, 332 and n., 337
and 1914 estimates in Cabinet, 341–345
and 1914 estimates in Commons, 345
mobilisation of Fleet for war, 387, 397
on Commons' attitude to intervention, July 1914, 403–4
sought as ally by neutralists, 411
(Mentioned), 13n., 21, 47n., 95, 164, 194, 213n., 225n., 238, 241, 288n., 289–90, 296, 299, 307–8, 317, 331n., 386, 390, 394–5, 401
Citizen Army, 104 and n., 360
Clemenceau, Georges, 42, 48, 170–1
Clifford, Dr. John, 262
Clynes, J. R., 131
Cobden, Richard, 2, 4, 110, 117n., 144, 304
Committee of Imperial Defence, 23 Aug. 1911, meeting, 287–91, 295–7
(Mentioned) 43n., 58, 77n., 78, 80n., 149, 229, 283, 318–19, 321–2, 359
Concert of Europe, 69, 183, 185, 191, 202, 229, 281, 353, 355–7, 361, 373, 378–9
Confidential print, Foreign Office, 33 and n.
Congo, 191–2, 194, 217 and n., 218, 237, 241, 246
Conscription, 71, 92–6, 170, 216, 287, 318, 321, 325, 331, 348, 360
Continuity of foreign policy, 23–4,
34, 277, 377
Conwell-Evans, T. P., 267–8
Cotton, Sir Henry, 88, 91, 244n.
Council of Union of Ethical Societies, 258n.
Courtney, Kate, 199n., 201n., 278, 305, 405, 410–11
Courtney, Leonard, 2, 19, 46, 98 and n., 107, 129, 181n., 185, 211, 234n., 246, 260–1, 265, 269, 279–80, 305, 309, 323, 405, 419
Courtney Committee on foreign policy, 269, 329
Cremer, Sir Randal, 10, 105n., 244n.
Crewe, Lord, 20, 84, 151–2, 222, 277, 288, 301, 341, 386, 397
Crowe, Sir Eyre, 44, 121, 173–4, 201, 221, 237, 284, 318, 385
Curzon, Lord, 216n., 258, 259 and n.
Custance, Admiral, 152

Delaisi, Francis, 274
Delbrück, Professor, 217
Delcassé, Théophile, 35, 45, 51, 53n., 239n., 245n., 316
Dickinson, W. H., 408n.
Dilke, Sir Charles, 89–90, 92, 95n., 121, 161, 185, 264n.
Dilke Return, 109n.
Dillon, E. J., 193
Dillon, John, 157–8, 164, 186–7, 230, 254, 258n., 262, 277, 331
Doumergue, Gaston, 369
Dreadnought, 106, 107n., 114, 121, 122–4, 144, 146–7, 149–53, 156, 158–9, 161, 163–5, 207–8, 214 and n., 215, 224, 225 and n., 230, 245, 270, 322, 324, 332, 336–7, 341–2
Dreikaiserbund, 53 and n.
Dubail, General, 283–4

Edward VII,
and Relugas Compact, 14, 15 and n.
on Balfour's resignation, 17
on Campbell-Bannerman's Cabinet, 21
dislike of Kaiser, 40
on Grey's fears for entente, 43–4
as inspiration of German encirclement, 51n., 169, 208 and n.
visits Kaiser and Francis Joseph, 51
visit to Reval, 176, 178, 180–1, 186
death of, 208
Edward 'the Peacemaker', 214–15
(Mentioned), 33n., 41, 45, 80, 113, 121n., 211, 213n.
Egypt, 170
Elections,
by-elections—constitutional significance of pre-1906, 13n.

general elections,
1906, estimates of result, 26
effect on Commons, 26–7, 33–4, 97–9, 323
Jan. 1910, 209–10, 244n.
Dec. 1910, 212–13, 215 and n.
Elgin, Earl of, 15, 20, 238
Ellis, J. Edward, 20n., 129, 157
Ellison, Col. Gerald, 73
Ensor, R. C. K., 269
Esher, Reginald Viscount,
on Haldane's appointment as War Minister, 72
on Churchill as an 'economist', 82–3
on Haldane's faults as a Minister, 81
and Kaiser–Tweedmouth correspondence, 133 and n.
on Ll. George as 'big navy' supporter, 140
on 1909 naval 'panic', 158
on Edward VII influence on foreign policy, 208n.
on the Kaiser, 214
on secret meeting of C.I.D., Aug. 1911, 288
discusses strategy with Asquith, Oct. 1911, 291–2
(Mentioned), 57, 73, 78, 125, 136, 138–9, 211, 214n., 277n., 309, 321–2, 337, 359
Eversley, G. L., 142 and n.
Expeditionary Force,
decision not to mobilise by Cabinet, 1914, 394–5
(Mentioned), 75–8, 80, 82, 87, 89, 283, 285, 289n., 291–2

Faber, W. V., 261n.
Fabians, 4
Fallières, President, 176
Fallows, J. A., 205
Farrer, J. A., 203, 334
Fez, Riots at, 1911, 235–6
Finn, Joseph, 263
Fischoff, Albert, 105n.
Fisher, Adm. Sir John, 107, 109n., 112n., 120 and n., 123n., 126–7, 140, 149 and n., 151n., 153, 159, 162–4, 180n, 214, 287, 290, 310n., 317, 322, 359, 387n.
Fitzmaurice, Lord Edmond, 37, 40, 103
Fitzroy, Sir Almeric, 240n., 256n., 277n., 297, 396
Foreign Office,
reorganisation, 29
anti-German prejudice, 41
concern at Campbell-Bannerman's views of entente, 43
Forster, Arnold, 71–2
Fowler, Sir Henry, 16

Fox, Charles James, 6
Fox, William, 305
Francis Ferdinand, Archduke, 374, 382–4
Francis Joseph, Emperor, 51
Franco-British Russian Loan, 1905, 177n.
Franco–German Accord, 1909, 175, 193, 195, 197, 235–6, 240, 246–7
Frank Ludwig, 352
'Free Hand', 356, 358, 370, 372, 405, 416
Free Trade, 1, 19, 20n., 22, 25, 98, 180, 203, 331
French, Gen. Sir John, 180n., 288
Fried, Alfred, 200n., 212n.
Friends of Russian Freedom, 66, 182n.
Fry, Sir Edward, 113n., 116, 118, 185
Fyfe, Hamilton, 419

Galsworthy, John, 64, 224
Gambetta, Leon, 334
Gardiner, A. G., 12, 374, 405–6
Garvin, J. L., 69n., 153, 159, 210, 333n.
George V,
visit to Paris, April 1914, 366, 368–369
(Mentioned) 234, 291, 297–8, 322 386, 388, 416
George, David Lloyd,
on the Cabinet and foreign policy 31
economy campaign on 1907 Army estimates, 81–5
friendship with Churchill, 81–83, 340–4
and 1908 Naval estimates, 127–8
appointed Chancellor of Exchequer, 139
aggressive nature, 140
and unemployment in shipbuilding, 142 and n.
and 1909 Naval estimates, 150–4
1909 Budget, 160, 164, 167, 243
evidence of German Dreadnought capacity, 149–51
suspects tricked over four extra Dreadnoughts, 163
as 'economist' leader in Cabinet, 224
illness, April 1911, 225n.
Mansion House speech, 239 and n., 241–50 and n., 255, 259–60, 276, 286, 307, 310, 340n., 341
'darling' of Foreign Office, 240 and n.
prevents General Strike, 1911, 242
changing attitude to Germany, 1911, 300
fears of war, July 1911, 286

George, David Lloyd—*contd.*
Criccieth interview, Jan. 1914, 340
and n., 363
concedes fight over 1914 Naval
estimates, 345
and Balkan Wars, 352
statements on Anglo-German relations, 1914, 374, 377
and civil strife in Ulster, 376
pro-French leanings, 387–8
and Belgian neutrality, 391, 396, 400
rejects leadership of neutralists,
390, 399 401
astonishment at Morley's resignation, 400
(Mentioned), 6, 20, 23n., 125n., 126,
209, 211, 212n., 215n., 222, 227,
251, 265, 288 and n., 294, 296,
299, 308, 310n., 394, 415
German Navy League, 121
German Navy Law,
1900: 122, 133
1908: 151, 208–9, 213, 227, 230
1912: 305, 307, 309, 311, 324
German Peace Society, 212
Gladstone, Herbert, 17, 20, 238
Gladstone, W. E., 4, 6, 9, 29, 180, 253,
266n., 283, 348, 354, 400, 416
Gooch, G. P., 98, 124, 182, 244n.
Goschen, Sir Edward, 237, 260, 392–3
Gosse, Edmund, 13
Graham, R. Cunninghame, 64, 171–2
Gree, J. F., 226–7
Greenwood, Frederick, 2
Grey, Sir Edward,
and Relugas Compact, 14–16
initial refusal to serve as Foreign
Secretary, 18
claim to be Foreign Secretary, 18–
19 and n.
Radical estimates of in 1905, 22
public expectations on his appointment, 23 and n.
on 'continuity' in foreign policy,
23–4
as an orator, 23n., 52, 276–7 and n.
City speech, Oct. 1905, 23, 52–3
character, 29, 37n.
relationship with F. O. officials, 29–
30
ignorance of Germany, 40
and Kaiser's visit, 43–4
and questions in Commons, 64, 65
and n.
independence in Cabinet, 30–2
deviousness with Cabinet colleagues,
29, 33, 39
relationship with Campbell-Bannerman, 32, 42–3
and Algeciras Conference, 36, 39
and military conversations, 36–8,
290–1, 297, 370, 372–3

exaggerated concern for French
opinion, 42–4
Russian policy postulates, 52–5,
58–9, 65, 377
and Radical critics of Russian
policy, 60–2
his secrecy, 52, 65, 69–70, 179, 230,
303, 377
on military implications of entente
policy, 72
speech on disarmament, May 1906,
101–2
fails to support Campbell-Bannerman in Commons, 113
on Kaiser–Tweedmouth correspondence, 134–5
and 1909 Naval estimates, 147–8
on retrenchment, 151n., 162
informed of true German Dreadnought programme, 161
concern about German shipbuilding
plans, 162–3
and Reval debate, 177–8
and Macedonian reform, 1908, 182
and Bosnian crisis, 183
Persian policy criticised, 186–7
Russian policy criticised, 177–80,
186, 190–2
on rumour of Anglo-French military agreement, 1911, 197–8
speech on reductionist motion,
March 1911, 227–9
concern over Cabinet's attitude to
Agadir, 238–9
and Lloyd George's Mansion House
speech, 239
use of Press, 1911, 239n.
use of Blue Books to mislead critics,
257n.
and Shuster affair, 254–8
and Italian invasion of Tripoli,
253–5
concerned with Radical criticism,
255, 272, 303, 348–9
and secret articles of Anglo-French
entente, 274
defence of policies, Nov. 1911, 275–
277
on Germany's 'war-like intent',
278–9
exaggerated assessment of Russia's
strength, 284, 289n., 364
little enthusiasm for Anglo-German
rapprochement, 305–6
attitude to Haldane's Berlin Mission, 1912, 305–6, 308
and Grey–Cambon letters, 313–17
rejects idea of Anglo-French defensive alliance, 318–19
praised by Radicals, 352–3
unchanging fundamental postulates
of his policy, 358–9

anger at Ll. George's Criccieth interview, 363
fear of Russia joining Germany, 365
conversation with Sazonov, 1912, 364–5
and Anglo-Russian naval talks, 1914, 364–71
talks in Paris, April 1914, 366, 368–370
estimate of French motives re possibility of Anglo-Russian naval agreement, 369
ambiguous reply to Byles and King, 371–2
Tory support for, 378
on the efficacy of simple remedies, 381
and Sarajevo assassination, 384–5
and Austrian ultimatum to Serbia, 385 6
suggests Four Power conference, 387
anger at rejection of conference initiative, 388
and German initiative for neutrality, 392–3
decision not to mobilise Expeditionary Force, 394–5
and British Channel, 396–8
and Belgian neutrality, 396, 399–400
statements to Commons in final crisis, 403–4, 407
Ponsonby interview, 409
and back-bench critics in final crisis, 409–10
speech to Commons, 3 Aug. 1914, 415–18
sends ultimatum to Germany, 418
(Mentioned,) 80, 84, 91, 104, 107n., 111, 113n., 118n., 124, 135n., 137–8, 149, 151–3, 164 and n., 169, 174, 193n., 227n., 231n., 233, 237, 246, 248 and n., 249–51, 252, 260, 263, 264 and n., 269, 273n., 287–8, 295–6, 298–300 and n., 305n., 325, 327, 329, 334, 341, 343, 347

Haase, Hugo, 413
Hague Conference
the Second, 1907, 22, 50, 97–121, 122, 171, 232
the Third, 225, 351, 381
Hague Convention, 252, 254n.
Haldane, R. B.,
and Relugas Compact, 14–16, 18
claims to office, 18–19 and n.
Radical estimate of in 1905, 22
attitude to Germany, 32, 40–1
on faults in Cabinet organisation, 32–3

first discusses military conversations with Grey, 37
visits Berlin, 1906, 41–2
on his military reforms generally, see Chapter 2, *passim*
and army reform in Cabinet, 78–84
and army reforms in Commons, 84–96
style of oratory, 86–7
on military strategy, 75–7
importance of Campbell-Bannerman's support, 71, 78, 81, 95–6
distrusted by Radicals, 73, 84
difficulties upon taking War Office, 72–3
weaknesses of his parliamentary critics, 74
offers resignation to Asquith, 82
use of Cardwellian argument, 82, 94–5
Tory criticism of, 89, 94
threatens resignation unless W.O. strategy accepted, 291
presses Asquith to change First Lord of Admiralty, 293
covets Admiralty for himself, 293
chosen for Berlin Mission, 1912, 308–9
comments upon Mission, 310, 311 and n.
concern about Churchill's fleet plans, 318–19
(Mentioned), 43–5, 49n., 54n., 107n., 127, 137–8, 151–8, 216, 260, 280n., 282, 284–5, 289–90, 292, 294, 297, 305, 307, 341, 388, 400
Hankey, Maurice, 290
Harcourt, Lewis V., 82, 126–7, 139, 140, 150, 152, 225n., 288, 296, 300–1, 308, 311, 319 and n., 343, 389–90, 396–8, 401–2
Harcourt, Sir William, 5, 7
Hardie, J. Keir, 27, 108, 110 and n., 130, 175–6, 177 and n., 205–6, 227, 263n., 277 and n., 352–3, 413–14, 420
Hardinge, Sir Charles, 30, 33n., 41, 58, 62, 137, 176, 193n., 221, 257n.
Harris, Sir Charles, 73, 76–7, 84
Harvey, A. G. C., 115n., 151 and n., 266n., 327, 338–9, 380, 419
Harvey, T. E., 266n., 404, 411
Heaford, William, 216n.
Henderson, Arthur, 157–8, 206–7, 263n., 278, 414
Hirst, Francis, W., 8, 112, 117 and n., 141, 232, 263, 303–5, 323, 326–30, 338–9, 346
Hobhouse, Charles, 341, 343
Hobhouse, L. T., 12, 269
Hobson, J. A., 1–3, 4 and n., 64, 172, 269, 279, 412

Holt, Richard, 404, 410
Home Rule, 215, 331, 338–9
Horne, C. Silvester, 254, 266n.
House, Col. E. M., 381
Hugo, Victor, 110
Huguet, Major, 38n., 283–4
Hutchinson, Dr, 14n.
Hyndman, H. M., 104 and n., 200n.,
    202n., 205, 360

Imperialism, 1–7, 26, 97, 124, 171–3,
    175, 252
Imperialism (I. L. P. pamphlet), 4
Imperial Maritime League (the 'Navier
    League'), 123 and n.
Imperial Union, 13
Independent Labour Party, 4, 206–7,
    215n, 331n., 420
India, 75, 80n.
Indian Army,
    functions of, 83–4, 90
    Haldane on, 84, 87–8, 95
    Radicals on, 88, 90–1
    Kitchener on, 77n., 87n.
Indian Government, 55–7
International Arbitration and Peace
    Association, 68, 69n., 73n., 100n.,
    135n., 190, 198, 206, 212 and n.,
    251, 258n., 324
International Arbitration League,
    231n., 352
International Prize Court, 118
International Socialist Bureau, British
    Section of the, 413–14
Inter-Parliamentary Union, 62, 103,
    105n., 201
Ireland, 16, 18, 376, 383, 386–7, 404
Irish party, 27, 157–8, 177n., 187,
    330–1, 417
Isolationism, 36, 107n., 180
Isvolsky, A. P., 51, 53, 187, 191, 195,
    369

Jagow, G. von, 372–3, 384–5
Jaurès, Jean, 158, 175, 340n., 362, 413
Jellicoe, Adm. Sir J. R., 149
Johnson, Sir Harry, 382
Jones, Kennedy, 210
Jones, Leif, 339
Joffre, General, 284
Jowett, Fred, 197 and n.

Kautsky, Karl, 201
Kiderlen-Wächter, A. von, 195, 220
    and n.
King, Joseph, 226, 266n., 371
Kitchener, Sir Herbert, 72, 77n., 87n.,
    288 and n.
Knollys, Sir Francis, 14–15, 43, 53
Koss, Professor Stephen E., 270 and n.
Kronstadt, proposed visit of Baltic
    Fleet to, 60–1

Kruger, Paul, 3
Krupp, 148, 163, 334

Labour Party,
    gains in 1906 election, 27
    as revolutionaries, 27–8 and n.
    and foreign policy, 27–8
    pre 1900 links with Radicals, 1
    and internationalism, 34, 49
    as critics of Haldane, 95
    and 1909 Naval estimates, 157–9
    and continued support for pacifists,
        168
    and Anglo-Russian Convention, 176
    and Bosnian crisis, 183, 185–6
    views on Tsarist régime, 176–9
    and Reval visit, 1908, 176
    as critics of Grey's Russian policy,
        177–80, 187
    on Tsar's visit to England, 188–91
    parochialism, 205
    claim distinctive voice from Radi-
        cals, 204–7, 215n., 227
    condemn Grey's anti-German pol-
        icy, 1911, 263–4
    claim leadership of anti-Grey move-
        ment, 263n.
    view of Radicals, 264n., 336 and n.
    as a provincial interest group, 272
    and Anglo-German friendship cam-
        paign, 1912, 306
    and divisions in Army and Navy
        votes, 336
    and pacifism, 1913–14, 352–3, 361
    maintain criticism of Grey, 1912–
        1913, 357–8
    and final crisis, July/Aug. 1914,
        412–14
    (Mentioned), 97, 99, 105
Lamsdorff, Count, 51, 53
Lansdowne, Lord, 22, 36, 41, 51, 124,
    191, 212n., 276
Lascelles, Sir Francis, 223, 233, 262–3
Laurier, Sir W., 337
Lavisse, Ernest, 366–7
Law, Andrew Bonar, 276–7, 326, 397
    and n., 417
Lawrence, F. W. Pethick, 27
League of Peace, 85, 97, 99, 110, 119,
    136, 191, 367
Lee, Arthur, 107–8, 109 and n., 112n.,
    128, 141, 143, 146, 165, 326, 339
Ledebour, Georg, 201
Lefevre, G. Shaw, 8, 109n.
Leopold II, 194, 217
Liakhoff, Col., 186
Liberal Imperialists (Limps), 4, 5,
    16, 20, 30, 73, 84, 125n., 136, 138,
    260, 296
Liberal League, 16, 389
Lichnowsky, Prince K. M., 373, 380,
    384–5, 391

London, Declaration of, 219, 232
London Conference, 1913, 353–4
Long, Walter, 403
Lords, House of, 213, 215, 241, 244n.
Loreburn, Lord (Sir Robert Reid), 20, 22, 117 and n., 181n., 221–3, 288, 295–6, 298–9, 300, 305 and n., 308, 311, 316–17, 319n.
Lough, Thomas, 408n.
Lupton, Arnold, 93
Lynch, H. F. B., 186, 244n.
Lyttleton, Alfred, 296
Lyttleton, Arthur, 160

Macdonald, J. A. Murray, 8, 126, 129–130, 143, 164, 226–7, 229, 324, 330
MacDonald, J. Ramsay, 4n., 27 and n., 64, 118, 176, 178–9, 201, 205–6, 232, 242, 244n., 245, 249, 268n., 277 and n., 317, 329, 335, 415, 418
Macedonia, 182–3
Mackarness, F. C., 91, 265
MacNeill, J. Swift, 357
Madison, Fred, 4, 108, 178n., 219n.
Mallet, Louis, 23n.
Manchester Doctrine, 180
Marrakesh, riots at, 1907, 171
Marx, Karl, 2, 4n., 204, 227
Mason, D. M., 244n., 253–4, 258n., 266n., 311, 330, 354, 408n.
Massingham, H. W., 12, 45, 48, 86, 108n., 206, 230, 240, 265, 304, 317, 325–6, 329–30, 339, 356, 406
Masterman, C. F. G., 139, 152, 224, 390, 415
Masterman, Lucy, 152
Mauchamp, Dr, 171
Maurice, C. E., 170, 203–4
Maurras, Charles, 236
Maxse, Leo J., 21, 47, 52, 85–7, 109n., 121 and n., 180, 196, 209, 233, 295n., 303
May, Adm. W. H., 151
McKenna, Reginald,
appointed First Lord of Admiralty, 139
appointment welcome by Radicals, 140
ambivalent attitude to retrenchment, 143
and Ll. G's scheme for shipyard employment, 142 and n.
agrees to Sea Lords' demands, 1908, 142
on German shipbuilding capacity, 147
encourages Asquith's concern re gun mountings, 149 and n.
and 1909 Naval estimates in Commons, 156, 159–60
contingency plan criticised, 164
and discussion with Asquith over footnote to 1909 naval estimates, 162–3
defeats 'economists' in Cabinet, 1911 estimates, 225
admits incorrect statement on German dreadnoughts, 225, 230
and 1911 Naval estimates in Commons, 227
loyal supporter of Admiralty views, 292
removed from Admiralty, 293, 295, 301
leads opposition to Churchill in Cabinet, 320–2
(Mentioned), 21, 141, 148, 150–2, 166–7, 174, 214n., 229, 286–8, 300, 311, 317, 343–4, 394–5, 397
Messimy, A. M., 283
Metternich, Count P. W. von, 36, 41, 49n., 133, 147, 161, 212–13, 237, 239n., 249, 286, 307, 311
Mévil, André, 174n., 236
Meyer, Rev. F. B., 232
Military conversations, 36–7, 38 and n., 39, 42, 43 and n., 48 and n., 49, 78, 137, 197 and n., 283–4, 290–1, 293, 297–8, 301, 313, 317, 370, 372, 375, 395
Milner, Viscount, 79 and n.
Milyoukov, 59
Minto, Earl of, 54, 56–8
Mohammed Ali, 186, 188, 241, 255
Molteno, Percy, 330, 339, 408n.
Monis, A. M., 236, 245n.
Moore, W. A., 182
Morel, E. D., 194, 217n., 420
Morley, John,
personality, 30, 56
importance of his support for Grey's Russian policy, 30, 55n., 57, 70
and Indian government, 54 and n., 57
doubts concerning Haldane's reforms, 78–79
consulted by Loreburn re secret C.I.D. meeting, 296
raises secret meeting of C.I.D. in Cabinet, 297
incompetence and conceit in old age, 297, 300
and resignation, 1914, 389, 394, 397–401
(Mentioned), 2, 5, 6, 17–18, 20, 22, 77, 79–80, 82–3, 88, 104n., 138–9, 150–3, 223, 238, 249, 267, 277n., 280, 288, 299, 301, 305, 309–10, 311n., 313–14, 317, 319n., 326–7, 343, 415

Morocco, 35–6, 39–40, 75, 170–5, 197, 235–8, 240–1, 245 and n., 246–50, 255
Morrell, Philip, 186, 258n., 266n., 329, 408 and n., 420
Moscheles, Felix, 190, 231, 251, 281
Mulai, Hafid, 172–3
Mulliner, H. H., 148 and n., 149 and n., 150, 334n., 336
de Mun, Albert, 236
Murray, A. C., 240
Murray, Gilbert, 59

Napoleon, Louis, 1
Nathan, Paul, 312n.
National Liberal Club, 304
National Liberal Federation 125, 155, 157, 269, 270 and n., 271, 304–5, 326–7, 330, 338 and n.
National Peace Congresses,
　1906, 97–8, 103
　1907, 84
　1910, 218–19
　1913, 334
　1914, 379, 381
National Peace Council, 97 and n., 142n., 211, 253n., 254n., 260n., 262–3, 327, 351, 380, 401
National Service League, 96, 277n., 331
Naval staff, 293 and n.
Navy,
　as a defensive force only, 111, 113 and n., 117
　and unpreparedness at time of Agadir crisis, 285–6
　and British sea power in Mediterranean, 314, 318–20
　Estimates,
　1906, 106, 121
　1908, 82, 123–8, 130–2, 134
　1909, 140, 150–3, 154 and n., 156–158, 162 and n., 163, 201–2, 208
　1910, 164–6, 213 and n.
　1911, 224–5, 227
　1912, 318, 323 4
　Supplementary,
　　1912, 324, 326–7
　　1913, 225, 330 and n., 340–5
　1914, 403
Navy League, 123 and n., 141–2, 339–340
Neutralists, in Cabinet, July 1914, 397–402
Neutrality League, 411–12
Nevinson, H. W., 60, 62–3, 68, 115–116, 179, 349, 361
Nicholson, C. N., 408n.
Nicholson, Field Marshal (C. I. G. S.), 282, 288, 291, 300
Nicolson, Sir Arthur, 33n, 36, 53–4, 63, 193 and n., 196, 222–3, 237,

240n., 245, 256, 308, 311, 313–14, 318, 319n., 320, 364, 384–5, 387n., 395
Non-resistance, doctrine of, 204
Northcliffe, Lord, 214
Nuttall, H., 408n.

Official Secrets Act, 1911, 241–2
Osborne, judgment, 215n., 244n.
Ottley, Adm. Sir. C., 288

Pacifism and pacifists, 71, 74, 97, 104, 105 and n., 109, 110 and n., 118, 131, 155, 166–8, 190, 198n., 201–204, 212, 223–4, 227, 229, 231, 233, 234n., 254n., 260, 305, 306 and n., 350n., 352, 361, 367–8, 379–81
Palmerston, Lord, 179–80, 257n.
Paris, Declaration of, 1856, 219
Parliament Act, 1911, 241, 243
Parliamentary Persia Committee, 186, 241, 258 and n.
Passy, Frédéric, 50
Paulton, Henry, 17
Peace Day Meetings,
　1908, 129
　1911, 234
　1914, 380
Peace Party, in Cabinet, 1914, 380
Pease, J. A., 178n., 238, 343, 380–1, 389, 396–8, 401
Perris, G. H., 8, 103, 109, 114, 159, 177–8, 189n., 190–1, 209–13, 280, 335, 367, 379
Perris, H. S., 98n., 104n., 137n.
Persia, 186–7, 190–2, 195, 241, 251, 255–9, 277, 303
Pichon, Stephen, 51, 173, 191, 197
Poincaré, R., 313–16, 368
Ponsonby, Arthur, 26, 29n., 62, 178n., 186, 199n., 226–7, 229, 258n., 261 and n., 264–6, 267n., 330, 339, 357, 378–9, 408–11, 419–20
Potsdam Agreement, 1910, 195, 207n, 208, 242, 255
Pratt, Hodgson, 98
Press, 12, 13 and n., 32, 46, 47 and n., 52, 74 and n., 81, 85, 94 and n., 102, 120n., 130–1, 134–5, 144–6, 153, 155, 159, 173–6, 184, 192, 196, 198, 205, 214, 223, 229, 233, 234n., 236, 239n., 246–7, 250n., 252n., 262, 270–2, 278, 281, 304, 317, 325, 328–9, 336, 368, 378, 382–4, 404–6, 412, 419
(Individual journals quoted in text)
Albany Review, 52, 63, 68, 93, 111–112, 114n., 116, 119, 120n., 124, 132, 182
Arbitrator, 380

Christian Commonwealth, 231, 281
Clarion, 202n.
Concord, 10, 11, 22, 47–8, 51, 61,
  64n., 68n., 69 and n., 74n., 85–6,
  92n., 99n., 102–3, 105n., 110 and
  n., 113–14, 116n., 120, 123 and n.,
  126, 128, 130, 136, 155, 166, 170,
  172–3, 178, 189n., 190, 192, 194–5,
  199n., 200, 202n., 203–4, 207,
  209, 212, 215, 223–4, 226–7, 229n.,
  231, 234, 245–6, 253–4, 263, 274,
  280, 325, 334n., 335, 346, 351–2,
  354, 362, 367–8, 379
Contemporary Review, 1, 3, 45, 88,
  119n., 217, 261, 355
Daily Chronicle, 49, 246, 261, 340,
  404, 406
Daily Mail, 112n., 122–3, 126, 131,
  141, 210–11
Daily News, 49n., 85–6, 93, 159,
  176, 179, 213n., 217, 225, 231,
  245, 253n., 274, 277 and n., 326,
  346, 368, 374
Daily Telegraph, 160
Economist, 123n., 232, 263
Edinburgh Review, 5, 198
The Globe, 109n.
Labour Leader, 138–9, 158–9, 165–6,
  170, 174, 176, 179, 183, 188, 190–
  191, 264n., 273n., 276n., 332n.,
  335n., 336 and n., 337n., 338n.,
  340n., 358–9, 368, 412–13,
  420
Manchester Guardian, 21, 45, 48,
  50, 66, 86, 87n., 93–4, 99, 108,
  113n., 118–19, 142–3, 145, 165,
  170n., 173 and n., 179, 182n., 193,
  197, 198n., 210, 213, 215–16, 218,
  225, 230–2, 234, 245, 248, 258–9,
  262, 266, 272–3, 306, 312, 324–6,
  329–30, 339, 348–51, 360, 367,
  372, 406–8, 413–14, 418
Morning Post, 11, 49n., 259n.
The Nation, 28n., 50–2, 66, 68n.,
  69, 70 and n., 85, 87n., 94n., 95,
  111, 114, 116–18, 124–6, 128–9,
  131, 133, 138, 142, 145, 160, 167,
  170 and n., 171–6, 180–3, 185,
  187, 190–1, 197n., 206, 209, 211,
  212 and n., 216, 217 and n., 218,
  230, 240, 245–6, 250, 255, 259,
  270, 272, 304–5, 309, 312, 324,
  326, 328–9, 331, 339, 348–9, 351,
  355, 360–2, 372–3, 404, 419
National Review, 21, 86, 109n., 112
  n., 233
Navy League Journal, 123
New Age, 4n., 28, 63, 66 and n., 95n.,
  101n., 104n., 105n., 116n., 118,
  120n., 158–9, 170, 173, 176, 179–
  180, 183, 189–90, 197n., 199n.,
  200n., 208, 227n., 245n., 261n.,
269n., 274n., 306n., 317, 357–8,
  360, 368, 383, 419
News Weekly, 383
The Observer, 159
Pall Mall Gazette, 310n., 332
Review of Reviews, 21, 114
The Speaker, [21, 40n., 45n., 48–9,
  60 1, 99n., 102, 108n.
The Standard, 4n., 109n.
The Times, 2, 27n., 46n., 64, 69,
  86, 103n., 104n., 134, 143, 160,
  175n., 185, 266n., 340 and n.,
  349, 366, 368, 393n.
Tribune, 86, 99
Westminster Gazette, 24, 69, 80, 86,
  144, 162, 246, 325, 384, 404
Yorkshire Observer, 89
Princip, Gavrilo, 382
Provincialism, 271–2

Quakers, 4, 129, 204, 251, 303, 401,
  404
Quelch, Harry, 4n., 120n., 205 and n.
Questions in Commons, 64, 65 and n.,
  108, 109 and n., 143, 146, 176–7,
  197n., 356–8, 405

Radicals and Radicalism,
  optimism, 8–9, 11, 97, 118–19, 135,
  192, 281, 376, 420
  primacy of domestic reform, ix, 9,
  26
  and 'League of Peace', 24–5
  loyalty to Liberal leadership and
  party, 9, 129–30, 154–5, 259, 309,
  331, 345–6, 376
  distrust of ententes as alliances,
  170–1, 179–80, 260, 274–5, 305
  faith in Campbell-Bannerman, 22,
  32, 85, 95, 100, 106, 113, 115n.,
  118, 126, 129, 136–7
  and 'secret diplomacy', 52, 175,
  265, 267n., 274 and n., 352–3
  stipulatory definition, 5n.
  divisions among, 5–6
  initial pro-French attitude, 10
  on Imperialism's connections with
  Protection, 19
  and morality, ix
  and nonconformist conscience, ix,
  11–12
  and tradition, 5–6
  and alliance with Labour, 27–8
  as pro-Boers, 6
  and patriotism, 6
  and disarmament, 7–9
  concern with Grey and relationship
  with F. O. officials, 29 and n.
  concern with 'patriotic' press, 46, 52
  hopes of German Socialism as a
  force for peace, 49–50
  views on Russia, 1907, 59–64

Radicals, and Radicalism—*contd.*
  criticism of and divisions of opinion over merits of Anglo-Russian Convention, 67–9, 177–81, 185
  attitude to Army reform, 71–2, 84–96
  distrust of Haldane, 73, 84
  on experts, 91–2, 95, 130, 144
  aggressive demands for peace 1906–1907, 97
  penchant for resolutions, 101 and n.
  plans for Hague Conference, 102–3
  on failure of Hague Conference, 119–21
  confusion of attitude to Navy, 108, 143, 144, 161
  on Asquith's Cabinet, 1908, 138–9
  and contractors, 141, 158, 160, 165
  and 1909 panic, 154, 157–8, 160–2
  critics of McKenna's 'contingency' plan, 164–5
  on Imperialism, 171, 175
  on 'lending' Powers, 172
  on Reval visit, 176–7, 181
  changing view of Bosnian crisis, 183–6
  as critics of Grey's Persian policy, 185–8
  and Tsar's visit to Cowes, 189–91
  and Balance of Power, 191–2.
  and Potsdam Agreement, 196
  on rumours of Anglo-French military agreement, March 1911, 197 and n., 198
  on German Social Democrats as force for peace, 200n.
  estimates of Bethmann-Hollweg, 208
  and King Edward's death, 214–15
  support for Congo reform, 217n.
  and Bagdad Railway project, 217n, 218
  and 'open markets', 218
  and Declaration of London, 219 and n.
  advocate political agreement with Germany, 1910, 223
  concern with increasing naval costs, 224–5
  and 1911 naval estimates, 226–9
  confused attitude towards navy, 226–7
  response to Grey's reductionist speech, 1911, 227–30
  on influence of 'Jingo' press, 233, 234 and n.
  reasons for delayed reaction to Agadir crisis, 242–3, 246
  and Agadir crisis, 248–50
  and House of Lords question, 243
  strength in Commons, 1911, 243, 244 and n.

  strength in Cabinet, 1911, 238
  indecision over intervention, 1911, 251
  as sentimental pacifists, 5n., 251
  and support for Young Turks, 253 and n.
  and Tripoli massacres, 253–5
  and Persia, 255–9
  criticism disarmed by Grey's threats of resignation, 257, 265
  and information on Persia, 257–8
  alliance with Tories over Persia, 258–9
  and military preparations, Autumn 1911, 261–2
  on parliamentary control of foreign affairs, 264–7
  and incubus of provincialism, 271–2
  on Grey's fears of German 'menace', 275, 279–80
  'Grey must Go' campaign defeated, 1911, 277–8
  determination to 'smash Grey' 1912, 303 and n., 304 and n.
  desire special Berlin mission, 305–6
  hopes of Haldane's Berlin Mission, 1912, 309–10, 312
  anger at Churchill's jingoism, 310
  expectations of Anglo-German agreement, 1912, 311
  and Grey-Cambon letters, 315–17
  their apocalyptic vision, 323
  armaments and policy, 325–6
  disarmament campaign, 1912–13, 327–3
  self-centred group, 329, 330 and n.
  and 'Naval Holiday' proposal, 332, 337
  and praise of Grey, 1913, 334
  and armament manufacturers, 335–336
  censure Asquith for lack of zeal on disarmament, 338
  criticise 1914 Naval estimates, 345
  criticism of Grey prior Balkan Wars, 348–9
  changing view of Young Turks, 348–50
  enthusiasm for Balkan League, 1912, 350
  insist on British neutrality in Balkans, 351–3
  impatience with London Conference, 353
  differences over intervention in Balkans, 354
  and Grey's 'conversion', 355–7
  why easily deluded by Grey, 359
  and rumours of Anglo-Russian naval agreement, 371–2
  ambivalent attitude in foreign policy, 1914, 374–5

reasons for apparent complacency, 1914, 376–8
political naivety, 376
forced to adopt passive rôle, 379
and idea of 'continuity' in foreign policy, 377
and Anglo-German relations, May 1914, 380
sympathy for subject nationalities, 384
afforded little information in Commons during the last crisis, 403
bewilderment, and fixity of ideas, 404
belief that no Liberal government would wage war, 404
plead for British neutrality, 404, 407–10
public activities against Britain's entry into war, 412–15, 419
reaction to Grey's speech, 3 Aug. 1914, 417–18
Radical Foreign Affairs Committee, 265, 266 and n., 267 and n., 268–269, 408–11
Radolin, Prince, 41, 174
Reay, Lord, 117–18
Red Cross, 101
Redmond, John, 330, 417
Reduction of Armaments Committee, 125, 142n., 144–6, 154, 166, 323, 326
Reform Club Concordat, 1901, 6
Relugas Compact, Oct. 1905, 14–16, 18, 71
Repington, Charles à Court, 47n., 52n., 72–3, 90n., 92, 134–5, 210, 309
Rhodes, Cecil, 6
Richard, Henry, 9, 105n., 266n.
Richter, Adolf, 212
Riddell, Lord, 415
Right of Capture at Sea, 117 and n., 120, 218, 219 and n., 329–30
Ripon, Lord, 17, 20, 33, 37–40, 44, 78, 238
Roberts, Lord, 72n., 277n., 331, 360
Roberts, Samuel, 160–1
Robertson, Edmund, 106–7, 108n., 112n.
Robertson, J. M., 91, 127–8, 132, 139
Rosebery, Lord, 4–5, 11, 13, 17, 19–20, 71, 84, 135–6, 138, 194
Rowntree, Arnold, 244n., 266, 408n., 419–20
Rowntree, Joshua, 253, 334
Rouvier, Maurice, 23, 35, 39n., 51
Runciman, Walter, 21, 151–2, 222, 238, 343, 395–6, 400, 405
Russian Committee, 182n., 190
Rutherford, Vickerman, 186

Salisbury, Lord, 5, 22, 132, 273n.
Samuel, Herbert, 21, 238, 342–3, 398
Sanders, Liman von, incident, 365
Sanderson, Thomas, 23n., 39n.
Sandjak railway project, 181
Sarajevo, 374, 382–3
Sardar assad, 187
Sazanov, S. D., 195, 233n., 314, 364–365, 369
Schlieffen, Count von, 402
Schuster, Ernest, 304
Scott, A. McCallum, 190, 254, 266n., 272
Scott, C. P., 225, 238–40, 246–7, 248n., 250n., 265, 305 and n., 343–4, 372, 387–8, 412
Seely, J. E. B., 95n., 360
Sembat, Marcel, 225
Shaw, G. B., 4 and n., 64, 189
Shuster, Morgan, 255–8
Simon, Sir John, 342–3, 390, 394, 396, 398, 401, 415
Sinclair, John, 20, 80
Smith, E. G., 199n.
Smith, F. E., 241, 340
Smith, L. G. Horton, 123
Snowden, Philip, 166, 207, 231, 242, 281, 336, 345
Social Democratic Federation, 104–5, 200n.
Socialist International,
    Brussels, 1906, 99
    Stuttgart, 1907, 104n., 120n., 418
    Copenhagen, 1910, 206, 418
Socialism, 3, 4n., 28, 49–50, 95n., 100, 101 and n., 102, 105, 130, 306n., 309
Sorel, Georges, 242
Spencer, Earl of, 6, 13–14
Spender, J. A., 18, 20, 24, 76, 80, 88, 161–2, 196, 258n., 270, 278, 326, 359, 372, 383, 405–6
Splendid isolation, 23, 273n., 276
Spring Rice, Sir Cecil, 53
Stanley, Venetia, 386, 395, 398
Stead, W. T., 20–2, 110, 114–16, 119 and n., 123, 142, 253
Steed, Henry Wickham, 382
Stein, Ludwig, 312n., 323
Stevenson, Frances, 391
Stokes, Major, 256 and n.
Strike, as an anti-war measure, 206–7, 242
Stumm, W. von, 41, 133
Suicide Club, 333–7
Sydenham of Combe, Lord, 117n.
Syndicalism, 242

Tabriz massacres, 258
Taft, President, 228–9, 231
Tardieu, André, 169–70, 195
Tariff Reform, 13

Taylor, A. J. P., ix, 250
Taylor, T. C., 404
Territorial Army,
 debates in Commons, 1907–08, 87–92
 Radical criticism of, 91–3
Thorne, Will, 205
Tirpitz, Alfred von, 122, 161–2, 220, 307, 331 and n.
Tisza, Count Stephen, 383–4
Trevelyan, C. P., 395, 401, 405, 409, 412, 417, 420
Trevelyan, G. M., 280
Triple alliance, threaten strike, 1914, 376
Triple entente, 169–234, 240, 358–9, 363–4, 366–8, 385
Tripoli, 251–4, 256n.
Tsar Nicholas, 176–7, 180, 182n., 186, 188–91, 195, 208
Tschirschky, H. von, 42
Tweedmouth, Lord, 18, 20, 107n., 112n., 123–5, 127–8, 133–5, 139, 295 and n.
Two power standard, 109n., 135, 143, 146 and n., 214

Union of Democratic Control, 34, 217n., 420
Universal Peace Congresses,
 1905, 45–6
 1908, 202n., 214

Vanderveldt, Emile, 413
Vereeniging, peace of, 7
Vincent, Sir Howard, 105n.
Vivian, Henry, 101–2, 104n.

Wallace, Robert, 3
Wallas, Graham, 412
War Office,
 Propaganda Department, 74n., 283, 286–7, 289, 291–3
Ward, Dudley, 304
Ward, John, 92, 105n., 158
Ward, Sir Joseph, 232
Weardale, Lord, 105n., 218, 232–3

Wedgwood, J. C., 109n., 266n., 267n., 419
Weinroth, Howard, 251
Wells, H. G., 386
Weltpolitik, 212–13, 333–4
West, Algernon, 8
White, Sir William, 152
Whitehouse, J. H., 244n., 259–60, 266n.
William II, 15, 40–3, 49 and n., 51, 133–5, 169, 174n., 175, 180n., 189, 192, 195, 199n., 208, 214–15, 231, 233–4, 270, 278, 285, 306 and n., 307, 311
Williamson, S. R., jr., 317
Williams, W. M. J., 325
Wilson, Adm. Sir A. K., 283, 286, 288–9, 291
Wilson, Charles, 101n.
Wilson, General Sir Henry,
 character and disposition, 282
 on size of Expeditionary Force, 283
 on importance of military conversations, 283
 demands British intervention on continent, 284–5
 and W.O. strategical concept explained to Committee of Imperial Defence, 288–9
 on Radical members of Cabinet, 300–1
 not obliged to inform Cabinet of frequency of meetings with French Staff, 301
 estimate of Grey, 285
 (Mentioned), 290, 292, 318, 395
Wilson, H. J., 103
Wilson, P. W., 334n.
Wilson, President, 381
Wolf, Lucien, 253n.
Wolff, Theodor, 371
Wood, T. McKinnon, 398
Wyatt, H. F., 123
Wyndham, George, 159

Young Turks, 182–3, 253

Zabern incident, 361